AMERICAN
URBAN
COMMUNITIES

Harper's Social Science Series
Under the Editorship of
F. STUART CHAPIN

AMERICAN
URBAN
COMMUNITIES

by

WILBUR C. HALLENBECK

Professor of Education
Teachers College
Columbia University

HARPER & BROTHERS PUBLISHERS · NEW YORK

AMERICAN URBAN COMMUNITIES

G-C

Library of Congress catalog card number: 51–11920

To
my father

EDWIN FORREST HALLENBECK,

who reared me in cities
and from whom I learned
to respect and appreciate
city people and their institutions

and to

HARLAN PAUL DOUGLASS,

in whose companionship and
under whose tutelage for
many years I pursued
the serious study of
American urban communities

Contents

Part V. Patterns of Urban Structure

Part VI. People in Cities

Part VII. Cities and the Future

Preface

THIS book had its beginnings many years ago during a period when the author was responsible for the direction and development of a number of different kinds of urban organizations. It was early discovered that many forces were at work in urban life and these must be understood and appraised before these organizations could define their tasks and plan their fulfillment. It also became clear that no organization can stand on self-made foundations, but that they have their place by virtue of a role in community life and in their relations to the whole pattern of organizations. This brought the need for understanding cities very close not only to the multiplicity of institutions but also to the people who made and operated these institutions and to all those who made their lives within the cities.

Nearly a decade of professional research into the various problems of institutions and the urban milieu in the major cities across the United States added greatly to the understanding of cities and their institutions through more detailed analysis of problems and the practical application of the knowledge which was acquired.

During the last decade and a half it has been the author's good fortune to have had the opportunity of working with graduate students who sought a more comprehensive knowledge and understanding of American urban communities. Through this coöperative search there has accumulated a constantly increasing resource of details, analyses, and illustrations of the manifold aspects of urban life, its organization, and its problems. Many have participated in this search and each has added his part, some more, some less.

In this day when so many different kinds of professional people must do their work within the framework of cities and such a large proportion of American citizens live and work in cities or under the direct influence of cities, knowledge about and understanding of cities has become of great importance. As a resource toward the end of a more intelligent and effective citizenry the accumulations of knowledge and understanding have been set down herein.

In writing this book not only have college and graduate students been in mind but also the increasing numbers of conscientious citizens who have dedicated significant portions of their time and energy to making cities better places in which to live, to work, and to find the fuller satisfactions of living. This book seeks to give recognition to these people as the great hope for the remaking of our American urban communities in new and better patterns and to bring them some measure of help in meeting the challenge and responsibilities which they face.

To inventory and acknowledge the great number of individuals who have contributed to making this book is beyond the power of recollection of the author, but their help is appreciated none the less. Some students, however, intrigued by one or another aspect of city life, have searched for facts and struggled with their organization far beyond the call of requirements. The results of their efforts have been incorporated in the various chapters on which they worked, though they may not recognize their handiwork in its present form. Naming them here is but a small token of the gratitude held for their diligent and gracious help: Florence Beatty Brown, Margaret Shreffler Wingert, Paul B. Gillen, Benjamin Shangold, Morris Grumer, Harold Goldstein, William N. Martin.

Special mention must be given to Oliver E. Loud, who, while a student, wrought out and organized the ideas presented in Chapter 6 and who later as a professor in Antioch College assisted in preparing the manuscript of the chapter.

From among my colleagues in Teachers College and Columbia University a number have given graciously of their time to discuss problems and ideas, locate materials, read manuscript, and offer most helpful criticism. I am deeply indebted to George T. Renner, Harold F. Clark, Paul R. Mort, Ernest G. Osborne, Paul L. Essert, Robert D. Calkins, and J. Marshall Miller.

I am greatly indebted to Harold S. Buttenheim and Eric Carlson of The American City for their careful reading of the whole manuscript and for the very valuable suggestions and criticisms which they made.

A number of secretaries have most graciously done the many things required to prepare the manuscript for publication. I am deeply grateful to them all: Jean Weiss Ziering, Aileen Karppinen

Johnson, Doris Berg, Florence Miller Anderson, Esther Grossmark, and Ruth O'Donnell.

Dr. F. Stuart Chapin, editor of Harper's Social Science Series, read my manuscript in both preliminary and final versions, and I am greatly indebted to him for many helpful criticisms and suggestions.

My gratitude is greatest to my close friend and colleague, Edmund deS. Brunner, who challenged me to do the job, urged me on through the many years of writing, read countless drafts, spent untold hours in discussing problems and offering suggestions, and gave generously of his insight and scholarship.

WILBUR C. HALLENBECK

New York
July, 1951

INTRODUCTION

CHAPTER 1

THE STUDY OF CITIES

CITIES affect the lives of most Americans. More than half of the people live in cities. At least another quarter live in suburbs or so close to cities that they can use the cities whenever and in whatever way they may desire. Of the balance, only a very small percentage live in places so remote that they have no contacts with cities. The rest, though they live in rural areas and are occupied with the business and associations of rural life, find that the influence of cities through the modern means of communication and transportation, especially the radio and the automobile, insinuates itself into their patterns of living, into their wants and interests and even into their ideas.

How did cities come to be? What are they? What do they do? Why are they so important? How do they operate? Why do they have so many problems? What can be done about them? Most people cannot escape being concerned about these questions. Citizens of the cities must cope with them day after day, either to be overwhelmed by the forces of the city, or to accommodate themselves to the cities' ways, or to aggressively participate in making the city a better place in which to live. Most young people will find their work, their family life, and their pursuit of leisure-time activities in cities. They must know how to meet the requirements and use the resources of the city. Many young men and women brought up on farms or in the villages will seek opportunities in cities. Whether they succeed or fail will depend not only on their abilities, but also on their knowledge of how to use these abilities in the complex life of a modern American city. Retired people, and especially widows from the country, make their way to cities to find ease, comfort, freedom, and happiness, but disillusionment and despair can also be found in cities; which ends are obtained depends partly on an understanding of cities.

3

For these people and all who need to know what cities are like, even those who have had much experience living in cities, but whose experience has been largely unintegrated, this book is written. It undertakes to answer the questions of major importance about cities, to the extent that the accumulation of experience and knowledge provides the answers. It presents a great deal of information about cities, but its chief purpose is to present that information in such a way that it will give a comprehensive idea of cities—that is, to show the many facets of city life in their various relationships, so that the reader can see the city as a whole.

This book is not for long-time students of cities. It makes no pretense of adding to the knowledge of cities, although it contains some material which has not been made available before and other material which has not been used in its connection with cities. It is hoped, however, that it will be useful to various specialists in cities whose preoccupation has precluded their looking at the city as a whole, or whose specialization has dulled their perception of the many other aspects of city life to which their specialization must be related. Especially should it be helpful to those who, in their respective ways, are endeavoring to make cities more effective instruments for the better living of their people.

LIMITATIONS OF THIS BOOK

The purposes and character of the book, therefore, set certain limitations which should be indicated at the outset so that they may be fully recognized and taken into consideration by the readers.

First, the discussion is limited to American cities. In ancient times, people built their cities, and in each succeeding cycle of history, other people, in other places, for other purposes, have added their cities. Some of the oldest still survive because of their strategic positions, their continued growth, and their capacity to adapt to the evolving needs of each new age. Others have been passed by in the stream of history because they were no longer important, or because they lacked the capacity to adapt to a new age; they remain as crumbling monuments in the backwash of civilization. Still others have disappeared, buried by the deposits of conquest, of disease, or of nature. Even the ancient city of Troy, which arose nine times from its own ashes, finally succumbed to the changing world.

The dominant purpose of ancient cities was protection. They were surrounded by walls with small gates. They had fortifications and implements of war. Soldiers were in readiness, and watchmen made their tours. Safety and security from outside enemies was found in these concentrations of people, but the developments of civilization were not ready to take care of them, and the price of the concentration of so many was often slavery, hunger, and death.

Medieval cities kept the walls, but as much to hem the people in as to protect them from the destruction of wars. Feudalism, the developing crafts, guilds, a growing community organization, the increasing merchant group, all played a part in holding people together. In some instances, feudal lords facilitated the development of cities to strengthen their control; in other cases, it came as an expression of the growing power of a people revolting from such power and control. At any rate, in time, the city-states came into being; these finally gave way to the formation of the nation-states. Cities, with all of their problems, held a central place in the Middle Ages.[1]

With the expansion of industry, a broad outreach of trade, and the formation of national states within which and between which commerce could be carried on, cities of the modern era came into being. These cities were predominantly service centers.

The transition from one stage of development, with its predominant purpose, to another, with another purpose, was gradual, as was the transition from one era to another. It was rather a pattern of purposes that changed because of changing circumstances which imposed new needs on cities. Social organization and controls were not absent from ancient cities, but they were relatively simple, largely for the purpose of obtaining coöperation to meet the main problem of protection. They became of paramount importance, however, in modern cities, not so much as a matter of control, as of making cities work in their complex job of service. Protection, which became secondary in the cities of the Middle Ages, changed its character completely in modern times, becoming protection not against external enemies, but against internal enemies such as disease, confusion, fire, crime, and conflict. Traffic in goods was essential in the life of ancient cities; but, as goods were increased in quantity and variety in the Middle Ages, it became more significant

---

[1] Lewis Mumford, *The Culture of Cities* (New York: Harcourt, Brace and Company, 1938). Chap. I gives a penetrating analysis of the rise, character, development, and decline of the medieval cities.

as a factor in the organization of city life. Not until the Industrial Revolution had taken hold, however, did commerce play the dominant role.

American cities belong to the modern age. They have had their development largely in response to the forces which the industrial age has unloosed. Because they have not been encumbered by the patterns and traditions of a long past, they have had a better chance to develop to meet the needs of modern trends. Whether or not they have done better than cities in other parts of the world is another question. Because of this uniqueness in their story and because American students and urbanites are concerned primarily with understanding the circumstances and problems in the midst of which they must live and work, this book is confined to the consideration of American cities. Some of the past experience is involved, however, inasmuch as American cities came into being and developed across a span of years which marked the change from an essentially agricultural, rural age to a predominantly industrial, urban era.

A second limitation is found in the purpose of the book—a comprehensive treatment that is an introduction to American cities. To include a discussion of the major facets of cities precludes an exhaustive treatment of any one. The extent of treatment will, however, vary from topic to topic, partly in terms of relative importance and partly because of differences in the amount of material which has been developed. Books could be written, as they have been, about most of the topics. Treatment of the various aspects of some fills whole libraries. A few have never been dealt with as such, but have been touched upon in many writings. Any of the topics might be an area for years of specialized study.

To prepare this kind of book, consequently, a process of selection of material is required. This is not an easy task because it involves several things. In the first place, there is a vast literature in some of the areas which are considered. One who is not a specialist in such an area could not possibly be adequately familiar with this literature; consequently, there may very well be important material which has entirely escaped the writer. Major works are readily located, but significant secondary material in lesser works can easily escape attention. In the second place, the basis for the selection of material is established by the purposes of the book. The first purpose is to present the various aspects of city life, but no such presentation can avoid highlighting the problems in each area. This, in turn, calls for indications of the possibility for the solution of problems. Choices must be made, and interpretations are involved; in the final analysis, it is a matter of the judgment of the writer. In the third place, judgments and interpretations are influenced by the author's ideas and concepts. At this point, bias inevitably creeps in. Bias is a matter of opinion and is always subject to controversy. The bias of this book may be accepted or rejected by the reader; that is his responsibility. In order to help him face this responsibility squarely, however, it is only fair that the author set down his point of view at the outset.

HYPOTHESES AND ASSUMPTIONS

Prolonged study and observation of American cities result not only in some measure of understanding of them, but also in some strong convictions about them. Such convictions form the point of view with which this book has been written. They are expressed here in two groups. The first is a series of hypotheses around which the material of the book has been arranged to provide an exposition of their meaning and significance, and to give an argument for their substantiation. The second group is made up of a number of general assumptions, the application of which is in some cases explained, but the validity of which is taken for granted as sufficiently self-evident to need no argument.

The hypotheses are as follows:

1. The growth and development of cities is part and parcel of the development of America; consequently, cities play an indispensable role in American society. This accounts for their increasing importance and dominance in the American culture, society, and economy.
2. Cities represent a type of organization and a way of life created and sustained by the continual operation of industry and commerce. Their character and variations are functions of the general and particular roles they play in the whole society.
3. Because cities are the focal points in the dynamics of American society, their various relationships are crucial. Although these relationships are inadequately defined either in theory or in social mechanisms, nevertheless they engender basic responsibilities to the whole society on the part of cities.
4. As urbanization has spread throughout American society, it has profoundly modified the functional patterns and the organizational structure not only of city life, but also in the operation of nonurban communities.

5. Cities, technically, are highly artificial political units; the social unit is the much larger urban community. To make the political and social units conterminous is desirable for effective operation.

6. The pattern of functions which is required to make cities work and play their roles is the basis of their institutional structure and their organic life. With reference to this pattern, the inadequacies of cities can be identified.

7. The inexorable force of rapid change compels a high degree of adaptability, which cities have failed to attain. The hope of American urban communities lies in a more comprehensive, scientific planning, democratically conceived and executed.

The assumptions are self-evident but are mentioned because they bear upon the point of view from which this book is written. There are four of major importance:

1. A culture determines the character and the limitations of its various social forms. American cities, therefore, must be seen in the light of American culture. Since the dominant factors in American culture are democracy—the acceptance of the preëminence of human values and the democratic principle of social and political organization—and rapid change growing out of great technological advance and its impact upon all aspects of the society, these factors in turn become both the controls and the objectives of cities.

2. In the community, individuals and their families find their relationships to society. The function of the individual in his community has come more and more to replace family and wealth as the basis of status. The use of human resources, consequently, comes to be of paramount concern both to communities and to people.

3. The urban community is a social organism; thus its effectiveness is in terms of the adequacy of its organization and the integration of its many parts into a working whole.

4. Social forms and, consequently, urban communities are subject to control, manipulation, and purposeful development by their own members; this is to say that the citizens of any city can, within limits, make of that city what they will.

The last two assumptions will be subjected to further exposition in the proper place in the chapters which follow.

ORGANIZATION OF THE BOOK

The book is divided into seven parts, each representing a phase of the study of American urban communities.

Part I, "The Rise of American Cities," lays the basis of study by relating the development of cities to the development of the country; it points out what cities are and why, how, and where they have grown; and it indicates the basis of the variations in cities.

Part II, "External Interrelationships of Cities," proposes a basic theory of the manifold relationships of cities in American society, followed by an analysis of the major patterns of relationships, and points up the responsibilities which rest on cities as a result of their position in these areas of interdependence.

Part III, "The Form and Structure of Cities," deals with the geography, topography, growth, real estate development, and other factors which have determined the physical form of cities, the social structure which has developed around the physical form, and the recent trend toward suburbanization and decentralization, which has eventuated in metropolitan communities.

Part IV, "Organized Life in Cities," discusses the basic principles of organization in cities, describes the overall phases of organization (government, politics, and economic life), points out the significance of the impact of the process of urbanization on social organization, and considers some of the major urban problems.

Part V, "Patterns of Urban Structure," takes as illustrations five of the important areas of organization in cities—welfare, health, education, recreation, and religion—and describes their structure and operation. Each one is dealt with in a different way, partly because each story takes its own form and partly to show that there are various ways in which they can be viewed.

Part VI, "People in Cities," endeavors to show what cities do to people in that they require a new pattern for families and impose a multitude of relationships, the conditions for crises and maladjustments, and social stratification on their people.

Part VII, "Cities and the Future," describes the backgrounds, present status, and potentialities of planning in cities, shows the assets and liabilities of democracy in cities, and closes with a summary chapter showing the place and obligations of cities in the American scene.

Following each chapter are suggested supplementary readings for any who may desire to pursue, in further detail, the important points of the chapter, or who may desire to get on the track of specialized study.

Those who are interested not only in general knowledge about cities, but also in better understanding of their own cities, can readily pursue the study of a particular city in the pattern of this general analysis and so see their own cities against the backdrop of the general picture which is presented here.

The points of interpretation which are to be found in all sections involve issues concerning which opinions differ. They can, therefore, become the basis of fruitful and enlightening discussion.

Supplementary Reading

Chase, Stuart. *The Proper Study of Mankind: An Inquiry into the Science of Human Relations.* New York: Harper & Brothers, 1948.
> This is a comprehensive and organized survey of the social sciences. It forms an important background for understanding the phases and relationships of any social science.

Lundberg, George A. *Can Science Save Us?* New York: Longmans, Green and Co., 1947.
> This is a plea for more adequate use of the social sciences in the light of the many problems which might have been solved and the potentialities which the various social sciences hold for practical use.

Mumford, Lewis. *The Culture of Cities.* New York: Harcourt, Brace and Company, 1938.
> An erudite historical background for the sociological study of modern cities.

PART I

THE RISE OF AMERICAN CITIES

CITIES have been a product of the industrial and commercial economy which has developed in America (Chap. 2). Inherent in functions which cities have been called forth to perform is that which makes cities cities; by virtue of what they are, cities have developed many characteristics (Chap. 3). The great growth of cities and the changing patterns of growth are among the most interesting and significant social phenomena in America (Chap. 4). The development of cities has been unequal and has resulted in different kinds of cities; the differences which can be determined seem to be a measure of the relative potentialities of cities (Chap. 5).

CHAPTER 2

THE DEVELOPMENT OF CITIES
IN AMERICA

THE earliest settlers in the territory that is now the United States built their dwellings huddled close together at various points along the Atlantic seaboard. They had come to the New World inspired by a desire for freedom—freedom to worship God according to the dictates of their own consciences, freedom to make their living in their own way on their own initiative, freedom from an overpowering burden of taxation and practical enslavement to landed aristocracy, freedom to own their own land, and freedom to set up new political forms, in which they might have a voice, and which would guarantee them the freedoms which they sought.[1]

Two problems immediately faced the colonists. The first was to protect their families from the Indians, and the second was to provide for their sustenance. Relatively soon, the first problem became less serious and the second more acute. Families began to make their way farther and farther into the wilderness to clear land and develop farms. Agriculture, to provide the materials to meet their needs, and the simple crafts, to turn the materials into food, clothing, shelter, and utensils, occupied most of the time of all members of these early family units. The things which they could provide by their own work and ingenuity went into the process of their own living.[2]

THE EMERGENCE OF CITIES

With the clearing of more land, the improvement of routines, the invention of devices and gadgets for simplifying work, and the more

[1] Charles A. Beard and Mary Beard, *The Rise of American Civilization* (New York: The Macmillan Company, 1927).

[2] Jane de Forest Shelton, *The Salt Box House* (New York: Charles Scribner's Sons, 1929).

13

efficient use of resources, surpluses began to appear on the farms. The increasing efficiency of agricultural production also released a substantial part of the population from the farms to engage in other vocations. In the meantime, new needs and wants which could not be supplied on the farms came into being. The surpluses, the new needs, and the availability of people to carry on new activities were the essential ingredients for trade and industry. Trade, which began in the simple form of barter, could not meet the conditions of commerce, for many of the goods which were wanted were not produced locally. Currency and banking were required, and the means of exporting and importing goods were necessary.

Ships brought needed goods and supplies. There were many jobs to be performed in connection with the landing, repair, building, unloading, loading, and also the manning of the ships. Goods had to be made available to potential purchasers. Produce had to be sold and shipped. Villages grew up composed of the people who did these jobs.

People depended upon villages for other things also. Schools and churches were there. The beginnings of government were there. The mills for grinding the grain, the blacksmiths and their shops, the other artisans—cobblers, coopers, cabinetmakers, and the rest—also found it more convenient to render their services from the villages.

This was the beginning of American cities. The eighteenth-century villages, though a far cry from the great cities of the twentieth century, became, in effect, the cities of their day. This gathering of relatively large numbers of people who lived and worked in close proximity began a new way of life and brought new kinds of problems.

Cities come into existence as products of and as focal points in the social and economic life of a people that has reached a certain stage of development. The resulting division of labor presupposes and furthers urbanization. When a civilization arrives at such a stage of maturity that its life is no longer local and self-sufficient but is intertwined in a nexus of national and world commerce, technology, population movement, social and intellectual intercourse and cultural and political contact, cities emerge because they discharge certain vital functions. The very existence and the growth of cities in turn sets into operation forces that create problems both within the city and in the Nation at large.[3]

[3] National Resources Committee, *Our Cities: Their Role in the National Economy*, Report of the Urbanism Committee (Washington: Government Printing Office, 1937), p. 31.

There are two major points to consider. First, the development of cities is a concomitant of a developing nation, and, consequently, the major factors in national development are the keys to urban development. In the social and economic evolution of a nation there comes a time when certain functions require cities. When cities arise to take their essential place in the nation, they become focal points of national culture and from then on, in a very real sense, hold the center of the stage, from a sociological point of view.

The second major point is that the large and complicated urban communities in their very nature generate new, extensive, and complex social problems. While each city is responsible for the solutions of its own problems, the solutions frequently involve the whole nation in one way or another. These involvements, in turn, extend the social influence and social importance of cities.

CONDITIONS OF DEVELOPMENT

The impetus for the settlement of America did much to set the stage and condition the people for a great development in the New World. The dissatisfactions with the Old World were very strong and had accumulated over a long period of time. The people who were to migrate had come to regard them as so intolerable that no sacrifice or hardship could be too great in exchange for escaping from them. These dissatisfactions were political, social, economic, and religious.[4]

These dissatisfactions provided a negative base for developments in the New World; they represented things the people did not want. They did more than this, however; they gave readiness for consideration of new, constructive ideas and plans for social organization.

Reports of the great resources and possibilities of the New World had reached the restless souls of the Old World and given them courage to make the adventure. In spite of the early struggle and disappointments of the settlers, the resources and potentialities of America which unfolded in the fullness of time were far beyond their wildest hopes and dreams. There was a wealth of natural resources—fertile soil, water, lumber, stone, coal, iron, copper, silver, gold, oil, and many other minerals.

[4] H. J. Carmen, *Social and Economic History of the United States* (Boston: D. C. Heath and Company, 1930), Vol. I, pp. 1–41.

Small but increasing quantities of capital from Europe, paid for by the agricultural exports of the colonies, made possible the expansion of the early home industries soon after the beginning of the nineteenth century. Inventions and importation of machinery from Europe greatly increased the utility of the resources. The demands for raw materials, the expanding needs of the people, and the acquirement of new skills made the way for developments in transportation and communication. The importation of Negroes and the influx of immigrants provided the necessary labor supply. An expanding frontier, coupled with the willingness of the colonists to break away from medieval patterns of trade, was a constant stimulus to rapid development.[5]

PRINCIPAL FACTORS IN AMERICAN URBAN DEVELOPMENT

Changing economic conditions were largely responsible for initiating cities, but certain additional factors in the development of America stand out as especially significant in the making, location, and expansion of cities. These factors may be grouped under several headings.

Geographic Factors. The geographic factors in the location and development of cities were always very significant and in combination with primary factors were determinative. For example, the necessity for port cities to handle trade and communication with other lands was a primary cause for many cities, but the geographic factors of protected harbors conveniently accessible to their hinterland and to deep-water seaways determined the location that port cities would have. The chief seaport towns of the early colonies through which the two worlds kept in contact were Boston, Newport, New York, Philadelphia, Charleston, and Savannah.[6]

The Spanish cities of the Pacific coast and the Southwest were established as missionary posts and operated simply for this purpose. Some of them, located on harbors and at other strategic places, became cities when the settlers from the East reached them.

The geographic factors changed in relative importance as other

---

[5] Harry Elmer Barnes, *The History of Western Civilization* (New York: Harcourt, Brace and Company, 1935), Vol. II, pp. 213, 356 ff., 406.

[6] E. Churchill Semple, *The Influence of Geographic Environment* (New York: Henry Holt and Company, 1911), pp. 1–101; Carl Bridenbaugh, *Cities in the Wilderness* (New York: The Ronald Press Company, 1938), p. 22.

factors changed; in the earlier years they had greater influence than in later years. In the settlement and growth of practically all American cities, however, the matter of geography was of outstanding importance. A number of different aspects of geography were significant.

Fertility of the soil has always been a primary element in settlement, but in the beginning of colonial days it was all-important because family life then depended upon agriculture for food and other needs.[7] In addition, however, the degree of fertility determined the number of families which could make their living in any area, and, in turn, the relative density of population determined the extent of hinterland which required a city.

Inasmuch as transportation in early years was largely by waterways, those which made trade with the interior possible set the pattern of the first urban developments. Here were the gateways from the interior to the Atlantic and the rest of the world. The more important were Long Island Sound and the Connecticut River, New York Bay and the Hudson River, Delaware Bay and the Delaware River, Chesapeake Bay and the Susquehanna and Potomac Rivers. Where navigation up the rivers was interrupted by the fall line, another group of inland commercial cities and transfer points sprang up—Hartford, Albany, Trenton, Richmond, Raleigh, Columbia, and Augusta.

Farther in the interior, the Mississippi River and its great tributaries extended navigation to the greater Mississippi River Valley; the St. Lawrence River and the Great Lakes served a great section of what is now the northern part of the United States and the southern part of Canada; these greatly assisted early settlement and trading. Where different waterways were separated by relatively short land distance, portages developed; with them forts and trading posts came into being. These were the beginnings of cities and to a large extent set the patterns of highway systems that have continued through the years. These portages were of sufficient importance to be the centers of the French and English wars for supremacy in the New World.[8]

Colonial Charters.   The colonies were established on charters given by the European kings who sponsored the enterprises. These charters designated certain areas of land within which settlement

[7] Bridenbaugh, op cit., p. 6.
[8] Ernest L. Bogart, Economic History of the American People (New York: Longmans, Green and Co., 1935), pp. 114, 115.

was to be made. This imposed geographic limits upon each colony. In the early years, however, this limitation was less significant than two incidental results of the procedure by charter. First, the people of each colony came from the same country, had the same backgrounds in tradition and custom, and spoke the same language. Second, familiarity with Old World social forms, and continued contacts with their former countries, made it natural and convenient to copy the type of life in the parts of Europe from which they had come.

Villages and their uses were already a part of the colonists' former experience; so, when the time was ripe, they began to establish this form of social arrangements in their new world. Consequently, their villages and towns, as they came into being, had patterns of life and custom very similar to those in the Old World.[9]

Independence and Expansion. The removal of restrictions enforced upon the colonists by the British system in the form of Navigation Acts (1740–1760), and the American Revolution (1775), gave strength and ambition to the new republic to establish economic and political independence of England (1789). Then, upon a better political and economic foundation, the Republic gave its attention to westward migration and settlement.

The migrants moved overland by the Cumberland Road and down the Ohio and Mississippi Rivers, starting settlements and developing trade. They left on their trail the beginnings of Pittsburgh, Wheeling, Zanesville, Columbus, Springfield, Indianapolis, Terre Haute, Vandalia, St. Louis, Cincinnati, Louisville, Memphis, and New Orleans. Others moved westward along the Hudson, the Mohawk, the St. Lawrence Valley, and the Great Lakes and established the settlements that have developed into the large cities of the present.

Even before many of these places were founded, Lewis and Clarke had ascended the Missouri River, crossed over to the Columbia River, and reached the Pacific, disclosing the resources of the Northwest.

Several things encouraged this migration. Population along the Atlantic seaboard was getting to what then seemed the saturation point. This was particularly true in the rocky, less fertile soil of New England. To get more room, more land, more fertile fields to sup-

---

[9] John Spencer Bassett, *A Short History of the United States* (New York: The Macmillan Company, 1935), pp. 1–75.

port more people, Connecticut sent out settlers to open up the Western Reserve.

Among the people of the early colonies there were restless souls, seeking adventure, wanting to be on the frontier. As things settled down into more regularized and routinized community life and neighbors came closer, these "Daniel Boones" were off to follow the frontier westward. It was easy for them to go in the greater freedom and democracy of the New World, where primogeniture had been discarded and the bonds which held "great" families together around ancestral homes were lessened. Brothers, sisters, and cousins, with their respective families, became scattered far and wide.

Once begun, the winning of the West continued for about two centuries as the frontier was pushed farther and farther westward until it reached the Pacific. Pioneer days were prolonged, and during most of this time, without easy communication and transportation, the experience of developing communities and cities was recapitulated again and again.

Transportation.   The key to the development of cities is to be found specifically in the extension of transportation more than in any other one factor. The full significance of transportation, however, can be seen only in connection with other factors: the economic necessity for trade, geography, the expansion of the hinterland, and the development of industry.

Cooley made a study of the location of cities in terms of transportation and the connections with the outside world and the rest of the country. He concluded: "Population and wealth tend to collect wherever there is a break in transportation."[10] These breaks varied in importance in terms of what was involved in the transfer of goods. If it was merely the moving of materials, the settlement was likely to be less than where trading and change of ownership took place.[11] This accounts for four groups: the seaport towns, the places along the waterways, the fall-line villages, and the portage settlements.

McKenzie has divided the development of America into three periods on the basis of the predominant type of transportation: water-

---

[10] Charles Horton Cooley, "The Theory of Transportation in Sociological Theory and Social Research," first published by the American Economic Association, May, 1904.

[11] For an extended discussion of this theory and the location of cities, see Noll P. Gist and L. A. Halbert, *Urban Society* (New York: Thomas Y. Crowell Company, 1941), pp. 78–88.

ways, railroads, and motor vehicles.[12] "From the beginning of colo‑
nial times to about the middle of the nineteenth century the natural
systems of water highways—including the seaboard and navigable
rivers and lakes, supplemented from time to time by canals and
other artificial extensions—determined the main outlines of settlement, expansion and the location of the principal centers of com‑
merce."[13] In later years, the extensive development of air transport
bids fair to have its influence upon urban development, although the
particulars cannot yet be defined.

Of the man-made extensions of transportation ways, the turnpike
and the Cumberland Road were important at the beginning of the
nineteenth century. The steamboat, from about the same time, was
widely used for many years.[14] Canals, beginning with the building
of the Erie Canal connecting Lake Erie with the Hudson River in
1823, were a great impetus to the birth of cities. This led to the
building of other canals in Pennsylvania, Massachusetts, Maryland,
Virginia, Ohio, Indiana, and Michigan. The great importance of the
Erie Canal, however, lay in the fact that it completed the great east-
west waterway. Up to this time, the outlet for the West was by the
north-south, Mississippi-Ohio system. Competition between the two
systems was strong, but the nearer access to the Old World through
New York, the disorganization of the shipping on the Mississippi-
Ohio system during the Civil War, and the development of railways
along the east-west way gave increasing advantage to the Hudson–
Erie Canal–Great Lakes system. Along the latter, many of the great
northern cities developed. During the first half of the nineteenth
century, forty-six of the ninety-four cities that in 1937 had over
100,000 population were incorporated.[15]

The fact that transportation facilities are of first importance in the
development of centers of population was well recognized in America. Baltimore determined to hold on to her commercial supremacy
and to counteract the advantages of the canal by a most revolutionary and spectacular scheme, the building of America's first railroad,
the Baltimore and Ohio. The era of railway transportation origi-

[12] R. D. McKenzie, *The Metropolitan Community* (New York: McGraw-
Hill Book Company, 1933), Chaps. I and X.
[13] By permission from *The Metropolitan Community*, by R. D. McKenzie,
Copyrighted, 1933. McGraw-Hill Book Co., Inc., p. 129.
[14] Bogart, *op. cit.*, pp. 311–315.
[15] Bureau of the Census, *Financial Statistics of Cities over 100,000 Population, 1937* (Washington: Government Printing Office, 1940), Table I.

nated about 1830 and began its dominant role by the middle of the century. The steel rails reached Chicago in 1852 and the Pacific coast in 1869.[16] When Chicago was taking over the supremacy of St. Louis, a newspaperman expressed the formula that has been successfully demonstrated again and again in the building of cities: natural advantages plus transportation plus aggressive men make cities.[17]

The Central Pacific, and the other railways related to it, played important roles in the development of Denver, San Francisco, Los Angeles, San Diego, Portland, Tacoma, Seattle, and Spokane. The promoters of these railroads often played one existing settlement against another in their efforts to raise capital for the development of their enterprises. As a member of the California Constitutional Convention in 1879 put it:

> They start out their railway track and survey their line near a thriving village. They go to the most prominent citizens of that village and say, "If you will give us so many thousand dollars we will run through here; if you do not we will run by"; and in every instance where the subsidy was not granted, that course was taken, and the effect was just as they said, to kill off the little town. Here was the town of Paradise, in Stanislaus County; because they did not get what they wanted, they established another town four miles from there. In every instance where they were refused a subsidy in money unless their terms were acceded to, they have established a depot near to the place, and always have frozen them out.[18]

The railroads were manipulable, as the waterways were not, and brought a new element into the development. In spite of certain difficulties related to special interests, this has been, in the long run, a great advantage. The railroad period, comprising approximately the second half of the nineteenth century, brought the greatest development of American towns. The early rivalry between seaboard towns was shifted to a race for western markets; and the areas of settlement were greatly extended.[19] Rivalry between railroads brought duplication of feeder lines to lakes and rivers and of branches to the main lines.[20] Many of these ceased to function later,

[16] McKenzie, op. cit., p. 131.
[17] G. C. Quiett, They Built the West (New York: D. Appleton-Century Co., 1934), pp. 83 f.
[18] Ibid., p. 83.
[19] Bogart, op. cit., pp. 328 ff.
[20] George R. Leighton, Five Cities (New York: Harper & Brothers, 1939), pp. 100–110.

and some new lines were added, but by the turn of the century the main outline of the present railroad systems was established, with nearly a half million miles of trackage.

Three things of importance in the urban development of America occurred in the process of the extension of railways during this period. First, the dominance of the east-west movement became established. The bulk of settlement which came during these years was along the east-west transportation line. Nearly half a billion acres were added to cultivation. There was a tremendous increase in population. The number of people west of the Mississippi increased many fold. The number of cities was rapidly multiplied. The increase in urban population far outran the increase in rural population. Not only were the railroads the greatest influence in the pattern of this development, but the greater convenience and dependability of shipments by rail added greatly to its stability.

The second thing of importance was that those places situated so as to be accessible to a large hinterland, at rail junction points, and at freight-rate breaking points, became increasingly important. The outstanding example is Chicago, which in 1840 had a population of only about 4000 but by 1890 had increased to 1,000,000 to become the second-largest city in the United States, far exceeding New Orleans and St. Louis in size and importance.

The third significant element in urban development in this railroad period was the closer integration of larger regions. In the years of waterway preëminence, areas related to one part of the transportation system were relatively isolated and developed a sectionalism and many cultural differences. The railroads, on the other hand, not only tended to bring these areas into closer relationships, but also developed regions around the cities which were closely integrated through their economic and social relationships as well as through closer communication. This pattern of city regionalism which developed has increased throughout the country and continues to be the basic pattern of American life.[21]

The period of motor transportation came with the twentieth century. While it did not change the basic pattern of urban development, it did serve to make several important modifications. The first great increase in hard-surfaced highways tended to center on the cities, especially in the more thickly settled areas. As arterial high-

[21] McKenzie, *op. cit.*, pp. 131–140.

ways have developed, however, their courses have been laid without regard for railway routes. As a result, many smaller cities have been given new impetus.

The most important aspect of this development has been to make short hauls by motor truck convenient and inexpensive. This has multiplied the avenues of contact within local areas and increased the significance of metropolitan regions.[22] This use of motor trucks, in combination with the development of electric power in industry, made it no longer necessary for manufacturing establishments to be located within the larger cities; consequently, during this period, urban decentralization began, a trend whose ultimate results cannot yet be foreseen.

While these aspects of transportation development just reviewed have been highly important, the full significance of transportation in the development of American cities can be seen only in its relation to the opening up of new natural resources and the development of industry.

New Natural Resources. The agricultural developments—wheat lands of the Northwest, corn lands of the west-central section, and the cattle of the West and Southwest—brought cities for markets, trading, storage, and processing. Points where the cattle trails crossed the transcontinental railroads became important cattle market and shipping points as Newton and Dodge City.[23]

Mineral resources, as they were discovered, added their influence to the location and development of cities. Coal made its cities in Pennsylvania, Colorado, and Wyoming. Iron, with the steel mills and the manufacturers using steel, had its influence in developing such cities as Pittsburgh, Bethlehem, Cleveland, Detroit, Duluth, Gary, and later Birmingham.[24] There were also silver and gold in Colorado and California, copper in Montana, and later the most spectacular of all, the oil cities—Los Angeles and Bakersfield, Tulsa and Oklahoma City, Dallas and Fort Worth, and others.

Industry. By 1812, the influence of the Napoleonic Wars, through the Nonintercourse Acts, gave a great impetus to the development of American manufacturing. "The immense capital which had been employed in commerce previously to the restrictions, was trans-

[22] *Ibid.*, pp. 140–143.
[23] Bogart, *op. cit.*, p. 518.
[24] *Ibid.*, p. 562; Leighton, *op. cit.*, pp. 100 ff.

ferred to manufacturers and workshops; mills and machinery for the fabrication of commodities were erected, as if by enchantment."[25] For the first time the new American republic had its own industrial market to itself. These new circumstances were met with a new type of industrial development. "Concentration of all the processes of manufacture in a factory involving their withdrawal from the household and shop where they had previously been carried on; use of specialized machines, driven by non-human power, and the organization of the workers under skilled management, for stipulated wages and fixed hours, with production for the general market and not upon order."[26]

The first American protecitve tariff was passed in 1816. At the same time the factory system was expanding. Factory towns sprang up on the streams of New England and the middle states. Lowell, Lawrence, Holyoke, Fall River, Cohoes, Paterson are examples.

Through the early part of the nineteenth century, water power ran the factories; then came the application of steam to factory machines. The Industrial Revolution, so called, did not take hold in the United States until after the Civil War. The industrial cities of the South did not come into being until a later time.

Steam had a centripetal influence upon the development of cities. "Since steam is most cheaply produced in large quantities and must be used close to where it is produced, from which point the power it generates can be extended only over limited distances by means of shafting, belts, and pulleys, it fostered the concentration of manufacturing processes and large units of production."[27] So steam vastly increased the potentialities of living for the people, but it also drained off an increasing proportion of the population from tilling the soil; and it made possible, through the railroads, the transportation of adequate foodstuffs and raw materials to cities, and manufactured commodities away from the cities. So more and more people, drawn from rural America and from across the sea, came to the cities to supply the needs for industrial and civic labor.

For the first time the essentials for the development of great cities were brought together: sufficient experience in civic and social organization, power, labor supply, capital, inventive agencies, transportation, freedom from restrictions on interstate commerce, leaders

---

[25] Bogart, *op. cit.*, p. 383.
[26] *Ibid.*, p. 384.
[27] National Resources Committee, *op. cit.*, p. 30.

in civic, commercial, and industrial enterprise. Cities grew by leaps and bounds. In 1850 there were only six cities of 100,000 population or over, with 5.1 percent of the total population; by 1900 there were thirty-eight cities of this size, with 18.7 percent of the total population.

The next major development in American industry, the application of electricity to machine production, came during the second decade of the twentieth century. This made a much more flexible use of machinery possible, so that plants could be laid out for the most efficient production, taking advantage of all the potentialities of line production. The necessity for the concentration of industry near the sources of power in the centers of the cities was removed because electricity was easily transmitted by means of cables and wires. Electric power, combined with motor-truck transportation, as already noted, started the removal of industry from the big cities, a fact which has been markedly reflected in the reports of the 1940 Census.

More recently the photoelectric cell has been combined with electric power to make automatic machinery. This had three effects upon industrial production. First, machines could do things which could not be done before, and do them more rapidly and more efficiently. Second, industry required fewer workers, so that jobs became less stable and technological unemployment more frequent. Third, the release of workers from industry made a greater development of the service occupations possible. This marked a great advance, but made many acute problems for cities.

One further aspect of industry has had an equivocal effect upon the development of cities. This is its nomadic character. "The very forces which made for localization tended also to cause the migration of industry when these advantages showed themselves more strongly in other localities."[28]

Agricultural implement factories moved from New York to Ohio and Illinois to be nearer the areas of their distribution. Following the retreat of the forests, the lumber industry moved along the northern boundary of the United States from Maine to Washington. With the opening of the great grain-producing lands of the Northwest, flour-milling shifted from Rochester to Minneapolis. Slaughtering and meat-processing centralized in Chicago and then dispersed to Omaha and other places nearer the cattle ranges. Paper

[28] Bogart, *op. cit.*, p. 569.

mills formerly used rags in Holyoke, but now use wood pulp in Wisconsin, Canada, and the southern states. Although industrial development in the South still lags far behind the North, since the depression many textile factories have moved from New England to the southern states to be nearer raw materials and a cheap labor supply, as well as to be able to operate with less capital outlay.

THE URBAN WAY OF LIFE

Village life was a new kind of life. In the first place, the people who lived in villages carried on the new functions and provided the new services which the villages required for their activities. These were particular jobs and had little, if anything, to do directly with the people's lives. This marked the beginning of specialization. So the villages were made up of different kinds of people in terms of vocations, of interests, and of activities. Foreigners also began to drift in from the Old World and from other sections of the New World, which further complicated village life. In the second place, new patterns of human relationships arose. No longer were families self-sufficient; they became dependent upon others for the very essentials of living. In contrast to those engaged in agriculture, whose homes were relatively isolated and whose contacts with other people were relatively rare, village people lived in houses which were right next door to each other; and they had daily contacts with those outside their immediate family groups.

Living in such proximity immediately imposed a whole range of social problems entirely outside the experience of farm people. In turn, the solution of these problems created the need for community or public service, and also the need for additional commercial services to supply the needs of village families which they were no longer in a position to supply by their own direct efforts.

The problems of this new type of living and the social inventions which were developed to meet them were exceedingly important elements in the development of cities. They established certain characteristics of urban life which have persisted through the years. While these problems seem perfectly obvious and matter-of-fact today, in the beginning of our cities they were baffling and serious. Some of the more important, by way of illustration, were fire, streets, crime, poverty, disease, and community property.

Social Problems. The hazard of fire took on a new aspect. So long as houses were far removed from each other, when one burned down, it was a great calamity to the family which owned it, but the loss and the concern were theirs alone. Neighbors might sympathize and assist in taking care of the family burned out, and even give them materials and labor for the construction of a new house, but this was their only concern. When the neighbor's home was next door, however, it was a different matter. A fire in one house was a direct danger and usually brought partial or total loss to the houses adjacent to it. Protection against fire became a community problem. This led to certain required specifications for buildings. Chimneys built of wood and plaster were forbidden. In some cases, houses had to be built of brick or stone. Then provision for a water supply for fighting fires was necessary.

Individual care of the sections of street in front of each house did not work out satisfactorily, because responsibility was accepted unequally and streets were used by all. The construction and maintenance of streets became a community problem.

As the towns grew and gathered within them more and more people to participate in their increasing functions, they also collected some who were parasites on the community and some who were criminally inclined. Opportunities for theft, exploitation, and violence were greater in places of concentrated population. So crime and delinquency grew, and the necessity for maintaining order and protection increased. This, again, was a community concern and called for organization and planning.

Pauperism developed partly as a concomitant of the drift of undesirable elements from the wars and from the ships to the towns, and partly because there was no place in the households of town families for the distant kin. There were some unemployed, and the unfit from illness and accident also increased. These people could no longer be taken care of on a family basis.

Disease became a community problem, primarily because of the increased danger of contagion, with more people living in closer contact. Sanitation and other matters of health also had to be dealt with on a community basis.

Each community had certain equipment that was needed for its convenience and business—pumps for the wells, fire-fighting equipment, bridges, wharves, harbors, and others. These were of benefit to all, to some directly and to others indirectly. All of these things had to be paid for and maintained. Coöperative participation broke down because those who did not directly benefit were reluctant to pay their share in money and work; consequently, the enterprises had to be carried out by community organization and taxes.[29]

The solutions of these problems brought a much greater development in organized community life, both in government and in private enterprise; and they brought the villages further on the road toward becoming cities. The people took over those methods and means of the Old World which were useful and practical in the New World—for example, the curfew which required that in all houses fires must be banked or put out between the ringing of the bells at nine in the evening and five in the morning. The ingenuity of the colonists, however, soon went far beyond the Old World methods, particularly in the development of coöperative organization. Most of the American towns were well in advance of European towns of the same period in the development of their corporate life. The New England town meeting was a new venture, and exceedingly effective, in the advance of community life, and it laid the foundations of democratic government.

Some of the problems were taken care of by private organizations. Churches formed societies to furnish assistance to the indigent. The taverns, to a large extent, took care of the need for recreation. So the pattern of both public and private enterprise in the solution of social problems was begun. As cities have become larger and the problems more extensive and more complicated, this pattern has persisted, with a corresponding development of complexity in organization. More and more people became necessary to conduct community affairs, from the early days, when citizens were conscripted for the tasks of night watch and constable, to later times, when many people were employed full time for the work of the various activities of government and private agency activities.

The social advance of cities, which came under the pressure of necessity, brought prestige. As the process has continued, this prestige has grown, and the influence of cities has been greatly extended.

Tackling the vexing social problems of city life stimulated intellectual leadership. The closer contacts with the Old World, the concentration of skilled and professional people in cities, and the relatively greater educational opportunities which cities afforded have continued this leadership throughout the history of America.

Appearance of Social Cleavages. A distinctive society developed in American urban communities out of their unique circumstances of life.

[29] Bridenbaugh, *op. cit.*, pp. 55–94, 100–107, 257–265, 418–419.

The accumulation of economic resources and their concentration in urban units, their direction in commercial venture which attracted and supported large populations within these units, and the problems of providing for the physical and social well-being of those who thus became city-dwellers, all these aspects of urban development succeeded in bringing forth in America a distinctive society. In constitution, spiritual life, recreational activities and intellectual pursuits, it differed from types of society to be found in other sections of the continent.[30]

One of the results of the distinctive character of city life was its separation from the kind of life which continued in the country. People in farm families went on being busy with the many kinds of work which were centered in their own families; village people, on the other hand, were engaged in specialized work, with the focus of their concern in the community. Rural people were still, for the most part, isolated in their immediate environments, while people in the towns were brought more and more in contact with the outside world. These different experience worlds made it increasingly difficult for farm and village people to understand each other. Cleavages arose and conflicts deepened; and they increased into the twentieth century. Only through the impact of the development in communication and transportation have the lines of separation begun to break down in the last decades.

Social cleavages also tended to develop within the embryonic urban centers. The economically more enterprising and more fortunate, and the professional and better-educated people, tended to associate more closely and formed cliques. The indigent and the ne'er-do-wells were far removed in their associations and ways of life. In between were the business people and artisans, who began to form what has been called the "middle class." Immigrant and racial groups, Negroes and Indians, made up their own groupings. Each group took on partial separateness, and cleavages of many kinds began to develop.

Not the least significant of the groupings were caused by religious differences. Not only were religious cleavages at the bottom of many of the interesting happenings and tales of colonial days, but they were sufficiently acute to have been the reason for the founding of cities like Portsmouth, Providence, New Haven, and later Salt Lake City.

[30] Carl Bridenbaugh, *Cities in the Wilderness,* Copyright 1938, The Ronald Press Company, p. 477. See also Carmen, *op. cit.,* pp. 170 ff.

Stabilization. Although the relationships between the New World and the Old were close up to the middle of the eighteenth century, the new kind of life developing in America continued to draw them spiritually apart. Communal life fostered a coöperative spirit and a social consciousness which was less individualistic. The colonists in the towns were constantly widening their outlook toward material progress and commercial expansion. Contact with the larger world of interests made them more susceptible to outside influences. They became more polished, urbane, and sophisticated, more aware of fashion and change. As a result, they could meet the representatives of the outside world as equals.

In their positions as centers of transit between the Old and New Worlds, the towns were the channels through which commodities of all sorts flowed; not the least of these commodities were world thought and knowledge, which were assimilated and redistributed throughout the countryside. The outlook of the people continued to be eastward, and their contacts with Europe were strong.

The people in the rural agricultural areas went on in relative isolation and self-sufficiency. They were, for the most part, ignorant of outside developments and distrustful of new ideas from abroad. So the diverging ways of rural and urban America carried them farther and farther apart.[31]

In this process, the urban way of life took form and became stabilized. In the early years, its influence was out of all proportion to the small part of the population it involved. The power of urban influence has continued, although not until the end of the second decade of the twentieth century did the urban population reach a majority in the United States. Even now, however, the distribution of representation in government puts the balance of power in the rural population. In the middle of the twentieth century, nevertheless, it can be realistically said that America is an urban nation.

SUMMARY

This is the background against which American cities have developed. The story is a "piece" of the story of the development of the country. Many factors have entered into the increase in urbanization. There is no simple or single explanation.

Cities had their beginnings in the economic pressures which cre-

[31] Bridenbaugh, *op. cit.*, p. 481.

ated commerce and later industry. Their locations and respective developments and importance came as a result of various combinations of a group of factors: geography, original colonial charters, independence and expansion, transportation developments, the opening up of new natural resources, and the expansion of industry.

As cities developed, there appeared an urban way of life, due to the impact of conditions out of which social problems arose and to the necessity for solving these problems through community-organized efforts. The result of this new way of life engendered cleavage, both between cities and the rest of the country, and also between the various segments of population within the cities. As the country has developed, however, the urban way of life has increased in its influence and scope until it has become predominant in America.

A more detailed analysis of the growth of cities gives further point to these considerations. Before this, however, it seems wise to see what cities are.

Supplementary Reading

Allen, Robert S. (editor). *Our Fair City.* New York: The Vanguard Press, 1947.
> Brief sketches of selected cities emphasizing serious problems and political manipulation and control.

Bridenbaugh, Carl. *Cities in the Wilderness.* New York: The Ronald Press Company, 1938.
> A history of the United States built around the development of cities. Especially valuable for the sections on the emergence and development of social problems.

Leighton, George R. *Five Cities.* New York: Harper & Brothers, 1939.
> Historical and analytical articles about five unique and interesting American cities.

Perry, George Sessions. *Cities of America.* New York: McGraw-Hill Book Company, 1947.
> Descriptive portraits of various American cities emphasizing unique characteristics and individuality.

Schlesinger, Arthur Meier. *The Rise of the City: 1878–1898.* New York: The Macmillan Company, 1938.
> Deals with that period in American history during which cities began to be of great importance.

CHAPTER 3

WHAT IS A CITY?

ANY attempt to define a city encounters serious difficulties. The factors of definition are relative, not absolute, so that they indicate quantitative rather than qualitative differences. Some have escaped the difficulties by stating what a city is not; others have by-passed the difficulties by pointing out the predominant characteristics of cities. Neither of these is satisfactory, for they fail to indicate what makes a city a city.

The threads of the distinctive character of a city, however, have already been picked up in the exploration of how cities emerged and developed in the American scene. These are the clues to definition.

DEFINITION OF A CITY

Many people came together in strategic places to engage in the various kinds of work which were necessary to carry on commerce and industry. These were specialized occupations; and people with other specialized occupations found these places convenient and congenial for the pursuit of their work. This necessitated other specialized services to make it possible for the specialists to live, but it also was necessary to develop complex overall organization to enable the whole community to operate successfully. These are the factors of what a city is. No one of them alone, but all of them, in combination with their interrelationships, make a city. To put it in the form of a definition:

A city is a community consisting of a large concentration of population in a relatively limited geographical area, activated by the production of manufactured goods and/or the distribution of various kinds of goods and services, involving a high degree of specialization and complicated social and political organization.

32

A city is a community. "A community is a population aggregate, inhabiting a contiguous territory, integrated through common experience, possessing a number of basic service institutions, conscious of its local unity, and able to act in a corporate capacity."[1] But a city is not only a highly developed community; it is a particular kind of community.

The factor which appears to distinguish cities more than any other is the kind of production that forms the basis of economic life. People are engaged in fabricating and exchanging things—artifacts made out of raw materials brought from the outside. This is in striking contrast to the production, in the more fundamental sense of creation, in the agriculture of rural America. Even in the few cities that have grown up around mining, life is dominated by highly mechanized processes. Not only does this fundamental factor of urban life make a different set of vocations for its people, but it also makes a great difference in the character of all phases of living. It removes people from any dependence on, or direct relation to, the land and the natural processes and puts them in the midst of entirely artificial, in the primary sense of man-made, surroundings. So land is valuable only as space, and operations are carried on according to convenience and not by nature—the sun, the seasons, and the weather.

Cities exist for the purposes of commerce and industry. As in any community, there must be an economic base in production. Cities produce all sorts of manufactured goods and various kinds of services. The distribution of these commodities is quite as important as their production. In fact, the process of distribution involves not only those things which are made in a city, but things which are made in other cities as well as those raw materials and foodstuffs which are produced in agriculture, fishing, and mining.

The city . . . is the workshop of American civilization. In 1929 there were concentrated in 155 counties, containing the larger industrial cities, 64.7 percent of all the industrial establishments, 74 percent of all industrial wage earners, 80.7 percent of all salaried officers and employees. Moreover, 78.8 percent of all wages and 82.9 percent of all salaries in the country were paid in these counties. The value of the products of these establishments produced was 79 percent of the country's total. They had installed 64.2 percent of the total horsepower classed as "prime movers"

[1] From *Community Backgrounds of Education*, by Lloyd Allen Cook. Copyright, 1938. Courtesy of McGraw-Hill Book Co., p. 27.

and 72.5 percent of the electric motors. They were credited with 80.2 percent of all the value added to products by manufacturing. Eighty-three percent of all of the wholesale trade in the United States was carried on in 127 counties, and the counties containing the 11 largest cities alone accounted for over one-half of the total, while the 93 cities over 100,000 reported over three-fourths of the total. Not only are the cities and especially the great cities, the industrial workshops of the Nation that produce the bulk of its manufactured products and employ and support the majority of its working population, but they are also the managerial, service, and commercial distributing centers.

It is in the cities, furthermore, that the transportation and communication lines converge, and it is from the cities, which are the traditional home of invention, that the technical facilities characteristic of modern civilization are diffused to other areas. Thus, 73 percent of all railway traffic terminates in urban areas; the single metropolis of New York contains over 500 freight stations within a radius of 35 miles of the city. Half of all railroad passengers either begin or end their journeys in 12 metropolitan cities. The use of electric energy is confined almost entirely to cities, since 86 percent of the population for whom electric energy is available live in urban communities. The urban areas make the most use of aviation, of rapid transit, of telephones, and the telegraph. Nearly 40 percent of all the mail in the United States originates in 12 metropolitan cities.[2]

All of these things act as a centripetal force which draws a large number of people into the city and holds them there, not temporarily gathered together, but maintaining families, supplying daily needs, worshiping, and carrying on the affairs of the community—so keeping in operation the major social institutions of family, church, government, and business.

The organization of business takes many forms, from large complex establishments with many employees, down to many one-man concerns. It engages in manufacturing, processing, trade, communication, transportation, and the dispensing of all sorts of services. Government in cities is no longer simply administration, legislation, courts, and protection, but extends also to streets and highways, sanitation and health, education, parks and recreation, and many other things. Many people are engaged in these activities. The social service agencies—some public and some private—are many, in health, child welfare, social case work, group work, education, rec-

[2] National Resources Committee, *Our Cities: Their Role in the National Economy,* Report of the Urbanism Committee (Washington: Government Printing Office, 1937), pp. 2–3.

reation, and other areas; and they extend vocational opportunities to large numbers of people. Religion also is highly organized and uses additional professional people. Beyond all this, the organized life of cities contains almost countless associations of people related to special interests of all sorts.

The city's work is done in smaller space, demands more people for many different kinds of activity, and must have them readily accessible. The circumstances of city life make people dependent on others for the necessities of life, and also for their jobs, while larger cash incomes and greater opportunities give them the illusion of independence. The circumstances of life, the ways by which men make their living, the multiplicity of human relationships, and the variety of problems which must be met by virtue of the quantity of people living and working in relatively close quarters, make a different kind of people and a distinct way of life.

A further clue to understanding the fundamental differentiation of urban communities is found in a statement by Anderson and Lindeman:

A city is what a city does. A city is among other things, a state of mind, a way of behaving. When the primary relationships that characterize village and town life have yielded to something more complex, when the neighborhood has broken up into smaller and more isolated units which are separated according to their diverse interests, we can call a community a city. When a number of unlike groups gather, no longer related and kept in control by the old folk-craft, then we have the beginning of metropolitan life; formal control is initiated and law comes to take the place of custom. The work of the city, as of any impersonal institution, is the beginning of rules—when control comes through some intermediate agency.[3]

The legalizing and extension of social controls are evidences of the complexity of problems that arise where many people live in close proximity. In turn, the multiplicity of rules and regulations under which people must live conditions their living by forming habits of behavior and by shaping attitudes which leave their marks upon the character of people.

It is for people that cities exist and by people that they are made to operate as living things. Cities must be alive. The material aspects of cities loom so large that they can easily be mistaken for

[3] Nels Anderson and Eduard C. Lindeman, *Urban Sociology* (New York: Alfred A. Knopf, 1928), p. xxviii.

more important things. Clarence A. Dykstra has laid emphasis upon the life that is the city.

Cities are not alone legal, physical, and economic entities. They are—and this is, after all, their fundamental characteristic—made up of human beings. Whoever in his contemplation of cities thinks only of brick and stone, highways and buildings, industry and business, avoids many difficulties and thinks he settles many problems. In the last analysis, however, he settles nothing, for he has neglected all those psychological factors which, after all, are controlling in the history and growth of self-governing communities.

The city, besides all else, is a way of life, a method of living. It is a mechanism or device for getting satisfactions out of life. It faces the same problems in its planning that the individual does when he organizes his own life. The individual without a purpose finds little satisfaction in living, even if that purpose be as mundane as the search for financial security. The city, too, must have an objective—something to look forward to and work for if it is to be psychologically sound. In such an objective may be included comfort, beauty, happiness, or distinction in some field of joint endeavor.[4]

So the beginning and the end of the city is the people. Cities are not ends, but rather means—means to provide the facilities for good living to their people. The *raison d'être* of cities is to be found in the needs and wants of people. A city is good or efficient or beautiful or successful to the degree that it provides the opportunity for a good life and makes it possible for all of its people to experience the good life. It is only against this fundamental fact that the many aspects of cities make any sense.

One further practical matter in the definition of cities: the United States Census has designated places having 2500 inhabitants or more as urban.[5] The Census definition must of necessity be followed in all of the statistical treatment of urban populations.

CHARACTERISTICS OF CITIES

While the definition of cities gives the clue to an understanding of what cities are, it gives very little help in knowing what cities are

---

[4] Clarence A. Dykstra, Introduction to George W. Robbins and L. Deming Tilton (editors), *Los Angeles: Preface to a Master Plan* (Los Angeles: The Pacific Southwest Academy, 1941), p. 3.

[5] Bureau of the Census, *Sixteenth Census of the United States, 1940: Population: First Series: Number of Inhabitants* (Washington: Government Printing Office, 1941), p. 3.

like. It is necessary, therefore, to find some common descriptive qualities of cities. What things would an alert person who had never seen a city before observe? Many of the phenomena which mark the peculiarities of urban life are clearly apparent. City people, however, are so accustomed to them that they take them for granted; it would never occur to them to point them out as characteristics of cities, but they are important. These phenomena may be grouped under three headings: physical characteristics, activity characteristics, and human characteristics.[6]

Physical Characteristics. First observations take in the distinctive material aspects of a city.

Built Up. Cities are built up. The larger the city, the greater the concentration of structures. Buildings touch each other; they are separated here and there by paved streets bordered by narrow cement sidewalks. Open spaces are conspicuously absent. Sunlight makes its way to the ground with difficulty. Here and there one may find a park pressed in on all sides by buildings. Even in the sections where people live, space is lacking. In some parts of the cities, dwellings are also solidly built; farther out, detached family residences are for the most part on narrow lots, with little more space between them than is taken up with automobile driveways. Only in the suburbs can space be found.

Quantity and Variety of Buildings. A number and variety of buildings are on every hand. In the great cities are the stores, block after block, street after street, all kinds and sizes from the great department stores, sometimes a block in extent, with many floors where almost anything can be had, to the little hole in the wall with only cheap jewelry or hot dogs. There are many different kinds of stores, each with its particular lines of goods, and sometimes a number of the same kind within the same block. Large buildings filled with offices of all sorts are to be found one after another on some streets; business offices, lawyers' offices, railway and steamship offices, doctors' offices, salesrooms, offices of organizations and clubs,

[6] S. A. Queen and L. F. Thomas, *The City: A Study of Urbanism in the United States* (New York: McGraw-Hill Book Company, 1939), pp. 4–9. Here are gathered together the various "criteria" which urban sociologists have used in defining cities. Most of these are here designated as characteristics of cities. While it is true that wherever we find a city these factors are present and that wherever these factors are found there is a city, nevertheless, these phenomena are not so much what makes cities cities as they are characteristics which cities manifest.

artists' studios, and lofts which turn out to be small manufacturing establishments. Then there are factories, the large ones by the railway tracks or along the rivers, the small ones tucked away in most unexpected places. Warehouses and storage buildings are sometimes away off on the side streets, at other times right in the midst of things.

Apartment houses line blocks and streets in some sections, modern cliff dwellings in which many city people live. Then there are rows of houses all just alike, reaching their climax in Baltimore, with its hundreds of white marble steps. Other sections have streets of small detached houses, all built from the same plans. There are districts with the more spacious individual houses of the well-to-do and, finally, the mansions of the wealthy.

Flow of Materials. The constant flow of materials cannot escape notice. In the business districts, trucks are backed up to the curbs, loading and unloading boxes. In the residential sections, delivery wagons stop here and there to deliver goods that have been purchased. Downtown, in some places, boys can be seen pushing hand trucks or carrying large packages. Among the apartment houses, boys will be pushing three-wheeled carts of grocery orders. On the main traffic ways will be seen huge trucks with all sorts of labels, and motor-tanks filled with gasoline or milk. Small delivery trucks dart in and out with their bundles of newspapers at almost any hour. Long trains of freight cars roll in and out of the depots every day.

Transportation Facilities. Means of transportation are in evidence on every hand, not only those that are engaged in the constant flow of goods, but also vehicles for the movement of people. Streetcars of various types and age are still found in some cities, although they are rapidly being replaced by buses. There are buses of all kinds and sizes, from small affairs in the outlying sections to great double-deckers plying the main thoroughfares of the largest cities. Express highways have been built in some cities to expedite the movement of private passenger cars, which can be seen by the thousand plying the streets by day and parked at the curbs by night. Elevated trains rattle along overhead, and subways speed their way underneath the streets. In a number of cities, notably San Francisco, cable cars are still in use. Hundreds of trains of commuters roll into the larger cities each morning between 7:30 and 9:00 and out again in the afternoons from 4:30 to 6:00.

Contrasts. One cannot long be in any city without being impressed by the contrasts of all sorts. In the large cities, contrasts are very striking. Almost beside the new modern skyscrapers can be seen the ancient tenements without any of the present-day conveniences. There are buildings going up and buildings falling down. The palaces of the rich are not far from the slums of the poor. Magnificent hotels are matched by flophouses. Looking in any direction, one can see the beautiful and the ugly. The bare, cold, asphalt streets, surrounded by cement and walls of stone and brick, are not a great distance from green grass, trees, and flowers in parks. The avenues along which people clothed in the latest styles walk and ride across the side streets where others in rags make their way. Palaces and hovels, riches and poverty, new and old, health and disease, beauty and ugliness, selfishness and service, love and hate, all make their homes in the cities.

Congestion. Everywhere there is congestion. Buildings in a solid mass, people crowded on the streets, automobiles and trucks so thick that they can scarcely move, hundreds waiting in line to enter the motion-picture theaters, people so closely packed in public conveyances that the doors will barely close. Every way you turn, things and people press in upon you. While such intense congestion has long been present in the largest cities, it is becoming true to some degree of even the smaller cities, as is evident when one must drive through these cities. There is a sense of being cramped and smothered, which city people are used to but people from the country find terrifying and oppressive.

Activity Characteristics. Activity is everywhere in cities. It encompasses people and carries them along in spite of their resistance.

Rapidity of Life. Life moves rapidly in cities. In the big city, everyone and everything seems to be in a hurry. People walk fast, automobiles and trucks speed along to make one more block before traffic lights change, streetcars and buses rush along, making their stops and starts quickly, subway trains rush at sixty miles an hour for three miles between stops, elevators ascend and descend fifty stories in a single flight. The lives of city people are habituated to movement and to speed.

Fluidity of Life. The crowds and this rapid pace converge to make a fluidity of life. East and west, north and south, up and down, the population constantly flows. Into the buildings of business in the morning, out to the streets at noon, into the buses, automobiles, and subways when the work is over, back to the Great White Way in the evenings. Into and out of the lower third of Manhattan Island of New York flow nearly four million people every working day.

Specialization. Apparent on every hand is a highly developed specialization of activity. People spend their lives at single jobs, many of which are not found away from cities: paper-sellers, traffic officers, motormen, bus-drivers, telegraph boys, doormen, elevator boys, white wings, salesmen, porters, waiters, cashiers, to name but a few of the more obvious of the hundreds.

Greater Opportunity. The great variety of opportunity which these specializations afford in many phases of life is the basis for the lure and fascination of cities. There are vocations to meet the interests and abilities of all sorts of people. Many jobs, different ways of making a living, some dull and routine, others challenging and exciting, are present in the city; many earn their livelihood doing the things that away from the cities can be only leisure-time hobbies.

A variety of amusement and entertainment is available: motion-picture theaters, large and small, with and without stage shows; the legitimate stage; baseball games and other professional athletic contests, including prize fighting; exhibitions; celebrations; special events; and countless others.

Opportunities for participating in recreational activities are afforded by parks, athletic fields, gymnasiums, skating rinks, bowling alleys, and like places. Recreation and education can be combined in symphony concerts, artist recitals, opera, historical and art and natural history museums, zoos and aquariums. Educational possibilities are many and varied, with all sorts of lectures, forums, and classes.

The social service organizations of cities have developed many services to afford greater human welfare: financial aid to different types of dependent people; family services; child welfare; counseling for social, psychological, and vocational adjustment; health services, with clinics, lectures, visiting nurses, and activities for the prevention of disease and accidents.

The many churches in the cities testify to the wide variety of religious expression that is to be found: famous preachers and professional music in the great churches on the avenues, little store-front churches on the side streets. Some churches confine their activities to traditional services of worship; others are highly developed social institutions, with community programs comprised of educational, recreational, and social as well as religious activities.

To illustrate the interesting opportunities which cities afford for varied experiences are the many different kinds of eating. The roster of restaurants includes the swanky and the plain, the expensive and the cheap, leisurely dining and quick lunches, those serving foreign foods of many kinds, others specializing in particular kinds of food; surroundings may be simple or bizarre, plain or atmospheric; meals may be with or without liquor, with or without music, with or without floor shows, with or without dancing; there are sidewalk cafés, night clubs, tea shoppes, roof gardens, lunch counters, and hot-dog and soft-drink stands.

Two other activity characteristics of cities can scarcely escape observation.

Being Built. Cities are never finished. Something is always being built. Old buildings are being torn down, new ones are being erected. Trolley rails are being torn up to clear the streets for bus lines. Pavements are being repaired or relaid. Stores and apartment houses are being remodeled. On every hand there are evidences of cities being built.

Cleaning Dirt. Cities are dirty. Those with many industries are dirtier than others. Constant accumulation of dirt inside and outside necessitates an everlasting process of cleaning. Men are cleaning streets, janitors are hosing sidewalks, sanitation trucks are collecting refuse. The fronts of buildings are being cleaned by steam or sand blast. Park attendants are spearing bits of paper from lawns and flower beds. Washings are hanging on lines between apartment houses or on roofs. Laundries and cleaning establishments are sometimes several to a block. Car-washing signs are seen in front of garages and service stations. Women are shaking dust mops out of windows. Dirt is always accumulating, and cleaning is forever going on in cities.

Human Characteristics. The characteristics of city people are in many respects subtle and difficult to understand, but there are several marks of urban humanity that will not escape an observer.

Heterogeneity. To look at the faces of those one passes on city streets or sees in a city crowd is to speculate on the background of the people. Many different types of features represent almost the whole range of nationalities. Some are very pronounced, others bear slight traces of another world. Names on store windows with their different endings, -itch, -ian, -son, -sen, etc., check the observations. Economic and social differences can also be seen in the faces and the clothing of the people. So also are good fortune, bad luck, the stresses and strains of life, worry, hope, despair, and determination clearly portrayed. The whole range of human personalities is laid out before one in a brief walk along the city streets.

Anonymity. With all the crowds, people are individuals, and cities tend to keep each person on his own. It is a rarity to see two persons speak on the street. Each goes his way, scarcely noticing the others about him, bent on his own course. People are jammed together in crowded streets; on public conveyances, bodies are in close contact; and yet people are oblivious of the nearness of others. There is an impersonality about persons. Life is strikingly anonymous. The most lonesome place in the world is in a crowd in a great city.

These appearances of anonymity have deeper roots, which have serious implications for the personalities and behavior of city people. When individuals are isolated from intimate continuous association with others and have to make their decisions and take their actions largely on their own responsibility, they do so outside the most powerful of social controls—what other people will think of them, and the gossip of the neighborhood. Many break under the strain of this responsibility, and others use the circumstances as protection for nefarious practices and immoral self-indulgence.

Similarity. In spite of the wide differences that mark city people and the individuality that they bear, there is also a striking similarity among them. There is a likeness about their clothes, which are more or less in the latest style. Women's hair-do's, their use of cosmetics, and the color of their stockings, give them a similar look. Men depart little from conventional attire and clean-shaven faces. The ordinary daily behavior patterns are alike; the automatic impersonal reactions to contacts with others, the general lack of courtesy and consideration, the indifferent pursuit of their own business are present.

City people seem to be forever reading newspapers, purchasing things in the many stores, riding the same transportation conveyances—always in a hurry. In spite of the differences in their faces, they appear much alike.

Obvious but Unobservable Characteristics. Other marks of cities can be readily deduced from the characteristics which are apparent, although, in themselves, they cannot be observed.

Highly Developed Government. The organizational machinery and controls that are essential to keep a city going smoothly are very complicated. Evidences of this are to be observed on every hand. Many types of protection are necessary; fire, police, and traffic are the most obvious. Protection of people against disease and accidents is clearly essential though somewhat less evident. Control and operation of public services such as transportation, communication, and the utilities must be taken care of. General movements and relations of people cannot be neglected where so many people in relatively small areas are concerned. All of these things, in addition to their coördination and integration, the administration of the many services that are made available, and the proper functioning of the political affairs of the people, could not be carried on without a well-established and legally supported government. Highly developed forms of government in cities are to be expected. (Cf. Chap. 15.)

Complicated Social Organization. The many needs of such large numbers of people, the complexity of human relationships, the necessity for simple grouping within the total life, make it clear that social organization must be exceedingly complex. Evidences of social organization are on every hand, but many agencies and associations, such as coördinating agencies, research institutes, and personal services, which one might well expect to exist, cannot be seen.

Cultural Centers. Although the diffusion of developments in American culture is much more rapid in this day of radio and rapid transportation, the hinterland is still sufficiently slow in the absorption of the new to give one who comes to the city an impression of an abundance of new things. New gadgets, new styles, new conveniences are to be found all about; but, more than this, there are new ideas in the air, and new habits of living, acting, and thinking can be observed.

Conditions are such in cities that new things have a better chance of acceptance. The adoption of the new in cities eventuates in cultural changes that are gradually diffused throughout the country. In a very real sense, the cities form the spearhead of cultural change.

In the narrower sense of the word, cities are also cultural centers, for in them the arts—music, drama, architecture, painting, sculpture, literature, and the others—have their greatest support and, consequently, their highest development, and their influence radiates from the cities.

These are the more marked characteristics which cities have, some more, some less. Their beginnings can be observed in smaller cities; they are developed to a high degree in the great cities. In addition, certain measurable differences between urban and rural areas can be pointed out.

URBAN-RURAL CONTRASTS

A quarter of a century ago, the chief characteristics of cities were found in the very clear differences between city and country, which could be seen in the comparison of urban and rural statistics. Sociologies have been written on this basis.[7] At that time, this type of analysis was a substantial basis for determining the characteristics of cities and their people. The changes which have taken place in recent years, however, make it clear that these differences are not real, for they are tending to grow less and less. Furthermore, the differences reflect regional differences more than they indicate differences between city and country.[8]

Differences between cities and country which might still be pointed out are not so much differences in themselves as they reflect differences in opportunities, conditions, and attitudes. For example: cities have a larger proportion of their children in school and young people there stay in school longer, but the opportunities for schooling are greater in cities. In the country, young people are needed for work on the farms; in the cities, however, opportunities for young people to work are relatively few. Then, city people put a higher value on "schooling" than do country people. The fact that there are more illiterates in the country reflects the further fact that circumstances of living put a greater pressure on city people to learn to read and write, and the opportunities to overcome these lacks are greater in cities. A larger proportion of the foreign-born in the country have become naturalized citizens, but this is largely because of the difference in the nationality backgrounds of immigrants who settled in the country and those who stayed in the cities.

It has frequently been pointed out that there are differences in health, but these differences are fading out. In fact, differences be-

[7] Pitirim Sorokin and Carle C. Zimmerman, *Principles of Rural-Urban Sociology* (New York: Henry Holt and Company, 1929); a notable example.
[8] W. F. Ogburn, "Regions," *Social Forces*, Vol. 15 (1936), pp. 6–11.

tween urban and rural death rates are less than the variations within states. It can be pointed out, however, that:

Cities, because of their relatively greater wealth, population, and technical and institutional resources, are better able to supply their residents with the more complex and specialized types of medical service than are rural communities.

Large cities are better equipped with physicians, dentists, nurses, and with medical facilities in general than are smaller and rural communities. Municipalities spend about twice as much per capita for public-health services as do counties in rural areas. Privately supported health organizations in cities offer nursing, health education, and other preventive services not readily available in rural communities.[9]

By city standards, rural people have, on the average, lower standards of living; that is, fewer homes have electricity, use electrical appliances, have mechanical refrigeration, and have running water and bathrooms. Cities, however, are not so superior in regard to such things, for all too many city families also live without these modern conveniences. The differences do reflect again the availability of the utilities which cities provide. At any rate, more rural families own their own homes.

Underlying the apparent differences, two factors have been significant. First, in the country there is less accumulated wealth as a resource for tax income, partly because the economic system tends to drain the wealth of the country into the city. (Cf. pp. 134–135.) Second, the per capita income is less in the country, but great advances have been made in equalization through the operation of the agricultural subsidies, which, with all the difficulties involved, have made the farmers' dollars and the industrial workers' dollars nearer the same size.

Population Differences. Several population differences between rural and urban areas continue to exist; so, as far as can be seen, they indicate real differences. The factors are closely related, but the basic one is the difference in net reproduction rates.[10] These

[9] National Resources Committee, *op. cit.*, pp. 12–13.

[10] "The net reproduction rate is a measure of the potential rate of increase or decrease of a population. This rate shows how much population might be expected to increase over a generation if present birth and death rates at different age levels should continue unchanged.

"More precisely, the net reproduction rate shows the number of daughters that would be born to the survivors of a group of 100 female infants during the course of their lifetime if present age specific birth and death rates should continue unchanged. A rate of 100 would indicate that, on the average, the sur-

rates change, but the disparity between city and country is clear, as can be seen in Table 1. The relative deficit of population in urban

TABLE 1. Net Reproduction Rates by Urban, Rural-Nonfarm, and Rural-Farm Residence, United States, 1930, 1940, 1947

Year	Total	Urban	Rural-Nonfarm	Rural-Farm
1930[a]	111.0	88.0	132.0	159.0
1935–1940[b]	97.8	72.6	115.0	166.1
1942–1947[b]	129.2	108.5	146.5	185.9

[a] Bureau of the Census, *Net Reproduction Rates, 1930 and 1940.*
[b] Bureau of the Census, Current Population Reports: *Population Characteristics*, P-20, No. 18 (June 30, 1948), p. 5.

areas and the surplus in rural areas are the basis for the continuing movement of people from country to city.

A second population difference is in the ratio of males to females. While the ratio varies from age group to age group in both rural and urban populations, in general there are more men in the country and more women in the cities. The ratios can be seen in Table 2.[11]

TABLE 2. Males per 100 Females in the Population of Urban, Rural-Nonfarm, and Rural-Farm Areas in the United States, 1920, 1930, and 1940

	1940[a]	1930[a]	1920[b]
Total population	100.7	102.5	104.0
Urban	95.5	98.1	100.4
Rural-nonfarm	103.7	105.0	106.5
Rural-farm	111.7	111.0	109.1

[a] *16th Census, 1940: Population:* Second Series: *Characteristics of Population:* "United States, Summary," Table 1, p. 3, and Table 5, p. 14.
[b] *14th Census, 1920:* Vol. II, *Population,* Table 1, p. 107.

vivors of such a group of 100 would give birth to 100 daughters. Since these 100 daughters would be just enough to replace the original cohort of mothers, the populations would remain stationary and would become neither larger nor smaller in the next generation. If the rates were higher than 100, however, it would indicate that population would increase from one generation to the next, and if it were lower than 100, it would indicate that the population would decline. All these assumptions are contingent upon the continuance of the same birth and death rates as those observed when the computation was made."— *16th Census, 1940:* Preliminary Release, Series P-5, No. 4 (Feb. 21, 1941): *Future Population Growth in the United States by Urban and Rural Residence as Measured by the Net Reproduction Rate, 1940.*

[11] Sample census studies indicate that for the first time, in the total U.S. population, the number of males per 100 females will drop below 100, but that there are still more single males than females in the "marriage age" group, 15–30. New York *Times,* Feb. 13, 1950, p. 23.

A third factor, which is a corollary of the first, is the size of families. Table 3 gives a percentage distribution of families by size in urban, rural-nonfarm, and rural-farm areas, which shows clearly that small families are more frequent in cities and large families are more likely to be found on the farms. While the trend in all areas is toward smaller families, urban families continue to be smallest. The differences show up in the median size, which, in 1949, was urban 3.00, rural-nonfarm 3.15, rural-farm 3.48, and total United States 3.11.

TABLE 3. Percentage Distribution by Size of Urban, Rural-Nonfarm and Rural-Farm Families in the United States, 1930, 1940, and 1949[12]

Size of Families No. of Persons	Total			Urban			Rural-Nonfarm			Rural-Farm		
	1949	1940	1930	1949	1940	1930	1949	1940	1930	1949	1940	1930
1	8.0	10.1	7.9	9.2	11.1	8.0	7.3	11.1	10.4	4.8	6.3	5.2
2	27.2	25.7	23.4	28.5	27.5	25.1	26.9	25.5	23.8	23.1	20.7	18.3
3	24.1	21.9	20.8	24.5	22.9	22.1	24.5	21.8	20.2	22.5	19.4	18.0
4	19.2	17.5	17.5	19.3	17.7	18.1	19.9	17.2	16.6	17.7	17.4	16.6
5	10.4	10.6	12.0	9.6	10.0	11.6	11.3	10.5	11.4	12.4	12.8	13.3
6	5.5	6.2	7.6	5.0	5.3	6.8	4.7	6.2	7.3	8.4	8.8	10.0
7	2.7	3.5	4.7	2.0	2.7	3.8	2.7	3.5	4.5	5.2	5.8	7.1
8	1.3	2.0	2.8	0.9	1.4	2.1	1.3	2.0	2.7	2.6	3.8	4.8
9 or more	1.5	2.4	3.4	1.0	1.5	2.3	1.5	2.3	3.0	3.4	5.1	6.7
	100.0	100.0	100.0	100.0	100.0	100.0	100.0	100.0	100.0	100.0	100.0	100.0

The fourth difference is the age structure of the population, which can be clearly seen in the population pyramids shown in Figure 1. Rural-nonfarm areas have the nearest to a normal age distribution, while there are disproportionate percentages of those under twenty in rural-farm areas, and of those over twenty in urban areas. This reflects, on the one hand, the higher birth rates and larger families on the farms, and, on the other hand, the migration to cities of people from twenty to sixty years of age.

SUMMARY

The distinctive character of American cities grows out of two fundamental facts: first, they are built primarily around industry and commerce and/or the services such as education, government, and resorts; second, they are composed of many different kinds of peo-

[12] *16th Census, 1940: Population and Housing: Families: General Characteristics,* Table 8, p. 24. Current Population Reports: *Population Characteristics: Marital Status and Household Characteristics:* April, 1949. Series P-20, No. 26 (Jan. 27, 1950), Table 6, p. 14.

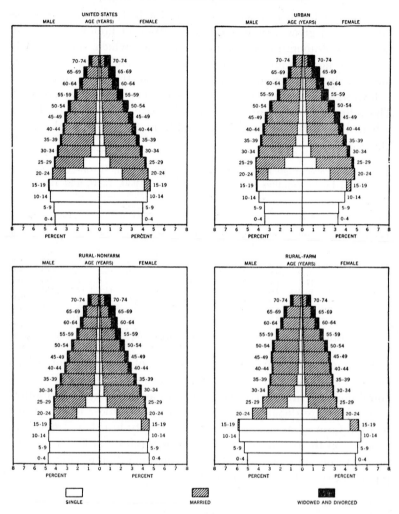

Figure 1. Age and Sex Structure of Urban, Rural-Nonfarm, and Rural-Farm Population in the United States, 1940. (16th Census, 1940: Population: Vol. IV, Characteristics by Age, p. x.)

ple living in close proximity, with many interrelationships. Out of these factors evolves a way of life that is distinctive to urban areas.

Cities have many observable characteristics. Some of these are physical. Cities are built up. They have a great quantity and variety of buildings. A constant flow of all sorts of materials is ever going on. Transportation facilities of many kinds are always on the move. Cities are filled with striking contrasts. There is congestion on every hand.

Activity characteristics are quite as obvious. There is a rapidity and fluidity of life. Evidences of specialization can be seen in the many vocations of individuals. Greater opportunities for good living and self-expression are apparent in the many different kinds of jobs that are necessary and in the abundance of places and occasions for amusement, recreation, entertainment, and education. There is also a wide variety of organizations for social service. A great diversity of experiences are always available. Then, too, cities are always being built, and many people are occupied cleaning dirt.

Human characteristics are no less striking. Tremendous heterogeneity in personality and backgrounds can be seen in the faces and bearing of the individuals. There are an anonymity of life and a similarity in the general appearance and behavior of people.

Observations of cities lead to the deductions that highly developed government is necessary, that complicated social organizations must exist, and that cities are cultural centers in both the broad and the narrow meaning of the term.

The differences between urban and rural people which have been traditionally thought of as significant are for the most part tending to disappear. There are, however, differences in the structures of the population which persist. The net reproduction rate is higher in the country; there are more men in the country and more women in the cities; families are larger in the country; and the age structure of the population differs markedly, with a much higher proportion of children and youth in the country and a larger percentage of young people and those of middle age in the cities.

Here, then, are the more important items around which can be built a reasonably comprehensive concept of what a city is. Over a long period of years, growth and its implications have been at the bottom of all considerations of American cities. How do cities grow? What changes have taken place in the patterns of urban growth? This is the next consideration.

Supplementary Reading

Burgess, Ernest W. *The Urban Community*. Chicago: The University of Chicago Press, 1926.

A symposium presenting many preliminary statements dealing with various aspects of urban communities.

National Resources Committee. *Our Cities: Their Role in the National Economy*. Report of the Urbanism Committee. Washington: Government Printing Office, 1937.

A brief statement of what modern American cities are like and what their problems are.

CHAPTER 4

THE GROWTH OF AMERICAN CITIES

THE growth of cities has been one of the most spectacular things in the development of America. Cities have grown in size, in number, and in the proportion of the population which they contain, until the United States has become a predominantly urban nation. The implications of the basic fact are profound; both as effect and as cause this growing urbanization of the nation marks a focal point of the changing culture.

EXTENT OF URBAN GROWTH

When the first United States census was taken in 1790, the United States was an overwhelmingly rural nation; only 5.1 percent of the population lived in places of 2500 or more population.[1] By 1950 there were 16¾ times as many rural people, but 436 times as many urban people. In 1790 there were 18½ times as many rural people as urban people, but in 1950 there were 1.4 times as many urban as rural people. The urban part of the total population had reached 58.7 percent. Table 4 shows the changing proportion of urban and rural people at each census since the first. The urban portion of America's people has increased continuously, but at a lessening rate in the more recent decades. It has, however, attained a substantial majority and bids to continue so, though it is likely that a balance between rural and urban population is being reached.

The growing nation has grown in all its parts, but not equally. A comparison of the growth curves of total population, rural population, urban population, and number of cities can be seen in Figure 2.

---

[1] The statistical treatment of urban growth necessarily depends upon data from the U.S. census and is based on the census definition of cities—places with 2500 or more population.

The percentage increase for each of these portions by decades is given in Table 5. With the exception of the decade 1810–1820, the increase in both urban population and number of cities has been at a higher rate than that of the total population and the rural population.

More Cities. The number of cities has increased from twenty-four, all under 50,000 population, in 1790 to 4270 cities, of which

TABLE 4. Percentage Distribution of the Urban and
Rural Population of the United States, 1790–1950[2]

Census Year	Percentage of Total Population	
	Urban	Rural
1790	5.1	94.9
1800	6.1	93.9
1810	7.3	92.7
1820	7.2	92.8
1830	8.8	91.2
1840	10.8	89.2
1850	15.3	84.7
1860	19.8	80.2
1870	25.7	74.3
1880	28.2	71.8
1890	35.1	64.9
1900	39.7	60.3
1910	45.7	54.3
1920	51.2	48.8
1930	56.2	43.8
1940	56.5	43.5
1950	58.7	41.3

106 were over 100,000 population and five over 1,000,000 in 1950. This growing up of the cities both in number and in size from the first to the last census can be seen in Table 6, p. 55.

New cities sprang up in the wake of the frontier, but also appeared where the population thickened up in the older areas. Older cities grew larger, but some of the younger ones outstripped them. Cities of all ages have experienced growth,[3] but cities have not

[2] Bureau of the Census, *Sixteenth Census of the United States, 1940: Population:* First Series: "U.S., Summary," Table 6, p. 10. 1950 Census of Population: Preliminary Counts: *Population of Urban Places:* April 1, 1950. Series PC-3, No. 8, Table 1, p. 2.

[3] National Resources Committee, *Our Cities: Their Role in the National Economy,* Report of the Urbanism Committee (Washington: Government Printing Office, 1937), facing p. 98, gives three maps with cities by location

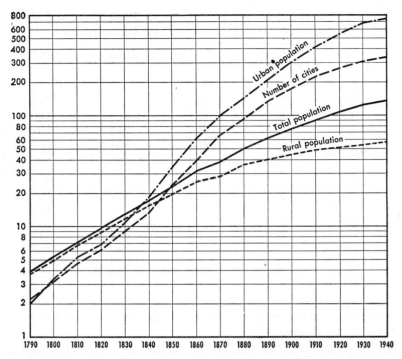

Figure 2. Comparison of Growth Curves for Total, Rural, and Urban Population and Number of Cities in the United States, 1790 to 1940. (*16th Census, 1940: Population: First Series: U.S. Summary, Table 6, p. 10.*)

grown because they were old. Only fifteen of 1790's twenty-four cities are found on the list of cities over 100,000 population in 1940. Several of the cities of 100,000 or more population in 1940 are less than fifty years old. Gary (Indiana) appeared first in the census of 1910, Miami (Florida) and Tulsa (Oklahoma) in 1900, and Oklahoma City (Oklahoma), Long Beach (California), Spokane (Washington), and Tacoma (Washington) in 1890. Nor does the fact that a city has attained a large population assure continuing growth. There was one less city of 100,000 or more population in 1940 than in 1930. This was the result of population changes in five cities. Three cities slipped back below the 100,000 mark, and two cities passed this mark in their growth. From 1940 to 1950 fifteen cities

and relative size as of 1930: older cities, which appeared in the census of 1850; medium-aged cities, which appeared in the census of 1900 but not in 1850; and new cities, which appeared in 1930 but not in 1900.

TABLE 5. Percentage Growth by Decades for Total, Rural, and Urban Population and Number of Cities in the U.S., 1790–1950[4]

Decade	Total Population	Rural Population	Urban Population	Number of Cities
1800	35.1	33.8	59.9	37.5
1810	36.4	34.7	63.0	39.4
1820	33.1	33.2	31.9	32.6
1830	33.5	31.2	62.6	47.5
1840	32.7	29.7	63.7	45.5
1850	35.9	29.1	92.1	80.1
1860	35.6	28.4	75.4	66.1
1870	22.6	13.6	59.3	69.1
1880	30.1	25.7	42.7	41.6
1890	25.5	13.4	56.5	43.5
1900	20.7	12.2	36.4	28.9
1910	21.0	9.0	39.3	30.2
1920	14.9	3.2	29.0	20.3
1930	16.1	4.4	27.3	16.3
1940	7.2	6.4	7.9	9.4
1950	14.5	9.7	18.2	23.3

grew into, and one slipped back out of, the group of cities of over 100,000 population.

The growth of cities of 25,000 population or over varies greatly during the four decades 1910–1950; some cities showed extreme gain (50 percent or more) and some moderate gain (from 1.1 to 49.9 percent), some were static (from −1.1 to 1.1 percent), and some lost population. This distribution is given in Table 7, together with the range of percentage gain or loss, the number and percentage of cities in each decade which more than doubled in population, and the number of states in which cities showing extreme gain were located. The decline in the rate of growth shows up as the proportion of cities with extreme gain decreases and the proportion of static and losing cities increases in the 1930–1940 decade. In 1910–1920 and 1920–1930 the cities showing extreme gain were widely scattered over the country, but in 1930–1940 they were all in three states, California, Florida, and Texas, except for three cities

[4] 16th Census, 1940: Population: First Series: "U. S., Summary," Table 6, p. 10, and Table 10, pp. 18–19. 1950 Census of Population: Preliminary Counts: Population of Urban Places: April 1, 1950. Series PC-3, No. 8, Table 1, p. 2. Note: In 1950 the U.S. Census included as urban for the first time unincorporated places of 2500 or more population. There were 397 such places with a total population of 1,984,630. Omitting these, the 1940 to 1950 increase in urban population was 15.5 percent and in number of cities was 11.8 percent.

TABLE 6. Number of Cities in the United States, by Size Groups, 1790–1950[5]

Year	1790	1800	1810	1820	1830	1840	1850	1860	1870	1880	1890	1900	1910	1920	1930	1940	1950
Total No. Cities	24	33	46	61	90	131	236	392	663	939	1,348	1,737	2,262	2,722	3,165	3,464	4,270
1,000,000 or more										1	3	3	3	3	5	5	5
500,000 to 1,000,000								2	2	3	1	3	5	9	8	9	13
250,000 to 500,000						1	1	1	5	4	7	9	11	13	24	23	23
100,000 to 250,000				1	1	2	5	6	7	12	17	23	31	43	56	55	65
50,000 to 100,000		1	2	2	3	2	4	7	11	15	30	40	59	76	98	107	125
25,000 to 50,000	2	2	2	2	3	7	16	19	27	42	66	82	119	143	185	213	246
10,000 to 25,000	3	3	7	8	16	25	36	58	116	146	230	280	369	465	606	665	780
5,000 to 10,000	7	15	17	22	33	48	85	136	186	249	340	465	605	715	851	965	1174
2,500 to 5,000	12	12	18	26	34	46	89	163	309	467	654	832	1,060	1,255	1,332	1,422	1,839
Cumulative number:																	
Places of 100,000 or more				1	1	3	6	9	14	20	28	38	50	68	93	92	106
Places of 25,000 or more	2	3	4	5	7	12	26	35	52	77	124	160	228	287	376	412	477
Places of 10,000 or more	5	6	11	13	23	37	62	93	168	223	354	440	597	752	982	1,077	1,257

[5] Ibid. Note: Of the 397 unincorporated places included in 1950, 3 were 25,000 to 50,000, 26 were 10,000 to 25,000, 82 were 5,000 to 10,000, and 286 were 2,500 to 5,000.

TABLE 7. Distribution of Cities of 25,000 Population or More,
by Rates of Growth, 1910–1950[6]

Rate of Growth	1910–1920		1920–1930		1930–1940		1940–1950	
	No. of Cities	Percent	No. of Cities	Percent	No. of Cities	Percent	No. of Cities	Percent
	405	100.0	410	100.0	412	100.0	477	100.0
Extreme gain (50% or more)	109	26.9	108	26.4	13	3.2	72	15.1
Gaining (1.1% to 49.9%)	278	68.6	276	67.3	268	65.0	348	72.9
Static (−1.1% to 1.1%)	6	1.5	5	1.2	53	12.9	22	4.6
Losing (−1.1% or more)	12	3.0	21	5.1	78	18.9	35	7.4
Range of change								
Greatest gain %		1266.0		2485.9		331.4		319.7
Greatest loss %		−49.4		−16.0		−15.4		−13.2
Over 100% growth	41	10.1	47	11.5	4	1.0	21	4.4
No. of states containing cities with extreme gain		30		29		6		28

whose growth can be clearly explained. Gadsden (Alabama) was enlarged by the annexation of Alabama City. Teaneck (New Jersey), just across the Hudson River from Manhattan, became easily accessible for commuters to New York when the George Washington Bridge was opened in 1931. Arlington (Virginia) was a convenient place for the location of many of the additional employees of the federal government in the thirties. Geographical location in itself does not appear to be a primary determinant of growth. From 1940 to 1950 the wider distribution of rapidly growing cities reflects the higher rate of total population growth, but thirty-three of the seventy-two cities increasing 50 percent or more in population were located in California, Texas, and Florida.

Cities and Their States. There is a wide variation in the proportion of the urban population in the states. In 1940, ten states had more than 60 percent of their populations in cities (Rhode Island 91.6, Massachusetts 89.4, New York 82.8, New Jersey 81.6, Illinois 73.6, California 71.0, Connecticut 67.8, Ohio 66.8, Pennsylvania 66.5, Michigan 65.7), and, on the other end of the scale, five states had less than 25 percent of their population in cities (South Dakota 24.6, South Carolina 24.5, Arkansas 22.2, North Dakota 20.6, Mississippi 19.8). A wide range is also found in the percentage increase of urban

[6] Data from *16th Census, 1940: Population: First Series:* "U.S., Summary," Table 13, pp. 26–28. 1950 Census of Population: Preliminary Counts: *Population of Urban Places:* April 1, 1950. Series PC-3, No. 8, Table 2, pp. 3–31.

population from 1930 to 1940. When the ranking of the states on the percentage increase of urban population is statistically compared with the rank on the percentage of urban population in 1930, the correlation is found to be −.66, which would seem to indicate that there is a strong tendency for increase in urban population to come where the percentage of urban population is low. Since there is a correlation of .54 between the percentage increase of total population and the percentage increase of urban population by states, the inference is that the causes of total population growth and urban population growth are much the same. Urban population increase has been in the preponderance except for the Pacific coast states, where there is still agricultural expansion, and in the states of the great industrial triangle, which already had a saturation of urban people.

PATTERNS OF URBAN GROWTH

Cities have grown in different ways, in different places, for different reasons at different times.

In the Nineteenth Century. When Weber published his exhaustive study of the growth of cities at the close of the nineteenth century, he stated: "Lavasseur's hypothesis that 'the power of attraction of human groups is, in general, proportionate to their mass' was nearly everywhere sustained. . . . Urban growth is essentially a great-city growth."[7] Weber noted what he called a suburban development, but explained with certain facts showing that the centers of the great cities were slowing up in their growth and the outlying sections were growing rapidly. At that time the means of transportation which have since made suburbs possible were not yet available, but Weber saw in rapid transit and "the rise of the suburbs . . . the solid basis of hope that the evils of city life, so far as they result from overcrowding, may be in large part removed."[8]

Although it was not apparent at the turn of the century, it has become clear from the perspective of the present that the phenomenon of clustering of cities is of importance and of long standing. Clusters of cities began to appear as early as 1840 along the Atlantic seaboard. By 1900 the clustering of lesser cities around the major

[7] Adna F. Weber, *The Growth of Cities in the Nineteenth Century* (New York: The Macmillan Company, 1899), pp. 446, 448.
[8] *Ibid.*, p. 475.

cities had become an established phenomenon. By 1930 intense clustering of urban communities had spread throughout the whole United States, showing up even at places where cities were small thirty years before. By 1940 and since, the phenomenon of the clustering of cities has become more intensified.

With the beginning of the twentieth century a selective process of city growth became more definite, although no single category of cities nor any single factor of growth can explain the increase. The factors of size, regional location, and relationship to other cities continue to be significant, but always in relation to the function of the particular city. Cities grow where and when society needs cities.

From 1900 to 1910. The decade 1900–1910 marked the last big spurt in the increase of the number of cities and the growth of the population they contained. There were 525 cities added to the total number, an increase of 30.23 percent, by no means up to the percentage gains in the decades of the nineteenth century, but the largest increase in the twentieth century and the largest number of cities added in any decade in the history of the United States. Medium-sized cities, those between 25,000 and 100,000, had the largest increase in number, 45.9 percent.

The greatest gains in the proportion of urban population were in the West, especially the Pacific states, the mountain region (chiefly in Idaho and Arizona), and the west-south-central region (chiefly in Oklahoma). North Dakota and Florida had large urban growth. New England, however, fell far behind the national average. The cities of phenomenal growth were Tulsa, Oklahoma City, Birmingham, Flint, Seattle, and Fort Worth, all reflecting industrial development, and Seattle the expansion of shipping.[9]

From 1910 to 1920. From 1910 to 1920 the number of cities continued to increase. Large cities (100,000 population and over) showed the greatest gain, but chiefly by virtue of the fact that eighteen cities grew into this group, increasing the total number by more than one third (36 percent). The number of cities between 500,000 and 1,000,000 population changed from five to nine.

Growth was more definitely a matter of states than of regions. Nine states increased their urban population more than 50 percent:

[9] For increase in urban population by areas, divisions, and states between each census and the next, see *16th Census, 1940: Population:* First Series: *Number of Inhabitants:* "U.S. Summary," Table 8, pp. 12–16. For growth of population for urban places of 25,000 population or more, from 1910 to 1940, see the same, Table 13, pp. 26–28.

West Virginia (61.7), North Carolina (54.0), Florida (61.4), Oklahoma (68.7), Texas (61.2), Idaho (70.3), Arizona (90.9), California (58.5), and Michigan (68.9). New England fell even farther below the average urban population growth, as did a few other scattered states. The cities which grew at high rates are mostly located in those states where explanations are clear; for example, in Oklahoma it was the oil city of Tulsa; in California largely the small cities around Los Angeles as the trek to that state got up momentum; in Florida the winter resort cities Miami, Orlando, St. Petersburg, and West Palm Beach; in Michigan the automobile-manufacturing cities Detroit, Dearborn, Flint, Hamtramck, Highland Park, and Pontiac, and the residential suburb of Detroit, Royal Oak.

From 1920 to 1930. In the next ten-year period, 1920–1930, the pattern did not greatly change. The cities over 1,000,000 population increased from three to five, and the total number of large cities (100,000 and over) increased from sixty-eight to ninety-three, 36.76 percent. Cities were still growing up and small places becoming cities.

The geographical pattern of urban population growth did not change, although there were shifts within the pattern. In the south Atlantic states the large urban growth was in North Carolina (65.2 percent) and Florida (114.9 percent), both materially increasing their rate of growth; the east-south-central states grew at a moderate but above average rate; in the west-south-central states Oklahoma (52.7 percent) and Texas (58.0 percent) maintained the lead, but growth was somewhat more general. In the West there was a shift in major growth to Nevada (125.9 percent) and New Mexico (64.4 percent); California (78.8 percent) represented the center of growth on the Pacific coast. The New England states fell farther behind and were joined in below-average increases by most of the middle Atlantic and west-north-central states. The particular cities which grew show about the same situations. In California and Florida growth was more widely spread. All cities of 25,000 population or more, but one, in North Carolina grew more than 50 percent. In Michigan, Dearborn grew 1938.8 percent (the Ford plant had been built there), and some other communities continued their growth. Scattered widely over the country, however, residential suburbs of the large cities showed very large growth.

From 1930 to 1940. The decade 1930–1940 showed a radical change in the pattern of the growth of American cities. Not only did the large cities decrease one in number, but many of them lost population, and their total rate of growth, 4.6 percent, was far below the total urban population growth of 7.9 percent. This was in part due to the declining rate of total population growth, which fell to 7.2 percent. Urban population growth, still slightly above the rate of total population growth, declined 71.1 percent while rural population growth increased 45.5 percent. This redistribution of population growth hit the large cities hardest. The medium-sized cities still

TABLE 8.   Percentage Increase in Population and Number of Cities, for Large, Medium, and Small Cities in the United States, by Decades, 1900–1950[10]

	1940–1950		1930–1940		1920–1930		1910–1920		1900–1910	
	Population	Number	Population	Number	Population	Number	Population	Number	Population	Number
Large cities 100,000 population and over	15.7	15.2	4.6	−1.1	32.4	36.8	35.1	36.0	42.9	31.6
Medium cities 25,000 to 100,000 population	17.7	15.0	14.3	13.1	24.9	29.2	26.0	23.0	48.9	45.9
Small cities 2,500 to 25,000 population	13.9	−1.5	10.0	9.4	20.3	14.5	21.4	19.7	29.3	29.0
Total urban population	15.5	11.8	7.9	9.4	27.3	16.3	29.0	20.3	39.3	30.2

grew 14.3 percent and the small cities 10.0 percent. The percentage increase of urban population and number of cities by large, medium, and small cities for each decade of the twentieth century is given in Table 8.

The increase in urban population by states also showed the redistribution of growth; some states with little growth from 1920 to 1930 had above-average growth from 1930 to 1940: for example, Delaware jumped from 2.0 percent to 13.2 percent, Montana from 5.2 percent to 16.8 percent, and Idaho from 8.8 percent to 36.4 percent. On the other hand, the reverse was true in other states: for

[10] *16th Census, 1940: Population:* First Series: *Number of Inhabitants:* "U.S., Summary," Table 6, p. 10, and Table 10, p. 18. 1950 Census of Population: Preliminary Counts: *Population of Urban Places:* April 1, 1950. Series PC-3, No. 8, Table 1, p. 2. *Note:* Unincorporated places not included in computing 1940–1950 percentages.

example, New Jersey dropped from 32.4 percent to 1.7 percent, Illinois from 28.0 percent to 3.1 percent, Michigan from 47.3 percent to 4.6 percent, West Virginia from 33.2 percent to 8.7 percent, Oklahoma from 52.7 percent to 7.1 percent, and a number of others with less striking differences. The states with more than twice the average urban growth were in the South and Southwest (Virginia 20.3, North Carolina 20.3, South Carolina 25.6, Georgia 19.9, Florida 37.6, Mississippi 27.8, Louisiana 17.6, Texas 21.8, New Mexico 65.1, Arizona 16.1, and California 17.8) and in the north-central and mountain area (North Dakota 16.4, South Dakota 20.8, Montana 16.8, Idaho 36.4, Wyoming 33.5, and Nevada 25.6). Several of these states had not been in the group of those with the largest rate of urban population increase since the turn of the century.

In this decade a pattern of urban growth in the 140 metropolitan districts became clear. The districts as a whole grew 9.4 percent in population, slightly more than the total population (7.2 percent) and the total urban population (7.9 percent). When this is broken down, however, the population in the central cities grew 6.1 percent, considerably below the growth of urban population from 1930 to 1940, and the population residing in the districts outside the central cities increased 16.9 percent, more than twice the rate of growth of the total urban population. Not all of these districts followed the pattern, however, indicating that other selective factors were also at work. Thirty-six of the central cities actually lost in population, and fifty others increased less than the average (6.1 percent), while eighty-eight of the areas outside the central cities grew more than their average (16.9 percent) and sixty-four of them by more than 25 percent. This pattern had partly appeared in the 1920–1930 decade, when in a smaller number of designated metropolitan districts the areas outside central cities increased 39.2 percent while the central cities increased only 19.4 percent. During this period, however, the growth in the central cities was still above the increase of the total United States population (16.1 percent), though it was less than the total increase of urban population (27.3 percent).[11]

An inspection of cities of all sizes which grew at a higher rate than the national growth of urban population between 1930 and 1940 shows certain tendencies, but also that no single explanation is sufficient to account for the growth of particular places. Geographically, there appears to be a tendency for places near large urban centers to

[11] Further statistics of metropolitan districts are given in Table 26, p. 261.

grow. Sometimes these are within metropolitan areas, sometimes just beyond the limits of the accepted metropolitan district, and in a few cases this influence of the urban center seems to reach as far as fifty miles. Then, also, places at the crossing of a number of highways, especially if they are county-seat towns, appeared to have been more likely to grow. Both of these tendencies imply functional relationships. By no means all of the cities which met these conditions, however, grew, and in many cases the cities with such locations which had a large growth during the previous decade did not increase above the average during this decade. The inference seems to be that cities grow primarily because and where people are needed. Sometimes a large urban center needs more people, and outlying residential suburbs grow up. The decentralization of industry from large cities to smaller communities, or the expansion of industry in a smaller city, makes the respective places grow. The expanding use of outlying but accessible places as service centers causes them to grow up. The secondary factor would then be accessibility, especially by highways for motor transportation.

Cities During the War.   The selective character of city growth was confirmed during the period of the war. Some American cities had tremendous gains in population while others lost population. The need for workers where war industries were concentrated was the key to the redistribution of people which made the increases.

Hauser found that between April 1, 1940, and March 1, 1943, the 137 metropolitan counties in the United States gained 2.4 percent in population, against a loss of 2.4 percent in the country as a whole, while the part of the county outside these metropolitan areas lost 7.3 percent. The major part of the gains were in the West, where fifteen metropolitan counties increased 12.5 percent, and the South, where 48 metropolitan counties gained 12.2 percent. There were 81 metropolitan counties which gained 9.6 percent, while the remaining 56 lost in population. This was the "result of an extensive in-migration of civilians from the rest of the country."[12]

In April, 1947, sample surveys were made of thirty-four metropolitan districts by the Bureau of the Census.[13] Some of the areas showed

[12] Philip M. Hauser, *Changing Markets: Changes of a Geographic Nature in Wartime with Some Consideration of Postwar Population Prospects of Metropolitan Areas* (Washington: Bureau of the Census, Nov. 11, 1943, mimeographed), pp. 4, 5, and Table 1, p. 62.

[13] Bureau of the Census, Current Population Reports, Series P-21, No. 35 (Washington, Aug. 24, 1947), pp. 1, 5, 18.

particularly large percentage increases over the population recorded by the 1940 census; for example, Norfolk–Portsmouth–Newport News increased 43 percent, San Francisco–Oakland 39 percent, Los Angeles 35 percent, Seattle and Washington each 33 percent, Portland (Oregon) and San Antonio 31 percent. Most of the places which showed exceptional gains were centers of war production or other war activities.

Since these were largely war years, when many were drawn out of the civilian population by the armed services and natural increase was below normal, it is clear that the increase came from the movement of people into the metropolitan districts. A comparison of the percentage increase in total population from 1940 to 1947 and the percentage of the population increase by migration from 1940 to 1947 gives a correlation of .81 (rho), which is indicative of a high degree of relationship.

Perhaps the most important aspect of these facts is that they show to what a great extent population in the United States is maneuverable. Not that individual people can be moved around, but that where the forces which draw people are localized and the facilities for assisting people to move easily are set up, great shifts of population can be accomplished. This is what was done, for example, when the Kaiser shipbuilding plants were established in Pacific coast and Gulf cities. Advertisements calling for workers were placed in newspapers around the country, and offices were opened at strategic centers to employ people and assist them in arranging for transportation.

Whether or not the population gains in cities during the war period will be permanent remains to be seen. On the basis of his study compared with the trends in population growth in the 1930–1940 decade, Hauser grouped the metropolitan areas on the basis of their relative potentialities for postwar growth into four categories and five subgroups as follows:

Class A-1 areas: those which have grown most rapidly since 1940 and in the preceding period and which are, therefore, on the basis of past growth alone, adjudged to have *superior* prospects of retaining wartime growth. Atlanta, Charleston S.C., Columbia, Columbus Ga., Corpus Christi, Dallas, Galveston, Houston, Jacksonville, Miami, Mobile, Phoenix, San Antonio, San Diego, Tampa–St. Petersburg, Washington, D.C.

Class A-2 areas: those which grew at above average rates during the course of the war and in the preceding period and which are adjudged, therefore, to have *excellent* prospects of retaining wartime population growth. Amarillo, Augusta, Baltimore, Beaumont–Port Arthur, Charleston, W. Va., Denver, Detroit, Durham, Evansville, Fort Worth, Indianapolis, Jackson, Little Rock, Los Angeles, Macon, Madison, Memphis, Montgomery, Nashville, New Orleans, Norfolk–Portsmouth–Newport News, Oklahoma City, Portland, Me., Richmond, Sacramento, Salt Lake City, San Francisco–Oakland, San Jose, Savannah, Seattle, Spokane, Stockton, Tacoma, Wilmington.

Class A-3: those which grew at above average rates during the course of the war, with moderate increase in the preceding period, and which are believed to have *good* prospects for retaining wartime population growth. Birmingham, Bridgeport, Canton, Cincinnati, Columbus Ohio, Hamilton–Middletown, Hartford–New Britain, Pueblo, St. Louis, Springfield, Ohio.

Class B metropolitan areas. These are the metropolitan areas which have grown most rapidly since the onset of the war but at a substantially lower relative rate in the preceding decade; and whose wartime growth is expected, therefore, to be transient unless special effort is made after the war to convert their wartime facilities to peacetime pursuits. Akron, Dayton, El Paso, Erie, Kansas City, Mo.–Kansas City, Kans., Louisville, Portland, Ore., Rockford, Tulsa, Waco, Wichita.

Class C-1 areas: those which lost population or increased relatively little during the course of the war but which grew at above average rates between 1930 and 1940 (and in most cases between 1920 and 1930) and which are, therefore, believed to have *excellent* postwar prospects of "coming back." Asheville, Austin, Binghamton, Cedar Rapids, Charlotte, Chattanooga, Davenport (Ia.)–Rock Island–Moline (Ill.), Des Moines, Fresno, Kalamazoo, Knoxville, Lansing, Minneapolis–St. Paul, Peoria, Shreveport, Springfield, Mo., Waterloo, Winston-Salem.

Class C-2 areas: those which lost population or increased relatively little during the course of the war and between 1930 and 1940, but which grew at relatively rapid rates between 1920 and 1930; and which, therefore, are believed to have *fair* prospects of "coming back" in the postwar period. Atlantic City, Chicago, Cleveland, Decatur, Flint, Fort Wayne, Grand Rapids, Huntington (W. Va.)–Ashland (Ky.), Milwaukee, New York–Northeastern New Jersey, Roanoke, South Bend, Toledo, Topeka, Youngstown.

Class D metropolitan areas: those which lost population or grew relatively little during the war and in each of the two preceding periods of observation and which, therefore, cannot be expected to grow rapidly or even to recoup their losses in the postwar period. Albany–Schenectady–Troy, Allentown–Bethlehem–Easton, Altoona, Boston, Buffalo–Niagara, Duluth (Minn.)–Superior (Wis.), Fall River–New Bedford, Harrisburg, Johnstown, Lancaster, Lincoln, Manchester, New Haven, Omaha (Neb.)–Council Bluffs (Ia.), Philadelphia, Pittsburgh, Providence, Racine–Kenosha, Reading, Rochester, Saginaw–Bay City, St. Joseph, Scranton–Wilkes-Barre, Sioux City, Springfield, Ill., Springfield–Holyoke, Mass., Syracuse, Terre Haute, Trenton, Utica–Rome, Wheeling, Worcester, York.[14]

From 1940 to 1950. In the main the patterns of city growth which became apparent in the preceding decade continued. The higher rate of population growth in the whole country and the concentration of this growth in cities, however, made the patterns less clear. Not all cities grew, however, as Tables 7 and 8 have shown. Small cities fell below both the rate of total population growth and the rate of total urban population growth. The population in medium-size cities increased most, but that in large cities showed the most unexpected increase.

Of the 168 metropolitan areas seven lost in population, eighty gained less than the average (21.2 percent), and eighty-one grew more than the average of which twenty-two increased more than 50 percent. Hauser's predictions were borne out on the whole although a number of individual cities did not grow as anticipated. The median percentages of growth were: A-1 areas 50.0 percent, A-2 areas 31.9 percent, A-3 areas 20.5 percent, B areas 27.2 percent, C-1 areas 17.0 percent, C-2 areas 14.4 percent, and D areas 8.9 percent. All A-1 areas grew considerably above average and all D areas lost in population or increased much less than average. The chief error in prediction was in A-3 and B areas largely because cities held their war-worker families to a greater extent than was expected and because the tendency of cities which had not been growing to pick up in rate of increase and those which had been growing rapidly to slacken off in rate of increase was not recognized.

SOURCES OF URBAN GROWTH

People to make cities grow can come from only three possible sources: natural increase, migration, and immigration.

Immigration has largely ceased except for a relatively few refugees and some displaced persons who are being afforded a haven in America; so the immediate past and probabilities in the future make

[14] Hauser, *op. cit.*, pp. 8–14.

this source practically insignificant. There have been periods in the past, however, when this source has been a large factor. The twentieth-century immigration tended to settle disproportionately in the cities. The first decade was the all-time peak of immigration to the United States—in four of these years the number exceeded one million. The total for the ten years was a little over 8,750,000, the equivalent of more than half the total increase in population during that decade and three quarters as much as the increase in urban population. From 1911 to 1920, with only two years over one million and a big decrease with the coming of World War I, the total dropped to just under 5,750,000 but still represented 42 percent of total population growth and 47 percent of urban increase. In the decade 1921–1930 the total was a little more than 4,000,000 and the percentages 24 and 28 respectively. In the 1931–1940 decade there were just over half a million immigrants, which represented 6 percent of the total population increase and a little less than 10 percent of the urban population growth.[15] Since 1940 even smaller numbers have entered America, except for Puerto Ricans, who, being United States citizens, are not considered immigrants. They have, however, been coming in considerable numbers during recent years, and they have settled for the most part in cities, especially New York.

Natural increase has been failing American cities as a source of growth. For many years birth rates have been decreasing and families have been growing smaller. Historically, the urban population has been growing increasingly infertile. The earliest urban net reproduction rate available was 93.7 for the period 1905–1910. From this time there has been a persistent decline to 72.6 for the period 1935–1940. During the next five years, 1941–1946, however, the net reproduction rate rose to 97.6, the nearest it had come to 100.0. Commenting on this rise, the census bulletin said: "It is doubtful that urban fertility will continue at this level, however, because this high rate is partly a consequence of the fact that there are greater proportions married among people at most ages than have prevailed at any time for which we have census records on this subject (since 1890). . . . If economic conditions become less favorable in the next few years, the proportions married may be expected to fall again." Net reproduction rates "are merely gauges of the balance of fertility and mortality conditions of a particular date and do not take into

---

[15] *World Almanac*, 1946, "Aliens Admitted from All Countries: Fiscal Years," p. 668.

account the degree of normality or abnormality of existing conditions."[16]

When, however, net reproductions were computed for the period 1942–1947, the urban rate was found to be 108.5. This unexpected increase seems to be the result of a continuation of favorable economic conditions and "abnormal increases in the proportion of the population who are married, and in the proportion of annual births which are first births and second births." This is a prolonged effect of delayed marriages caused by the war. The report comments: "A value for the net reproduction rate that is above 100.0, such as the one of about 108.5 for the period 1942 to 1947, is most unusual for an urban population in modern times."[17]

There appears to be no prospect of continued growth of cities by natural increase of population. At best, they can produce only enough children to partially compensate for their mortality losses.

This leaves the major source of population growth to migration. Since declining net reproduction rates have still left those in the rural nonfarm areas, and especially in the rural farm areas, above 100.0, it is clear that continuing population deficits in cities provide a suction which will draw the surplus of rural people cityward. The rural-urban population movement is inevitable. To what cities people will go in overbalancing numbers, however, will depend upon the needs of particular places, primarily for an increased labor force. The highly developed mobility of people makes possible extensive selection of great numbers of people, as has been demonstrated, especially during the war years. Of those who migrated to cities from 1935 to 1940, 59.2 percent were between the ages of twenty and fourty-four, in the prime of their working life; that is, ambitious workers and their families made up the bulk of those who came to the cities, for only 9 percent were fifty-five years of age or above.

PATTERNS OF GROWTH WITHIN CITIES

The overall percentage of increase or decrease in population of a city gives no indication of the geographical redistribution of people which is taking place within the city. When population change is computed by small geographical units such as census tracts, it is in

[16] Bureau of the Census, Current Population Reports, Series P-20, No. 8 (Washington: Dec. 31, 1947), pp. 5, 6; also Series P-47, No. 2, p. 1.

[17] Bureau of the Census, Current Population Reports: *Population Characteristics:* Series P-20, No. 18 (June, 1948), pp. 4–5, also note 3.

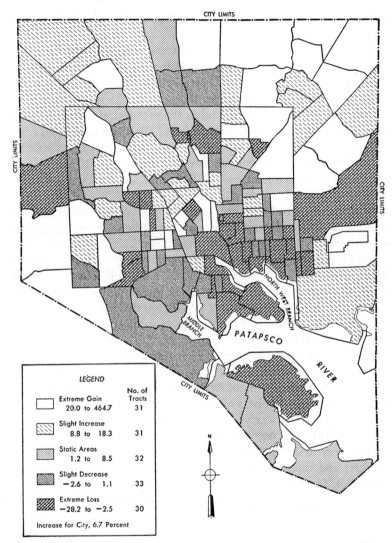

Figure 3. Growth of Population in Baltimore, by Census Tracts, 1930–1940. (*16th Census, 1940: Population for Individual Cities by Census Tracts.*)

most cases found that some of the areas showed an extreme loss in population and others an extreme gain, while the rest are fairly well distributed in between. For example, see Figure 3, which is a map of Baltimore by census tracts on which is indicated the relative growth of each tract in five groups: those showing large loss, those showing slight loss, those remaining about the same, those showing moderate gain, and those in which a very large increase took place in the decade 1930–1940. The city of Baltimore increased in population 6.7 percent, but the range of growth in its tracts was from a loss of 28.2 percent to a gain of 464.7 percent.

The pattern is basically loss of population in the central, dense, and older areas, with areas of slight loss just beyond fading into static areas, with areas of moderate and extreme gains on the outer fringes beyond. Divergencies from the precise pattern are usually easily explained. Areas of loss may be away from the center because they are made up of old settlements which may be surrounded by the later expansion of the city. Areas of slight growth may be beyond the areas of extreme growth because the crest of expansion has not yet reached them. Areas of extreme gain may be near the center of the city because of recent replacements of single-family dwellings with new multiple-family structures. The sixteen areas comprising the metropolitan area of Baltimore beyond the city limits, which grew 29.9 percent during this decade, all show extreme growth except the area contiguous to the northwest corner.

This pattern is apparent in all cities of moderate or large size, no matter whether the city is gaining, is static, or is losing population.[18]

PRINCIPLES OF URBAN GROWTH

It becomes clear that Lavasseur's hypothesis, "the power of attraction of human groups is, in general, proportionate to their mass," and Weber's conclusion regarding the nineteenth century, "urban growth is essentially a great-city growth," do not account for the growth of cities in the twentieth century. This theory is not entirely without significance, however, as can be seen by the major movement of urban growth in the metropolitan areas.

The growth of cities has become a selective process. Only certain places grow. The basis of selection seems to be functional; that is, cities grow where cities are needed, not just because they are cities. In some cases this is a part of a regional population growth where more adequate and better distributed service centers are required. Again, places may be selected as the location of new activities of

[18] For additional maps of urban population increase and further interpretation, see Figures 16–19, pp. 170–173.

production or service and draw to themselves workers and their families and those to operate the facilities and services of community living. In other places the decentralization of industry operates in a similar way.

Throughout the study of the geography of urban growth these tendencies are increasingly evident: the tendency toward balancing the urban and rural population as urbanization in America continues to increase; the tendency toward the wider distribution of people in urban centers, seen both in the extension of the geographical area of occupation of cities and in many cases in the development of suburban residential places within the immediate metropolitan areas; and, third, the tendency of focal points in the relationships of cities to their hinterlands and regions to be the places of growth.

One of the most important aspects of city growth, which has become clear in the patterns of the war period, is the possibility of controlling the distribution of population and so the growth of cities. Here are potentialities not before apparent for a purposeful redistribution of the population of the United States on the basis of a more efficient use of people and a greater possibility of satisfactory living for people, through a process which fully preserves democratic freedom.

The selective process of urban population growth leads naturally to a consideration of the varieties of American cities.

Supplementary Reading

Census reports include a great many data about cities and their populations, both general and for individual cities and metropolitan districts. Study of these materials can reveal many fascinating details about the growth of cities.

CHAPTER 5

VARIETIES OF AMERICAN CITIES

CITIES differ in many ways, and each way is important in some respect. Some differences may, however, be superficial, while others are fundamental. Are there factors which can be measured so that a classification built upon objective differences can be determined? This is the crux of the problem. The process of trying to determine significant degrees of difference makes the problem more complex.

INDIVIDUALITY OF CITIES

It is well to recognize at the outset that every city is different from every other city. Each is as individual as a person. Historical developments, physical and social environments, relationships, and many other factors enter into the pattern of individuality. Some cities have characteristics of obvious uniqueness.

San Francisco began as a Spanish settlement around the old Franciscan Mission and was within the territory of Mexico for a number of years. This left an imprint of the old, aristocratic, Roman Catholic society of Spain. The first big development was at the time of the gold rush, with its reckless abandon, adventure, and distorted values. The great Pacific harbor facilitated its contacts with the Far East and brought an influx of Orientals. The moderate climate, the sightly location, the development of transportation, and the opening up of the valleys of northern and central California to agriculture by irrigation contributed to the growth and importance of San Francisco.

All of these, and many other elements, made this city the cultural and commercial center of the Pacific coast, with a unique tradition expressed in a fostering of the arts in its museums, symphony orchestra, and opera, in a bohemian spirit with a multiplicity of entertainment, plays, and restaurants, even a Bohemian Club, in a cosmopolitan character with its Chinatown, North Beach Italian

section, and Russian Hill, with the Presidio, a financial district, headquarters of big business and industry, many piers for the stream of
ships, its bridges, ferries, and railroads, and a large and varied suburban area.

So Boston took unto itself the tradition of the sons and daughters
of the *Mayflower;* its leadership during Revolutionary days brought
the title "the cradle of liberty." During the nineteenth century the
concentration of men of letters made it the literary capital of the
United States. During the years of large immigrations many foreign-
born, specifically Irish and Italians, settled in the city to man its expanding industry. Their numbers have had a great democratizing
influence, making this a cosmopolitan center. No longer does the
quip

> The land of the bean and the cod,
> Where Lowells speak only to Cabots
> And Cabots speak only to God

describe the city whose cultural aristocracy has slipped more and
more into a minority, and whose new majority has entirely changed
the political make-up.

New Orleans, the old French city with a large early Spanish population, has a Latin tradition which has persisted through the years
and is expressed in the annual Mardi Gras and the wrought-iron
balconies of the old city. Its strategic location as the point of en-
trance and exit for the Mississippi Valley through most of the nineteenth century, and as the terminus of the Mississippi steamboats,
brought wealth and made it the commercial center of the South and
also a great center of Southern society and culture. Though its commercial importance has diminished, its uniqueness continues.

The old Dutch settlement of New Amsterdam became the English
New York. Its central location and great harbor made it a crossroads
of the world. The Erie Canal, linking the Great Lakes with the
Mohawk and Hudson Valleys, completed the east-west line of transport, whose continued dominance has helped to make New York
America's largest city, filled with people from the whole world as
well as all parts of the United States. It has become the financial,
commercial, and cultural center of America, and the most cosmopolitan and most highly urbanized city in the world, with all aspects of
urban life developed to a high degree.

Birmingham is a young city, founded by a group of industrialists and speculators in 1871 because of a combination of natural resources unique in the world, all the essentials for the production of steel—coal, iron, and limestone—lying side by side. With promise of becoming the industrial center of the South, the industrial supremacy of Birmingham has been thwarted by political and financial manipulation, absentee landlords, racial conflict, competition of Northern industry, and the general economic conditions in the South.

Such characterizations could go on: Richmond, the capital of the Confederacy; Chicago, the transportation center of the nation; Charleston, the seat of Southern aristocracy; Seattle, the center for the great Northwest; Cleveland, with its background of the Western Reserve; Miami, the winter playground of America; Atlantic City, the seacoast summer resort; the Salt Lake City of the Mormons; the Providence of Roger Williams and the Baptists; Tulsa, the city that oil built; Hollywood, capital of the movies. Each city is unique, and its peculiar characteristics are important for an understanding of its behavior, organization, and problems.

Even the small cities have distinctive character, brought about by the particular combinations of such factors as the type of people who were their settlers, the kind of hinterland and its produce, the relationship to other places through transportation, and special historical circumstances. When any city is being studied, the analysis of all such factors should be the beginning, for the unique characteristics give the clues to a city's peculiarities and problems.

CLASSIFICATION OF CITIES

For a general study of American cities, however, similarities as well as differences are of great importance. It is clear from observation that there are different kinds of cities and that the cities of each kind have many similarities. If a relatively small number of groups could be determined, it would materially assist in the understanding of urban America. A classification of cities requires a method which will put like cities into groups which have sociologically significant and measurable differences. Many attempts at such classification have been made, and each has contributed something. Several of the more significant will be reviewed briefly.

Size Classification. The United States census classifies cities by size of population into nine groups. The division is arbitrary. Table 9 gives the number of cities and populations in each group, with the

TABLE 9. Distribution of Urban Places and Population, by City Size Groups, 1950[1]

Size Groups	Cities			Percent of Total Population	Percent of Urban Population
	Number	Percent	Population		
Total United States	—	—	150,697,361	100.0	—
Total Urban	4,270	100.0	87,992,647	58.4	100.0
Places of:					
1,000,000 or more	5	.1	17,302,538	11.5	19.7
500,000 to 1,000,000	13	.3	9,110,922	6.0	10.4
250,000 to 500,000	23	.5	8,131,010	5.4	9.2
100,000 to 250,000	65	1.5	9,410,440	6.3	10.7
50,000 to 100,000	125	2.9	8,826,709	5.9	10.0
25,000 to 50,000	246	5.8	8,644,050	5.7	9.8
10,000 to 25,000	780	18.3	11,962,110	7.9	13.6
5,000 to 10,000	1,174	27.5	8,123,192	5.4	9.2
2,500 to 5,000	1,839	43.1	6,481,676	4.3	7.4

percentage distributions of total population and also of urban population.

This classification has the value of showing the relative importance of the various sizes of cities in terms of the number and proportion of cities and people in each size group. For example, knowing that the degree of complexity of urban organization is related to size of city, the number of cities and the number of people involved in various degrees of complexity of urban life can be seen. The largest cities, with extremely complex organization, are only five, or .1 percent of the cities, but they have 11.5 percent of the total population of the United States and 19.7 percent of the urban population. At the other end of the scale, the simple small cities number 1,839, or 43.1 percent of the cities, but they contain only 4.3 percent of the total population and 7.4 percent of the urban population. The largest part of city people have to cope with the greatest complexities of urban life in the smallest group of cities.

A more usable size classification divides cities into three groups, large, medium, and small, as in Table 10. Comparisons between large, medium-sized, and small cities are important for throwing certain differences into perspective. The more significant differences,

[1] Bureau of the Census, 1950 Census of Population: Preliminary Counts: Population of Urban Places: April 1, 1950. Series PC-3, No. 8 (Jan. 11, 1951), Table 1, p. 2. Note: Unincorporated places included.

TABLE 10. Number and Population of Large, Medium, and
Small Urban Places, 1950

Size Class	Cities			Percent of Total Population	Percent of Urban Population
	Number	Percent	Population		
Total	4,270	100.0	87,992,647	58.4	100.0
Large cities, (100,000 and over)	106	2.4	43,954,910	29.2	50.0
Medium-size cities, (25,000 to 100,000)	371	8.7	14,470,759	11.6	19.8
Small cities, (2,500 to 25,000)	3,793	89.9	26,566,978	17.6	30.2

however, are qualitative rather than quantitative, and these must have primary consideration in classifications of cities.

Historical Classification. Another way of classifying cities is essentially historical. Different periods in which cities have developed have left distinguishing marks in physical structure, types of architecture, and traditional modes of living. The purposes of cities, differing at various stages of the development of the American civilization, their location in relation to means of communication and transportation, the degree to which planning had come into use, all indicate that cities can be grouped according to similarities.[2]

Another classification of this general type, built on the environmental factors of a city, is used by geographers. It relates American cities to their regions and deals with those differences which arise out of the climate, produce, and economy of the regions and the corresponding relationships and influences that are imposed on the cities of the respective regions and subregions. This is of major importance for understanding cities, but it deals more with the *cause* of the differences than with the *differences* themselves and consequently falls within the scope of the following division of this book, which is concerned with the external interaction of cities.

Functions of Cities. Many urban sociologists have resorted to a functional classification of cities, based upon the dominant functions

[2] Louis Wirth, "A Bibliography of the Urban Community," Chap. 10 in Robert E. Park, Ernest W. Burgess, and Roderick D. McKenzie (editors), *The City* (Chicago: The University of Chicago Press, 1925), pp. 175–182.

which cities perform in their society. Gist and Halbert use a six-group classification, with explanations, subgroupings, and illustrations:

1. Production centers.
2. Centers of trade and commerce.
3. Political capitals.
4. Cultural centers.
5. Health and recreation centers.
6. Diversified cities.[3]

Such a classification of cities is empirical, and the necessity for subclasses and qualifications testifies to its lack of exactness. It serves to point out an exceedingly important aspect of the relationship of cities to their society and indicates differences that have many important implications. It is useful, however, only as a descriptive classification of cities. Its chief difficulty lies in the fact that American cities perform many functions and tend more and more to fall into the diversified class.

Harris added to the force and validity of the functional classification of cities by resorting to a means of measurement by which he determined which cities fell into what groups. He was able to differentiate nine types of cities: manufacturing cities (with two subtypes), retail centers, diversified cities, wholesale centers, transportation centers, mining towns, university towns, resort and retirement towns, and political centers. He used the statistics of employment from the 1935 census of business and of manufacturing, and classified each city by its disproportionate percentage in the employment group indicated by the designation. The 605 functional units which were classified contained 988 cities of 10,000 or more population, and each type of cities showed a distinctive geographical pattern in the United States.[4]

In the *Municipal Year Book*, the International City Managers' Association has used two classifications of cities. The first is based on the status of cities in the metropolitan complex and uses six categories: independent cities, central cities, and three types of suburbs —employing, balanced, and dormitory. Their distribution by regions is given in Table 11. The second, similar to the Harris classification,

[3] Noel P. Gist and L. A. Halbert, *Urban Society,* third edition (New York: Thomas Y. Crowell Company, 1948), pp. 8–15.
[4] Chauncy D. Harris, "A Functional Classification of Cities in the United States," *Geographical Review,* No. 23 (Jan., 1943), pp. 86–89.

TABLE 11. Metropolitan Status of Cities over 10,000, by Geographic Regions[5]

Geographic Region[a]	(I) Independent		(C) Central		Suburbs						Total[b]	
					(E) Employing		(B) Balanced		(D) Dormitory			
	No.	%	No.	%	No.	%	No.	%	No.	%	No.	%
New England	39	29.5	16	12.1	29	22.0	10	7.6	38	28.8	132	100
Middle Atlantic	69	31.2	30	13.5	49	22.2	26	11.8	47	21.3	221	100
South	176	71.8	51	20.8	1	0.4	5	2.1	12	4.9	245	100
East North Central	127	54.7	34	14.7	26	11.2	12	5.2	33	14.2	232	100
West North Central	63	70.8	17	19.1	1	1.2	1	1.1	7	7.9	89	100
West	69	56.6	17	13.9	3	2.4	8	6.6	25	20.5	122	100
Total	543	52.2	165	15.8	109	10.5	62	5.9	162	15.6	1,041[b]	100

[a] The states in the several regions are: New England—Conn., Me., Mass., N.H., R.I., Vt.; Middle Atlantic—N.J., N.Y., Pa.; South—Ala., Ark., Del., Fla., Ga., Ky., La., Md., Miss., N.C., Okla., S.C., Tenn., Tex., Va., W.Va.; East North Central—Ill., Ind., Mich., Ohio, Wis.; West North Central—Iowa, Kan., Minn., Mo., Neb., N.D., S.D.; West—Ariz., Calif., Colo., Idaho, Mont., N.M., Nev., Ore., Utah, Wash., Wyo.

[b] Excludes Washington, D.C., and 35 urban places (chiefly towns and townships) for which the data were not available.

[5] International City Managers' Association, *Municipal Year Book, 1949*: "Economic Classification of Cities," by Grace Kneedler Ohlson, Table 1, p. 38.

TABLE 12. Economic Base of Cities over 10,000[6]

Metropolitan Status	Min-ing (Mg)	Trans-porta-tion (T)	Manu-fac-turing (Mm)	In-dus-trial (M)	Di-versi-fied Mfg. (Mr)	Di-versi-fied Retail (Rm)	Re-tail (Rr)	Whole-sale (W)	Re-sort (X)	Edu-ca-tion (S)	Gov-ern-ment (G)	Dor-mi-tory (D)	Total
A. By Metropolitan Status													
Independent (I)	20	9	112	55	57	106	111	11	15	28	13	6	545
Central (C)	2	3	47	13	30	47	13	0	5	1	4	0	163
Suburbs:													
Employing (E)	1	0	88	10	4	2	3	1	0	0	0	0	109
Balanced (B)	6	0	20	11	7	8	8	1	0	0	1	0	62
Dormitory (D)	0	0	0	0	0	0	0	0	0	2	0	160	162
Total cities	29	12	267	89	98	163	135	13	20	31	18	166	1041
B. By Geographic Region													
New England	0	0	66	14	4	9	1	0	0	0	0	38	132
Middle Atlantic	14	3	84	20	21	18	10	0	1	1	2	47	221
South	6	2	38	5	28	60	60	5	12	8	6	15	245
East North Central	5	1	72	41	37	31	3	0	0	7	1	34	232
West North Central	1	4	4	9	3	24	25	1	1	7	3	7	89
West	3	2	3	0	5	21	36	7	6	8	6	25	122
Total all regions	29	12	267	89	98	163	135	13	20	31	18	166	1041
C. By Population Group													
Over 500,000	0	0	2	0	7	4	0	0	0	0	0	0	13
250,000 to 500,000	0	0	3	0	5	14	1	0	0	0	0	0	23
100,000 to 250,000	0	0	18	6	10	9	4	0	1	0	3	3	54
50,000 to 100,000	1	2	30	12	10	21	10	0	4	2	1	13	106
25,000 to 50,000	3	1	57	25	24	28	25	4	5	4	0	26	202
10,000 to 25,000	25	9	157	46	42	87	95	9	10	25	14	124	643
Total all c.	29	12	267	89	98	163	135	13	20	31	18	166	1041

uses the economic base for classification into twelve categories, which are given in three breakdowns, metropolitan status, geographical regions, and population groups, in Table 12.

Leiffer had earlier subjected this basis of classification to measurement, using as his data the enumeration of employed people in cities by industrial grouping in the 1930 census.[7] This study was confined to "Mediopolis," the 140 cities between 50,000 and 150,000 in population.

Examination of the occupational data assembled . . . affords a basis for classification of all cities in our population grouping. Five types can be clearly differentiated:
1. The Commercial City: The Prototype of Mediopolis
2. The Industrial City: Mediopolis in Overalls
3. The Industrial Suburb: The Workshop of the Nation
4. The Residential Suburb: The Parlor of the Metropolis
5. The Resort City: The Playtown of the Nation
On the basis of this classification twenty-seven cities, representing each of the above types, and also all geographical sections of the country, were selected as a sample for more intensive study.[8]

The cities within each group show striking similarities in the pattern of their occupational distribution, and the averages for each group show distinct differences from the others. Table 13 gives the percentage distribution of employed persons by major industrial groups for each group of cities and the range of percentages found within each group in the sample. While the sample is small, the differences are sufficiently clear to indicate that each type of city has its particular pattern of occupations. Taking commercial cities as a norm, and considering them to have a balanced distribution of people by occupations, the determinative divergencies are chiefly in the items of manufacturing, trade, professional services, and domestic services. Commercial cities have less than a quarter of their employed people in industry, while industrial cities have over a third, and industrial suburbs have half. Residential suburbs have the highest proportion in trade and professional services, with a relatively large group in domestic service. Resort cities stand highest in domestic service and fairly high in trade.

Certain other accompanying facts are noted by Leiffer. Industrial

[7] Murray H. Leiffer, *City and Church in Transition* (Chicago: Willett, Clark and Company, 1938), tables, pp. 27–33.
[8] *Ibid.*, pp. 32–33.

TABLE 13. Average and Range of Occupational Distribution by Types of Cities[9]

Urban type	Commercial		Industrial		Industrial Suburb		Residential Suburb		Resort	
Sample cities	Des Moines, Duluth, El Paso, Montgomery, Salt Lake City, Wichita		Altoona, Binghamton, Evansville, Scranton, Tacoma, Winston-Salem		Cicero, Dearborn, Gary, Lynn, McKeesport, Paterson		Cleveland Hts., East Orange, Evanston, Mt. Vernon, Newton, Pasadena		Atlantic City, Miami, San Diego	
Total employed	278,667		245,849		221,837		167,810		148,223	
Occupation	Per-cent	Range	Per-cent	Range	Per-cent	Range	Per-cent	Range	Per-cent	Range
Agriculture and fishing	1.8	1.3–2.9	1.1	.2–3.0	0.4	.0–.8	2.0	.6–5.4	2.8	.5–3.6
Building	6.3	5.5–7.8	5.4	4.5–6.2	5.2	3.6–6.0	7.5	5.2–10.3	9.0	7.7–10.7
Manufacturing, mechanical and Education	22.0	18.2–24.8	39.7	32.7–48.6	49.8	46.2–55.0	14.8	12.3–17.2	13.2	10.9–14.4
Transportation and communication	10.3	8.6–13.5	10.1	5.7–20.2	6.5	5.4–7.4	6.2	3.4–7.6	7.5	6.7–8.2
Trade	20.0	16.6–23.5	15.1	11.6–17.3	12.1	9.2–13.6	21.8	19.2–26.6	19.6	16.7–20.8
Public service	2.3	1.5–3.3	1.8	1.2–2.1	1.8	1.5–2.2	1.7	.8–2.1	7.2	2.0–13.3
Professional service	9.0	6.9–10.5	6.8	5.4–7.9	6.0	4.3–6.7	15.0	12.1–18.5	8.7	7.0–10.3
Domestic and personal service	15.1	11.9–28.8	10.7	7.9–14.6	7.5	5.1–9.2	17.0	11.6–20.9	23.5	14.7–37.2
Clerical	13.3	8.7–16.9	9.3	6.6–10.6	10.7	7.1–18.3	14.1	9.5–20.3	8.5	7.7–9.1
Total	100.1		100.0		100.0		100.1		100.0	

[9] Ibid., Tables I, II, III, V, VI, pp. 45, 64, 85, 102, 117, and Appendix II, p. 282.

cities have more foreign-born, more younger men and women, and a larger proportion of women workers. Industrial suburbs have the same characteristics to a greater degree and are apt to have large concentrations of people of the same nationality backgrounds. Residential suburbs have an excess of women, fewer single males, and more single females. There are also a larger proportion of older people and a smaller proportion of foreign-born. Illiteracy rates are low, and school attendance is unusually high. Evidence of higher standards of living is found in high value of homes, larger proportion of professional people, and amount and quality of retail trade. In the resort cities, the native white population is dominant, and literacy is higher. There is a higher percentage of widowed and divorced men and women.

This method of classification has enabled Leiffer to detect the social circumstances of each type of city, to locate community needs, and to show the pattern of community organization and the program which were required to meet the problems. The grouping of cities carried out in this study not only is significant as such, but has many practical implications. Whether or not a more adequate sample would lessen the differences, or whether this classification would be as valid for the smaller or larger cities, the data have not been compiled to determine.

Goodness of Cities. In spite of differences in tradition, size, history, and functions, the opportunities for good living that are afforded by various cities differ widely. Thorndike has made a statistical analysis of the cities in the United States over 30,000 in population,[10] and also of the cities between 20,000 and 30,000 population,[11] in order to rate their relative "goodness."

Three hundred items susceptible of statistical measurement were obtained for each of the cities. From these, "thirty seven all or nearly all of which all responsible persons will regard as significant for the goodness of life for good people in a city,"[12] were found to be most indicative of differences and, consequently, were selected for use in measuring the relative goodness of the cities. These items were arranged in six groups: first, five items concerning health; second, eight items concerning education; third, two items concern-

[10] E. L. Thorndike, *Your City* (New York: Harcourt, Brace and Company, 1939).

[11] E. L. Thorndike, *144 Smaller Cities* (New York: Harcourt, Brace and Company, 1940).

[12] Thorndike, *Your City,* p. 12.

ing recreation; fourth, eight social and economic items; fifth, five items dealing with creature comforts; sixth and last, a group of six miscellaneous items.

The differences between cities on each item were very great. The chances that a baby would die within a year from its birth were found to be four times as great in some cities as in others. The probability of a girl between the age of ten and fourteen having to work were fifty times greater in some cities. In some cities about every family has electricity installed, while in others less than a third of the families do. Nearly a tenth of the young people between fifteen and twenty-four are illiterate in some cities, while others have fewer than 0.2 percent who cannot read or write. A composite picture of wages shows a range of 100 percent. In like manner, the variations appeared in all the items.

The cities were rated by a composite score which was made up by weighting and combining the thirty-seven items. There was a marked tendency for "good traits to go together in cities."[13] Those cities which were good on one point were likely to be good on the other points, and vice versa, although there was much variation. The final scores were derived from a scale which made zero a combination of the lowest scores on each item found in any city, and the top 1541 the highest scores; the G (goodness) scores ranged from 1110 for the best city to 330 for the worst city.[14]

Thorndike carried his statistical process further in an effort to isolate the various causes of the variation among cities. He studied the relationship of the per capita value of taxable property (W), a combination of items indicating the per capita incomes of the inhabitants of the cities (I), and a combination of other items indicating as closely as possible the intelligence, character, and other personal qualities of the citizens (P). A wide variation among the cities was found also in the scores which were obtained for these factors.

[13] *Ibid.*, p. 29.

[14] This brief summary is taken from the study of the larger cities. The results were essentially the same in the study of the smaller cities.

There is a great difference of opinion among sociologists as to the validity and significance of the Thorndike studies. The criticism has centered on the method, especially in the selection and weighting of items, and also on the results. The fact that differences within cities are greater than those between cities is a problem of any attempt to classify cities on the basis of measurement. If, however, the studies are accepted as an exploratory attempt to discover the possibility of determining measurable differences, and if they are used only in the limited way for which they were intended, the very general conclusions which Thorndike made can be used as a basis for further study.

The correlations between the various scores brought the following results: there was a correlation of +.28 between W (wealth) and G (goodness) which was entirely accounted for by association between per capita taxable wealth and per capita private income, since the correlation between G and per capita taxable wealth in cities identical in per capita income was zero. The correlation between I (income) and G (goodness) was +.56, and the correlation between P (personal qualities) and G (goodness) was +.69. An explanation of the relationship of many other factors singly and in combination added little except to define somewhat and increase the significance of these results. Thorndike's final statement is:

> I estimate that if perfect measures of every fact about these cities and their inhabitants were available, the differences among the 295 cities in the goodness of life for good people would be attributable:—
>> about 60 percent to difference in the mental and moral qualities of the populations
>> about 3 percent to difference in their physical health and energy
>> about 25 percent to differences in their incomes
>> about 2 percent to differences in the works of previous generations (other than giving birth and training to the present generation)
>> about 5 percent to differences in the work of the government
>> about 1 percent to differences in homogeneity of race and culture
>> about 4 percent to causes at present unknown
>
> The surest and most important fact is the relative unimportance of everything except the quality of the citizens and their incomes.[15]

So, by a factual and statistical study, Thorndike demonstrates that a relatively large proportion of good people who have fair incomes makes good cities. Good people are indicated by such things as "citizens who live decently, care about education, read books, and are able to progress well in school, who spend their private money to buy a home, have a telephone, and care for their children's teeth rather than engage in litigation, and who spend public money for teachers, schools, libraries and parks rather than for politicians, city halls, court-houses, jails, streets and sewers. Some cities attract and support artists, physicians, trained nurses and teachers and get along with few male domestic servants."[16]

The reason why good people precede incomes in importance is that the difference comes in what the incomes are spent for. "Good people, rich or poor, earning much or earning little, are a good

[15] Thorndike, *Your City*, p. 117.
[16] *Ibid.*, p. 64.

thing for a city, but the more they have and earn, the better."[17] This means, and the analysis bears it out, that disparity of income is not of primary importance so long as the proportion of very poor families is very small. Factory cities are no worse, as such, than the general cities, but "We may be suspicious of a business enterprise which can maintain itself only by importing cheap labor."[18]

While Thorndike's statistical analysis extracted the factors of principal significance in the relative goodness of cities, it could not determine the underlying conditions in which the variations between cities thrive. This is of major importance in classifying cities. The chief significance of Thorndike's work is that it indicates the relative weaknesses of each city and the potentialities of cities by showing that other cities have been able to make a much better record.

Occupational Constituency.   The clues derived from the functional classifications of cities and the ranking of cities on their relative goodness can be explored further by means of a new breakdown of employed workers fourteen years old and over in cities, given in the 1940 census. In addition to the former breakdown by industrial groups, there is a breakdown by major occupational groups. For the purpose of classifying cities, this has distinct advantages. When workers are classified by industry groups, all grades from unskilled workers to managers are included in the industry or business in which they work. In occupational grouping, however, all professional workers, all clerical workers, all laborers, and so forth in a city are grouped together.

These occupational groupings have important implications. There are differences in the income received by people in the different occupations. While there is a great range in income within most of the groups, the common impression that there is an increase in the amount of income from laborers to professionals is borne out by the facts reported by the census. Table 14 gives the median incomes by major occupational groups from the census distribution of incomes for workers in the predominantly urban occupational groupings, for the United States in 1948.

Occupation also carries significant overtones of intelligence and education. A number of researches have demonstrated a high relationship between these three. Pond, in her sample, found a correlation coefficient of $+.77$ between the intelligence test scores and the

[17] *Ibid.*, p. 67.
[18] *Ibid.*, p. 81.

TABLE 14. Median Income for Persons Fourteen Years of Age and Over with Incomes in 1948, by Major Occupation Group, Male and Female, for the United States[19]

Occupational Groups	Median Income	
	Male	Female
Professional	$3,913	$2,191
Proprietors, managers, and officials	3,548	1,941
Semi-professional	3,202	———
Craftsmen, foremen, and the like	3,081	———
Clerical and kindred	2,940	1,944
Salesmen	2,793	1,208
Operatives	2,685	1,590
Service workers	2,154	1,052
Laborers	1,918	———
Domestic workers	———	425

intelligence demanded by various occupations and a coefficient of +.74 between occupations and length of schooling.[20] Beckman found that, in the persons he studied, the length of education correlated directly with the occupational grades which had been attained.[21] Lorge and Blau, by correlating former intelligence measurements according to occupation with a scale of intellectual requirements of the various occupations, were able to establish a scale of ascending intellectual demands of the major occupational groups.[22]

Intelligence and education are by no means all that is involved in what Thorndike called "the quality of the citizens," but they are the most important and the most measurable factors of "quality."

Occupations, therefore, provide a single index which combines the most important factors of difference between cities—namely, the income and the quality of the employed people. The pattern of occupations also involves directly the characteristics which have led to the various descriptive schemes of classifying cities.

A Basic City Yardstick. On the basis of the data in the United States census giving the distribution of the labor force by major oc-

[19] Bureau of the Census, Current Population Reports: *Consumer Income*, Series P-60, No. 6 (Feb. 14, 1950), Table 14, p. 25.

[20] Millicent Pond, "Occupations, Intelligence, Age and Schooling," *Personnel Journal*, Vol. 11 (1933), pp. 378–383.

[21] R. O. Beckman, "A New Scale for Gauging Occupational Rank," *Personnel Journal*, Vol. 13 (1934), pp. 225–233.

[22] Irving Lorge and R. D. Blau, "Broad Occupational Groupings by Intelligence Levels," *Occupations*, Vol. 20 (March, 1942), pp. 419–423.

cupational groups for American cities, Gillen devised a yardstick by which cities can be measured. He accepted the evidence which indicates that descriptive classifications do not give fundamental differences between cities. His measuring device, consequently, was one to be applied to individual cities, resulting in a scale by which the relative standing of cities could be seen.

The first step was to show by occupational profiles of sample cities that great variations in occupational patterns were to be found. Figure 4 reproduces the illustration of differences in pattern. These

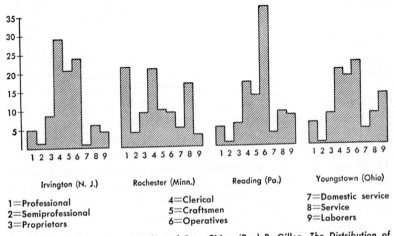

Figure 4.   The Occupational Profiles of Four Cities. (Paul B. Gillen, *The Distribution of Occupations as a City Yardstick* [New York: King's Crown Press, 1951], p. 24.)

differences were put into an occupational score for each city, based on the proportions of the labor force in each occupation group and derived by the use of weighted income ratios.[23]

The cities were divided into four groups, on the basis of the size of their populations, as follows:

Group I	91 cities	100,000 and over
Group II	107 cities	50,000 to 99,999
Group III	213 cities	25,000 to 49,999
Group IV	664 cities	10,000 to 24,999

The distribution of the scores within each of the four size groups is given in Table 15. As might be expected, there is a much greater

[23] Paul B. Gillen, *The Distribution of Occupations as a City Yardstick* (New York: King's Crown Press, 1951), Chap. 4.

TABLE 15. The Distribution of Occupational Indices Among 1073 Cities According to City Size Groups[24]

Occupational Indices	Number of Cities			
	Group I	Group II	Group III	Group IV
150–159				2
140–149		1	1	10
130–139		5	7	18
120–129	1	4	11	47
110–119	19	15	27	127
100–109	35	36	72	165
90– 99	19	21	55	134
80– 89	13	13	22	74
70– 79	3	7	13	55
60– 69	1	3	4	17
50– 59		2	1	11
40– 49				1
30– 39				1
20– 29				1
10– 19				1
0– 9				
Totals	91	107	213	664
Means	100.22	99.85	100.46	100.37
Sigmas	10.94	16.37	16.38	18.58

range in scores among the smaller cities, which can be and often are given over to single industries. The largest cities, on the other hand, have become more and more diversified. Figure 5 shows the occupational profiles of the high-score cities and the low-score cities in each of the size groups. This method of scoring does give a distribution of cities, but does the score give an index of what the city is?

If the assumptions are correct and occupations designate income and education, then the combined occupations should provide an index of the ability of a city to support its institutions and also an indication of the degree to which a city is likely to accept superior standards. Gillen checked the significance of the city scores with education and with health. He used an education index which combined the median years of schooling of the population twenty-five years of age and over, the percentage of youth aged from sixteen to twenty who were attending school, and the percentage of those eighteen and nineteen years of age who were high-school graduates, from the data in the 1940 census. These data were available only for

[24] *Ibid.*, Table 5, p. 42.

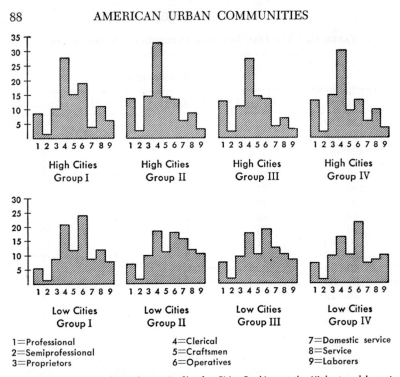

Figure 5. Occupational Distribution Profiles for Cities Ranking at the Highest and Lowest Ten Scale Points on Occupational Score, by City Size Groups. (Paul B. Gillen, *The Distribution of Occupations as a City Yardstick* [New York: King's Crown Press, 1951], p. 45.)

cities above 50,000 population, so that indices for cities only in the first two groups of cities were possible. When correlated with the occupation index, the correlations were: Group I cities, +.78; Group II cities, +.90.[25]

Since infant mortality has been generally found to be the best single index of a community's health, the infant death rates were correlated with the occupation indices, with the result of −.65 for Group I cities and −.70 for Group II cities. The corresponding correlations between education and health were: Group I cities, −.54; Group II cities, −.81.[26]

The occupation index has predictive value for education and health. When the occupational pattern of a city is such that it produces a high occupational score, the standards of education are

[25] *Ibid.*, pp. 54–61, 63.
[26] *Ibid.*, pp. 81, 82.

likely to be high and the health conditions good. When the score is low, the reverse would be true.

When he compared his method of scoring cities with the descriptive classification of Harris, Gillen found that Harris' types were not mutually exclusive[27] and consequently could have no significance for social characteristics or institutional standards. He therefore designated six city types by dividing the range of indices for individual cities into six equal parts, as shown in Table 16. As he states, "regardless of size, location, special function (so-called) and other factors, we should with confidence expect to find that cities falling within a given typing would have many similarities."[28]

TABLE 16. Six Types of Cities Based on
Occupational Scores[29]

Type of City	Occupational Score Range
A (h^1)	118 plus
B (h^2)	109–117
C (h^3)	103–108
D (h^4)	95–102
E (h^5)	84– 94
F (h^6)	0– 83

Not only is this a classification which is readily usable, because the score for a city is easily determined, but it is an indication of many things about a city and its people. It is important for administrators in education, health, social service, and community organization because it indicates problems and needs, the level of understanding of the population, and also the inherent potentialities of the city for development.

It is of greatest importance to city planners and to organizations such as chambers of commerce, whose business is the expansion and development of their cities. Many an agency of this type, in the past, with all good intentions, has brought new enterprises into its city which have lowered the standard of living in the city and decreased its actual potential for development because, through a rearrangement of the occupational pattern, it has lowered the level of the city's occupational make-up. If such activities are approached through this occupational yardstick with an understanding of its

[27] Ibid., pp. 96–99.
[28] Ibid., p. 105.
[29] Ibid., p. 105.

significance and implications, mistakes of this type are not likely to happen.

On the basis of this relative standing of cities through their occupational patterns, the varieties of cities become an important factor in the understanding of cities.

Supplementary Reading

Gillen, Paul B. *The Distribution of Occupations as a City Yardstick*. New York: King's Crown Press, 1951.

The theory, method, and application of a simple measuring scale for cities which has basic implications for city development.

Harris, Chauncy D. "A Functional Classification of Cities in the United States." *The Geographical Review,* No. 23 (Jan., 1943), pp. 86–89.

The best presentation of the functional classification of cities.

Lieffer, Murray H. *City and Church in Transition*. Chicago: Willett, Clark and Company, 1938.

A practical demonstration of the usefulness of a classification of cities.

Thorndike, E. L. *Your City*. New York: Harcourt, Brace and Company, 1939.

The details and rationale of the first major attempt to devise a scale for the measurement of cities.

PART II

EXTERNAL INTERRELATION-
SHIPS OF CITIES

CITIES play an important role in American culture, and their manifold interrelationships are of great importance. The basis of these interrelationships is the flow of energy and materials in which cities are at the focal points (Chap. 6). Urban and rural areas have come to be mutually interdependent in a great variety of ways (Chap. 7). The great natural regions of the United States are increasing in their significance in the operation of American society, and the central cities of the regions are the instruments of this operation (Chap. 8). In consequence, cities become responsible in many ways for the development of their regions (Chap. 9).

CHAPTER 6

CITIES IN RELATION
TO THE FLOW OF ENERGY
AND MATERIALS

In the discussion of the development of cities, it became clear that cities are in strategic situations. Surpluses of material, both agricultural and fabricated, flow through urban centers, where they are exchanged as commodities of commerce. This phenomenon, which underlies the rather obvious historical and continuing connection between cities and trade, needs to be looked at in a more comprehensive and fundamental way.

Human life is, of course, the basis of the urban community. Life, however, cannot be considered apart from its environment. The fact that the maintenance of human life requires food, clothing, and shelter makes this obvious, for these necessities are derived from the environment by the unremitting use of human capacities. That the environment for civilized man is largely his own artifaction may obscure, but can never end, this relationship. Perhaps any realistic concept of community takes into account the manifold interrelations of life and environment.

LIFE AND ENVIRONMENT

Ecologists[1] have had opportunity to study the interrelations of living things and their environment in situations varying all the way from what might be considered a minimum, to what might be considered a maximum, of human intervention. They have learned to recognize *communities* of living things and to classify communities among several distinct types. They have also learned to identify sev-

---

[1] Ecology is "that division of biology which treats of the relations between organisms and their environment" (*New College Standard Dictionary*).

eral distinct patterns of community development and to determine trends therein by attention to each of several critical factors in community development. In all of this inquiry, it has been of crucial importance to keep clearly distinct the ways in which human-dominated communities differ, and do not differ, from other communities of living things.

The surface of the world itself turns out to be a vast community, composed, in turn, of great regional communities. Each of these, in turn, is composed of subregional communities, and so on—to almost any degree of analytical detail. A research ecologist may choose to deal with a community as extensive as the arctic tundra or to focus upon a community as delimited as the southern slope of a Connecticut pasture abandoned from agricultural use and reinvaded by red cedars. The great regional communities are defined by correlating several interrelated kinds of data, climate, topography, the dominant vegetation, and the resulting soil type proving to be the most significant and convenient. As evidence that communities so defined are not obscured by human occupation, certain striking relationships become apparent when cultural data are matched with these physical and ecological data. For example, the greatest prevalence of illiteracy in the United States is largely coextensive with the southern pine area, and cotton-growing with both. The abandonment of farms as a result of wind erosion locates closely the high plains area. Speculative cereal farming and its accompanying distress are, in general, found in the grass lands.[2]

What are the critical factors that determine the character of a community? Six such factors have been isolated by ecologists. Before listing them, two points need emphasis: first, each factor is, in itself, a variable, a process; second, all of the factors interact continuously, so that they are at any point of time simultaneously causes and effects of one another. The factors are: (1) the evolution of new plant and animal species; (2) the migration of species from the locality of their origin; (3) the climate, slowly shifting over long geological periods of relative stability, during which the climate operates more nearly than any of the other factors as the basic determinant; (4) the topography, also slowly remodeled as the processes of gradation run their diverse local courses, to establish everywhere, together with climate, the drainage phases of the water cycle;

[2] Paul B. Sears, *Life and Environment* (New York: Bureau of Publications, Teachers College, Columbia University, 1939), p. 84.

(5) the soil, an intricate process resulting from the interaction of the living community with its inorganic context; and (6) the patterns of biological interrelations that develop, in the general direction of stabilization.[3]

If no cataclysm occurs in any of these factors, a community develops toward what is called a *climax condition*. This condition has characterized any community developing in its natural course without interruption by the artifactions of man. Toward the appropriate climax condition a community runs its predictable course through a sequence of phases summarized by ecologists as the *succession* to be expected in that area.

The climax condition is an identifiable community pattern representing a *dynamic equilibrium* at a maximum *biological potential*. The community is identifiable in terms, usually, of the dominant plant species. The phrase "maximum biological potential" implies a maximum abundance of life in terms of the particular combination of factors involved in any situation—a maximum conversion of the inflowing energy into the energies of living processes, a maximum turnover rate of materials through living processes, through the "chemical cycles." (As will be subsequently seen, this is a very different concept from that of maximum production, familiar in the industrial world.) The phrase "dynamic equilibrium" means that stabilization has been achieved, so that a durable community pattern is revealed in which the relative populations of living species are in adjustment to each other and to the available supplies of energy and materials. But, as has been pointed out, more is actually happening in the climax community than in any preclimax phase of succession. This is not a static, but rather a dynamic, condition, in which change continues to take place and growth always goes on because of the inherent variable qualities of all of the factors enumerated. So long as none of the determining factors changes disruptively, however, changes will produce adjustments that maintain an equilibrium.

If human intervention is withdrawn from an area, it will revert to this natural process of succession leading toward the appropriate climax condition—unless the dislocation of factors has been too severe. In that case, even an impressive civilization can vanish and leave a wasteland so impoverished that nature cannot catch hold. In such cases, if the wasteland can be reclaimed at all, it can be only

[3] *Ibid.*, pp. 86–97.

by the most intensive modern techniques. Perhaps there is no more striking illustration of this course of events than the eastern Mediterranean littoral, where the Jewish people have currently undertaken the great task of reclamation.[4]

MAN'S INTERVENTION

Prior to what historians call the Agricultural Revolution (in other words, before man had equipped himself with the techniques essential to domesticating herd animals and hard cereals), he fitted into any community he invaded as just another species. The techniques which brought the Agricultural Revolution, later reinforced by the rapidly developing technology of the Industrial Revolution, however, gave man the power to intervene so much more powerfully in community processes that we might concede a seventh determining factor in community development—man's productive techniques. The science of ecology is new, but it has seen that man's intervention has been, so far, generally a disruption. Temporary, impressive productiveness has made possible great expansions of human populations and the nourishment of each of several cultures. But over and over again the interaction of factors in community development was only imperfectly understood. Natural resources, such as soil, forest, grass, fish, and other wild life, that under proper handling are now considered potentialy self-renewing were more or less rapidly exhausted because, while they were recognized as exhaustible locally, they were considered limitless continentally as men proceeded to wear out farm after farm, raze forest after forest, and the like. In the tropical or arctic extremes the scars of mismanagement are less impressive. In temperate or subtropical areas, however, men either have made deserts or have stabilized their existence on the basis of unremitting labor and continuing poverty. Nowhere in history, probably, has the damage been swifter, severer, more ominous, than in the continental United States—for all our deceptively continuing abundance.

The stake of the urban dweller in the arresting and reversing of these trends is clear today to every literate person. The city is still as dependent upon its rural base as it ever was in the river valleys of the classical Middle East. This dependence is equally real, whether

---

[4] W. C. Lowdermilk, *Palestine, Land of Promise* (New York: Harper & Brothers, 1944).

seen in terms of long-range trends in the use of resources (for instance, the water or milk supplies from the countryside) or in the operation of the economy (for example, the supplementary markets for farm and factory products) or in terms of intermittent hazards (such as the menace of flood waters from mismanaged watersheds to congested cities). Sooner or later, the citizens of the cities will need to join in planning for the adoption of more scientific procedures which will take account of the principles which have been induced by ecologists from the study of successions toward the climax community and the conditions for its maximum biological potential. The importance of this proposition will be clearer when the place and the function of cities in our culture are considered.

URBAN COMMUNITIES

The factors determining community development have two applications in the case of urban communities. The first is in direct dealing with these factors as they operate in the urban community. The second is in the role of the urban community in the productive processes of the economy.

Before developing further these two applications, it is necessary to emphasize that they are *applications*, not *analogies*. It must be pointed out further that the use of ecological science in this chapter is an enterprise quite distinct from the work of the "ecological school of sociologists," who have adapted from ecology the search for recognizable patterns, in space and time, of community development. There is no occasion here for suggesting either the power or the limitations of that effort.

The City as a Biological Community.   To pass in review the factors in community development, with our attention directed to the city, will forcefully remind us that even there, where human intervention has been most extreme, man is still involved in a community that an ecologist would recognize as such.

The evolution and migration of plant and animal species include the appearance of pathogenic microörganisms which cause epidemics among shade trees, pets, or the human population. So, too, the deliberate breeding of new or preferred plant and animal varieties, as well as the continuous hybridization of humans, is included. The immigration or emigration of families or individuals of the human species, carrying with them their particular arrays of genes and their particular cultural conditionings, is of special significance since people of rural and foreign origins have settled disproportionately in American cities.

City-dwellers have become surprisingly independent of the immediate inconveniences or perils of weather and climate by an extensive use of shelter and other techniques for controlling internal environments. On the other hand, their congestion renders them peculiarly vulnerable to extreme events of storm or flood and harasses them with periodic or perpetual conditions of air pollution. The engineers have made over the given topography in many instances to fit the superimposed urban pattern; they have created the artificial water cycle of water supply, sanitary sewer, and storm sewer, a system which has made them assailable by deficiencies in water due to the terrific waste in these systems. The soil has largely lost its significance, for land has become a resource not for agricultural production but as site. In built-up areas of continuous pavement this is obvious, but even in those portions where soil has a designated use for growing things it is also true.

The pattern of biological interrelations in the city includes, of course, the incredible congestion of the human population and that most peculiar association of living things: man, his pets, his vermin, and his parasitic microörganisms. The last two engage him in unrelenting struggle, for the housefly, clothes moth, cockroach, bedbug, rat, mouse, and the like can be more concentrated in numbers per square mile than he is, and health and medical experts work to suppress disease epidemics resulting from explosive reproductions and migrations of microbes. In fact, the improvement of sanitation techniques is regarded as one of the significant preconditions of the very existence of the modern city. These techniques comprise the chief measures that for more than a century have enabled most cities in the Western world to maintain their populations.[5]

Parks and lawns are thoroughly administered communities, designed and maintained by human vigilance and labor in weeding, planting, fertilizing, spraying, cutting, and the like. Such is the cost of designing a nonclimax community, arrested from pursuing its natural succession.

The humans themselves are most interdependent in their many interrelations. The division of labor has been carried to such an ex-

[5] National Resources Committee, *Our Cities: Their Role in the National Economy* (Washington: Government Printing Office, 1937), p. 31.

treme that countless people are involved in supplying anyone's needs. Almost every conceivable good and service has become a commodity. Social and political organization is correspondingly complex. Cultural interchange and innovation reach their most distinctive intensity. Nowhere so much as in the city are man's productive techniques so visibly and so inescapably evident in his works. "What man hath wrought" here replaces the original community so completely that both failure and promise are equally convincing.

Appreciating this paradox, Lewis Mumford could celebrate the city in these words: "It is in the city, the city as theater, that man's more purposive activities are formulated and worked out, through conflicting and cooperating personalities, events, groups, into more significant culminations. Without the social drama that comes into existence through the focusing and intensification of group activity there is not a single function performed in the city that could not be performed—and has not in fact been performed—in the open country."[6]

Productive Processes in the Urban-Rural Community.   Because of the interdependence of the urban nucleus and the adjacent countryside, it is impossible—ecologically, economically, or politically—to divorce the urban from the rural aspect of a community or to consider either singly with any possibility of genuine understanding. For that reason, the phrase "urban-rural community" represents a more realistic concept of this single larger unit that must be understood and, in the final analysis, administered as a whole. One pattern which significantly integrates this urban-rural community is the flow of energy and materials within it.

In any community, an ecologist finds an analytical description of the flow of energy and materials a powerful device for understanding not only what is going on but what is likely to go on and even what could go on, with some skillful intervention, at some time in the future. The great physical laws of thermodynamics and the modern theory of evolution are effectively restated in such terms. For instance, as early as 1886, Boltzmann remarked that the "struggle for existence" is a struggle for free energy available for work. A present-day ecologist, Oliver Pearson, carrying the principle into his research, has compared the competitive performances of species in the forests of eastern Pennsylvania. Using data such as the average

[6] Lewis Mumford, *The Culture of Cities* (New York: Harcourt, Brace and Company, 1938), p. 480.

weight of the individual organism, the number of organisms of each species per acre, and the metabolic rate of each species, he was able to calculate the "kilogram-calories per acre per day" captured and converted in the diverse specific protoplasms: long-tailed shrew, earthworm, deer, aboriginal Indian, modern Pennsylvanian citizen, and the like. In accounting for contemporary man, he found it necessary to consider the larger-than-local area from which materials flow to the consumer, and he had to supplement the energy converted in human metabolism with the several times greater share of energy technically controlled in the processes of our industrial culture.[7]

The engineer has devised the *flow chart* as a device for describing in detail the flow of energy and materials through productive processes. Simplified flow charts are probably familiar to many laymen as effective graphic presentations of industrial processes, to the public, for public relations purposes. The significance of the flow chart is lost to view, however, unless it is appreciated as more than merely an educational device, to show a picture of operations. It is used by engineers at the same time as a measuring instrument for appraising the performance of an industry and for suggesting further developments in the rationalization of the process. It would seem to be a fruitful hypothesis that the flow-chart device could be adapted for the appraisal of the performance of the urban-rural economy, not only to understand, but to improve, that performance.

Such an analysis would reveal two complementary aspects of the urban-rural economy: first would be the appropriate uniqueness of the local economy in relation to the larger economy, the basis for import from and export to the wider world, in terms of natural resources, productive techniques, human labor reserves, and consumer markets; second would be the feasible degree of self-sufficiency whereby certain goods and services are exchanged internally.

The city also proves to be a regional community in the flow and conversion of energy and materials under increasing technical and administrative controls. Largely outside the nucleus, in the countryside, are the extractive processes whereby raw materials are gained from natural resources, together with those two great natural processes, photosynthesis and the water cycle, which provide any com-

---

[7] Oliver Pearson, "Metabolism and Bio-energetics," *Scientific Monthly*, Vol. 66, No. 2 (Feb., 1948), pp. 131–134.

munity with the basic energy and material conversions. To mention two consequences only: each day two quarts of milk and a hundred gallons of water per urban dweller need to be diverted from "milkshed" and "watershed" into the city.

In or near the population center, the most spectacular success in the processing of materials, the fabrication of artifacts, and the maintenance and facilitation of good living is evident. Converging upon the city, ramifying through it and diverging from it, can be traced the actual physical routes of this flow. Most apparent of all, although often skillfully concealed, are the utility networks: electric power, telephone, telegraph, fuel gas, water, sewerage, and public carrier routes of all kinds. Along the transport lines, people move to and from work, shopping, recreation, public service, and the like, and the distribution of raw materials, finished goods, supplies, and services takes place. A flow chart of one phase of this movement is shown in Figure 6. Along the lines of communication go the dissemination of ideas and the routing of administrative decisions. To follow this flow of energy and materials through the urban-rural community by engineering-economic analysis is to understand critically the processes that maintain the community.

Since our undebated overall criterion of community performance is the quality of living achieved in the community, the flow of energy and materials must be traced ultimately to each consuming unit. It is in terms of the amplitude of the goods and services which actually reach individuals that the good life can be, in part, defined. Some of this definition, in this era, is inescapably technical, assuming, for example, the form of the energy and material requirements of human nutrition[8] or of the properly conditioned internal environment now technically possible in good housing.[9] An ample flow of energy and materials through a community does not of necessity mean a good life to all or even to many people—witness Gary (Indiana), even in boom times. A community, however, through which the flow is feeble or capricious cannot possibly provide for its people a good life consistent with our technical potential.

[8] National Research Council, Food and Nutrition Board, *Recommended Daily Dietary Allowances,* revised, Circular Series, 129 (Washington: Government Printing Office, 1948).

[9] National Association of Housing Officials, *Practical Standards for Modern Housing* (Chicago, 1939); American Public Health Association, *Thirty Criteria of Healthful Housing* (New York, 1938).

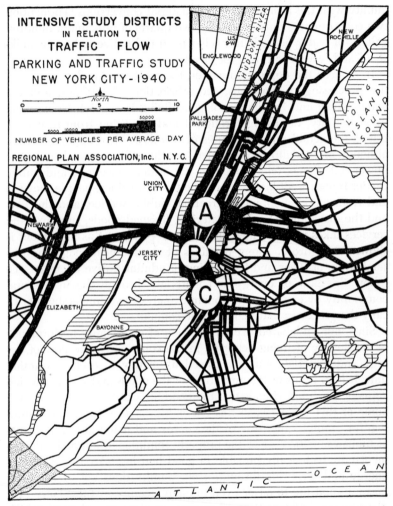

Figure 6. Traffic Flow, New York City, 1940. (Regional Plan Association, Inc., New York City.)

IMPLICATIONS FOR CITIES

In looking briefly at some of the implications for cities that can be derived from the preceding argument, the concluding chapters of this book are unavoidably anticipated. For the implications point to the future, and discussion shifts, consequently, into advocacy of how men can collaborate not only to ensure their common survival, but to improve everywhere to equivalent levels their diverse ways of life.

Ecologists, appraising the climax community (that stage, in the ecological succession or evolution of a plant-animal community, which is stable and self-perpetuating), see its stability and its great abundance. Engineers, appraising the performance of a productive process, measure it against the ideal of the completely rationalized process, where the flow of energy and materials is continuous and automatic and ingeniously preventive of waste. It would seem that an idealized urban-rural community might be envisaged which would meet, among other requirements, those of the ecologist and engineer. And it seems likely that, from ecological and engineering knowledge concerning the development of natural communities and productive processes, some of the effective working principles needed for the design and administration of more advantageous human communities can be adapted.

For one thing, men need to replace the naturally established climax communities which they have invaded and destroyed as well as the inadequate communities which have developed (according to inept, if any, planning) with *administered communities,* which, separately and together, should comprise an evolving design, perhaps the culminating artifaction of the species. As always, these communities will be communities within communities, on every level of detail or scope, from the immediate residential neighborhood or contour-cultivated slope to the unified river valley, to the larger region, to the one-world community itself.

Vast areas of the earth's surface may be permitted or even assisted to remain in, or revert to, climax conditions for interrelated purposes of scientific inquiry, aesthetic or recreational use, and engineering economy. A beginning has been made in the national forests and the large national parks left undisturbed.

Other vast areas will be laid out for agricultural production as soil building, plant and animal breeding, sustained-yield forestry, and chemurgic techniques are refined, and as man learns to intervene as powerfully to conserve his resource base and improve his standards of living in the countryside as in the city. Here the labor of men and power machines will maintain in stable balance and unfailing productiveness the artificial (because arrested in succession) communities of cropland, pasture, orchard, vineyard, plantation, and range.

Finally, residential, industrial, service, administrative, and cultural zones will be designed as those community nuclei where men have chosen to focus their social endeavors—the immediate and appropriate environment for their association as homemakers, as workers, and as free citizens. A fundamentally significant planning unit will be the integral urban-rural community defined earlier in this chapter.

The development of such communities would seem to require the coördinated findings of diverse scientific investigators, natural and social, and the refinement of comprehensive planning procedures. Such procedures include: the survey and appraisal of biological, mineral, technical, and human resources; the survey and appraisal of community performance as evident both in the flow chart of energy and material transformations and, ultimately, in the quality of living of individuals; the location of problem areas by comparing community performance with emerging criteria of possible performance; the projection of a comprehensive, time-scheduled, yet flexible plan for closing the gap between performance and possibility; the education and organization of people for participation in planning and in carrying plans into effect; the provision for democratic processes in the making of social policy—in the making of value choices among the predicted consequences of alternative proposals. All of this might closely integrate public educational processes with those of community planning.[10]

Careful consideration would have to be given to determining tentatively, on the one hand, the feasible measure of self-sufficiency for the urban-rural community and, on the other hand, the unique role of the urban-rural community in the larger economy and culture.

There are at least two validities in the concept of a climax condition as the model for the administered community of the future. First, the maximum potential in the flow and transformation of energy and materials is the basis for both stability and prosperity. This is a very different principle from maximum production with unconsidered exploitation of energy and materials. In the administered community, this flow can come increasingly under technical control. Man stands today on the threshold of an era when he can extricate himself from his recent dependence on the burning of exhaustible mineral fuels. Whether a technically managed photosynthetic proc-

[10] Mumford, *op. cit.*, pp. 391–401.

ess or the development of nuclear energy or a combination of the two techniques will first secure the long future for the species is debatable as yet.

Second, stabilization does not mean the cessation of change but increasingly the provision of the very context within which the adventure of cultural innovation will freely engage the energies of increasing numbers of human beings. And the criterion of prosperity is no longer the neutral measuring of the rate of energy flow and material circulation through living processes but the quality of living, both material and cultural, for the individuals of the permanently dominant species, man, the culture-conditioned creator of culture.

Certain suggestions emerge concerning the relationship of individuals to their communities. First, the meaning of a man's work can be clarified and validated by revealing his role in maintaining the flow of goods and services in the community. Productive labor can resume its proper prestige in this social perspective. Second, no man should work with techniques that persist unnecessarily on a level lagging behind those of the advancing technology. Primitive processes should not be permitted to hold men anywhere to obsolete levels of poverty and hardship. Third, since each community is part of a larger community, which, in turn, is part of a larger community still, and since there must, therefore, be produced a hierarchy of master plans within master plan, the citizen needs to acquire a community-consciousness on every level, from neighborhood to world.

Thus a theory of community development under human control for emerging human purposes is suggested. Progress can continue unshackled, no longer on the assumption of a providential natural law by naïve optimists who disregard the equivocation of experience, but on the basis of the continuous fulfillment of a vast system of master plans whose schedules and revisions are determined with full regard to reliable data and democratically effected value judgments. When and if man assumes control of his further destiny in these terms, he becomes a citizen in a world community that is inherently democratic. His struggle will no longer be that of class against class or of nation against nation, but the struggle of man to revise upward continuously the conditions of living for himself and his fellows and so to explore the endless frontier of his further development. The winning of freedom to take up this challenge is the essence of the vast social revolution through which man is now pain-fully attempting to pass.

As this profound change in the ordering of communities comes toward accomplishment, it will record and inaugurate the mutual fulfillment of the discipline we call scientific and the commitment we call democratic. The integration of scientific and democratic pro-cedures seems now to be the most promising basis for resolving the grave problems already crowding the current agenda of history and for moving ahead into the single world society in which the peoples of the earth can participate on truly equivalent terms—enjoying equivalent standards of living and contributing equivalently to cul-tural change.

The bases of this whole new world structure must be, surely, the thinking and acting of free men who understand the interaction of factors in community development and participate coöperatively in ordering both their own immediate communities and the interrela-tions of these communities with others within the hierarchy of com-munities that is our world.

THE PLACE OF THE CITY

The city holds, then, a strategic place in this perspective. It be-comes the nucleus of a well-integrated urban-rural community, the efficient and stirring site for certain kinds of work and play and in-teraction, the strategic center for the patterned flow of energy and materials, as of men, their goods and services and ideas. Such an integration requires new concepts and objectives as well as new forms of social, economic, and political organization. The city-as-nucleus would no longer dominate in the sense of exploiting its rural environs, either in fact or in attitude. The resultant culture would be inextricably urban and rural. Sociologists have listed the diverse advantages and disadvantages common or peculiar to urban *and* rural living. Conceivably the advantages of both could be preserved, refined, and extended to all members of the urban-rural community; while the disadvantages could be discarded for all. The extension of electric power to the countryside is a partial step in this direction. The development of metropolitan regional planning looks in this di-rection. Other steps are the city-planning effort to bring green and open spaces within walking distance of every city-dweller and the proposed reorganization of metropolitan areas into identifiable and

bona-fide neighborhood communities.[11] The historic and still continuing cleavage between city and country can be erased.

In working toward this end, cities would be expected to take a
large measure of leadership because of their location, resources, and
specialists. But the process would need to be wholly coöperative.

These last few pages have been, as earlier conceded, an anticipation of the concluding chapters of the book. The bulk of the book,
which comes between, should provide a detailed, comprehensive,
and, so, substantial foundation for this advocacy. The task of the
sociologist in a world in trouble is not merely to describe that world,
but to develop some of the techniques which men can employ for
moving it in the direction that men learn to want it to go.

Supplementary Reading

Hartford, Ellis Ford. *Our Common Mooring*. Atlanta: University of
Georgia Press, 1941.

    Note especially the preface by Walter Cocking.

Perry, Clarence A. *The Neighborhood Unit: A Scheme of Arrangement
for the Family-Life Community*. Monograph 1 in *Neighborhood and
Community Planning* (Vol. 7 of the Regional Survey of New York and
Its Environs). New York: Regional Plan of New York and Its Environs,
1929.

    The basic and most complete description of neighborhoods as the
basis for city-planning.

Sears, Paul B. *Life and Environment*. New York: Bureau of Publications,
Teachers College, Columbia University, 1939.

    Dealing with the basic relationships of human beings to their en-
vironment as the foundations of social development.

[11] This has been advocated by the New York Regional Plan Association in
its bulletin. It was accepted as the basis of the London County Plan. See p. 554.

CHAPTER 7

RURAL-URBAN RELATIONSHIPS

THE basis of the interdependence of rural and urban areas has been stated in the preceding chapter. Now for a more specific reference to the details of interrelationships. For convenience these interrelationships are grouped under five headings, though their differentiation is neither clear-cut nor easy: physical and demographic relationships, economic interdependence, social interdependence, cleavages in ideas, and problems of communication.

PHYSICAL AND DEMOGRAPHIC RELATIONSHIPS

A map showing the distribution of population in the United States clearly indicates that around each concentration of population marked by a city the density grows less as the distance from the city increases. The location of the cities is both cause and effect of this pattern of population distribution: effect, because one of the primary determinants in the location of cities has been convenience for collection and distribution of agricultural produce, and consequently cities have grown up at places which combined accessibility to large hinterlands under agricultural cultivation and access to transportation systems; cause, in that growing cities need more food and so create a pressure on adjacent farm lands to meet these needs directly through intensive production, especially of vegetables and dairy products, so that more valuable crops make more valuable land, intensive cultivation makes smaller farms, and smaller farms use more people.

Another aspect of rural-urban relationships in connection with population is very significant. Since cities can no longer reproduce themselves, they must, in the nature of the case, draw the people they require from the rural farm areas, where population increases

at a rate which produces a surplus. The inevitable rural-urban movement of population is of two kinds. The sporadic, but larger, shifts
are due to the suction of the city in times of rapid industrial expansion, such as occurred during World War II, which brought many
Negroes and poor whites from the rural South into the northern cities, or to the expulsion of farmers from deteriorated soil, such as occurred when migrants from the Dust Bowl went to the Pacific coast.
The steady, continuous shift to maintain population balance, however, is from the agricultural hinterland to the nearby city, often
through the villages.[1] This interdependence has to do with the very
existence of both city and country. There are economic implications
of this population movement which will be considered presently.

Brunner and Kolb, in their study of rural social trends, made comparisons of concentric zones extending out from cities on a large
number of factors. Taking the city county as the center, the adjoining counties as tier one, the next counties as tier two, and so forth,
they found measurable differences between the tiers on most
points.[2] The results of these comparisons were, in part: City and tier
one counties tended to have small farms with truck crops, fruit, and
intensive dairying, and consequently more compact communities,
more dense population, and contacts of all sorts with their cities.
Urban characteristics, such as lower birth rates, fewer children, and
more persons in the productive age range, were showing up in these
areas. The *second* and *third* tiers showed particularly a great increase in dairy products and less influence of urban characteristics,
especially tier three. The outer zone of tier *four* had larger farms,
but a smaller proportion of acreage under cultivation, with crops
such as cereals and cotton. Outer tiers experienced greater fluctuations of land values in both inflation and depression. The high ratio
of children to women from twenty to forty-five years of age in the
outer zones makes adequate education difficult and more subject to
economic depression, as evidenced by the analysis of educational
expenditures through 1934, which revealed that "the more rural the
area, the harder was public education hit."[3]

[1] J. H. Kolb and Edmund deS. Brunner, *A Study of Rural Society*, third
edition (Boston: Houghton Mifflin Company, 1946), Chap. III, especially pp.
38–45.
[2] E. deS. Brunner and J. H. Kolb, *Rural Social Trends* (New York: Mc-
Graw-Hill Book Company, 1933), Chap. V and Appendix D.
[3] From *Rural Social Trends*, by E. deS. Brunner and J. H. Kolb. Copyright, 1933. Courtesy of McGraw-Hill Book Co.

The results of these comparisons clearly show the influence of nearness to cities on rural areas. The nearer rural areas are to cities, the greater is the influence of the cities.

ECONOMIC INTERDEPENDENCE

The economic interdependence of city and country has essentially two parts. The first is made up of the city's need for food, fiber, and other raw materials, on the one hand, and, on the other hand, the country's need for markets. The second is reciprocal, the farmers' need for manufactured goods and the industrialists' and their workers' need for purchasers for their products.

Agricultural Markets. The influence of cities upon the use to which agricultural land in their vicinity is put, already referred to, is first of all the result of the food needs of the city people. The process of supplying these needs, however, raises problems. Farmers may find their land best fitted to produce grain, but if the demands for fresh vegetables and dairy products in the nearby city offer them higher prices for these things, they raise vegetables and operate dairy farms the best they can. Though transportation has developed so that fruits and vegetables from all over the country and many parts of the world can be, and are, brought especially to the larger cities, still, because it is more economical, the bulk of these products come to the cities from their own environs.

Milk and other dairy products are also, in the main, produced and consumed in local areas. The milkshed of the great cities is very extensive. A farmer in New Hampshire may have his herd and barns inspected by a Boston organization which sets the standards for his milk and the conditions under which it must be produced. So cities reach out to impose health and quality standards upon the farmers in their vicinity.

Similar relationships are found with respect to agricultural products of food and fiber that are processed or used as raw materials in the city factories. Kind and quality of the products of the land are controlled by the demand of the city industries. For example, many farms in the South continue to raise cotton after the soil is worn out for this crop, because the cotton mills in the cities are established purchasers of their produce.

These relationships, however, are mutually advantageous; in fact, they are an inevitable interdependence without which neither country nor city could survive.[4]

Industrial Markets. The case for the products of industry is not so obvious, but it is just as vital, nevertheless. The balance which makes for success and profit or failure and loss to the manufacturers is the amount of goods which rural areas can absorb. The need for goods is there. The trend toward increasing mechanization of agriculture has created a demand for a great variety of farm machinery; the extension of rural electrification has opened the way for many uses of electrical power and household appliances; the growing awareness on the part of rural people of city standards of living has created a demand for the same sort of manufactured articles that city people use. The determining factor as to whether or not the rural market is available to industry is the farmers' ability to pay for goods. This depends upon the income from agricultural production. The depression which hit agriculture in the early 1920's was a significant factor in the financial collapse of 1929 and the ensuing depression. The Agricultural Adjustment Act, whose first principle was the equalization of the farmers' dollar, was as important to the city people as to the farmers. The effect of the increased farm purchasing power was seen, for example, in the fact that freight-car loadings to rural states doubled almost immediately following the receipt by the farmers of the first AAA checks.[5]

This economic interdependence of rural and urban America is basic to prosperity; and if city people must in the future pay higher prices for their food in order to maintain a parity of income of farmers with industrial workers, the extra cost will continue to come back to the cities as the farms and their families absorb more and more manufactured goods. This will result in more stable employment in the factories and a higher standard of living all around.

Commercial Relationships. As the demands for a greater variety of goods on the part of farmers increased, the crossroads and small-town retail establishments became less and less adequate to serve them. This resulted in two developments. Village merchants mod-

---

[4] Carl C. Taylor and others, *Rural Life in the United States* (New York: Alfred A. Knopf, 1949), pp. 414, 416, 431–432, 436, 441, 490.

[5] Department of Agriculture, first report, Agricultural Adjustment Administration, March 26, 1934. For a brief but comprehensive analysis of the AAA and its results, see Kolb and Brunner, *op. cit.,* pp. 187–197.

ernized their stores and their business methods, and a greater number and variety of stores were opened. In 1910 there was an average of 44.9 commercial establishments in each American village; in 1920, 49.3; in 1930, 56.2.[6] Farmers also came to use the more highly specialized shops in the cities for certain of their purchases. Kolb and Brunner quote a 1930 study by *Successful Farming* of Des Moines to the effect that farm families traveled average distances of from 5.9 to 7.8 miles to purchase hardware, farm machinery, groceries, and automobile accessories, 14 miles for furniture, and 19.5 miles for women's apparel.[7]

In either case the cities profit, for wholesale distribution is a city function, and whether rural people use their automobiles to make their retail purchases in the nearby cities or more goods are distributed through the intermediary of local stores, some of the money they spend makes its way to the city. As banking has tended to be dominated increasingly by cities through branches, the return of money to cities is further facilitated.

SOCIAL RELATIONSHIPS

Within the range of social organization the relationships between cities and their rural environments are manifold. These relationships may be characterized in the main by the influence exerted by cities because of their greater advance in social organization and the techniques of social services and by services which cities have extended to rural people.

Education. Although half the children and young people of America have been enrolled in rural schools, according to present standards of education they have received an inferior training, principally because the resources of rural areas have not been sufficient to pay for modern buildings, well-trained teachers, and the other essentials, especially for a scattered population. The advances which have been possible in urban areas because of more concentrated population and larger available funds have, however, had an influence upon rural education. One-teacher schools have decreased 42 percent from 1929–1930 to 1945–1946, to 86,563; the Office of Education reports that by 1950 the number had further decreased to 75,000. This change was accelerated by the assistance of the federal

[6] Kolb and Brunner, *op. cit.*, pp. 282–289.
[7] *Ibid.*, p. 380.

government through the Public Works Administration for the building of new schools. Some advance has been made toward the equalization of educational opportunity through the increase in state funds for public education and through federal funds for vocational education under the Smith-Hughes Law and for special projects such as school lunches under the Lanham Act. Developments have, in the main, followed the patterns set by city schools. The newer developments in curriculum have been especially effective in the rural situation when they have been under competent teachers.

On the secondary level many country young people attend the central high schools in the nearby smaller cities. While on the whole this provides better opportunity, it has the disadvantage of educating those from the farms and villages in the secondary schools made for the city's children.

In adult education, rural America has far surpassed the urban areas, largely by the very practical and well-organized program of the Coöperative Extension Service in agriculture, homemaking, and 4-H clubs. Through state organizations with a staff of specialists and county organizations with paid staffs and the well-developed use of volunteer leadership, most of the rural areas have been covered. In fact, in a few states, notably New Hampshire, New Jersey, New York, and Connecticut, workers have been employed to operate in cities. So in adult education the influence has been reversed, though the response to this influence in cities has been, to date, all too meager.[8]

It should be noted that the influence of rural America on city schools can be seen in the school terms, the vacations of which, coming at the time farmers' children are most needed in the fields, have little relationship to conditions of urban life.

Religion. Rural churches have been even more subject to the impact of their social environment than schools. The conservatism of rural people, with persistent denominational loyalties, has tended to maintain many feeble churches, with programs in many cases consisting of preaching services and Sunday School.

Under the impact, however, of national denominational organization and the growing knowledge of the more adequate services of well-developed city church programs, there have been in some places developments of various forms of united churches, in which

[8] A comprehensive summary of rural education is given in Kolb and Brunner, *op. cit.*, Chaps. XVIII, XIX, and XX.

larger memberships and greater resources have made possible
broader programs and a greater variety of group organizations.

On the other hand, the continued rural-urban migration has had
an influence toward conservatism in organizations, methods, and
teachings on most urban churches. It has partially accounted for the
increase in reactionary small churches in cities and has resulted in
a considerable proportion of city churches (some 25 percent) being
essentially rural churches in size and organization.[9]

Social Services. Social welfare in rural areas consisted largely in
the barest minimum of relief, doled out by local agencies, until the
collapse of local relief in the depression. With the coming of federal
subsidies of various kinds, used through state administration, not
only the same resources, but also the same procedures and standards, became available to rural as to urban areas. In addition, special programs such as that of the Farm Security Administration were
devised for the rehabilitation of farmers. Perhaps the most important result of the experience of these years was that rural people became aware of the problems of social welfare and the necessity of
doing something about them for the good of the community. It is a
real advance, for example, when local welfare officials carry on their
operations by using the techniques of family case work and have as
their objective the rehabilitation of families rather than simply passing out groceries and fuel for temporary subsistence.

Health. Up to the turn of the century people in the rural areas of
the United States enjoyed a higher level of health than those in the
cities, if morbidity and mortality rates are accepted as an index. As
public health programs in the cities were extended and medical
services increased, the rates of illness and death in urban areas decreased to below those in rural areas. Where public health has been
organized in rural communities, rates have also improved. Many
studies reveal that the number of doctors in rural areas has been
decreasing over a long period. The number of hospitals has never
been adequate, although there has been some increase in recent
years. Inadequacy of services and facilities for medical care in the
country makes rural people dependent on their nearby cities.

Government and Community Organization. Because the problems and interests of rural people are distinctly related to their
agricultural environment, their government and community organi-

[9] H. Paul Douglass and Edmund deS. Brunner, *The Protestant Church as
a Social Institution* (New York: Harper & Brothers, 1935), pp. 29, 83.

zation has developed its own patterns. The growth of local government has taken some lessons from urban experience. In New England many of the towns have organized as municipalities. In other rural parts of the country, county government has had greater development. Where there are medium or large cities, their government overshadows that of their counties. While some rural people participate in some organizations, such as churches, lodges, and women's and men's clubs, especially in their county-seat cities, by and large the organized life tends to keep rural and urban people apart and to magnify their respective special interests.

CLEAVAGES IN IDEAS AND VALUES

The definition of a city which has been proposed was based on the artificial processes of industrial production, while by contrast the life of rural people was centered on the creative production of agriculture. The influence of these very different environments has a profound effect on the patterns of living, the ideas and the values of the people.

Farmers are dependent on natural conditions: the soil and the weather. Their days are regulated by the sun, and their seasons are those of nature, which dictate the demands of their crops. Farmers are essentially individualists, and even their increasing use of cooperation is built on their sense of individual initiative, perseverance, and responsibility. On the other hand, the lives of city people are regulated by clocks, working hours, and schedules. Their seasons are matters of arrangement and convenience. They are dependent upon the facilities which men have devised. Weather is only a matter of convenience in most occupations. People are so used to their dependence upon others and their complexity of human relationships that they take them for granted.

Rural people quite naturally lay great stress on characteristics and qualities of individuals. Because there are fewer people in rural communities, each one knows a great deal about his neighbors' behavior, and all are forced to regard highly the respect of their fellows. Convention holds a firm grip on people. Consequently, such things as drinking, smoking by women, and even laziness and procrastination become generally frowned on, and, because of these strong pressures for conformity, such "vices" are less frequent. On the other hand, city people, even in the midst of high population

density and a myriad of human relationships, can and do live anonymously. As persons, they have great freedom to do as they please.
This puts a serious strain on an individual's integrity and principles,
which sometimes is too much for him. Individual virtues, therefore,
do not have the same degree of importance in cities. Capacities and
abilities are regarded more highly. The impact of these differences
is increased by the greater degree of homogeneity generally found in
rural communities.

Kolb and Brunner point out that city residents have a broader
range of experience than country people because they see more people, find themselves in more situations, and are exposed to a far
greater number of environmental action-patterns. At the same time,
however, their occupational experience is more limited than that of
farmers or villagers. The latter's wider range of occupational activities tends to make them sterner, more virile, persevering, patient,
and dependent upon facts.[10]

Again, because city people must, in the nature of the case, live
entirely by the intermediary of money, money as such has come to
be considered of great value, and the tendency is to measure success
in terms of how much money a person has. In the country a man's
success is more apt to be measured in terms of his character and his
service to his community.

These differences are not clear-cut, and their variation is great.
The important point is that the environmental factors surrounding
the lives of country and of city people are of such a different character that their respective ideas, values, and patterns of thinking are
different. This is a fundamental problem in the development of understanding and coöperation on any broader-than-local basis.

PROBLEMS OF COMMUNICATION

Developments of communication in its many and varied aspects
have had a profound effect by bringing rural and urban people into
like habits of living. They read the same newspapers, listen to the
same radio broadcasts, and see the same movies, all of which have a
predominantly urban tone. They get around in the same kinds of
automobiles for the same kinds of purposes. They are subject to the
impact of the same advertising in newspapers and periodicals, radio
commercials, and billboards. They use the same products, whether

[10] Kolb and Brunner, *op. cit.*, pp. 83–84.

soap, toothpaste, breakfast food, or cigarettes. They even wear clothes of the same type and style.

This is all to the good, except that the influences are largely urban, whereas turnabout would also be advantageous. But the standardization of life which results is, in the main, in its more superficial aspects, and rural and urban people can grow to be much alike and yet make no progress toward mutual understanding. Lack of understanding will continue so long as rural and urban people see their interests in conflict. It is still too often true that city workers think that farmers are conspiring to keep the cost of food so high that they cannot maintain a decent standard of living, and farmers think that organized workers fighting for shorter hours and higher wages are trying to make a greater inequality in standard of living by keeping farm incomes low and making the prices of manufactured goods rise. There is still far too little realization that in terms of a prosperous country the problems are all one and the same.

The weak spot in communication between rural and urban America lies in the fact that their respective peoples seldom work together on common problems and by so doing build a broader basis for mutual confidence and understanding. The problems of communication, therefore, are problems of a social organization through which rural and urban people can coöperate in building better communities on a broader base.

Rural-urban relationships are becoming increasingly close because the character of the modern world tends to multiply interdependencies. Some relationships facilitate understanding; others emphasize cleavages. But a coöperative life is essential to both rural and urban people.

Supplementary Reading

Kolb, J. H., and Brunner, Edmund deS. *A Study of Rural Society,* third edition. Boston: Houghton Mifflin Company, 1946.

A comprehensive analysis of American rural communities, with consideration of the relationships to cities.

CHAPTER 8

CITIES AND THEIR REGIONS

THE implication of the two preceding chapters, that cities cannot be profitably considered apart from the areas surrounding them, should be carried one step further. Before doing so, however, it should be noted that difficulty in understanding the United States often arises from the fact that this vast country is usually examined either as a whole or in terms of its component states. Sociologically, neither the country nor any one of the individual states is a homogeneous unit. The latter, indeed, are mere accidents of history and possess highly artificial boundaries. In contrast to the states, there are farily well-defined areas or regions in this country which, when used as units of study in examining people in their areal relationships, provide a much sounder basis for sociologically understanding American society. Use of the regional approach to the study of urban communities is usually highly fruitful because the character and function of cities can thereby be clearly determined in terms not only of their setting in American society but of their relationships to the resources and forces which support them.

AMERICAN REGIONALISM

The idea of the *region* as an area worthy of study and useful as an instrument of analysis has grown primarily out of the field studies of geographers, and to a lesser extent out of those of geologists, biologists, and soil scientists. The closely related concept of *regionalism*[1] as the sum total of the effect of a region upon its floral, fau-

[1] There are certain drawbacks attendant upon the use of any term of analysis ending in "ism" because it smacks of a doctrinaire point of view (which certainly is not an attribute of American students of regionalism). The term "regionality" has been proposed, but it is hardly applicable, for its structure connotes merely the "regional-ness" inherent in a region itself. Indeed,

nal, and human inhabitants, originated in the thinking of geographers, historians, and economists. It was introduced into sociology in 1920 by Warren H. Wilson, whose classification Morse and Brunner used in their study *The Town and Country Church in the United States* in 1923. McKenzie published his *Regional Sociology* in 1924. Howard W. Odum, however, popularized and extended the concept and its utility in his monumental study *Southern Regions of the United States*[2] and in the later, more general work *American Regionalism*.[3]

The concept of regionalism has been simply expressed by Renner and Renner as follows: "regions . . . originate in the process of man adjusting himself to his natural environment. In this process of adjustment, a social environment slowly develops to fit the underlying natural one. The result is to create in turn a force called regionalism. This force is part natural, part socio-economic, and part psychological."[4] Following this definition, seven great regions of the United States are outlined fairly definitely (despite a few marginal uncertainties) as shown in Figure 7. Despite numerous equalizing factors at work, such as migration, mobility, the facility of transportation, movies, and the radio, it is stated: "As long as the various parts of America differ in climate and soil, water and minerals, fauna and flora, geographic location and landscape character, just so long must man think and behave differently in dealing with such factors. Despite standardization in certain aspects of American life, diversity in other aspects must not only continue, but actually increase."[5] This diversity is fundamental and has profound implications with respect to the character of the life and work of people. This diversity involves physical differences, economic differences, separate histories, different sociologies, different political philosophies, different leaders and eminent men, different heroes and leg-

---

Renner used it in this latter sense as early as 1935 (see *Annals* of the Association of American Geographers, Vol. 25, No. 3). Furthermore, Renner suggests that a better word to denote the dynamism of areas might be "regionocracy" or "regionarchy."

[2] Howard W. Odum, *Southern Regions of the United States* (Chapel Hill: The University of North Carolina Press, 1936).

[3] Howard W. Odum and Harry Estill Moore, *American Regionalism* (New York: Henry Holt and Company, 1938).

[4] George T. Renner and Mayme P. Renner, "Regionalism in American Life," *Teachers College Record*, Vol. 43, No. 5 (Feb., 1942), p. 338.

[5] *Ibid.*, p. 340.

ondary figures, unique social types, different dialects, regional music and song, prose literature, poetry, and art.[6]

Odum and Moore say: "It is not possible, therefore, to understand or to direct society except through the regional approach. Somewhere within the realistic bounds of regional science and arrangement will be found both the elements and tools of any great totality

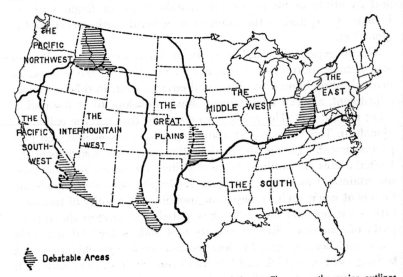

Figure 7. The Seven Great Regions of the United States. These are the major outlines of the differentiation of American culture. (George T. Renner and Mayme P. Renner, "Regionalism in American Life," *Teachers College Record*, Vol. 43, No. 5 [Feb., 1942], p. 339.)

and unity of national development."[7] They go on to give an exposition of a variety of definitions of regionalism[8] and summarize five general types of regions commonly recognized in the United States:

first, the natural region, such as mountain range, river valley, or plain; *second,* the metropolitan region, where the city is the center and focus of the radiating territory adjacent; *third,* a generally loosely used designation which implies the section or provincial area from which loyalties, patriotism, folkways radiate [had they pursued their analysis further, they would probably have found this to be the geographic or human-ecological region described by Renner and Renner and actually underlying their

6 *Ibid.,* pp. 340–353.
7 Odum and Moore, *op. cit.,* p. 13.
8 *Ibid.,* pp. 13–28.

own group-of-states divisions]; *fourth*, the region based on administrative convenience, as for instance territorial divisions used by national organizations or governmental bureaus or departments; and *fifth*, the group-of-states region, which, if state lines be used primarily as the arbitrary margins of measurement, may comprehend in varying degrees most of the other types.[9]

They discard the first four types of regions, not because they consider them unimportant, but because they seek a practicable division of the United States which would give promise of being used.

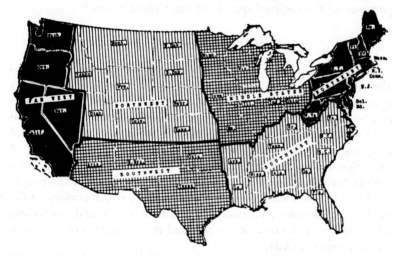

Figure 8. The Six Major Societal Group-of-States Regions. These are utilized in *American Regionalism* as having approximately the largest available degree of homogeneity measured by the largest number of indices available for the largest possible number of purposes. (From *American Regionalism* by Howard W. Odum and Harry Estill Moore. Copyright, 1938, by Henry Holt and Company, Inc. Used by permission of the publishers.)

Their primary goal is the delineation of the "composite societal region" made up, with due attention paid to all pertinent considerations, of a "group of states" and with due allowance for subregions and districts.[10] The resulting six regions are shown in Figure 8.

The Stanford University group under the direction of Professor Paul R. Hanna, which coöperated with the Progressive Education Association in their program and publication on "The Role of Education in Utilizing Regional Resources," working toward the same

[9] *Ibid.*, p. 29.
[10] *Ibid.*, pp. 30–32.

objective of delineating societal regions made up of groups of states, arrived at an eight-region division of the United States. Idaho was placed with Washington and Oregon to make a greater Pacific Northwest, Utah and Arizona with Nevada and California to make an enlarged Pacific Southwest, and New England was made a region separate from the remainder of the eastern states.

There is no intention here of debating the relative merits of any particular pattern of regions, or to argue whether there be six, seven, or eight American regions. The point, rather, is to indicate the importance of the regional quality of the United States.[11]

REGIONS IN OPERATION

The development of the use of regions is far greater than is usually supposed. Almost all federal and many national organizations operate in one way or another on a regional basis. A regional map can be found on the walls of almost all high officials of the federal government, large industrial establishments, or national social and religious organizations, showing the areas by which the affairs of the office are carried on. The United States has been divided into regions for administration and operational purposes, but the people are loath to acknowledge either the regionality of the country or the existence of the many barriers of tradition, loyalties, and institutions which stand in the way of the political reorganization of the country on a regional basis.

More than one hundred departments, bureaus, and other major agencies of the federal government have established regions of various sizes and shapes. Each has devised its regional arrangement on the basis of convenience for administration and services, with the result that there are as many patterns as there are offices using regions, even differing sets of regions for bureaus and agencies being used within the same departments, without coördination or coöperation.[12]

The large business establishments which serve the whole nation

[11] Those interested in exploring further the geography of natural and socio-economic factors will find a whole series of regional delineations presented by Renner, Gans, Dimock, and Crane, in a report of the National Resources Committee, *Regional Factors in National Planning* (Washington: Government Printing Office, 1935), pp. 171–177.

[12] Odum and Moore, *op. cit.*, Chap. VIII. Selected maps of various regional patterns of federal government agencies are shown in National Resources Committee, *op. cit.*, pp. 206–223.

have found it expedient to organize their sales and distribution by some sort of regions. By so doing, they have been able to operate an otherwise unwieldy business, render better and more rapid service, develop good will, and, when necessary, adapt their products to special regional needs. Industry usually shows natural regionalism owing to the environmental relationships of raw materials and facilities of production and transportation.

In similar manner, churches have their bishoprics, and colleges and schools their regional associations, as do trade, fraternal, and professional organizations, and historical and learned societies. All in all, these areal schemata are legion. More coöperative relationships and operations can be carried out where there are proximity and a better mutual understanding due to the similarity of conditions, problems, and interests.[13]

Only one real experiment in operative regionalism has been tried in the United States, the Tennessee Valley Authority. The Tennessee was a river of extremes: its valley suffered from severe floods and soil erosion, and, as a result, its people were constantly in distress; great numbers lived in poverty, and their problems were beyond their ability to solve. Transportation was a serious problem, and power was unavailable, and yet the potential of the river for the improvement of transportation and for the generation of electric power was great.

A prior start had been made by the construction of Wilson Dam and the Muscle Shoals power and nitrate plants, one of the projects of World War I. To salvage this enterprise and carry on and expand the plans then evolved, Congress established the TVA in 1933 at the request of President Roosevelt, whose message to Congress requesting it contained these statements:

It is clear that the Muscle Shoals development is but a small part of the potential usefulness of the entire Tennessee River. Such use, if envisioned in its entirety, transcends mere power development; it enters the wide fields of flood control, soil erosion, afforestation, elimination from agricultural use of marginal lands, and distribution and diversification of industry. In short, this power development of war days leads logically to national planning for a complete river watershed involving many states and the future lives and welfare of millions. It touches and gives life to all forms of human concerns. I, therefore, suggest to the Congress legislation to create a Tennessee Valley Authority—a corporation clothed with the

[13] Odum and Moore, *op. cit.*, Chaps. IX and XV.

powers of government but possessed of the flexibility and initiative of a private enterprise. It should be charged with the broadest duty of planning for the proper use, conservation, and development of the natural resources of the Tennessee River drainage basin and its adjoining territory for the general social and economic welfare of the Nation. This authority should be clothed also with the necessary power to carry these plans into effect. Its duty should be the rehabilitation of the Muscle Shoals development and the coordination of it with the wider plan.[14]

This flexible organization with power to act included parts of seven states in its scope. It called on the resources of engineers and experts throughout the range of modern skills of science and organization. It carried out its plans with the active democratic participation of the people in all of the developments. The technical achievements have been substantial and are reported with care and detail in many volumes of scientific reports by TVA engineers, agronomists, town-builders, chemists, biologists, foresters, public health experts, architects, and others.

These technical reports will interest the experts. The average citizen will measure the change through reports of another kind: in the records of new private industries established in the valley, of failing enterprises revived, more money in people's hands, less tax delinquencies, increased bank deposits, a greater volume of buying at the stores—trends clearly established before the war. The citizen may read of the decade's change in records of new public library service or state parks established where none had been before, more hospitals, county health units almost doubled, less tuberculosis and malaria and other "low-income" diseases. He may read of the number of miles of lines built to bring power to the farms of the area and the rapid increase in the amount of electricity used by the people—unprecedented in this country. He may reflect on the better quality of food produced and the increased yield per acre on the land, or analyze the ton-miles of traffic increase on the river. He may figure the potential value of the millions of seedlings planted in farm woodland and forest. He may see the newly created "Great Lakes of the South," the beauty of their thousands of miles of wooded shoreline unmarred, deep blue waters set among high mountains and abounding with game fish.

Such sights and such records reflect the ways in which, as this beautiful valley has changed, the lives of several million fellow Americans have also changed.[15]

[14] Quoted in National Resources Committee, *op. cit.*, p. 85.
[15] David E. Lilienthal, *TVA—Democracy on the March* (New York: Harper & Brothers, 1944), pp. 9–10.

Lilienthal believes, however, that the greatest accomplishment was the demonstration that a genuinely democratic process can use modern technology in the service of all men to the accomplishment of greater individual freedom and the development of individual personality.

Odum and Moore, concerned primarily with the value of the TVA from the standpoint of American regionalism, say:

The chief significance must be found in the TVA as a great experiment in the twin motivation of developing and utilizing both the physical and human resources and as a type of subregion.

The three-fold significance . . . as a subregional symbol is: first, its availability for a national-regional laboratory, revolutionary in its methodology, heroic in its sweep; second, its tremendous significance in the framework of realistic regional analysis and planning; and, third, its reality as a type of actual subregion of the national scene.[16]

This consideration of regionalism is for the purpose of indicating the reality of this phenomenon in America and the potentialities of regional development when organized and planned, and principally for the purpose of pointing out the framework within which cities must be considered.

CITIES AND REGIONS

In relation to the various regions of the United States there are cities which both historically and functionally are important. In discussing the separate histories of the seven regions, Renner and Renner present a map showing the early settlements. This is reproduced in Figure 9. The authors' inventory of these regional beginnings is as follows:

The settlement of the East dates back to Plymouth in 1620, but it also dates back to Fort Weston in 1607 and Nassau in 1614. Its story is also told at Nieuw Amsterdam (1623), Pemaquid (1625), Boston (1630), Fort Christina (1638), and Fort Duquesne (Pittsburgh, 1754).

The story of the South, on the other hand, begins at Port Royal (1562), St. Augustine (1565), Roanoke Island (1584), Jamestown and Williamsburg (1607 and 1633), Fort Prudhomme (1682), Biloxi (1699), Mobile (1702), Natchitoches (1717), San Antonio and New Orleans (1718).

Settlement in the Middle West is scarcely younger than in the East, but derives from different sources. Ashland, Wisconsin (1665), Michili-

[16] Odum and Moore, op. cit., pp. 105–106.

mackinac and Green Bay (1669), Fort Miami, Peoria and South Bend (1680), Prairie du Chien, Wisconsin (1685), East St. Louis (Cahokia—1698), Kaskaskia, Illinois (1700), Detroit (1701), Vincennes, Indiana (1735), St. Louis (1764), Marietta and Cincinnati (1788), and Independence, Missouri (1831).

Two thousand miles beyond the Middle West, the Pacific Southwest began with San Diego (1769), San Francisco (1776), Jedediah Smith's

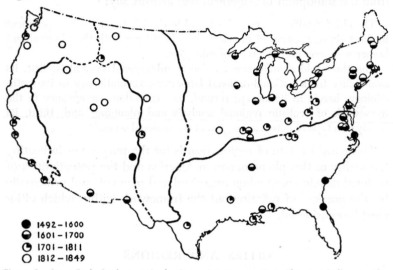

Figure 9. Some Early Settlements in the Seven American Regions. This map indicates quite graphically that the history of each of our periods is rather venerable. (George T. Renner and Mayme P. Renner, "Regionalism in American Life," *Teachers College Record*, Vol. 43, No. 5 [Feb., 1942], p. 343.)

arrival in Los Angeles in 1826, and gold at Sutter's Mill (1848). In this same far western theater, settlement in the Pacific Northwest began at Astoria (1811), Fort Vancouver (1825), Salem (1834), Walla Walla (1836), and Tumwater on Puget Sound (1844).

In the Intermountain Country, the story opens with Santa Fe (1597), El Paso (1682), Tucson (San Xavier and Tumacacori, about 1700), Fort Ashley, Utah (1825), Fort Hall and Boise (1834), Salt Lake City (1847). In the youngest region, the Great Plains, the drama starts with the first trip on the Santa Fe trail (1805), the fur station at Three Forks, Montana (1808), Bents Fort (circa 1809), the opening of traffic on the Santa Fe Trail (1822), Fort Laramie (1834), Denver (1858), the first transcontinental railway (1869), the cattle kingdom in the 1870's and the coming of the dry land farmers (1880's).[17]

[17] Renner and Renner, *op. cit.*, pp. 342–344.

Many of these places are important cities in their regions today, but some have been passed by and replaced by other centers in the development of the regions.

The Committee on Regional Planning of the National Resources Committee later known as the National Resources Planning Board, in their report,[18] point out at length the basic fallacies in defining regions with reference to metropolitan centers, or basing them on administrative convenience, or making their boundaries conform to

Figure 10. Possible Planning Regions Based upon Major Metropolitan Influence. (National Resources Committee, *Regional Factors in National Planning* [Washington: Government Printing Office, 1935], Fig. 16, p. 158.)

state lines, and quite rightly so, for the whole concept of regionalism is based on making areal units in which people have common problems, like conditions, and similar interests. The Committee, however, do go so far as to present a map showing possible planning regions based upon the dominent influence of major cities (see Figure 10). However, as is pointed out, metropolitan spheres of influence are only partial elements in the total regional picture and not its fundamental outline. And further:

Some large cities are created by the regions which contain them and for which they are in many respects centers of integration, but many other cities are not products of regional forces. These instead are created

[18] *Regional Factors in National Planning*, pp. 157–167.

by larger factors in the total national economy. Most of the million-cities are probably of this latter type. To identify regions with such cities, therefore, is to create a regionalism of somewhat dubious validity. Many of the smaller cities do exhibit a certain areal control, but their application as regional criteria results in a great number of divisions, whose use could only result in planning upon a district rather than a real regional scale.[19]

The Committee's map showing twelve regions as they were worked out to indicate "maximum homogeneity of social, economic and environmental elements," and consequently "regarded as one of

Figure 11. Possible Planning Regions Based upon Composite Planning Problems. (National Resources Committee, *Regional Factors in National Planning* [Washington: Government Printing Office, 1935], Fig. 20, p. 166.)

the best possible segregations of composite planning problems," is shown in Figure 11. "Particular weight was assigned to the factor of land-use problems because of its preëminent significance in underlying any possible planning program. Some consideration was also paid to the insistence of that general sectional consciousness which is apparent in general thinking and reference." On this map are indicated certain urban centers whose relationships indicate them to be integrating centers of their respective regions.

[19] *Ibid.*, p. 159.

TYPES OF RELATIONSHIPS

Through the lines of communication and transportation which stem from cities, the patterns of movement of the people, of distribution of goods, of channeling of produce, are formed. In these same patterns are also to be found the lines of administration, consultation and discussion, planning and coöperation. There are, however, different types or orders of cities in terms of their relationships within the regions. These types can be clearly designated, although in the case of any particular city the type may not be clear-cut, or it may be a combination of types.

First, the district city—those cities which are directly related to areas of significant size and some degree of natural and social unity which are less than regional in extent. The size of the area will vary greatly. Where population is dense, especially in the northeastern and Atlantic seaboard sections of the country, where the cities are relatively close together, the districts will be smaller. Often the district city will be a county-seat city, though the districts will seldom be smaller than several counties. In the western part of the country, a district city is more likely to be a state capital with a district as large as, or larger than, a state, but usually the district area will not be conterminous with a state. This is the center of the metropolitan community discussed in Chap. 13.

Second, the regional city—those cities which by functions and relationships are the focal points of the region and through which the region tends to operate. These centers will be the logical place for whatever regional headquarters may be developed. It is possible that some regions may be bifocal and so have two centers.

Third, the supraregional city—those cities which are more than regional in their significance; that is, whose functions and relationships are national in their scope, and which are involved in the processes of interregional relationships rather than the integration of a region. The largest American cities are for the most part of this kind, although it is possible that some cities may be both regional and supraregional at the same time.

Even those cities which do not seem to fit precisely into any of these categories will inevitably have many relationships to the region of which they are a part, and an understanding of these relationships is essential to the understanding of the city. These relationships are of such a character that they impose definite responsibilities on the cities, which the next chapter will consider.

Supplementary Reading

National Resources Committee. *Regional Factors in National Planning.* Washington: Government Printing Office, 1935.

This gives basic information important to the consideration and development of regions as functioning units in the United States.

Odum, Howard W., and Moore, Harry Estill. *American Regionalism.* New York: Henry Holt and Company, 1938.

This is the comprehensive work in this field, written by those who developed the field.

White, C. L., and Renner, G. T. *Human Geography.* New York: Appleton-Century-Crofts, 1948. Especially Chaps. 1, 40, 41, and 42.

This presents a geographical theory of human society based on the philosophy of regionalism. An important approach, to be taken into consideration by the sociology student.

CHAPTER 9

RESPONSIBILITIES OF CITIES FOR REGIONAL DEVELOPMENT

IN a number of respects cities have profited greatly through their relationships to the regions in which they are located. This has come about, on the one hand, through the increasing services which cities perform for their areas, and, on the other hand, through the intensification of the organized life of the cities as concentrations of population have grown.

CITIES DRAIN THEIR REGIONS

The circumstances involved in the development of cities have, in the very nature of the case, created and continued a drain of their regions both in population and in economic resources.

Population Drain. With the great increase in the mobility of people, the shifting of population has become a significant element in the United States. There were 15,734,798, or 12.0 percent of the total 1940 population, who had changed the communities in which they lived from 1935 to 1940: 11.1 percent of the urban population, 16.5 percent of the rural nonfarm, and 10.1 percent of the rural farm. The moves were in all directions and to and from all types of areas. Table 17 shows where the 1935–1940 migrants came from, and Table 18 shows where these same migrants went to. More than half the migrants came from the cities, but nearly two-thirds of these went to other cities, while half of those leaving the villages and a quarter of those leaving the farms went to cities. Farmers moved to other farms, and many villagers moved to other villages. In the shifts cities suffered a net loss of around 8 percent, which was chiefly in the larger cities, for of the ninety-five cities of 100,000 population or over in 1930 or 1940 only ten had a net gain from migration from 1935 to 1940. It is, however, the large numbers who come into cities which are of concern here.

TABLE 17.   Where 1935–1940 Migrants Came From[1]

	Number	Percent
Total migrants	15,734,798	100.0
From cities	8,895,255	56.5
From rural nonfarm	2,982,627	18.9
From rural farm	3,014,932	19.2
From rural (nonclassified)	658,578	4.2
No report, rural or urban	183,406	1.2

TABLE 18.   Where 1935–1940 Migrants Went To, in Percentage[2]

To	From		
	Urban	Rural Nonfarm	Rural Farm
Cities	63.7	49.4	25.4
Rural nonfarm	27.2	38.3	21.4
Rural farm	9.1	12.2	53.1

The in-migrants are indispensable to American cities, for without them the cities could not go on. "It is probable that the urban population of the nation as a whole has produced less than 50 per cent of its present members."[3]

Although the rate of population growth of cities decreased significantly after 1930, migration continued. Table 19 gives an analysis of migration to cities from 1935 to 1940.

The most significant fact here is that cities draw people mainly from their regions (72.9 percent from their own and the contiguous states) and from urban areas, usually smaller cities, and villages (86.7 percent). The total of two and a half million from rural areas, making 30 percent of the 1940 urban in-migrants, is, however, no small proportion.

The age distribution of the migrants into cities is significant. "Approximately 40 per cent of the farm boys and girls who were 10 to 20 years old in 1920 left the farm between 1920 and 1930. A smaller proportion of those 20 to 50 years of age migrate to the city. In late

[1] Data are from Bureau of the Census, *Sixteenth Census of the United States, 1940: Internal Migration 1935–1940,* "Age of Migrants," Table 12, p. 54.
[2] *Ibid.*
[3] National Resources Committee, *The Problems of a Changing Population* (Washington: Government Printing Office, 1938), p. 109.

TABLE 19.   Population Migrating to Cities, 1935–1940[4]

	Number	Percent	
1940 urban population	74,423,702	100.0	——
1935–1940 migrants	8,230,003	11.1	100.0
From within state	4,226,712	*5.7*	51.3
From contiguous states	1,774,734	*2.4*	21.6
From noncontiguous states	2,228,557	*3.0*	27.1
From urban centers	5,663,353	7.7	68.8
From rural areas	2,464,246	3.3	29.9
nonfarm	1,474,970	*1.9*	*17.9*
farm	765,797	*1.2*	*9.3*
nonclassified	223,479	*.2*	*2.7*

adult life, however, migration from farms is resumed and continues at a rapid rate, especially among elderly women."[5] The age pattern changed somewhat from 1935 to 1940, as shown in Table 20. Two-thirds of those who migrated to cities during this five-year period were at the beginning or in the midst of their full productive period of life. So the city drains its region of its human productive power.

TABLE 20.   Comparative Age Distribution of Urban and
Rural Migrants to Cities, 1935–1940, by Percentage[6]

Age Group	Total Migrants to Cities	Urban Migrants	Rural Migrants
5–14	14.1	13.8	15.0
15–24	22.7	19.6	29.8
25–34	28.1	29.2	25.4
35–44	16.6	18.2	12.8
45–54	9.5	10.1	8.1
55–64	5.1	5.2	4.8
65 and over	3.9	3.8	4.1

This is in itself not so serious because rural areas raise more people than can be used effectively in productive work, although it does tend to raise the median age of the rural labor force. There are those who hold that the rural-to-urban shift of population tends to drain the best workers from rural areas, though this supposition cannot be

[4] Data are from *16th Census, 1940: Internal Migration 1935–1940:* "Age of Migrants," Tables 8 and 9, pp. 24 and 29.
[5] National Resources Committee, *op. cit.*, p. 110.
[6] Data are from *16th Census, 1940: Internal Migration 1935–1940:* "Age of Migrants," Table 9, p. 29.

proved from facts that are available. There are, however, some economic implications of this drain of people which are important.

Economic Drain. The bulk of the rural-urban migrants have been between the ages of fifteen and twenty-five. So the city gains large numbers at the very beginning of their productive lives, but it gains them after the cost of their care and education has been borne by the rural areas. It has been estimated that during the 1920's the gain to the city, translated into terms of money, approximated $1,400,000,000 a year.[7]

The economic drain on the rural areas by cities includes a number of other items. The value of the productive power of the people would be impossible to estimate. A significant number of these migrants are older people who have come to the age of retirement. They bring their life savings to spend in the city during their remaining years. Widows sell the family farms, collect their life insurance, and take the money to town. Then also, in the settlements of estates of rural people, a large part of the inheritances go to relatives who have gone to the cities. The cash value of these inheritances has been estimated at from $300,000,000 to $400,000,000 a year.[8] This is largely money made in the country and spent in cities.

In addition, there are the profits of finance and banking, especially the interest on farm mortgages, which go to cities because these are largely city services. Wholesale distribution is also a city function through which cities make a part of their profits from the country. There is a part of retail trade, also, from which cities make their profit from money earned in the country. This consists particularly of larger items of durable goods which are available for the most part only in cities.

There are some offsets in this accounting. Cities must furnish supplementary educational, health, and social services to compensate for background deficiencies of rural people they absorb. The distribution of state tax income is to the advantage of rural areas. The same is true in some respects of federal funds which help pay for vocational teachers, the coöperative agricultural extension services, and the like. These, however, in no sense compensate for the financial drainage from rural to urban areas.

Cities profit in many ways at the expense of the country with no

[7] O. E. Baker, "Rural-Urban Migration and the National Welfare," *Annals* of the Association of American Geographers, June, 1933.

[8] *Ibid.*, p. 87.

apparent realization that this is so, nor any sense of reciprocal obligation, nor even recognition that many extra costs in the operation of cities are the result of rural inequalities which grow out of the situation.

ADVANCED SOCIAL DEVELOPMENTS IN CITIES

Social organization has reached a much higher stage of development in cities. This is by virtue of facts inherent in the situation. There is a greater concentration of social needs in cities which is a concomitant of a greater bulk of population. If rates of morbidity, of dependency, of delinquency, and so forth, were the same in rural and urban areas, which they seldom are, the numbers of cases involved would be much greater. With a rate of five cases of anything per thousand: in a village community of 1000, there would be five cases; in a city of 10,000, fifty cases; in a city of 100,000, five hundred cases; and in a city of 1,000,000, five thousand cases. It is obvious that five cases might be handled without any special to-do about it, but where there are five hundred cases special organization to handle the situation becomes necessary, and where there are five thousand cases the special organization has the opportunity of becoming highly specialized, well equipped, and efficiently organized and of using a thoroughly trained professional staff of specialists. The very size of the problem demands, and usually receives, reasonably adequate support from the community, through either public or private funds.

In the field of social work the cities have many agencies. Not only do most of them carry on very particular functions, but often there are a number of separate agencies carrying on the same function. In the larger cities agencies with like functions operate for special groups such as Jews, Catholics, Protestants, Negroes, seamen, and foreign-born. Services are also organized by community areas within the cities.

The directory of social work of New York City lists around 1100 organizations. The listing is on the basis of a functional classification with twenty-eight separate types of services: aged; child health; chronically ill, hospitals and homes; clinics (forty different kinds of medical clinics); common services and federations, including regional councils of social agencies; convalescent care; day care of children, including day nurseries, nursery schools, kindergartens;

dependent children; employment and vocational guidance; family service and relief; foreign-born and travelers; handicapped; health administration and education; homeless and unattached, resident and transient; homemaker services; hospitals, general, including medical social service; housing; information services; legal aid; maternity services, including hospitals, prenatal and postnatal clinics, special nursing services; mental hygiene, clinics and agency services; nursing services; protective and correctional care; recreation, group work, settlements, neighborhood centers; seamen; sheltered workshops; shelters, temporary, for children; vacation services, including day camps. Some are state agencies operating in the city. Both public (tax-supported) and private agencies are listed, and special services of universities, courts, churches, and so forth are included.[9]

In the area of health the extent of the demand and the ability to pay have brought forth a great variety of specialized services in cities, specialized hospitals of many kinds and also professional specialists among doctors, nurses, and technicians, and, in addition, the many clinics already referred to, and also broadly developed public health services with health centers, health education, visiting nursing services, and so forth. No rural community could support such a variety of services even if there were enough need for them. Rural people who need such services must either get them in the nearest city or get along as best they can without them.

In education the story is the same. Only by consolidating school districts and carrying the children long distances by buses can the country provide a well-rounded basic secondary education with some of the broader special opportunities. But in a city whole schools of specialized studies can be provided, not only commercial and technical high schools in addition to the more traditional academic high school, but also music and arts high school, food trades high school, aviation trades high school, needle trades high school, and so forth. In addition, cities offer higher education. New York, for example, has four colleges, one with two separately located centers, all of which are a part of the system of public education. Then, too, there are often many private schools and commercial ventures which add to the educational opportunities, to say nothing of vari-

<hr/>

[9] *Directory of Social Agencies of the City of New York,* prepared under the direction of the Committee on Information Services of the Welfare Council (New York: Columbia University Press, 1948).

ous kinds of museums, special libraries, and a variety of adult education activities. The New York Adult Education Council has listed in its information file some 24,000 adult education offerings of about 2000 different organizations.

The story could be multiplied with all sorts of institutions, services, and programs. Cities yield such extensive social development, not because of any superior virtue or intelligence, but of necessity and by dint of circumstances. In the process cities have produced or imported great numbers of professionally trained and highly skilled people.

CONCENTRATION OF TECHNICAL AND PROFESSIONAL PERSONNEL

The complex organization of the institutions for social services of all sorts, business, industry, and government which are found in cities can be operated only by a large number and great variety of technical and professional personnel. In 1940, of the employed workers, 9.4 percent were professional or semiprofessional in urban areas and 4.9 percent in rural areas.[10]

Not only need for specialists, but also opportunity for the capable and ambitious, as well as the possibility of higher incomes, draws this type of people to the cities. Among them are the famous people of the United States such as it is the intention of *Who's Who in America* to list. Table 21 gives a comparison of the percentage of urban population and the number of persons listed in *Who's Who in America* per 100,000 population by states. There is a rank order correlation (rho) of .612, which shows a significant positive relationship; that is, the higher the proportion of urban population in a state the larger the proportionate number of its citizens listed in *Who's Who*. An analysis of the women listed in *Who's Who in America* for 1948–1949 shows that leading women have tended to gravitate to cities. While 32 percent were found to have been born in communities of less than 2500 population, only 12 percent resided in rural areas in 1948; 30 percent were born in cities of 100,000 and over, but 53 percent lived in 1948 in the large cities.[11]

[10] *16th Census, 1940: Population: Second Series: Characteristics of Population*, "U.S., Summary," Table 18, p. 42.

[11] Clyde V. Kiser and Nathaliel Schacter "Demographic Characteristics of Women in 'Who's Who,'" *Milbank Memorial Fund Quarterly*, Vol. 27, No. 4 (Oct., 1949), reprint, p. 15.

TABLE 21.   Comparison of Percentage of Urban Population, 1940, with Number of Names in *Who's Who in America, 1940–41*, per 100,000 Population, by States

Rank	State	% Urban Population[a]	No. Names, *Who's Who*, per 100,000[b]	State	Rank
1	Rhode Island	91.6	76.3	Connecticut	1
2	Massachusetts	89.4	61.7	Nevada	2
3	New York	82.8	59.5	New York	3
4	New Jersey	81.6	59.0	Massachusetts	4
5	Illinois	73.6	53.7	New Hampshire	5
6	California	71.0	44.0	Maryland	6
7	Connecticut	67.8	42.8	Delaware	7
8	Ohio	66.8	42.6	Vermont	8
9	Pennsylvania	66.5	38.8	California	9
10	Michigan	65.7	35.2	Rhode Island	10
11	Maryland	59.3	33.1	Colorado	11
12	New Hampshire	57.6	31.9	Maine	12
13	Utah	55.5	31.7	New Jersey	13
14	Florida	55.1	30.5	Illinois	14
15	Indiana	55.1	27.4	Florida	15
16	Wisconsin	53.5	26.1	Arizona	16
17	Washington	53.1	25.0	New Mexico	17
18	Colorado	52.6	24.9	Virginia	18
19	Delaware	52.3	23.9	Wyoming	19
20	Missouri	51.8	23.4	Pennsylvania	20
21	Minnesota	49.8	22.4	Utah	21
22	Oregon	48.8	22.2	Minnesota	22
23	Texas	45.4	21.2	Ohio	23
24	Iowa	42.7	21.1	Washington	24
25	Kansas	41.9	20.1	Nebraska	25
26	Louisiana	41.5	19.7	Missouri	26
27	Maine	40.5	19.5	Montana	27
28	Nevada	39.3	17.3	South Dakota	28
29	Nebraska	39.1	17.2	Tennessee	29
30	Montana	37.8	16.5	Iowa	30
31	Oklahoma	37.6	16.3	Wisconsin	31
32	Wyoming	37.3	15.8	Michigan	32
33	Virginia	35.3	15.4	Idaho	33
34	Tennessee	35.2	14.9	Kansas	34
35	Arizona	34.8	14.8	Indiana	35
36	Georgia	34.4	14.4	North Carolina	36
37	Vermont	34.3	13.5	Georgia	37
38	Idaho	33.7	13.0	South Carolina	38
39	New Mexico	33.2	12.7	Alabama	39
40	Alabama	30.2	12.6	Oklahoma	40
41	Kentucky	29.8	12.6	North Dakota	41
42	West Virginia	28.1	11.9	West Virginia	42
43	North Carolina	27.8	11.5	Oregon	43
44	South Dakota	24.6	11.0	Kentucky	44
45	South Carolina	24.5	10.8	Texas	45
46	Arkansas	22.2	10.6	Louisiana	46
47	North Dakota	20.6	7.7	Arkansas	47
48	Mississippi	19.8	6.1	Mississippi	48

[a] *16th Census of the United States, 1940: Population:* First Series: U.S. Summary, Table 7, p. 11.
[b] *Who's Who in America, 1940–41*, Geographical Index.

It is inevitable that cities should accumulate a high proportion of technical and professional personnel as our society and economy operate, but the very fact itself increases the difficulties of the country because social problems exist in the country as they do in cities.

Though quantitatively they are smaller, qualitatively they are no less serious, and without adequate resources or trained specialists to solve the problems it is quite impossible to expect rural services to meet the standards of urban services.

This is not to say that rural areas are entirely without well-organized specialized services. In some places, through private endowments, coöperative organization, or state services, splendid work has been done. In fact, the Coöperative Extension Service in homemaking, agriculture, and youth organization, previously mentioned, by means of coöperative financing by county, state, and federal governments, has provided in most of the counties of the United States adult education services which have better organization, staffs, and programs than those in American cities.

Some of the cities make certain of their services available to the surrounding country. Private enterprise has been more flexible in this respect. Business, professional medical services, and hospitals are seldom constricted by municipal boundary lines. Case work and group work organizations are usually pretty well confined to the areas from which their support comes or which they are organized to serve. Tax-supported agencies find great difficulty in crossing the city limit. There are cities where a house which catches on fire on the outside of a city boundary street will be allowed to burn down while fire engines and firemen stand by on the city side of the street to protect the homes within the city. In other places, the adjoining community pays the city for certain of its services.

The situation is not as simple, however, as might be inferred from this description. Another side to the issue involves the suburbs, where much of the wealth derived from cities is located, and where it becomes unavailable to the cities as taxable resource or support for private agencies.

Under the authority of a special state law passed in 1932, Philadelphia was given wide freedom to levy taxes. The major experiment made by the city was suggested by the bankers—a tax on wages, collected at the source by checkoff, so that all who earn their living in Philadelphia must pay regardless of where they live. Originally 1.5 percent, it has been reduced to 1 percent, and in spite of some opposition the tax now produces about one-fourth of the city's income. In 1947 another Pennsylvania state law extended this broader city authority to the other cities in the state. In 1949 there were 152 local governments in Pennsylvania and six more in Ohio and Missouri which had income pay-roll taxes.[12] This is recognition of metropolitan interdependence.

RESPONSIBILITY OF CITIES

Since cities are inextricably enmeshed in a complex of relationships, not only with their immediate environs, but also with the regions in which they are located, it seems clear that, for the efficient operation of these relationships and the welfare of the people of the cities and of the country areas involved, these channels of interaction should be recognized as a basis for the structure of organized life. Because of their central position, their dependence upon their regions, and their concentration of essential personnel and resources, it seems logical to assume that responsibility for taking the initiative in working out a more adequate social organization is with the cities.

Some experiments have been made to do something about parts of this problem. The recognition of the great regions, however, has so far been confined largely to analysis and theory. Subregions have fared better. The Tennessee Valley Authority has made an important demonstration. A Missouri Valley Authority has been laid out, but political conflicts have prevented it from getting into operation. In the Columbia River Basin, much has been accomplished, but full coördination still remains to be achieved. In New England, there have been talk and some study.

Most cities which have gone far in their planning have recognized the necessity of going beyond city boundaries. In a number of places, privately organized agencies have made plans for the metropolitan areas or regions. Official regional planning commissions now exist in a number of areas. Cleveland has a regional planning commission. St. Louis has a bistate development agency responsible for both planning and building metropolitan projects. There is also an active Detroit Metropolitan Area Regional Planning Commission. Official planning agencies for limited regions also exist in Virginia, California, and Northern Westchester County in New York.[13] Some experience, both negative and positive, has been accumulated as a basis for beginning to tackle this major problem.

[12] Public Administration Clearing House, *News Bulletin*, Feb. 21, 1949; Pennsylvania State Department of Internal Affairs, *Bulletin*, Feb., 1950.
[13] See Chap. 13 for a discussion of these developments.

Though the ways and means are yet to be discovered, the problem and the general objectives are clear—making a geographical social unit which includes the inevitable interrelationships of human life and building social organization and institutions so that it can function adequately. The problem ultimately must be faced in whatever terms are recognized, be they the replanning of services and operation, the building of more organizations with increased budgets, or even radical changes in social and political structure. The problem is fraught with tremendous difficulties. Cities may wait until they are forced by circumstances to take the initiative in its solution, or they may coöpt their best intelligence to make studies and prepare plans so that the solution can come by way of wisdom rather than by way of necessity. But the solution must come, for the welfare of cities and their people is at stake.

Supplementary Readings

Bureau of the Census. *Social Characteristics of Migrants* and *Economic Characteristics of Migrants* and *Age of Migrants*. Washington: Government Printing Office, 1946.

> Source data on migration which can be used for many different types of further analysis.

National Resources Committee. *The Problems of a Changing Population*. Washington: Government Printing Office, 1938.

> A basic analysis of the very significant problems in the United States arising out of various changes which are taking place in its population.

PART III

THE FORM AND STRUCTURE OF CITIES

GEOGRAPHY, topography, lines of communication are determinative in the physical development and forms of cities (Chap. 10). On this base the social structure of cities develops with profound implications for all phases of city life and all kinds of city problems (Chap. 11). The development of suburbs and the growing decentralization of cities into both residential and production satellite communities have further significance in city patterns (Chap. 12), of which metropolitan communities have the greatest potentialities (Chap. 13).

CHAPTER 10

THE PHYSICAL FORM OF CITIES

THE size of a city is usually measured by the number of people it contains. When one asks how big such and such a city is, the expected answer is its population, not the number of acres or square miles within its boundaries. And yet people must have space, and as cities grow in population they must also grow in the land area which they occupy. Geography, therefore, becomes important in several respects. Since the site of every city is unique, the influences of the site will account in part for each city's individual character.

Geography affects not only the physical form of cities, but also their organization and pattern of business. Then it sets the limitations on the development of the city as far as its shape, size, and rapidity of growth are concerned. It is no accident that city-planners begin their work with a study of the geography of a city, and the implications drawn from this consideration are the basis of their plans.

An example can be found in the new Cincinnati city plan. Chapter 2, entitled "Background," begins with a consideration of topography, which is followed by sections entitled "Brief History of Cincinnati," "Regional Status of the Area," "Economy of the Area," and "Population Trends and Estimates." So the basis of the plan is laid in geography, people, production, and relationships.[1]

SOME GEOGRAPHICAL TERMS

A number of geographical terms are used with reference to cities. Various people, however, use these terms to mean different things. To forestall confusion, the definitions to be used in this analysis are indicated.

[1] *The Cincinnati Metropolitan Master Plan and the Official City Plan of the City of Cincinnati* (Cincinnati: City Planning Commission, 1948), pp. 13–23.

Region. The word "region," which has come into use as a socio-logical term, has already been defined and discussed (Chap. 8). The term is used to designate the great regions of the United States that are differentiated because "each region has some characteristic which tends to unify that area and to distinguish it from the sur-rounding areas."[2] These great regions are made up of many subre-gions of common characteristics and problems. One type of sub-region is the metropolitan region, which has become more widely known because of the activities of various regional planning asso-ciations which have done much planning in the areas of some of the larger cities.

Metropolitan community. The geographical areas including cities and the adjacent areas which are closely related to the cities have been given several designations. "Metropolitan region," already men-tioned, is the most widely used. "Metropolitan district" is the census term, with a definition of area on the basis of density of population. Another term is "greater city."

The most comprehensive study of the important interrelationships which bind the cities and their immediate hinterland together was made by R. D. McKenzie. He called the social phenomenon and the geographical area involved a "metropolitan community."[3] Conse-quently, this is the term to be used to indicate the larger area in-cluding cities and their environs, which function in many respects as a social unit.

City. The term "city," as it involves space, is necessarily defined as that area which lies within the boundary lines officially set to in-clude the area incorporated in a municipality. Many of the data essential for the analysis of a city are reported in these terms. Among these data are census, social, health, and similar statistics.

Urban community. The term used in the title of this work, "urban community," is by intention somewhat flexible. It is confined in many instances to "city" on account of the use of available data. It is in-tended, however, to have no rigidity and wherever possible reaches out to include the area and people of the social unit represented by the designation "metropolitan community."

Neighborhood. Those areas within cities which have a clear en-

[2] Willmarth W. Drake, *The New Frontier,* University of North Carolina Library Extension Publications, Vol. VI, No. 1 (Chapel Hill: The University of North Carolina Press, 1939), p. 14.

[3] R. D. McKenzie, *The Metropolitan Community* (New York: McGraw-Hill Book Company, 1933).

tity and social significance are often called "communities." They do not, however, meet all of the specifications of a community, so that the use of the term in this connection is misleading. Another term frequently used to designate part of cities is "district." There are health districts, social work districts, police districts, and others. Often the boundaries are arbitrarily set for administrative convenience and have little social significance.

The term "neighborhood" is not wholly satisfactory to designate these areas within cities because they are much larger than the traditional concepts of neighborhood. They are, however, recognized as the smaller social units of the community and as such have an appropriate meaning. To use "neighborhood" for this purpose, therefore, seems desirable, especially when a definition of urban neighborhood is made. Such a definition is to follow.

"Ghetto" is a European term used for the area in cities which has been set aside for the Jewish people. It is often used by American sociologists with a broader meaning to indicate those neighborhoods composed largely of foreign-born, foreign-speaking people who maintain many of their Old World traditions, habits, and ceremonies and live very much to themselves in a relatively close-knit community life. It indicates, therefore, only a particular kind of neighborhood.

LOCATION

Location determined the early settlements which became American cities (see pp. 16 f.). The hinterland which was served and which in turn served a city was a primary consideration. This was a matter of natural resources, the soil and its agriculture first, but soon minerals, lumber, fish, and others.

The second consideration was accessibility in the relationship of the city to the outside world. This was a matter of transportation and has varied as transportation has developed from natural waterways and trails through corduroy roads, canals, and railroads to highways and airways.

These two factors of geography have increased in importance as interdependence between the cities and their surrounding country and between the cities and the nation has increased. The orderly operation of the urban community depends on planning in order to facilitate this interdependence.

Assets and Liabilities of Location.   The location of a city is good if it enables that city to do its job efficiently. Popularly, a location is thought good in terms of beauty, sightliness, climate, natural facilities for recreation, and the like. These are important because they have to do with the welfare of the people of the city, but the matter of function comes first.

Many of the early assets of a city have later become liabilities. For example, the cities along great rivers depended upon these waterways for their very life. The transportation which they afforded and the water they supplied were essential. But new methods of transportation replaced the old, and better means of water supply have made proximity to the rivers of little importance. Since the assets of the rivers have largely disappeared, the liabilities, in the floods which frequently occur and which cause great expense for control, may greatly outweigh them.

The newer knowledge concerning the conditions of health have shown at least parts of most cities to be very undesirable for residence. As the location of cities has become more flexible and less dependent upon purely natural conditions, such things as climate have become in some cases great assets and in others great liabilities.

Out of the geographical factors of a city's location have come, in many instances, some of its greatest problems. The first Cincinnati city plan recognized the far-reaching implications of its difficult terrain.

The outstanding physical characteristic of Cincinnati is the rugged topography. . . . [This] is a disadvantage from the City Planning standpoint, in that it forces the city to spread out abnormally and involves the city in exceptionally heavy cost for public works and public services, due to the unusual distances that have to be covered and the difficulty of surmounting the steep slopes. This is the chief reason for a relatively high per capita cost of city government in Cincinnati in proportion to the results. From a City Planning standpoint, it presents the problem of so planning the future growth of the city as to avoid, or at least to counteract, these two setbacks to economic development.[4]

Similar problems, for the same geographical reason, exist in Pittsburgh and San Francisco. Rochester and Los Angeles found it necessary to extend the city boundaries in a long narrow strip to include points, in the first instance, on Lake Ontario, and, in the second, on

[4] *The Official City Plan of Cincinnati, Ohio* (Cincinnati: City Planning Commission, 1925), pp. 9–10.

the Pacific Ocean, for harbors. New York, with its business and political centers on the island of Manhattan and its residential areas extending in all directions, has been put to great expense to provide
transportation facilities, such as ferries, bridges, and tubes. So, many
other cities have had to meet problems arising out of their geography. These have become, on the one hand, the incentives and, on
the other, the headaches, of city-planning.

GEOGRAPHICAL EXPANSION OF CITIES

As population increases, cities expand in a natural, not a conventional, pattern. If water is gradually poured on a spot on the ground,
it slowly creeps out along the edge to occupy more and more ground
around the spot made by the first drops. When the flow of the water
is at a steady rate, the fringes of the puddle will creep outward more
and more slowly because of an increasing circumference. Since all
ground is uneven, the actual expansion will not be symmetrical.
High spots will become islands as the water flows together around
them. Abrupt, high rises of the ground will hold the water back a
long time. Low spots will fill more rapidly. If the start was made at
a low spot, the minute lines of drainage will draw the water out into
points of advance, taking on the configuration determined by the
topography of the particular ground. In a similar way cities expand.
The star design is quite characteristic of American cities, in some
cases in a very pronounced form. Figure 12 shows the expansion of
several American cities by indicating the area of settlement at various periods.

A theory of city expansion in the form of a concentric circle pattern was offered by the Chicago sociologists in 1923.[5] Since the
presentation, it has been the subject of much criticism, largely on
the ground that every city showed many exceptions. This is obviously the case and was so noted in the original presentation. The
various barriers which make every city have its own individual pattern are important because of the sociological significance in the
geography of its people, which grows out of the geography of the
land. The actual form of expansion in any particular city, however,
must be interpreted against the concentric circle pattern.

[5] Paper presented at the meeting of the Sociological Society in Washington
in 1923; published as Chap. II, "The Growth of the City," in Robert E. Park,
Ernest W. Burgess, and Roderick D. McKenzie, *The City* (Chicago: The University of Chicago Press, 1925), pp. 47–62.

SETTLED AREAS AT DIFFERENT PERIODS

GROWTH OF SETTLED AREAS, 1830–1936

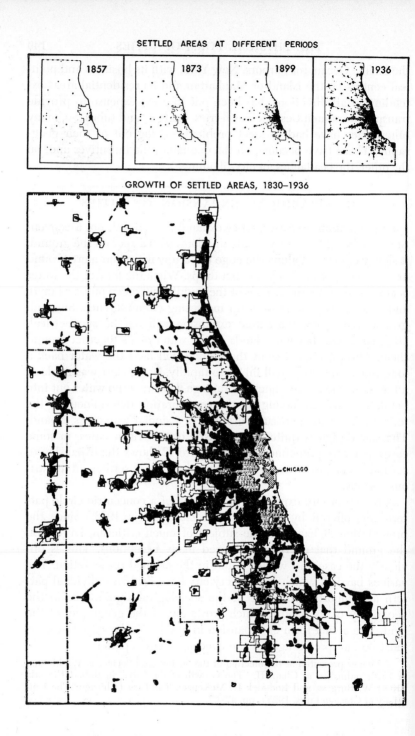

THE PHYSICAL FORM OF CITIES

Maps Show Extent of Growth at Indicated Dates

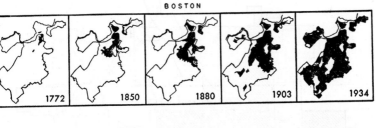

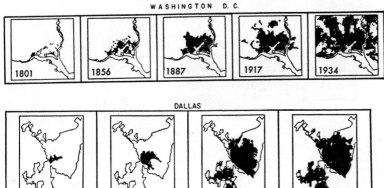

Figure 12. Growth of Settled Areas of American Cities: Chicago Metropolitan Region, Boston, Washington, and Dallas. (Federal Housing Administration, *The Structure and Growth of Residential Neighborhoods in American Cities* [Washington: Government Printing Office, 1939], pp. 98, 158, 159.)

Many cities were originally located on rivers, on lakes, or on the sea. These barriers cut off half the circle of expansion and cause a semicircular pattern of expansion. Chicago, Cleveland, Cincinnati, St. Louis, Detroit, and many others illustrate this type of situation. Usually the land is low and level adjacent to the water and then rises —sometimes abruptly, as in Pittsburgh and Cincinnati. Sometimes the high ground is cut by the valley of a tributary to the big water. This happens, for example, in Cleveland, and so the way of the railroads is set, and the location of heavy industry, which depends on transportation and sometimes on water power, is established.

Roads follow the contours of the land and have their influence on the expanding city. Railroads entering some cities have been laid on filled roadbeds and have become important barriers. Streets that

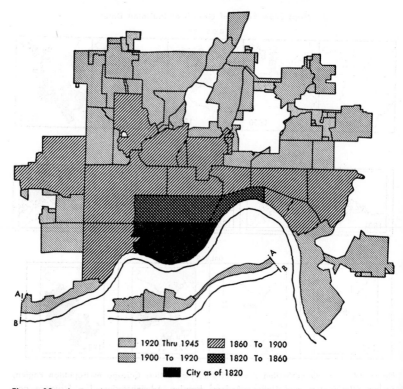

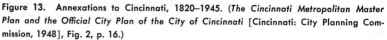

Figure 13. Annexations to Cincinnati, 1820–1945. (*The Cincinnati Metropolitan Master Plan and the Official City Plan of the City of Cincinnati* [Cincinnati: City Planning Commission, 1948], Fig. 2, p. 16.)

carry increasing motor traffic also influence the development of most cities.

Real estate promoters capitalize on the natural lay of the land, influence the extension of streets, buses, streetcars, and public utilities and so accentuate the rapidity of expansion in the direction of their developments.

Cities expand, not by blocks or miles, but by sections, often well built up before their annexation to the city. In Figure 13 an illustration of additions to a city over a little more than a century can be seen. The picture has something of the appearance of a patchwork quilt.

When the concentric circle concept of city expansion was applied to Chicago, the details of the social geography fitted into the scheme

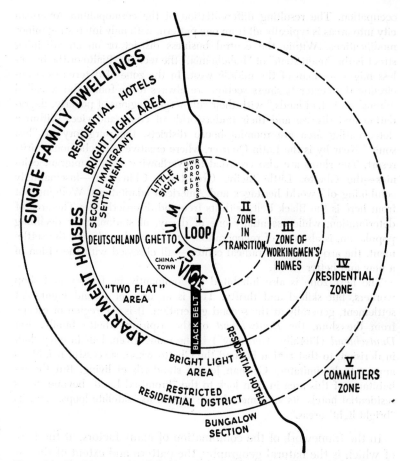

Figure 14. The Diagram of Radial Urban Expansion Applied to Chicago. (Robert E. Park, Ernest W. Burgess, and Roderick D. McKenzie, *The City* [Chicago: The University of Chicago Press, 1925], p. 55.)

in such a way as to add materially to the understanding of the concept itself. The diagram of the scheme in Chicago is reproduced in Figure 14. The study of this diagram while thinking of another city emphasizes the uniqueness of detail that will be found in each city.

Burgess described what happens within a city as it expands in this way:

In the expansion of the city a process of distribution takes place which sifts and sorts and relocates individuals and groups by residence and occupation. The resulting differentiation of the cosmopolitan American city into areas is typically all from one pattern, with only interesting minor modifications. Within the central business district or on an adjoining street is the "main stem" of "hobohemia," the teeming Rialto of the homeless migratory man of the middle west. In the zone of deterioration encircling the center business section are always to be found the so-called "slums" and "bad lands," with their submerged regions of poverty, degradation and disease and their underworlds of crime and vice. Within a deteriorating area are rooming-house districts, the purgatory of "lost souls." Near by is the Latin Quarter, where creative and rebellious spirits resort. The slums are also crowded to overflowing with immigrant colonies—the Ghetto, Little Sicily, Greektown, Chinatown—fascinatingly combining old world heritages and American adaptations. Wedging out from here is the Black Belt, with its free and disorderly life. The area of deterioration, while essentially one of decay, of stationary or declining population, is also one of regeneration, as witness the mission, the settlement, the artists' colony, radical centers—all obsessed with the vision of a new and better world.

The next zone is also inhabited predominantly by factory and shop workers, but skilled and thrifty. This is an area of second immigrant settlement, generally at the second generation. It is the region of escape from the slum, the *Deutschland* of the aspiring Ghetto family. For *Deutschland* (literally "Germany") is the name given, half in envy, half in derision, to that region beyond the Ghetto where successful neighbors appear to be imitating German Jewish standards of living. But the inhabitants of this area in turn look to the "Promised Land" beyond, to its residential hotels, its apartment-house region, its "satellite loops," and its "bright light" areas.[6]

In the framework of the combination of many factors, at the base of which is the natural geography, the pattern and extent of the expansion of each city take place. An important aspect of this development is the formation of natural areas, some with very definite boundaries, others with boundaries that are less obvious. But these areas tend to have much social significance in the analysis of a city.

NEIGHBORHOODS

A tradition of neighborliness exists in the United States, which consists of intimate acquaintances and friendly relationships, such as kitchen visiting, borrowing back and forth of supplies or implements, exchange of products of the cookstove, taking care of the other

[6] Park, Burgess, and McKenzie, *op. cit.*, pp. 54–56.

family's children, helpfulness in cases of emergency, and many similar things. Dictionaries, however, in their definitions of the terms "neighbor" and "neighborhood" confine themselves to the ideas of nearness of dwelling and the common characteristics of a district.

Conditions of urban life discourage the development of neighborliness in the neighborhoods; yet young children soon become acquainted, and school children who live near together often become close friends. Parents follow their children into acquaintance and association. Adults with baby carriages or dogs often become friendly as they meet on the street. Areas of single-family homes, home-ownership, and stability encourage neighborliness, while apartment houses, and especially rooming houses, discourage acquaintances. War work and common problems draw people together. In fact, the more forward-looking urban leaders are putting great importance on the organization of people in their neighborhood relationships. While some neighborhoods tend to be made up of people disposed to neighborliness, and others have people who are not so disposed, neighborliness does exist to some degree in most city neighborhoods. This would seem to contradict the view of many people that neighborhoods have broken down in cities.

The difficulty is that circumstances modify the expression of neighborliness and many of the conditions of urban life are not conducive to such expression. There is a limit, however, even under the best circumstances, to the numbers of families with which one can be neighborly. In small communities it is probably from one to six, but where homes are separated in spacious lots, those few families may be scattered over a considerable area. An equivalent space in densely populated areas of cities would house thousands of people. With from twenty-four to two hundred families in one building and from a thousand to two thousand on a block, there must be a high degree of selection of those families with which one is "neighborly" in a city.

Generally speaking, it is probable that within the area of neighborliness city people will have as many neighborly families as rural people, though hundreds of families may live in between. This can be true while one may never have seen a large majority of the people who live in the same building.

People in cities are very conscious of neighborhoods, however. They select the places they will live with much care. First, perhaps, it is a matter of rents, of where they can afford to live and where shops provide the types and prices of merchandise and food which are in accord with their standard of living. Secondarily, they will seek an area where friends live or, at any rate, a place where their kind of people are located. Sometimes this is a matter of language or nationality backgrounds, at other times of vocation or age of children or social status. Wide previous acquaintance with people is apparently of little importance.

Segregation.   In relation to neighborhoods in cities comes the phenomenon of segregation, around which there has been much controversy and out of which have come many unsolved problems. Three things can be recognized as a basis for dealing with these problems.

In the first place, segregation is a positive factor in the city's life. This is stated by Burgess: "This differentiation into natural economic and cultural groupings gives form and character to the city. For segregation offers the group, and thereby the individuals who compose the group, a place and a rôle in the total organization of city life. Segregation limits development in certain directions but releases it in others. These areas tend to accentuate certain traits, to attract and develop their kind of individuals, and so become further differentiated."[7] In the eclectic culture of democracy the preservation of various groups not only is possible but is also one of the important factors in preserving balance and virility.

In the second place, among the neighborhoods which take form in cities are those made up of people of lesser privilege. Some are people who are less familiar with the American principles of social organization and idealism because of their backgrounds in other cultures. Others are of races or religions other than those dominant in America. Frequently these people also have low economic status and limited educational backgrounds, which tend to make them more subject to political manipulation and more susceptible to economic exploitation, even in such everyday matters as the cost of food, merchandise, and rent.

Where other than American customs are obvious, or physical characteristics make people clearly discernible, prejudices against them come into play, discrimination in many forms is exercised, and social distance deepens. Such experiences tend to solidify the group and encourage it to develop its own institutions and the greater self-sufficiency of its neighborhood. This, in turn, increases the separate-

---

[7] Park, Burgess, and McKenzie, *op. cit.*, p. 56.

ness of groups, makes them more competitive with other groups, and so weakens the whole community.

When the number of people in these groups is increasing and the area occupied is expanding, tensions are apt to be great, and conflict frequently becomes acute at the points of invasion. When one of these groups replaces another in a neighborhood, prejudices and discriminations are usually transferred to the new group in the succession.

In the third place, not only does the competition which develops as a part of segregation weaken the cohesiveness of the community, but the concomitant slowness of integration of people into the larger community puts serious limitations on the potentialities of the city. The statements Mumford makes about smaller cities with a limited variety of people apply also to neighborhoods within larger cities:

Communities that are so small that the essential differences between people and groups must be prudently glozed over, or so large that they cannot intermingle and clash without violent disorder, fail to provide the best environment for the development of human character. . . .

. . . the city, if it is to function effectively, cannot be a segregated environment: the city with a single class, with a single social stratum, with a single type of industrial activity, offers fewer possibilities for the higher forms of human achievement than a many-sided urban environment.[8]

Significance of Neighborhoods in Cities.   Neighborhoods in cities are significant not only because of the general characteristics of people which differentiate the areas, but also because of their importance to the people who live in them. While mobility is a characteristic of cities, only a small fraction of people is involved. The lives of more people than is supposed are confined to the neighborhoods in which they live. The facilities for daily life are there. The homemakers can do their shopping and find their associations in the vicinity of their homes, and elementary schools are scattered so that children can go to school in their own neighborhoods. Even the men who operate the local shops and offices need not range beyond the neighborhood in their occupations.

Economic patterns tend to follow the habits of people. Drug stores and specialty shops follow the grocery stores and meat markets into the local areas. Where two or more neighborhoods come together in

[8] Lewis Mumford, *The Culture of Cities* (New York: Harcourt, Brace and Company, 1938), pp. 485–486.

some relationship to transportation facilities, business subcenters develop, and other institutions, such as churches, health centers, book stores, motion-picture theaters, take their locations. So the tendency toward the constriction of people's movements is intensified.

Social workers were the first to become aware of the great differences in neighborhoods. They discovered that problems differed from neighborhood to neighborhood, and consequently programs of service and types of personnel had to be adapted to neighborhood circumstances. Settlement and neighborhood houses are testimony to the necessity of serving people where they are, in terms of their particular needs. Adaptation of school programs and development of community centers for recreation and adult education have more lately added to the testimony.

Social work organizations and health agencies long since divided cities into districts, as did also police, welfare, and other municipal departments, for the purpose of administration and program. But operation by geographical areas made necessary an accurate analysis of the population and its characteristics as a basis for understanding needs and problems and for planning services. Census data, however, were available only by city totals or by wards, whose boundaries were frequently changed.

CENSUS TRACTS

The first efforts to establish permanent small areas, on the basis of which the decennial United States census would be reported for cities, was made some forty years ago by Dr. Walter Laidlaw, at that time a member of the staff of the New York Church Federation. Howard Whipple Green, Director of the Health Council of Cleveland, added much to the development of this work during his long years as Chairman of the Committee on Census Enumeration Areas of the American Statistical Association. The Local Community Research Committee of Chicago, after its formation in 1923, added further influence. The whole-hearted coöperation of Dr. Leon E. Truesdale, Chief of the Population Division of the Bureau of the Census, and the active efforts of Dr. Clarence E. Batschelet, Geographer of the Bureau of the Census, have made possible the extension of the list of census tract cities and the local use of tract data.

The task was approached on an experimental basis, and in 1910, for cities over 500,000 in population, square miles or, in more dense areas, smaller squares were used. New York, where there were 708 large tracts, was the only city to use the tract data. In 1920 the plan for tracts was somewhat modified and prepared for the cities of New York, Chicago, Philadelphia, Boston, Cleveland, St. Louis, Pittsburgh, and Baltimore. The data were used extensively in New York, Chicago, and Cleveland. Under Dr. Laidlaw a stupendous volume with many special tabulations of data for 3427 districts was published. By 1930 a wider interest had been developed, the principles of determining tracts were clarified, and eighteen cities had tracts defined and census data prepared. A number of them obtained special tabulations of data from the Census Bureau, and several published their census tract data in some form. During the ensuing decade a great deal of study was put on the problem, and the idea was propagated widely. The 1940 census, as a result, published tract data for sixty cities and had a well-established policy. This census also published housing data by blocks for 191 cities which had 50,-000 or more population in 1930.

Two essential principles have been recognized. First, cities must have local census tract committees which work in collaboration with the Census Bureau in defining the tracts. Second, the tracts should, as far as possible, be areas of sociological significance, including people of some degree of homogeneity; they should be, roughly, of a geographical size that will result in nearly equal total populations; and they should be so small and so bounded that they can be fitted into many of the various administrative districts and political units that have been established.

Because census tracts are usually small areas, a neighborhood area will, in most cases, be a combination of several census tracts.

NEIGHBORHOOD AREAS

When the boundaries of neighborhood areas in cities have been determined, a basis for sociological analysis has been established. Such a geographical basis makes possible not only an analysis of all sorts of demographic and social data, but also a continuity of study. These are the bases for all planning.

This was the first major task undertaken by the Local Community Research Committee of Chicago after its formation in 1923. The Committee operated in coöperation with the social science departments of the University of Chicago and various organizations of the city.[9] The Committee undertook to find out if there were significant areas and, if so, to determine the boundaries of the neighborhood areas of Chicago. The project began in 1924 under the direction of Vivien M. Palmer and was carried on for several years with a number of field workers. A tremendous amount of all kinds of data was collected and carefully analyzed, with the result that a base map of eighty neighborhood areas with local or appropriate names was drawn up. Minor changes decreased the number of areas to seventy-five for the 1940 census, which are shown in Figure 15. A book[10] was prepared which outlines and illustrates the methods used in considerable detail.

Factors for Determining Neighborhoods. An abbreviated outline of the elements that are most important in determining the boundaries of neighborhood areas in cities may be arranged in three groups of factors:

I. Physical factors.[11]
  A. Radial patterns developed in the growth of the city: especially the areas of the central business district, of the zone of deterioration and transition, of the older residences, and of the newer residences.
  B. Topography and barriers: hills and valleys, waterways, bays, lakes and major rivers, elevated railway tracks, and parks and parkways.
  C. Street plan and transportation: checkerboard and radial street patterns, especially the elements of accessibility and transportation flow.
II. Organizational factors.[12]
  A. Economic organization: the distribution of business and industry, especially the location and extent of secondary and tertiary business centers.

[9] The purpose of this committee is to plan, coördinate, supervise, and undertake social research, especially in the urban community of Chicago. Its philosophy, organization, equipment, and early program are reported in T. V. Smith and Leonard D. White (editors), *Chicago: An Experiment in Social Science Research* (Chicago: The University of Chicago Press, 1929).

[10] Vivien M. Palmer, *Field Studies in Sociology: A Student's Manual* (Chicago: The University of Chicago Press, 1928). The outline and explanation of the methods used in determining the Chicago community areas are given in Chap. II, pp. 47–101. This is illustrated by a case study of one of these areas in Appendix A, pp. 211–236.

[11] Smith and White, *op. cit.*, pp. 113–123.

[12] *Ibid.*, pp. 125–135.

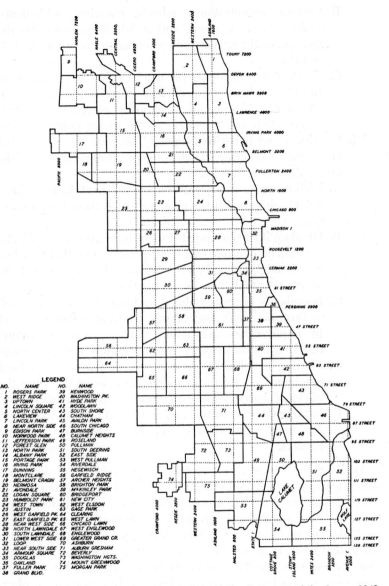

Figure 15. Community Areas of Chicago, as Adopted by the Bureau of the Census, 1940.

    B. Cultural organizations: schools, churches, settlements, community associations, and social clubs; especially the location of the agency with reference to the location of its constituency.

    C. Political organizations: the official political geography of the city and the groups which exist for the purpose of affecting legislation and social policy, especially the actual organization and operation of the strong political party.

III. Ideational and behavior factors.[13] These are the factors that check the relationship between the physical patterns and the social patterns of the city.

    A. Well-recognized historical names and boundaries of local neighborhoods and the changes which these have undergone.

    B. Dividing lines that are at present recognized by residents, as when on one side of a street persons state that they live in one neighborhood and persons on the other side of the street state that they live in another neighborhood.

    C. Boundaries of areas claimed by local organizations, such as business men's associations, by local newspapers and by improvement associations, and in cases of dispute, checking claims by plotting memberships of these groups.

    D. Plotting membership, attendance, or patronage of local neighborhood institutions or enterprises and noting the effect of barriers like parks and elevated railway lines.

    E. Plotting the distribution and movement of cultural groups, like immigrant colonies, and noting the effect of these barriers.

Applying the Process. The detailed study made in Chicago resulted not only in a neighborhood area map of the city, but also in some generalizations that are important for any American city: ". . . the lines of physical separation, with some few exceptions, were also the dividing lines between local communities. It was also found that while these local communities were in a state of change, more or less rapid as the case might be, the changes taking place were more or less localized by the effects of these permanent physical barriers. These and other considerations led to the conclusion that the eighty local communities, as determined by this study, were

[13] *Ibid.*, p. 58. The five items are quoted, with "neighborhood" substituted for "community."

basic social units in the present organization of the life of the city."[14]

On the basis of this type of generalization the assumption can be made that the same would be true in other cities, so that a much shorter process can be carried out which will check the assumption and determine neighborhood boundaries at the same time. In more and more cities this job has been done, and once neighborhood areas are defined, the same boundaries should be maintained for all possible purposes. Comparability of data is more important than exactness in boundaries. Minor errors, in most cases, will fade out in the analysis.

The dividing lines between neighborhoods are not always clear-cut. Many times one fades gradually into another. In most cases the geographical units by which demographic data are available are determinative of the lines, and occasionally these lines must be arbitrarily drawn. A person with a sound knowledge of the structure of cities will be able to determine neighborhood boundaries by observation if he knows the geography of a city and has a map of population unit areas.

There are some general remarks which are of assistance in making and interpreting observations. People flow downhill. They will climb the hill to get home, but their natural movement otherwise is down. So, also, people customarily move more easily in the direction of downtown, as wise merchants know and accordingly plan their locations in reference to the area to be served.

Streets carrying heavy traffic flow become as significant barriers to the movement of people as major physical barriers. Even schools in some cities have found that they could draw their students across such streets only by erecting overpasses or underpasses. Where two heavy traffic streets cross, business centers develop. There will be traffic lights, and the center will serve the quadrants, though they will likely be separate neighborhoods.[15]

The degree to which the life of people, especially women and children, is confined to the neighborhoods in which they live is always a surprise. The larger the city, the truer this statement will be. The subsidiary business centers become of great importance as they also tend to intensify this condition. Schools, playgrounds, and neighborhood houses have found it essential to operate their programs on the basis of this fact. It has been found that most churches

---

[14] *Ibid.*, p. 59.
[15] Park, Burgess, and McKenzie, *op. cit.*, p. 149.

in American cities are neighborhood institutions with compact parishes.

The consideration of the physical form of cities has led to the recognition of neighborhood areas, which, in turn, form the link between physical and social geography and are the basis of the social understanding of cities.

Supplementary Reading

Palmer, Vivien M. *Field Studies in Sociology: A Student's Manual.* Chicago: The University of Chicago Press, 1928.

>Plans and methods of sociological field studies in urban communities, including a case study in the historical and sociological methods of determining city neighborhoods.

Smith, T. V., and White, Leonard D. (editors). *Chicago: An Experiment in Social Science Research.* Chicago: The University of Chicago Press, 1929.

>The story of how an organization was developed in one city to carry on continuous research in the many aspects of urban life, and a description of some of the earlier research processes.

CHAPTER 11

THE SOCIAL STRUCTURE
OF CITIES

"But the question may be fairly raised: Why is it necessary or even desirable to subdivide the city into units for social science studies? . . . In scientific research an object is studied not as a whole but by breaking it up into its parts which are then described and analyzed in their interrelationships."[1] That is, the understanding of a city depends upon the factual analysis of its parts. Any statistical facts about a city as a whole are only averages which wash out the real meaning to be found in the great variation between neighborhoods within the city. The scientific study starts on this geographical base, the neighborhoods, which form the immediate environment of the city's people. Here are to be found the needs of people, their organizations, the agencies which serve them, and the problems they face—all localized with particular characteristics in city neighborhoods.

It is the study of individual cities which is important. A general analysis such as this, however, can show the way to go at such a study, point out the kinds of data which are required, indicate general patterns of cities, with which particular cities can be compared, and provide a few generalizations regarding American cities in so far as comparable studies in a number of cities make them available.

In the study of cities, neighborhood areas are used in four ways. The most important is the study of the neighborhood itself because it is there that new patterns can be developed and problems can be solved. To understand the neighborhood fully, however, the social configuration of the whole urban community must be seen in order

[1] T. V. Smith and Leonard D. White (editors), *Chicago: An Experiment in Social Science Research* (Chicago: The University of Chicago Press, 1929), p. 59.

that the significance of the facts about neighborhoods can be appraised in relation to each other. Then a comparison of the configurations of different cities indicates divergencies from the usual patterns which can be used as clues to understanding the peculiar circumstances of each city. Much is added to the understanding of cities and their neighborhoods by an analysis of the social changes which are taking place within cities. This chapter will deal with these four things: first, the general basis for urban social patterns; second, the social configuration of a city; third, the analysis of neighborhoods as such; and fourth, the patterns of social trends in a number of American cities.

BASIS OF SOCIAL PATTERN IN CITIES

The design of urban social geography, which begins with the radial pattern of city growth, has already been presented (pp. 149–154). This, however, has a number of important aspects to be considered.

Types of Dwellings and Their People. The most obvious aspect is the distribution of type, age, and condition of dwellings. In the center of a city which has become predominantly given over to retail business, with spots of wholesale business and industry, those dwellings that are left are usually old and decrepit. In these areas hotels and fairly modern buildings with small apartments are also found. The zone of transition surrounding the business center contains the one-time fine residences which have grown old, have been abandoned by their owners and allowed to run down. While owners of this kind of property await the advance of business to gain unearned increment on their land, the old houses, when taken over for business use, are used for furnished rooms and light-housekeeping quarters. This area sometimes has sections occupied by modern high-class apartment buildings. Beyond are the bulk of the residences, built during the middle period of the city's history, representing the dominant style of their era, and of an age reckoned from the years of that city's greatest growth. On the fringes of the built-up area—this varies in location from well within the city limits to beyond them—are the newer, modern residences. This pattern may be significantly changed during the years in which the extreme deficit of urban housing, resulting from the depression and World War II, is overcome, especially if slum-clearance, city-planning, and government housing projects are a part of future activities in home-building.

There is an affinity of kinds of people for the various kinds of dwellings. The newer residential areas house families with high incomes. Here the families of men of large business, industrialists, and specialists among the professionals usually reside. In recent years new developments of more modest homes have added younger families of the more successful newer people in the professions, business, and industry. In a few cases sections of small inexpensive homes have brought low-income people to the fringes of cities. The largest group of the stable, middle-class people, composed of white-collar workers, owners of small businesses, foremen, shop superintendents, and the like, especially as they represent the older residents, will be found in the older residential sections. In the rooming-house areas are the unstable elements of the population, a large proportion of which are unattached individuals. Many are the poorly equipped who work at any job and who are apt to be unemployed when jobs are scarce. Among them are those who have failed, on the farms and in the villages, and have made their way to the city for a last try with the knowledge that if they fail the city will take care of them. Housing projects of the multiple-dwelling type have sometimes, through slum-clearance, provided better housing for low-income people in approximately their former locations, and at other times have preëmpted poor, centrally located housing areas for a return of the people of higher economic status to locations adjacent to downtown.

But the "comers" are also here—the young men and women with ambition and ability who have come to the city to make their fortune. Strange contrast, those going up and those coming down the social and economic ladder living side by side.

Nationality and racial groups, especially of the lower economic level, are huddled together in their respective spots, scattering along their radial lines, with the second and third generations reaching out toward the newer residential areas. Somewhere in most cities the process of invasion and succession is clearly in operation.

Factors of Urban Expansion. These characteristic areas of American cities differ in particulars from city to city and, within a city, from time to time. The variations are due primarily to the rate and extent of population growth in any city. Growth of population may

come, on the one hand, in the form of increased density of population, or, on the other hand, in the form of the extension of the
built-up area. Many factors enter into determining what happens in
a particular city, but two factors fit into the analysis at this point
because either can accelerate or deter expansion.

The first of these is real estate subdivision. It is a long, complicated, and expensive process to transform land from the open
fields of a rural status to usability in an urban community. It involves
the planning of lots and streets and preparing them for use. Legal
procedures must be carried through and approval by the city authority obtained. In most cases, however, no adequate provision is
made to clear subdivision activities with planning agencies. A further difficulty is that the timing of subdivisions is related to periods
of speculation rather than to need. These two difficulties are problems of city-wide social interest and call for a more regulated procedure. After a study of subdivision and utilization in a number of
American cities, Fisher makes these observations:

(1) Utilization lags far behind subdividing as far as geographical distribution of the sites involved is concerned. (2) Compared with the
tendencies in subdividing, utilization tends rather to creep from the already built-up fringes into the penumbra with occasional sorties deeper
into it. Utilization shows some tendencies, however, to jump from the
periphery of the built-up area into isolated and detached locations,
gradually filling up the interstices. But this tendency is far less pronounced than it is in subdividing. (3) The geographical distribution of
utilization is much more uniform than that of subdividing. Whereas subdividing activities are grouped with heavy masses falling in some spots
and practically none in others, utilization is more evenly spread over the
penumbra with the principal grouping tending to fall near the inner
edge.[2]

The second determining factor is the extension of the utilities that
have become essential to urban life: water, sewer, gas, electricity,
telephone, and transportation. The process of preparing new land
for settlement is not complete without provision for these facilities.
They are not always provided, however, with equal adequacy or
contemporaneously because responsibility for them rests with different groups. The municipal government is responsible for some and

---

[2] Ernest M. Fisher, "Experiment of the Urban Land Area," from *The
Metropolitan Community*, by R. D. McKenzie. Copyright, 1933. Courtesy of
McGraw-Hill Book Co., p. 209.

private enterprise for others. Negotiations with the various agencies are, of course, carried on by the real estate concern responsible for a subdivision, but the great cost of the installation of utilities, because "preparation is wholesale, while utilization is piecemeal," makes the whole process very difficult. It has been suggested that subdividers "be obliged to secure from a properly constituted authority, such as a city or regional planning commission, a certificate of public convenience and necessity, similar to that required of a public utility, before they can offer subdivided lots for sale" and/or "that subdividers be required to install throughout a subdivision all the necessary public utilities, or file a bond guaranteeing their installation. . . . Some power to exercise social control or regulation of the amount of subdividing appears to be necessary."[3]

SOCIAL CONFIGURATION OF CITIES

The social configuration of cities shows up in the variations in density of population, the distribution of many population characteristics, the geography of the city's social ills and problems, and the concentrations of social services to meet people's needs.

Distribution of Population.   Great variation in density in the distribution of population over an urban community is usually present, but the variations are not haphazard. As might be expected, the pattern of density follows the general radial development. A spot map depicting density, as in Figure 16, shows the persistence of this pattern and its continuance over a long period of time. When the area of habitation is defined by marking off the space occupied by industry, railroads, cemeteries, parks, and public property, the spots indicate that the greatest density is in the central part of the city and that population thins out more and more as the distance from the center increases. There are, however, subcenters of concentration from which the phenomenon is repeated.

Growth of population is in the same pattern. The more dense sections are, in general, losing population, and the areas on the outskirts of cities are gaining. In between the area is predominantly static, though there are often sections of moderate growth and of slight decline in relation to the particular circumstances in each city. Several examples of the distribution of population growth shown by census tracts can be seen in Figures 17, 18, and 19. These maps have

[3] *Ibid.,* p. 212.

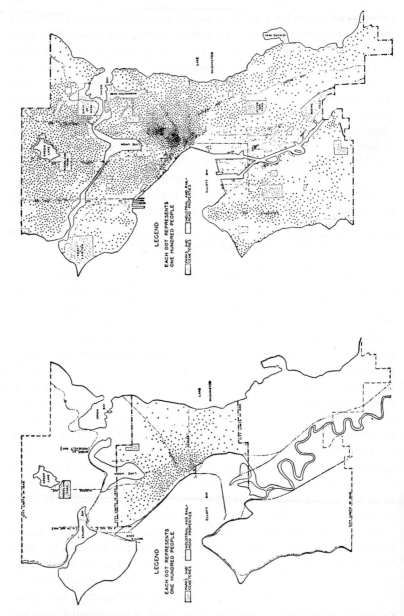

Figure 16. Distribution of Population in Seattle, 1890 and 1940. (Calvin F. Schmidt, *Social Trends in Seattle* [Seattle: University of Washington Press, 1945].)

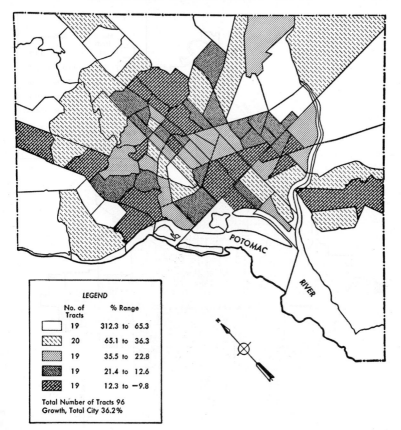

Figure 17. Change in Population in Washington (D.C.), by Census Tracts, 1930–1940. (Data are from *16th Census, 1940: Population and Housing*. Statistics for census tracts, Washington, D.C.)

been prepared by taking the percentage increase or decrease for all census tracts, arranging them in order from greatest gain to greatest loss, then dividing the whole number in five equal parts and giving all of the tracts in each part the same growth characteristic. This shows the pattern of each city in terms of its own rate of growth. The three cities show the same basic radial pattern, though as cities they differ widely in their growth from 1930 to 1940: Washington, the most rapidly growing city in the United States, 36.2 percent; Indianapolis, growing slightly less than the total population of the

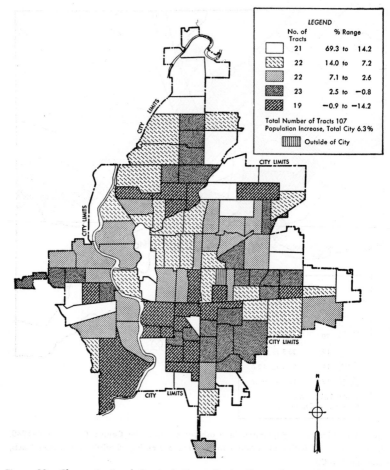

Figure 18. Change in Population in Indianapolis, by Census Tracts, 1930–1940. (Data are from *16th Census, 1940: Population and Housing.* Statistics for census tracts, Indianapolis.)

United States, 6.3 percent; and Cleveland, losing slightly, 2.5 percent, though its county is increasing, 12.6 percent. The releases of the Bureau of the Census giving census tract population data for both 1930 and 1940 carry this statement: "The majority of the tracts that increased five percent or more in population between 1930 and 1940 were located near the boundaries of the city, whereas most of the tracts that decreased ten percent or more were situated near the

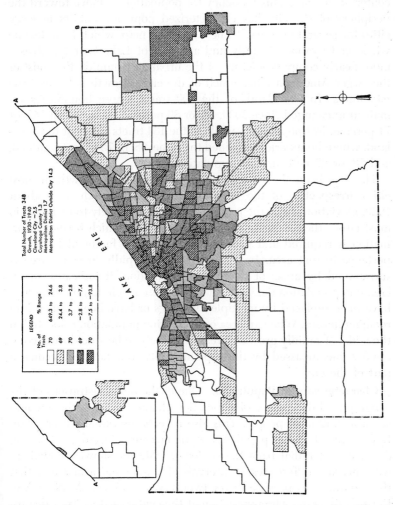

Figure 19. Change in Population in Cleveland and Adjacent Areas, by Census Tracts, 1930–1940. (Data are from *16th Census, 1940: Population and Housing.* Statistics for census tracts, Cleveland.)

center of the city. This tendency for population to move toward the periphery of the city has characterized population shifts in large cities for several decades."[4] The Cleveland map, which includes the whole of Cuyahoga County and a corner of Lake County, gives a more nearly complete picture of the urban community. For most of the larger American cities much of the city's growth is beyond the city limits. In Cleveland, of the 200 tracts whose boundaries remained unchanged since 1930, 58, or 39 percent, gained, and 142, or 71 percent, lost population, while in the 134 tracts adjacent to Cleveland, where boundaries remained the same, 98, or 73 percent, gained, and 36, or 27 percent, lost population.[5]

This has been the pattern of urban population growth in most cities, irrespective of the variation in rates of growth since about 1920. Deviations from the pattern, however, are likely to be found in most cities; they indicate the areas concerning which further information is required and generally lead to some factor of basic importance in that area. In general, when a rapidly growing area is surrounded by areas of decreasing population, it indicates an increase in population density, usually because single-family dwellings have been replaced by multiple dwellings or have been turned into rooming houses. When an area of decreasing population is located in the midst of rapidly growing areas, it is likely to be an old rural community encompassed by the expanded city, but not yet become a part of the city.

Characteristics of Population. One of the best illustrations of the geographical differences of population characteristics is the age and sex distribution of people. This also reflects the radial pattern. McKenzie, by means of population pyramids for selected tracts along the east-west radial from the center of Chicago, showed that there were marked differences at intervals of a mile and a half and that these differences persisted over twenty years. Figure 20 gives McKenzie's diagram. The population at the center of the city is disproportionately male and middle-aged, and a balanced distribution, indicating a more normal family structure of population, is approached toward the periphery of the community.

Social ills have their geography too. The general pattern is similar

---

[4] Bureau of the Census, *Sixteenth Census of the United States, 1940:* Released Series PH-2, Nos. 3, 16, 30, etc.
[5] *Ibid.,* No. 30.

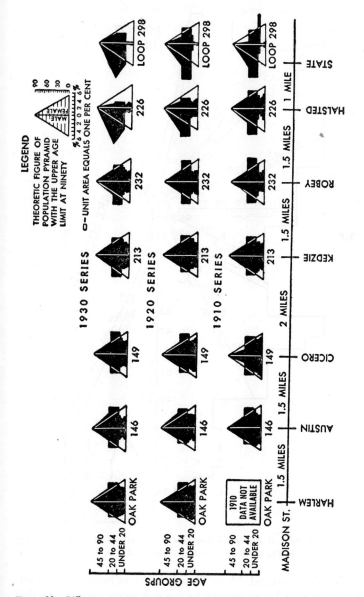

Figure 20. Differences in Age and Sex Composition in Census Tracts Along the East-West Radial in Chicago, 1910, 1920, and 1930. (From *The Metropolitan Community*, by R. D. McKenzie. Copyright, 1933. Courtesy of McGraw-Hill Book Co., p. 181.)

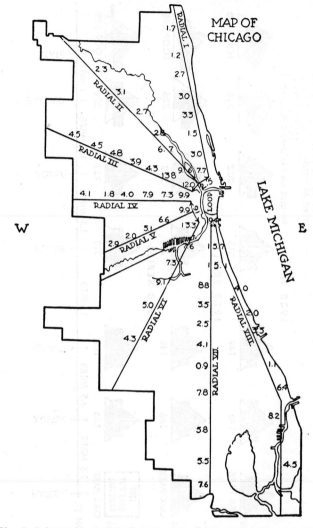

Figure 21. Radial Pattern of Juvenile Delinquency in Chicago. (Clifford R. Shaw, *Delinquency Areas* [Chicago: The University of Chicago Press, 1929], p. 91.)

to those already discussed. Many illustrations can be given, and additional details will be presented in the following sections of this chapter. One of the most comprehensive studies of the geography of social ills was that of delinquency made by Shaw in Chicago. One of a number of maps in his study is reproduced in Figure 21. The radial pattern is clearly shown. The principal findings of this study are these:

1. There are marked variations in the rate of school truants, juvenile delinquents and adult criminals between areas in Chicago. Some areas are characterized by very high rates, while others show very low rates.

2. Rates of truancy, delinquency and adult crime tend to vary inversely in proportion to the distance from the center of the city. In general the nearer to the center of the city a given locality is, the higher will be its rates of delinquency and crime.

3. There is a marked similarity in the distribution of truants, juvenile delinquents and adult criminals in the city. Those communities which show the highest rates of juvenile delinquency also show, as a rule, the highest rate of truancy and adult crime.

4. The differences in rates of truancy, delinquency and crime reflect differences in community backgrounds. High rates occur in the areas which are characterized by physical deterioration and declining population.

5. The main high rate areas of the city have been characterized by high rates over a long period.[6]

The councils of social agencies, often in coöperation with sociology departments of local universities, in Pittsburgh, Rochester, Minneapolis, St. Louis, and other cities, have brought together demographic data and social statistics for their cities and published them in a form to be readily usable by social and health workers, community planners, educators, businessmen and industrialists. From among these the series of booklets from Rochester[7] is selected as best suited to illustrate the sociological configuration of an American city.

Two series of maps were prepared. The first was to show what the population *is* (that is, the characteristics of the population), taking data from the United States census tract enumeration. The eight factors used, with the weighting assigned to each, were: density per acre (4), average rental (1), overcrowding per room (4), foreign-born ratio (1), children under five years (2), unemployment (3), educational status of adults (2), advanced schooling of children over

---

[6] Clifford R. Shaw, *Delinquency Areas* (Chicago: The University of Chicago Press, 1929), pp. 198, 202, 203.

[7] *Rochester, New York, 1940 (I): A Graphic Interpretation of Population by Census Tracts; Rochester, New York, 1940 (II): An Atlas of Population Variables by Census Tracts; Rochester, New York, 1940 (III): An Atlas of the Ecological Patterns of the City's Social Problems.* Published by the Research Department of the Council of Social Agencies, Rochester, New York, 1942, 1943, and 1944 respectively.

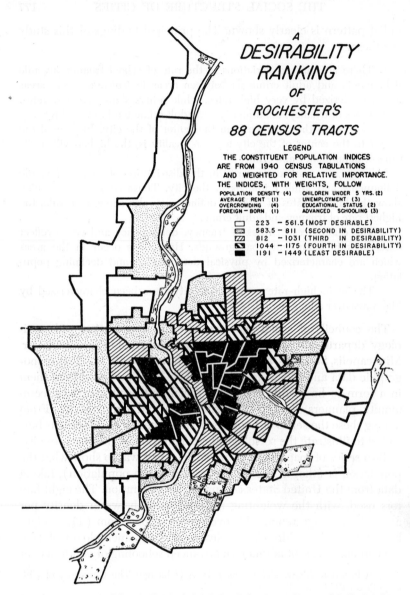

Figure 22. A Desirability Ranking of the Eighty-Eight Census Tracts of Rochester (New York). (Earl Lomon Koos, *Rochester, New York, 1940 [III]: An Atlas of the Ecological Patterns of the City's Social Problems* [Rochester: Research Department of the Council of Social Agencies, 1944], Chart 2.)

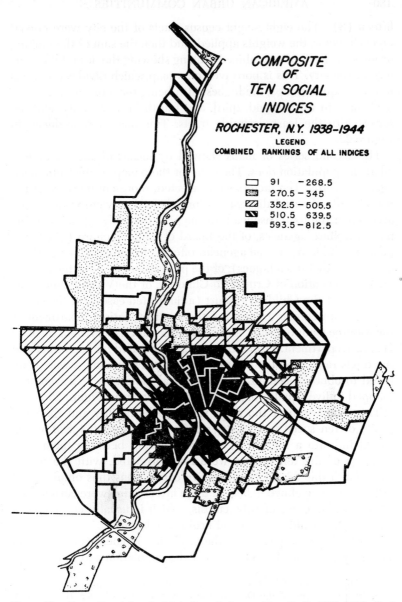

Figure 23.   Composite of Ten Social Indices, Rochester (New York), 1938–1944. (Earl Lomon Koos, *Rochester, New York, 1940* [*III*]: *An Atlas of the Ecological Patterns of the City's Social Problems* [Rochester: Research Department of the Council of Social Agencies, 1944], Chart 3.)

fifteen (3).[8] The eighty-eight census tracts of the city were ranked on each factor, the weights applied, and then the sum of the ranking used as the basis of a combined ranking showing the desirability pattern of the city. This is portrayed on a map which divides the tracts into five equal groups, the highest fifth being the most desirable, the next three in turn second, third, and fourth in desirability, and the lowest fifth the least desirable tracts. This map is reproduced in Figure 22.

The second series of maps showed by means of various indices what the population *does*. The data for these maps came from social agency records. Ten factors were selected, representing some of the major fields of social disorganization where data were most readily accessible: the total case loads of the private family agencies, of the public welfare agencies, of the Board of Child Welfare (aid to dependent children), of the agencies offering foster care (for children away from their own homes), of the protective service of the Society for the Prevention of Cruelty to Children, of the Visiting Nurse Association, of the Children's Court (adjudicated cases), of the courts dealing with chronic truancy, of the adult probation department of the Monroe County Court, and of the tuberculosis service of the City Health Department. Proper ratios were computed for each tract and the tracts ranked on the basis of the ratios. The rankings were combined to obtain a composite of ten social indices,[9] which were also mapped in five equal groups of tracts, as shown in Figure 23.

The comparison of the maps showing desirability and the composite of ten social indices has a rank correlation of +.839, which would indicate a high degree of relationship between them. The rankings of the ten indices were intercorrelated, with the results shown in Table 22. Of the forty-five correlations thus obtained, all but fifteen were above +.500; of these fifteen, nine were correlations with the new cases of tuberculosis, which is usually considered a relatively poor index of general health conditions.

The basic radial pattern of the city's development is apparent in the analysis of the characteristics of the population and in the map-

---

[8] The selection of factors and the weighting were determined by a special committee consisting of the Dean of the University of Rochester, the Research Director of the Chamber of Commerce, and the Director of the Department of Research of the Council of Social Agencies. These were subjective judgments and "therefore open to the usual criticism of all subjective methods."

[9] *Rochester, New York, 1940 (III)*: explanation, pp. 12–13; table of rankings, pp. 14–17.

TABLE 22. Correlations Between the Rankings of Census Tracts on Ten Social Indices, Rochester, New York[10]

	Chronic Truancy	Adjudicated Juvenile Delinquency	County Court Probation	Tuberculosis New Cases	Visiting Nurse Case Load	SPCC Protective Care	Foster Care	Aid to Dependent Children	Public Family Agency
Private family agency	.450	.325	.509	.461	.528	.372	.619	.369	.626
Public family agency	.685	.568	.699	.433	.646	.671	.747	.711	
Aid to dependent children	.637	.607	.669	.423	.681	.579	.564		
Foster care	.635	.655	.707	.478	.633	.659			
SPCC protective care	.637	.671	.555	.365	.485				
Visiting nurse case load	.707	.482	.576	.250					
Tuberculosis new cases	.389	.445	.454						
County court probation	.616	.676							
Adjudicated juvenile delinquency	.618								

[10] *Rochester, New York, 1940 (III)*, Table III, p. 18.

ping of the social ills. There is a high degree of relationship between them, which would be expected as a result of the natural manner of expansion of a city. It is clear that characteristics attributed to a city are averages of a wide variation within the city and have value only for purposes of rough comparisons of different cities. A study of a city itself necessitates breaking down the various characteristics to neighborhoods, for every factor has its geography within a city. This process makes it possible to locate problems, determine the characteristics of the environment of the problems, and lay the basis for planning and program. A further consideration of neighborhood study is in order.

CHARACTERISTICS OF NEIGHBORHOODS

Three parts are involved in the detailed study of neighborhood areas, the first two of which grow directly out of an analysis of the social configuration of the whole city. The first is putting together the various items of demographic and population-characteristic data from the census material; the second is assembling all social, economic, and housing data from census reports and records of social agencies; and the third is a neighborhood case study.

Demographic Data.   The basic demographic data for neighborhoods are of such importance that in many cities they have been published in graphic form for the use of community agencies and workers. The Bureau of Social Research of the Federation of Social Agencies of Pittsburgh and Allegheny County for many years has kept a cumulative file on each neighborhood area, which is always available for use.

One of the most readily useful of these publications was gotten out by the Department of Public Health and Preventive Medicine in Cornell University Medical College for the Kips Bay–Yorkville section of New York.[11] In this district the Department has its offices and laboratories, together with the office of the district health education committee in one of the city's health centers. The booklet contains a series of maps of the whole district showing graphically, by census tracts, predominant land use areas, population from 1910 to 1940, major age groups, and major nationalities; then follow a section

[11] Earl Lomon Koos (editor), *Kips Bay–Yorkville, 1940* (New York: Department of Public Health and Preventive Medicine in Cornell University Medical College, 1942).

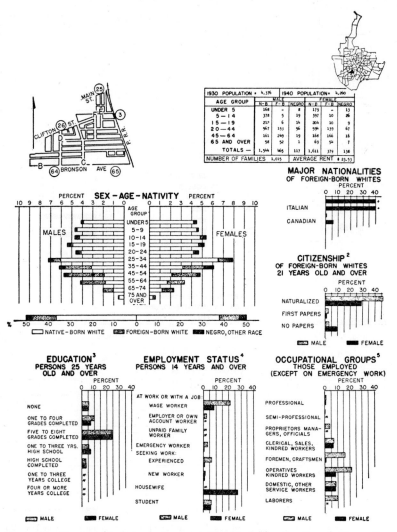

Figure 24. Demographic Data as Presented Graphically for the Use of Community-Workers in Rochester (New York). At top left, B = George M. Forbes School #4, 198 Bronson Ave.; C = Trinity Presbyterian Church (Negro), Reynolds St. and Bronson Ave.; D = Epiphany Episcopal Church, 309 Jefferson Ave.; E = St. Lucy's Roman Catholic Church, 253 Troup St.; F = Community Home for Girls, 293 Troup St. (*Rochester, New York, 1940 [1]: A Graphic Interpretation of Population by Census Tracts* [Rochester: Research Department of the Council of Social Agencies, 1942].)

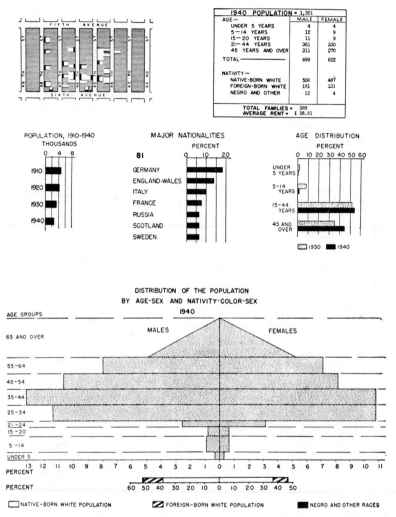

Figure 25. Nativity, Color, Age, and Sex Composition of the Population in Census Tract 96 in the Kips Bay–Yorkville Section of New York City. (Earl Lomon Koos, editor, *Kips Bay– Yorkville, 1940* [New York: Department of Public Health and Preventive Medicine in Cornell University Medical College, 1942].)

for each health area, with a narrative description; a page for each census tract, showing the basic population data; and a summary page for the area, showing sex-nativity-race of major age groups, citizenship, school attendance, education, citizenship, major occupa-

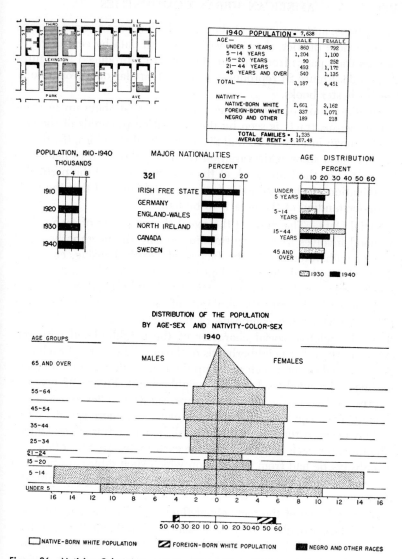

1940 POPULATION = 7,638		
AGE —	MALE	FEMALE
UNDER 5 YEARS	860	792
5—14 YEARS	1,204	1,100
15—20 YEARS	90	252
21—44 YEARS	493	1,172
45 YEARS AND OVER	540	1,135
TOTAL	3,187	4,451
NATIVITY —		
NATIVE-BORN WHITE	2,661	3,162
FOREIGN-BORN WHITE	337	1,071
NEGRO AND OTHER	189	218

TOTAL FAMILIES = 1,235
AVERAGE RENT = $ 167.48

POPULATION, 1910-1940

MAJOR NATIONALITIES

AGE DISTRIBUTION

DISTRIBUTION OF THE POPULATION
BY AGE-SEX AND NATIVITY-COLOR-SEX
1940

NATIVE-BORN WHITE POPULATION   FOREIGN-BORN WHITE POPULATION   NEGRO AND OTHER RACES

Figure 26. Nativity, Color, Age, and Sex Composition of the Population in Census Tract 120 in the Kips Bay–Yorkville Section of New York City. (Earl Lomon Koos, editor, *Kips Bay–Yorkville, 1940* [New York: Department of Public Health and Preventive Medicine in Cornell University Medical College, 1942].)

tion groups, and employment status. In the back are a series of maps of the whole district, showing various health data by census tracts. Census tract pages from this publication are reproduced in Figures 25 and 26. Figure 24 reproduces a page of similar data from one of the Rochester books.

An illustration of the striking differences that show up in comparing census tracts is seen by the population pyramids of the two tracts shown in Figures 25 and 26. Through all the cities, the demographic facts show wide variation from neighborhood to neighborhood. It is in the framework of these differences and the particular combination of characteristics in every neighborhood that the basis of understanding of the area is to be had.

Social Data. The study of the social circumstances of each neighborhood involves its relative standing among the neighborhoods of its city with reference to the factors of health, housing, economic status of people, deliquency, dependency and the like, and also the specific rates applying to the particular neighborhood. Such a map as Figure 23, showing the rankings of census tracts in Rochester (New York) on the composite of ten social indices by fifths will show the relative social character of the neighborhood with reference to the other neighborhoods of the city. The maps of each particular social factor which make up the composite picture add more particular knowledge about the neighborhood. Figure 27 gives as illustration two of the Rochester maps, showing relief and juvenile delinquency. The tables behind such maps give more specific information because they are usually published in terms of rankings.[12] The rates for each neighborhood for each factor are important and can always be had from the data on which such tables are built. In some cities a great number of social factors have been geographically analyzed.

A compilation of the facts about the social ills of a neighborhood reveals the particular problems of that neighborhood. These in turn become the clues for further study to discover the relationships between circumstances and social problems and among the various social problems, and to understand the people themselves and their attitudes. A great deal more has to be known before the planning and remedial action stages can be reached.

Neighborhood Case Study. The purpose of a case study of a neighborhood is to record all that is possible about everything and

[12] See *Rochester, New York, 1940 (III)*, pp. 14–17.

everybody in the area. As a matter of fact, however, all case studies have particular purposes so that in actual practice the purpose sets certain limitations on the investigation. In some cities a great many case studies of particular phases of neighborhoods have been made. These will be complementary and can be fitted together with other needed information when there is a broad purpose of neighborhood planning.

The statistical correlations between the ranking of neighborhoods or census tracts on various factors indicate the relationships that are probable. In St. Louis census tracts were ranked on thirty-one factors and the intercorrelations worked out.[13] All of the 465 correlations—some high and some low, some positive and some negative—reveal where the important relationships may be expected. For example, there is no relationship between percentage of males married and percentage of males employed, which might be unexpected; there is a high relationship between rents and ownership of radios and between single-family dwellings and home ownership, which in turn is related positively to males employed and negatively to females employed. The factors of disease, illiteracy, relief, and delinquency are all positively related to each other and negatively related to median rentals.

Each factor needs intensive study. For example: If the problem is delinquency, "get full records of the crimes committed over a longer period. What kinds of crimes were they? What ages were the boys and girls? What nationalities or social backgrounds were represented? How much schooling did the delinquents have? Were they related to any social or character-building agencies? Did they attend any church school? What was done with those committed? Were there other cases or complaints not resulting in conviction? Visit the probation officer and discuss the problems of your community with him. Go to the police department and get whatever information is available about adult arrests and convictions from your community."[14]

The detailed analysis of the facts bearing on the problems which have been revealed leads to the study of schools, churches, and other agencies of the neighborhood, their organization, their facilities and

[13] Ralph Carr Fletcher, Harry L. Hornback, and Stuart A. Queen, *Social Statistics of St. Louis by Census Tracts* (St. Louis: School of Business and Public Administration, Washington University, 1935), p. 18.

[14] Wilbur C. Hallenbeck, *My Community, My Church and Me* (New York: Friendship Press, 1938), p. 44.

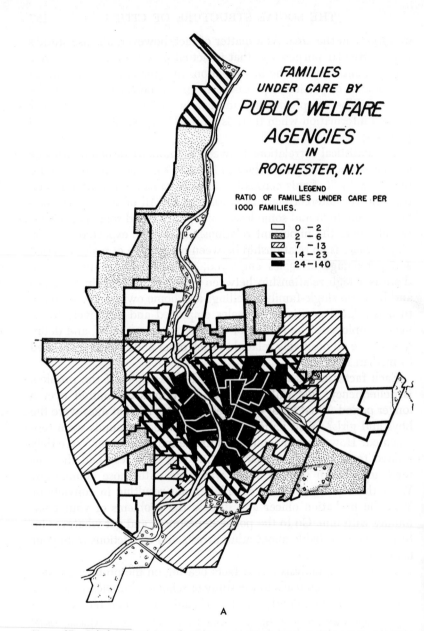

FAMILIES
UNDER CARE BY
PUBLIC WELFARE
AGENCIES
IN
ROCHESTER, N.Y.

LEGEND
RATIO OF FAMILIES UNDER CARE PER
1000 FAMILIES.

0 — 2
2 — 6
7 — 13
14 — 23
24 —140

A

Figure 27. Relief (A) and Juvenile Delinquency (B), by Census Tracts, Rochester (New York). (Earl Lomon Koos, *Rochester, New York, 1940 [III]: An Atlas of the Ecological Pat-*

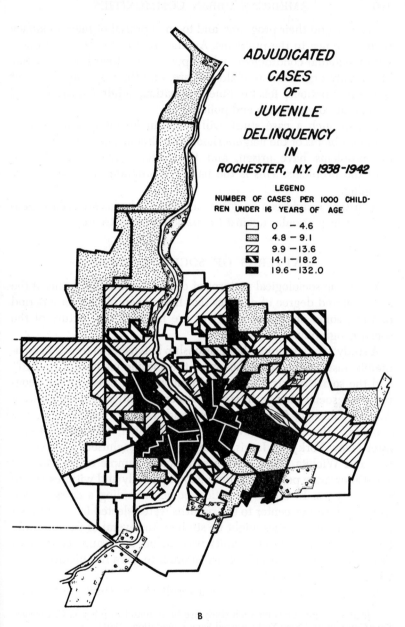

ADJUDICATED
CASES
OF
JUVENILE
DELINQUENCY
IN
ROCHESTER, N.Y. 1938-1942

LEGEND
NUMBER OF CASES PER 1000 CHILD-
REN UNDER 16 YEARS OF AGE

0 – 4.6
4.8 – 9.1
9.9 – 13.6
14.1 – 18.2
19.6 – 132.0

B

terns of the City's Social Problems [Rochester: Research Department of the Council of Social Agencies, 1944], Charts 5 and 12.)

personnel, and their programs, and to an appraisal of their adequacy with reference to the problems. Another part of the study will deal with the actual conditions in which people live, their housing, home life, family organization, child welfare, and the way they use their time—occupations, leisure time, recreation, adult education, and community organization and politics.[15]

Out of such a case study will come an inventory and analysis of the problems of the neighborhood, the circumstances out of which the problems have arisen, and the factors involved in dealing with the problems. This is the basis for program and constructive planning.

A further insight can be gained as neighborhoods are seen in general and in particular against the background of trends.

PATTERNS OF SOCIAL CHANGE

When the sociological patterns of cities are viewed in terms of the direction and degree of changes that have taken place over a period of time, some important additions are made to the picture of the social geography.

A study[16] to determine the relationship between the trends in community institutions (churches were the specific institution studied) and the social trends in their environments was based on the geography of social change in sixteen American cities. The cities were Albany, Chicago, Cincinnati, Cleveland, Detroit, Indianapolis, Los Angeles, Minneapolis, New York, Philadelphia, Pittsburgh, Rochester (New York), St. Louis, Springfield (Massachusetts), Washington, and Wichita. They were a satisfactory sample of the cities of 100,000 or more population, both geographically and with respect to general types. In the larger cities sectors including a cross section from the business center to the suburbs were selected in order that a larger number of cities might be studied. In several of the cities the territory beyond the city limits was included because continuous development made this necessary in order to get a fair picture of the whole urban community.

Factors of Measurement. As a result of city studies carried on

[15] Many suggestions for such study are to be found in Johanna C. Colcord, *Your Community* (New York: Russell Sage Foundation, 1939).

[16] Ross W. Sanderson, *The Strategy of City Church Planning* (New York: Institute of Social and Religious Research, 1932). The material for this section was drawn from this report and from the files of the data collected in the field work.

over a decade, there had come to be a conviction on the part of the research staff that there were a series of major areas of human life in cities which, when considered in combination, would give a relatively comprehensive and accurate analysis of human fortunes. Eight major areas of living were selected empirically, and this selection proved satisfactory in use and had the approval of many sociologists, students of cities, who were consulted during the study. Four of the factors dealt with population and housing: aggregate quantity, composition, stability, and desirability of residence; four dealt with the conditions of the people themselves: economic status, dependency, delinquency, and health.

After the sector of each city was divided into neighborhood areas, they were subjected to measurement on the basis of the best available index of the trends in respect to each factor:

1. Population increase or decrease—census data for small areas within cities for 1920–1930.

2. Change in composition of population—census data to show change in population composition.

3. Increase or decrease in stability of population—change in proportion of population occupying furnished rooms or light-housekeeping quarters, or turnover in public-school enrollments.

4. Improvement or deterioration in desirability of residence— changes in land use on a zoning basis.

5. Change in average economic status of people—median rents.

6. Increase or decrease in dependency—percentage of families receiving relief.

7. Increase or decrease in delinquency—change in rates of juvenile delinquency.

8. Changes in health—rates of infant mortality at the beginning and the end of the decade compared.[17]

Ranking of Neighborhoods. When rates of change had been computed, neighborhoods were ranked from the greatest improvement to the greatest deterioration, on each factor. The districts were then divided into four equal groups, designated best area, above-average area, below-average area, and worst area. These groupings were mapped as illustrated by the series of maps of Detroit shown in Figure 28, based on the Strategy of City Church Planning study data. Table 23 gives the ranking of the neighborhoods on each factor.

---

[17] Sanderson, *op. cit.*, Appendix A, note 3, p. 203, explains how the difficulties incurred in the use of these indices and the measurements involved were met.

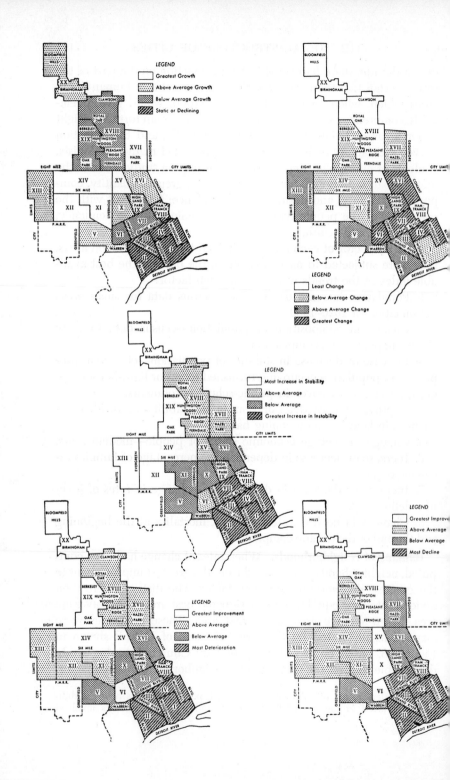

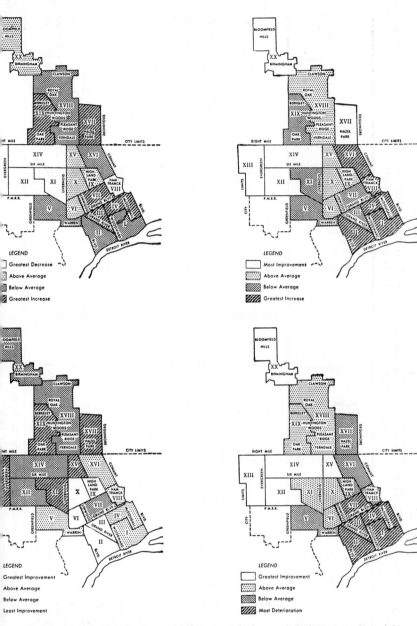

Figure 28. Maps Showing Areas of Relative Social Change on Eight Factors, Central Sector, Metropolitan Detroit, 1920–1930. **Opposite page:** upper left, population increase or decrease; upper right, change in composition of population; center, increase or decrease in stability of population; lower left, improvement or deterioration in desirability of residence; lower right, change in economic status of people. **This page:** upper left, increase or decrease in dependency; upper right, increase or decrease in delinquency; lower left changes in health; lower right, composite of eight factors of social change.

TABLE 23. Ranking of the Twenty Neighborhood Areas of the Central Sector of Detroit on Eight Factors of Social Change, and the Combined Ranking[19]

Neighborhood Area	Total Population	Composition of Population	Stability	Desirability of Residence	Economic Status	Dependency	Delinquency	Health	Total of Rankings	Combined Rank	Designation
I	20	8	16	20	20	14	20	8	126	19	Worst
II	16	15	17	19	16	15	18	5	121	17	Worst
III	19	14	19	16	17	16	15	4	120	16	Worst
IV	18	19	18	18	19	19	16	7	134	20	Worst
V	8	12	13	14	15	11	11	10	94	14	Below Average
VI	15	18	8	5	2	7	6	3	64	6	Above Average
VII	14	17	20	15	18	18	12	11	125	18	Worst
VIII	17	5	7	17	11	4	19	6	86	11	Below Average
IX	13	16	14	12	14	8	14	1	92	13	Below Average
X	10	13	12	13	4	10	10	2	74	9	Above Average
XI	4	6	11	9	7	5	8	16	66	7	Above Average
XII	2	4	2	6	8	2	4	13	41	2	Best
XIII	6	11	3	7	9	1	1	17	55	5	Best
XIV	3	7	1	1	6	3	2	12	35	1	Best
XV	1	3	6	3	1	6	7	20	47	3	Best
XVI	7	20	15	11	13	13	17	9	105	15	Below Average
XVII	5	10	10	10	12	20	5	19	91	12	Below Average
XVIII	11	2	9	8	3	12	9	14	68	8	Above Average
XIX	12	9	4	2	10	17	13	18	85	10	Above Average
XX	9	1	5	4	5	9	3	15	51	4	Best

[19] Data are from the files of the study for Sanderson, *op. cit.*

While there are wide differences at some points, there is a strong tendency toward a similarity of pattern from one factor to another. The widest differences seen in the health rankings are likely related to a combination of the rapidity of growth, changes in age structure of the population, and the availability and recognition of established health services.[18]

Composite Picture. For each city the rankings on the eight factors were combined to make a composite picture. The process of adding the ranks and re-ranking the neighborhoods is also shown in the table 23. The same procedure of dividing the neighborhoods into four groups on the basis of the combined ranking was followed. Ranking and dividing into quarters were used for the purpose of compensating for minor inaccuracies and to emphasize the relative character of the groupings in broad terms. Figure 29 shows the composite picture for thirteen cities.[20] Again there is the reflection of the radial pattern which showed up so clearly in the demographic and social data maps.

The picture of trends dealing with the relative degree of change shows some differences from the static picture. The groupings in which neighborhood areas are expected to appear is reversed in a number of instances. Where the front of most rapid development is well within the outer limits of expansion, areas of greatest improvement are found inside of areas of above-average improvement; for example, in Chicago, Detroit, and Indianapolis. The reverse of this is also true. Areas at the center of a city long since badly deteriorated and still the worst are surpassed by adjoining areas in the rate of deterioration. The Pittsburgh map shows the "golden triangle" below average and the adjacent areas most rapidly deteriorating. When there is a secondary center of expansion, as in South Chicago and East Liberty in Pittsburgh, there is a tendency for a partial duplication of the pattern of the city's center.

Occasionally islands show up in the pictures, as Mt. Adams in Cincinnati, above average surrounded by areas of greatest deterioration. This is due to the topography, which to an appreciable degree isolates this area and enables it to withstand the impact of the outward

---

[18] A considerable discussion of the rankings on each of the social factors, their significance, and the problems and disparities, can be found in Sanderson, *op. cit.*, pp. 40–69.

[20] Los Angeles, New York, and Philadelphia are omitted because the maps are based on very limited data, though they show essentially the same pattern.

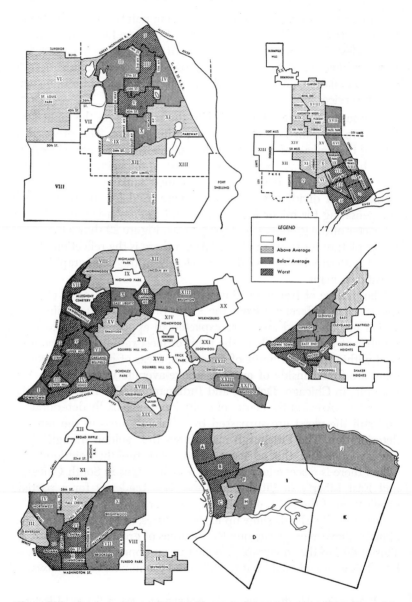

Figure 29A. Composite Picture of Social Change in Thirteen American Cities. Upper left, Minneapolis (South Sector, survey districts); upper right, metropolitan Detroit (Central Sector); left center, Pittsburgh (East Sector); right center, Cleveland (East Sector); lower left, Indianapolis (Northeast Sector); lower right, Springfield (Mass.).

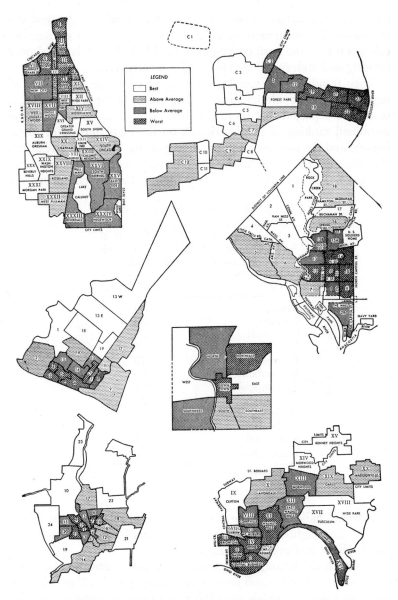

Figure 29B. Upper left, Chicago (South Sector); upper right, St. Louis (West Sector); left center, Albany (approximate ward boundaries); center, Wichita; right center, Washington (Northwest and Southwest Sector, census tracts); lower left, Rochester (N.Y.) (wards); lower right, Cincinnati (East Sector). (Data from files of the Strategy of City Church Planning study.)

movements of deterioration. In Pittsburgh an area of greatest deterioration is surrounded by areas of less unfavorable change because it is near the business center of East Liberty and has had poor housing and underprivileged people from early days.

Since trends in the social geography of cities are a corollary of expansion, and population growth is the major factor of expansion, it would be expected that there would be a relationship between the combined ranking of neighborhoods on the eight factors of social change and the ranking on population growth. That such a relationship does exist is borne out by the rank-order correlations shown in Table 24. The correlations are very high, with only one below 80.

TABLE 24.　Rank-Order Correlations Between Combined Ranking of Neighborhood Areas on the Eight Factors of Social Change and Rankings on Population Growth in Twelve Cities

City	Correlation
Albany	.90
Chicago	.83
Cincinnati	.87
Cleveland	.98
Detroit	.75
Indianapolis	.93
Minneapolis	.87
Pittsburgh	.87
Rochester	.88
St. Louis	.82
Springfield	.91
Washington	.96

Range:　.75 to .98
Median:　.875
Mean:　.88

This would indicate that the general picture of relative social trends among the neighborhood areas of a city can be inferred from the geographical analysis of population change.

To return to Detroit, which shows the lowest correlation between the combined ranking and population change (+.75), if we examine in detail Table 25, which gives the rankings on all factors, it will be noted that there are a number of inconsistencies and that the ranking on health is most out of line. Table 25 gives the correlations between each factor and the combined rankings. It should be noted

TABLE 25. Rank-Order Correlations Between Combined Ranking and Rankings on Each Factor for the Twenty Neighborhood Areas of Detroit

Factor	Correlation (p) with Combined Ranking
(1) Population change	.75
(2) Change in composition of population	.55
(3) Increase or decrease in stability	.90
(4) Improvement or deterioration in desirability of residence	.87
(5) Change in average economic status	.89
(6) Increase or decrease in dependency	.78
(7) Increase or decrease in delinquency	.83
(8) Changes in health	−.45

that the index of health used was infant mortality rates per total population. True rates could not be used because the number of infants under one year of age was not available. Thus a considerable error is involved, due to the differences in age and sex structure of the population in different parts of the city, which has already been discussed. Leaving this factor out of the combined ranking, and computing the correlation with population change, however, raises the correlation only from .75 to .78.

To illustrate the value of studying the discrepancies revealed in the table showing the Detroit rankings, one neighborhood is further analyzed. Neighborhood Area VIII is the city of Hamtramck. Its rankings appear in all four quarters of the scale, two in greatest improvement, two above average, one below average, and three in greatest deterioration. Hamtramck is a limited area completely surrounded by Detroit, which, having experienced its great growth of population before the beginning of the decade studied (1920), stands low (17, worst) in population change. Low-cost housing, many multiple dwellings, already old and inevitably deteriorating, and increasing industrialization make for decreasing desirability of residence (17, worst). Hamtramck contains, and is adjacent to, some of the large industrial establishments of Detroit. A large proportion of its residents are industrial workers. There are many foreign-born with their native-born children; hence the improvement in composition of population (5, best) as second generation replaces foreign-born.

Such a population is moderately stable (7, above average), of moderate but steady income (11, below average) and consequently is subject to decreasing relief needs for dependency (4, best). As an older area, its health services are established and recognized, and since this type of area characteristically has a declining birth rate, health by the index used is improving (6, above average). Many of the factors that are usually noted as concomitants of delinquency are present in this area: below-average income, poor housing, clash between foreign-born parents and native-born children. Hamtramck was increasing its juvenile delinquency at next to the highest rate (19, worst).

The combined ranking, with population change as a close index, gives a generalized picture of the geography of the social trends in a city, but the rankings of neighborhoods give clues to the neighborhood picture, and the explanation of inconsistencies in the rankings highlight problem areas.

The social geography of a city is the background of its problems, its program, and its potentialities. These general patterns show what may be expected in an American city and may be the basis of analysis of any particular city and its neighborhoods. Here planning begins. Understanding and constructive activities in a city's neighborhoods are of great importance because within the framwork of these small areas a city molds its people and their institutions.

Supplementary Reading

Colcord, Johanna C. *Your Community,* third edition. New York: Russell Sage Foundation, 1949.

> An extensive outline for the sociological inventory and study of a community adequate for use in urban situations.

Hallenbeck, Wilbur C. *My Community, My Church and Me.* New York: Friendship Press, 1938.

> A handbook for guidance of groups concerned with making sociological studies of urban institutions in their community setting.

Sanderson, Ross W. *The Strategy of City Church Planning.* New York: Institute of Social and Religious Research, 1932.

> The report of an intensive study of the relationship of urban institutions to their social environment in sixteen major American cities.

Shaw, Clifford R. *Delinquency Areas.* Chicago: The University of Chicago Press, 1929.

> The report of a comprehensive study of the social geography of delinquency and crime in Chicago.

CHAPTER 12

SUBURBANIZATION AND DECENTRALIZATION

THE social geography of cities reveals that it is necessary to go beyond municipal boundary lines in order to get an analysis of the whole urban community. In some cases this is because settlement is spilling over too narrow city limits, but more often the reason is quite different. There are distinct communities that stand apart. They are not city, though they have many marks of cities, which in turn separate them from the country. They are clearly related to their cities, but they have made it clear that they are not a part of them. Such communities have come to be called suburbs.

SUBURBANIZATION

Who it was, where it was, or when it was, as a family first made its escape from the growing congestion of some American city to take up its abode in a village or the countryside adjacent to the city, no one knows. The why, however, is clear. People wanted to have the advantages and escape the disadvantages of both country and city: to have the fresh air, sunshine, open spaces, and natural surroundings which cities decreasingly offer, and to enjoy the resources, conveniences, opportunities, and services which only cities can afford to provide.

Suburbs were a corollary of the industrialization, growth, and increasing wealth of cities. Sometime before the turn of the century, moreover, industrialists had discovered some advantages in getting their establishments away from cities. An indication of this can be found in the fact that in the suburban areas of the thirteen largest American cities there was a 98 percent increase in wage earners between 1898 and 1909, while in these same cities themselves the increase was only 41 percent.[1] Some of the increase in suburban wage-earners undoubtedly was due to the location of factories in the suburbs.

One of the phenomena of American cities of any size is a suburban zone which lies between city proper and country. It is not precisely definable by municipal or other boundary lines. In some instances it looks much like a country village, in others like a miniature of the city's modern mode, but its people are unmistakably of the city.

Extent and Growth of Suburbs.   A precise accounting of suburban population is not possible. Douglass, however, on the basis of the 1920 census, made a careful estimate of the suburban population as approximately fifteen million.[2] As nearly comparable as possible, an estimate for 1940 would be in the neighborhood of twenty-three million suburban population. An estimate for 1950 is about thirty-five million.[3] This would seem to indicate that from 1920 to 1940 the population in the suburbs of American cities increased at nearly twice the rate of the total population and went from about one-seventh to one-fifth of the total population. From 1940 to 1950 suburban population increased nearly two and one-half times the rate of total population gain and six times the rate of increase of the population outside standard metropolitan areas to become nearly one-quarter of the population of the United States. The rapid growth of suburban areas is attested by the fact that from 1930 to 1940, in the metropolitan districts, the area outside cities increased

[1] Bureau of the Census, *Thirteenth United States Census, 1910,* Vol. X, Table 6.

[2] H. P. Douglass, *The Suburban Trend* (New York: The Century Co., 1925), pp. 52–60.

[3] Estimate of suburban population from the 1940 census:

Population outside cities in 140 metropolitan districts	20,169,603
Fourth of population in cities of from 25,000 to 50,000, as estimate of suburban population additional to that included above	1,854,274
Additional balance on account of suburban population inside some city limits and nonsuburban population in some metropolitan districts	1,000,000
Total	23,023,877

The estimate for suburban population for 1950 is even more difficult because of the more inclusive definition of metropolitan areas. Assuming that suburban population not included in metropolitan areas and nonsuburban population which is included approximately balance, the suburban population can be taken as that of the outlying parts of standard metropolitan areas which is 34,905,928 in the preliminary count.

16.9 per cent in population, while the population of the area inside cities increased only 6.1 percent and from 1940 to 1950 the outlying parts increased 34.7 percent and the central cities only 13.0 percent.

The changing patterns of urban growth discussed in Chapter 4 have already indicated the increasing significance of suburbs. Not only are the number of suburbs and the number of people who live in suburbs increasing, but the proportion of urban people and the proportion of people in the United States living in suburban areas have been increasing and will probably continue to increase.

Douglass gives as the chief reason for the growth of suburbs the fact that homes and industries are crowded out of cities. "Suburbs grow because cities grow and because cities grow more crowded." "Going out" was found roughly proportionate to "going up"; that is, "in proportion as congestion increased beyond the average the suburban movement is accelerated and with but little delay."[4] The circumstances surrounding the location and growth of suburbs in 1920[5] continue to be essentially the same in 1950 (see chapters 4 and 13). In the regions where the proportion of urban population is high, the suburban population is also large. There is a relationship between size of city and extent of suburbs and between size of suburbs and rate of growth, which in each case indicates a tendency in the direction of balancing density; that is, the movement of people is from places of high density to places of low density. In general, this indicates that small suburbs near large cities are most likely to grow.

The variation in the immediacy and degree of response to this pressure in different situations is very great. People seem to have a tolerance of congestion, which may be high or low according to four factors; that is to say, there are four things which facilitate the development of suburbs in American cities.

The first is a psychological factor. It has to do with ideas and concepts. When people have not thought of the disadvantages of close quarters or the lack of adequate play space for children, or the inadequacies of schools, if they do not know that sunshine and fresh air are essential to health, or that noise, traffic congestion, and crowds provide intense nervous strain, if the characteristics that make housing bad have not been brought to their attention or they are unconscious of neighborhood deterioration, then they have developed

[4] Douglass, *op. cit.*, pp. 44–46.
[5] *Ibid.*, pp. 46–52.

no motivation for escaping from cities. In recent years, through all sorts of publicity, these and related points have been increasingly reiterated to the public.

A second factor is the development of transportation and communication. Since a significant part of the suburban population is made up of commuters, they must be able to get to and from their cities conveniently, rapidly, and comfortably. As a matter of fact, distance from the city is reckoned in time rather than miles; so, as the speed of transportation has increased, the radius of suburban development has also increased. Other contacts with the city must also be readily available: the city newspapers at the door, cheap and adequate telephone service,[6] parcel delivery by city stores, and other such things. These things have all been greatly improved in recent years. The use of the automobile and the extension of express highways have been important elements in suburban development.

A third factor is the stage of community organization to which the suburb has developed. This represents certain important aspects of the standard of living in terms of the facilities, goods, and services which are available. Many of these things, in spite of nearness to cities, have to operate in the locality itself: food stores, schools, churches, etc. Without these things available, one of the basic purposes of suburbs is unfulfilled. It is almost necessary for new suburbs to "spring full fashioned from the mind of Jove"—the mind of Jove being the planning boards or real estate speculators.

The fourth factor is the cost of living in the suburb. For many years it was taken for granted that suburban life was for the economically favored families. Living costs have been relatively high in residential suburbs. In recent years, however, considerable attention has been given to the accommodation of familiies of more moderate incomes in the development of new suburbs. This has been notably true of housing projects, resettlement projects, and the green-belt towns.

Character and Laws of Suburbs. Suburbanization seems to revolve around the factor of density—the motivation, the behavior patterns, the conditions and extent of development, and the rela-

---

[6] In February, 1950, a new telephone service was inaugurated in one of the northern New Jersey suburbs of New York City by which it became possible to dial any New York telephone number from any local telephone. It has been promised that this service will soon be made available to many other suburban communities.

tionship of suburbs to their cities are in one way or another affected by the degree of thickening up of population.

Douglass has recognized two laws of suburbanization. The first is "that its magnitude is generally proportionate to the congestion of the city center." Except where physical barriers limit in some way the spreading out of a city, or where its type of economic life necessitates a disproportionate spread, the pressure built up by the crowding in the central areas of cities is proportionately reflected by the extent to which suburbs have developed. The second law of suburbanization is "that its relation to the city tends to vary directly as its distance from the center." Except for those communities near cities which exist in their own right and have not yet become real suburbs, the farther suburbs are from their cities, the less dependent they are upon the cities and the more completely developed is their own community life.[7]

These laws are reflected in the characteristics which can be observed in suburban communities. Four such characteristics of suburbs are particularly worthy of note. The first is that fewer people occupy more land. This finds expression in a larger proportion of single-family dwellings, fewer families per dwelling, larger families, homes of higher value, and more spacious surroundings, with landscaping and gardens.

A second characteristic is that suburbs decentralize only a fraction of the city's total functions and so are fragmentary and dependent communities. They make available the goods and services which are essential to daily life, but leave the supplying of goods for occasional needs and the specialized services to their cities. So business centers are small, with a limited number and variety of shops, industry is less apt to be present, and no great variety of professionals, as a rule, are available.

Closely related to this is the third characteristic: there are fewer major institutions than in independent towns of the same size. Such agencies as hospitals, social service organizations, and special schools are usually left to the cities near by, where people go for their services.

The fourth characteristic, then, is that going to the city and the means of getting back and forth must be readily accessible and convenient, for a suburb can exist only by virtue of a set of continu-

[7] Douglass, *op. cit.*, pp. 24–32.

ously active connections with the city. The very reasons for which suburbs exist make such relationships essential.[8]

All of these characteristics, however, vary greatly among suburbs, depending in the last analysis on which kind of suburb is under consideration.

Varieties of Suburbs.   The classification of suburbs can be made on the basis of many different criteria, depending on what is most important at the moment. There are rich suburbs and poor suburbs. There are suburbs with concentrations of foreign-born, with almost entirely native-born, and with large proportions of Negro population. There are children's suburbs and old people's suburbs. There are workers' suburbs and bosses' suburbs. There are suburbs with and without previous community tradition. There are successful and unsuccessful suburbs. There are suburbs that are economically or socially specialized and those which are heterogeneous in their make-up. Some suburbs have distinct unity and are built around a definite center of community life; others are a series of detached neighborhoods. There are suburbs that are planned and suburbs that are unplanned.

In the last analysis, however, a suburb depends upon the kind of people that live there, and the best index to the kind of people is what they do. Douglass found that there was a wide variation in the percentage of industrial wage-earners in various suburbs.[9] This was particularly striking when compared with the parent cities. Some had a very much lower percentage of wage-earners, some had a very much higher percentage, and some had just about the same percentage.[10] These differences became the basis of his classification. The three kinds are (1) residential, or suburbs of consumption, (2) industrial, or suburbs of production, and (3) mixed suburbs. Lundberg, Komarovsky, and McInerny use the same classification, but have changed the the terms to "the wealthy residential suburb, the middle class and poor residential suburb, and the satellite city or mixed suburb."[11]

[8] H. Paul Douglass, "Suburbs," in *Encyclopedia of the Social Sciences.*
[9] *The Suburban Trend,* pp. 87–89.
[10] Median percentages of wage-earners in total population for a sample of ten cities and fifty-seven suburbs: parent cities, 12.4; suburbs, first group, 2.6; second group, 25.5; third group, 11.9. *Ibid.*
[11] George A. Lundberg, Mira Komarovsky, and Mary Alice McInerny, *Leisure: A Suburban Study* (New York: Columbia University Press, 1934), pp. 37–42.

Just what the relative numbers of the three types of suburbs may be is not known, for an inventory has not been made. Because people generally think of suburbs as the bedrooms of the city, they consider the residential the predominant type. The clearest examples of this type are usually found adjacent to the largest cities. Over a long period, in many instances, industrial suburbs have become mixed suburbs, and they in turn have grown up to become major cities in their own right. Few would now think of Yonkers (New York), Newark (New Jersey), Gary (Indiana), and Hollywood (California) as industrial suburbs. In recent years, especially during the war, however, the industrial type has increased because many of the new and enlarged industrial plants were located in areas outside of, but adjacent to, cities. This development has been somewhat equivocal, as far as increasing the industrial type of suburb is concerned, because in many instances workers came to the factories daily from homes scattered over a wide area rather than settling adjacent to the plants, where housing was not available. There is an apparent tendency for both residential and industrial suburbs to develop in the direction of the intermediate, mixed type. There are also great numbers of small communities of long standing, mostly agricultural, but some industrial, on which suburban features have been engraved as expanding urban communities have engulfed them. Such communities tend to retain their more balanced character as they become suburbs. It is likely, therefore, that a large proportion of the suburbs of American cities are more or less of the mixed type. The few suburban studies which have been made are devoted to this type.

The studies of suburban communities in Connecticut[12] and the study of Webster (New York),[13] as well as the study of Westchester County,[14] in so far as data are comparable, agree that the influx of suburbanites has changed the complexion of communities mate-

[12] Studies of Suburbanization in Connecticut (Storrs: Department of Sociology, Connecticut State College): 1, N. L. Whetten and E. C. Devereux, Jr., *Windsor, a Highly Developed Agricultural Area* (1936); 2, N. L. Whetten and R. F. Field, *Norwich, an Industrial Part-Time Farming Area* (1938); 3, N. L. Whetten, *Wilton, a Rural Farm Area near Metropolitan New York* (1939); 4, H. W. Riecken, Jr., and N. L. Whetten, *Rural Social Organization in Litchfield County, Connecticut* (1948).

[13] Earl Lomon Koos and Edmund deS. Brunner, *Suburbanization in Webster, New York* (Rochester: Department of Sociology, University of Rochester, 1945).

[14] Lundberg et al., *op. cit.*

rially. Since the in-migrant families are predominantly lately formed,[15] the communities have come to have a larger proportion of young adults and children. "On the whole, the outstanding feature of the suburban family is the frequent presence of young children."[16] The natural concomitant of lowering the median age—raising the median years of schooling—is also found.

But the suburbanites have been primarily concerned with the improvement of the living conditions of their own families. "Apparently the desire for owned homes, for single homes, for more room and for better equipped homes, is one of the motivating forces in bringing families from the city to the suburb. Since this move occurs most frequently in the period just preceding or immediately following the birth of the first child, the housing adjustment that these families make may probably be regarded as an attempt to provide a better setting in which to realize the traditional values of home life."[17]

The largest proportion of the in-migrants to these suburban communities come from the central cities, and so the householders, continuing their city jobs, become commuters. In Wilton 55.5 percent of the working householders were found to be commuters,[18] in Windsor 48.8 percent,[19] in Webster 39.8 percent,[20] and in Norwich, which is an industrial suburb only, 22.9 percent.[21] In Westchester County it was found that in certain districts as many as 68.3 percent of the gainfully employed commute to New York City. When, however, the commuters were figured in terms of all of the adults and the whole county, the most accurate estimate possible showed that "only about 10 per cent of the adult population (in 1930) commute to New York City."[22] This last is a more realistic picture of the usual suburban situation, but commuters are an important factor in suburban life. "The commuting population sometimes wields an influence in their suburban community quite out of proportion to their numbers."[23] In other places the reverse is true, but in any case they make for a divisive element in the suburban communities. "As

[15] Koos and Brunner, *op. cit.*, p. 35.
[16] Lundberg et al., *op. cit.*, p. 36.
[17] Whetten and Devereux, *op. cit.*, p. 100.
[18] Whetten, *op. cit.*, p. 52.
[19] Whetten and Devereux, *op. cit.*, p. 56.
[20] Koos and Brunner, *op. cit.*, p. 29.
[21] Whetten and Field, *op. cit.*, p. 52.
[22] Lundberg et al., *op. cit.*, p. 48.
[23] *Ibid.*

reflected in the places patronized for various social and economic services and the places where organizational memberships are held, it appears that the interests of the newcomers are largely focused upon the city."[24] In Webster, Koos and Brunner found that "56.2 per cent of the commuter families have put down no grass roots into the community through organization membership and this is of even more importance when it is noted upon detailed analysis that the only memberships in many families are those of the children in Girl Scout or Boy Scout troops; in other words, participation in community life by the adults in these families is substantially absent."[25]

In the Webster study, Koos went to considerable lengths to get an understanding of the feelings of the farmers and villagers toward the suburbanites, and vice versa. He found a consciousness on the part of the old settlers of difference in cultural backgrounds, in values, in behavior patterns, and in standards of living, which were expressed in terms of disapproval and suspicion of the newcomers. The suburbanites felt that they were unwelcome and that their participation in the life of the community was opposed all the way from attending church to politics.[26]

Liabilities of Suburbs. The liabilities of the suburbs start with the cleavage between the old and the new settlers within the same community when suburbanites move into an established village, or between the people of a suburban community which is started *de novo* and those living in the rest of the township. This results in weak and underdeveloped community organization, accentuated by the fact that continuing dependence on the central cities allows community functions to be only partially localized. Homes, religion, primary consumption, the education and recreation of children, and, to some degree, the activities of women are carried on in the suburban community. On the other hand, business, production, specialized services both economic and social, higher education, recreation of adults, and, to a considerable extent, youth center in the cities. New suburbs sometimes compensate for the weaknesses in total community structure by an overdeveloped organization of their people in community associations, highly developed community church activities, clubs with recreational and social programs, and adult

[24] Whetten and Devereux, *op. cit.,* p. 6.
[25] *Koos and Brunner, op. cit.,* p. 52.
[26] Koos and Brunner, *op. cit.* Part Two gives an extended analysis of this sense of difference, in quotations from people on both sides.

education, to the point where free evenings are few and far between. With fathers off daily to their work and interests in the cities, and with responsibilities of home and children left to the women, there tends to develop a neomatriarchal family.

Suburbs are segregated communities in that they usually develop some degree of exclusiveness for one type of people. At any rate, they mark the separation of consumption and production, which in itself prevents the development of a "whole" community. This factor is specially emphasized by Mumford.

The suburb was . . . a specialized urban fragment. . . . Hence it lacked the necessary elements for extensive social co-operation, for creative intercourse, for an expansion of the social heritage as a whole. Consuming much, it produced little, created less. The stimulus of variety, the shock and jostle and challenge of different groups, were largely absent from its life. For the inhabitants of the suburb lived divided lives. Their purses were in the central city; their domestic affections were concentrated one or two hours away, in the villa. Neither side of their lives could be wholly active, wholly efficient. The necessary routine, with its daily shuttling between home and workplace, between nest and market, undermined life at both extremes. Spatial concentration has an essential part to play in psychological focus—and that above all was lacking in this new regime.[27]

This dependence on their cities is not confined to the residential suburbs. "The industrial suburb is more independent of the parent city than is the residential one because the workers work near home as well as live there. Nevertheless, marked relations to the city continue and subordination is definitely a fact although taking different forms. The city constitutes the major center where the trains, credit facilities, the docks and railroad terminals, which are the ultimate factors of transportation and the primary labor markets, all remain."[28]

This dependence is a liability to cities as well, for it makes suburbs parasites on them. Each family and each factory that moves from a city to a suburb decreases the tax base of the city. They often move to escape the high taxes of the city, and they may be willing to put up with fewer municipal services in the suburb. They still depend on the city in many ways, but are unwilling to help

[27] Lewis Mumford, *The Culture of Cities* (New York: Harcourt, Brace and Company, 1938), p. 217.
[28] Douglass, *The Suburban Trend*, p. 86.

maintain the city, without which they could not exist satisfactorily. So cities find it necessary to provide increasing services on a relatively decreasing income. Or, even if the taxes are no less in the suburbs, the situation is the same, for suburban taxes are spent for the benefit of suburban people and make possible in some instances superior services; for example, the suburban communities around New York City have a large proportion of the best public schools in America, while New York City has to continue to plead with the state legislature for funds to keep its school system going.

Another serious liability to cities is the loss to their coöperative life of some of their best citizens. "Interpreters of urban life have been particularly disturbed over the withdrawal of large numbers of the more competent and successful members of the urban community from responsibility and participation in the life of the central city in which they make their living. This withdrawal has been blamed for the notoriously bad government of cities."[29]

Assets of Suburbs. The assets of suburbs are, however, very great—health, freedom, natural surroundings for living, especially a decent chance for children. But the realization of the assets is involved in the solution of the problems, toward which, as yet, only a little has been done. Douglass summarizes the situation in a paragraph entitled "The Suburbs, the Hope of the City."

Because they constitute an unscrambling of an over complex situation, because they are largely composed of like-minded people to whom coöperation should not be difficult, and because of the environmental advantages of roominess, the suburbs, in spite of their limitations, are the most promising aspect of urban civilization. By the very experience of revulsion by which they have taken themselves out of the central congestion of city life they are committed to finding or creating a solution of the city's problems, as well as of their own. Formed out of the dust of cities, they wait to have breathed into them the breath of community sentiment, of neighborly fraternity and peace. They reflect the unspoiled and youthful aspect of urban civilization, the adolescent and not yet disillusioned part of the city, where, if at all, happiness and worthy living may be achieved, as well as material well-being.[30]

The destinies of the suburbs and their cities are inextricably interwoven. The solution of their reciprocal problems can be worked

[29] *Encyclopedia of the Social Sciences*, Vol. XIV, Copyright, 1934, by The Macmillan Company and used with their permission. "Suburbs" by Douglass.
[30] Douglass, *The Suburban Trend*, p. 36.

out only in coöperation and with mutual confidence in and respect for each other's people.

DECENTRALIZATION

Suburbs of American cities have been developing over a long period of time. Their increase and growth have marked a decentralization of cities. But the concept of decentralization, for the most part, came after the fact. It is a term which has come to be used to connote a philosophy and theory of urban development to be carried out in a purposeful procedure. So this section deals with the rationalization of the suburban trend and shows its various applications to certain urban developments and the values of both theory and experience for wiser developments in its future. The growing acceptance of the philosophy of decentralization is, in large measure, due to the fact that through the growth of suburbs people were ready for it even before its prophets arose.

Mumford traces the beginning of the concept of decentralization to the ideas of Robert Owen, expressed around the beginning of the nineteenth century. Owen was a successful industrialist who believed that man's life and character were influenced almost entirely by his early environment. A number of industrialists put these ideas into practice about the middle of the nineteenth century in France, Belgium, Germany, and England.[31] These men built communities for the workers in their factories which were directly related to the industry, which made provision for the social life of the workers, and which tended to be well-rounded communities.

Somewhat later Prince Kropotkin proposed "the marriage of agriculture and industry" which developed into a plan for decentralization in England in 1872.[32] This idea had considerable influence on the subsistence homestead plan which developed during the depression of the 1930's in the United States.

Thomas Jefferson, even before Robert Owen, had bemoaned the development of cities: "When we get piled upon one another in large cities, as in Europe, we shall become corrupt as in Europe, and go to eating one another as they do there."[33] He was particularly con-

[31] Mumford, *op. cit.*, pp. 392–393.

[32] P. Kropotkin, *Fields, Factories and Workshops* (New York: G. P. Putnam's Sons; London: Swan, Sonnenschein & Co.), pp. 177–183.

[33] Letter to James Madison, Dec. 12, 1787, quoted in Saul K. Padover, *The Complete Jefferson* (New York: Duell, Sloan and Pearce, 1943), p. 123.

cerned that the United States continue to be an agricultural nation and leave manufacturing to Europe because he believed that manufacturing and its accompanying urbanism were inimical to democratic government. "The mobs of great cities add just so much to the support of pure government, as sores do to the strength of the human body."[34]

Garden Cities.   The first comprehensive statement of the idea of decentralization was made by Sir Ebenezer Howard in his book *Garden Cities of Tomorrow*, published at the very beginning of the twentieth century.[35] Howard proposed building completely new cities some distance from London, constructed according to a general pattern and organized and maintained on fundamentally different and unique principles.

The pattern given in Howard's book is shown in Figure 30. It is, in general, a radial layout, with recreation areas at the center and farm lands on the periphery. Industry is located on the outskirts of the residential areas, in the midst of which are business and other community institutions. Transportation comes to the industrial area and in turn may be used to connect a series of garden cities. The plans were laid out to procure convenience, utility, and beauty, with accessibility in terms of walking, as the maximum distance between places in the community was a mile and a half.

The first principle was a balanced community based on self-sufficiency. The farm land was to produce the agricultural products needed by the city, and the city was to provide a steady accessible market for the farmers. Industry was for the basic production of wealth for the community and was to provide jobs and income for the citizens. Business, education, recreation, the social services, and people's organizations were to be developed in accordance with the needs of the people and in their operation were to give employment to the required numbers. This meant a stable city with a point of maximum social and economic services.

So the second principle, in reality a corollary of the first, was controlled growth and limited population. The band of open country around the garden city was not only for agriculture and recreation,

[34] "Notes on the State of Virginia," Query XIX, Manufacturers (1781), *ibid.*, p. 679.
[35] Ebenezer Howard, *Garden Cities of Tomorrow*, third edition (London: Swan, Sonnenschein & Co., 1902). The first edition, under the title *Tomorrow*, was published in 1898.

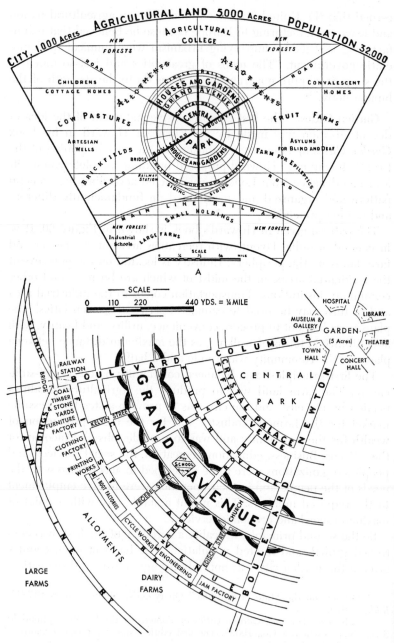

A

B

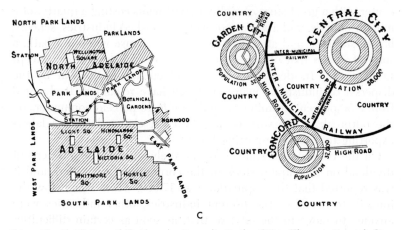

Figure 30. The Pattern of Sir Ebenezer Howard's Garden Cities. (Ebenezer Howard, *Garden Cities of Tomorrow*, third edition [London: Swan, Sonnenschein & Co., 1902], pp. 23, 128.)

but also to prevent the expansion of the community beyond its maximum and to prevent the encroachment of other communities. Howard's estimate of the size of the whole community was a tract of approximately 6000 acres, with an area having a radius of three-quarters of a mile—a little over 1000 acres, including a park of some 145 acres at the center—for the city. The maximum population, he estimated, would be 32,000. Any growth beyond this point would take place by starting another garden city and not by spreading or overcrowding the first.

The third principle had profound implications for the control of the other two. All of the land was to be owned by the corporate community, with administration and control vested in an elected board of trustees. None of the land could be parceled out to individual ownership, but would be granted for approved use to individuals or groups and the use paid for by an established scale of ground rentals. By this plan Howard believed that democratic control could be maintained, the balance of the community assured, and speculative land value prevented.

In 1904 a private association interested in the experiment established a garden city, Letchworth, and some years later a second was founded, Welwyn.

After a slow and discouraging start, Letchworth began a solid development with a civic and social center, a well-developed shopping center with a great store of eighty departments costing a quarter of a million pounds, and a variety of well-established industries, schools, health services, and attractive houses—"no house without a bath, a state of affairs that obtains in no other town in the country except Letchworth." Its development was helped during the war by the dispersal of industries, many of which have remained. It changed from a 50 percent dormitory population to 15 percent commuters by the outbreak of the war, during which it changed from a labor-exporting to a labor-importing town.[36]

On the twenty-fifth anniversary of Welwyn, in 1946, a 5 percent dividend on the capital stock of the corporation was voted, and it was reported that the population was 17,000, which was below the immediate needs of the present industries; other industries were anxious to move to the city, so that, as soon as certain difficulties were cleared up with the Greater London plan, the residents would go forward with the plans to extend the town to a population of 50,000.[37]

American Experiments.   Some industrialists in the United States undertook to decentralize their establishments to some degree. Most of them were small and developed into desolate industrial villages. Henry Ford's plans had, and continue to have, the greatest publicity.

The influence of Howard's ideas spread from England to the Continent and to America, but they were never adopted completely. Garden City (Long Island) took the name, but apart from planning the layout of the community and the coöperative ownership of apartments, the ideas were unused. Radburn (New Jersey), "the city of the motor age," was another example of this influence. It was started from open country, planned by Henry Wright and Clarence Stein, architects and town-planners.

Here was the first town built anywhere that consistently abandoned the corridor avenue lined with houses, that divorced the functions of domestic living from the noise and traffic of the street, and that provided a continuous belt of park space within the residential super-blocks, instead of placing the park on the outskirts. Each super-block was planned in relation to a school, a playground, and a swimming pool: open spaces were treated as part of the original cost of the development. By means

[36] Charles Dalton, "A New Town Grows," *Town and Country Planning Quarterly*, Autumn, 1945.

[37] Chairman's speech at the twenty-sixth Ordinary General Meeting of Welwyn Garden City Limited, July 10, 1946.

of footpaths with underpasses and bridges one can walk from one part of the community to another without encountering a motor car.[38]

During the depression of the 1930's the idea of subsistence farming came into vogue. This involved communities with homes having a small acreage on which families could produce part of the food necessary for their own use. The communities were to be accessible to industry, where the family heads could earn money whenever work was available. The purpose was to reëstablish a basic partial security for family units in an uncertain economic order. The federal government established a number of resettlement communities on this basis, which were only partially successful. Some of the resettlement communities, such as Arthurdale (West Virginia), operated with a high degree of democracy; but, when the communities were built and organized, the workers had little to do because industrial opportunity was not accessible; as a result, many difficulties in the communities developed.

Another federal experiment was the establishment of several green-belt towns. Three were actually built, the best-known, Greenbelt (Maryland), just outside Washington. There were also Greendale, near Milwaukee, and Greenhills, on the outskirts of Cincinnati. These were a new type of government-financed housing projects for families with maximum incomes of $1800 for three, $2200 for six, members. They were carefully planned, architecturally progressive and unified, and financially sound. The unity of ownership—the federal government, with the intent to transfer it to a local community agency—and the surrounding area of open country were taken from the garden cities, and the motor-age superblock from the Radburn plan.[39] They had two fundamental weaknesses, however—they depended on the nearby cities for the employment of the workers, and they were occupied by families within a limited income range. As a result, they became parasite suburbs, like most other suburban communities. Actually, a social stratification did develop along occupational lines: management, professionals, and various types of workers.[40]

The nearest to success of all the American projects of decentrali-

[38] Mumford, op. cit., p. 437.
[39] O. Kline Fulmer, Greenbelt (Washington: American Council on Public Affairs), p. 11.
[40] William H. Form, "Status Stratification in a Planned Community," American Sociological Review, Vol. 10, No. 5 (Oct., 1945), p. 605.

zation was the Tennessee Valley Authority. This region has been organized as a functioning unit taking in parts of seven different states, under a special act of Congress. In working out the building of a whole series of dams for flood control, electric power production, irrigation, and recreation, it was necessary to completely reorganize the region on a new industrial base and to relocate a large proportion of the people whose farm lands and villages were inundated by the water impounded by the dams. In the process of development new people came to live and work under the TVA, new vocational patterns were developed for the people already there, new land was put under cultivation, submarginal land was removed from agricultural use, new cities were built, and people engaged in democratic discussions and activities in building their communities and their institutions. A higher standard of living was established, consumer co-operative enterprises were organized, new conveniences for living were made available, and richer patterns of living through education were developed.

Lilienthal, in writing about this experiment, has this to say:

The chief purpose of such methods of decentralization is to provide greater opportunity for a richer, more interesting, and more responsible life for the individual, and to increase his genuine freedom, his sense of his own importance. Centralization in administration promotes remote and absentee control and thereby increasingly denies to the individual the opportunity to make decisions and to carry those responsibilities by which human personality is nourished and developed. I find it impossible to comprehend how democracy can be a living reality if people are remote from their government and in their daily lives are not made a part of it, or if the control and direction of making a living—industry, farming, the distribution of goods—is far removed from the stream of life and from the local community.[41]

He further gives the essential factors in making such circumstances possible: "You do not get decentralization as we know it in the TVA unless you meet two tests: First, do the men in the field have the power of decision? Second, are the people, their private and their local institutions, actively participating in the enterprise?"[42]

The TVA towns were not adequately planned in terms of layout, function, and balance; and the architectural imagination in the

[41] David E. Lilienthal, *TVA: Democracy on the March* (New York: Harper & Brothers, 1944), p. 139.

[42] *Ibid.*, p. 147.

towns and homes was not comparable to that beautifully manifested in the dams, powerhouses, etc.

Philosophy of Decentralization.   Many apostles of decentralization as a philosophy of life have propagated their ideas with conviction and enthusiasm. In general, they can be divided into three groups.

First are the proponents of rural life as the best way of life. This has been a call to people to settle on farms, engage in agriculture, and enjoy the independence of farm life and the health of the open air in the country.[43] It has stemmed in part from a fear lest the continued rural-urban population movement would deplete rural America and break down its weakening community institutions. Activities supporting this idea got their start with President Theodore Roosevelt's American Country Life Commission and the important rural sociological studies brought about by Charles J. Galpin when he became executive of the Commission after his work in the Wisconsin College of Agriculture.

A second group emphasizes the escape from the city and its great accumulations of evils, materialism, and dependency to a life partly rural, with the opportunity to establish some measure of independence through subsistence agriculture under circumstances conducive to the development of human personality. Ralph Borsodi has been one of the most vocal proponents of this philosophy.[44] He established a very small community of a few families interested in trying out its precepts, outside of Suffern (New York). The center of the community was the School for Living. The former director expressed the philosophy in these terms:

Basic laws of decentralization:
1. Self-realization as the freedom to be oneself, improve oneself, express oneself.
2. Personal access to the use of the means and materials necessary for the production of all the consumer goods necessary for life, health, comfort and happiness.
3. Socialization as the right to volunteer to associate or dissociate in extending group control over arrangements for shared enterprise.
4. Conscious assertion of personal inner integrity and as the inevitable

---

[43] Paul H. Landis, *Rural Life in Process* (New York: McGraw-Hill Book Company, 1940), pp. 233–254 and bibliography.

[44] Ralph Borsodi, *Flight from the City* (New York: Harper & Brothers, 1933); *Prosperity and Security* (New York: Harper & Brothers, 1938).

corollary of the same, conscientious objection against whatever sullies it or thwarts its growth.[45]

Principles and practices of decentralization:

I. Production of goods for consumption
II. A conception of the wholeness of life
III. A new attitude toward technological improvement—technological considerateness
IV. The development of community through the extension of neighborliness.[46]

A symposium under the editorship of Elmer T. Petersen undertakes to "offer some measure of diagnosis for the ills which beset us domestically": "From almost every angle that we view urban life in America, the decentralization of cities seems desirable—public health, economic betterment, economic logistics, moral welfare, better local utilization of natural resources, better distribution of manufactured products, a better conceived military defense, a more rational architecture, and, in general, a happier adaptation to the changing mores."[47] In addition to analyzing the evidence supporting this generalization, facts are presented indicating the extent to which decentralization has already taken place. One of the basic concepts of decentralization is offered by Sears: "The idea of balance—of a flexible system of give-and-take—seems implicit throughout nature. It is the basis of physical and chemical theory. It is fundamental in biology. There is no reason to think that human activities are exempt from its control."[48] The book closes with a review of seven points of American folklore inimical to decentralization but open to serious question: the saga of bigness; the legend of efficiency; the cult of statistics; the myth of the farm as service station; independence as in itself virtuous; the theorem that, if large aggregations of specialists are good, larger and larger aggregations, to an infinite degree, are still better; the failure to differentiate between durable satisfactions and sensory or neurotic stimuli as goals to be attained.[49]

[45] Ralph T. Templin, "A School of Living," unpublished Doctor of Education Project (Teachers College, Columbia University, 1946), p. 3.

[46] Ibid., pp. 63–65.

[47] Reprinted from Elmer T. Peterson, Cities Are Abnormal, Copyright 1946, by the University of Oklahoma Press. Reprinted by permission of the publisher.

[48] Paul B. Sears, "The Ecology of City and Country," in Petersen, op. cit., p. 38.

[49] Petersen, op. cit., pp. 251–256.

A third group of apostles of decentralization is made up of architects and city-planners. They range in their points of emphasis from those who belong more in the second group to those who present fundamental plans for a new decentralized city. Saarinen presents much history and many data about European cities and emphasizes his philosophy of the evils of the city.[50] Sert presents the mature findings of the Congrès International d'Architecture Moderne, with some details of the construction of cities around a functional concept.[51] Frank Lloyd Wright propounds the idea that great cities are not consistent with democracy and gives three words—organic, integration, democracy—to express his philosophy for cities of the future. He lays out plans for "Broadacre," a community to be built much like Greenbelt except that it provides for a small acreage for each family, where it can produce much of its food.[52] Mumford is the encyclopedist of decentralization.[53] Hilberseimer deals more extensively with the various aspects of planning involved in new cities.[54] Churchill makes his approach from the consideration of rebuilding the old cities,[55] as does also Justement, who goes further with the implications of decentralization, working out his analysis of city-building in terms of space, time, and money.[56] These last will be discussed more extensively with the consideration of city-planning.

Conditions and Limits of Decentralization.   The evidence that has been accumulated depicting the ills of cities and city life and the degree to which decentralization has already taken place makes it clear that the law of diminishing returns has been passed in the accumulation of population in big cities. It has become possible only within recent years to plan purposefully the decentralization of cities. Four modern developments make this practical by mitigating

[50] Eliel Saarinen, *The City: Its Growth, Its Decay, Its Future* (New York: Reinhold Publishing Corporation, 1943).

[51] J. L. Sert, *Can Our Cities Survive?* (Cambridge: Harvard University Press, 1942).

[52] Frank Lloyd Wright, *The Disappearing City* (New York: Payson, 1932); *When Democracy Builds* (Chicago: The University of Chicago Press, 1945).

[53] Mumford, *op. cit.*

[54] L. Hilberseimer, *The New City: Principles of Planning* (Chicago: Paul Theobald, 1944).

[55] Henry S. Churchill, *The City Is the People* (New York: Reynal and Hitchcock, 1945).

[56] Louis Justement, *New Cities for Old* (New York: McGraw-Hill Book Company, 1946).

the primary cause for the necessity for cities in an industrial age. First is the use of electricity for industrial power; electricity is easily transmissable to any point where it is needed. Second is the use of motor trucks for short haulage, which removes the necessity for a factory to be located on a railway. Third is the extensive use of the automobile, so that a factory is no longer compelled to be immediately accessible to a large number of workers. Fourth are the availability and the low cost of telephone communication, which enables industrial executives to be immediately in touch with whoever is required. In addition, the developments of transportation, especially by motor bus as well as railway, and the use of automobiles for personal movement have greatly facilitated the decentralization of residence.

So decentralization has been accelerated. It is beginning to have more purpose and plan. It is not yet adequately conceived, however, and it is by no means the complete final formula for American urban communities, important as it is in part.

Wholesale decentralization, which is being advocated by some, does not seem to be compatible with the effective performance of the economic and cultural role of the urban community in the life of the Nation. Neither does it appear practicable under the existing equipment that we could afford. Widespread dispersion would be wasteful also because it would probably increase the cost of production and distribution and the cost of providing public facilities and services, thus rendering the attainment of a higher standard of material and cultural well-being more difficult for the whole population.[57]

No longer is it possible to conceive of a single community in terms of its decentralizing effect upon a city. The multiplex interrelationships must be taken into account and the place of each community in the larger community given complete consideration. Mumford's comment on the garden cities is a fair appraisal of the whole decentralization concept and process:

The slowness of the garden city in taking root is due to the fact that it is, so to speak, the native form only for a co-operative and socially planned society: one in which agriculture is on a parity with industry, and in which the necessary social basis in land ownership and land control is lodged in the community. To be built successfully, the garden city should be the product of a regional authority, with a wider scope of

[57] National Resources Committee, *Our Cities* (Washington: Government Printing Office, 1937), p. 84.

action than the municipality, and with greater local concentration than a centralized bureau operating from Washington, London, or Paris. The garden city can take form, in other words, only when our political and economic institutions are directed toward regional rehabilitation. What is important to recognize is that these new principles of urban development, as demonstrated by Sir Ebenezer Howard and his associates, are universal ones: they point toward balanced urban communities within balanced regions: on one hand, a wider diffusion of the instruments and processes of a higher human culture, and on the other the infusion into the city of the life-sustaining environment and life-directed interests of the countryside.[58]

In the more adequate consideration of both suburbanization and decentralization the metropolitan community has an exceedingly important place.

Supplementary Reading

The footnote references throughout the chapter present materials helpful for supplementary reading, especially Douglass, Lundberg et al., the Connecticut Studies of Suburbanization, Koos and Brunner, Howard, Fulmer, Lilienthal, Saarinen, Sert, Wright, Hilberseimer, Churchill, and Justement. Clues to their respective points of importance can be found in the text at the point of reference. The most important single suggestion is:

Howard, Ebenezer. *Garden Cities of Tomorrow,* third edition. London: Swan, Sonnenschein & Co., 1902. Reprinted in London by Faber and Faber in 1946 with an Introduction by Lewis Mumford.

Additional readings are:

Firey, Walter. *Social Aspects of Land Use Planning in the Country-City Fringe: The Case of Flint, Michigan.* Special Bulletin 339 (June, 1946). East Lansing: Michigan State College, Agricultural Experiment Station.

Kimball, Solon T. *The New Social Frontier, the Fringe.* Special Bulletin 360 (June, 1949). East Lansing: Michigan State College, Agricultural Experiment Station.

These two are studies of what is happening and of the problems arising in the fringe areas in the vicinity of American cities.

[58] Mumford, *op. cit.,* p. 401.

CHAPTER 13

METROPOLITAN COMMUNITIES

ONE result of the processes of suburbanization and decentralization has been the development of areas around cities with which the cities have manifold interrelationships, so making larger communities of which the cities are the centers. These metropolitan communities became the concern of students of cities around the turn of the century. Many studies have been made and many data collected with reference to these communities, though not much has yet been accomplished toward making them functioning social units.

DEFINING METROPOLITAN COMMUNITIES

Determining the extent of this "greater city" has been a difficult problem, and the final answer has not yet been reached, but a working basis has gradually evolved which for practical purposes is reasonably satisfactory. The first definite steps toward the definition of metropolitan communities in the United States were taken by the Bureau of the Census.

Metropolitan Districts of the Census. In the report of the fourteenth decennial census of the United States, 1910, a section entitled "Cities and Their Suburbs" appeared for the first time, with an account of these larger metropolitan communities. Two sets of computations were made: (1) cities and adjacent territory, comprising each city of 100,000 inhabitants, together with the civil units all or a major portion of which fell within ten miles of the city boundary; (2) metropolitan districts, comprising each city of 200,-000 inhabitants and the civil units within the ten-mile zone which had a density of population not less than 150 per square mile. There were twenty-five that came in the classification of metropolitan districts and nineteen others in the first group. The total of forty-four had a population of slightly over twenty-seven million, of which nineteen and a half million were in the forty-seven central cities, leaving 27.7 percent in the adjacent territory. The population growth of these districts in the decade 1900–1910 was 33.8 percent, with both central cities and adjacent territory growing at practically the same rate.

The 1920 census used the same basis of accounting and enumerated a total of fifty-eight communities, of which it designated twenty-nine as metropolitan districts. The total population was 36,-886,961, with 28.8 percent in the adjacent territory. The growth of population in the whole area had slowed down to 26.4 percent, and the distribution of the growth had changed so that the adjacent territory was growing at a slightly more rapid rate, 27.4 percent compared with the 26 percent growth in the central cities.

In the 1930 census the single basis for determining metropolitan districts became a central city or cities together with all contiguous or surrounding civil divisions with a density of not less than 150 inhabitants per square mile which had an aggregate population of 100,000 or more. Ninety-six such districts were designated, with a total population of 54,753,645, of which 30.9 percent was outside the central cities. In the decade 1920–1930 the total population growth of these districts was 24.9 percent. The central cities grew 19.4 percent and the territory outside the cities 39.2 percent. The growth pattern that appeared during the preceding decade was intensified.

The 1940 census continued the same basis of determining metropolitan districts except that *all* cities of 50,000 or more population were included. The number rose to 140, with a total population of 62,965,773, of which 32.0 percent was outside the central cities. Total growth slowed down in proportion to the slowing up of the population growth in the nation. For the total of all districts the growth was 9.3 percent; in central cities it was 6.1 percent, outside cities 16.9 percent.

For the 1950 census the basic principle of the two preceding censuses was retained with some refinements to facilitate the use of the areas designated by other departments of the federal government and to make them more readily useable in the local situations. This involved dealing with county units (towns in New England) and including with the county containing the central city or cities of 50,000 population or more the contiguous counties, on the basis of two types of specific criteria. The first was concerned with the character of the county as a place of work for nonagricultural workers and with the density of population. The second was concerned with the extent to which contiguous counties are socially and economically integrated with the central city. The designation was changed to metropolitan areas and 168 were designated. The increase in number was made up of twenty not formerly recognized and the balance of the separation of former combinations because, in most cases, where central cities were more than twenty miles apart, they have been considered to be two separate metropolitan areas.

TABLE 26.   Metropolitan Districts: Number, Population, and Growth, 1910–1950[1]

	1910	1920	1930	1940	1950
Number of districts[a]	44	58	96	140	168
Population—Total	27,020,818	36,886,961	54,753,645	62,965,773	83,929,863
In central cities	19,538,782	26,254,645	37,814,610	42,796,170	49,023,935
Outside central cities	4,482,036	10,632,316	16,939,035	20,169,603	34,905,928
Percentage outside	27.7	28.8	30.9	32.0	41.6
Percentage of total U.S.	29.4	34.9	44.6	47.8	56.0
Percentage of growth in decades[b]					
Total districts	33.8	26.4	24.9[c]	9.3	21.2
In central cities	33.8	26.0	19.4[c]	6.1	13.0
Outside cities	33.9	27.4	39.2[c]	16.9	34.7
Total U.S.	21.0	14.9	16.1	7.2	14.3

[a] Note that the basis of determining metropolitan districts differed. For 1910 and 1920 these figures are for cities of 100,000 or more population and adjacent territory (ten miles from city limits).

[b] Growth computed on areas the same at beginning as at close of decade.

[c] Does not include metropolitan districts for which comparable figures were not available.

A few new combinations were also made. The total population of the 168 metropolitan areas was 83,929,863, an increase of 21.2 percent and representing more than four-fifths of the national population increase. The central cities increased 13.0 percent and the outlying parts, 34.7 percent. The areas of the United States outside the metropolitan areas increased only 5.7 percent. The outlying parts contained 41.6 percent of the population of the metropolitan areas and in the growth in these parts nearly half of the population's increase of the entire country took place.

Table 26 gives a series of data for metropolitan districts for the five censuses in which they were reported. Though the data for the different censuses are not directly comparable because of the

[1] Data are from Bureau of the Census, *Fourteenth Decennial Census of the United States, 1920: Cities and Their Suburbs; Fifteenth Census of the United States, 1930: Metropolitan Districts; Sixteenth Census of the United States, 1940: Population,* First Series: "United States Summary"; *Seventeenth Census of the United States, 1950: Preliminary Counts: Population of Standard Metropolitan Areas:* April 1, 1950. Series PC-3, No. 3.

changing basis of determining the metropolitan districts, several important facts can be noted: first, the importance of metropolitan districts has been increasingly recognized as the basis for determining them has broadened to include a larger number of centers; second, a corollary to the first, an increasing proportion of the population has been recognized as living in metropolitan communities, so that in 1950 more than half the nation's people were listed as belonging to these important centers; third, since 1910 the area outside the central cities has had a greater proportionate growth than the area inside city boundaries; fourth, these metropolitan districts have increased in population more rapidly than the total United States. This was true for both outside and inside cities except between 1930 and 1940 when the rate of growth inside the central cities fell below the rate of national increase.

Figure 31 shows the geographical distribution of the 140 metropolitan districts of 1940 in the United States. While they are widely scattered, there is a large concentration in the northern and eastern sections of the country, where industry is also concentrated and the greatest total density of population is to be found. Eight states have no metropolitan districts, and eleven have one each. On the other hand, two have eleven each, and one has ten. Twenty-three of the districts include land within two different states.

What Is a Metropolitan Community? While density of population is a characteristic of metropolitan communities, it is the reason for the density that is important. The Bureau of the Census had to have a basis for determining metropolitan districts that was consistent, uniform, and simple and that made comparable districts. It found a high degree of relationship between density of population and analysis of a composite of many other factors. More fundamental definitions have been attempted by a number of writers.

Duffus made a single, yet comprehensive, statement which describes metropolitan communities generally, though it was applied to New York: "all that territory in which people's ways of living and working are directly affected by the presence of the metropolis."[2] McKenzie emphasizes the "functional entity," especially of the metropolitan community which is "organized around a central city or focal point of dominance in which are located the institutions and services that cater to the region as a whole" and which creates the

[2] R. L. Duffus, *Mastering a Metropolis* (New York: Harper & Brothers, 1930), p. 2.

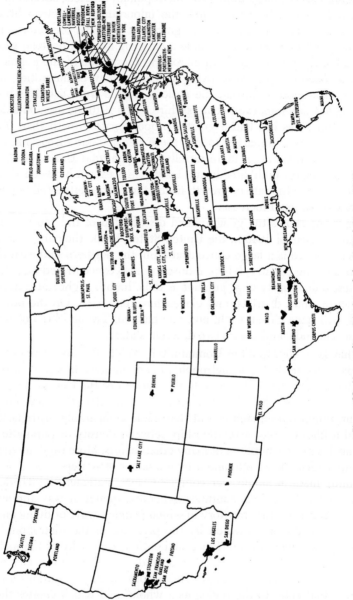

Figure 31. Metropolitan Districts of the United States, 1940.

patterns in which subcenters perform their complementary and local functions.[3] This idea of the dominance of the central city in the
metropolitan community was recognized by a committee of the industrial bureaus of chambers of commerce in a 1927 report. "It is an
area within which the conditions of manufacturing, trade, transportation, labor and living, in brief the daily economic and social life,
are predominantly influenced by the central city."[4] The basic assumption on which the regional plan for New York was worked out
was expressed in the first of the series of survey reports: "In recent
years the emphasis in city planning has rested less and less upon
artistic conceptions of 'The City Beautiful,' and more and more
upon efforts to prepare a 'productive piece of economic machinery'
designed to attain desirable ends within and beyond the city's limits. The economic character of a city plan has changed from that of
a 'consumption good' to that of a 'production good.' "[5]

It might be said, then, that the metropolitan community is the
urban community as it is taking form. It consists of a city of quantitative importance, together with that part of the surrounding area
wherein the activities and people are inextricably woven together in
a complex of interrelationships in the process of daily living. The
development of metropolitan communities is tending to make functional sociological units which are increasingly significant in the operation of American society.

CHARACTERISTICS OF METROPOLITAN COMMUNITIES

McKenzie, after further study of metropolitan communities, said:
"The movements of people to a given urban center seem to have
considerable stability and to constitute the phases for regional social
consciousness. I have, therefore, come to the tentative conclusion
that the retail shopping area about a metropolis represents the practical or optimum type of regional unit to use in social and economic
planning."[6] On the basis of this statement, the primary character-

[3] From *The Metropolitan Community*, by R. D. McKenzie. Copyright,
1933. Courtesy of McGraw-Hill Book Co., p. 70.
[4] *15th Census, 1930: Metropolitan Districts* (Washington: Government
Printing Office, 1932), p. 5, footnote.
[5] *Regional Survey of New York and Its Environs*, Vol. I: *Main Economic
Factors in Metropolitan Growth and Arrangement* (New York: Regional Plan of
New York and Its Environs, 1927), p. 9; cf. p. 19.
[6] National Resources Committee, *Regional Factors in National Planning
and Development* (Washington: Government Printing Office, 1935), p. 149.

istics of metropolitan communities are: the movement of people, which is primarily commuting, and the outreach of retail trade, represented by the extension of services of major retail establishments. There are, however, two other characteristics which are implicit in the phenomenon of metropolitan communities: the pattern of industrial production of the area in relation to the central city, and the social relationship of people in their range from simple social intercourse to the patterns of social services which have developed.

Commuting. The total picture of commuting in any metropolitan community is difficult to get. While the bulk of commuters continue to use railroads in daily journeys to the center of the large cities, the automobile plays a major role in the smaller metropolitan communities. However, when one watches the express highways, the bridges, and the ferries at about eight o'clock in the morning and five-thirty in the afternoon, even in New York, it is clear that those traveling by automobile are no small number. Then there are buses which carry great numbers during the commuting hours, and in New York there has been initiated a commuting service by airplane.[7] And what shall be said of the large numbers of people who spend an equivalent of time traveling by rapid transit from their homes to their work—from Woodlawn, South Shore, Rogers Park, or Forest Glen to the Loop in Chicago; from Shaker Heights to the Public Square in Cleveland; from Grand River to Grand Circus in Detroit; or from Riverdale, Pelham, or Jamaica to Times Square, New York?

The New York Regional Plan Association has used this broader basis of daily population movement to analyze the persons and vehicles entering Manhattan south of Sixty-first Street during the twenty-four hours of a typical business day. The principal results of this analysis are shown for passengers in Table 27 and for vehicles in Table 28.

The bulk of the passengers come from within the city limits via rapid transit lines, but there was a marked increase in the number which comes by railroad—the commuters—from 1940 to 1948. The large increase in the number of buses and bus passengers is partly offset by the replacement of trolleys by buses.

The backbone of commuting, however, is the railroad, and it is likely to continue to be for some time to come. An analysis of railroad commutation, therefore, is important. One of the great com-

[7] New York *Times,* July 17, 1946.

TABLE 27. Passenger Movements into Lower Manhattan on a
Typical Business Day, 1948[8]

Via	Number of Passengers	Percentage of Passengers	Percentage of Change, 1940–1948
Rapid transit	2,389,000	63.5	+10.1
Autos	626,000	16.6	+24.5
Buses and trolleys	314,000	8.3	+50.2
Railroads	283,000	7.5	+37.4
Trucks	105,000	2.8	−9.5
Ferries	48,000	1.3	−29.4
Total	3,765,000	100.0	+15.1

muting areas in the United States is Long Island, and one of the
railroads given very largely to commutation service is the Long Island Railroad, running out of the Pennsylvania Station in New York
City. Table 29 shows the extent of this commuting service over a
period of thirty years.

The large drop in number of passengers between 1930 and 1935
was due to the opening of the extensions of the New York City subways and the addition of bus lines, operating from the end of the
subway, which served many areas formerly served almost entirely
by the Long Island Railroad.

The percentage distribution of commuters by the distance of their
daily travel is given for selected years from 1922 to 1944 in Table

TABLE 28. Vehicle Movements into Lower Manhattan on a Typical
Business Day, 1948[9]

Type	Number	Percentage	Persons per Vehicle	Percentage of Change, 1940–1948
Autos	304,300	79.7	2.1	+10.6
Buses	10,000	2.6	29.0	+72.4
Trucks	67,700	17.7	1.6	− 3.7
Total	382,000	100.0	2.7	+ 8.8

[8] Regional Plan Association of New York, Bulletin No. 74 (Oct., 1949),
Table 2, and Supplement (mimeographed), Dec., 1949; The Port of New York
Authority, Department of Port Development, Planning Bureau, *Persons and Ve-
hicles Entering Manhattan South of 61st Street 1924, 1932, 1940, and 1948,*
Table 2.

[9] Regional Plan Association of New York, Bulletin No. 74 (Oct., 1949),
Table 3, and Supplement (mimeographed), Dec., 1949; The Port of New York
Authority, Department of Port Development, Planning Bureau, *Persons and
Vehicles Entering Manhattan South of 61st Street 1924, 1932, 1940, and 1948,*
Table 4.

TABLE 29.   Commutation Traffic, Long Island Railroad[10]

Year	Number of Commuters	Percentage of Total Passengers Carried
1911	10,262,950	30.31
1915	14,074,975	33.02
1920	28,891,350	39.72
1925	56,176,920	55.66
1930	83,348,220	70.52
1935	55,457,068	71.40
1940	47,661,469	70.01
1941	48,112,465	67.59

30. Since the opening of the extension of the New York subways, the largest numbers of commuters have been from communities which are situated between fifteen and twenty-five miles from the New York terminal. In 1944, 82.70 percent of all commuters traveled twenty-five miles or less. Beyond twenty-five miles there is a sharp drop. A rough check of some other railroads which provide commuter service to New York City, on the basis of the peak of train service, shows a   similar pattern, with slight variations due to the speed that is possible. For example, the peak service on the New York, New Haven and Hartford Railroad is from Stamford (Connecticut) to New York, with sixty-seven eastbound trains per day. It is a distance of 33.1 miles, the express running time is about fifty minutes, and the monthly commutation cost is $17.15. This is beyond the peak of commuting, but there are many commuters from farther out in Connecticut. The higher cost in time and money reflects a selective process in which income, standard of living in the

TABLE 30.   Percentage Distribution of Commutation Tickets Sold on Long Island Railroad, by Distance from Pennsylvania Station, New York City, for Selected Years, 1922–1944[11]

Miles	1922	1927	1931	1936	1937	1939	1940	1941	1942	1943	1944
0–10	15.3	12.2	12.3	6.5	2.8	2.1	1.1	.7	.67	.83	1.16
10–15	18.7	30.5	30.5	18.3	12.9	12.2	11.8	10.7	11.11	12.54	13.82
15–20	21.2	21.0	21.0	32.0	35.7	30.1	32.8	33.1	33.56	34.43	34.70
20–25	29.5	24.3	24.3	29.3	32.8	36.3	35.9	36.4	35.23	34.05	33.02
25–30	5.0	4.3	4.3	5.1	5.8	7.7	6.5	6.8	6.95	6.51	5.99
30–35	2.7	2.2	2.2	2.6	3.0	3.4	3.5	3.6	4.04	3.94	3.55
35–60	5.7	4.3	4.3	5.0	5.6	6.6	6.8	7.0	6.74	6.08	6.10
50	1.9	1.2	1.1	1.2	1.4	1.6	1.6	1.7	1.70	1.62	1.66

[10] *The Long Island Railroad, Its Problems and Future* (New York: Long Island Railroad, 1942), p. 54.

[11] *Ibid.*, p. 55; additional data furnished by the Assistant Chief Clerk in the Passenger Traffic Department.

community, and vocations play a part. There are occasionally people who commute long distances because of unique circumstances, but there is a practical limit to commuting distance. The major factors are apparently time and cost rather than distance. There is, however, little likelihood that any appreciable speed can be added to the relatively short distances involved in commuting. The average commuter on the Long Island Railroad spends less than three-quarters of an hour on the train each way between home and work, and spends a little less than ten dollars a month for his commutation ticket.[12] The practical limit of commuting is approximately thirty miles from the center of the city.

This limit, however, does not mean that all communities within this area are resdential suburbs from which the majority of the working population commute to the city. All sorts of communities can be found. In Nassau County, contiguous to New York City, and in the fringe of Suffolk County, up to a distance of fifty miles on Long Island from the Pennsylvania Station in New York City, there are seventy-six stations on the Long Island Railroad. The percentage of commuters in the population of the communities served by these stations varies from zero to 59.4. Communities with a small percentage of commuters lie adjacent to communities with a large percentage. There is, however, a slight relationship between distance from the city and proportion of commuters, if Nassau County, New York, is a fair illustration. Though the variation is very great, the average commuting percentage of the population tends to decline as the distance from the city increases, and three-quarters of the percentages over 20 belong to communities within the thirty-mile radius. Table 31 shows these comparisons.

Table 32 distributes the same communities on the basis of size. As would be expected, smaller communities have a larger percentage of commuters because, as communities increase in size, they require an increasing proportion of their population to operate the activities that are needed to serve the people. There is no relationship between size and distance from the city in terms of proportion of commuters. In general, commuters make up a small part of the population, although they may be a large proportion of the labor force of a community. Of the communities in this Long Island sample, only one-fifth have over 20 percent of the population commu-

[12] The actual average cost: 1941, $10.01; 1942, $9.47; 1943, $9.48; 1944, $9.82. Present costs have increased proportionately to other costs.

TABLE 31. Percentage of Total Population in Communities of Nassau
County, New York, Commuting on Long Island Railroad, by
Distance from Pennsylvania Station in New York City[13]

Miles from Penn. Station	No. of Communities	Range of Percentage	Median Percentage	Average Percentage
15–20	15	6.0–59.4	14.6	20.0
20–25	23	.5–38.0	10.0	20.1
25–30	10	2.1–32.2	12.9	14.6
30–35	12	.0–31.1	6.9	8.8
35–50	16	1.0–24.5	9.6	13.3

ters. Of the fifteen such communities, three are under 1000 population, four are from 1000 to 2500, six are from 2500 to 10,000, and
the remaining two are from 10,000 to 25,000.

This illustrative analysis of commuting is significant in that it
seems to indicate that there is a real limit to the outreach of the
metropolitan community. Some light is thrown on the problems of
mobility of people as they go to and come from work to their homes
by a study that was made of the journey to work by those employed
in a number of large industrial establishments of Greater London.[14]
This study found that a large proportion of workers traveled short
distances with relatively small cost, on the public transportation systems, but that the time of the journey was approximately the same
as that of New York commuters. There is an implication that com-

TABLE 32. Percentage of Total Population in Communities of Nassau
County, New York, Commuting on Long Island Railroad, by
Population of Communities[15]

Population of Communities	No. of Communities	Range of Percentage	Median Percentage	Average Percentage
Under 1,000	13	.0–57.5	10.0	14.9
1,000 to 2,500	15	1.1–59.4	12.8	18.0
2,500 to 10,000	30	.5–35.4	11.1	12.9
10,000 to 25,000	15	1.0–25.5	8.9	10.3
Over 25,000	3	5.5– 8.6	6.0	6.7

[13] Computed from population estimates for 1943, based on the 1940 census,
and the number of commuters in May, 1943, on the Long Island Railroad, as
given in *Long Island: the Sunrise Homeland* (New York: The Long Island Association, 1944).

[14] Kate Lipeman, *The Journey to Work* (New York: Oxford University
Press, 1944), especially Part A, Chap. IV, and Part B, Chap. II.

[15] From the same sources as Table 31.

muting has relationships to social and vocational groupings, and that among lower-income workers cost supersedes time as the most important factor.

Retail Shopping Area. The large retail establishments in New York City make their deliveries of purchased goods through a single organization, the United Parcel Service. An analysis of its operations gives a rather accurate picture of the retail shopping area of New York City.

The principle of operation is similar to that of the distribution of the mail. Parcels are distributed by areas; those for each area are taken to its subcenter from all the other subcenters, sorted by routes, and then delivered. There are thirty-two substations in the New York area.

The radius of daily delivery from New York City (Manhattan) is approximately fifty miles, a much larger area than the commuting area. The deliveries in the outer fringes of daily routes are disproportionately on telephone and mail orders.

The United Parcel Service operates also in twelve metropolitan areas in the United States. The plan and pattern of operations are the same, although a smaller proportion of the retail outlets are served. The radius of operation varies somewhat, but approximates the same size, regardless of the size of the central city, except where the area approaches the outreach of another large city.

Industrial Production. The types of industry which technology has developed are highly interdependent. Modern industrial processes culminate in the assembly line, so that the accessibility of the many factories which contribute to the final product and the facility of short-haul transportation, primarily by motor trucks, are of paramount importance. Then the industries in a metropolitan community are all operating under the same conditions, which gives them common concerns and problems. The centralization of markets and of distribution points is also important to manufacturers. In the final analysis, the welfare and prosperity of urban communities depend upon an efficient productive base in industry, both for the production of the great variety of manufactured goods which urban people need, and for the use of the many kinds of human resources which urban communities have.

These considerations indicate a necessity for coöperative planning as a first concern of the whole urban community. In fact, the extensive survey which was made as a basis for the Regional Plan of New

York and Its Environs began with an economic study of the industries of the area. The principal reason for this basis for planning was stated as follows: "The metropolis, in one of its aspects, is essentially a piece of productive economic machinery competing with other metropolitan machines. It will prosper or decline as compared with other metropolises roughly in proportion to the relative efficiency with which it can do economic work—that is produce economic goods and services."[16] The survey goes on to show the importance of the location of industrial establishments, of the adequacy of port and terminal facilities, of congestion of traffic, etc., for the efficiency of the community as a productive "factory." This became the basis of planning and the principle on which zoning was worked out, and in turn the basis on which an appraisal of progress toward the accomplishment of the plan has been made,[17] although the actual terms of the appraisal are highways, transportation, parks, housing, etc.

Patterns are still to be worked out. In only a few metropolitan communities has the problem of industrial coördination even been considered. Private enterprise, which is highly individualistic, has not yet been able to establish a basis for coöperation. The principles of coördination, and the means of measuring attainment in terms of efficiency of operation and of welfare of the metropolitan community, are still to be determined by a kind of research not yet undertaken. There are a few people, however, in the great cities who recognize this problem and are working toward more adequate study and planning.

Social Relationships. The increasing mobility of urban people has lessened the significance of proximity as a basis for their associations. McKenzie uses the increase in local telephone calls and the preponderance of short automobile trips as evidence of the broadening social contacts of people in urban areas.[18] The Westchester County study included sample data on how families spend their

[16] Robert Murray Haig (in consultation with Roswell C. McCrea), *Main Economic Factors in Metropolitan Growth and Arrangement: A Study of Trends and Tendencies in the Economic Activities Within the Region of New York and Its Environs* (New York: Regional Plan of New York and Its Environs, 1927), p. 18.

[17] Staff of the Regional Plan Association, *From Plan to Reality:* Vol. I, *Four Years of Progress on the Regional Development of New York and Its Environs;* Vol. II, *Eight Years of Progress;* Vol. III, *Twelve Years of Progress* (New York: Regional Plan Association, 1933, 1938, 1942).

[18] McKenzie, *op. cit.*, pp. 81–83.

evenings.[19] It found that the suburban families engaged in many activities, a considerable proportion of which were centered in New York. Competition for the use of the family car is common experience in both suburban and city families. How far social contacts can reach is not known, nor is it clear what, if anything, a study of such relationships would add to understanding of the metropolitan community beyond the obvious fact that its facilities and opportunities give wide range to the possibilities for personal relationships.

For the most part, even private social agencies operate within the geographical limits of political boundaries. Here and there, however, in response to needs that know no such limits, wider areas of operation are recognized, as, for example, by the Federation of Social Agencies of Pittsburgh and Allegheny County.

Outreach of Metropolitan Communities. The characteristics of metropolitan communities so far discussed include factors which limit the expansion of urban communities. Three additional factors, involved in the outreach of their influence, must be mentioned. They are, first, the relation of the great cities to the geography of urban population growth; second, the influence of the metropolises on their agricultural hinterlands; and, third, the extent of communication, as seen in metropolitan newspaper circulation.

One of the important results of the analysis of urban population growth in the decade 1930–1940 (see p. 61) was that those cities which showed exceptional growth tended to be located within the penumbra of metropolises. The radii of the areas adjacent to the large cities within which the smaller, rapidly growing cities were located differed from city to city. In the case of New York a fifty-mile radius included most of the rapidly growing cities of New York State and New Jersey. In the case of the smaller metropolitan centers the radius of inclusion was much shorter. The evidence was clear, however, that growth of cities in this period was in some way related to the factor of proximity to a large urban center. Although evidence to define this relationship is lacking, it is unmistakable that the immediate influence of a city goes beyond the area of its daily operations. One might surmise that the explanation, at least in part, might be that the widespread use of the automobile has made it possible for many people to obtain the varieties of services and fa-

[19] George A. Lundberg, Mira Komarovsky, and Mary Alice McInerny, *Leisure: A Suburban Study* (New York: Columbia University Press, 1934), Chap. IV, pp. 178 f., 188.

cilities of city life, but at the same time live some distance away from the oppressive bigness of the great cities. This is probably combined with the increasing vocational opportunities in the smaller cities, both because of their growth and because of the tendency of industry to select such cities for their location.

The second factor recalls a fact already discussed—that the needs of the city rather than what the soil is fitted for dictate the use of the farm land adjacent to the metropolises (see p. 109). This interrelationship, made up, on the one hand, of the control of the city over the agricultural patterns, and, on the other hand, of the provision of relatively stable markets with good prices to the farmers, is mutually advantageous. The cities get the fresh food they need, and the farmers gain a standard of living that is above average. To what extent it is reasonable to consider this rural hinterland a part of metropolitan communities is difficult to determine; it is, however, certainly a more specific relationship than the general matters of rural-urban interrelations.

"Communication is fundamental to the existence of every form and type of society, and one form of communication, namely, the newspaper, has been found to circulate over the natural areas within which society is organized." In addition, newspapers are a commodity to be distributed and sold quickly if their value as communicators of news is to be preserved. Their circulation is the basis of their value as an advertising medium, which is another form of communication. Since it has been shown that there is a close relationship between newspaper circulation and trade areas, the extent of the circulation can be used as an index of an area of social organization.

These are the premises on which Park and Newcomb divided the United States into forty-one metropolitan regions,[20] which are shown in Figure 32. They took the Federal Reserve cities, later supplemented by five other cities which became clearly necessary, and analyzed the geographical distribution of the leading incoming newspapers in each city. The boundaries of each metropolitan region were drawn to include all cities and towns in which more than 50 percent of the local circulation of metropolitan newspapers came from the central city. The areas varied greatly according to the relative density of population and proximity of cities, but the regions

[20] McKenzie, *op. cit.*, Chap. VIII, especially pp. 98–99, 107–108. See also Fig. 5, p. 102.

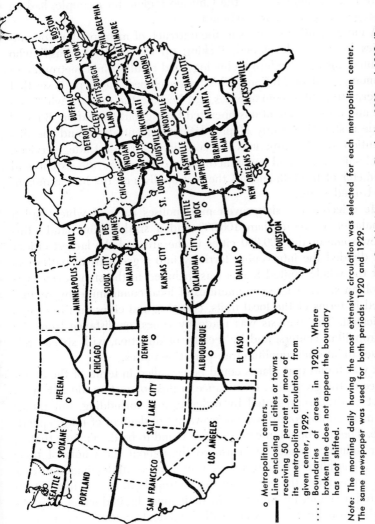

o Metropolitan centers.

— Line enclosing all cities or towns receiving 50 percent or more of its metropolitan circulation from given center, 1929.

···· Boundaries of areas in 1920. Where broken line does not appear the boundary has not shifted.

Note: The morning daily having the most extensive circulation was selected for each metropolitan center. The same newspaper was used for both periods: 1920 and 1929.

Figure 32. Metropolitan Regions in the United States as Defined by Newspaper Circulation, 1920 and 1929. (From *The Metropolitan Community*, by R. D. McKenzie. Copyright, 1933. Courtesy of McGraw-Hill Book Co., p. 107.)

were of considerable size; the Chicago region, for example, had an average radius of about two hundred miles.

A more detailed analysis of the outreach of metropolitan communities has been developed. Picking up the work of Gras,[21] who pointed out that modern technology had resulted in a metropolitan economy, and of McKenzie,[22] who developed the hypothesis that supermetropolitan communities had become the units in which social and economic relations operated throughout the nation, Bogue[23] made a statistical study of population concentrations and the distribution of the functions of sustenance—retail trade, services, wholesale trade, and manufactures—to determine the extent and character of the influence of the metropolises on the hinterlands of the United States.

He selected the sixty-seven metropolises each of which had a population of more than 100,000 and a sizable hinterland (this threw some of the 100,000 cities in the areas of the largest cities) and divided the intervening territory into a geometrical pattern so that the whole United States was included in the sixty-seven metropolitan areas. These communities of local communities were analyzed in terms of the local units, counties, and cities on the factors indicated. The analysis was made by zones, or distance from the metropolitan centers, and by sectors, or direction, with special reference to intermetropolitan transportation routes.

It was found that places could be classified in terms of the dominance of the great city. Dominance in this connection did not mean overt control, represented by ordering and forbidding, but rather the more subtle control which grows out of degrees of interdependence. The metropolitan centers were found to be dominants; that is, their influence could be measured throughout the whole of their areas. The hinterland cities were found to be subdominants in that they were under the control of the metropolitan center, but in turn exerted a significant influence in their more limited areas. The villages (rural nonfarm) were called influents because to a much more limited extent and degree they also exerted influence in their

[21] N. S. B. Gras, *An Introduction to Economic History* (New York: Harper & Brothers, 1922).
[22] McKenzie, *op. cit.*
[23] Don S. Bogue, *The Structure of the Metropolitan Community: A Study of Dominance and Subdominance* (Ann Arbor: University of Michigan, Horace H. Rackham School of Graduate Studies, 1949).

vicinities while they operated under the dominance of the cities. The rural farm areas were found to be subinfluents under much domination and with very limited influence. Dominance is, therefore, a variable, not an attribute, and is a matter of the kind and extent of relationships. The patterns are to be regarded, not as static or permanent, but as subject to change as conditions change.

Concentration of population was found to be clearly related to the metropoltan centers, for throughout the whole United States the number of persons per square mile decreases as the distance from the metropolis increases. This distance pattern encompassed all of the hinterland, with suburban and distant zones showing only different aspects of the same phenomenon. Within this framework the other cities showed similar, though much less extensive, patterns of secondary population concentrations.

The four sustenance activities also showed a distance pattern, but it differed from the pattern of population, and each activity had its own peculiarities, which indicated specialization of function. While there is a greater specialization in retail trade, service, and wholesale trade in central cities, the influence of the city in retail trade is largely confined within a thirty-five mile radius. The services exert a pull on the surrounding area to about forty-five miles. Although there is a tendency for wholesale trade to be dispersed within the twenty-five mile zones of the central cities, its influence can be seen throughout the metropolitan communities, with a slight revival in the forty-five to sixty-four mile zone. Manufacturing is spread within the forty-five mile zone rather than concentrated in the central cities, but from this location it serves the hinterland. Calculated in terms of the requirements of the population, up to forty-five miles the population is dependent upon the metropolis for retail trade, but throughout the whole hinterland, even to five hundred miles or more when it extends that far, the populations depend very largely on central cities for wholesale trade, business services, and financial matters. In manufacturing, the area beyond sixty-five miles depends upon the area within that distance.

The sectors along the intermetropolitan transportation routes and those with subdominant cities tend to disperse populations farther and support more remote concentrations of population. The former are more specialized in retail trade, in services, and in wholesale trade, while the latter are more inclined to manufacturing. In all cases the activities are supplementary and related to the metropolitan centers. The local sectors have the lowest average level of land occupancy and are much less specialized.

Bogue concludes that "a metropolitan community is an organization of many subdominant, influent, and subinfluent communities, distributed in a definite pattern about a dominant city, and bound together in a territorial division of labor through a dependence upon the activities of the dominant city," that this "has come to be a characteristic pattern by which at least one urbanized commercial-industrial society, the United States, is organized," and that "in the foreseeable future the element of intercommunity exchange remains the basis for the metropolitan pattern of population distribution."[24]

This factual study establishes the importance and extent of metropolitan communities throughout all of the country. Much still remains to be done to define more precisely the relationships which are involved. One important extension of the study is to determine the interrelationships of metropolitan centers in terms of the natural regions of the United States. The results of such an analysis should contribute greatly to defining the functional regions as effective administrative and perhaps political units for the decentralization of federal governmental operations.

METROPOLITAN COMMUNITIES AS FUNCTIONING SOCIAL UNITS

It is quite clear from the evidence already recounted that in many respects these metropolitan communities are actually operating as such; but the extent to which they can operate as social units is very limited because they are not yet organized as political entities. Several steps, however, have been taken in the direction of developing metropolitan communities as functioning units.

Annexation. For many years, as cities expanded beyond their boundaries, the boundaries were pushed out by the annexation of the settled land. The picture of the annexations of many cities over the years is a veritable checkerboard, like the map of Cincinnati shown earlier (Fig. 13). McKenzie made a study of the annexations in the larger American cities and found that since the middle of the nineteenth century there was a distinct trend toward more, but

[24] *Ibid.*, pp. 61–63. Chap. I gives the hypothesis, Chap. II the methods of the study, and Chap. III the findings.

smaller, annexations.[25] He concluded that annexation had in no way kept pace with the growth of metropolitan areas.

As population began to nucleate in subcenters beyond city limits and local governments developed in these outlying communities, it became less and less possible to make the central city inclusive by annexing additional areas. In 1898 New York City met this problem by a consolidation of New York (Manhattan), Brooklyn, the Bronx, part of Queens County, and Staten Island into the present city with its five boroughs. The boroughs retain some governmental function. This took place about thirty years after a period (1857–1870) in which various functional metropolitan districts (police, fire, sanitary) were experimented with and found unsatisfactory. It still leaves, however, a growing area within which people and communities which are a part of the metropolitan community are still outside the reach of organized governmental coördination.[26] In 1907 the city of Allegheny was annexed to Pittsburgh. The political repercussions were widespread and have served to discourage similar plans. But this did not solve the problems of metropolitan Pittsburgh. In fact, almost constantly since that time there have been activities to devise and put into effect a plan by which the many other municipalities adjacent to the city might be included in a coördinating organization. Between 1910 and 1920, Los Angeles annexed territory more than two and a half times the area the city had at the beginning of the decade, including, principally, the then sparsely settled San Fernando Valley to the northwest of the city. It was not possible even at that time to include the municipality of Beverly Hills to the west, or to add the more settled areas to the east made up of many municipalities, the largest of which was Pasadena, or Long Beach to the south.[27] These are illustrations of many similar situations. It is clear that this method cannot cope with the need in decentralized metropolitan communities.

Annexation continues, however, to take care of the bulging cities. Since the war, many cities have added territory (see Table 33). In most cases the additions were incorporated residential land; 20 percent of them were one-half square mile or more. Some made large proportionate increases in population; for example, Palquemine (Louisiana), with population of 7500, added five square miles to its

[25] McKenzie, *op. cit.*, pp. 195–197.

[26] Victor Jones, *Metropolitan Government* (Chicago: The University of Chicago Press, 1942), pp. 86, 94, 123.

[27] *Ibid.*, pp. 123, 124, 127, 128.

one square mile and increased its population 500 percent; El Paso, with 135,000, added two and one-half square miles and gained 42 percent in population; Milwaukee, with 627,000, annexed slightly more than three square miles and added 7 percent to its population. Even this type of annexation brought serious problems in the extension of public services.[28]

TABLE 33. Annexation to Cities, 1945 to 1948[29]

	All Cities over 5,000		Cities of 5,000 to 10,000		Cities over 10,000	
	Total No. Annexing Cities	No. Cities Annexing ½ Sq. Mi. or Over	Total No. Annexing Cities	No. Cities Annexing ½ Sq. Mi. or Over	Total No. Annexing Cities	No. Cities Annexing ½ Sq. Mi. or Over
1948	289	59	95	7	194	52
1947	298	68	128	15	170	53
1946	259	43	105	13	154	30
1945	152	25	63	3	89	20

Special Functional Districts. In spite of such failures as that in New York, already mentioned, special *ad hoc* functional districts continue to be formed in metropolitan areas to deal with particular problems which require immediate solution. McKenzie classifies these districts into three groups: "(1) those which are agents of the central government, the governing body being appointed by and responsible to the governor or legislature; . . . (2) those which are agents of the various local units within the district, the governing body being made up of representatives chosen by the governing bodies of these units; . . . (3) those which are themselves distinct units of local government, the governing body being elected directly by the people of the district."[30]

An example of the first kind is the Massachusetts Metropolitan District, whose background development is: Metropolitan Sewage District, 1889; Metropolitan Park District, 1893; Metropolitan Water District, 1895; Sewage and Water combined, 1901; these combined with Park, 1919. McKenzie calls attention to this process of joining functions in a single organization as moving toward metropolitan community government. This type of district, however, was

[28] John C. Bollens, "Changes in City Areas," in *The Municipal Year Book, 1949* (Chicago: The International City Managers' Association, 1949), pp. 92–99. This reports a special survey of land annexations to cities made in 1949.

[29] *Ibid.*, Table 1, p. 93.

[30] McKenzie, *op. cit.*, p. 305.

severely criticized by a special investigating commission of the Massachusetts legislature as early as 1896:

A system of metropolitan control which permits the legislature, representing the entire commonwealth, to tax the people of the district not for state but for local purposes, and then, having deprived them of all but a fractional voice in the levying of the tax, decrees that the money shall be spent by those whom the payers of the tax have no voice in appointing and over whom they can exercise no control, is not a system that can be reconciled with the American political methods. That good work has been done under it is not an argument in its defense.[31]

The Metropolitan Water District of Southern California, established in 1930, illustrates the second type of district. This is one of many federated special authorities. Los Angeles, together with other southern California municipalities, has carried on stupendous operations, involving Boulder Dam, land rights, water rights, and power rights in Arizona and Nevada, as well as California. This type of organization, however, is subject to the whims and delays of its component local governments and may easily be stymied in its operation.

The third class is illustrated by the Chicago Sanitary District, organized in 1889, which has carried on the complicated and expensive activities involved in water supply and sewage disposal, but has not extended its operations, except for the development of the Chicago River as a part of the Lakes-to-Gulf navigation project, and of electric power from the channel current. Beyond this the district has been unable to function, though many other metropolitan problems have developed. Besides this, its charter compels it to serve municipalities under specified conditions, but makes no provision for the coöperation of, or reimbursement by, these municipalities.[32]

This method is a functional approach to the solution of specific problems and as such in most cases has been successful within these narrow limits. It seemed quite impossible to build the two vehicular tunnels under the Hudson River and the George Washington Bridge over it, until the job was given to the Port of New York Authority, which had already evolved a method of working for the two states of New York and New Jersey in the development of the port of New York. The method, however, even though it could be greatly extended, is no solution to the basic problems of operating a metropol-

[31] Quoted by Paul Studenski, *The Government of Metropolitan Areas in the United States* (New York: National Municipal League, 1930), p. 316.

[32] McKenzie, *op. cit.*, pp. 305–306, and Jones, *op. cit.*, pp. 66, 96.

itan community, for it would only multiply independent functional units.

Rise of Metropolitan Planning. The need for organization of metropolitan communities is further seen in the development of regional planning associations. City plans often state that to finish the job of planning it is necessary to go beyond the city limits and include those areas which are a part of the larger community, but this reaches beyond the city's jurisdiction. In many of the metropolitan communities private agencies have been formed to study the metropolitan community and draw up plans for its development. The most noteworthy and the pioneer of these organizations is the Regional Plan Association of New York. It was organized in 1929 and subsidized by a large grant from the Russell Sage Foundation. It published a report in two volumes, containing the proposed plans: one volume of maps and a second of details and descriptions.[33] This plan has had a great influence on the developments in the New York area; in fact, three volumes at four-year intervals have been published by the Association, recording the accomplishments toward working out the plan. The difficulty in working out the plan, as in all similar situations, has been that there was no authority by which activities could be coördinated to bring the plan to reality. The results obtained have been by virtue of the general recognition of the importance of planning for the whole area and of the soundness of the plan, so that many local governments have tried, in so far as possible, to make their developments accord with the master plan. How much more might have been accomplished if there had been a united implementing government is a matter of conjecture. Certainly, however, the job might be done with greater facility. The development of planning activities in many of the American metropolitan areas is an indication that, in spite of serious problems, metropolitan communities are being recognized and are beginning partially to function as such.

PROBLEMS OF METROPOLITAN COMMUNITIES

Three groups of problems[34] are inherent in the development of metropolitan communities: first, problems of function; second, prob-

[33] See also p. 236 for the list of supplementary reports and pp. 550–552 for a discussion of the significance of the New York Regional Plan in the development of city-planning and also its shortcomings.

[34] Much additional detail will be found in Jones, *op. cit.*, Chap. III.

lems of finance; and third, problems of structure or organization. The first two deal with the acute matters which are largely going by default because the metropolitan communities are powerless to act as such, their powerlessness being due to the circumstances of the third group of problems.

Problems of Function

Communication. This is one of the prime necessities of a metropolitan community. If people are unable to get around, severe limitations are put upon the functioning of these communities. A serious lag exists between transportation needs and facilities. Most means of transportation have been privately operated and tend to confine their operations to the main line of access to the center of the city. This has been a major factor in the star-shaped development of metropolitan communities already referred to and has left large interstitial areas, often nearer to the main business center, without means of transportation and consequently undeveloped for residence purposes. Frequently there is very little, if any, means of going from one outlying community to another, so that it is necessary to go into the city and out again to reach a place nearer than the city itself. The large and powerful transportation companies negotiate their franchises with each local government and are not subject to unified control. New patterns of routes and coverage need to be worked out, not only on the basis of present traffic flow, but also on the basis of potential use to the people of the whole community.

Highways suffer the same difficulties because they are built and maintained in pieces by local governments. Somewhat less practical limitations exist, however, because the users of automobiles seek out convenient routes, and their growing use is responded to quickly with improvements. The most serious needs are related to the relief of the intense traffic congestion in the business sections of the central cities. Such solutions as the express highways in Pittsburgh and New York are in large measure for the benefit of those living outside the city, but their cost has had to be met by the city itself. In the states of California and Pennsylvania these problems have been summarily met by designating city streets as state highways, which makes their development and maintenance the responsibility of the state governments.[35]

[35] *Ibid.,* p. 107.

Protection. This cannot be effectively carried on in the midst of a maze of municipal boundary lines. Criminals find it easy to operate under these conditions. Police are severely limited in their service when they are needed beyond the line that stops their operation. Jurisdictional disputes are frequent in situations such as the Chicago area, where 522 different agencies have police forces in operation. Specialized services, training of police personnel, modern equipment, are possible only in wealthy or large communities. Crime-prevention efforts are futile without coördinated activities.[36] Fire-fighting is somewhat better because obvious emergencies facilitate the interchange of equipment, but inequalities are very great, not only in equipment, but also in salaries and consequently in personnel. In the matter of water supply and pressure, building codes and their enforcement, differences are tremendous.

Health protection is one of the most serious problems. Epidemics do not stop at city limits. The most thorough work of an efficient health department can be undone quickly by indifference and negligence in another municipality across the street. Inequalities in the inspection and testing of water, milk, and food and in sanitation make the chain only as strong as its weakest link. Sewage and garbage disposal, again, need the same standards. Water pollution in recreational areas is important. With all of the work of the Chicago Sanitary District to protect the waters of Lake Michigan, they are still polluted by the municipalities across the Indiana line.[37] These are but some of the health-protection aspects of urban life which can only be provided for in the metropolitan community on a unified basis.

Facilities and Services. Those which are essential to satisfactory living in urban areas also vary greatly. Good water is expensive to provide for cities. Suburban communities, unless they can catch on to their city's water system, must pay a disproportionately high price or get along with inferior water. Health services are notoriously divided, unequal, and confused in metropolitan communities. The agencies providing health services often number in the hundreds, sometimes as many as a hundred governmental agencies having supervisory responsibility. What can be expected in a health program under a part-time $200 health officer compared with that under a high-salaried, full-time Doctor of Public Health? Only large cities

[36] *Ibid.*, pp. 68–71.
[37] *Ibid.*, p. 97.

can support well-equipped general and special hospitals, specialized clinics and treatment centers, x-ray programs for the detection of tuberculosis and free treatment centers, school lunch programs, pre-natal and well-baby clinics, health centers, health education programs, visiting nurses, and so forth. Those who live beyond the limits of the central cities in most cases either do not get these services or bootleg them from the city. A few wealthy suburbs have some exceptionally well-developed and highly efficient health services.

TABLE 34. Variations in Taxable Wealth Behind Each Child Enrolled in Cook County School Districts, as Shown by Assessed Valuation for 1934[38]

Measure	All Districts (192)	Elementary School Districts (175)	High School Districts (17)
Poorer district	$ 906	$ 906	$ 7,966
Lower quartile	4,874	4,799	9,673
Median	8,513	7,724	10,680
Upper quartile	13,017	13,389	13,972
Richest district	53,437	53,437	20,631

One glance at Table 34 shows the inevitable inequalities in educational services in the various communities in the Cook County part of the Chicago metropolitan community. In fact, the range is even greater in the whole Chicago metropolitan area, as it is in the New York and Los Angeles metropolitan areas, because most of the costliest and best schools of America are in the favored communities of these areas. Many schools within metropolitan areas, because of their smallness and their lack of resources, are deprived of the ability to offer the broad opportunities of modern schools, the well-trained teaching and administrative staffs, and the buildings and equipment which are provided in the larger, wealthier communities. But no metropolitan community can afford anything less than the best in education and training for its children, who will soon be responsible for its affairs.

Efficiency in government is impossible where so much duplication exists. The cost, the variety of personnel, the equipment, the pro-

[38] John Albert Vieg, *The Government of Education in Metropolitan Chicago* (Chicago: The University of Chicago Press, 1939), p. 175, Table 23, as quoted in Jones, *op. cit.*, Table 10, p. 75. The data were secured from an auditor on the staff of the Cook County superintendent of schools. Chicago's per pupil valuation was $4352. Enrollments for 1934–1935 have been used for all computations.

gram can be far more effective in one well-supported, properly organized department than in a hundred small departments with little if any coördination or coöperation. The fiscal problems of policy, budget, and accounting are hopeless under the circumstances that exist. Bigness *per se* is not necessarily the solution of the problems, but bigness with planning and organization for efficiency, operated democratically, makes the solution possible.

Problems of Finance. Tax resources from community to community in metropolitan areas vary greatly and inevitably so, as any sociological analysis will show. But in the last analysis local municipalities build their organization and operations on their own tax resources. This is to some extent true where state funds are available when they are distributed in proportion to the local community's investment. What must be the results when one district must make a levy four times as large as another to get the same amount of tax income?

Within the great cities the concentration of tax resources in the retail business center does not deprive the people in underprivileged areas of the services of the city's departments. But in the metropolitan communities the wealth of an Evanston, Wilmette, or Oak Park out of Chicago, a Bronxville, Montclair, or Locust Valley out of New York, a Grosse Point out of Detroit, a Shaker Heights out of Cleveland, or a Beverly Hills or Pasadena out of Los Angeles, provides the tax resources for its own use, regardless of the helplessness of the communities that may be situated beside it.

Overlapping of taxing units is very confusing, especially where many special districts have been established. Sanitation, park, water, high school, elementary school, street lighting, library, etc., etc., are types of districts with power to tax, and they usually have differing boundary lines, which can be found in varying combinations in metropolitan communities. When their levies are added to city or village, township or county taxes, the amount of taxes on each particular piece of property must be figured out by consolidating the rates that apply. The individual property owner is in a bad position either to understand his taxes or to have anything to say about them. The impossibility of anything but fiscal chaos under such circumstances is obvious.

Problems of Structure. The problems already referred to have their roots in the organization of government throughout urban areas. "The greatest obstacle to the full emergence of a metropolitan community is the great number of conflicting and overlapping political and administrative units into which the area is divided."[39] This is particularly true of the metropolitan districts with largest area and population. In 1940 the district of New York and northeastern New Jersey had 284 incorporated places in addition to the central cities; Pittsburgh, 136; Chicago, 117; Philadelphia, 92; St. Louis, 69; Los Angeles, 55; Boston, 54. The 17 metropolitan districts with populations over 700,000 in 1940 had 1103 incorporated places in addition to the 27 central cities. This was 71 more than in 1930 and 240 more than in 1920. Of the 71 increase from 1930 to 1940, 61 were new municipalities and 10 were added by extending the metropolitan district areas. Most of the places were small: 113, or 10.2 percent, under 500; 122, or 11.1 percent, from 500 to 999; 224, or 20.3 percent, from 1000 to 2499; 180, or 16.3 percent, from 2500 to 4999; and 199 or 18.0 percent, from 5000 to 9999; that is, 76.0 percent were under 10,000 population. The number of these minor municipalities continues to increase.[40] These do not include the multiplicity of special districts and authorities already discussed.

The situation is further complicated by the fact that, of the 140 census metropolitan districts in 1940, twenty-three straddled state lines (see Fig. 31). This is particularly significant because, legally, cities are subject to their states and must operate and develop their organization within the framework of all sorts of restrictive state statutes, or gaps in state statutes, which have been the basis for court action in many cases. Even in those states where home rule for municipalities has been constitutionally established, the court decisions have interpreted the powers of cities narrowly. In some instances states have taken over city licensing, fees, and inspectional functions where the cities already have successful experience. Recently the federal government has increased its relationships to cities and its activities in their behalf, but procedures have not yet been able to by-pass state laws and legislatures.[41]

Progress in intermunicipal understanding and relations has come through voluntary state and national associations of municipalities and municipal officials as they have coöperatively studied fiscal and administrative policies. The National Municipal League in New

[39] National Resources Committee, *Our Cities* (Washington: Government Printing Office, 1937), p. 67.
[40] Jones, *op. cit.*, pp. 16–23.
[41] National Resources Committee, *Our Cities*, pp. 48–52, 64–67.

York has carried on studies and published reports on a great many aspects of city government and publishes monthly the *National Municipal Review*, containing important current material on municipal problems and activities. In Chicago there are twenty-two different associations of municipal officials popularly known as the "1313 Group" because they all have their offices in a building at 1313 East 60th Street which was constructed for the special purpose of housing them. Each of the organizations is separate and distinct and entirely independent, but they coöperate in many ways through the Public Administration Clearing House. Each organization serves its membership in many ways, carries on research in its special field, publishes news letters and other periodicals as well as special reports, one of the most comprehensive of which is the annual *Municipal Year Book* of the International City Managers' Association. In Washington there is another group of organizations located at 730 Jackson Place, composed of the Conference of Mayors, the National Institute of Law Officers, purchasing offices, and others which operate in similar ways. Another approach is by a private enterprise, the monthly magazine *The American City*, which covers a wide variety of matters of interest and concern to city people. The staff have also continued to be involved in many of the activities for the development and improvement of cities. Thus the consideration of common problems and the development of acquaintance are paving the way for far-reaching coöperation in the solution of the basic problems of metropolitan communities.

METROPOLITAN GOVERNMENT

It is already clear that there is no such thing as government of metropolitan communities. Some few efforts in this direction, however, are worthy of note.

Various Principles. Jones makes a classification of the experience with and proposals for metropolitan government in two groups:

A. Devices involving no structional changes in local government.
    (1) extension of jurisdiction and services of central cities beyond their boundaries;
    (2) establishment of *ad hoc* authorities;
    (3) intergovernmental arrangements;
    (4) extension of state administration;
    (5) extension of federal administration.

B. Plans requiring fundamental changes in structure of local units.
   (1) annexation and consolidation of adjacent municipalities;
   (2) city-county consolidation or separation;
   (3) merger of special authorities with central government;
   (4) reorganization of urban county with assumption of metropolitan functions;
   (5) establishment of a "federated" municipal government for metropolitan area;
   (6) creation of a metropolitan city-state.[42]

Some of these have already been discussed. The first group have at best only limited possibilities. Extension of jurisdiction, authorities, and intergovernmental arrangements are, in the nature of the case, confined to special functions and consequently become only temporary measures; in fact, by multiplying governmental agencies, they further complicate the basic problem. To turn over administration of metropolitan community affairs to state governments is obviously completely unsatisfactory because it moves far away from the democracy of local control. The same would hold for extending federal government administration although the federal government can make many contributions in the right direction through demonstration, experimentation, research, surveys, statistical reporting, and setting of standards, and perhaps by grants-in-aid under certain specific limitations. A federal agency which provided services to industry and urban life comparable to those provided through the various activities of the Department of Agriculture to agriculture and rural life could be of tremendous assistance.[43]

Within the second group there are greater possibilities. It is hardly likely that an adequate solution of this problem of metropolitan government can be made without fundamental changes in the structure of local government units. Annexation seems to have gone by the board because the situations have reached a stage of complexity beyond the reach of such a simple process. Any readjustment of city and county governments would be effective in only a very few cases because metropolitan community areas do not, and certainly would not continue to, correspond to county areas. A merger of special authorities would be in the right direction, but it is likely that it would be almost as difficult as a more comprehensive step and at best still be only a partial solution. The idea of the city-state is

[42] Jones, *op. cit.*, p. 87. These items are discussed at length in the same work, pp. 85–154.

[43] National Resources Committee, *Our Cities*, pp. 78–79, 82–84.

challenging, for it would seem to be the most complete solution to the problems of metropolitan government. It has, however, two basic difficulties. The first is that it would disrupt the political structure of the nation and quickly rally the political forces against it. The second difficulty, which is more fundamental, is that it would cut apart the urban and rural areas in complete disregard of the facts of regionalism already discussed; but, more than that, it would segregate the areas of greatest wealth and organize them with reference to their own immediate interests rather than the welfare of the whole society.

This leaves the principle of "federated" municipal government as the most practical and promising. It has the advantages of preserving the identity of the various communities, of being easily effected even across state lines, and of having a flexibility that would enable it to develop functionally in the direction of a more complete metropolitan government. In fact, many proposals of this type have been under consideration in a number of the metropolitan areas in recent years.

Metropolitan Councils. Prompted by the difficulties in implementing metropolitan planning, the American Society of Planning Officials in 1942 held a nation-wide competition for the best "Proposal for the Organization and Operation of a Regional Council in a Metropolitan Area." The first-prize essay and three second-prize essays were published.[44] The first-prize essay proposed a nine-man council including two representatives each from the federal, state, and central city governments, to be nominated by the official planning agency of each and appointed by the chief executives of the governments concerned. The appointees were to be statesmanlike, mature, experienced, and progressive, with a knowledge of planning, and were to have full-time status at high salaries. The secretariat was to be made up of technicians in the fields of economics, engineering, and administration. Wide use was to be made of advisory bodies in the various areas of operation.

One of the plans, built on an entirely different principle, starts with a group of citizens interested enough to promote the idea and the calling of a convention of the "power holders and decision makers" from government, enterprise, and labor to work out policies and plans of organization and finance. Operation was to be by spe-

---

[44] *Organization for Metropolitan Planning: Four Proposals for Regional Councils* (Chicago: The American Society of Planning Officials, 1943).

cial committees. A central agency and personnel was to administer, to provide technical service, and to carry on public relations. Another plan "represents stage one in the development of a metropolitan government planning agency" by a planning commission appointed or elected by the communities involved, an officials' advisory council chosen by the legislative bodies of the coöperating local units, a citizens' advisory council appointed by the chairman of the planning commissions from the leaders in various civic organizations, and an operating organization of functional departments headed by technicians. The last published plan calls for a volunteer council made up of "any individual, government agency, or corporation sufficiently interested to pay dues," a board of directors "related to population, political units, and economic interests," and a staff composed of executive secretary, technical director, field consultant, and membership secretary. The program determined by the council was to operate through advisory committees. "The regional council should include as a major part of its program certain types of activity designed to promote and facilitate coöperation and coördination throughout the metropolitan area."

This contest called for principles, and the plans published represented different approaches to the solution of the problem. In the words of the Executive Director of the American Society of Planning Officials, in the foreword, "We do not believe that these are the final words on the subject." In fact, perhaps the best of each proposal does not even give adequate principles of operation. The most important result is that the proposals make clear that there are a variety of ways of going at the problem.

The "Boston Contest." In 1944 another contest was held for a plan of organizing Metropolitan Boston. The "Boston Contest" was initiated by the Boston Society of Architects, administered by Boston University, and sponsored by these organizations and the Boston Chamber of Commerce, Harvard University, and the Massachusetts Institute of Technology. Ninety plans were submitted, three prizes awarded to teams, and honorable mention given to nine individuals for meritorious suggestions. The plans are developed specifically to fit the Boston situation and are worthy of study.[45] The first-prize program proposes the organization of "a Metropolitan Authority to exercise those joint functions which are clearly metropolitan in na-

[45] *The Boston Contest of 1944: Prize Winning Programs* (Boston: The Boston University Press, 1945).

ture." This would take over the functions of the existing special bodies. "The government structure of the Metropolitan Authority should be of the city manager type. In other words, a representative council, possibly elected on the basis of proportional representation, with the pre-existing communities as electoral units (federal principle), would choose and appoint a business manager, well-paid ($25,000), and chosen on the basis of an open competition. His term of office would be indefinite, and the responsibility for most of the District's business would be his. . . . The council retains the authority to enact ordinances, to make appropriations, and to enact comprehensive plans for metropolitan development. . . . While the cities and towns would retain their separate entity and autonomy, a measure of reduction in municipal activities and expenditures would take place, especially in the City of Boston proper."

The second-prize proposal is similar except that it is based on a governing assembly composed of "one member elected from each city and town except that Boston would elect four"; the assembly, in turn, would elect a council of seven members as its executive body. The third-prize plan has three stages: a Boston Regional Planning Authority, an independent State Commission appointed by the Governor; a Boston Region Administrative Authority on the basis of a charter prepared by the Planning Authority, also appointed by the Governor and making the Planning Authority a department; and, finally, a Boston Region Administration, established through public elections as the unified regional government, with district commissions, and supplanting the counties involved.

Much emphasis is put on citizen participation in the Boston plans. The first quotes the Special Commission of 1896: "popular representative institutions are maintained even more for their general effect upon the people than for the high quality of government work which they secure." No matter is greater in the development of metropolitan government than the re-creation of citizen participation in the affairs of the community.

For no community in a democratic society can long remain a sound functioning organism if those among its members who gain the greatest benefits from it escape from most of the obligations communal life imposes and if those who obtain the least returns in the way of the necessities and amenities of life are left to bear the brunt of civic responsibility and taxation. If an orderly development and a higher level of life for the people of the imposing supercities are to be attained, some measures cal-

culated to endow them with the capacity to act collectively as a political
unit are indispensable.[46]

SUMMARY

Making metropolitan communities into social units which will
effectively operate as such is perhaps the most difficult and complicated problem of American urban communities. It involves, on
the one hand, devising new patterns of government which will enable these great populations covering large areas to operate as a
single consolidated unit, and, at the same time, to preserve the integrity of the many local units in the process. On the other hand, it
involves the revision of the whole structure of government in the
nation, taking into consideration the rural hinterland that is closely
involved in the life of metropolitan communities, though not quite a
part of them, the regions that have their operational centers in the
metropolises of the country, the great regions of the nation which
are already struggling to take form, and the federal government
itself, which has become too greatly centralized for effective service.
The recognition of the great regions, already operational in part, can
become the basis of the functional decentralization of federal government.

This readjustment of government may perhaps produce five levels,
all with distinctive forms and functions: the federal government,
which makes possible the operation of the nation as such and enables
it to be part of a world organization; regional organizations, functional in character, with thoroughly devised relationships to federal
and local governments on a basis of making things work; subregions
(metropolitan regions), perhaps largely political, but combining a
few functions of present state and community governments; metropolitan community organization, predominantly functional, with
whatever political aspects are found after careful study to be essential; and, finally, neighborhood organizations built primarily on the
basis of democratic participation and small enough to make this
possible, not only preserving local autonomy in the lesser municipalities, but also creating small operating communities in the larger
cities, these to be so integrated with the political and functional
structure that the local autonomy becomes real and functional operation can proceed on a highly technical basis.

[46] National Resources Committee, *Our Cities*, p. 68.

An enlightened citizenry, with politics conducted on the highest level, could bring about this reconstruction of the social and political structure of the United States in between a quarter and a half century. The great social forces in the nation are pushing in this direction; it behooves the people of the nation to gain control of these forces, to make them work to their own ends—a democratic society.

Supplementary Reading

Bogue, Don J. *The Structure of the Metropolitan Community: A Study of Dominance and Subdominance.* Ann Arbor: University of Michigan, Horace H. Rackham School of Graduate Studies, 1949.

> An extensive analysis of the basis of determining metropolitan communities and the patterns of interrelationships on which they function.

Bureau of the Census. *Sixteenth Census of the United States, 1940.* Washington: Government Printing Office.

> The volumes Population Series I–IV and Housing Series I–IV contain many data for the 140 metropolitan districts. From this material a detailed demographic study may be made for any of those districts.

Duffus, R. L. *Mastering a Metropolis.* New York: Harper & Brothers, 1930.

> A popular presentation of the New York Regional Plan, with suggestions for an analysis of any metropolitan regional plan or for outlining a proposal for such a plan.

Jones, Victor. *Metropolitan Government.* Chicago: The University of Chicago Press, 1942.

> A comprehensive treatment of the subject, with much detail and illustration; a basis for appraising the organizational status of any metropolitan community.

McKenzie, R. D. *The Metropolitan Community.* New York: McGraw-Hill Book Company, 1933.

> The basic work in this field, though by no means adequate or comprehensive in organization and treatment. Contains many clues for interesting special studies of a metropolitan community.

National Resources Planning Board. *Urban Government.* Washington: Government Printing Office, 1939. Part I, Section 4, pp. 27–35.

> Statement of the problems of metropolitan government.

The Boston Contest of 1944: Prize Winning Programs. Boston: The Boston University Press, 1945.

> Presents a wide variety of proposals for the development of metropolitan government in Boston. Suggestive for developing proposals for consolidated government in other metropolitan communities.

PART IV

ORGANIZED LIFE IN CITIES

CITIES are highly organized social forms, and their organization is not haphazard; it is based on the functions which must be carried out to keep alive the organism of the city (Chap. 14). The integrating force which holds the organism together is municipal government (Chap. 15), which operates through city politics (Chap. 16). The life of cities is made possible, however, through production, commerce, and the services which form the economic base of cities (Chap. 17). The growing force of urbanization determines, in large measure, the functions and forms of all aspects of social organization (Chap. 18). Urbanization has saddled some serious problems on American cities: poverty, disease, crime (Chap. 19), and the complicated and acute problem of housing (Chap. 20).

CHAPTER 14

FUNCTION AS THE BASIS OF THE ORGANIC LIFE OF CITIES

THE villages and towns of the eighteenth century which were destined to become the cities of America, even while in the form of embryonic cities, found it necessary to develop a coöperative life. The people who made up these communities had more specialized occupations, and consequently they had less independence, than those who lived in self-sustaining family units in the rural areas. The artisans, those engaged in trade, the preachers and teachers, the constables and community officials, and the rest became increasingly dependent upon others for food, clothing, and shelter and upon each other for their respective services.

The broader group needs which came into being as a part of living in close-knit communities made it necessary to have new regulations, different controls, and more extended services. These needs had to be met coöperatively because they were common to all the people.

These were the circumstances in which many varieties of organized life took form. This development of organization, gradual, to be sure, was the process of forming urban communities into distinct entities on their own account, with the possibility of existing and operating as units of society. In present-day psychological terms, the urban communities were becoming social organisms.

Carpenter wrote that "cities and towns probably arose whenever and wherever men developed sufficient technical knowledge and social organization to live together. . . . The city . . . was in large measure embedded in the advancement and diffusion of culture. It was, in a sense, a product of cultural growth."[1] The growth of technical knowledge, as it manifested itself in specialization, was one of the factors that brought cities into being. The understanding of so-

[1] Niles Carpenter, *The Sociology of City Life* (New York: Longmans, Green and Co., 1931), p. 18.

cial organization accumulated rapidly through experience in the building of American cities. The long history of cities in the Old World was a great resource to the city-builders. Many techniques of handling problems were imported: the curfew, means of preserving the public peace, the systems of poor relief. The ideals of freedom and democracy on which the New World was founded, however, dominated the developments of social organization and made them indigenous. The town meeting in New England, for example, was the form of organization by which the government of towns was operated democratically.

THE URBAN COMMUNITY AS AN ORGANISM

The interpretation of the community as a living organism is far older than formal sociological theory. It goes back at least to Aristotle and St. Paul. Medieval writers and some of a later date, also, extended the analogy between the human body and society to an obvious absurdity.

MacIver points out the falsity in such analogy between a community and a biological organism because of complete differences in purpose and consciousness, reaction to environment, definiteness of entity, and mortality.[2] Two further major differences can be pointed out. Biological organisms change within very narrow limits; there are no limits to the extent or kind of change that can take place in a community. Furthermore, the evolution of a biological organism is subject to control to only a limited degree, and that control not by itself, but by external human intelligence; a community can be planned and manipulated by its members—that is, from within the organism itself—to make it whatever is desired. Consequently, the application of the term "organism" to the community can be made only in a philosophical sense, though certain comparisons to the human body are suggestive.

Webster's dictionary defines organism philosophically as "anything or structure composed of distinct parts and so constituted that the functioning of the parts and their relation to one another is governed by their relation to the whole." This definition fits an urban community—an entity which has life and operates by means of an array of functions which are essential to the on-going process and to

[2] R. M. MacIver, *Community: A Sociological Study* (London: Macmillan & Co., 1924), pp. 72–76, 207.

which all individuals and all groups in the community are related; "the integrity of the organism as a whole rests on the integrity of its individual elements, and the elements, in turn, are impotent and useless save as parts of the organized whole."[3]

This mutual dependence is often unrecognized because the cooperative processes which are fundamental to urban life are taken for granted; the many competitive aspects of city life are much more apparent. This suggests a further comparison between the conditions of a healthy body and those of a healthy community. The human body is made up of a tremendous complexity of different kinds of tissue, a variety of diverse organs, and a number of functional systems, and the remarkable thing is that they all are thoroughly coordinated in their relationships and so articulated as to make a healthy and efficient human being. This purpose of health and activity is central. Coördination, in the nature of the case, must have a purpose: "the social organism, like the bodily organism, cannot be vigorous and efficient unless its elements are assured the essential minimal conditions for healthful life and activity. And the possession of a mind by the human elements would require that these conditions include not only provision for the elementary needs . . . but also reasonable satisfaction of desires."[4]

COÖRDINATION THE BASIS OF ORGANISM

An important aspect of this coördination of human health is the bodily equilibrium as regards temperature, chemical reaction, fluid content, etc., for which the medical term is "homeostasis." This indicates that coördination and equilibrium in the human body are made possible by large reserves and the capacity for replacement. These qualities need to be taken into account in social administration and planning if the social organism is to be able to meet unusual and unforeseen circumstances. "The success of the body physiologic would seem to intimate that in the body politic there should be a thorough coöperation of functional groups, with the administrative groups dependent, like the others, on a common welfare. And the failure of the body physiologic to survive would seem to emphasize the importance of adequate replacement of functional groups as an

[3] Walter B. Cannon, *The Wisdom of the Body* (New York: W. W. Norton & Company, 1932), p. 309.
[4] *Ibid.*, p. 322.

elementary necessity for the social body's persistence. Its finest basis for longevity and stability would appear to be a generally accepted mode of replacement socially sponsored as being orderly and just."[5]

An urban community is an amazingly complex phenomenon. Many observers, including some sociologists, have been more impressed by the evidences of disunity in cities than by the more fundamental unity in which the varied aspects of city life operate. Much of the coöperation is impersonal and unconscious, but it is essential, and it works. The high degree of specialization and division of labor "means that the unity that exists within any modern group must be an organic unity, a functional cohesion of unlike parts."[6] At any rate, the analysis of our American urban communities is an exceedingly difficult task and calls upon the resources of research method in many different fields. "It has become necessary to resort to all the means of research at our disposal, both old and new, in order to know our cities thoroughly. This knowledge could not be sought in the manner of the past, ignoring the mobility, the changing structure, and the future possibilities of cities, but *by considering cities as living organisms.* In its academic and traditional sense, city planning has become obsolete. *In its place must be substituted urban biology, or the study of the life of cities and of the living conditions within them.*"[7]

One way, then, to gain an understanding of cities is to look at them as living organisms and to seek out the pattern of functions which is essential to their on-going processes and operation.

FUNCTIONAL PATTERN

Functions are the processes of meeting needs. Needs, however, in urban communities are various and complex. There are the basic needs of living, food, clothing, and shelter, which are common to all people. The processes of supplying these needs in cities have become exceedingly intricate. In addition, there are the needs which arise by virtue of the fact that many people live and work in close proximity

[5] Walter B. Cannon, "The Body Physiologic and the Body Politic," *Science,* Jan. 3, 1941, p. 9.

[6] Cecil C. North, "The City as a Community," in Ernest W. Burgess (editor), *The Urban Community* (Chicago: The University of Chicago Press, 1926), p. 234.

[7] José Louis Sert, *Can Our Cities Survive?* (Congrès International d'Architecture Moderne) (Cambridge: Harvard University Press, 1942), p. 2.

and with a high degree of interdependence. These necessitate social controls and the machinery for their administration as well as highly organized coöperative activity. Other functions grow out of the social problems which have become acute because of the concentration of people. Then there are the functions involved in the operation of the productive machinery of the city. In addition are the functional operations of education, and the training of individuals to fit into the cultural, social, political, and economic life of their urban communities.

To facilitate the analysis of the essential functions of an urban community, a classification is desirable. Establishing a basis of classification, however, is not easy. When a classification based on various human needs is considered, the complexity of the interrelationships of functions confuses rather than simplifies the analysis. For example, clothing is a universal human need, but it involves the assembling of raw materials, their processing into the goods used, the manufacture of the articles of clothing, wholesale distribution, and retail distribution. All of these are distinct functions. A classification on the basis of the auspices under which functions are carried out, public or private, fails to reveal any generally applicable pattern because urban communities differ so widely in the developments of public enterprise. In the field of city-planning a classification of the broad areas of human needs has been devised as a basis of planning activities. Four functions of the city were recognized in the Town-Planning Chart of the Fourth CIAM (Congrès International d'Architecture Moderne), meeting in Athens in 1933: (1) dwelling, (2) recreation, (3) work, (4) transportation.[8] While such a classification is doubtless very useful for city-planning, for this purpose it is subject to the difficulties already mentioned with reference to needs and in addition has the limitation of not allowing place for many important functions of cities; for example, where could the functions of control be accounted for under these headings?

A workable classification can be based on broad categories of functions in terms of their similarity of purpose and operation. Such a classification is used here not because it is without difficulty, but because it permits a clearer differentiation and a more comprehensive analysis. Four groupings are used: (1) *control:* the basic functions of government, involving the processes by which an urban community is held together and operated; (2) *administration:* the func-

[8] *Ibid.*, pp. 246–248.

tions which provide the universal services which are essential to the operation, maintenance, and protection of the city—these are also a part of government; (3) *economic functions:* industry, business, and the many services which form the productive base of community life and the means of distributing goods and services to people—for the most part carried on by private enterprise; (4) *social utilities:* the

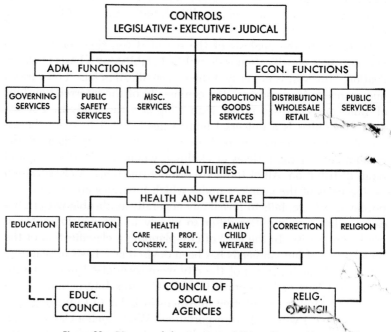

Figure 33. Diagram of the Functions of Urban Communities.

great variety of social services, health, recreation, education, religion, and others—a very broad and inclusive category.

The analysis of the functions which operate in American urban communities is presented in two ways: first, Figure 33 is a diagrammatic form intending to show the total pattern more clearly; second, Table 35 gives a classified list in some detail.

The purpose of this analysis is to give a comprehensive concept of the great variety of things that go on in cities to "make them tick." The items of function are not always mutually exclusive, and there is some repetition. Moreover, many close relationships exist between certain functions which the analysis cannot indicate. There are some

TABLE 35. An Analysis of Urban Functions

I. CONTROL

A. *Legislative*
1. Municipal council or commission
2. Legislative committees and special bodies
3. Clerk of council
4. Ordinances and proceedings

B. *Executive*
1. Chief executive (Mayor)
2. Commissioners
3. Boards and commissions

C. *Judicial*
1. Criminal courts
   a. Felonies
   b. Misdemeanors
2. Civil courts
   a. Chancery
   b. Probate
   c. Law
3. Domestic relations courts
   a. Juvenile
   b. Family, etc.

II. ADMINISTRATIVE FUNCTIONS

A. *Governing services*
1. Municipal management
2. Elections
3. Finance
4. Budgeting
5. Legal
6. Recording and reporting
7. Planning and zoning
8. Personnel administration
9. Research and investigation
10. Vital statistics and health control
11. Licensing

B. *Public safety services*
1. Police protection
2. Fire protection
3. Protective inspection
4. Sanitation and waste-removal
5. Smoke-clntrol

C. *Miscellaneous services*
1. Engineering
2. Public works
3. Streets and highways
4. Street lighting
5. Building supervision
6. Community promotion
7. Pensions, etc.
8. Cemeteries, etc.

III. ECONOMIC FUNCTIONS

A. Production

1. Goods

a. *Manufacturing[a]*
Food and kindred products
Tobacco products
Apparel and other fabricated textile products
Lumber, furniture, and wooden goods
Paper and allied products
Printing, publishing, and allied industries
Chemicals and allied products
Rubber products
Leather and leather products
Stone, clay, and glass products
Iron and steel and their products
Nonferrous metals and their products
Machinery
Transportation equipment
Other manufacturing industries

b. *Mining*
A few cities have mining as a major enterprise—e.g., Scranton, coal; Helena, copper.

c. *Agriculture*
Some cities with much land not yet built upon use it for truck gardens to supply their own markets—e.g., the fertile San Fernando Valley, within the city limits of Los Angeles.

d. *Fishing*
Fishing is a major industry of Gloucester (Mass.) and is important in other coastal cities.

[a] Main headings under manufacturing in the accounting of employed persons by industry in the 16th census of the U.S., 1940.

TABLE 35. An Analysis of Urban Functions (*Continued*)

2. *Services*

a. *Professional*	b. *Semiprofessional*	c. *Business and repair*	d. *Clerical and sales*	e. *Craftsmen*	f. *Domestic*	g. *Service workers*
Actor	Athlete	Accountant	Auctioneer	Blacksmith	Cook	Barber
Artist	Aviator	Automobile	Bookkeeper,	Cabinet-	House-	Beautician
Assayer	Dancer	rental	etc.	maker	keeper	Bootblack
Author	Designer	and repair	Canvasser	Carpenter	Laundress	Charwoman
Chemist	Draftsman	Cleaning	Demonstrator	Cement	Servant	Elevator
Chemical	Embalmer	Consultant	Huckster	worker		operator
engineer	Funeral	Dyeing	Insurance	Decorator		Hostess
Civil	director	Hotel	agent	Electrician		Janitor
engineer	Laboratory	lodging	Newsboy	Furrier		Manicurist
Editor	technician	Laundry	Office-	Gold-silver		Porter
Electrical	Photographer	Miscellane-	machine	smith		Receptionist
engineer	Radio	ous repair	operator	Mason		Steward
Industrial	operator	Statistical	Salesman	Optician		
engineer	Showman		Secretary	Painter		
Lawyer	Sports in-		Solicitor	Piano and		
Mechanical	structor		Stenographer	organ tuner		
engineer	Sports official		Traveling	Plasterer		
Metallurgist	Surveyor		salesman	Shoemaker		
Mining	Technician		Typist	Tailor		
engineer	(misc.)			Upholsterer		
Musician				Watchmaker		
Reporter				Window-		
Teacher				dresser		
(misc.)						

B. *Distribution*

1. *Wholesale*

The pattern of wholesale trade differs widely from city to city. In general, the larger the city the greater the number and variety of wholesale establishments.

Some cities operate as distribution centers for large areas. In these cities there is a disproportionately large number of wholesale concerns.

Smaller cities tend to have wholesalers who handle a variety of goods, while the largest cities have wholesale places of even greater variety than their retail stores; for example, a haberdashery will handle a variety of personal items for men, while there may be separate wholesalers for suspenders, socks, neckties, shirts, jewelry, etc., etc.

On this account the U.S. census, in its analysis of employed workers by industry, lumps all wholesale trade personnel in a single item.

2. *Retail*[b]

Apparel and accessorie
Dairy products and milk
Drugs
Eating and drinking places
Filling stations
Florist
Food
Fuel and ice
Furniture and house
  furnishings
General merchandise
Hardware and farm
  implements
Household appliances and
  radio
Jewelry
Limited-price variety
Liquor
Lumber and building
  material
Motor vehicles and
  accessories
Shoes
Miscellaneous

[b] This is the common-denominator list used by the 16th census of the U.S., 1940.

TABLE 35. An Analysis of Urban Functions (*Continued*)

C. *Public Services*

1. *Land use*	2. *Finance*	3. *Utilities*	4. *Communication*	5. *Transportation*	6. *Storage*	7. *Salvage*
Zoning	Banking	Water	Newspapers	Street car	Merchandise	Junk
Real estate	Brokerage	Gas	Periodicals	Bus	Food	Fats
Rentals	Clearing	Electricity	Telephone	Subway	Supplies	Rubber
Sales	house	Steam	Telegraph	Railway	Private	Cloth
Construction	Loans		Radio	Air	goods	Paper
Architecture	Credit		Mail	Water	Archives	
Contracting	Financing		Messenger	Delivery	Records	
Building	Pawn			Hauling	Historical	8. *Waste*
trades	brokerage			Taxicab	material	*disposal*
Building				Express	Art	
management				Freight	Valuables	Garbage
Transient				Lighterage	Money	Rubbish
hotel				Moving	Cold storage	Dirt
Garage				Steamship	Warehouses	
Engineers				Pipe line		

D. *Coördination*

Chamber of commerce
Industrial associations
Boards of trade
Better business bureaus
Employment agencies
Consumer services
Consumer coöperatives

IV. SOCIAL UTILITIES
A. *Health and Welfare*

1. *Health*			2. *Welfare*		
a. *Care*	b. *Conservation*	c. *Professional services*	a. *Family and child welfare*	b. *Institutional care*	c. *Misc. social services*
General hospital	Public health	Medical	Public welfare	Orphans	Vocational
Special hospital	programs	Surgical	Family case	Aged	guidance
Clinic and	Child health	Nursing	work	Chronically	Travelers' aid
dispensary	Prenatal care	Therapy	Family relief	ill	Vacation
Convalescent	Day care of	Pharmacy	Care of dependent children	Handicapped	Room registry
care	children	Osteopathy	Unattached and	Mental	services
Mental hospitals	Health education	Optometry	homeless	defectives	Services to
Nursing services	Medical social	Technicians		Epileptics	special
	service	Veterinary			groups
	Mental hygiene				
	Maternity care				

3. *Recreation*		4. *Correction*	5. *Coördinating services*
Settlement work	Outdoor activities:	Supervision	Council of social agencies
Group work	Swimming	Institutional	Social service exchange
Comptetitive sports	Golf	operation	Community fund
Playgrounds	Tennis	Industrial	Research
Parks	Boating	activities	Functional committees
Gymnasium	Picnicking	Delinquency	Special projects
Auditorium		services	
Commercial amusements		Probation	
Pool and billiards		Parole	
Bowling			
Dancing			

TABLE 35.   An Analysis of Urban Functions (*Continued*)

B. *Education*

1. *Formal schooling*	2. *Adult education*	3. *Community services*	4. *Cultural dissemination*	5. *Social life*
Nursery	Remedial:	Library	Art	Informal
Kindergarten	Citizenship	Museum:	Music	associations
Elementary	English to	Historical	Dramatics	Men's clubs
Junior high	foreigners	Natural history	Literary	Women's clubs
Senior high	Common branches	Science & industry	Theater	Group activities
Commercial	Vocational:	Art	Civic monuments	
Trades	Training	Zoo	Historical events	
Technical	Retraining	Aquarium		
Special	Rehabilitation	Botanical gardens		
Junior college	Relational:	Celebrations		
College	Personality	Expositions		
University	development			
Professional	Parents' education			
	Workers' education			
	Political:			
	Forums			
	Discussion groups			
	Liberal:			
	General education		C. *Religion*	
	Arts		Worship	
	Hobbies		Religious education	
	Interest groups		Community service	
	Community participation		Age and sex groups	
			Service groups	
			Missions	

coördination
city mission societies
church councils

inconsistencies in the level of detail; in some sections, where detail is obvious or is a standardized breakdown, it has been omitted; in other sections it has seemed desirable to show the extreme detail of function that is a result of the high degree of specialization developed in the largest cities.

Several other difficulties appear. Is the analysis a composite of American cities, or does it give a skeletal outline of the pattern of functions in urban communities? It is intended to be the latter, but at some points compromises with the former. For example, the list of functions under manufacturing is taken from the main headings of the census classification of persons employed in industry. Consequently, no city can be expected to function in all of the categories. Each city has its own pattern of industry. Some cities have one outstanding major industry, with many small industries: Detroit, automobiles; Akron, tires and rubber goods; Pittsburgh, steel; Hartford, insurance. Others have diversified principal industries: Rochester (New York), cameras, optical goods, telephone and radio equipment, men's clothing; Springfield (Massachusetts), firearms, motorcycles, automotive electrical equipment.

The items given under Retail Distribution make a similar case. The common-denominator list from the 1940 census gives little indication, for example, of the high degree of specialization which has been developed in retailing in the largest cities, where from 150 to 200 distinct varieties of retail establishments can be found.

The list of those who produce the services is also far from complete for the great cities. It will doubtless be noted that certain kinds of people who render services in all cities are not on the list: judges, firemen, professors, clergymen, social workers, librarians, bankers, foremen, bakers, printers, and so forth. The reason for this omission is that these people function only in connection with their respective institutions, while those on the list function as individuals receiving their income in payment for their direct services. Another omission from these lists is those engaged in health services. Inasmuch as these people are more important in the life of the community as functionaries of health than as the individual producers of services, they are made a part of health functions even though the services of most of them can be bought individually.

FUNCTIONS OF INDIVIDUAL CITIES

While this pattern of functions is one into which any city will fit, there are wide variations from city to city. This was revealed in the differences in the occupational make-up of cities on which the classification of cities in Chapter 5 was based. The analysis of employed workers by industry and by occupations in the census, with the classified telephone directory, will give an understanding of the functional analysis of a particular city.

Three questions arise about the variations in functions from city to city: What kinds of variations are found? What accounts for the variations? What is the significance of the variations?

While the needs of urban people are essentially the same in all cities, and consequently the functions which meet these needs are also similar, there are differences in the ways by which, and the extent to which, the needs are met. In some places certain needs are barely met, and in other places they may be met very elaborately.

In some instances this will be due to the kind of city. A specialized function will be highly developed on account of the service that a city renders to a large area—for example, the care and feeding of transient people in a resort community like Atlantic City, or the very extensive medical services and care in a place like Rochester (Minnesota). Variations also arise in the addition of special functions created by particular circumstances, as the services to seamen found in port cities where there are many ships and much shipping.

The size of a city also accounts for variations. Many jobs which have to be done in a city are quite incidental so long as the city is small, but sheer bulk of population may make an incidental problem become actually very large. So a function which is highly developed in a great city may be carried on in a small city as an accessory of another function, as churches, in carrying out the function of religion, may take on responsibility for needed relief. Sometimes a substitute is made for an essential function; where sewers are not provided, each home has its own septic tank. Occasionally a function is borrowed from another community, as when a city without a hospital will arrange to have needed hospitalization taken care of in a neighboring place.

It costs money to carry on the functions of a city, so that a city can afford only what it can pay for. Since there is a tremendous range in the median income in American cities, there is bound to be a great difference in the extent to which cities can pay for carrying out the essential functions.

Variations are accounted for further by cultural differences in cities. Whether these differences arise out of regional traditions, educational backgrounds, provincialism, or all of these together with other factors, there are marked differences from city to city. These cultural differences become evident in the techniques that are locally available for carrying out functions, the awareness of the population of problems that exist, the standards which are accepted for services, the importance or value given to the improvement of the circumstances of living, and the leadership that emerges in the community. A city which does not place high value on the welfare of its youth will be unaware of tendencies toward delinquency, will lack leadership, methods of organization, and programs for youth services.

Variations in the functional patterns of particular cities can be determined only by careful study. The meaning of overdevelopments or underdevelopments of function will be found to be either in meeting unusual circumstances or in deficiences in the city's life. Deficiencies are pathological conditions.

PUBLICLY AND PRIVATELY OPERATED FUNCTIONS

One of the major changes in recent years has been the increase of publicly operated functions. Government operated for the benefit of all the people of the community and maintained by all the people through taxes has greatly extended the areas of its operation. As a result, most of the functional areas of cities have been entered by government somewhere, and in many instances the public operations have become extensive. Some cities have municipally operated public utilities, some have broad public health programs that offer many health services, etc.

Theoretically there is no limit to the extension of publicly operated functions. When public opinion recognizes a function as serving all the people and as beneficial to the social group as a whole, it is likely to become a public function. There are, however, three limitations to this recognition, generally considered inherent in American democracy: (1) the precept that a place for private enterprise is an essential element of freedom; (2) the fact that a law of diminishing returns in the size of any enterprise establishes a point in bigness beyond which efficiency diminishes; (3) the ideal that the direct controls and operation of most enterprise should be retained by people themselves.

Within these limitations cities have operated, considering each specific function as circumstances raise the issues, but applying them for the most part negatively on the basis of an assumption that certain functions can best be operated privately. The differences in application as problems arise and in different communities, however, make for changing patterns of public and private functions, and no standards of comparison from city to city are possible.

RELATION OF FUNCTION TO ORGANIC STRUCTURE

Around these functions cities build their organized life. Institutions are formed to carry out the functions. Each institution has its right to existence and its relation to its community in the function which it performs. So the primary responsibility of an institution is to carry out its function by means of a constant readaptation to the changes which have their impact on both functions and structures in community life. Frequently institutions fail to meet this obligation and so find themselves extraneous to the life of their communities or discarded by their communities. One of the most famous examples is the home in New York City for those retired from the crews of sailing ships. While the institution is heavily endowed with property that has increased in value and income, there are no more sailing ships to retire their sailors.

Any inventory of institutions in an urban community is constantly changing, and the character of institutions also changes, although there is a strong tendency for an institution to continue in its established form of organization and pattern of operation. All cities have many examples of this form of cultural lag.

The discussion turns now to the structure of cities as it is found in their organized life, their institutions. No attempt will be made to consider the whole range of the operation of urban functions. A few areas, however, are selected because of their particular importance or interest by way of illustration. Some will embrace a broad functional area, others a very narrow area; and still others will be presented with reference to significant current problems.

Supplementary Reading

Dahir, James. *Communities for Better Living.* New York: Harper & Brothers, 1950.

How many communities are planning to meet the needs of their people.

Queen, Stuart A., and Thomas, Lewis F. *The City: A Study of Urbanism in the United States.* New York: McGraw-Hill Book Company, 1939.

Part II, "Urban Institutions and Folkways," deals with how cities have organized to carry out their functions.

Sert, José Louis. *Can Our Cities Survive? Congrès International d'Architecture Moderne.* Cambridge: Harvard University Press, 1942.

A functional approach to the study of cities, though limited in its scope.

CHAPTER 15

MUNICIPAL GOVERNMENT

A COMPREHENSIVE introduction to a consideration of the government of cities in the United States can be found in the first finding of the National Resources Committee's report on urban government:

Practically all of the problems facing the American urban community take us sooner or later into the American city hall. For it is at the city hall and its related governmental offices, like the urban county court house, where the questions of the city's physical plan, of its population and industry, its business and transportation, its health, education, crime, and recreation, are ultimately translated into social policy and administrative action. The urban governments of the United States perform those essential public services without which the concentrated urban centers, containing the majority of our citizens and the bulk of our enterprise, could not continue to exist. These governments provide water, dispose of sewage, prevent epidemics, guard public health, protect life and property, control traffic, and regulate and facilitate trade and industry.[1]

The business of urban government has increased as cities have grown in number and in population, but the functions and activities have also expanded. Large numbers of people are employed, an increasing proportion of whom are trained specialists. City budgets have multiplied many-fold in the last half century. By 1932 the expenditures of cities of 8000 population and over had reached $4,250,-000,000 a year, and by 1948 the cost of the 397 largest cities was about the same amount. Urban government is one of the nation's major industries.

The great significance of urban government in America, however, does not rest so much on its bigness as on the importance of its place in American life. While the principles of social and eco-

[1] National Resources Committee, *Urban Government,* Vol. I of the Supplementary Report of the Urbanism Committee (Washington: Government Printing Office, 1939), p. 3.

nomic operation are largely determined by national and state policies and laws, it is in the cities that enforcement is carried out and
services are rendered. "The American city performs those functions
which are among the most urgent public services in modern life."[2]

The sociological interest in this situation lies in the fact that the
services performed by the city government are those delegated to it
by the citizens. In other words, the community takes over, for all individuals, functions no individual can, under urban conditions, perform for himself. As more and more such functions pass from individuals to the community, the social institution called government
increases its activities, its cost, and its powers.

The first question of interest in a sociological study is, consequently: What is the character of the expanding scope of urban government? This leads directly to the further questions: What is the
cost of city government? What are the forms of city government?
What are the conditions of good government?

SCOPE OF CITY GOVERNMENT

One of the most important factors in the development of American cities, already pointed out (p. 28), is the gradual expansion of
the operations of government. This was a natural and inevitable development, which came partly because the increase in the numbers
of people living in cities made more of a job for government, partly
because these concentrations of people created problems which
could only be solved as all worked together through their government, partly because better and better techniques and methods were
developed for rendering essential services for all the people through
government, partly because more government could be paid for by
the increasing wealth resulting from the exploitation of scientific
discoveries, partly because of changing concepts of social justice and
community responsibility for the amelioration of poor social and
economic conditions, and partly because public opinion continued to
find more and more activities desirable and acceptable for public
operation.

Pattern of City Government. The general pattern of the functional area of city government was set at an early stage in the development of cities. In terms of broad categories the areas of operation were established a century ago. General government, protection,

[2] *Ibid.*, p. 8.

highways, health, welfare, education, and recreation have been, and still are, the principal functions of government in cities. Within these functional areas, however, the subsidiary functions and activities have been greatly expanded, so that some of the subordinate functions have become of such great importance that they have taken their place as principal functions.

The functional analysis now used as the basis of the analysis of the activities of municipal government is as follows:

I. General Control
    1. Legislative
    2. Executive
    3. Judicial
    4. Election
    5. Staff services
       a. Finance
          (1) Accounting, auditing and budgeting
          (2) Assessment and levy of taxes
          (3) Collection, custody and disbursement of funds
          (4) Other
       b. Law
       c. Municipal clerk and recording and reporting
       d. Administrative offices and boards
       e. Planning and zoning
       f. Personnel administration
       g. Other
II. Public Safety
    1. Police
    2. Fire
    3. Protective inspection
    4. Other
III. Highways
    1. Supervision
    2. Roadways
    3. Snow and ice removal
    4. Street lighting
    5. Bridges, tunnels, viaducts and grade separations
    6. Other
IV. Sanitation
    1. Sewers and sewage disposal
    2. Street sanitation
    3. Waste collection and disposal
    4. Other

V. Health
   1. Supervision
   2. Vital statistics
   3. Food and sanitary regulation
   4. Control of communicable diseases
      a. Tuberculosis
      b. Venereal diseases
      c. Other
   5. Child health services
   6. Other
VI. Hospitals
   1. General municipal hospitals
   2. Tuberculosis
      a. Municipal
      b. Patients in other
   3. Other communicable disease hospitals
   4. Mental disease hospitals
      a. Municipal
      b. Patients in other
   5. Other hospitals
      a. Municipal
      b. Patients in other
VII. Public Welfare
   1. Supervision
   2. Care in municipal institutions
   3. Public assistance
      a. Administration
      b. General relief
      c. Old age assistance
      d. Aid to dependent children
      e. Aid to blind
      f. Veterans aid
      g. Other
   4. Other
VIII. Correction
   1. Supervision
   2. Adults
   3. Minors
   4. Probation and parole
IX. Education
   1. Schools
      a. Administration
      b. Nursery schools

      c. Elementary schools
      d. Secondary schools
      e. Vocational and special schools
      f. Colleges and universities
      g. Adult education
      h. Special projects
   2. Libraries
      a. Supervision
      b. Accessions
      c. Library services
 X. Recreation
   1. Cultural and scientific recreation
      a. Galleries and museums
      b. Zoos and botanical gardens
      c. Others
   2. Organized recreation
      a. Outdoor play areas and activities
      b. Recreation buildings and indoor activities
      c. Golf
      d. Other
   3. Municipal parks
   4. Auditoriums and Stadiums
   5. Other
 XI. Miscellaneous
   1. Judgements and losses
   2. Compensation for employee injury
   3. Gratuities
   4. Contributions to state administered retirement systems
   5. Municipal service enterprises
   6. Commercial activities
      a. Markets
      b. Warehouses
      c. Other
   7. Other[3]

The details of activities, all more or less specialized, which would come under each of the subheadings of this outline give some clues to the variety: for example, under IX, 2, Libraries: Supervision would include administration; budgeting; planning and maintaining

---

[3] Bureau of the Census, *City Finances, 1943:* Vol. 3, *Statistical Compendium* (Washington: Government Printing Office, 1945), Tables 18–27, pp. 71–81. The subheadings under "Schools" have been supplied and those under "Libraries" and "Organized recreation" taken from the analysis in the 1941 report.

buildings and equipment; employing, assigning, and training professional, clerical, and maintenance help; Accessions involves selecting appropriate books, periodicals, pamphlets, visual materials, and recordings; purchasing materials from various sources; cataloguing and arranging the materials for use; Library services include circulating material to readers, providing information, advising adults in the use of materials, helping children to explore the world of print, and stimulating the use of resources by group activities. This gives something of an idea of the complexity and extent of the operations of municipal government.

Expanding Functions. The functions have multiplied over the years by a constantly accelerating stream of additions. Upson studied this growth in the city of Detroit and found that, when the city was established in 1815, with less than 1500 population, there were 23 functions of the city government; fifty-five years later, in 1870, the number had a little more than doubled, at 59; at the close of the century, 1900, there were 132; the next decade added 38 more than were added in the first half century, making a total of 170; 1910–1920 added 81 more, making 251; and 1920–1930 brought 55 new activities, totaling 306 in 1930, an increase of 1230 percent in 110 years.[4] As Upson comments, "some of these activities are distinctly new, such as municipal landing field and an airplane hanger. Most of them resulted from the diversification of the old services of public health, education, recreation and safety. Some are trivial and inexpensive; others are important and costly."[5]

While the functions of local government have increased in response to expanding needs in urban community life and as science and technology have made possible more ample solutions to the needs, they have not multiplied in what would at first glance seem a logical manner. This is due largely to the increasing interrelationship between functions and the consequent involvement of various departments of city government.

The automobile came as a new facility for the convenience of individuals and their families in increasing their mobility and pleasure, so raising their standard of living, and also as an instrument to extend the services and ease of operation of business. But the auto-

[4] Lent D. Upson, *The Growth of a City Government* (Detroit: Bureau of Governmental Research, 1937), pp. 208–210.

[5] Lent D. Upson, *The Growth of a City Government: An Enumeration of Detroit's Municipal Activities* (Detroit: Bureau of Governmental Research, 1931), p. 12.

mobile, as its numbers and uses have increased, has had a profound effect upon the operation of municipal government by causing a number of departments to extend their responsibilities and activities. The license bureau has the job of licensing taxicabs and their drivers, trucks, and in a few cities private cars; the inspection department has added the testing of gasoline and checking of gasoline pumps and oil measures; the legislative branch has enacted a whole code of traffic laws and regulations; the police department has organized a new branch of the force for traffic control and has the responsibility for the enforcement of the traffic laws; the engineering department has had to plan wider streets, to install traffic lights, to provide areas for off-street parking and truck loading and unloading; the highway department has greatly increased miles of paving, has widened and straightened streets, has multiplied the maintenance service; hospitals have had to increase their emergency and ambulance services; the judicial branch has organized special traffic courts; the planning departments have had to lay out new streets, express highways, and parkways, and finally to replan the whole layout of the cities. In addition to such things, the use of motor vehicles by most departments has increased the range of their activities and has enabled police and fire departments to accomplish what was impossible before. This, however, has made necessary a department for the service and maintenance of trucks, cars, and motor machinery.

Another of the many possible illustrations can be taken from the expansion of city services in the single aspect of health dealing with child care. The problem of contagious diseases, early met only by quarantine, later came to involve health supervision in schools, inoculation, and clinics. The services of clinics soon were expanded to deal with health as well as disease; this involved problems of food, especially of milk, and required additional inspection reaching out to the checking of herds of cows for bovine tuberculosis, and dairy barns and equipment for cleanliness, on the distant milk shed. More adequate family relief became involved. Then came care of mothers, both prenatal and post-delivery, through visiting nurses and clinics, as well as extended services for family health. Other uses for clinics, visiting nurses, and health centers were found extending the whole program of service to adults and young people. More lately, community health education has been developing rapidly.

So, in a perfectly obvious and natural way, the functions of government have multiplied and continue to multiply in the social process by which the institution of government adjusts to meet changing conditions and emerging needs. One of the important concomitants is the effect that these changes have had on the kind of people that are employed by municipal governments.

Changes in Personnel. It should be clear even from this limited reference to the kinds of things that are done by city governments in this day and age that the people who are responsible for the activities must have a high degree of specialized ability. Two types of personnel have become particularly important, those equipped for scientific management and those trained as professional technicians. From the head of the city government, mayor or manager, through the department heads and bureau heads, and even through several levels lower in the organizational scheme, the primary responsibility is that of management; the actual operations are of an increasingly technical nature and call for trained specialized technicians with professional status.

Pfiffner uses the term "management" as synonomous with administration and coördination. As he says, "it involves the control of operations so as to secure the maximum results with the minimum expenditures; the elimination of waste, duplication, and excess effort." He goes on to analyze municipal management into four elements: "In the first place, it utilizes technology and the services of technicians; secondly, it tries to act intelligently by proceeding on the basis of research and planning; thirdly, it definitely tends toward an integrated executive control, and lastly, it is groping toward a scientific personnel policy."[6] A somewhat more detailed analysis of the administrative techniques in municipal affairs is given in *Urban Government:* (1) budgeting of finances; (2) cost accounting; (3) personnel techniques; (4) centralized purchasing; (5) investigation and research; (6) public reporting; (7) public relations techniques; and (8) planning.[7]

The number of specialists in urban government is constantly growing, though the actual figures of growth are not possible to obtain because data are lacking. "In Detroit, for example, one of the few cities for which personnel records are available over a long

[6] John M. Pfiffner, *Municipal Administration.* Copyright 1940 by The Ronald Press Company, pp. 5–8.

[7] National Resources Committee, *op. cit.,* pp. 37–40.

period of time, the professional and technical employees increased from 41 persons in 1907 to 2,170 in 1935."[8] Most of the recognized professions are represented; by way of illustration: medicine, in its many branches, with increased numbers; law with a considerable number; engineering with an estimate of almost 50 percent employed by government;[9] school administrators, teachers, and librarians are almost all city employees; social work and recreation have the majority of their professionals operating in city government. In addition, urban, along with federal and state, governments have produced new professional technicians: detectives, sanitary engineers, highway and safety engineers, health inspectors, public finance specialists, tax experts, social psychiatrists, probation officers, city planners, and others. "The new municipal executive, the city manager, represents in conception and operation one of the most daring creations of American skill. . . . It should be obvious even to those who have not done field research in municipal government that no city could perform the whole imposing series of municipal services unless it carried on its pay roll many of the best experts in the community untouched by spoils appointment and political interference."[10]

These changes have been accompanied and facilitated by developments of tenure, civil service selection, uniform classification schemes, retirement allowances, and training in municipal administration. While these developments are very unequal, and in some instances quite scattered, the larger cities are paving the way, and the trends are established.[11]

THE COST OF MUNICIPAL GOVERNMENT

Some idea of the relative extent of operations under the various functions of municipal government can be got from a functional analysis of expenditures. A somewhat less accurate idea of the relative significance in which the various functions are regarded can be obtained in the same way provided it is borne in mind that some functions, in the nature of the case, are more costly. At any rate, the relative expenditures indicate a hierarchy of the pressure of needs in

[8] *Ibid.*, p. 46.
[9] *Ibid.*, p. 45.
[10] *Ibid.*, p. 46.
[11] See *Urban Government*, pp. 45–50, for analysis of the status of these developments up to 1932. For a discussion of the theory and operation, see Pfiffner, *op. cit.*, pp. 129–155.

the awareness of the citizens and their government. But, first, how big is city government?

Big Business. Any way you look at it, urban government is big business. It has a great variety of operations; it employs many people; it uses a large number and many kinds of specialists, professionals, and experts; it owns a tremendous amount of property of all kinds; and it costs a lot of money.

Through the early 1930's urban government was also big government. In 1932, for example (Table 36), the expenditures of cities of

TABLE 36.   Expenditures for Various Levels of Government, 1932[12]

Level of Government	Amount	Percent
National	$ 3,906,556,000	29.0
States	2,505,838,000	18.6
Local non-urban	2,805,888,000	20.8
Local urban[a]	4,250,892,000	31.6
Total	$13,469,171,000	100.0

[a] Includes cities of 8000 population and over and other urban units.

8000 population and over was greater than the expenditures of the federal government; and, when the cost of other local governments, including small cities, towns, villages, and counties, are taken into consideration, more than half the total cost of government in the United States is accounted for.

As federal government activities and expenditures mounted with the depression program and then soared to the sky during the war, they dwarfed the proportions of local government expenditures, as shown in Table 37. When the costs of war (national defense, veterans' services and benefits, and interest on the public debt) are deducted from federal expenditures for 1947, however, the percentage of expenditures for local government is just about doubled.

The amount of city government expenditures changed very little during the war period, but since 1945 has been increasing, the expenditures of the 397 largest cities almost 10 percent from 1945 to 1946, about 18 percent from 1946 to 1947, and approximately 16 percent from 1947 to 1948; from 1942 to 1948 the increase was just over 51 percent. Revenues also increased 7.6 percent from 1945 to 1946, and 130 percent from 1946 to 1947. During the war and until

[12] National Resources Committee *op. cit.*, Table 5, p. 7.

TABLE 37. Percentage Distribution of Government Expenditures, Federal, State, and Local, for Selected Years, 1913 to 1947[13]

Year	Total	Federal	State	Local
1913	100.0	28.6	15.3	56.1
1927	100.0	26.8	18.4	54.8
1937	100.0	48.4	19.6	32.0
1940	100.0	51.8	20.3	27.9
1942	100.0	80.6	8.7	10.7
1944	100.0	92.1	3.5	4.4
1946	100.0	85.8	6.3	7.9
1947	100.0	75.1	11.3	13.7

1946 gross indebtedness was decreased 14.8 percent. It increased 1.2 percent from 1946 to 1947 and 3.7 percent from 1947 to 1948, leaving a net decrease of 7.8 percent from 1942 to 1948. During this period there was a nearly tenfold increase in borrowings.[14] The trends from 1942 to 1948 are shown in Figure 34. The analysis of the finances of the 397 cities for 1948 is given in Table 38.

With expenditures increasing at a more rapid rate than revenue, and with the necessity of borrowing an amount equal to 12 percent

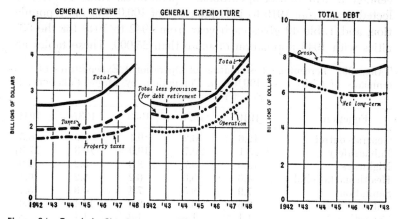

Figure 34. Trends in City Government Finances, 1942–1948. Data are for the 397 cities having 1940 populations over 25,000. (Bureau of the Census, *Summary of City Government Finances in 1948*, G-CF48-No. 1 [Oct., 1949], p. 1.)

[13] *Facts and Figures on Government Finance, 1948–49* (New York: The Tax Foundation, 1949).

[14] Bureau of the Census, *Summary of City Government Finances in 1948*, G-CF48-No. 1 (Oct., 1949); *Summary of City Government Finances in 1947*, G-CF47-No. 1 (Oct., 1948); *Historical Review of State and Local Government Finances*, G-SS-No. 25 (June, 1948).

of the revenue in 1948, it would not appear that city finances are in very good shape; in spite of very large debt retirement in the last few years, stupendous needs for capital expenditures have piled up.

Where the Money Goes. Eleven broad classifications are used by the Bureau of the Census to annually account for the expenditures

TABLE 38.   Finances of the 397 Largest Cities in the United States, 1948[15]

Revenue and borrowings		$4,200,102,000
Borrowings	$ 449,869,000	
General revenue	3,750,233,000	
Total general expenditures		4,048,467,000
Debt retirement	289,338,000	
Operations	2,849,976,000	
Capital outlay	467,051,000	
Aid to other governments	24,731,000	
Interest	119,203,000	
Contributions to trust funds and enterprises	298,168,000	

of cities. Two series of these analyses are presented to show the percentage distribution of operational expenditures. Table 39 gives selected years from 1910 to 1941 for cities of 100,000 or more population, and Table 40 gives each year from 1942 to 1948 for the 397 cities with 1940 population of more than 25,000. These tables are

TABLE 39.   Percentage Distribution of Operational Expenditures of Governments of Cities over 100,000 in Population, by Major Functions, for Select Years, 1910–1941[16]

Function	1910	1921	1930	1937	1941
General control	12.6	10.2	9.1	7.9	6.5
Public safety	25.1	20.7	19.9	16.3	17.3
Highways	12.0	9.7	8.3	5.2	4.9
Health and hospitals	4.6	5.0	6.2	6.2	6.1
Sanitation	7.9	8.5	7.4	4.9	5.4
Public welfare	3.5	3.7	2.9	16.4	13.4
Correction	1.1	1.2	1.2	1.1	.8
Schools	26.5	32.0	34.5	29.4	32.2
Libraries	1.4	1.2	1.3	1.2	1.2
Recreation	4.0	3.4	3.7	2.9	3.1
Miscellaneous	1.3	4.4	5.5	8.5	9.1

[15] Bureau of the Census, *Summary of City Government Finances in 1948*, Tables 2, p. 5, and 3, p. 6.

[16] Data are from Bureau of the Census, *Financial Statistics of Cities*, for the corresponding years.

TABLE 40. Percentage Distribution of Operational Expenditures of the 397 Cities Having 1940 Populations over 25,000, by Major Functions, 1942–1948[17]

Function	1942	1943	1944	1945	1946	1947	1948
General control	8.3	8.3	8.6	8.7	8.6	8.4	8.0
Public safety	23.9	24.9	24.9	24.3	24.7	24.3	23.9
Highways	7.2	7.3	7.4	6.8	7.6	7.4	7.6
Sanitation	7.1	7.4	7.9	8.1	8.5	8.3	8.1
Health and hospitals	7.5	7.6	8.3	9.2	8.8	8.7	9.0
Public welfare	13.9	11.2	9.8	10.2	9.5	10.8	11.2
Correction	1.0	1.0	1.0	1.1	.9	1.0	1.0
Schools	23.5	24.2	23.8	23.3	22.5	22.2	22.2
Libraries	1.5	1.6	1.6	1.6	1.6	1.6	1.6
Recreation	3.5	4.1	4.1	4.3	4.5	4.5	4.5
Miscellaneous	2.6	2.8	2.6	2.8	2.8	2.8	2.7

not comparable, not only because they cover different groups of cities, but also because in 1941 the basis of accounting was changed. In the years 1941 and before the figures include prorated amounts for overlying independent local governments; from 1942 on only the expenditures of city corporations are given. This difference shows up particularly in the expenditures for schools.

Two important observations can be made from these tables. The principal change occurred at the time of the depression, when private family relief broke down and public welfare was reorganized and began to operate on a more inclusive basis with higher standards of professional service and of family relief. This item of expenditure increased by five times between 1930 and 1937, and the other items of expenditure were adjusted to meet this increase. The higher standards of operation having been attained, they have been continued, and expenditures for public welfare have remained on a higher level. Since 1942 the distribution of expenditures has remained relatively stable, with slight shifts reflecting economic conditions through the call on public welfare funds.

Differences between the distributions for different size groups of cities can be seen in Table 41. The most notable differences are found by comparing Group I cities (excluding New York) and Group VI cities. The large cities spend more for general control and public safety and less for schools. New York saves on general control and public safety and invests the savings in public welfare and

[17] Bureau of the Census, *Historical Review of State and Local Government Finances*, Table 18, p. 26; *Summary of City Government Finances in 1947*, Table 4, p. 7; *Summary of City Government Finances in 1948*, Table 4, p. 7.

schools. The smallest cities have greater calls on their resources for highways and schools, which they meet by making smaller expenditures for health, hospitals, public welfare, and correction.

While the distribution of expenditures of cities tends to become relatively stable, differences do appear from time to time, reflecting changes in the patterns of need for services which come with changes in conditions. Differences between the size groups of cities

TABLE 41. Percentage Distribution of Operational Expenditures, by Major Function and by Population Group, for Cities over 25,000 in Population in 1940, for 1948[18]

Item	Total 397 Cities	Group I 5 Cities 1,000,000 & Over All 5	Group I 5 Cities 1,000,000 & Over Excluding New York	Group II 9 Cities 500,000 to 1,000,000	Group III 23 Cities 250,000 to 500,000	Group IV 55 Cities 100,000 to 250,000	Group V 105 Cities 50,000 to 100,000	Group VI 200 Cities 25,000 to 50,000
Total	100.0	100.0	100.0	100.0	100.0	100.0	100.0	100.0
General Control	8.0	8.1	10.1	8.1	7.9	7.6	8.2	8.3
Public Safety	23.9	22.3	33.4	23.0	25.4	25.1	26.7	24.9
Police	13.0	13.5	20.9	12.9	13.0	12.2	12.8	12.0
Fire	9.8	7.7	10.8	9.0	11.3	11.6	12.7	11.8
Other	1.2	1.1	1.7	1.1	1.2	1.3	1.1	1.1
Highways	7.6	5.4	6.5	6.2	8.5	9.5	10.6	12.4
Sanitation	8.1	7.4	10.0	8.1	9.1	8.7	8.6	8.5
Health	2.1	1.7	2.4	2.5	2.7	2.6	2.2	1.8
Hospitals	6.9	7.9	5.5	10.1	7.2	4.6	4.8	3.0
Public Welfare	11.2	16.5	8.3	11.4	6.7	7.9	6.3	6.1
Correction	1.0	1.4	1.8	1.8	.8	.3	.1	.2
Schools	22.2	23.4	13.8	19.4	22.2	22.4	20.0	24.0
Libraries	1.6	1.2	2.2	1.8	1.9	1.7	1.8	1.7
Recreation	4.5	3.1	3.9	5.4	5.9	5.3	5.4	5.2
Miscellaneous	2.7	1.7	2.2	2.2	1.8	4.1	5.1	4.0

also show differences in requirements for city government activities as population aggregates increase in size. Marked differences can also be found from city to city, which give an additional clue to the relative values which the people of a particular city place on the various categories of service.

What the best distribution of city funds may be, only a thorough appraisal of each particular city, including a careful matching of needs with resources, can determine. There are, of course, wide differences in distribution from city to city which would seem to indicate that to some extent this process is being carried out. This is the

[18] Bureau of the Census, *Summary of City Government Finances in 1948*, Table 4, p. 7.

average distribution, a base against which variations can be determined and studied.

Where the Money Comes From. Cities have two major sources of income: taxes, which in 1948 amounted to almost 70 percent, of which taxes on property comprised nearly 80 percent; and about 20 percent which is euphemistically called "aid received from other governments." The latter consists mostly of what cities can beg back from taxes their state governments have collected in large part from city people.

TABLE 42. Percentage Distribution of Income for the 397 Largest United States Cities, by Sources, for Each Year 1942–1948[19]

	1942	1943	1944	1945	1946	1947	1948
Total general revenue:							
Dollars in millions	2,598	2,591	2,663	2,714	2,921	3,306	3,750
Percentage	100.0	100.0	100.0	100.0	100.0	100.0	100.0
Taxes, total	74.6	75.1	74.0	72.6	70.7	69.8	69.9
Property	64.9	66.0	64.8	63.1	60.4	56.4	54.8
Sales and gross							
receipts	4.7	4.3	4.4	4.7	5.0	8.0	9.2
Licenses and other	5.0	4.8	4.8	4.8	5.3	5.4	5.8
Aid from other							
governments	17.2	16.9	17.0	17.9	18.7	19.4	19.7
From state governments only	16.1	15.5	15.8	16.6	17.6	18.4	18.5
Charges and miscellaneous	8.2	8.0	8.9	9.5	10.6	10.8	10.4

There has been a proportionate lessening of property taxes in recent years, which has been due principally to increased income from sales taxes and new forms of taxation in the larger cities, a general increase of grants from state governments, an increase of charges for current services, and contributions from enterprises in the cities under a quarter of a million population. A percentage distribution of income, by various sources, for each year 1942–1948 is given in Table 42.

The comment of the Urbanism Committee of the National Resources Committee, made some years ago, is still pertinent to the problem of financing cities, which continues serious and unsolved.

The confusion and inadequacies of American municipal finance arise in large part from unplanned and uncoordinated State financial control.

[19] Computed from Bureau of the Census, *Summary of City Government Finances in 1948,* Table 1, p. 4.

The city is forced to depend upon the shrinking general property tax as the major source of municipal income, while the State has been preempting most of the newer sources of taxation and of the available public revenues. It is true that cities have in many instances been ineffective in local tax administration. On the other hand, the States have continued to handicap the cities by doling out under strict and sometimes arbitrary regulations grants-in-aid and local shares of State-collected taxes to cities. Recently property tax limitations have been reestablished in some States and these seriously threaten to curtail urban services. The anomaly in the situation is that the 48 State governments which dictate the systems of local taxation are, from the standpoint of total expenditures, only half as important as all of the local governments they are presumed to control. Our largest cities alone, like New York, Chicago, Boston and Detroit, have larger budgets than the States which contain them. The problem of municipal finance is becoming even more complicated with the extension of Federal and State taxation to support the newer services, such as social security.

These problems of municipal revenues are thus not merely problems of State-local relationship. They are problems requiring national planning as well, for a Nation which in its economy has come to be an interdependent whole, cutting across the differences between State and State, city and region, or town and country, cannot afford to compartmentalize rigidly the distribution of public revenues any more than it can compartmentalize the planning of the use and development of its natural resources, its industries, and its commercial activities, which in turn constitute the fountain of public revenues.[20]

The report from which this quotation comes was made in 1937. Since that time a few states have broadened somewhat their legislation permitting increased taxing powers to their cities. Pennsylvania in 1947, in Act 481, gave local units the power to tax practically everything not taxed by the state. This followed after fifteen years an experimental act applying only to Philadelphia. The experience under both acts has been good. In the annual meeting of the United States Conference of Mayors in May, 1950, the president found it necessary to say:

By and large, however, our cities find themselves in a fiscal straightjacket, bound to a governmental system under which there is widespread and almost complete pre-emption of available tax sources by the Federal and state governments; a system under which state legislatures may

[20] National Resources Committee, *Our Cities* (Washington: Government Printing Office, 1937), pp. 68–69.

arbitrarily impose upon us additional responsibilities without regard for our capacity to meet the financial burdens which normally follow, and a system under which there is demonstrated favoritism to rural and smaller corporate entities in the distribution of state grants-in-aid and of state collected locally shared taxes. We want to make it crystal clear that we are not fighting our rural citizens but we do ask for equal treatment with them in each state legislature . . . give us the representation we are constitutionally entitled to in our state legislatures—give us independence commensurate with the governmental functions and services it is necessary for us to perform—give us home rule to the extent necessary for us to make our own decisions in strictly local affairs. Having these, we will be in a position to put and keep our own houses in order.[21]

There is growing sentiment and pressure for the establishment of a Joint Congressional Tax Commission, to be composed of members of the House and Senate and official representatives of federal departments, states, and cities, which would make a nation-wide survey of the existing federal, state, and local tax structure as the initial step in the elimination of tax conflicts, the division of tax revenues, and the allocation of proceeds among the federal government, the forty-eight states, and the cities. This has the support of the President of the United States.

The Problem of Taxes. So far cities have for the most part temporized with the very serious problem of taxes; not that the problem has been unrecognized, but under the present conditions no adequate or practical solution has been found. Property taxes, the basis and bulk of city income, have proved thoroughly inadequate as the tax base shrinks proportionately and the costs of city governments increase. Resorting to increase in tax rates has more and more discouraged building and improvements for both business and residence, especially since, in most cities, improvements are taxed at the same rate as land.

The Urbanism Committee of the National Resources Committee recommended a reduction of the rate of taxation on buildings and an increase on land. There have been many supporters of this recommendation. Harold S. Buttenheim, editor of *The American City*, has pointed out that there is no scientific or ethical reason for mixing the taxes on land and on improvements; the former are based on socially created values—national advantages, population concentra-

<hr />

[21] News Service The United States Conferences of Mayors, 730 Jackson Place, N.W. Washington, D.C. Thursday Morning, May 11, 1950.

tions, and available government services—while the latter are the products of human labor. He further states that increasing taxes on land and decreasing taxes on improvements would reduce specula-tion by stabilizing land values and encourage improvements by placing a premium on improved and used land. He describes the partial achievement of this change in Pittsburgh and Scranton since 1914, where the tax rates on buildings are fixed at one-half the tax on land.[22] Pittsburgh has consistently shown per capita building per-mits markedly higher than those of many other large cities.

Many experiments have been made with various nonproperty taxes. Those of any importance, together with the states in which they are used by cities, are shown in Figure 35. No one of the taxes is used by as many as 10 percent of the cities, and the returns are small in relation to the total revenue, although even these small ad-ditions to city income have helped.

Only one of the special taxes is in any way a radical departure from traditional methods—the income and pay-roll taxes instituted by twenty-two municipalities over 10,000 in population and four be-tween 5000 and 10,000, all in Pennsylvania and Ohio, except St. Louis, Washington, and Louisville. The total collection in 1948 was $56,511,300, of which $31,166,800 was in Philadelphia; of the others, only St. Louis, Washington, Toledo, and Louisville exceeded the million mark, collecting all together $23,061,800. The rates range from 0.3 percent to 1 percent, with over half at 1 percent.[23] This tax has the advantage of being related to the source of income of the city, and it reaches all people who earn their living in the city, re-gardless of where they live. It therefore tends to compensate to some degree for the city's continuing loss of tax potential as its workers move to the suburbs. For the same reason, the suburbanites have objected to the tax—hardly, however, with justification. The serious drawback of the pay-roll tax is that it is, in effect, an addi-tional income tax, on the source of revenue which has been pre-empted by the federal and state governments. It could hardly be expected that it would be generally acceptable unless there was a unification of federal, state, and city taxes. A small pay-roll tax to

[22] Harold S. Buttenheim, "Differential Taxation of Land and Buildings," a paper presented at the Fourth Annual Conference of the National Association of Assessing Officers, New York, October 20–22, 1937; reprint from *Municipal Finance*.

[23] *The Municipal Year Book, 1949* (Chicago: The International City Man-agers' Association, 1949), pp. 195, 196, 203.

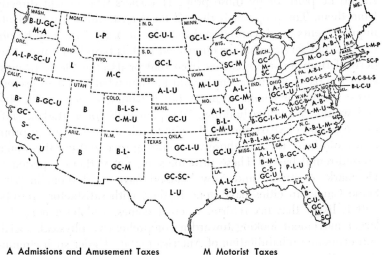

A Admissions and Amusement Taxes
B Business Gross Receipts Taxes
C Cigarette and Tobacco Taxes
GC Garbage and Refuse Collection Charges
I Income and Payroll Taxes
L Liquor and Beverage Licenses

M Motorist Taxes
O Occupancy Taxes
P Poll and Street Taxes
S Sales Taxes
SC Sewer Rentals and Service Charges
U Public Utility Gross Receipts Taxes

Parking Meters in Alberta and Ontario, Canada, and all states except North Dakota.
Contributions from city-owned utilities in all states and in Alberta, Ontario, Quebec, and
Saskatchewan, Canada.

	Canadian Provinces
Alberta	SC, O, P, U
British Columbia	A, B, P
New Brunswick	O, P
Nova Scotia	P
Ontario	A, O, P
Quebec	A, GC, O, P, S
Saskatchewan	A, P

Figure 35. Selected Nonproperty Taxes Used by Cities in Canada and the United States.
(*Municipal Finance News Letter* [Chicago: Municipal Finance Officers Association], Vol.
XXIV, No. 13. Data also from *Municipal Year Book, 1949* [Chicago: International City
Managers' Association], pp. 193–203.)

supplement the present property taxes would be only further tem-
porizing with the problem.

One proposal more radical than the earlier suggestion is based on
two assumptions: first, that the value of land is in its uses, and, second, that it is the great city improvements and the growth of population which increase the value of city property. Consequently, the
rise in value of property which accrues to the profit of the owners is
in reality at the expense of the city, so that these improvements

should be paid for by those property owners who benefit directly from them. The proposal is that all taxes on buildings and private improvements be discarded and that the income of the city be obtained from service charges on ground rentals based on a use value derived from income received from rent or its equivalent. In most cases the payment to the city would be somewhat less than present taxes; in some it would be more, but it would be fair and flexible and would encourage building. The plan calls for a gradual shift over a period of years and for the city to take over delinquent properties and lease them to those who will improve and use them on a ground-rental basis.[24] These principles are not without experience. Denmark, Australia, and New Zealand have tried them in part. Some Canadian cities have gone further, with satisfactory results.

It is likely that tax reform, when it comes, will be a part of a larger movement looking toward a comprehensive physical, social, and economic rehabilitation of American cities. Under such circumstances the necessity for a new tax structure as one of the means for making useful and beautiful cities will be clear. Just such an approach has been suggested by Justement in his plan for the reconstruction of American cities.[25] This plan involves the gradual rebuilding of the cities on the basis of obsolescence, with an established period of life for all building. The city would purchase all land marked for redevelopment and retain the ownership. Thereafter the land would be granted on long-term leases for use at a modest ground rental. Taxes on the property would be at their maximum when buildings were new and would decline 2 percent a year to nothing when the period of obsolescence was reached. In a gradual but continuous redevelopment, new buildings with maximum taxes would compensate for declining taxes as buildings grew old, so that there would be stability of income for cities.

A great spur to beginning an orderly change in this direction is provided by the Housing Act of 1949. By April, 1950, eighty-five communities had taken official action toward participation in the federal aid program for slum-clearance and urban redevelopment and had received reservations of capital grant funds to the total of $120,253,410 for projects to be intiated by July 1, 1951. There remains the balance from the $200,000,000 allocation for the first two

[24] Gilbert M. Tucker, *The Self-Supporting City* (New York: Robert Schalkenbach Foundation, 1946).

[25] Louis Justement, *New Cities for Old* (New York: McGraw-Hill Book Company, 1946), Chaps. 6, 7, 8, and 9.

years and the $300,000,000 available in three subsequent annual installments.

These are but illustrations of possible ways by which the question of taxes might be solved. Perhaps there is no single way. At any rate, it is a problem which every city must face in its own terms, for the solutions cannot wait much longer.

FORM OF CITY GOVERNMENT

The 2033 American cities of over 5000 population in 1949 have three principal forms of government: the mayor-council form accounts for 58.7 percent of the cities, the commission form for 15.1 percent, and the council-manager form for 22.5 percent. The re-

TABLE 43.   Form of Government in 2033 Cities over 5000 in Population, by Population Groups[26]

Population Group	Total Number of Cities	Mayor-Council No.	Mayor-Council %	Commission No.	Commission %	Council-Manager No.	Council-Manager %	Rep. Town-Meet. No.	Rep. Town-Meet. %	Town Meeting No.	Town Meeting %
Over 500,000	13	13	100.0	—	—	—	—	—	—	—	—
250,000 to 500,000	23	9	39.1	8	34.8	6	26.1	—	—	—	—
100,000 to 250,000	55	25	45.5	13	23.6	17	30.9	—	—	—	—
50,000 to 100,000	106	39	36.8	34	32.1	33	31.1	—	—	—	—
25,000 to 50,000	212	106	50.0	41	19.3	60	28.3	4	1.9	1	0.5
10,000 to 25,000	662	347	52.4	118	17.8	163	24.6	18	2.7	16	2.4
5,000 to 10,000	962	654	68.0	92	9.6	179	18.6	5	0.5	32	3.3
All cities over 5,000	2,033	1,193	58.7	306	15.1	458	22.5	27	1.3	49	2.4

maining 3.7 percent is made up of forty-nine New England towns of smaller size with the town-meeting form of government, in which the final legal authority rests in the assembly of the whole citizenry, and of twenty-seven with a representative town meeting, which is a development in the direction of a council. The distribution of cities by form of government according to city size groups is given in Table 43.

The nineteenth century brought a slow increase in the strength of municipal executives through the popular election of mayors, delegating to them responsibility for city administration, and granting them power to appoint the heads of administrative departments; yet the turn of the century found most of the heads of city governments in rather weak positions. The tradition of divided power and checks

[26] *The Municipal Year Book, 1949*, Table 1, p. 41.

and balances still prevailed. With the great growth of the cities and the increase in the scope of their governments, many American cities had fallen into the hands of political bosses and their henchmen, were filled with graft and corruption, and had become utterly ineffective in crises of either a major or a minor nature.

This impotence of city government was brought home to the people of Galveston as they tried to recover from their tragedy of September, 1900. Their efforts to overcome the situation resulted in the establishment of a commission form of government the following year. This experience showed the way for others, and the example of the new city government in Galveston was followed by many American cities.

Another water-borne tragedy started a further experiment in city government in Dayton in 1913. This was the first city of any size to establish the city-manager form of government. To an even greater extent cities fell in line with this experiment.

It is likely that the determining factor in the great improvement in city government was the rallying of the people to a concern in civic affairs rather than the particular new form of government which was established. In fact, many cities accomplished the same result by clarifying the organization of their governments and strengthening the administrative power and responsibility of their mayors, without resorting to such radical means as change in form of government.

Mayor-Council Government.   The mayor-council form of city government consists of a city council made up of aldermen, selectmen, council delegates, or whatever they may be called, elected by the people and making up the legislative body of the community. The members of the council are paid. In smaller cities there is only a small annual salary or a stated sum per council meeting because the relatively limited amount of time required does not usually interfere with the members' regular occupations. On this basis a higher quality of people are willing to be council members. In larger cities, however, salaries are as high as $7500 or $8000 because the work is arduous, involving not only council sessions, but many committee meetings, investigations, and conferences with hundreds of people regarding requests or grievances, as well as the continuance of political activities.

Since the abandonment, in most cities, of bicameral legislative bodies, there has been a constant tendency toward smaller councils.

Nine has become the established number in many cities; some have numbers in the twenties, and a few go even into the fifties.

Most cities still elect councilmen representing wards or districts. There is a strong tendency, however, to elect councilmen from the city at large. This seems to provide more able people who have a broader vision of the problems of the city as a whole, and to lessen the pressure for political patronage. To overcome the difficulty of a clean sweep for the majority party and the consequent denial to the minority group or groups of a voice in civic affairs, the Hare system of proportional representation has been adopted in a few cities.[27] This, by a system of voting which expresses preference and by a complicated method of tallying votes, gives minority groups representation on the council proportionate to their strength in the city. This makes a council which has the same complexion as the community itself and brings into council deliberations the differences of opinion and the conflicts of interest which really exist. As a result, the deliberations, the bargaining, the compromises, and the coalitions represent the actual process of the city's life.

The function of the council is to form the policy for the operation of the city. It does this by the enactment of the laws under which the city operates. The validation of this function is in the fact that the members of the council are the elected representatives of the people; hence the importance of its being as really representative as possible. The powers of the council are limited by the city charter, and its actions must be in harmony with the constitutions and laws of the state and nation, as well as the common law of the state.

The work of the council is done through committees. Each proposal must run its course of consideration, revision, and recommendation in the committee to which it is referred before coming before the council for action. In most cases committee recommendation is followed. The number of committees varies from city to city. From five to nine would include most situations. The finance committee heads the list in importance; then, under various names, are usually committees on public works, safety, health, welfare, and water supply. Each councilman is a member of several committees, and, especially in the larger cities, committee work takes a great amount of time.

[27] For a full explanation of proportional representation, see Austin F. Macdonald, *American City Government and Administration* (New York: Thomas Y. Crowell Company, 1941), pp. 260–269, and other references at the end of the chapter.

Mayor-council city government is of two types: the weak-mayor and the strong-mayor. In the weak-mayor plan the mayor has very little power. Departments are administered by boards elected by the people or appointed by the council. Even the few appointments which are left to the mayor must be approved by the council. He usually has veto power, which can be overridden, however, by a two-thirds majority of the council. He presides over the council and has supervisory responsibility over the various administrative areas, but this is almost entirely ineffective without administrative power, since the various administrative officers are not responsible to him.

The strong-mayor plan, on the other hand, vests the administrative responsibility and power in the hands of the mayor. He appoints and removes heads of departments and, through civil service processes, the range of city employees. He is responsible for the city budget. He usually does not act as the chairman of the council, which elects its own president. The mayor is the focal point of responsibility for city government to the people of the city. Since he is an elected official, he is also the political head through whom policy is expressed. As such, he is involved in many social duties, such as welcoming distinguished visitors, presiding at civic affairs, and speaking to numerous organizations. Political leadership is a disadvantage, as well as an asset, because it makes it necessary to maintain a strong political organization behind him in order to assure his reëlection or his advancement in political life.

The cities which hold to this form of government are, for the most part, neither clear-cut weak-mayor nor strong-mayor, but rather lie somewhere between the extremes, each with its own combination of the elements of both.

Commission Government. The commission form of city government consists of a small group, commonly five, elected at large by the people, and forming the legislative body. Each commissioner is in charge of a department of the city government. The distribution of responsibility is sometimes by agreement of the total body and at other times by specific election. One of the commissioners is designated as mayor to preside over the sessions of the commissioners and carry out the social responsibilities of such an office. For this he is paid a slightly higher salary. The salaries of commissioners range from $1200 to $7500 a year. A commissioner determines the policies and supervises the operation of his department. Under him, and responsible to him, is the department superintendent—a full-time city employee—who administers and provides the technical service required.

Theoretically, all other city officials and employees should be appointed by the commissioners. Actually, in most cases, other officials, such as the school board and the controller, are also elected.

Very early in the development of commission government the merit system, the direct primary, the initiative, the referendum, and the recall were added. These features significantly enhanced the popular appeal of this type of government, though they are by no means exclusive to it.

Commission government has been most widely accepted by smaller cities of 3000–4000 population. A few larger cities have tried it, although none with a population of over 500,000.

"The commission plan is merely a device for simplifying government by putting it completely in the hands of a small group of directors or commissioners of approximately equal rank and power."[28] The concentration of responsibility has been advantageous both in the more direct relationship between the people and the government and in the greater workability resulting from the smaller number of people involved in the governmental processes. Its simpler form enables voters to understand the operation of their government, especially as the short ballot has become a reality.

Experience revealed, however, that this plan divided administration too much to be effective, that it became government by amateurs, that the commission was too small to be representative of communities of any size, and that the small number of fixed departments was inflexible and artificial. It was partly to overcome these weaknesses that the city-manager plan was developed.

Council-Manager Government. The manager plan was an attempt to adopt the principles of modern business organization to city government. The council, elected by the people as their representative body to determine policy, operates as a board of directors which passes ordinances and resolutions, employs a technical expert as manager to administer all phases of municipal activity, and holds him responsible for their operation. A mayor is elected either by popular vote or by the council to be its presiding officer and to act as the political and social head of the city, but without any administrative powers.

[28] Austin F. Macdonald, *American City Government and Administration,* Thomas Y. Crowell Company, 1941, p. 188.

Employed as an expert at the will of the council, without designated term of office, the manager need not be a resident of the city, usually is paid a high salary, and exercises extensive powers, including the selection of his subordinates, with or without the aid of a civil service commission.

The manager has no direct part in the determining of policy, although he exerts an important influence on the actions of the council in his advisory relationship because of his expert knowledge of the community, its needs, and its problems, as well as the inadequacies of government functions and operations.

City charters do not specify the technical qualifications for a city manager because little was known, when they were adopted, of the body of knowledge that such an office required. However, experience has produced many able city managers and has built a sufficient understanding of the knowledge that is required so that a number of universities have established courses for the training of public administrators. There has been great advance as the need for expert administration in city government has been recognized, as the effectiveness of trained administrators has been demonstrated, and as the spoils system has been greatly diminished under the manager plan.

One important problem is yet unsolved. The manager plan has not been able to produce adequate political leadership. The manager who becomes directly involved in advocacy of policies or who goes over the head of the council to the people is ceasing to be a technical expert. The mayor, on the other hand, is not sufficiently important to lead community thought or to head political operations. The way out of this dilemma is not clear. Possibly a certain increase in the power of the mayor, together with some plan of effective collaboration between mayor and manager, can be worked out.

While the manager plan at first was adopted chiefly by small cities, gradually larger and larger cities have taken it up. Since the first city adopted council-manager government in 1911, it has been accepted by a little less than one-quarter of the cities over 5000 in population. In 1948–1949 alone twenty-seven additional cities have been added to the list, twenty-three changing from mayor-council government, three from commission government, and one from town meeting. Two cities changed from council-manager to mayor-council form. All in all, counting villages, townships, and counties, a total of 810 places in the United States have adopted the council-manager plan.[29] In many ways this is the most promising development in city government.

These types of governmental organization are illustrations of the various ways in which communities can produce different patterns of social organization to accomplish similar social purposes or objectives. Some forms may be better instruments, but the measure of effectiveness is the degree to which the functions of the city are carried out.

EFFICIENCY OF CITY GOVERNMENT

The efficiency of city government is difficult to estimate, let alone measure. In certain broad terms, the type of organization, the degree of authority and responsibility placed in administrative heads, the extent to which trained and experienced personnel are used in the great variety of technical jobs, the amount of money that is available and the controls upon its use, and other such things, can give a substantial index of the potentiality of efficiency. Efficiency finally depends, however, upon a number of other factors.

The chief administrator, be he mayor or manager, may have all of the authority and responsibility that are necessary, but, unless he is highly skilled in the techniques of administering a very complicated organization, truly has the welfare of the people of his city at heart, unselfishly uses his authority consistently for this objective, and has a political sense by which he can win the confidence and support of the people and the coöperation of his colleagues and the employees of the city government, the very authority which is essential may eventuate in highly inefficient and bad government.

A city's personnel administration may be thoroughly satisfactory; its civil service commission may have effective procedures for the selection of well-qualified people, with a salary scale that enables it to compete fairly with private enterprise for people of training and experience; the merit system may be well established; and yet, if the personnel do not understand the problems and operation of public administration, cannot work coöperatively and creatively at their jobs, do not have sympathetic and understanding attitudes to-

[29] *The Municipal Year Book, 1949,* pp. 40–41, 241–244.

ward the people of the city, and do not have the service they can render as their primary motive, the city government will fail in its efficient operation.

Public opinion is the final determinant of good and efficient government. This involves not only the values which the people have, but the understanding with which they consider and face their city's problems. The growth in recent years of municipal public relations, the appointment by cities of public relations officials, and the activities of the Association of Municipal Public Relations Officers testify to a growing recognition of the fact that "the city tells its story." In addition to this, an organization through which public opinion can be consolidated, made articulate, and brought to support those in authority and to influence their decisions, is essential.

It can be said with considerable conviction that educational processes, a community organization which involves all the people, the quality of the people, and the sincerity and capabilities of city government personnel are more important for efficient and good government than the form of government a city has. With these factors, good government can be had with a poor organization, but without them good government cannot be attained, even with the best form of organization.

Government in the American democratic system operates through politics, which is the next consideration.

Supplementary Reading

Anderson, William, and Weidner, Edward. *American City Government*. New York: Henry Holt and Company, 1950.
> Good for the details of city government and administration.

Bureau of the Census. *City Finances*.
> Published each year, formerly under the title *Financial Statistics of Cities;* basic data for all studies of revenue, expenditure, debt, and operations of American cities.

MacDonald, Austin F. *American City Government and Administration*. New York: Thomas Y. Crowell Company, 1941.
> Good for the details of city government and administration.

Municipal Year Book. Chicago: International City Managers' Association. Published annually.
> Contains a great number of current data about American cities; a very important source book and reference work.

National Resources Planning Board. *Urban Government*. Washington: Government Printing Office, 1939.

An analysis of the problem of urban government; a basis for the study of any city.

Pfiffner, John M. *Municipal Administration.* New York: The Ronald Press Company, 1941.

Good for the details of city government and administration.

Read, Thomas. *Municipal Management.* New York: McGraw-Hill Book Company, 1941.

Good for the details of city government and administration.

Upson, Lent D. *The Growth of City Government.* Detroit: Bureau of Governmental Research, 1937.

Upson, Lent D. *The Growth of City Government: An Examination of Detroit Municipal Activities.* Detroit: Bureau of Governmental Research, 1931. Pamphlet, 22 pages.

A basis for the study of the expanding functions of municipal government.

CHAPTER 16

CITY POLITICS

AMERICAN cities have been notorious for political corruption and graft. The stories of the bosses and their henchmen made infamous by plunder, violence, and manipulation are exciting, though disheartening, reading. The better-known Tweed, Ruff, Vance, Pendergast, and Thompson, and others, too, are gone—some forgotten, some deposed, and some imprisoned; yet today bosses call the tune for many cities. Though Tammany in New York has been discredited and defeated periodically over the years, even after a fearless and constructive "fusion" administration, Tammany went back into power in the 1945 election, as did machine politics in Hartford, Springfield (Massachusetts), and other cities.

City politics is exceedingly complicated; each city has its unique features, but the general pattern is much the same. It behooves students of cities and workers in cities to make a thorough study both of the general principles and methods of politics and of its organization and operation in their particular cities. Political machines are forms of social organization, essential in the life of an urban community, but all too often perverted to the selfish advantage of the politicians in control of them. Politics as such is neither "good" nor "bad"; it is the politicians and their purposes which make the difference.

THE SHAME OF THE CITIES

Just after the beginning of the century the muckrakers turned up much devastating information about politics in a number of American cities. The chief of the muckrakers was Lincoln Steffens. The report of his studies, *The Shame of the Cities,* is a journalistic, though factual, report of what he found in the cities he studied. It was written with the purpose "to sound for the civic pride of an apparently shameless citizenship" and was "dedicated, in all good faith, to the accused—to all the citizens of all the cities in the United States."[1] Later, in Steffens' autobiography, an interpretive account of his experiences in the cities was given.[2] Several of his convictions, developed over the years, are of particular significance for understanding city politics.

First there was the close relationship between politics and business: "back of the political boss was the business boss whose agent he was, and . . . the business boss was back also of the politics of business and business graft."[3] It was privilege which was central to the problem and operations of politics: "If it was privilege that caused what we called evil, it was privilege that had to be dealt with, not men. . . . To shift our votes from one to another of the political parties, both of which were organized to serve the privileged or the privilege seekers, was folly."[4] Then Steffens was convinced that much so-called crookedness developed because the significance and implications of individual actions were not understood, not even thought of. He suggested to President Eliot of Harvard that college students should be instructed in "the forms in which the first steps to bribery and corruption came to young men in all walks of life." He said: "All I want to do is to make it impossible for them to be crooks and not know it. Intelligence is what I am aiming at, not honesty. We have, we Americans, enough honesty now. What we need is integrity, intellectual honesty."[5] This quality Steffens found more frequently in the bosses and their lieutenants than among the so-called "good men" of the city.

This was partly so because he became convinced "that the ethics and the morals of politics are higher than those of business." In explanation he offered this illustration:

No general ethical principle known to me held in practice; or could hold. Only special, professional ethics limited the conduct of men, and these differed so fundamentally that a "good merchant," like Mayor Strong of New York, might be a "bad politician." One reason for this was that while a business man is trained to meet and deal with the tempta-

[1] Lincoln Steffens, *The Shame of the Cities,* new edition (New York: Peter Smith, 1949), pp. 3, 26.
[2] *The Autobiography of Lincoln Steffens* (New York: Harcourt, Brace and Company, 1941), pp. 357–627.
[3] *Ibid.,* p. 533.
[4] *Ibid.,* p. 493.
[5] *Ibid.,* p. 608.

tions of business, he is a novice and weak before those of politics. Another reason is that what is right in business may be wrong in politics.
Richard Croker, the Tammany boss, was not so "bad" in business as
Mayor Strong was "bad" in politics. Nay, Croker was not so "bad" in
business as he was as a politician. When he confessed under public cross-
examination that he "worked for his own pocket all the time" he was
denounced and politically doomed. But W. L. Strong, as a merchant, had
done that all his life and he was not condemned for making a profit. That
was a matter of course in commerce. As a successful profiteer, the rich
merchant was promoted to be mayor of New York and failed as a reform
official because his business ethics . . . did not fit him for the job.[6]

The inherent evils of politics as it operates are three. First, it is
based on the traditional ethics of individualism, which are vastly
different from the social ethics demanded by a democratic society.
Honesty, wealth, morality, success, individual achievement, re-
spectability, privilege, and freedom are outmoded, sterile, and con-
tradictory for group relationships in the modern world.[7] Second, it
inevitably takes the actual governing power out of the hands of the
people and puts it into the hands of the powerful few. "Political
corruption is, then, a process. It is not a temporary evil, not an acci-
dental wickedness, not a passing symptom of the youth of a people.
It is a natural process by which a democracy is made gradually over
into a plutocracy. Treason, in brief, is not a bad act; it is an inevitable, successful policy."[8] And third, politics is built on disloyalty.
Leaders gain the trust and loyalty of the common people and organize into a powerful machine which acquires rights and privileges
which are sold to those with special individual interests, who in
turn use them, not for the good of the people, but to the accumulation of their own wealth and power. So the politicians become
traitors to their own.[9]

The price paid for corrupt politics is not so much the graft and
the spoils, expensive and evil though they are, but rather that it
builds up municipal governments with puppets who are insensitive
to the ever new emerging needs of their cities, who are incapable of
coping with the acute and difficult problems which constantly arise,
and who are thoroughly ineffective in the first responsibility of urban government—facilitating the operation of a highly complex
community.

[6] *Ibid.*, p. 408.
[7] *Ibid.*, pp. 492–494.
[8] *Ibid.*, p. 413.
[9] *Ibid.*, pp. 417–421.

Many of the modern developments in municipal government, however, have put severe limitations on the spoils system and the other forms of corruption: the direct primary, the short ballot, the recall, civil service, the increasing use of technicians, management, budget control, and the like; also the municipal research agencies and the federal agencies which render service to cities have done their part. Some of these, especially the primary and civil service, have been susceptible of manipulation, but as their operation becomes perfected they can become the most effective of all.

POWER OF POLITICAL MACHINES

Why is it that bosses continue to exist and political machines are strong in cities? The answer is not difficult. The reasons are organization, personal relationships, and direct rewards.

The large city is organized by precincts, and each party has a precinct executive who is appointed by the ward executive. He is the key man in the machine and is responsible for delivering the votes in his precinct. These precinct captains, and their committeemen, are people who have demonstrated their ability to get votes through a long apprenticeship in minor jobs in the party. A large number of them, especially in large cities, are municipal employees who have obtained their jobs by reason of political patronage and consequently have a loyalty to their parties and a self-interest in rendering faithful service. Among the captains are also usually to be found some attorneys, a number of merchants, and representatives of the "lesser employments."[10]

The center of the political activities of precinct captains is the canvass of their district to keep track of the votes and to persuade people to vote and vote "right." They make the arrangements for the election, including the appointment of the people who conduct the voting in their precincts. They see that their party voters get to the polls. Formerly they were responsible for the execution of the various fraudulent procedures, from buying votes and stuffing the ballot boxes to strong-arm methods and falsifying returns. These have largely disappeared, however, because of the modern election methods.[11]

The primary election is the precinct captain's most important job,

[10] Harold F. Gosnell, *Machine Politics: Chicago Model* (Chicago: The University of Chicago Press, 1937), pp. 51–68.
[11] *Ibid.*, pp. 81–90.

and he must see that the candidates selected by his machine are nominated. This is not difficult. Each precinct has, roughly, 600 voters, approximately 250 of whom would be registered in each of the two main parties, Democratic and Republican. Not more than half of these vote in the primary, which means that the control of sixty-five votes controls the election. The precinct executive is responsible for the appointment of the election judges and clerks and of the runners, as well as for the renting of the place of voting. With all the people involved, plus the others in the precinct who have their jobs by virtue of the executive's political influence, together with the members of their families, the required votes are usually exceeded. The ward executives supervise and assist and are the channels through which precinct executives reach the city boss. There are many volunteer workers in each precinct who keep in touch with the voters.[12]

One of the greatest aids in maintaining personal relationships is the ward club. The club has a place with recreation equipment, space for meetings and the use of groups, and the ward executive's office. Primarily the clubs are political, but there are many social activities which are very popular with the members of the party, especially in those areas where such gathering places are scarce. Field days, picnics, benefits, card parties, shows, dances, and the like are used in many places to provide social opportunities for people and to keep in touch with them.

The direct services to individuals are taken care of by the precinct executive. There are regular times when he can always be found in a specific place. The requests for help that come to him are legion, and through these services he lays the basis for live relationships to his constituency. The extent of these services can be seen in the results obtained by Gosnell from questioning Chicago precinct captains. The list of the benevolent services and the percentage of those answering who rendered each service in 1936 were as follows: *goods*—food (70), coal (32), rent (37), Christmas baskets (39); *advice*—juvenile guidance (35), adjusted domestic difficulties (25); *brokerage agency for*—local governments: governmental jobs (51), governmental jobs formerly (43), miscellaneous jobs (47), streets and alleys (74), taxes adjusted (36), permits secured (43), scholarships provided (10), building and zoning regulations (20), con-

---

[12] Frank R. Kent, *The Great Game of Politics* (New York: Doubleday, Doran and Company, 1935), Chaps. I–VIII.

tact with social agencies (67), medical aid of some sort (57), of which 44 percent was with public medical agencies, relief agencies (66); courts: legal aid (62), trouble with law (53), traffic violations (27); federal government: aid in naturalization (69), veterans' bonus (38), HOLC (52); *Deference*—funerals (62), weddings (52). The development of gratitude and loyalty among the recipients of such help needs no comment.[13]

The whole system is built on personal advantage, and the rewards to individual service are quick and direct. The successful precinct executive is in line for a vacancy as ward executive and more direct relationship to the machine and its power and rewards. He may be stepped up to a better position in the city government, where he is often already employed. Outstanding ward executives may be the boss some time and in the meantime may be candidates for a higher political office, or at least they have the say as to who the candidate will be. Faithful workers get jobs working for the city. In addition, the various workers in the organization, one way or another, get their share of the campaign funds.[14]

Not only is personal advantage the basis of political activity, but it is also the basis for the support of political parties. Election campaigns cost money, and the maintenance of organizations, headquarters, and so forth require funds continuously, and those who are the beneficiaries of political patronage are expected to contribute to the party. As earlier indicated, there is always an alliance between business and politics, and this is the point of its pay-off. This is the source of the large contributions. While the "shakedown" is far less frequent than it was a quarter of a century and more ago, there are still cities in which special protection for illegitimate enterprises provides in one way or another a part of the support of political machines. Small business concerns are expected to do their part, and they are sometimes seriously harassed by the close application of many city ordinances, usually for the most part forgotten, if they do not come across. The manipulation of assessments and taxes has been a most useful means of encouraging generous support of the party. Another roundabout source of sizable contributions is through various inside tips and profitable contracts, which have enabled individuals to make a large amount of money. Only small amounts from the party funds get down to the precincts. The cap-

[13] Gosnell, *op. cit.*, p. 71; see also Kent, *op. cit.*, Chaps. VI and IX.
[14] Kent, *op. cit.*, Chaps. XVII–XXII.

tains may get as little as $25 or $100 for precinct use, and sometimes they have to pay canvassers or watchers out of their own pockets.[15]

This is the way politics operates in American cities. The questionable elements are fading out of the picture, but political parties maintain their strength by organization built on personal contacts and services, specific responsibilities for active party members, and direct rewards to the faithful. The result of political strength may be good government or it may be bad government depending on what kind of people the politicians are. One of the most encouraging things which have happened since the war is the increase in the number of city mayors and municipal administrations which are doing good, honest, and clean jobs.

The primary elections are of first importance because, if they are controlled, they permit the machine to run the city. Only in the primaries can the machine be beaten, for here candidates are nominated. The party may be defeated in the general election, and that does not seriously injure the machine; but, if the machine loses in the primaries, it is out of business. The indifference of most voters to primary elections makes their control easy.[16]

One thing should be very certainly understood. Politics as such is neither good nor bad; it is the method by which democratic government works. In the words of Kent: "The truth is that political organizations are absolutely essential to the conduct of government— city, state or national. This is a government by parties. Parties can no more be held together and made to function without organization than any great business can be run without organization. Without organization there would be no parties. Without parties there would be no government."[17]

The amount of corruption that exists in political machines is proportionate to the tolerance of the people of the community. It is the excesses and abuses of political organization that are bad; the organization itself is sound and essential.

REFORM OF CITY GOVERNMENT

Many attempts have been made to reform municipal government. Most of them have not been reform at all; witness their failure to make changes stick. Highly developed propaganda and a strong

[15] Gosnell, *op. cit.*, pp. 4–7, 38–43, 59, 89.
[16] Kent, *op. cit.*, Chap. II.
[17] *Ibid.*, p. 352.

campaign to elect nonpartisan or fusion candidates may succeed in placing better men in the elective positions in the government of a city, but they accomplish little in terms of genuine reform and are usually only temporary because they do not have the backing of a strong organization of voters, an adequate ideational basis, or the use of real leaders of the people.

A genuine reform of city government is based on the establishment of new and adequate concepts regarding the function and objectives of government and the responsibilities of citizenship. It must also involve the principles of social ethics and the values consistent with social organization in a democracy. Then it must use in its structure the true leaders of people, those who are known, respected, and trusted to such an extent that they are followed by the people.

The methods of reform are the methods of politics. One of the most successful reforms of city government took place in Cincinnati in the 1920's. Taft commented on its methods: "The Charter Committee was to organize completely in wards and precincts to elect them [the candidates] and run one campaign for them all. That was an epochal decision . . . it represented a political method theretofore unknown in municipal reform and marks the most distinctive feature of the whole Cincinnati experiment. If we have contributed anything to the permanent good of our nation, politically speaking, it is this plan, rather than the service of any particular individual."[18] This plan involved the people in an actual block organization. It built up within the city the kind of organization which more naturally occurs in rural and suburban America, where, through broadened personal acquaintance and face-to-face contacts, the basis for democratic action is established.

The campaign was also a thorough educational job, made possible by the organization. People developed an understanding of the new charter and its significance and implications. The organization and the education have been maintained, and the new government has lived and operates so that Cincinnati is one of the best-governed cities in America.

The acceptance of responsibility on the part of citizens is essential to good city government. Political organization is essential and must be operated by devoted people who are willing to invest time,

[18] Charles P. Taft, *City Management: The Cincinnati Experiment* (New York: Rinehart and Company, Inc., 1933), p. 76.

energy, and money to maintain good government. Citizens must participate, not only in political campaigns, but also in the regular life and work of the city. A continuing program of education is necessary to keep understanding abreast of change and its problems.

As Martin Lomasny once said to Lincoln Steffens: "I think there's got to be in every ward somebody that any bloke can come to—no matter what he's done—and get help. Help, you understand; none of your law and your justice, but help."[19]

Steffens had great faith in the usefulness of the professional politicians in good government: "they seem to be as eager to do great good as great evil. They are simply not asked to do good; the drift of things, the rewards, the applause and education, are all the other way."[20]

From government and politics, through which urban communities hold together and are able to operate as social units, we turn to the economic base by which cities are able to live.

Supplementary Reading

Gosnell, Harold F. *Machine Politics: Chicago Model.* Chicago: The University of Chicago Press, 1937.

A scientific study of political organization in Chicago under the impact of the depression.

Kent, Frank R. *The Great Game of Politics.* New York: Doubleday, Doran and Company, 1935.

A comprehensive analysis of the purposes, function, organization, and operation of politics.

Steffens, Lincoln. *The Autobiography of Lincoln Steffens.* New York: Harcourt, Brace and Company, 1931.

Containing the penetrating analyses of an experienced observer of political machinery and operations in the large American cities in the 1920's.

[19] Steffens, *Autobiography,* p. 618.
[20] *Ibid.,* p. 417.

CHAPTER 17

THE ECONOMIC LIFE OF CITIES

THE economic life of cities is of great importance, for without it there could be no city at all. It involves the production of wealth, which is the foundation of a city's existence, and commerce, which was the original impetus for the development of cities. It includes the vocations by which people earn their living, find the basis of their relationship to their cities, and experience their potentialities for usefulness and satisfaction in living. Economic affairs are largely the field of private enterprise.

To analyze the economic life of cities is artificial at best because its various aspects are intertwined and it involves many activities which are not themselves a part of the economic structure. It is necessary, however, to consider the major aspects of the economy of cities. This will be done, with little more than inference regarding the complex interrelationships, under four headings: production, distribution, jobs, and taxes.

PRODUCTION

Since the things produced by man's hands, machines, and brains are his wealth, this production of wealth is the basis of the life of cities. This wealth consists of the goods and services which are produced in the factories, the stores, the shops, and the offices.

Since our modern, highly urbanized civilization operates almost entirely on the basis of specialization, those engaged in the productive processes give their working time to particular operations related directly to the production of this and that without any relation whatever to their own or their families' needs. It has become necessary, consequently, to use an instrument by means of which productive work can be exchanged for those things which meet people's needs. Money is indispensable in a highly urbanized civilization.

Not only do people in their individual and family lives have to have money, but also industry, business, education, social services, government, and all the rest have to operate by means of this medium of exchange. Financial services of all sorts—banking, credit, exchange, brokerage, etc.—are essential services in making cities operate.

So there are two levels of production—the actual production of goods and services, which makes up the basic wealth by which the urban community lives, and the great variety of services which make it possible for large numbers of people to live and work together in a city. While this distinction is clear in theory, it is often difficult or even impossible to classify particular services according to these categories. For example, education has a foot on each side of the line. At any rate, in the last analysis, all of the things in which men and women invest their thought, strength, and time through work become a part of a city's productive life.

Manufacturing. Organization for the production of goods has many patterns. In recent years the trend has been toward mass production by use of the assembly-line technique in large factories with many employees. Some plants, however, using automatic machinery, produce large quantities of goods with relatively few employees. The majority of manufacturing establishments are small affairs; nearly half (48.6 percent) have less than ten employees, and 82.1 percent have less than fifty employees, but the ten-man factories have only 3.3 percent of the employees and 3.2 percent of the value added by manufacture. Those with less than fifty employees account for only 15.9 percent of the workers and 14.8 percent of the value added by manufacture. On the other hand, less than 1 percent of the establishments, those with 1000 or more employees, have one-third of the workers and produce one-third of the value added by manufacture. Table 44 gives the distribution by size of establishments. It will be noted that the smallest plants have the largest value added by manufacture per employee.

These facts are for the whole United States; but, since manufacturing is predominantly an urban phenomenon, the analysis is essentially that of the patterns of organization for the production of goods in cities. Not only is industry largely urban; it is also concentrated in a relatively small area. There are 127 counties in thirty-two states which had 20,000 or more manufacturing employees in 1947. Together, they had 60 percent of all manufacturing establish-

TABLE 44. Percentage Distribution of Manufacturing Esta
Employees, and Value Added by Manufacture in the United Sta
of Establishments, 1947[1]

Establish-ments with Average No. of Employees	Establishments		Employees		Value Added by Manufacturer		Added per Employee $
	No.	%	No.	%	Dollars in Thousands	%	
1–4	70,384	29.22	161,007	1.13	905,693	1.22	5,625
5–9	46,621	19.35	310,880	2.17	1,446,896	1.94	4,654
10–19	40,646	16.87	561,911	3.93	2,600,693	3.49	4,628
20–49	40,016	16.61	1,243,931	8.70	6,051,171	8.13	4,865
50–99	18,672	7.75	1,300,719	9.10	6,592,661	8.86	5,068
100–249	14,323	5.95	2,228,615	15.59	11,794,687	15.85	5,292
250–499	5,555	2.31	1,932,366	13.52	10,459,178	14.05	5,413
500–999	2,729	1.13	1,883,464	13.18	10,185,817	13.69	5,408
1000–2499	1,431	.60	2,155,727	15.08	11,691,170	15.71	5,423
2500 and over	504	.21	2,515,684	17.60	12,697,859	17.06	5,047
Total	240,881	100.00	14,294,304	100.00	74,425,825	100.00	5,207

ments in the country, 66 percent of those employed, and 69 percent of the value added by manufacture for the year. This shows a slight decrease in the concentration over 1939, when the corresponding percentages were 61, 65, and 71.[2]

The *Census of Manufactures* lists some 450 different kinds of manufacturing establishments, each of which is reported in some detail. These are brought together in twenty major industrial groups, which, with the summary data on establishments, employees, and value added by manufacture, are given in Table 45.

In general, the predominance of small establishments holds through the various groups; seventeen of the twenty have the largest number of establishments in the group with 1–4 employees, the other three in the 20–49 group. In number of employees and value added by manufacture, however, the industrial groups are divided. Nine—food, apparel, lumber and its products, furniture, paper, printing and publishing, stone and clay and glass products, fabricated metal products, and miscellaneous manufactures—are in the group with 100–249 employees; one—leather and its products—is in the 250–499 group; one—textiles—is in the 500–2499 size; and nine—tobacco, chemicals, petroleum and coal products, rubber,

[1] Bureau of the Census, *Census of Manufactures, 1947: Manufacturing Establishments Classified by Size:* Preliminary Report, Series MC100–6 (Aug. 1, 1949).

[2] Bureau of the Census, *Census of Manufactures, 1947: Summary Statistics for Principal Industrial Counties in the United States:* Preliminary Report, Series MC100–2 (June 8, 1949), p. 1.

TABLE 45. Rank of Major Industry Groups by Percentage of Establishments, of Employees, and of Value Added by Manufacture, 1947[3]

Industry	Establishments			Employees			Value Added by Manufacture		
	Number	%	Rank	Number	%	Rank	Am't in Thousands	%	Rank
1. Food and kindred products	39,933	16.58	1	1,441,847	10.09	2	9,024,912	12.13	1
2. Tobacco manufactures	1,086	.45	19	111,782	.78	20	641,356	.86	20
3. Textile mill products	8,185	3.40	10	1,233,431	8.63	3	5,340,876	7.18	6
4. Apparel or related products	30,960	12.85	2	1,081,844	7.57	6	4,433,373	5.96	8
5. Lumber and products (except furniture)	26,231	10.89	4	635,708	4.45	10	2,497,192	3.35	12
6. Furniture and fixtures	7,687	3.19	11	322,384	2.26	16	1,377,908	1.85	17
7. Paper and allied products	4,103	1.70	14	449,833	3.15	14	2,874,958	3.86	11
8. Printing and publishing industries	28,986	12.03	3	715,450	5.01	9	4,269,416	5.74	9
9. Chemicals and allied products	10,073	4.18	9	632,319	4.42	11	5,365,201	7.21	5
10. Petroleum and coal products	1,387	.58	18	212,003	1.48	19	2,015,307	2.71	15
11. Rubber products	875	.36	20	259,092	1.81	17	1,302,863	1.75	18
12. Leather and leather products	5,308	2.20	13	383,175	2.68	15	1,532,803	2.06	16
13. Stone, clay, and glass products	11,650	4.84	8	462,072	3.23	13	2,306,480	3.10	13
14. Primary metal industries	5,363	2.23	12	1,157,124	8.09	5	5,765,434	7.75	4
15. Fabricated metal products	16,734	6.95	6	971,461	6.80	7	4,921,476	6.61	7
16. Machinery (except electrical)	17,906	7.43	5	1,545,323	10.81	1	7,812,455	10.50	2
17. Electrical machinery	3,973	1.65	15	801,359	5.61	8	3,894,115	5.23	10
18. Transportation equipment	3,711	1.54	16	1,181,680	8.26	4	5,869,196	7.89	3
19. Instruments and related products	2,599	1.08	17	231,997	1.62	18	1,080,336	1.45	19
20. Miscellaneous manufactures	14,131	5.87	7	464,420	3.25	12	2,090,168	2.81	14
	240,881	100.00		14,294,304	100.00		74,425,825	100.00	

[3] *Census of Manufactures, 1947:* Preliminary Report, Series MC100–6 (Aug. 1, 1949).

primary metal, machinery, electrical machinery, transportation equipment, and instruments—are in the group with 1000 or more employees.

The ten most significant industry groups in terms of number of establishments, number of employees, and value added by manufacture are shown in Table 46. These are not unrelated in order of

TABLE 46. The Ten Most Significant Industry Groups in Terms of Number of Establishments, Number of Employees, and Value Added by Manufacture, 1947[4]

Rank	No. of Establishments	No. of Employees	Value Added by Manufacture
1	Food	Machinery	Food
2	Apparel	Food	Machinery
3	Printing and Publishing	Textiles	Transportation Equipment
4	Lumber and Products	Transportation Equipment	Primary Metal
5	Machinery	Primary Metal	Chemicals
6	Metal Products	Apparel	Textiles
7	Miscellaneous	Metal Products	Metal Products
8	Stone, Clay, Glass Products	Electrical Machinery	Apparel
9	Chemicals	Printing and Publishing	Printing and Publishing
10	Textiles	Lumber and Products	Electrical Machinery

importance, although there are important differences. From the report of the 1939 *Census of Manufactures,* in which more data were given, the highest relationship in the order of importance was found to be between total wages paid and value added by manufacture ($r = .93$). This would seem to indicate that high wages are important to the profitableness of manufacturing as they have already been seen to be to community welfare.

Services. The production of services has been on the increase for a number of years, especially in urban communities. The combination of technical advance and a rising standard of living has made it possible to support more services and made more people available for service occupations.

Patterns of the services are more varied than those of industry. Many in the service occupations work as individuals. This is true of

[4] Census of Manufactures: 1947: Preliminary Report. Series MC100–6, August 1, 1949.

many professionals. Doctors, nurses, dentists, engineers, lawyers, etc., for the most part, practice alone or in small partnerships, although some work in large institutions. On the other hand, most teachers work in schools, which tend to be large establishments in American cities, while only a few operate as individuals. The same is true of other professionals, such as social workers and recreational specialists. Domestic servants, waiters, bootblacks, and newsboys work alone or in small groups, but charwomen, chambermaids, window-washers, bellboys, etc., work for large establishments. Barbers, beauticians, plumbers, and morticians work alone or in small shops. Secretaries, stenographers, and clerks may be found in all sizes and kinds of organizations. Actors work in casts, athletes in teams, musicians in orchestras. Great numbers work for telephone, telegraph, and radio companies, as they do for the various transportation concerns; so do many other types of workers in many kinds of work in all sorts of arrangements. Exceptions can be found to all the general statements which have been made, and many other patterns are to be found.

Services are essential to the operation and convenience of city living. This is the work which only people can do. The potential extensions of the service occupations are very great and undoubtedly in considerable measure still unforeseen. The United States census, in reporting on service establishments, classifies them into seven major groups:[5] (1) personal service establishments, such as barber shops, beauty parlors, power laundries, cleaning and dyeing plants, and photograph studios; (2) business service establishments, such as adjustment and credit bureaus and collection agencies, advertising agencies, billboard advertising service, dental laboratories, sign-painting shops, and other establishments rendering a service to business; (3) services allied to transportation, such as stevedoring, stockyard service, and warehousing; (4) automotive repairs and services, which include automobile repair shops, automobile paint shops, automobile top and body repair shops, battery and ignition repair shops, tire repair shops, and automobile laundries; (5) other repair services (except automobile, apparel, and shoes), which include blacksmith shops, piano and organ tuning and repair service,

[5] Bureau of the Census, *Sixteenth Census of the United States, 1940: Census of Business: Vol. III, Service Establishments, Places of Amusement, Hotels, Tourist Courts and Tourist Camps, 1939* (Washington: Government Printing Office, 1942).

radio repair shops, refrigerator service and repair shops, and watch, clock, and jewelry repair shops; (6) custom industries, which include cabinetmaking shops (including woodworking), printing and publishing shops, and other custom and manufacturing establishments not covered by the census of manufactures, since the value of the products of each is less than the minimum necessary for classification as a manufacturing plant; (7) miscellaneous services, which include circulating libraries, landscape gardening and tree surgery, livery stables, and other services which could not logically be classified in any of the other six groups.

In all, ninety-six specific types of establishments have statistics reported for them, and as many more are included in the miscellaneous group in each classification.

In 1939 there were 646,028 such establishments, which had total receipts of $3,420,417,000, an increase of 2.3 percent in the number of establishments and 14.0 percent in receipts over 1935. There tends to be from city to city plus or minus half as many service establishments as retail business establishments.[6]

These, too, were small affairs; in 1939, 56.5 percent had no employees, and 22.9 percent had only one employee, who may work either full or part time. Two-thirds of them (67.7 percent) had annual receipts of less than $3000, and more than nine-tenths (91.4 percent) had receipts of less than $10,000. Individual proprietorships accounted for 86.1 percent and partnerships for 9.4 percent.[7]

The relative importance of the various classifications can be seen in Table 47.

In the 1948 Census the accounting of service trades was limited to the personal, business, and repair service trades. A comparison with 1939 on the basis of the 1948 enumeration shows a decrease of 2 percent in the number of establishments, an increase of 42 percent in the number of employees to a total of 1,342,496, and an increase in annual receipts from $3.0 billion to $8.6 billion or 188 percent. The most striking fact in the change from 1939 to 1948 was the increase in per capita expenditures in service establishment from $23. to $59.

---

[6] The report gives statistics for cities over 2500 in population and for individual cities over 25,000 in population, but no summaries for urban communities are included. Service establishments, however, are more indigenous to cities than to the country.

[7] Ibid., pp. 12–15.

TABLE 47. Relative Significance of the Various Types of Service Establishments, 1939[8]

| | Percentage Distribution | | | |
	No. of Establishments	Receipts	Av. No. of Employees	Total Pay Roll
United States	100.1	100.1	100.1	100.1
Personal services	60.3	53.5	58.0	53.6
Business services	4.4	16.1	14.6	20.7
Services allied to transportation	.6	5.0	8.7	8.1
Automotive repairs and services	12.2	12.9	8.4	9.1
Other repair services except automobile, apparel, and shoe	11.2	5.8	3.0	3.2
Custom industries	10.2	5.0	5.7	3.3
Miscellaneous services	1.0	1.7	1.6	2.0

Nearly half of the total trade receipts in the United States (48 percent) were accounted for in the five highly urbanized states New York, Illinois, California, Ohio, and Pennsylvania. In 1939 these states accounted for a full 50 percent of the service trade dollars. The states which showed the greatest percentage increase in receipts from 1939 to 1948 were mainly in the South and West corresponding in part to the areas which have shown the greatest gain in urban population.[9]

The distribution of services is at the point of their production, but in the case of goods a wholly different structure and machinery are required.

DISTRIBUTION

One of the characteristics of our modern urban civilization is that it takes very complicated organizations to get things which are pro-

[8] Sixteenth Census of the U.S., 1940. Census of Business. Volume III, Service Establishments, Places of Amusement, Hotels, Tourist Courts and Tourist Camps. 1939, (Washington, D.C. Government Printing Office, 1942).

[9] 1948 Census of Business: Retail, Wholesale, Service Trades, Preliminary. Selected Service Trades, Comparative State Summary: 1948 and 1939. Release Series BC-1P-S-0, July 16, 1950. 1948 Census of Business: Selected Services: Personal, Business, and Repair Services; Comparative United States Summary: 1948 and 1939. Release Series BC-2-S-0, January 7, 1951.

duced to the people who need and want them. These organizations are wholesale and retail trade. They include in their operations places for storage and dispensing of goods, many kinds of transportation, materials and equipment for packaging and shipping, a variety of sales arrangements, accounting and finance, display and advertising, and the many kinds of people which these varied operations require.

Wholesale. Wholesale trade is found mostly in medium-size or large cities which are centrally located and accessible by transportation to large areas. Wholesale firms usually confine their operations to one line—for example, groceries or men's furnishings. The bulk of their business is relatively large, and their operations consist chiefly of warehousing, transhipping, and itinerant selling.

This essentially urban function of wholesale trade is a large as well as important affair. In 1948 it employed 2,626,923 persons of whom 2,463,433 were paid employees and 163,490 were proprietors —owners of unincorporated businesses. The pay roll totaled $8.3 billion. The number employed increased 49 percent over 1939.

The 243,366 wholesale establishments was an increase of 21 percent over the number in 1939. In addition, there were 1339 administrative offices or auxiliary units supervising or servicing the wholesale establishments. Sales of the wholesale establishments totaled $188.7 billion for the year 1948, which was 245 percent greater than for 1939; an additional $1.8 billion of sales was reported by the administrative offices and auxiliary units, making a combined total of $190.5 billion.

The major components of the 243,366 establishments in 1948—together with the amount of the sales of each and the percentage increase in sales over 1939—were: 146,518 merchant wholesalers, $79.8 billion, 254 percent; 23,768 manufacturers' sales branches, $52.7 billion, 270 percent; 29,451 petroleum bulk stations, $10.6 billion, 179 percent; 24,361 merchandise brokers, $34.6 billion, 194 percent; and 19,268 assemblers of farm products, $11.0 billion, 337 percent.[10]

The concentration is shown in the analysis of fifty highly urban counties, the location of the large cities. These fifty counties accounted for $127.7 billion of the national total wholesale sales or 68 percent; 118,444 of the total wholesale business establishments or

[10] 1948 Census of Business: Wholesale Trade: United States Summary: Release Series BC-2-W-0, January 7, 1951.

49 percent; and 1,367,277 of those employed in wholesale trade or 56 percent.

The increase in wholesale sales in the fifty counties from 1939 to 1948 was 224 percent which fell slightly below the national average of 245 percent which would indicate a tendency toward a somewhat greater decentralization of wholesale distribution. Furthermore, those counties which showed the largest increase in wholesale sales were not the largest cities. The counties highest on the list of increase—together with their central cities, the percentage growth, and their rank according to total sales—were: Woodbury County (Sioux City), Iowa, 392 percent, 34th; St. Clair County (East St. Louis), Illinois, 387 percent, 38th; Alameda County (Oakland), California, 374 percent, 33rd; Mecklenburg County (Charlotte), North Carolina, 370 percent, 29th; Queens County (Queens Borough, New York City), New York, 363 percent, 31st; Dallas County (Dallas), Texas, 358 percent, 14th; Tarrant County (Fort Worth), Texas, 343 percent, 39th; Fulton County (Atlanta), Georgia, 341 percent, 15th; Franklin County (Columbus), Ohio, 341 percent, 35th; Jefferson County (Louisville), Kentucky, 339 percent, 30th; Shelby County (Memphis), Tennessee, 337 percent, 16th; Duval County (Jacksonville), Florida, 308 percent, 42nd; Multnomah County (Portland), Oregon, 302 percent, 25th; and Dakota County (St. Paul), Minnesota, 301 percent, 50th.[11]

Wholesale trade is one of the important links which hold the hinterlands to the cities as well as the means through which supplying the great variety of needs of city people is made possible. It does not, however, reach to the consumers of goods.

Retail Business in Cities. Through retail business establishments the people of the cities procure their goods. Stores are on every hand. The larger stores and the specialty shops are customarily located in the business centers of the cities, but the vendors of supplies for daily use, such as groceries, meats, fruits, vegetables, drugs, tobacco, newspapers, magazines, are scattered throughout the residential neighborhoods.

Nearly one-fourth (24.3 percent) of the total retail business in the United States is conducted in the 14 cities of more than 500,000 population. One-half of the business (50.9 percent) is in cities of more than

[11] 1948 Census of Business: Retail, Wholesale, Service Trades. Preliminary. Wholesale Trade in 1948: 50 Largest Counties. Release Series BC-1P-W-1 August 6, 1950.

50,000 population. On the other hand, more than one-half of the stores (53.6 percent) are in places of less than 20,000 population.

The cities of more than 50,000 population in which more than one-half of the total retail business of the country is conducted contain 38.1 percent of the stores, which account for 36.6 percent of the proprietors, 55.1 percent of all retail employees and 60.7 percent of the total retail payroll.

Not only are the larger stores to be found in the larger places, but both the number of employees per dollar volume of sales and the average earnings per employee are definitely higher in large cities than in small cities and rural areas.[12]

The details, by ten city-size groups and rural areas, can be seen in Table 48.

These averages cover up the differences which are to be found by states and by geographic divisions. The variations in some instances are very great. This will serve to illustrate: In the New England and Pacific divisions one-half of all retail stores are located in cities of 30,000 or more population; in the Middle Atlantic division, in cities of 75,000 or more population; in the East North Central division, in cities of 20,000 or more population; in the West North Central, South Atlantic, West South Central and Mountain divisions, in places of 2500 or more population and in the East South Central divisions, in places of less than 2500 population.[13]

Varieties of Retail Stores. The variety of retail stores is very great, as already noted (p. 268). The census of retail trade has enumerated them in sixty-four kinds in fifteen groups. The groups are listed in Table 49. It is clear that the needs of people for different kinds of goods vary greatly. This is reflected in the ratio of the number of each kind of store to population. Food and eating, as would be expected, head the list. The table also gives the average sizes of stores in terms of sales and indicates how the average city person distributes his expenditures for retail goods.[14] The significance of these averages, of course, is limited because of the great variations

[12] *Census of Business, 1939: Retail Trade: Analysis by City-Size Groups* (Washington: Government Printing Office, 1942), p. 2.

[13] *Ibid.,* p. 3.

[14] Other retail stores include such diverse stores as those selling fuel, ice, and fuel oil, hay, grain, and feed, farm and garden supplies, jewelry, books, stationery, cigars, flowers, gifts, novelties and souvenirs, news, office and school supplies and equipment, optical goods, photographic supplies and cameras, sporting goods.

TABLE 48. Distribution of Retail Business by City-Size Groups, 1939[15]

City-Size Groups, Places of	Stores		Sales (add 000)		Proprietors		Employees		Pay Roll (add 000)	
	Number	%	Amount	%	Number	%	Number	%	Amount	%
500,000 or more	334,378	18.9	10,229,426	24.3	298,009	18.5	1,188,079	25.8	1,378,884	30.4
250,000 to 499,999	113,314	6.4	3,936,086	9.4	98,528	6.1	436,127	10.6	505,590	11.2
100,000 to 249,999	116,795	6.6	3,748,761	8.9	99,858	6.2	445,998	9.7	457,570	10.1
75,000 to 99,999	43,424	2.5	1,347,800	3.2	37,461	2.3	166,135	3.6	160,601	3.5
50,000 to 74,999	66,123	3.7	2,123,961	5.1	56,211	3.5	248,845	5.4	247,465	5.5
30,000 to 49,999	85,069	4.8	2,636,883	6.3	72,965	4.5	297,423	6.5	291,056	6.4
20,000 to 29,999	61,795	3.5	1,863,623	4.4	54,148	3.4	206,842	4.5	199,092	4.4
10,000 to 19,999	127,379	7.2	3,539,916	8.4	113,731	7.0	385,063	8.4	350,536	7.7
5,000 to 9,999	122,236	6.9	3,019,582	7.2	112,032	6.9	319,684	6.9	274,619	6.1
2,500 to 4,999	108,070	6.1	2,340,658	5.6	100,989	6.3	237,803	5.2	193,777	4.3
Other (rural)	591,772	33.4	7,255,094	17.2	569,741	35.3	618,218	13.4	470,309	10.4
Total U.S.	1,770,355	100.0	42,041,790	100.0	1,613,673	100.0	4,600,217	100.0	4,529,499	100.0

[15] *Ibid.*, p. 2.

TABLE 49.   Stores and Sales of City Retail Establishments, by Kinds of Business, 1939[16]

	No. of Stores	Popula- tion per Store	% of Stores	Total Sales	Sales per Store	Sales per Person	% Sales per Person
All city stores	1,178,583	63.1	100.00	34,786,696,000	29,515	467.41	100.00
Food group	383,693	194.0	32.56	8,178,257,000	21,314	109.88	23.51
General stores (with food)	2,289	32,513.6	.20	112,369,000	49,090	1.51	.32
General merchandise group	35,959	2,069.7	3.05	5,372,161,000	149,396	72.18	15.44
Apparel group	97,145	766.1	8.24	3,159,403,000	32,522	42.45	9.08
Furniture-household- radio	42,670	1,744.2	3.62	1,633,253,000	38,276	21.95	4.70
Automotive	41,836	1,778.9	3.55	4,734,048,000	113,154	63.61	13.61
Filling stations	112,338	662.5	9.53	1,843,028,000	16,406	24.76	5.30
Lumber-building group	25,021	2,974.4	2.12	1,329,005,000	53,115	17.86	3.82
Hardware group	20,165	3,690.7	1.71	619,615,000	30,727	8.33	1.78
Eating places	121,612	612.0	10.32	1,842,784,000	15,152	24.76	5.30
Drinking places	86,068	864.7	7.30	1,046,402,000	12,157	14.06	3.01
Drug stores	42,743	1,741.2	3.63	1,356,531,000	31,732	18.23	3.90
Liquor stores (Pkgd.)	13,909	5,350.8	1.18	512,641,000	36,856	6.88	1.47
Other retail stores	133,048	559.4	11.29	2,922,277,000	21,964	39.27	8.40
Second-hand stores	20,086	3,705.3	1.70	124,922,000	6,219	1.68	.36

from region to region, from city to city, and even among different sections of the same city.

It is difficult to make meaningful comparisons between 1939 and 1948 because of the great differences which prevailed in economic conditions and especially in the value of the dollar. For the total United States, however, increases were very great. The total of retail sales rose from $42 billion in 1939 to $130.5 billion in 1948 an increase of 212 percent. The number of paid employees in 1939 was 4.9 million and in 1948 7.1 million, a 44 percent increase. The number of retail stores remained just about the same. The pay rolls of over $14 billion were three times those of 1939 and represented about 11 percent of the total paid to all wage earners and salaried employees in the United States in 1948.

The percapita expenditures in retail stores in the United States rose from $319 in 1939 to $893 in 1948, a gain of 180 percent. In terms of the decrease in the value of the dollar, however, the increase if any is relatively small. The fact that the percentage increase in total sales is greater than the percentage increase in percapita expenditures would seem to indicate a somewhat more equal distribution of buying power. Sales increases from 1939 to 1948 were considerably above average in the trades handling consumer du-

[16] *Ibid.*, Table 12c, pp. 8–9.

rable goods: in the automotive trades sales increases from $5.5 billion to $20.1 billion; in the lumber-building-hardware group from $2.7 billion to $11.2 billion; and in the furniture-furnishings-appliance group from $1.7 billion to $6.9 billion.[17]

Independent and Chain Stores. Chain stores appear to be on every hand in cities. They are made to be conspicuous, but in reality they represent only a small proportion of city stores, 9.1 percent, although they do 24.4 percent of the total business. Table 50 com-

TABLE 50.   Comparison of Independent and Chain Stores in Cities, 1939[18]

	Total	Independent	Chain
Number of stores	1,178,583	1,071,346	107,237
Percentage of stores	100.0	90.9	9.1
Total sales (add 000)	34,786,696	26,317,558	8,469,138
Percentage of sales	100.0	75.7	24.3
Sales per store	29,516	24,560	78,976

pares independent and chain stores. Chain stores are larger, with more than three times the sales per store. The number and proportion of chain stores have been decreasing, while the sales per store have been increasing and the total sales increasing slightly.[19]

Large and Small Stores. "More than 54 per cent of all retail stores stores in the United States did less than $10,000 of business in 1939. In sales, however, the 958,972 stores in this size group accounted for $3,820,532,000, or only 9.1 percent of total retail sales. They provided employment to 933,603 proprietor-owners and nearly 400,000 employees, with a total payroll to the latter of $208,500,000. The compensation of proprietors is frequently arbitrary and uncertain and the amount is not available." At the other end of the scale, 12,630, or 0.7 percent, of the stores, with a business of $300,000 or more each, did a total of $9,855,631,000, or 23.4 percent of the retail business.

Table 51 gives comparisons of stores and sales by size groups for the years 1929, 1935, and 1939. It will be noted that stores with less than $10,000 are the only group which has increased in number of

---

[17] 1948 Census of Business: Retail Trade. United States Summary. Release Series BC-2-R-0. January 7, 1951. Retail Trade—Comparative State Summary: 1948 and 1939. Release Series BC-1P-R-0, July 2, 1950.

[18] Data from *Census of Business, 1939: Retail Trade: Analysis by City-Size Groups,* Tables 12c, 12d, 12e, pp. 8–13.

[19] *Census of Business, 1939: Retail Trade: Analysis by Sales Size* (Washington: Government Printing Office, 1941), p. 2.

TABLE 51. Analysis of Retail Stores in the United States by Size Groups, with Comparisons, 1929, 1935, and 1939[20]

Annual Sales Size Group	Stores		Sales Amount (add 000)	Percent
	Number	Percent		
300,000 and over				
1939	12,630	0.7	9,855,631	23.4
1935	8,443	.5	6,879,155	20.9
1929	15,029	1.0	12,323,766	25.5
100,000 to 299,999				
1939	50,097	2.8	7,955,285	18.9
1935	37,196	2.4	5,828,224	17.7
1929	62,009	4.2	9,786,669	20.2
50,000 to 99,999				
1939	93,318	5.3	6,394,703	15.2
1935	72,562	4.6	4,989,553	15.2
1929	127,148	8.6	8,631,797	17.9
30,000 to 49,999				
1939	133,221	7.5	5,077,007	12.1
1935	119,705	7.5	4,581,413	14.0
1929	173,269	11.7	6,617,169	13.7
10,000 to 29,999				
1939	522,117	29.5	8,938,632	21.3
1935	415,165	26.1	7,114,216	21.6
1929	468,885	31.8	8,349,491	17.3
Less than 10,000				
1939	958,972	54.2	3,820,532	9.1
1935	935,634	58.9	3,486,428	10.6
1929	630,025	42.7	2,620,760	5.4

stores and total sales in the decade (the 10,000–29,999 group increased in total sales). "Despite the great number of smaller stores, the size of the average store increased nearly 15 percent ($20,653 to $23,748) between 1935 and 1939, though it is still 27 percent below the average for 1929 ($32,736)."[21]

With almost 85 percent of retail establishments doing an annual business of less than $30,000, it must be said that the characteristic of trade in American democratic society is small business. Such business, according to modern standards, is inefficient. Profits are small, longer hours and harder work are required, and solvency is precarious. It has been estimated that approximately 300,000 concerns go out of business every year; some 5 percent of them are

[20] *Census of Business, 1939: Retail Trade: Analysis by Sales Size*, p. 2.
[21] *Ibid.*, p. 2.

failures involving loss to suppliers; some are liquidations of profitable enterprises; but the bulk involve the loss of personal capital or funds borrowed from relatives and friends.[22] At best, this is a large social loss.

Small business, however, has more than quantitative significance. Former Dean Robert D. Calkins of the School of Business, Columbia University, as a result of his studies and observation, is convinced that it is a way of life for many people, that operating on their own initiative, resources, and responsibility means more than income, ease, and leisure. This is an important aspect of urban life.

In this connection reference should be made to a report made to the Senate committee on small business. This was a comparative study of three pairs of cities, large, medium-sized, and small. One city of each pair was a big-business community and the other a small-business community. The broad conclusions suggested by the study are the following:

(1) The small-business cities provided for their residents a considerably more balanced economic life than did big-business cities;
(2) The general level of civic welfare was appreciably higher in the small-business cities;
(3) These differences between city life in big- and small-business cities were in the cases studied due largely to differences in industrial organization—that is, specifically to the dominance of big business on the one hand and the prevalence of small business on the other.[23]

Senator James E. Murray, chairman of the Senate committee, says in the Foreword:

It appears that in the small-business cities is found the most favorable environment for the development and growth of civic spirit. A more balanced economic life and greater industrial stability is provided in small-business cities. There the employment is more diversified, the home-owning middle class is larger and self-employment greater. Public health is better in the small-business communities investigated; the study reveals that a baby has a considerably greater chance to survive his first year in the small-business city than in the one dominated by a few large firms. In small-business cities public expenditures for such facilities as

[22] A. M. Sullivan (Advertising Manager, Dun and Bradstreet), "You, Your Retailers and the Future," *Printer's Ink,* March 19, 1943.
[23] *Small Business and Civic Welfare,* Report of the Smaller War Plants Corporations to the Special Committee to Study Problems of American Small Business, U.S. Senate, 79th Congress, Second Session, Senate Document No. 135 (Washington: Government Printing Office, 1946), pp. 1–2.

libraries and education are substantially above such expenditures in big-business cities. Where big business predominates slums are more prevalent. The small-business cities studied provide for their residents a more balanced economic and social life and on the whole a higher level of civic welfare than big-business cities.[24]

In the light of these facts the assistance which has been given to small business seems eminently justified. Further help and services to strengthen this base of democracy would be highly appropriate.

JOBS

In the midst of the economic life the workers of the cities have their jobs and earn a living for themselves and their families. Many people, with a great variety of skills, responsibilities, and functions, are required to keep cities in operation. Not only do people need jobs, but cities need workers; they cannot exist without them in tremendous variety. These jobs are all specialized.

The United States Employment Service of the Department of Labor, after an extended research into some 130 industries, produced over 50,000 job-analysis schedules, on the basis of which the *Dictionary of Occupational Titles*[25] was prepared. This dictionary defines 17,452 separate jobs, with 12,292 alternate titles, making a total of 29,744 titles defined. A supplement several years later added 3064 new job definitions. This was recognized as incomplete, but it gives important evidence of the expanding variety of the ways in which people make their living in cities, for the jobs defined are for the most part city jobs.

The occupational analysis of the labor force in American cities by the United States Census has already been presented in terms of the main groupings to show the difference that the occupational distribution in cities makes for the classification of cities in terms of their relative welfare characteristics (see pp. 84–90). The variety of occupations which cities require to get the essential work done remains to be pointed out. Table 52 lists the main occupational classifications together with the number of subclassifications under each and the number of separate occupations which are enumerated. Three of the main classifications have to do with farming, a strictly

TABLE 52.   Classification of Occupations in Urban Communities[26]

Main Classifications	Subclassifications	Occupations
Professional workers	20	27
Semiprofessional workers	14	18
Farmers and farm managers	2	2
Proprietors, managers, and officials, except farm	13	63
Clerical, sales, and kindred workers	28	28
Craftsmen, foremen, and kindred workers	45	75
Operatives and kindred workers	32	119
Domestic service workers	3	3
Service workers, except domestic	24	25
Farm laborers (wage workers) and farm foremen	2	2
Farm laborers (unpaid family workers)	1	1
Laborers, except farm	6	83
Total number (12)	190	451

nonurban occupation, but some people with these occupations are found in cities.

Here, it would seem, are enumerated a sufficient variety of occupations to meet the tastes and capacities of almost anyone. Such a breadth of opportunity only cities can afford. And yet the mechanisms of channeling people according to their interests and abilities through the proper kinds of training to actual jobs in their chosen occupations are still almost entirely undeveloped in American cities. This is a problem, many believe, of first priority.

TAXES

Taxes have already been considered from the standpoint of income for city government and public services (pp. 289–295). There remains, however, a consideration of taxes from the point of view of those who pay them, for city taxes are paid by the people of cities, and they are a part of the economic life of cities.

There is much complaint about high tax rates in cities, and well there may be, for taxes are a heavy burden on some city people. As has been pointed out, however, the trouble is that no city has been able to raise sufficient funds to adequately operate city government

[26] *16th Census, 1940: Population:* Third Series, *The Labor Force,* "U.S., Summary," p. 8 and table 58, pp. 75–80. See also *Population:* Second Series, *Characteristics of the Population,* "U.S., Summary," pp. 9–11.

and public services on the basis on which city taxes are levied. If each city had its own way, unhampered by state restrictions on its revenue sources or the competition of state and federal taxes, city budgets could be made ample for all the needs.

Most cities have organizations of citizens whose purpose it is to lower taxes. This is an impossible task. There is a proper function for such organizations to perform, however—to develop a sound basis for the tax structure of a city, to be the everlasting watchdogs for wise expenditures from the public treasury, and to aid in the improvement of the economic status of the city by participation in economic development activities such as employment committees for the better use of the human resources, activities for the development of needed services and business, and planning for new enterprises to expand the productive base of the city.

The urban community must exist and operate at least with some measure of efficiency to provide the framework within which the people of the city can earn their living and live their lives. It is the essential "overhead" of city life. This factor of overhead is recognized in homes, in business and industrial organizations, in education, in clubs, in churches, etc., but it is seldom recognized as such in cities.

The cost of overhead in all organizations depends, in the first place, on production; that is, there is a limit to the cost of overhead in terms of the amount of production or the gross income. As production or gross income increases, the leeway increases and permits additional services up to a certain point, where overhead costs must be considerably increased, but if the planning is well done production takes on corresponding jumps.

We have tried to run our cities without relation to the productive capacity of their people and have levied the charges for the operation and maintenance of the community against the accumulations of property. As a result, people have considered all but the barest cost of government as luxury items.

When people begin to see how important the maintenance of their city is to them, when they see their part of the responsibility for operating their city because of a direct relationship with their productive capacity, there will be new possibilities for successful cities. As it is, city people get more for the money they pay in taxes than for the money they pay for anything else. They can, and they should, get even more.

Supplementary Reading

Dictionary of Occupational Titles: Part I, *Definitions of Titles.* Washington: United States Government Printing Office, 1939; and Supplemental Edition II, 1943.

Much understanding of the great variety of jobs at which city people earn their livings can be obtained from exploring this work.

16th Census 1940 and *17th Census 1950: Population:* Third Series, *The Labor Force.*

Census of Manufactures 1939 and *1947.*

Census of Business 1939 and *1947.*

These are important resources of data which can be used in analyzing particular cities.

CHAPTER 18

URBANIZATION AND SOCIAL ORGANIZATION

Underlying the broadening scope and the changing character of the functions of urban community life which were illustrated in the discussion of city government (Chap. 15), and which permeate all of the organized life in cities, is the process of urbanization. This has been implicit in all of the considerations thus far, but must be summarized explicitly as part of the background for the specific considerations of some of the major parts of the organized life of urban communities.

Urbanization is the extension of what has come to be called urbanism, "that complex of traits which makes up the characteristic modes of life in cities."

URBANISM

A concise statement of urbanism is found in the summary of an article by Louis Wirth:

The urbanization of the world, which is one of the most impressive facts of modern times, has wrought profound changes in virtually every phase of social life. The recency and rapidity of urbanization in the United States account for the acuteness of our urban problems and our lack of awareness of them. Despite the dominance of urbanism in the modern world we still lack a sociological definition of the city which would take adequate account of the fact that while the city is the characteristic locus of urbanism, the urban mode of life is not confined to cities. For sociological purposes a city is a relatively large, dense, and permanent settlement of heterogeneous individuals. Large numbers account for individual variability, the relative absence of intimate personal acquaintanceship, the segmentalization of human relations which are largely anonymous, superficial, and transitory, and associated characteristics. Density involves diversification and specialization, the coincidence of close physical contact and distant social relations, glaring contrasts, a complex pattern of segregation, the predominance of formal social control, and accentuated friction, among other phenomena. Heterogeneity tends to break down rigid social structures and to produce increased mobility, instability, and insecurity, and the affiliation of the individual with a variety of intersecting and tangential social groups with a high rate of membership turnover. The pecuniary nexus tends to displace personal relations, and institutions tend to cater to mass rather than to individual requirements. The individual thus becomes effective only as he acts through organized groups. The complicated phenomena of urbanism may acquire unity and coherence if the sociological analysis proceeds in the light of such a body of theory. The empirical evidence concerning the ecology, the social organization, and the social psychology of the urban mode of life, confirms the fruitfulness of this approach.[1]

Each of these factors creates problems of living for city people which in turn affect the city's organization. Here are some far-reaching changes underlying urbanism.

Urbanization and Invention. The high development of technology in our modern civilization has been possible because of an urbanized society. Here the proper environment for invention has been established.

There is no indication that any individual's genius has been necessary to any invention that has had any importance. To the historian and social scientist the progress of invention appears impersonal.[2]

The creative personality, in medicine as in other sciences, does not effect change by the mere exercise of a powerful will, as most biographic histories suggest, but by synthesizing elements in his tradition into new forms slightly different from those that preceded them.[3]

Necessity, although acting as a stimulus to research, cannot produce an invention or discovery without the existence of the requisite social, technical and intellectual conditions. It may, however, in a limited sense, focus efforts on a technical problem which must be solved before further progress is possible.[4]

[1] Louis Wirth, "Urbanism as a Way of Life," *American Journal of Sociology*, 45: 743–755 (March, 1940).

[2] S. C. Gilfillan, *The Sociology of Invention* (Chicago: Follett Publishing Company, 1935), p. 10.

[3] Bernhard J. Stern, *Society and Medical Progress* (Princeton: Princeton University Press, 1941), p. 44.

[4] *Ibid.*, p. 43.

An invention is essentially a complex of most diverse elements. . . . The achievements of the inventor himself, and of his compeers, are a major cause of changes in the milieu out of which is compounded the inventional complex. . . . Some other chief changes causing invention are growths of wealth, education, population, industrialism and commercial organization.[5]

The great industrial establishments taking these things into account have established research laboratories in which highly trained people make invention their business.

More significant, however, is the large place artifacts have come to have in urban life and the extent to which people have come to depend upon them. Urbanization creates an ever-increasing expansion of human needs and opportunities; in response to the demands of these wants and purposes there has been a multiplication of artifacts. The way of life which has been engendered places increasing responsibility upon man for developing and utilizing tools to meet his expanding needs. The successful reliance upon man-wrought tools and instruments, which has given people increasing control of their environment, has also played an important part in the secularization of society.

The proliferation of artifacts, however, is not a simple matter of adding gadgets to daily life, for these instruments and conveniences cause changes in habits of living, in patterns of human relationships, and in the character and functions of social organizations. While people accept new artifacts with comparative ease, they resist changes in their social environment. Attitudes toward social relationships and social institutions tend to be dominated by acceptance of and reverence for established patterns.

The utilization of tools as consciously controllable means toward achievement of ends has only recently been extended into the social sphere, as MacIver points out.

. . . one difference between a primitive and a civilized society is that in the latter a great many things become merely or purely utilitarian, merely instruments or means. Now when anything is thought of merely as a means people try to improve it as a means—they constantly experiment with it to make it more efficient. An automobile engine is such a means, and it is changed almost every year. But a constitution is not regarded in the same way because of its cultural implications; only in times of crisis and then with difficulty is it liable to change in any im-

[5] Gilfillan, *op. cit.*, pp. 6, 7.

portant respects. The primitive mind regards the techniques and instruments of everyday use in the way that, among ourselves, the majority of people regard the Constitution. But with us technology has become detached, for the most part, from cultural limitations. It changes very rapidly. One indication is that in the five years ending 1845 the number of patents in the United States was 2,425, whereas in the five years ending 1930 the number was 219,384. One consequence of this free application of inventiveness is, for reasons we have already suggested, a more unstable and changeful social system.[6]

Regardless of pleas for moratoriums on invention by those who fear man is incapable of controlling the instruments of his invention, the progress of invention continues with increasing speed, and social scientists plead for speeding up the process of recognizing the necessity for social change, of carrying on social experimentation, and of devising new social forms to meet the pressures exerted by the material inventions. It should be noted that it was several years after the cotton picker was invented before it was made available, in order that something could be done about the social disruption it would cause by throwing Negroes out of employment in the South; also, in connection with the development of atomic power, there has been much preliminary consideration of its social implications, particularly with reference to its potential destructiveness for cities.

The interaction of physical and social invention and their effect upon human attitudes and behavior is an important part of the story of urban social organization.

Urbanization, Social Process, and Social Control. Urbanization has a profound effect upon the social process. New conditions of life develop. Human relationships become less direct and more extensive. The place of organization in community life has greater significance.

A simple rural community in the days before industry made its impact on American society was largely isolated from the rest of the country. The difficulties of transportation and the lack of any regular communication with other communities made it, in many respects, little different from primitive communities. This isolation was not only geographical; it was also social and intellectual. Under these circumstances there was no basis for comparison, criticism, or interpretation of community life. Behavior patterns, attitudes, and

[6] Robert M. MacIver, *Society: A Textbook of Sociology* (New York: Rinehart and Company, Inc., 1937), pp. 400–401.

relationships were established. Into such a situation each child was born, and he gradually adapted himself to the conventions and mores. Patterns of living were simple and continuing; they were accepted, in fact were regarded as sacred; divergences from the patterns were frowned upon; changes of any kind were feared.

Under these circumstances social control was simple. People lived under the close surveillance of their neighbors. Mores and conventions were the rules one lived by. Few laws were required.[7]

Urbanization has changed not only the patterns, but also the conditions, of the social process, and the basis of social control. The requirements of an industrial society, together with the developments of communication and transportation, have resulted in a high degree of accessibility, a continuous interchange of information and ideas, and a great mobility of population. So the pressures of circumstances have become diametrically opposite to those in the simple rural society.

In addition, the people in cities are engaged in specialized occupations; their primary human relationships are largely with reference to special interests, and, except in the incidental contacts of daily life, they are insulated from the opinions of their neighbors, in fact are for the most part unaware of them.

Under these circumstances any fixation of a behavior pattern is impossible; rather are diverse patterns recognized as desirable. There is a premium upon change of every kind; consequently, folkways and mores are subjected to analysis and criticism along with all patterns of behavior and all ideas. The basis of acceptance is rational: nothing is regarded as sacred, and social processes become secular and utilitarian. So social control becomes functional. It can no longer be informal pressure on individual behavior in accordance with accepted standards; instead, it deals with the matters which coöperative living requires and takes the formal character of law. Even offenses against the laws frequently involve no social ostracism.[8]

This makes for a high degree of freedom for the individual. People can and do live in cities without knowing their neighbors and without any formal ties to the organizations of the community ex-

---

[7] Howard Becker, "Vicinal Isolation and Mental Immobility," *Social Forces*, 9: 326–334 (March, 1943).

[8] Howard Becker, "Processes of Secularization," *Sociological Review* (London), 24: 140–144 (April, July, October, 1932).

cept for the money tie that relates them to their jobs. "The dweller in a large American city tends to be a highly developed roving predatory animal. His culture resembles a frontier boom-town, with everywhere the clatter of new buildings going up and disregard for the niceties of living in pursuit of the main chance. He is free—free to swim or drown, free to bet all his life on "the big money," free to turn on the gas as a lost and beaten atom in the anonymity of his furnished hall-bedroom."[9]

Urbanism brings to a focus such tendencies as rampant individualism, and the concept and feeling of community emerge with difficulty from the conflict of private interests, which are prevalent in the urban culture, because cities harbor the unrestrained egotistic qualities which the culture encourages. But this is not inherent in urbanism; rather is it the case that an urbanized society provides the environment which is conducive to the development of any qualities to which an individual is disposed.

Individualism and coöperation are constantly at war in city life. Freedom can lead individuals to try to "play it alone" or to become a part of the coöperative process by which a city lives. The "lone wolf" is either a helpless, frustrated person or a predatory parasite; it is those who find their places in the coöperative organizations who gain the advantages of the city and participate in its development.

There is, however, a striking paradox in this city freedom: many people seem always ready to follow the crowd. This gives a propaganda newspaper, an irresponsible radio commentator, a "witch hunt," an espionage trial, the opportunity to play on latent taboos and prejudices so that severe punishment can be inflicted by these people even on those merely suspected of deviation. Many illustrations of this reaction can be seen in recent years, when those whose names have been incidentally publicized in connection with "un-American" activities have been so harassed by people that their lives are precarious and their livelihoods are jeopardized, if not destroyed. Freedom can be dangerous without the balance wheel of social pressures and the integration of people in the associated life within their communities.

The integration of people into the organized life of the urban community cannot be taken for granted.

[9] Robert S. Lynd, *Knowledge for What?* (Princeton: Princeton University Press, 1939), p. 79.

Whereas the close, personalized contacts of the neighborhood encouraged spontaneous social cohesion in the rural, village, and small-town matrix in which our culture took shape, unguided spontaneity may not be relied upon to tie in the individual so securely as the population-base grows to city proportions. The rough generalization may be made that, as the size of a community grows arithmetically, the need for deliberate (as over against unplanned, casual) organization that weaves the individual into the group life increases in something like a geometrical progression. Urbanism in our culture has been almost entirely a matter of material change. As just pointed out, under the doctrine of casualness virtually no attention has been paid to the planning and perfecting of the non-material factor of social organization.[10]

While these last two sentences are true, they do not represent the whole story. Urbanization is a force which has compelled social organization to make some degree of adaptation for survival. In fact, problems which have had to be met are of such a nature that changes in, and the extension of, organization have gradually taken place. It is true, however, that these developments have in large measure been unconscious, without adequate rationalization, and, because of this, leave much to be desired in the adequacy and effectiveness of the organizational scheme and the operation of institutions.

Urbanization, even though it has been to a large extent an unconscious process, has in reality been the adaptation of society to modern man, whose experience worlds have been constantly enlarging, whose facilities for working and living have become highly developed, and whose opportunities for the enrichment of living have been greatly increased.

While this growing urbanization derives predominantly from economic causes, such as the concentration of industry in the "easy labor market" which a dense population affords and the resulting multiplication of retailing and other service activities among such a dense population, the growth of cities has also been influenced by other factors. Urban living represents the most favorable environment for those wishing to benefit by the resources of the culture. On the personal side, the city presents the opportunity for rich, selective acquaintanceship in the pursuit of personal growth. On the material side, the overhead cost of providing desirable modern services—from labor-saving utilities to schools and the arts—can best be borne when widely shared. Without, therefore,

[10] *Ibid.*, pp. 82–83.

by any means going to the extreme of Marx and Engels in speaking of "the idiocy of rural life," one may nevertheless say that the city is potentially a "natural" as a way of life for modern man. The inchoate character of urban life in one culture, which prompts some to characterize great cities as "wens of civilization," is not an evidence of the intrinsic weakness of urbanism, but rather of the pathologies that occur when urban units are allowed to develop casually as an adjunct to the individual scramble for wealth. We have not as yet addressed ourselves to the task of building urban *communities,* in the social sense.[11]

The planning and building of urban communities have to do with organizations and with institutions.

Urbanization and Institutional Development.   Not only do urban people have the needs of all humans, but by virtue of the kind of life they share there have been many additional needs, the meeting of which requires complicated organization. The fundamental social institutions, consequently, are to be found in highly developed form, but in addition to these there is a great variety of organizations, some of which have become or are becoming stable social institutions, others of which are transitory.

One of the marks of urbanization is a high degree of organization. It is the method of implementing ideas in a complex society; it is the means through which all operations take place. Its proliferation is the result of the greater breadth of freedom which has come with urbanization. Individuals are helpless in cities without organization. They get their food and other necessities through complex organizations. Their recreation, religion, education, and the rest are made available by highly developed organizations, and these organizations are always subject to modifications and development by the ingenuity of people. More than this, however, it is possible to accomplish almost any purpose or to achieve any determined end which human beings may desire if they build a proper and adequate organization. This is the freedom which cities provide.

Malinowski points out that even in the daily existence of an individual all of his purposes and concerns are brought to satisfaction through the organized life of the community. Even new ideas are sterile until they are made effective through organization.

. . . every group is organized for the satisfaction of one main need, to which all the other activities are subsidiary. It is for the satisfaction of this need that its material equipment, technical or otherwise, is developed.

[11] *Ibid.,* pp. 80–82.

It is around this need that the organization of the personnel centers, to this end the rules are always carried out; and the charter is connected with function, though it is never identical with it. The function of an institution therefore is the satisfaction of the need or needs for which that institution was organized. In other words, the function of an institution is equivalent to the enjoyment of the results of the activity by the group or personnel who performed it.[12]

Through its function an institution has its relationship to its community, just as the functions of community life are carried out by its institutions.

People are related to institutions in various ways around their several aspects, clearly defined by Chapin as the common reciprocating attitudes manifested in conventionalized behavior patterns, cultural objects of symbolic value around which emotional attachments develop, the utilitarian material objects which are the means of operation, and the particular code through which communication within the institutional framework is maintained. This configuration gives to the institutions the properties of relative persistence and relative rigidity as functioning units.[13]

Mannheim, who is particularly concerned with the development of rationalized collective behavior and a more thoroughly planned structure of the community, points out the difficulties involved in this tendency toward inflexibility in well-established institutions in the community. "In contrast to this traditional form of collective adjustment, rationalized collective behavior begins by abolishing the traditional symbolic elements in favor of those which are essential to the function of the body concerned, judged exclusively by the needs of the present situation."[14] He thinks of groups which have become rationally functional on the "cutting edge" of our developing urbanized society as associations which have not reached the stage of formalization and so maintain much flexibility. Rationality and flexibility, which are inseparable characteristics, are essential qualities of organized life in our urban community.

So urbanization provides new circumstances within which new

[12] Bronislaw Malinowski, *Freedom and Civilization* (New York: Roy Publishers, 1944), pp. 163–165; see also Part IV, Chap. 5, "Freedom Through Organization."

[13] F. Stuart Chapin, *Contemporary American Institutions* (New York: Harper & Brothers, 1935), p. 359; see also Chap. II.

[14] Karl Mannheim, *Man and Society in an Age of Reconstruction* (New York: Harcourt, Brace and Company, 1941), p. 291.

needs and new purposes compel action and so develop new patterns of organization. As men meet these situations and discover the necessity for thorough investigation, for appraisal of resources and methods, and for planning organizations and procedures, a new form of mentality develops. Evidences of this rational approach and clues to the impact of urbanization on the organizational framework of our society will be seen as we proceed to look at health services, social work, education, recreation, religion, and so forth.

SOCIAL LAG

Cities, by and large, are products of the concentration of population, materials, energy, and production resulting from the Industrial Revolution. So cities have become the foci of technological and social change. Urbanization, then, involves the adjustment of the whole range of social behavior, social relationships, and social organization to the conditions imposed by urban life, not only within cities themselves, but within the whole society as far as the influences of urban conditions reach. The discrepancies which develop by virtue of a time lag between changed circumstances and social adjustments are at the roots of many of the problems of cities.

This lag is inherent in the industrial age because new products of technology are constantly appearing on the scene. They do not spring into full use immediately, however, but are gradually absorbed into daily life. Consequently, it takes time for their effects on habits, relationships, and organizations to become evident. Disturbances in the usefulness of social forms intervene before it becomes apparent that social adjustments have to be made.

Prior to the impact of the Industrial Revolution, society was characterized by stability. Barnes says: "There were few changes in, or challenges to, the dominant social institutions. Custom, habit, tradition reigned supreme, with only faint protests."[15] Since the Industrial Revolution took hold, however, it has been a different world.

Inequalities in Change. The many forces at work in urbanization sooner or later have an impact on all aspects of life, individual and communal. It is in this matter of sooner or later that difficulties start. Material changes come easily and quickly, but it takes time for their social implications to become evident. The invention of the type-

[15] Harry Elmer Barnes, *Society in Transition.* Copyright 1939 by Prentice-Hall, Inc., p. 3.

writer, for example, was a material change in the form of a new tool which not only made work in a business office simpler and quicker, but also made a great many procedures possible which were not possible before. The social implications, however, such as making larger business establishments practical and providing a new kind of job, especially for women, did not become evident as far-reaching social changes for many years. But these social implications have had a profound effect upon the structure of American urban communities.

To take a more general example: One aspect of industrial development was that it took people out of their homes to work in factories and in offices; more members of families found a great variety of work opportunities and became independent. This, in turn, diversified the interests of the members of families; people began to associate on the basis of interests rather than proximity or family membership, and the independence of individuals replaced that of family groups. Cultural interests also increased in variety, and around these interests individuals formed other associations outside of the home. The increased significance of the operation of individuals in urban communities has changed the functions of the family. Yet in a hundred years urban families have not recognized the new patterns of function and organization which are required, and as a result the disintegration of urban families continues with increasing rapidity and scope. How could it be otherwise?

A more immediate illustration can be found in the growing use of television. It has already caused great disruption in the radio business and helped to cause a marked decline in attendance at motion-picture theaters, which has seriously affected the motion-picture industry. Family habits are being changed; in fact, children themselves report that the thing they like best about television is that the members of their families are getting together around this new interest and are working together more coöperatively in decisions about the programs to be seen. Teachers and school principals are beginning to report facts about the effects of television on children's schoolwork. Problems appear; solutions have not yet been found. The impact of this change hit hard and soon—changes come faster than they did and will come even more rapidly.

Rigidity of Social Institutions.   Change involves every phase of social organization. Social institutions, however, once they have established the pattern of their functions, organizations, and programs, have a strong, and easily accounted for, tendency to become rigid.

They become recognized in their communities and win prestige and support; they accumulate property; and they provide jobs for specialized personnel. The institution has become important and so must be maintained in traditional form and operation. This happens in business institutions, in schools, in churches, in social service agencies, in clubs and societies, and in all the rest of the many urban social institutions.

Changes come, functions disappear, new patterns of needs arise, old types of institution are outmoded. For example, products of certain factories are no longer useful, for people's tastes and needs change the things they buy; the population surrounding a church is completely replaced by people of different social and economic status, different backgrounds, and different needs, and the institution's patterns must be completely changed if it is to survive; some functions carried out by privately supported agencies become recognized as universally applicable in urban communities and are taken over by publicly supported agencies.

Social institutions are caught between two inescapable forces: the force of change and the force of inertia. Those which are youthful and vigorous tend to react to the former, and those which are senile and satisfied tend to react to the latter. In any city, institutions which have made each kind of response are to be found side by side. Strong institutional churches with a great variety of services and activities are not far from fine old edifices where small congregations, content with traditional patterns, struggle to keep alive against failing finances. A chain store with high prices and no services, except being open until 1:00 A.M., fails while just across the street a "coöp" with neighborhood membership grows in patronage. A neighborhood house, started to serve a special group, feebly struggles on as its constituency departs to other sections of the city, while another agency, located near by to serve the new people, can scarcely keep up with the demands for its services.

The tragedy is that cities never have enough institutions. There is work for them all, and those which live on though they are obsolete deprive the people of the cities of needed services, needed relationships, and needed participation.

Necessity for Planning. Experience has shown conclusively that institutions will not change themselves, but that they can be changed to meet changing circumstances and changing needs by scientific study and planning. The social sciences have reached a stage of development which enables them to predict, at least in part, what the effects of changes will be on individuals, institutions, and communities. It is not necessary to wait until the consequences of changes descend in full force, with serious problems of maladjustment in the community, before anything is done. Most problems can be solved before they arise.

PEOPLE AND URBANIZATION

The relationship of people to institutions, their ideas of freedom, and their difficulties in adjusting to a changing world create attitudes which intensify the problems of adaptability of institutions and produce concepts of, and attitudes toward, cities which contribute significantly to present problems.

In the development of the western frontier the traditional patterns were broken as frontiersmen had to make frequent readjustments to the circumstances of their new environment. The frontier philosophy, however, held that the free and happy man was the freeholder who was independent on his individual economic and political island. In the framework of farming, small handicrafts, and small shopkeeping, the idea of Jeffersonian democracy developed. This became the traditional ideal of democracy. It carried with it an antagonism to big government and big business because even in his freedom the frontiersman could not escape the controls of government and the exploitation of those who controlled the land, the goods, and the credit which he needed. But land speculators, merchants, and bankers were in the cities; so he damned the cities.

Complex society is precipitated by the wilderness into a kind of primitive organization based on the family. The tendency is anti-social. It produces antipathy to control, and particularly to any direct control. The tax-gatherer is viewed as a representative of oppression. . . . The frontier individualism has from the beginning promoted democracy. . . . So long as free land exists, the opportunity for a competency exists, and economic power. But the democracy born of free land, strong in selfishness and individualism, intolerant of administrative experience and education, and pressing individual liberty beyond its proper bounds, has its dangers as well as its benefits. Individualism in America has allowed a laxity in regard to government affairs which has rendered possible the spoils system and all the manifest evils that follow from the lack of a highly developed civic spirit. In this connection may be noted also the influence of frontier conditions in permitting lax business honor, inflated paper currency and wild-cat banking.[16]

And yet the frontier, with its loneliness and solitary ways of freedom, "has left a nostalgia often evident today."

Americans are coming to use collective agencies (technology among them) to fight intolerable collective conditions. Confine a modern American to a city and he will invent contrivances to burrow his way out, under rivers if necessary, to a suburb farther and farther away that he may "own his own home," his plot of land. Confine him too rigidly to that home and he devises a machine called a trailer to return him to the gypsy trail. Organize him too tightly in a factory or a union and he will often voluntarily go out of employment. Provide him with "relief" and he will sometimes cling to it though work is round the corner because relief, paltry as it is, gives him personal liberty which industry does not.[17]

Reaction Against the City.   When people find themselves in cities or within the orbit of the direct influence of cities (and a large majority of the population of the United States comes within one or the other of these categories), they tend to react against cities, some violently as against destroyers of men, others with the desire to escape the routine, the hustle and bustle, the confusion, the keeping up with the Joneses, the struggle for a place in the sun, to live the leisurely, unharried pace of the countryman.

This is an old story which goes back to the days of the ancient cities and breaks forth in times of stress and conflict such as the present. The classic critique of the city was pronounced by Oswald Spengler. "The period of civilization is that of the victory of city over country. It frees itself from the grip of the ground, but to its own ultimate ruin. Rootless, dead to the cosmic, irrevocably committed to stone and to intellectualism, it develops a form language that reproduces every trait of its essence. Not the language of a becoming and a growth, but that of a becomeness and completion—capable of alteration certainly, but not of evolution."[18] This statement is obviously only partly true and is inaccurate, especially in the last sentence, but it is believed by many people. The unrest awakened

[16] Frederick Jackson Turner, *The Frontier in American History* (New York: Henry Holt and Company, 1921), pp. 30–38.
[17] Roger Burlingame, *Engines of Democracy* (New York: Charles Scribner's Sons, 1940), p. 6.
[18] Edwin Franden Dakin (editor), *Today and Destiny: Vital Excerpts from The Decline of the West* (New York: Alfred A. Knopf, 1940), p. 227.

by the depression of 1929 and World War II has given vent to a prolific literature condemning the city and calling for a return to the rural village way.[19]

This is essentially a backward-looking philosophy and if widely accepted would be potentially dangerous. Cities have numerous defects and face serious problems. Drastic suggestions and strenuous efforts looking toward reform and the solution of the problems are being cautiously made by many health and welfare workers, city-planners, citizens' groups, and public officials. The positive values of urbanization and its contributions to human well-being must also be recognized. To accept a philosophy of despair and hopelessness is to turn mankind back from increased democratic and scientific control of his environment and his destiny.

The city has been a center of man's efforts to understand, control, and direct the world of nature and of spirit through his own intelligence and energy. The city is where man's struggle to master the unknown has found increasing fruition in the development of science, technology, and social organization. The city, historically, has been the battlefield of man's struggle against autocracies of supernaturalism, traditionalism, and aristocracy, where the self-appointed masters of men have received their greatest defeats. Because in the city man has discovered his own power, the city has been a dynamic force in the growth of democratic and scientific ideals. Consequently, it is reviled by those who fear the loss of their power over people.

The Basis of Fear.   Back of the social lag which is serious in cities, where changes in social structure need to correspond in rapidity to changes in circumstances, are the attitudes of people, which to a great extent have their basis in four fears.

First, the fear that human beings "are getting too big for their breeches," that men are fooling around with things best left alone. This fear grows out of deep-seated taboos regarding meddling with the unknown. When things get too complicated, when the play of forces seems incomprehensible, as it often does amid the complexities of urban life, the little man tends to revert to primitive and infantile modes of thought. He either accepts circumstances as in-

[19] Some samples of this literature are: Ralph Borsodi, *Flight from the City* (New York: Harper & Brothers, 1933); Arthur E. Morgan, *The Small Community* (New York: Harper & Brothers, 1942); Elmer T. Peterson (editor), *Cities Are Abnormal* (Norman: University of Oklahoma Press, 1946). Two of the periodicals are *The Decentralist* (Suffern, New York) and *Community Service News* (Yellow Springs, Ohio).

evitable and unavoidable or looks for some magical solution or a man on horseback to lead out of the morass of confusion and indecision. Or he may seek an escape to "the good old days" or a return "to simple farm life."

Second, the fear of facing and coming to grips with problems. This reflects, on the one hand, a sense of inadequacy and lack of resources in education and knowledge, on the part of the many who have never had the opportunity to develop self-reliance. On the other hand, it is an evidence of laziness and the desire to escape the work and the responsibility which thinking demands. Both of these fears are inimical to the conscious effort to understand and control a situation.

Third, the fear that social organization involves an increase of controls. The strange combination of vagabond and self-made man in many Americans, which is expressed in "I want to be my own boss" and "I don't want anyone telling me what to do," is an anachronism. It is built on an outmoded concept of freedom. "There was an American way, simple enough to formulate in the adolescence of the nation, but it has been lost. . . . The American way was the way of the solitary. . . . He was not an *individualist* as we now use the term—a product of frustration; he was an *individual* complete in himself. The suffix arrived when he was no longer so. Like all 'ists,' he was then a thwarted person."[20] Technology and an inherent gregariousness caused Americans to forsake the solitary way and become organized into collective bodies in order that they might build effective communities, and then they turned against the very process which they had found successful.

Fourth, the fear on the part of the authoritarian-minded that their power and prestige are being destroyed as people massed in cities organize popular movements to take power into their own hands and so break away from traditional authority. The power of elites, demagogues, industrial barons, is rationalized by them as necessary in order to do things for people. When people become strong enough to do things for themselves through organization, the self-appointed leaders revile the cities as "hotbeds of radicalism." This is well illustrated as late as 1945 by an article, circulated under the auspices of the Council on Medical Service and Public Relations of the American Medical Association, in its campaign against the Wagner-Murray-Dingell Bill, which states:

[20] Burlingame, *op. cit.*, pp. 4–7.

The most powerful single force responsible for the origin of the demand for compulsory health insurance is organized labor. . . . The place most conducive for formulation and pressing of such demand is the large city. . . . Illness apparently is not chiefly responsible for the demand for compulsory health insurance. If it were, recommendations would start in the medically least progressive states. However, they originate at the opposite end of the scale, where medical care and social services are most highly developed. . . . Mississippi is the antithesis of both California and New York. In industrial development it ranks among the lowest of the states. There are virtually no large cities; hence there is little opportunity for mass action.[21]

Another illustration can be found in the outspoken opposition of the National Association of Real Estate Boards to the big city's democracy even to the extent of fighting efforts to reapportion state legislatures to more adequately represent urban interests.

THE FIRST PROBLEM

The problem is to accept the changes as they come and to get into a position whereby people can control both the uses to which changes are put and the effects of changes upon individuals, institutions, and communities, rather than to allow the changes to control the welfare and destiny of people. This necessitates a simple, inclusive, coöperative, planning organization of the people themselves, which will always study and appraise what is happening and plan for what they want accomplished. But such an organization cannot work unless people have the will to make it work. Some city governments are contributing substantially to this educational job. Under the Welfare Department in Kansas City, citizen-official teamwork has been promoted through community councils and community coordinators. Many cities have established public relations departments to stimulate and encourage citizen participation and interest in local government.

Since the inability to meet change and the possibility of making change a constructive force both reside in the minds of men, the first problem deals with attitudes and understanding. It is a problem of

[21] Carl W. Strow and Gerhard Hirschfeld, "Health Insurance," *Journal of the American Medical Association,* July 21, 1945, pp. 870–878; reprinted by the American Medical Association under the title *The Factors Underlying the Demand for Compulsory Sickness Insurance.*

education and especially of adult education. An education, however, not of theory and textbooks, but of wrestling with real problems, building experience, and taking action. That is to say, the education should go hand in hand with "doing something about it."

Much is being done in American cities by public schools, neighborhood houses, libraries, labor unions, and other groups, but it is spotty and equivocal in its effectiveness.[22] A more consistent and far-reaching job in helping adults master the problems of change has been done in rural America through the Coöperative Extension Service.[23] There is great promise for cities, however, in the plans which are being developed for an extension service under the Department of Labor. One of the most constructive attacks on this problem in cities is being made by the Bureau of Adult Education of the New York State Department of Education. The members of the staff are spending their time and effort in helping people in the various urban communities to organize themselves for study and action.

At the foci of a world characterized by a constant stream of technological changes, which in turn require change in the social organization of human life, cities struggle to keep their social institutions adjusted to ever-changing needs. The inherent lag in social adjustments, the tendency of institutions to be inflexible, and the attitudes and fears of people hamper the process. A program of planning in which many people participate and experience the education involved in coöperatively working out problems gives promise of speeding up the process of adaptation.

Before considering important areas of organization in cities, it will be well to look at some of the major problems of cities which are concomitants of urbanization.

[22] One of the best illustrations is what happened "back of the yards" in Chicago, the story of which is told in Saul Alinsky, *Reveille for Radicals* (Chicago: The University of Chicago Press, 1946). Other types of adult education are reported in John W. Studebaker, *The American Way* (New York: McGraw-Hill Book Company, 1935); Watson Dickerman, *Outposts of the Public Schools* (New York: American Association for Adult Education, 1938); Alvin Johnson, *The Public Library—A People's University* (New York: American Association for Adult Education, 1938). Mary L. Ely, *Why Forums?* (New York: American Association for Adult Education, 1937).

[23] Edmund deS. Brunner and E. Hsin-Pao Yang, *Rural America and the Extension Service* (New York: Bureau of Publications, Teachers College, Columbia University, 1949).

Supplementary Reading

Barnes, Harry Elmer. *Society in Transition*. New York: Prentice-Hall, 1940.
    An exposition of the great changes which have taken place in American society.
Chapin, F. Stuart. *Contemporary American Institutions*. New York: Harper & Brothers, 1935.
    A comprehensive sociological analysis of social institutions and their place in American life.
Ogburn, William F. *Social Change*. New York: The Viking Press, 1922.
    Deals with the analysis and ramifications of social change. Has an exposition of the concept of cultural lag and a chapter on resistance to invention.

CHAPTER 19

SOME MAJOR URBAN PROBLEMS

CITIES are full of problems. In the considerations thus far they have been encountered at every juncture. *Our Cities*[1] reviews a list of thirty-six problems of urban America, taking nearly half of the report. There is no place here for reviewing the many problems, however; it is more important to analyze some of them in terms of their roots in urban life and their various implications for the welfare of urban communities. Some problems are of such magnitude that they eat at the heart of urban life and reach their tentacles into much of the organized life of cities. Of these, four will be briefly analyzed— poverty, disease, delinquency, and housing.

These problems are in part inherent in the very character of cities —that is, they are concomitants of the conditions and purposes in the development of cities; they are in part the results of the concentrations and precipitates in cities; in part they are amplified by inadequacies in the structure of city life; and in part they are expressions of deficiencies in one or another aspect of democracy.

The reason for considering these problems here is twofold: to show the basis on which organization is usually built, and through an analysis of the problems to give an indication of the complexity of their interrelationships and involvements. Most urban organizations and institutions get a negative start. They begin at a place where something is out of joint, where existent processes are not working smoothly, at the point of problems. The concerted effort to solve a problem, to overcome an evil, becomes organization. The most obvious illustration is in the field of health. No one realized the significance of health as a positive quality. It was the interruption of health by disease which was the important problem. So, at the point

[1] National Resources Committee, *Our Cities: Their Role in the National Economy*, Report of the Urbanism Committee (Washington: Government Printing Office, 1937).

of solving the problem of disease, attention was focused, activity concentrated, and organization developed. In early times the efforts were crude and filled with superstition, but, as knowledge and science developed, the attack on the problem became more scientific and successful.

A greater change than this, however, has taken place. The increased scientific knowledge and resources have also increased the understanding of the problems. As a result, the attack on the problem in more recent years has come to be positive. The preservation and enhancement of health and the prevention of disease are now the purposes of a developing organization of health services. Similar radical changes in the basis of organization are taking place, to a greater or less degree, in most areas of urban functions. But the shift from a negative to a positive approach to organization is exceedingly difficult. It involves changes in concepts and purposes and a consequent modification of organization and readjustment of practices. This is part of urbanization and growth.

Here is a job for the social sciences. It deals with the areas of their knowledge and theory and calls for the use of their techniques: the analysis of trends and their implications, the accumulation of pertinent facts about the community and about its institutions, the definition of the adjustments which are required and showing how they can be made. It is in such a scientific process that the possibilities for stepping up the response of institutions to the pressures of the changing circumstances in urbanization reside. Here, too, are the potentialities of projection by which problems can be anticipated and so prevented and the resources and energy of the community and its institutions can be directed positively, through planning, toward building a better and better environment for the lives of people.

POVERTY

"Poverty stalks the city streets in good times and bad. In spite of the increasing standard of living of the city worker, there still exists a large number of individuals and families who are without the essentials necessary to sustain life on even a minimum standard."[2]

There are those who argue that some people are inherently indigent, but this cannot be substantiated as long as an urban environ-

[2] *Ibid.*, p. 55.

ment exists which makes poverty. Until environment is changed, it is more reasonable to assume that poverty is the result of environment. The four horsemen of poverty in the urban environment are unemployment, sickness, old age, and slums.

The Urban Labor Pool. One of the reasons why industry located in cities and continues to operate to a large extent in cities is to be accessible to an abundant "supply of cheap labor." A concentration of people increases the chances for filling requirements for labor. But cities have continued to draw in new people because of the traditional notion that there were greater opportunities there—a treacherous idea, true in the sense that cities use more kinds of people, untrue in that cities have not used all their labor supply. Opportunity, however, has called the failures, the untrained, the incompetent, as well as the ambitious, the capable, the alert—the "comers." The competition which exists among the members of the labor force is the keenest at the lowest level of unskilled labor. An excess in the number employable over the number that is required to do the work leaves employers in the best position for bargaining and many laborers unemployed.

Depression and shrinking employment extend poverty not only to those on the margin of employment, but also into the realm of the ordinarily economically self-sufficient.

The causes of our economic cycles may be nation-wide or even international, but it is the city, as the nerve center of the country's commerce and industry, that is most immediately affected. The stock-market crashes, the banking house calls in its loans, the factory cuts production and wages, business offices slash their overhead, the city-workers lose their jobs, interest payments on home and farm are defaulted, the banks fail, purchases are curtailed, the retailer's business slumps, orders cease, the factory stops production, and the vicious circle is complete. The depression hits hard and suddenly in the city, which is precisely the spot where lives the mass of people, both factory and white-collared workers, who are dependent on their jobs and possess little beyond their ability to work.[3]

City people are completely helpless to do anything toward the maintenance of their own lives. In the country, though the land may be poor and a person unsuccessful as a farmer, he can at least produce a meager amount of food. But the person in the city is completely dependent upon the money which comes from his job to procure even the bare essentials of life. Consequently, the social

[3] *Ibid.,* p. 55.

responsibility for poverty is obvious and inevitable. For many years this social responsibility for "relief" has been carried in the "lady bountiful" tradition by those who were more fortunate. In recent years, however, beginning with the great depression period of the 1930's, when the problem became very acute, relief or family welfare has operated largely as a public responsibility even to the extent of calling on federal government funds.

Hazards to Individuals.   To those with small incomes and those without savings, accidents, sickness, and old age represent acute hazards. These hazards are not peculiar to cities, with the exception of old age, because of the larger proportion of older people in cities combined with the fact that cities tend to discard people from their labor force at an earlier age.

Many people find themselves not only unable to meet the high cost involved in these experiences, but also destitute when income stops. Carpenter makes much of the additional fact of the greater lack of family connection of city people, with the result that they have no one to turn to in an emergency.[4] Social responsibility for industrial accidents has been recognized for many years by the operation of compensation insurance laws in the various states, whereby the one who suffers an accident while employed must be given not only complete medical and hospital service but also compensation for loss of time from his job. Unemployment, sickness, and old age have more lately been accepted as social responsibility through the state and federal social security laws, which provide compensation and pensions that have been paid for jointly by the employee, the employer, and the state. There are many, however, who are not eligible for these benefits and whose only recourse is relief through public or private family welfare agencies.

Slums.   In the slum areas of our cities, where old and broken-down dwellings no longer fit for human habitation continue to be kept in use, where rents are less but still too high for what they buy, where physical and social decay are on every hand, where dirt, disease, and despair have accumulated—here the poverty-stricken have congregated. In homes of squalor without proper furnishings or conveniences, inimical to physical and mental health, the poor are to be found.

These areas are all too often devoid of the facilities for good living,

[4] Niles Carpenter, *The Sociology of City Life* (New York: Longmans, Green and Co., 1931), pp. 286–287.

recreation, parks and playgrounds, adult education, and other opportunities, and are the settling place of much delinquency and crime.

This is the environment into which generation after generation is born, and in which, amid the surroundings of despair and the admission of helplessness, it is raised, conditioned to poverty.

The Cost of Poverty. The urban community pays a high price for its poverty. The cost is levied in three ways. First, those who are unemployed either because there are no jobs or because they are unable to do a day's work deprive the whole community of their potential productive capacity. An idle person, as well as an idle machine or an idle factory, subtracts his capacity from the total production of wealth and by so much diminishes the standard of living of all. Second, those in poverty have none of the buying power which makes the economic wheel go round. "It is not merely the existence of large numbers of poor and underprivileged families, nor the philosophic implications of economic inequality, which constitutes a basic problem of urban life. An interdependent, mass production economy rests upon mass purchasing power. Widespread poverty, therefore, threatens the stability and even the survival of such an economy and the society based upon it."[5] Third is the cost of relief, which has been a sizable sum in city budgets. From 1926 to 1937, in the cities of 100,000 or more population in the United States, expenditures for relief rose from 3.1 percent to 16.4 percent of the government expenditures. During the same period the expenditures for schools dropped from 35.6 to 29.4 percent. In 1937 six of these cities (Minneapolis, Denver, Lowell, Fall River, and Somerville) had a larger per capita cost for relief than for education, and in a number of others the difference was very slight. For all of these cities the per capita cost was $8.81, but for the cities over 500,000 it was $11.86, and for New York City it reached the astounding sum of $20.82.[6] In addition are the expenditures of private agencies and individuals, which it is impossible to estimate.

This fundamental problem of urban communities is closely interrelated with other major problems, as has already been indicated and as will further be seen.

---

[5] National Resources Committee, *op. cit.*, p. 55.

[6] Bureau of the Census, *Financial Statistics of Cities of 100,000 Population, 1937* (Washington: Government Printing Office, 1940), p. 177 and Table 17, pp. 178–181.

DISEASE

The problems of disease in the early embryonic cities of the united States were obvious and simple. They came to be, however, both complicated and difficult. As cities have grown in size and complexity, as their knowledge of health and disease has increased, and as more and more ramifications of their health problems have become apparent, the solutions to the problems have little more than kept up with their increasing complexity. Disease has become one of the most intricate, difficult, and costly of urban problems.

The persistent problems of disease are grouped here for convenience of discussion, though they are inextricably intermingled, as contagion, sanitation, water supply, facilities for cleanliness, medical services, and health education.

Contagion. Contagion was the first to be recognized as a community problem. It was attacked by quarantine, keeping those who were ill out of circulation. Later quarantine was invoked against potential carriers of disease into the cities. Epidemics of many sorts, however, were rampant periodically in the cities until medical science discovered the nature of the transmission of infections, periods of incubation, and communicability, and had developed immunization for the various diseases. The last appearance in America of the plague, which had devastated many cities throughout the world for hundreds of years, was in San Francisco as late as 1900. This was checked because the offices of the federal health service stepped in and killed a million rats in the city and twenty million ground squirrels in the neighboring county, which had been infected. Most of the epidemic diseases, such as smallpox and even diphtheria, have been conquered. "The great pestilences no longer rage in the more civilized countries, but the fact that they are excluded does not mean that they have died out." Eternal vigilance is required to keep the cities free from them. The potentialities for devastation in cities are far greater than ever before because of the concentrations of people, the range of human contacts, and the means of rapid transportation, not the least of which is the world-spanning airplane.[7]

The virus diseases are still to be controlled. New epidemics con-

[7] Howard W. Haggard, *Devils, Drugs and Doctors* (New York: Harper & Bros., 1929), p. 190.

tinue to break out, such as the widespread influenza epidemic of 1918–1919 and the virus X in southern California in 1947–1948. Some of the most serious nonepidemic contagious diseases are not yet conquered. The techniques and knowledge necessary for the eradication of tuberculosis are at hand, but the rates of tuberculosis in American cities are still significantly high. The problem is the discovery of cases, acquainting people with the nature and care of the disease, changing attitudes toward it, making diagnostic services available to all people, and providing adequate facilities for proper care of those who are infected. A few years ago a concentrated campaign was carried out against tuberculosis in the city of Detroit. All forms of publicity and education, especially the radio, were used. Mobile units carried x-ray equipment throughout the city, and the facilities for care were expanded and used to the full. As a result, in the year 1938 the death rate from tuberculosis dropped 17.5 percent.[8] In 1947–1948 the United States Public Health Service, in coöperation with local boards of health and health agencies, planned a thoroughgoing educational, diagnostic, and treatment campaign for the whole country against venereal diseases. This was possible because of changing attitudes toward these diseases and simpler and surer treatment made possible by the newer drugs.

A most forward-looking attack on the problem of health has been made in Britain's pioneer health center, called the Peckham Experiment, outside of London, where a staff of doctors and other specialists are promoting health-building and studying health in a thoroughly well-equipped building.

So contagion continues to be a serious problem of health if we are to hold the gains which have been made, meet new problems, and put into use the means that have been developed. More and more it is being recognized as a social problem with particular acuteness in urban communities, and consequently it is entrusted increasingly to public agencies.

Sanitation. In the early days each family was considered responsible for its own sanitation. It was expected to build its own privy, take care of its own garbage and rubbish, and keep the street in front of its house clean. But increasing numbers of privies were found to pollute the land, the only way to dispose of garbage and rubbish was to dump it in the street, and people refused to clean

---

[8] Paul de Kruif, *The Fight for Life* (New York: Harcourt, Brace and Company, 1938), Chap. XI.

their parts of the streets. So the problems fell to the community. Cesspools were tried, but their emptying and cleaning at the expense of the householders was little improvement. Open drains in the streets became the chief solution, but they came slowly and persisted long. Modern sewers came into use during the last half of the nineteenth century, but "at the beginning of the twentieth century Philadelphia and St. Louis had twice as much street mileage as sewer mileage, while Baltimore, New Orleans, and Mobile relied mainly on open gutters for drainage."[9] Then came the problem of the pollution of streams, rivers, and lakes into which sewage was dumped, which necessitated the development of sewage disposal plants, which have not yet caught up with the need.

The removal of garbage and refuse was haphazardly cared for until almost the turn of the century. Even now the well-organized and well-equipped refuse disposal of a city like New York breaks down after a heavy snowfall, when trucks and men are turned to snow removal and ashes are dumped at the curb and garbage burned in the streets, which remain littered with filth for weeks.

As rental dwellings, especially in the form of multiple-family buildings, increased in cities, the sanitary conditions of family dwellings became a problem. Standards of sanitation were devised and made into law. These covered all kinds of buildings, including single-family homes owned by the occupants. Inspection was organized and inspectors appointed to check up on new buildings and all rental multiple dwellings created before the sanitary codes were adopted.

Specifications for buildings because of fire hazard go back to the early days of cities. It continues as a problem with increasing implications. Not only has the matter of sanitation been added, but also adequacy of structure, for stability and strength. Even the matters of ventilation and sunlight have resulted in specific building requirements.

Many other things have been involved in the widening complexity of sanitation problems in cities. Some illustrations are: the elimination of pests such as ants, bedbugs, and flies, which seem to thrive in city conditions; the maintenance of sanitary public facilities and the inspection of facilities used by the public; the inspection of foods; the control of disease-carriers. One of the most difficult and per-

[9] Bernhard J. Stern, *Society and Medical Progress* (Princeton: Princeton University Press, 1941), p. 116.

sistent problems is keeping high standards of sanitation in public restaurants and food-dispensers. As late as 1946 a clean-up campaign in "New York City where Health Department vigilance has always been eminently high" found conditions to be exceedingly bad even in some of the very expensive eating places. In many cities throughout the rest of the country filth has been found that is utterly unbelievable.[10] One large city which has solved this problem is St. Louis, where all restaurants are required to display grade cards prominently: a large blue A indicates top safety to the eating public; a green B shows that the establishment meets most of the important conditions; and a red C means that the place will be closed within thirty days unless drastic improvements are made. The ready cooperation of the public, the prestige accruing to employees, and the final approval of those who own and operate the restaurants have raised the standards and continued superior conditions.[11]

In recent years cities have attacked the problem of smoke, which has been a particularly serious health hazard in places where there are much heavy industry and many multiple dwellings. City councils have passed laws specifying the kind of fuel which was permitted and requiring devices for the elimination of smoke. Some cities have made great progress, but in many the pollution of the air is still very bad.

One of the most spectacular successes was in St. Louis, where conditions were extremely bad. "Up to 1939, St. Louis air was saturated with the fumes of high-volatile coal from the near-by Southern Illinois mines. An occasionally windy day gave the only relief. The smoke was ruinous to vegetation, to fabrics, to human respiratory organs. There was no getting used to it; it grew steadily. For half a century the city puttered with regulatory ordinances and educational campaigns, while the air grew denser and more poisonous, and choking motorists had to turn on their lights downtown at midday."[12] Then a newspaper campaign, a citizens' committee appointed by the mayor with strong leadership, pressure on the Board of Aldermen, which passed an ordinance making unlawful the sale and use of high-volatile coal except when used with effective smoke-prevention

[10] Howard Whitman, "Disease à la Carte," *Reader's Digest*, Aug., 1947 (condensed from *Woman's Home Companion*, Dec., 1946), pp. 1–4.

[11] Alberta Williams, "Report Cards for Restaurants," *Reader's Digest*, Nov., 1947 (condensed from *Survey Graphic*, Oct., 1947), pp. 133–136.

[12] From chapter by Carlos F. Hurd in Robert S. Allen, editor, *Our Fair City* (New York: The Vanguard Press, 1947), p. 242.

appliances, and continued vigilance and enforcement solved the problem. In spite of fuel shortages during the war and the pressure of mine interests, the atmosphere of St. Louis stays clear.[13]

Water Supply. The demands of American cities for water continue to increase, for drinking, for bathing, for washing, for cleaning endless things, for sewage, for steam heating and power, for solvents and many other industrial processes. Individual family wells and town pumps were followed by water mains of wood, which did not insulate the water from the seepage of contamination to which the wells had been subject. The later use of metal and terra cotta, however, eliminated this hazard. Steam pumps and, much more recently, electric power increased the potentialities for an extended water supply.

Early waterworks were mostly initiated, constructed, owned, and operated by private companies. In 1800, of the seventeen water systems, all but one were private concerns. At the time of the Civil War there were eighty private and sixty-eight publicly owned systems. The first major system to be planned and developed by a municipality was that of New York, with the Croton Reservoir, which began operation in 1862, but it was some time before the water was available to the tenement districts. Even at this time cities such as Portland, Providence, and Milwaukee had no publicly owned and operated water systems. By 1924 only 30 percent of the 9850 waterworks in the country were private concerns, and since that time the number operated by municipalities has increased further. There are still, however, many communities whose supply of water is inadequate, especially in times of drought.

The great advance in providing an adequate supply of pure water is illustrated by the Los Angeles system, which pipes its water several hundred miles from the high Sierra mountains, and the New York system, which is supplementing its water supply from the Catskill mountains with a new system whose pipe line comes through three states.[14]

Keeping water pure has never ceased to be a problem. This has been especially true as medical research has continued to increase knowledge, which has resulted in raising standards for the purity of water. The source of water for many cities continues to be the rivers on the banks of which they are located. These streams have been

[13] *Ibid.*, pp. 242–243.
[14] Stern, *op. cit.*, pp. 113–116.

subjected to increasing pollution through the emptying of sewage by towns upstream. Early methods of purification were sedimentation, disinfection (chiefly chlorination), and simple filtration. The first sand filter in a municipal water system was installed in Poughkeepsie in 1870, but by 1914 only 40 percent of the American urban population had filtered water, and large sections of the United States are still without it, with the consequent danger to public health.[15] Even today the citizens of Philadelphia draw from their spigots what is locally called "the chlorine cocktail" from the Delaware and Schuylkill Rivers, whose bacterial content is far in excess of what is considered acceptable by the United States Public Health Service. It is "safe" only because of its heavy chemical content.[16]

Family Facilities. The facilities for health in family living have widened greatly over the years. Running water, cookstoves, wood, coal, kerosene, electricity, flush toilets, bathtubs, central heating, improved bathroom and kitchen equipment, washing machines, and mechanical refrigeration are some of these facilities. To these should be added an adequate supply of inexpensive soap, disinfectants, and antiseptics.

The use of bathing facilities was delayed by the general opposition of the medical profession, who considered hot baths dangerous and bathing of any kind in winter the cause of such serious diseases as rheumatic fever; yet a far greater deterrent has been the economic state of a large part of the population.

The real property inventory in 1934 reported that in a sample of sixty-four cities, scattered throughout the United States and excluding the oldest cities with the poorest housing, one-fourth of the dwelling units were without installed bathing facilities. In some of these cities as many as one-half the dwelling units were without these facilities; in fact, in a number of the urban communities one-fourth of the units were even without running water, and 13 percent had no indoor flush toilets.[17]

The 1940 census reports the major deficits in the accepted facilities for family dwellings. There were 22.5 percent of urban dwelling units which had no private bathing facilities, 17 percent without private flush toilets, 6.5 percent without running water. Of the oc-

[15] *Ibid.*, p. 118.
[16] Allen, *op. cit.*, pp. 59–60.
[17] Department of Commerce, *Real Property Inventory, 1934* (Washington: Government Printing Office, 1934), p. 37.

cupied dwelling units, 44 percent did not have mechanical refrigeration, 6.7 percent had no facilities whatever for keeping food, 41.8 percent had no central heating, and 6.7 percent had no facilities for heating other than portable heaters, fireplaces, or kitchen stoves. On the other hand, there were only 8.1 percent of the occupied dwelling units which were without radios. That is to say, many more families had radios than had bathing facilities or flush toilets, almost as many as had running water, more than twice as many as had central heating, and one and two-thirds as many as had mechanical refrigeration. The record of cities of 50,000 or more population is slightly better. There is much to be desired in the health facilities of families in American urban communities; in fact, there is a strong inference that some other things are generally regarded as of more importance than health by city families.[18]

Health Services. It is a far cry from the public workhouses with their one-room infirmaries, which were the hospitals of the American cities in the early days, to the great, modern, scientifically planned and equipped buildings which are today's hospitals; from the poorly equipped doctors with their meager knowledge to the great number of well-equipped physicians and surgeons, the growing variety of specialists, the many well-trained registered nurses, and the many kinds of technicians; from the few simple natural remedies and medicines to an ever-increasing array of antiseptics, germicides, anesthetics, antibiotics, hormones, glandular derivatives, and many other kinds of materia medica; from the virtual absence of mechanical devices to many kinds of diagnostic, analytic, and therapeutic apparatus; from no laboratory facilities or chemical analysis to thoroughly equipped laboratories which make most complicated analyses of many sorts and are operated by highly skilled technicians.

Through these magnificent developments medical services beyond the wildest dreams of a century ago are at hand in American cities. But as the personnel, facilities, and techniques of medical service have increased, so also has the cost of medical care increased beyond the ability of most city people to pay for it. The private practice of medicine in all its forms, including hospital service, has increased the concentration of these services in cities, especially larger cities where there is a greater market. As a result, the rural areas, for

[18] Bureau of the Census, *Sixteenth Census of the United States, 1940: Housing:* Vol. II, Part I, "U.S., Summary," pp. 18, 42, 80, 82, 84, 92, 96, 100, 130, 138, 140.

the most part, are deprived of any such extensive services. This does not mean, however, that all is well in cities. Families with high incomes are able to purchase whatever services they may require. Those with the lowest incomes, if they are willing to accept charity and if they know how to obtain free services, can be well cared for in clinics and city hospitals. These free services, however, are, for the most part, made a responsibility of doctors who must otherwise earn their living. The great numbers of families whose incomes are in the middle range cannot obtain the services which cities offer because they do not know they exist, or do not know how to obtain them, or still believe in incantations or patent medicines, or cannot pay for them, or, if they do attempt to get them, find themselves hopelessly indebted by the costs.

The studies made by the Committee on the Costs of Medical Care revealed that, in spite of the large volume of free work done by hospitals, health departments, and individual practitioners, and in spite of the sliding scale of charges, half the individuals of the lowest income group receive no medical care whatever, and that the percentage decreases as the income increases, but that of all the people some 40 percent receive no medical, dental, or eye care.[19] The New York Academy of Medicine acknowledges that deficiencies in medical care account for more than half of the avoidable deaths of mothers at childbirth. The United States Public Health Service has stated that more than half of the sick in the crowded centers of our cities have no medical care.[20]

Cities, which have made possible highly developed medical services, have at the same time made these services unavailable to great numbers of their people. But they have done another thing which is perhaps of more fundamental significance.

Many experiments have been made in the prepayment of medical care under professional sponsorship in group practice, through cooperatives or other forms of consumer sponsorship, and under community sponsorship.[21] The Blue Cross and other hospitalization prepayment plans have been widely organized and have made needed hospital service possible for thousands of people. More recently surgical services have been added to the prepayment plans. These

[19] Committee on the Costs of Medical Care, *Medical Care for the American People* (Chicago: The University of Chicago Press, 1932), p. 9.

[20] *Doctors, Dollars and Disease*, Public Affairs Pamphlet No. 10 (Washington: Public Affairs Committee, 1937), p. 5.

[21] Committee on the Costs of Medical Care, *op. cit.*, Chap. IV.

experiments have, for the most part, been eminently satisfactory, though they have included only a very small part of the population. Federal legislation proposing to organize medical services throughout the nation on the prepayment basis has had bitter opposition from the organized medical profession and has been defeated. The problem of making medical services available to all the people is very acute.

This problem in the last few years has taken a new turn which reflects an important change in the general attitude toward health. During the war it became necessary to scrape the bottom of the barrel of the labor force to get the essential work done. Workdays lost were recognized as a serious problem because they cut down production. During the continued full employment after the war the situation has been essentially the same. Health has come to be recognized more than ever as a social problem. Not only because illness deprives society of the productive capacity of many people, but also because the cost of illness is a heavy burden on society, the prevention of disease has become a matter of grave public concern. This concern has expressed itself in a gradual expansion in the support of public health programs. In 1910 the cities of 100,000 or more population put 4.6 percent of their expenditures into health and hospitals; by 1945 the cities over 10,000 had doubled this percentage, and the expenditures continue in about this proportion (see pp. 286 f.). There is no evidence, however, to indicate that the amazing proportion of the expenditures for medical care that was spent for patent medicines, 10 percent, and cultists, 3.4 percent (as found by the Committee on the Costs of Medical Care),[22] has greatly declined since the studies were made. With an increased number of persons well trained in public health, with improved equipment and practical patterns of public health organization, the potentialities are present for extensive improvement in health and preventive medicine whenever city people are ready to accept and pay for them.

Health Education. The improvement of health depends upon the education of people in the area of health. If people no longer were deprived of medical service because they could not pay for it, and public health services were available to all, until their attitudes and understanding of health were changed they would still be unable to avail themselves of the services.

The job of health education in American cities is stupendous.

[22] *Op. cit.,* p. 15.

There are people of all kinds, of many social and economic levels, of many different cultural backgrounds, of many ages, and they all need some kind of health education. Positive attitudes toward health need to be developed. An understanding that health is far more than the absence of disease must be acquired. The principles of nutrition will have to be put into practice. The methods of disease prevention should be known. Good health habits need to be developed. Correct and effective methods of home treatment should be understood. How to recognize serious symptoms is necessary knowledge, as well as how to use the resources for medical service which the city affords.

A start has been made toward solving this problem. Health education is becoming a part of the curriculum of public schools. Health centers have devised many ways of reaching people with health information. Clinics are putting more emphasis on the educational part of their activities. Public health nurses are giving more and more attention to education in their work. Wherever common interests and problems such as care of babies make it possible, groups are given instruction. But the need is so great, and the resources, the facilities, and the trained health educators are so limited, that the problem grows faster than it can be met.

DELINQUENCY AND CRIME

Crime and delinquency are exceedingly complicated, as increasing knowledge and understanding have revealed. Along with better understanding has come a changed attitude toward crime, criminals, and delinquents. It is no longer tenable to think of crime simply as the overt behavior of individuals; rather, it is the manifestation of mental illness, for the most part the result of social conditioning—that is, the social illness of the community. Crime as such cannot be considered here, but some of the important sociological factors which are involved in crime and delinquency in urban communities will be discussed because here is a serious problem of American cities.

Characteristics of Urban Crime. Statistics of crime in cities have only recently been kept in anything like comprehensive fashion. It is difficult, however, to use these for more than very broad generalizations because they tempt anyone to easy analysis. A few of these generalizations, however, would seem to have significance here.

There is more crime and there are higher crime rates in cities. Crime follows the general pattern of concentration in cities, particularly because the circumstances of city life are more conducive to crime. There are evidences of a difference in the character of crime in urban and rural areas. A larger proportion of the crimes in cities are against property and in the country against persons. A large proportion of crimes of violence against persons in cities arise in situations in which crimes against property are primary, as, for example, when a man caught stealing may shoot and kill a policeman. This leads to two tentative interpretations.

First, basically people are much the same whether they live in cities or in the country. They are subject to the same emotions, jealousy, fear, hate, revenge, and so forth. They meet frustrations and conflicts. In the many areas of human relationships some, unable to cope with emotional stresses and strains, express themselves in acts of violence. In cities, however, human relationships, to a considerable degree, are impersonalized, which in turn tends to lessen the likelihood of reactions of direct personal violence.

Second, many things in cities tend to encourage and facilitate crimes against property. When anyone in the city desires food, clothing, shelter, transportation, recreation, or any of the other goods or services and has no money to purchase such things, the only other means of getting them by direct action is to take them. Cities are filled with property, from the vegetables and fruits on outdoor stands and valuable jewelry in store windows to money in the messengers' bags or behind the tellers' desks in the banks, or automobiles standing at the curb. Then standards of living in cities are so completely manifested by personal possessions—fine clothes, jewelry, fur coats, cars, and the rest—that the urge to possession is excited by the sights and sensations on every hand. Most of the crime is not so simple, however; it is devious and indirect—exploitation, extortion, bribery, fraud, falsifying of accounts, and many others. Cities are "a natural" for all sorts of crime; it is easier to escape detection and apprehension in the confusion and in the crowds and to sink into the oblivion which cities afford.

There is some evidence to indicate further that crime is related to economic conditions. The fluctuations of crime which occur in cities tend to correspond to the cycles of prosperity and depression. When there are much poverty and unemployment, there is more crime. Rising prices also tend to be accompanied by increases in crime. It would seem that the roots of crime are deep in urban society.[23]

It has already been seen that the geography of delinquency is very similar to that of the various other ills of city life in the social geography of cities (see pp. 191 f. and Fig 21). Shaw found in his studies that all crime in cities tends to fall into the same spatial patterns.[24] This would add further to the evidence that crime, to a considerable extent, has its roots in the many social evils that are present in city life.

Crime in cities is, in general, decreasing, though trends are not regular nor equal. In the major classes of crime the average numbers of offenses showed decreases from 1931–1934 to 1935–1939, except in three categories where there were increases—rape 31.8 percent, aggravated assault 1.2 percent, and larceny 8.1 percent. Explanations of these changes are difficult to make, although the decreases are no doubt due in part to the stimulation of law enforcement by the activities of the Federal Bureau of Investigation.[25]

Criminals of Cities. Facts which are available seem to indicate that crime rates are higher among migrants to the cities and their children than among those born and bred to the urban environment. Many people whose patterns of living and human relationships have been developed amid rural surroundings have great difficulty with the adjustment that it is necessary to make to life in cities. Cities crowded with people and with buildings are oppressive. The bigness of things and the rapidity of motion are terrifying. The impersonality of everything is disheartening and bewildering. How do you find your way around? Where can you get a job? How can you find a place to live? The newcomer soon learns that many people will try to cheat him. The policemen tell him to keep moving. Everything seems to be against him. Values are different. Carpenter makes

---

[23] Niles Carpenter, *op. cit.*, Chap. IX, contains a more extended discussion of most of these points in this section on crime. Some basic statistics are given in Noel P. Gist and L. A. Halbert, *Urban Society*, third edition (New York: Thomas Y. Crowell Company, 1948), pp. 347–351. Statistics of crime in cities are in the Uniform Crime Reports of the Federal Bureau of Investigation.

[24] Clifford R. Shaw, *Delinquency Areas* (Chicago: The University of Chicago Press, 1929), pp. 130–135.

[25] Mabel A. Elliott and Francis E. Merrill, *Social Disorganization*, revised edition (New York: Harper & Brothers, 1941), pp. 943–948, gives statistics on the varieties, trends, and costs of crime in cities of 25,000 population and over.

much of this "culture-shock," which, he holds, "evokes anti-social behavior, that is to say criminalism."[26]

Another group of criminals consists of those who take the "easy way" to get their living and find cities more profitable places to ply their trade—the pickpockets, loan sharks, burglars, "gold brick" sellers, and the rest. These are cold-blooded and ruthless, disregarding the rights or welfare of others and disrespectful of the law except to keep out of its clutches.

Then there are those who commercialize vice, especially gambling and prostitution. No longer are such businesses blatantly flaunted in the city's face, as they often were a half century ago. They operate under cover, sometimes with protection at a high cost. Gambling runs from the peddling of numbers in the streets for the number rackets and the illegal slot machine in the back rooms of pool halls and saloons to the magnificently furnished gambling places with all the equipment of a Monte Carlo. Prostitution no longer operates in segregated districts in American cities, and various forms of control which have been tried have been, for the most part, abandoned. Perhaps now more women operate as individuals than work for commercialized houses as formerly. Recent surveys show that since the war commercialized prostitution is coming back in many cities and that by 1949 the war gains had been largely wiped out.[27] Large numbers of visitors and young adults in cities, looser family ties, many mentally unstable individuals, the pecuniary basis of leisure activities in city life, and the high degree of mobility and anonymity are the explanations which Carpenter gives for the continuation of prostitution.

The three types of large-scale organized crime in modern times have been kidnaping, which has almost disappeared since the passage of the federal law making it a capital offense; bootlegging, which ceased to be extremely profitable after the repeal of prohibition; and racketeering, which had its heyday in the prohibition period but continues in old and new forms.

Racketeering is the big business of crime. It is the most insidious, the most involved, and the most difficult to deal with of all crime. Sixteen major varieties of rackets have been classified: pinball

[26] Carpenter, *op. cit.*, pp. 316–318, 325.
[27] Paul M. Kinsie, "To Combat the Return of Commercialized Prostitution," *The American City*, Aug., 1949, p. 102.

games, policy or number games, race tracks, commercialized vice, loan sharks, night clubs, union and industrial shakedowns, real estate, hot ice (diamonds), stocks and bonds, gambling (dice, cards, lotteries, etc.), produce and other goods, garages and automobiles, abortions, gun running and counterfeiting, narcotics.[28]

By organization and the control of certain essential materials or services, racketeers have been able to dictate whatever terms they chose to small businesses and exact their tribute in the process. The penalty for opposition to their system has been business failure, or bombing of the premises, or even killing in some cases. The violence has been easy so long as there have been gangsters who for a price would do anything.

Racketeering has entered the medical profession through venereal disease and abortion, and the legal profession through "ambulance chasing" and the defense of those involved in racketeering who are apprehended by the law. The police are constantly subject to the pressures and the temptations of the racketeers. The law has been largely impotent against them. This is due to the inadequacies of the laws to deal with the kinds of situations which are developed, the cleverness of organized groups in escaping detection, the great difficulty in finding people who will testify against them in court because of fear of direct retaliation, and the fact that it is practically impossible to get at those who are really responsible, carrying on as they do behind several echelons of accomplices. Consequently, though everyone may know that an Al Capone is the guilty person in crimes of many sorts, the only way that he can be reached is by the federal government through the FBI on charges of income tax evasion.[29]

In its more overt and violent forms racketeering has waned in American cities; but it still goes on, especially in the largest cities, though it has greater difficulties with the lessening of cutthroat competition among small business concerns, the greater vigilance of the police, and the greater consideration in the protection of the little man. During the war period, however, when goods were scarce, there was an upsurge in the form of black markets and tie-ins, and since the war many strikes have had elements of racketeering on both sides. The revelations of the Senate Crime Investigating Com-

[28] Morton Mooney, *Crime Incorporated* (New York: Whittlesey House, 1935), Chap. III; quoted by Elliott and Merrill, *op. cit.*, p. 939.
[29] See Elliott and Merrill, *op. cit.*, Chaps. VII and XXXIII.

mittee under the chairmanship of Senator Estes Kefauver in 1950 and 1951 astounded the American people. Crime was found to be organized on a nation-wide basis, and to have insinuated its power and influence into the political life, especially in the large cities.

Apprehension of Criminals. The detection of crime and the apprehension of criminals are complicated, technical, and expensive jobs in modern cities. They involve such things as a large and well-organized police force; a staff of detectives, with a bureau of criminal identification; many special groups for particular jobs, such as a pickpocket squad, a squad to search for stolen automobiles, a homicide squad, special emergency groups with special equipment; training schools; and technical research laboratories.

Flagrant and violent crimes are, in most cities, detected most expeditiously, and evidence is collected and scientifically analyzed with great rapidity. The records of city police departments are excellent. Minor and more recurrent crimes present a different problem. Policy, judgment, the adequacy of police personnel and equipment are involved. Keeping such offenses under control is considered the important thing. General corruption in city police forces, common a quarter of a century or more ago, is seldom found in American cities today. Occasionally, however, individuals may be guilty of extortion or receiving bribes, but their chances of carrying on such operations for long are very remote.

By and large it is becoming less and less possible to get away with crime of major significance in cities, though petty crime and racketeering still present difficulties. On the whole, the remedial part of the problem of crime has been reasonably well taken care of, but the prevention of crime, which necessitates getting at many of the very roots of society and its economic life, has made but little progress.

Juvenile Delinquency. The increase of delinquency among young people in the teen ages has become one of the greatest concerns in American cities. Much research has been carried on with respect to many aspects of the problem. Countless articles have been written and books published about it. Many activities have been developed to do something about it. In spite of all these, however, delinquency continues.

Failures have come, for the most part, because the character of urbanization and its effect upon the lives of children and young people have not been recognized. Urbanization has done several things to modify very radically the circumstances in which children live.

When the industrial age took work and earning a living out of homes, it did two things: it began the breakdown of the family unit with all its members as a coöperative group, in which each person had his or her responsibility to the work in hand and to each other as partners in this work; and it separated the basic economic provision for the welfare of the family and its members from the direct participation of the members of the family. As women and other members of the family group followed men out of the home to work, the coöperative unity was broken down still further. When child labor came to be frowned upon and later prohibited by law, children were completely separated from the circumstances of responsibility to the family group. Home came to be a place where shelter, food, and clothes were furnished in a more or less pleasant and satisfactory way, but a place which was run by adults who laid down the rules, set the specifications, and made certain demands. These demands were, for the most part, isolated jobs with no particular bearing, as far as the child was concerned, on his own interests or welfare and generally unpleasant, and they interfered with what usually seemed more important and more desirable things to do.

Other sections of living have also gone out of homes. Education has gone to schools, recreation to playgrounds, religion to churches, associations to neighborhood houses or other places, sickness to hospitals, etc., etc. As these experiences have gone out of homes into the community, the process of specialization that is fundamental to urban life has taken hold. Special organizations and institutions have arisen with their specially trained professional personnel, who with groups of adults run the institutions, establish the policies, and make the programs. So children and young people, wherever they go, find themselves in an adult-made world, with little if anything to say about what their experiences will be. There are exceptions, of course, in the way that programs are carried out, but in the main this is the way it is.

But "the normal child is individualistic, egoistic, thoughtless, and selfish. Only by patient effort, by precept and example, does the child learn to be unselfish, obedient, kind, and altruistic, and to respect private property."[30] And the circumstances of urban life are not conducive to such learning. Young people with but a feeble

---

[30] Elliott and Merrill, *op. cit.*, p. 114. See also John R. Ellingston, "New Police Methods with Children," *The American City,* Jan., 1949, pp. 91–93.

spark of initiative, enthusiasm, and capacity find it easy to conform, to abide by the rules, to slip into the adult-made patterns of living. But those in whom initiative is strong, and energy and capacity a flame, stand it so long and then revolt. Often this means breaking the school windows, stealing the things they want but cannot get, or stepping out of bounds from the conventional patterns.

There are many evidences which make it clear that young people revolt, fundamentally, in order to have something to say about the world in which they live. Thrasher found this in his extensive study of gangs.[31] He says: "Gangs represent the spontaneous effort of boys to create a society for themselves." Ganging is a natural phenomenon of human association. Where leadership emerges and the desire for new experience is strong, these tenuous associations become strongly organized. Thrasher found the gangs of Chicago in their destructive and antisocial forms in the areas where social ills of all kinds were concentrated and where constructive activities and facilities were largely lacking, just as later Shaw[32] found juvenile delinquency in the same kinds of areas (see pp. 176 f.). Gangs are not always bad. The differences seem to be in the general environment and in the kind of sympathetic and helpful adult associates which they háve. Predatory and terrorizing as many of the boy groups may be, they have their origin in the spontaneous play groups for which communities have made no provision.

"Cellar clubs" is the popular designation of the indigenous social clubs of young men past high-school age which are to be found in some sections of the large cities. It has been estimated that there are 5000 or more in New York City. To escape from their crowded tenements, the poolrooms, and the streets, these young men pool their resources to rent a basement of a tenement house so that they can have "rooms of their own." They clean it up, paint it, and equip it with the second-hand furniture they can afford, including a radio. Here they hold their weekly dances with their girls and guest couples. Most of their evenings are spent here talking, listening to the radio, playing ping-pong or cards. Sometimes there are other activities: talks, special parties, athletic events, or coöperation in community affairs. Some of the clubs may not be up to the generally

[31] Frederic M. Thrasher, *The Gang: A Study of 1,313 Gangs in Chicago*, second revised edition (Chicago: The University of Chicago Press, 1936), especially Chaps. II, III, and V.

[32] Shaw, *op. cit.*, pp. 202–206.

accepted standards of behavior, but they are far from being the "dens of iniquity" which they have been called by some unknowing newspaper reporters. A study made of those in the Henry Street district of New York[33] found these clubs to be important in the lives of their members, the center of most of their activities, the gathering place which enabled friends to stick together. Petty gambling went on in most of them, beer and wine were served at the big parties, but seldom was hard liquor permitted. Rules were strict about conduct. Girls could come in almost any time, but a single pair could not be there alone, and any misconduct would lose a boy his membership. A federation of the clubs was formed in this district to raise standards, to protect the groups against misunderstanding and police interference, and to arrange interclub athletics and other programs.

During the war period and since there have sprung up spontaneously all over the country "teen canteens" and "teen centers." They have come not only in communities which had no recreation programs for young people but also where recreation leaders had assumed that programs were adequate and sound. "Young people are breaking away from the type of program that comes all tied up in a neat little bundle, the planning of which is dominated by adults."[34] They want to be responsible, to plan and carry out on their own. They will take their communities as partners, but not as Santa Clauses. The young people want adult help, but not adult domination. They want the coöperation of their communities, not their paternalism. A sample study of the teen centers across the country revealed two important things: first, they were successful, and they continued to be so, in a direct relationship to the degree to which they were actually operated by the initiative and efforts of the young people themselves; second, as they continued, the young people became less and less interested in their own enjoyment, especially dancing to the music of their juke boxes and using their snack bars, as they became more and more absorbed in service activities in their communities. In localities where there are a number of teen centers, they have affiliated in youth councils to arrange events in which all the centers may participate, such as dramatics, song fes-

[33] Emeric Kurtaugh and George Stoney, *Rooms of Their Own* (New York: Survey Department, Henry Street Settlement, 1939).

[34] Louise D. Yuill, "Teen Centers and the Adult Community," *Sociology and Social Research,* Vol. 32, No. 1, p. 519 (Sept.–Oct. 1947).

tivals, talent shows, and excursions, and to participate with adults in community planning.[35]

This is by no means the whole of the problem of juvenile delinquency in American urban communities. Such factors as intelligence, physical limitations, and emotional disturbances in youngsters must also be recognized and dealt with. Many factors, also, in the community are significant. Probably the most deep-seated factor is the socio-psychological conditioning that grows out of the home and family life of children. The basic changes in the circumstances of the life of children which have been discussed here, however, are at the heart of this serious problem of cities.

Supplementary Reading

Cabot, Hugh. *The Patient's Dilemma: The Quest for Social Security in America.* New York: Reynal and Hitchcock, 1940.
> An analysis of the problems of health from the point of view of those who are ill.

Committee on the Costs of Medical Care. *Medical Care for the American People.* Chicago: The University of Chicago Press, 1932.
> The summary of a most extensive study of medical care in the United States.

Elliott, Mabel A., and Merrill, Francis E. *Social Disorganization,* third edition. New York: Harper & Brothers, 1950.
> A compendium of the basic problems of social life in terms of individuals, families, and communities.

Healy, William, and Bronner, Augusta. *New Light on Delinquency and Its Treatment.* New Haven: Yale University Press, 1936.
> A comparative study of urban delinquents and nondelinquent siblings, revealing the impact of urban conditions on the family in creating the attitudes and reactions leading to delinquent behavior.

Motley, Willard. *Knock on Any Door.* New York: D. Appleton-Century Co., 1947.
> Fiction, but an exceedingly realistic story of the impact of urban environment in the making of a criminal.

National Resources Committee. *Our Cities: Their Role in the National Economy.* Washington: Government Printing Office, 1937.
> A concise statement of the many important problems of American cities.

[35] *Ibid.,* pp. 519–526. Wilbur C. Hallenbeck and Louise D. Yuill, "Fitting the Adult Community into a Youth Recreation Program," *Teachers College Record,* Vol. 46, pp. 110–116 (Nov., 1944).

Pearse, Innes H., and Crocker, Lucy H. *The Peckham Experiment: A Study of the Living Structure of Society*. New Haven: Yale University Press, 1947.

The theory and description of this forward-looking experiment in community health development.

Smith, Bruce. *Police Systems in the United States*. New York: Harper & Brothers, 1940.

A basic work which looks at crime and delinquency from the point of view of the police and their operations.

Stern, Bernhard J. *Society and Medical Progress*. Princeton: Princeton University Press, 1941.

The story of the development of medical science and the train of emerging problems of health.

CHAPTER 20

PROBLEMS OF HOUSING

HOUSES are the shelter where the basic institution—the family—finds the locus of its life and functions; hence, in any society, they are of paramount importance. This is particularly true in temperate zones, where civilization is most advanced, and under conditions of city life, because houses must be more protective and more substantial. There is abundant evidence that inadequate and poor housing has greatly hampered family life and is among the roots of many of the acute problems of cities.

Shelter has always been one of man's serious problems. In the early days in America, building a house required gathering and preparing all the materials as well as the actual construction by the family itself. This took much time and energy away from obtaining the food and fiber that were essential to the life of the members of the families. In villages, craftsmen of various types began to be available for house-building, and so money was required to hire them. In cities, building became big business involving many specialists, and many houses were constructed for investment rather than use as an increasing proportion of dwellings were rented by the families which occupied them.

Housing has always lagged behind the need, both in quantity and in quality. The lag in quantity is inherent in the situation, for people need dwelling places before they are able to meet the costs of either ownership or rent. The lag in quality lies in the relationship between the rapid technical developments in building and in facilities of living, and the fact that dwellings last too long and are not usually considered expendable goods. The necessity for prolonging the use of outworn housing continues because a new supply is not provided with sufficient rapidity, because the amortization of capital investment is delayed too long, and because conditions of need for housing make it possible to extend use beyond the degree of deterioration which should require expendability. The result is an increasing gap between the housing in use and the technical possibilities of good housing. People in the cities became aware of the present housing problems as attention was directed to city slums and their very bad housing conditions through the persistent efforts of Jacob Riis and many others. Much has been written about these conditions, and a good deal has been done about them in one way or another, but city slums continue to exist and to be the focal points of the worst evils of city life.

The long-accumulating deficit in urban housing has been greatly accentuated in recent years. With all production, housing fell off during the depression years. Building of private houses practically stopped during the war because materials were not available except for emergency housing to take care of families whose workers were engaged in the expanding war plants. Following the war, there was a sudden increase in the number of families and children, due to the marriages delayed by the war. It has been estimated that some 4,000,000 homes were immediately needed for veterans and that from 12,000,000 to 18,000,000 homes would be required for the whole country in the ten years following the war.[1] And yet in 1946 only 453,800 permanent dwelling units were completed, and in the first six months of 1947 city building permits actually declined 14,000 compared with 1946.[2] By the close of 1947, however, 849,000 dwelling units had been started; in 1948, there were 931,000; in 1949, 1,025,000; and 1950 will, in all likelihood, see 1,200,000 dwelling units under way, although most of these houses are beyond the range of the vast body of moderate-income workers in cost.

This, in general, is the situation, and it raises several questions which should be understood: What are the basic problems in housing? What is good housing? Where are the difficulties in producing dwellings? Is home ownership possible and practical? What is the place of public housing?

BASIC PROBLEMS

As the deficiency in housing has become more acute in recent years, other aspects of the problems have been obscured, especially

[1] Charles Abrams, *A Housing Program for America* (New York: League for Industrial Democracy, 1946), p. 6.

[2] *Housing: Puny Giant* (New York: The Wall Street Journal, 1947), p. 3.

the increasing inability to produce houses for low-income families, the constant deterioration of dwellings, which tends to add to slums more rapidly than they can be removed, and the recognition of the characteristics of good housing. This consideration of urban housing will deal with these basic problems: obsolescence, speculative land values, taxes, and the instability of residential areas.

Obsolescence. The median age of urban dwellings in the United States in 1940 was 26.1 years; 13 percent were over fifty years old and 3 percent more than eighty years old, but this 3 percent was more than a million homes.[3] There were 11.5 percent of the urban dwellings in need of major repairs. This, with the 17.1 percent without private baths, was 28.6 percent which was certainly bad housing. In the cities, in 1940, 62.5 percent of the dwellings were occupied by tenants,[4] and the average monthly rent was $24.60. In 1930, 56.6 percent of families were tenants, and the median rent was $32.06. Tenants increased, but rents were almost 25 percent lower in 1940. The question arises, how could the average rents in cities be so low? There were about as many dwellings which rented for $4 per month or less (1.9 percent) as rented for $75 or more (2.1 percent).[5] The answer is that there were many old, dilapidated, and poorly equipped dwellings in cities which could only be rented for the smallest sums. There were 1,210,681 tenant-occupied urban dwellings in 1940 which rented for less than $10 per month.[6]

This matter of the aging and deterioration of housing beyond the point of decent use, the problem of obsolescence, is a concomitant of two other factors. First is the inadequacy of the supply of new houses. When the available dwelling units approach being occupied 100 percent (urban dwellings were 95.3 percent occupied in 1940),[7] it is obviously necessary to keep in use every possible unit. There must be some cushion of vacancy to absorb the constant movements in a mobile population. An additional important aspect of this factor in the problem is that the new dwellings which are produced are in the medium and upper rental cost ranges, leaving a pressure on the continued use of old and deteriorated housing to meet the requirements for low-rental housing. Second, no legal controls have

[3] Bureau of the Census, *Sixteenth Census of the United States, 1940: Housing:* Vol. II, Part 1, "U.S., Summary," p. 71.
[4] *16th Census, 1940: Housing:* First Series, "U.S., Summary," pp. 4, 5.
[5] *16th Census, 1940: Housing:* Vol. II, Part 1, pp. 54–56.
[6] *Ibid.,* p. 54.
[7] *16th Census, 1940: Housing:* First Series, "U.S., Summary," p. 3.

been established with regard to obsolescence per se; consequently, the only factors which in any way control obsolescence are entirely secondary. When housing has deteriorated to the point where major repairs and remodeling are necessary to make it habitable, it can be controlled by building regulations which require remodeled housing to meet the current standards. If the cost of the required alterations is greater than is economically justified by the potential rent of the remodeled dwellings, they are abandoned and "boarded up." Another contributory factor is so-called "slum clearance," which takes out of use all deteriorated dwellings, but this is contingent on changes in land use. City plans may call for the establishment of parks or playgrounds, or they may require land for other municipal uses. Occasionally the plans call for housing. In any case the land must be purchased from the many owners of the small parcels through condemnation procedures, the dwellings torn down, and the ground cleared for the new use. Sometimes the clearance of bad housing areas is done by private business to make way for a factory or a housing development. The difficulties in this instance are greater because the many pieces of land must be purchased in secret to avoid price-boosting, unless arrangements can be made to use the city's power of condemnation. In either case, when housing is built, rentals will be higher to cover the many items of cost, even though it is public housing or publicly subsidized private housing.

Other problems have significant influences as handicaps to solving the problem of obsolescence in American urban communities.

Speculative Land Values. Since urban land values are predominantly speculative rather than real, the owners of the land are always holding it to benefit from the unearned increment—that is, to sell it for a higher price than was paid for it. The condition is most acute in the area adjacent to the downtown retail business center, where expectation of financial gain through the sale of property for business purposes is greatest and where dwellings are allowed to deteriorate rapidly. In most situations the hope for big profits of this kind is entirely unjustified, but the situation fosters a disregard for aging dwellings either for residence use or for investment income.

Taxes. The basis of urban taxation is property, as has already been pointed out (p. 289). The greater burden of taxes is levied on the improvements which are put on the land; hence the profitableness of such improvements must be assured. When it comes to housing, this influence is all toward relatively high rents, especially as building costs have increased. Taxes are recognized as a deterrent to housing for low and medium rents, so that in the case of extensive development some kind of tax concession is often made for private as well as public housing. Since housing developments increase the number of available dwellings, they increase either populations or, at least, population concentrations. This inevitably necessitates the increase of many city services—fire and police protection, garbage disposal, schools, and many others—so that in turn the cost to the city is increased. So, when tax concessions are made, the increased cost must be distributed to other property. The present basis of taxation serves to discourage housing developments or to increase the inequality of urban taxation.

Instability of Residential Areas. Houses have been built one by one over a long period of time in most residential areas. Often the older houses have markedly deteriorated before the latest are built. Without restrictions as to land use, business and light industry have been interspersed with dwellings, making for earlier deterioration. Zoning laws in cities (see p. 547) have provided some protection to neighborhoods in recent years by designating the kinds of structures and their use which are permitted in each area. There are several difficulties in depending on zoning to accomplish neighborhood stability. The zoning specifications usually grow out of the use patterns which have already been established, so that they are of only limited help except in the areas of future development. The regulations are seldom drawn up with reference to comprehensive neighborhood planning, although in the places where this has happened a substantial stability has been established. Then zoning laws are subject to amendment and have been changed in many places where adequate pressure has been developed. The pressure always comes at the point where individual landowners consider that their potential profits from the sale of the land have been seriously limited by the use to which the land is restricted. The welfare and stability of the whole neighborhood are seldom the first criteria.

The most promising experiment for the stabilization of residential areas is by a combination of neighborhood planning and development as a unit through which a whole area is comprehensively planned and built up as a single project. In such procedures zoning is automatically taken care of. When dwellings are built in row units or in groups of detached houses, construction costs can be cut and provision made for wholesale purchase and distribution of utilities and coöperative maintenance. Under such plans stability can be established and continued over long periods while flexibility is maintained for public or private housing and for low-, medium-, or high-rental dwellings.[8] A good stable neighborhood is an essential part of good housing.

GOOD HOUSING

The primary factors influencing personality are the human relationships within the family group and the place where these relationships are centered.

Homes are the major factor in human environment—whether measured in terms of time, space, or the importance of functions carried on there.

To the individual it is the place where he belongs. It shelters him from the elements, protects his personal property, and is the only place he can expect to find privacy. For the family it is the housekeeping unit. The home must provide space and facilities for sleep and relaxation, for preparation of food and care of clothing, for personal cleanliness, for recreation and social life, for procreation and for the training of children, for every-day health requirements.[9]

Families are greatly concerned about their dwellings; they realize their importance and the satisfactions which they can contribute to living, so that obtaining a good home becomes one of the strongest incentives to the family members. But good housing is not only a matter of great concern to families; it is also an important concern of communities because the development and welfare of their people are their chief asset.

Under the circumstances of urban life many families are frustrated in their ambition to have good houses. Incomes, in a large proportion of urban families, are too small to permit the payment of rent for or the purchase of good houses in terms of the cost of current production. Even if incomes were sufficient, however, there would be nowhere nearly enough houses to go round. Underlying these important aspects of the problem is the fact that adequate and realistic standards and specifications of a good house are still to be

---

[8] For a fuller explanation and illustration, see Catherine Bauer, *A Citizen's Guide to Public Housing* (Poughkeepsie: Vassar College, 1940), pp. 53–63. The Neighborhood Unit Formula is explained in Clarence Arthur Perry, *Housing for the Machine Age* (New York: Russell Sage Foundation, 1939), Chap. III; the following chapters discuss the application.

[9] Bauer, *op. cit.*, p. 2.

worked out; a number of important partial specifications, however, have been made.

Houses for Family Living. What a good house is depends on what the house is to be used for. The answer to this question involves a comprehensive sociological analysis of the character, functions, and behavior of modern urban families, a job which so far has been done only in part.

One of the most helpful attempts to apply the available knowledge about urban families to the requirements for their housing was made by a conference of capable and interested people held at Rye (New York) in November, 1946, under the auspices of the Woman's Foundation, a report of which was published in a pamphlet under the title *Houses for Family Living*.[10] The pamphlet starts with a statement of the following characteristics of the "new family": The breadwinner goes out of the home to work and establishes the family standard of living by the amount of money he earns. Families are smaller, marriage comes later, but life expectancy is longer. Family incomes are spent for a wide range of necessary goods and services, and the wife is the purchasing agent. Children are economic liabilities and costly to raise. Families no longer have any importance as productive units. The family's unique reason for being is taken to be producing tomorrow's generation and being the major influence in forming the personality of the future citizens. The difficulties in bearing and rearing children are great; so our homes must be built and our cities rebuilt to offer the maximum advantages for family living.

There follows an analysis of the various periods in the "natural history of family living." The *early years* are the period during which the young couple live alone. The *crowded years* cover the period during which the babies arrive and last until the youngest has entered school. The *peak years* are crowded with people and with activity as children grow through their teens into adulthood. Then come the quiet *later years*, with their empty house. During each period the needs and the problems of families are different, and hence their requirements for their houses are different. Meeting these needs and providing the housing requirements must be the basis for making possible a satisfactory way of family living.

---

[10] Frederick Gutheim, *Houses for Family Living* (New York: The Woman's Foundation, 1948).

We must face up to the issue of housing as a vital element in family living. Without an acceptable solution to the housing question, all of the other remedies for family troubles—for divorce, the low birth rate, juvenile delinquency, maladjusted personalities, and the rest of the social problems we are now dumping on the next generation—the remedies advanced for these problems will be incomplete. Indeed, the very advice given to solve such problems can hardly be put into effect. We must attack the prime cause of major family difficulties: the obsolete house and the obsolete community in which it stands.[11]

When a house is thought of with reference to family use, it must no longer be considered as a collection of rooms. It must be regarded rather "as a pattern of spaces, each space designed for a special group of activities and each with its special size, shape and quality." The principal spaces for family use are the work center, the living area, and the sleeping areas. These should be put together in terms of their relationships, with entrances and corridors to provide ease of access and independence of operation, and with adequate and accessible space for the storage of both family and individuals' possessions—in other words, for maximum livability and privacy.

This basic formula is set down:

The house must be
    Flexible in plan and arrangement as the children grow
      It must change as human needs change
      It must change from time to time with different activities
    Planned to minimize waste
      There must be no waste space
      Each action must be efficient, each trip short
      Circulation patterns must reduce steps and give control
    Zoned for centers of family living
      There must be a place for noise and a quiet place
      There must be zones for getting together and for being alone
The family is the origin of the house[12]

Healthful Housing. Recognizing that healthfulness of shelter was of great importance, the American Public Health Association organized a Committee on the Hygiene of Housing. In May, 1939, a report of this Committee, containing a set of Basic Principles of

[11] *Ibid.*, p. 43.
[12] *Ibid.*, p. 50.

Healthful Housing, was published for study purposes. Thirty principles are given which the Committee considered to be minimum requirements for the promotion of physical, mental, and social health. The principles are in four groups, together with the specific requirements which are involved and the methods of attainment of these requirements. There follows the statement of these principles in the classifications under which they are given.

A. Fundamental Physiological Needs. 1. Maintenance of a thermal environment which will avoid undue heat loss from the human body. 2. Maintenance of a thermal environment which will permit adequate heat loss from the human body. 3. Provision of an atmosphere of reasonable chemical purity. 4. Provision of adequate daylight illumination and avoidance of undue daylight glare. 5. Provision for admission of direct sunlight. 6. Provision of adequate artificial illumination and avoidance of glare. 7. Protection against excessive noise. 8. Provision of adequate space for exercise and for the play of children.

B. Fundamental Psychological Needs. 9. Provision of adequate privacy for the individual. 10. Provision of opportunities for normal family life. 11. Provision of opportunities for normal community life. 12. Provision of facilities which make possible the performance of the tasks of the household without undue physical and mental fatigue. 13. Provision of facilities for maintenance of cleanliness of the dwelling and of the person. 14. Provision of possibilities for esthetic satisfaction in the home and its surroundings. 15. Concordance with prevailing social standards of the local community.

C. Protection Against Contagion. 16. Provision of a water supply of safe sanitary quality, available to the dwelling. 17. Protection of the water supply system against pollution within the dwelling. 18. Provision of toilet facilities of such a character as to minimize the danger of transmitting disease. 19. Protection against sewage contamination of the interior surfaces of the dwelling. 20. Avoidance of insanitary conditions in the vicinity of the dwelling. 21. Exclusion from the dwelling of vermin which may play a part in the transmission of disease. 22. Provision of facilities for keeping milk and food undecomposed. 23. Provision of sufficient space in sleeping-rooms to minimize the danger of contact infection.

D. Protection Against Accidents. 24. Erection of the dwelling with such materials and methods of construction as to minimize danger of accidents due to collapse of any part of the structure. 25. Control of conditions likely to cause fires or to promote their spread. 26. Provision of adequate facilities for escape in case of fire. 27. Protection against danger of electrical shocks and burns. 28. Protection against gas poisonings. 29. Protection against falls and other mechanical injuries in the home. 30. Protection of the neighborhood against the hazards of automobile traffic.[13]

This analysis, with the accompanying specifications and the considerations of family needs and uses, goes a long way toward laying the basis for good housing. The last section, however, needs further development.

Safe Housing. Accidents take a terrific toll in America, and household accidents head the list. In 1945 there were 33,500 deaths from accidents in homes and 5,000,000 nonfatal injuries, including 130,000 permanent injuries. These accidents cost the nation $600,-000,000 in wage loss, medical expenses, and insurance overhead. Falls caused 50.4 percent of the deaths, burns and explosions 18.8 percent, poisonings 5.4 percent, poisonous gas 4.5 percent, mechanical suffocation and firearms each 3.9 percent, and miscellaneous accidents 13.1 percent.[14]

Nothing can compensate for carelessness, but many hazards can be removed and many things can be done in the construction, arrangement, and specifications of houses to facilitate carefulness and safety. The National Safety Council has been working seriously on this matter. A series of safety suggestions for building and remodeling have been published. These deal with the site and its use areas, entrances and exits, structure of the house, interior planning (with the safety measures for hazardous spots), storage safety requirements, making electrical installations and appliances safe, and controlling the hazards from plumbing and heating. The Council has also prepared a check list for home safety and published other material making suggestions for a safe house and safe habits.[15]

Good Neighborhoods. When it is recognized that good neighborhoods are as important as good houses, the problem of providing good housing becomes even more complicated. Not only is the planning for homes extended to take in the whole neighborhood, but the whole matter of what is a good neighborhood is involved. Neighborhoods have already been discussed (pp. 154–164). Neigh-

[13] Committee on the Hygiene of Housing, *Basic Principles of Healthful Housing*, second edition (New York: American Public Health Association, 1946).

[14] *Facts About Home Accidents* (Chicago: National Safety Council, 1946).

[15] *Factors Influencing the Design and Construction of Safer Homes; Check List for Home Safety; Safe at Home.*

borhood planning—including not only housing and business centers, but also accessibility and transportation, community institutions and community organization—is the key to good neighborhoods and their stability. Many of the principles are involved in garden cities and the green-belt towns (see pp. 213–219).

The size of a community or a neighborhood is exceedingly important to planning. For the garden cities Howard worked out a formula in which geographical size and maximum population were related (see p. 594). This was the key to the whole plan. The basis was an assumption with regard to the desirability of low density of population. A decrease in the density of urban population has continued to be an assumption for all urban redevelopment plans. The validity of this assumption has been seriously challenged in recent years. Can the principle of decreasing the population be held for all urban redevelopment? Should different standards of density be accepted for different types of areas in cities—for example, neighborhoods of single-family houses and areas of multiple-family dwellings? Or should standards of density be abandoned altogether?

When the Metropolitan Life Insurance Company proposed the housing development of Stuyvesant Town, to be built in the area north of Fourteenth Street between First Avenue and the East River in New York City, an area of eighteen city blocks, there was much controversy about it. The plans for the project proposed closing a number of streets and erecting thirty-five fifteen-story buildings arranged so that there would be a total land coverage of 25 percent. The buildings would contain small apartments, mostly of three and four rooms, and on their completion would accommodate 8761 family units and a total population of approximately 24,000. During the public hearings many of the professional and lay city-planning groups from the universities and the city protested vigorously because the plan would more than double the density of population in that area, to 358 per gross acre or 598 per net acre, deducting the former street area absorbed in the project. This was sincerely considered a move in the wrong direction. The judge in the hearing asked: "What should the density in such an urban area be?" The groups were unable to give a substantial factual answer, and the plan was approved. This question is still unanswered. The significance of density may be entirely a matter of the character of the community plan, the adequacy of the essential facilities, the adequacy of community institutions, and the location with reference to accessibility to work and transportation, rather than of number of people to the acre.

An incentive of main importance for the simultaneous development of better neighborhoods and new housing was provided by Title I of the Federal Housing Act of 1949. This act provided grants and loans to cities for "the acquisition of land; the demolition and removal of buildings and improvements; installation, construction or reconstruction of streets, utilities and other site improvements essential to the preparation of sites for uses in accordance with the redevelopment plan; and making the land available for development or redevelopment at its fair value for such areas. Financial aid is available also for surveys and plans in preparation of a project which may be assisted under Title I." Adequate redevelopment plans are a requirement for assistance.[16]

PRODUCING HOUSES

The acute housing shortage following the war and the practically insurmountable difficulties in getting houses built have demonstrated the chaotic condition of the building industry which has been developing for at least a quarter of a century. The building business is one of America's greatest industries both in value of products and in number of persons employed. It has continued in the patterns of the crafts established a century ago, has built up procedures and protection fitted to these patterns, and now finds itself entirely unable to cope with the present-day demands for use of the technological developments which have been made.

Present conditions in the building industry have been vividly portrayed in many articles in current periodicals.[17] The principal factors in the chaos in the building trades are of considerable sociological significance, but they can be only briefly stated here.

[16] Housing and Home Finance Agency, *Slum Clearance and Urban Redevelopment Under Title I of the Housing Act of 1949* (Feb., 1950), pp. 3, 10, 11.

[17] For example: *Fortune*, Aug., 1947, "The Way to More—and Cheaper—Houses"; *Readers' Digest*, Oct., 1947, a digest of the *Fortune* article; *Wall Street Journal*, a series of articles on Oct. 9, 10, 13, 15, 16, 17, 20, and 21, editorials on Oct. 9 and 21, and news items on Oct. 10 and 20, all in 1947 (these were reprinted in a pamphlet entitled *Housing: Puny Giant*); *Saturday Evening Post*, March 6, 1948, "No New Houses for You," by Joseph M. Guilfoyle and John S. Cooper, members of the staff which procured the data and prepared the articles for the *Wall Street Journal*.

It is estimated that one billion dollars, about one dollar in five, was paid by the buyers of homes in the United States during the single year 1947 as an unnecessary toll for make-work labor practices, inefficient business methods, and obsolete building laws. These serious evils are not to be thought of in terms of viciousness and noncoöperation on the part of the groups involved, but rather as a result of urbanization and the changes which have come in the character and process of urban communities. Skilled workers who are dependent upon day wages in an industry where their median annual incomes as late as 1940 were under $1000 are forced to measures which spread work as far as possible. Home-builders who on the average put up no more than four homes a year, with 64 percent of single-family home-builders in 1938 producing only one house a year,[18] must be concerned with large profits. Manufacturers, jobbers, and dealers in a highly competitive economy are to be expected to seek all forms of protection. City councils and planning commissions, with all good intent to set requirements for safe and substantial houses, are subject to many group pressures which have political importance and are not always able to distinguish clearly between expert counsel and the pressure of special privilege.

Here are the areas of major difficulties reflecting the chaotic conditions in the housing industry.

High Cost of Distributing Materials. No matter whether a builder erects one house a year or ten houses a day, he must buy his materials at retail, for manufacturers will not sell direct to builders. This is what has been called "a bucket brigade of middlemen" —jobbers, wholesalers, retailers—which adds around 100 percent to the cost of materials. Imagine the cost of an automobile if the producer had to buy motors, tires, speedometers, spark plugs, etc., from a local automobile accessory store. Lumber, wall board, plumbing fixtures, electrical supplies, and the rest must be purchased this way, however, by those who build houses. Since houses are delivered well equipped with all sorts of appliances in recent years, the unreasonable additional costs through the prevailing system of distribution are tremendous. Since materials represent almost half the cost of a house, a 25–50 percent saving by direct purchase from the manufacturers would cut the cost of houses about one-fourth with no change in prices of materials.

[18] Charles Abrams, *op. cit.*, pp. 7, 8.

Union Make-Work Rules. Contractors testify that building workers are doing 30–50 percent less work than they did before the war. In many instances this goes back to a great variety of rules which unions have established to control their members. Bricklayers are laying 350–400 bricks a day in most places where before the war they laid 800–1000 and in a few places still do. Plumbers often take three times as long as is required to lay the pipe in a house. Lathers nail their daily allowance of thirty bundles between nine and two o'clock; it is obvious that they could nail sixty or seventy-five bundles. In some cities painters can use brushes no wider than four inches, while in other cities six and one-half inch brushes are permitted. In most places fewer apprentices than the union regulations permit are allowed on a job.

There are also various kinds of featherbedding practices. When machinery is used on the job in some cities, an $18-a-day man is required to check gasoline and oil; in other places a maintenance engineer must be hired to switch the machine on in the morning and off in the afternoon. There are cities where high-priced plumbers and steel workers must unload materials at the construction site, a job which could as well be done by laborers. In some situations skilled workers on the higher wage levels refuse to work except for wages considerably above the accepted wage scales.

Antique Codes. Building codes are essential to the maintenance of standards of dwellings and to the protection of neighborhoods from the deteriorating influence of jerry-built structures. But codes accumulate; it is difficult to repeal specifications which have been established; they tend to be a dead hand of the past as conditions and needs for housing change and as new knowledge makes old requirements outmoded.

These codes are mostly local. Two thousand cities have their own codes, fourteen states also have codes, and in addition there are some 1400 plumbing codes and 800 electrical codes, not to include the thousands of zoning ordinances and hundreds of state and local licensing laws. Most of them are different. There may be some reason for variations with the extreme differences in climate, but why should one city require three-quarter-inch sheathing when another, adjoining it, permits one-quarter-inch sheathing? Some cities openly ignore many useless provisions, while another enforces a code so vigorously that the smallest apartment would have to rent for $150 a month if the builder were to get his money back. Many requirements may cost only $20 or $25, but they can add up to 10 percent of the total cost; others may amount to almost as much in a single item.

One city requires in homes an oversize grease trap in kitchen sinks which would serve a restaurant. Another requires twelve-inch concrete foundations while others are satisfied with six inches. Asbestos shingles won't do if brick is specified in the code. Some places require solid sheathing rather than lath sheathing under shingles. Minimum thicknesses of brick walls vary from eight to sixteen inches. One city requires that roof drains of single-family dwellings be connected to sewers the same as in downtown solidly built areas. Some cities require three coats of plaster instead of the standard two coats.

Many new government-tested and approved materials are forbidden in hundreds of cities: light-gauge steel, reinforced gypsum, lightweight aggregate masonry block, plywood and metal skins for house walls, resin-bonded glues, prefabricated plumbing units, BX electric cable, and new insulation materials. Economy, speed, and low price go when such things are out.

A city in which many small houses of 600 square feet floor space had been built raised the minimum to 1000 square feet in a 1945 code. Another place requires thirty-foot expensively paved streets for even the side roads. Basements, made a thing of the past by the development of radiant heating, are still required by the codes in most cities.

Pressure Groups. A large number of cities have undertaken the revision of building codes, but it is not easy. Pressure groups are at work on every side. Labor groups want to retain or to increase their protection against what they see as labor-saving in new materials and methods. When labor is well organized, together with families and friends it makes a formidable political power. On the other hand, material manufacturers are also powerful. Some of the national associations keep staffs in various parts of the country to get quickly to the spots where codes are being reconsidered. These groups have large funds to put into their fights to preserve their protection.

Builders have unsuccessfully attempted a national research foundation. Building continues to be highly localized. Local licensing is effective in maintaining a scarcity of craftsmen and in keeping the business for local contractors.

Mass Production Sabotaged. Great hope was held for prefabricated houses, but the producers have run into insurmountable difficulties. Prefabricated houses cannot be completely built in a factory; they must be assembled on their permanent location. One city requires that a local architect draw the plans for its houses. The great differences in codes from city to city make it impossible to design a house that will meet all the specifications. Labor organizations either forbid their workers to work on prefabricated houses, or demand so much work that savings are more than overcome by the local labor costs, or make specific conditions for their work such as insisting that all windows be glazed on the job, or that doors cannot have hardware installed at the factory, or that plumbing must be assembled for each individual house. They also refuse to use modern tools: power saws, electric pipe-threaders, paint-spray guns, etc.

Lack of standardization continues; with great varieties of materials and supplies, dealers must have expensive stock inventories, which are finally paid for by the purchasers. Materials are cut and fitted on the job; this makes a waste of up to one-fifth, and the labor required to make the waste must also be paid for.

This is an illustration of how the social process gets bogged down. Solutions to many specific problems worked out independently combine to make a powerful force to hold the *status quo* and prevent changes which would solve a major problem.

Successful Experiments. Several large-scale builders have found different methods of coping with the adverse conditions with a reasonable degree of success. Each, however, has developed his own pattern.

One company with very large capital operates in a relatively small suburban area on Long Island. It owns a lumber mill in California, a cinder and concrete block plant near its operation, and much heavy grading and cement-mixing mobile equipment. It contemplates the purchase of factories producing some of the equipment for houses which is difficult to obtain. A preassembly plant has been built in its area which precuts lumber, bundles it, and delivers it to the site of each house so that there is a minimum use of a saw on the job. More complicated parts, such as plumbing systems, copper heating coils, cabinets, and stairways, are made in the factory by workmen who spend all of their time on the same kind of units.

This concern has eliminated the last and most expensive stage in the factory-wholesaler-jobber-retailer system of selling materials by setting up its own supply company. The inventories required by this type of operation run into the millions of dollars.

The company uses many subcontractors, whose fees are set by negotiations, not by bidding, and who work for no one else. An open shop is maintained, but wages are paid according to union wage scales and the key group of workers have year-round employment.

A concern operating in another city sets up a temporary assembly-line factory on the site of its operations. Entire walls, roofs, and other units are built and equipped in the factory with jigs and machine operations and moved to the house location with huge cranes. Operations are staggered so that factory and trucks and crews are constantly occupied and are able to place and assemble as many as ten houses a day. The shops use the most efficient methods with jigs and power machinery. Paint is sprayed. Subcontracts are on a piece-work basis; other work is paid for at union wage scales.

Another company, operating on the Pacific coast, has a city factory producing units of houses, but the actual building is largely conventional, with materials doled out for each house direct from the trainloads as received. The problem of retail purchase of materials has not been solved.

The unique features of a Middle West builder are operation in the smaller large cities, developing raw farm land, and operating in units of around two hundred houses. There is a special contract with building workers' unions whereby workers may perform more than one kind of job, with pay applicable to the work done; a large number of apprentices are used, and no limitations are put on the amount of work a worker can do nor on the use of labor-saving devices. Subcontractors are competent foremen, receive good salaries, and receive the profits of 49 percent of their business, which has been set up by the operator, who retains 51 percent of the stock.

So there are some rays of hope. When the problems are tackled in their own terms on a coöperative basis, solutions begin. There can be no doubt that the full solution of these problems is to the interest of all concerned; so, as the bases for solution are worked out, coöperation is bound to follow.[19]

---

[19] The material of this section was taken from the reports mentioned, where fuller details and illustrations can be found.

HOME OWNERSHIP

Home ownership is declining in cities. Whether or not it is a good thing for a family to own its own home is largely an academic question so long as the majority of families cannot buy houses. With the bulk of family incomes around $50 per week, homes cannot be purchased until a decently adequate home can be made available for $5000. This means that the problems of constructing moderate-priced houses must be solved first. The best that the most successful builders have been able to do so far under prevailing conditions is $7500 houses. The others are 15–20 percent over this price. When the building cost problems are solved, however, there remains the problem of financing.

Home ownership under the present system of financing is very largely fictitious. A purchaser is less concerned with the price of a house than he is with the monthly payments, which include interest, a small payment on principal, taxes, and carrying charges. If these amount to approximately what he can pay for rent, he considers he has a good buy and hopes that as equity builds up he will gradually attain ownership. Equity, however, builds up slowly and is usually offset by depreciation. The major item in payments is interest on the mortgage, which is very high compared with other fiduciary investments.

High interest charges are due to several conditions unique to the mortgage system. First, mortgages are not wholesaled through investment bankers and underwriters who have access to the money market for low-rate lending. Each mortgage is an individual transaction. Even with government guarantee of home mortgages neither the Federal Housing Administration nor the Home Loan Bank system has been permitted to offer them in group series to attract 3 percent money. Second, the builders, who themselves need money badly, are unable to bargain effectively and because of their very transient interest in a single house are largely indifferent to this problem of the purchaser. Third, the pressure of banking interests which have a stake in this source of high interest is against interest rate reduction. The many building-and-loan associations continue to borrow money for as little as 1.5 percent and then charge home purchasers 6 percent.

The rigidity of the mortgage system, coupled with high interest rates, makes unusual risks for the purchaser. Misfortunes, such as illness or unemployment, resulting in the default of even a single payment may cancel the home-owner's whole equity or perhaps even result in a personal judgment against him. The security of home ownership under these conditions is exceedingly precarious.[20] Coöperative housing, which has already been established successfully in some cities by new techniques of finance and organization to cut costs and lower monthly payments, is a promising middle way for extending houses in urban areas.

PUBLIC HOUSING

That housing is a social problem few if any will dispute. So also will most people recognize that it is a public responsibility to provide housing for low-income families. But how far public responsibility goes is a moot question.

In 1933 the federal government began its participation in housing through various agencies set up for the purpose. The aim was to reactivate building and not to reform the building industry. The Federal Housing Administration system of insuring home mortgages, the Home Loan Bank system of buying mortgages from building-and-loan organizations, insuring their deposits and buying their stock, and the FHA Public Housing Administration program for low-income families have accomplished a great deal and have survived. The first two were more effective in their basic purpose than "in bettering the lot of the homeowner, or making home buying sound, or stabilizing real estate patterns, checking blight, improving city planning, helping veterans buy or rent houses at reasonable prices, improving rural housing, or making progress in any of the aspects that so sorely and so long needed adjustment. . . . The idealism and the social objectives that inspired the early intervention by the government in housing gave way to an effort to employ the federal credit as a means of insuring profits and underwriting losses."[21] Builders, however, have been assisted and financiers given a greater range in protected investment. The public housing program added nearly a quarter of a million low-rental dwellings in addition to some fifty thousand war housing units. Of

[20] Abrams, *op. cit.*, pp. 11–13.
[21] *Ibid.*, p. 20.

the low-rental dwellings, 142,000 were built by local housing authorities. The low-rental houses cost, on the average, $4616 per unit.
The families housed in 1939 and 1940 had an average income of
$782 and paid an average gross rental of $18.26. In 1944 the family
incomes averaged $1237. The government contribution was approxi-
mately $8.38 per dwelling per month, or $2.00 per person. This was
only 69 percent of the maximum authorized by the law. In the process some 114,000 substandard dwellings were eliminated, 82 percent
of which were demolished. Studies of the improvement in conditions of the families provided for show that infant mortality, tuberculosis, communicable diseases, total home accidents, fires, and juvenile delinquency have been markedly reduced.[22] How much of
the reduction in social ills may be attributed to selection of tenants
it is not possible to estimate.

The most promising development in this program has been the
local housing activities which have been established in some 450
cities whose population exceeds 40,000,000. These organizations are
subject to the will of their cities, are directed by local people of
standing in their communities (54 percent are in business, banking,
and industry and 20 percent in the professions), and carry out their
programs with reference to local needs and conditions.

"The performance of these authorities has been one of the most
remarkable in the history of public operations. They faced the obstacles of the local political machine, inexperience in a new and difficult field, social problems, legal impediments, and all sorts of
pressures from real estate and other interests. Financing and management provided additional headaches. But by and large, these authorities have met the severest tests that a novel and untried field
can offer." Renters have met their social and contractual responsibilities remarkably well; arrears in rents are less than 0.2 percent. In
spite of lengthening the time of maturity of bonds and lowering the
interest rates to less than 2 percent, conservative financial concerns
are ready to back them with the money which is needed.[23]

A number of states do not have laws authorizing local housing
authorities, and only thirty states have enabling legislation for local
slum-clearance and urban redevelopment. Both of these types of
legislation are essential if cities are to benefit from the Housing Act
of 1949, which authorizes 810,000 public housing units in the next

[22] *Ibid.*, p. 23.
[23] *Ibid.*, pp. 22, 23.

six years and $1,000,000,000 in loans and $500,000,000 in grants for urban redevelopment during the next five years.[24]

Title I of the Housing Act requires community studies and community planning as prerequisites to assistance for redevelopment. Already some city neighborhoods which have developed programs of citizen participation in neighborhood planning have gained priorities thereby.

One of the serious problems of public housing is found in the underlying racial frictions and tensions which exist in many cities and which seriously impede redevelopment programs. Often the neighborhoods in greatest need of new housing are those where prejudices are acute and discrimination and segregation are practiced.[25] Cities in New York State are fortunate since state legislation bans racial discrimination or segregation in all future publicly *aided* housing or redevelopment projects.

SOME CONCLUSIONS ABOUT HOUSING

These are major problems of housing in American cities. They are the result of the intensification of urban patterns and of the slowness of the institutions involved in providing housing to adapt to changing circumstances and to changing needs. The solutions of the problems need not be too difficult. They depend, however, on a recognition that the public interest is fundamental. Everyone's welfare is involved in good houses, in stable neighborhoods, in employed workers, and in productive money. It is a coöperative job in which special interests of groups are dissolved in the larger interests through which all will gain. It is not a matter of public enterprise against private enterprise, but rather of both operating together with a flexibility that makes possible an adequate supply of good houses for all people.

The job cannot be done without careful and thorough planning for the development of good and stable neighborhoods. Better standards and specification for healthful, safe, and useful houses are the next requirement. Then manufacturers, distributors, workers,

[24] "What Cities Should Do Now to Qualify for Federal Redevelopment and Housing Aid," *The American City*, Aug., 1949, p. 93; "Does Your City Have the Necessary Powers to Participate Fully in Housing Act Benefits?" *The American City*, Sept., 1949, p. 138.

[25] See Robert Weaver, *The Negro Ghetto* (New York: Harcourt, Brace and Company, 1948).

builders, financiers, and city authorities will need to coöperate to work out the organization and processes which will establish economy, eliminate waste, use technical improvements, employ workers continuously at high wages, and enable families to purchase the kinds of houses they need at prices they can afford to pay.

SOME CONCLUSIONS ABOUT CITY PROBLEMS

These problems of poverty, of health, of delinquency and crime, of housing, and many more are especially problems of cities; not that they do not exist in rural areas, but the circumstances of urban living make them far more acute in cities. In spite of the concentration of resources in money, technical knowledge and skills, and organizational machinery in cities, the solutions of the problems come slowly, partly because of the very bulk of cities (big bodies move slowly), partly because the development of a supporting public opinion is required and public opinion develops slowly, and partly because even the resources of cities are inadequate to make a thorough solution possible. Any genuine solution of these problems involves such a far-reaching change in the foundations of urban social organization and economy that the terrific complexity of the implications is still baffling.

As much as cities have been able to accomplish in the solution of their problems (and the advances are great over the years), the problems have a way of keeping ahead of the solutions in the increasing complexity of modern civilization in its urban form. Like Alice and the Red Queen, cities have to run as fast as they can to keep up with the changing world, and twice as fast to get anywhere.

Supplementary Reading

Abrams, Charles. *The Future of Housing.* New York: Harper & Brothers, 1946.

Abrams, Charles. *A Housing Program for America.* New York: League for Industrial Democracy, 1946.

　　Statements of the current problems of housing and proposals for their solutions.

Committee on the Hygiene of Housing. *Basic Principles of Healthful Housing,* second edition. New York: American Public Health Association, 1946.

　　A presentation of the bases for good houses.

Dean, John. *Home Ownership: Is It Sound?* New York: Harper & Brothers, 1945.

An analysis of the desirability and feasibility of home ownership.

Gutheim, Frederick. *Houses for Family Living.* New York: The Woman's Foundation, 1948.

An analysis of the uses to which houses are put by families.

Housing: Puny Giant. New York: The Wall Street Journal, 1947.

Journalistic presentation of various aspects of the chaotic conditions in the building industry.

Perry, Clarence Arthur. *Housing for the Machine Age.* New York: Russell Sage Foundation, 1939.

An extended, well-illustrated treatment of housing with reference to planned neighborhood.

Recommendations for a Housing Program and Policy. New York: National Committee on Housing, 1944.

Suggested bases and plans for solving the problems of housing.

Straus, Nathan. *The Seven Myths of Housing.* New York: Alfred A. Knopf, 1944.

A discussion of the ideas and principles involved in the approach to the solution of the problems of housing.

PART V

PATTERNS OF URBAN
STRUCTURE

FROM the great complex of urban organization five major areas of organized life have been selected for analysis by way of illustration, each considered in a different pattern to show also that there are various ways in which any area of organization can be looked at: social services (Chap. 21), health (Chap. 22), education (Chap. 23), recreation (Chap. 24), and religion (Chap. 25).

CHAPTER 21

THE FUNCTIONS AND ORGANIZA-
TION OF THE SOCIAL SERVICES

In the early days of American society, the ever present desire to help those in difficulty and distress could be carried out in a simple and direct way. Those needing help had a relationship by kinship, by close association, or by acquaintance with those who could help them. Problems were simple—accident, sickness, improvidence, and the like. As cities began to take form, however, more people and different kinds of people, living in the narrow areas of specialization, made the range of personal contacts proportionally much smaller. The problems of people also took on a more complex character—unemployment, epidemic, vagrancy, poverty. This type of problem was not only the misfortune of individuals and families but also a disturbance and disruption of the community life, and it could not be solved by the efforts of individuals.

So the development of organized social services in American cities is part and parcel of the growing urbanization and inevitably so. As Shelby M. Harrison has expressed it:

What has come to be called social work dates back a long way. The expression in practical ways of the common human impulse to help another in distress was bound sooner or later to take organized form; and it did so markedly in this country during the last hundred years or more. One measure, in numerical terms alone, is the fact that approximately half the present annual expenditure of a majority of our states is devoted to the various services performed under the boards of welfare, health, corrections, and care of the insane; and fully half of the personnel of the states' employment is on these pay rolls. Including the large numbers in nongovernmental agencies, the total number of persons engaged in these and similar services in this country now almost certainly runs above one hundred thousand. Along with organized religion and education, social

403

work has taken its place as a major concern of the local community, state, and nation.[1]

In his study of the *Proceedings* of the National Conference of Social Work from 1874 to 1946, Frank J. Bruno reflects several things which are not only a part of the social history of America but also a part of the story of the development of American cities.[2]

First, new problems and old problems in new forms were constantly arising: care of the insane and feeble-minded; the protection of children; the treatment of the delinquent—probation and parole; the organization of charity for operation in urban areas; problems of migration, immigration, and transiency. These older problems were followed in the first quarter of the twentieth century by somewhat different kinds of problems, such as child labor, the use of juvenile courts, the establishment of mothers' pensions, and the beginning of coördination of the social services in cities through councils of social agencies and community chests. The second quarter of the twentieth century found the focus of attention on even broader and more fundamental problems: health, social insurance, social security, minority groups, and social reform.

Second, there was a growing necessity for a national clearing house. The problems encountered in the various cities were the same, but many different ideas with regard to their solution appeared, and so experimentation differed. The exchange of information and experience and the discussion of policies and differing opinions regarding responsibilities, principles, and methods become of great help and importance.

Third, there have been a broadening of the scope of social work and a definite trend from a remedial to a preventive attack on problems. The accumulation of experience has shaken down to accepted technique. The growing body of knowledge and skill and the increasing demand for trained people have established a firm basis for professional training of social workers.

Fourth, gradually more and more attention has been given to the principle of social work and the policies under which it should operate, looking toward uniformity of practice and the establishment of accepted standards for high quality of service.

---

[1] Foreword to Frank J. Bruno, *Trends in Social Work* (New York: Columbia University Press, 1948), p. vii.

[2] Bruno, *op. cit.*

All of these developments have left important deposits in cities. This has been especially true in the proliferation and expansion of organizations involved in carrying on social work. The variety and number of social service organizations in American cities are very great: some are large, and some are small; some are operated by public funds as a part of government, and others are operated by private groups, some of which, with broad community service, are supported by appeals to the people of the community, and others, serving sectarian or special interest groups, get support from those especially related to the groups or interests. Most of the agencies in the cities now operate according to the recognized principles and standards of social work, are recognized agencies and are well known; a few are small, feeble, and unknown, doing their work, as a rule, far below the established standard.

Each city has its own pattern of institution, which can usually be determined by the directory of social agencies. It is difficult to classify the types of agencies to be found in cities because categories of both function and organization are required. The basis of this problem, however, can be indicated.

SCOPE OF URBAN SOCIAL WORK

What is included in social work and what is excluded—this is a matter of definition.

What Is Social Work? After a very thorough study and analysis of social work, Helen L. Witmer wrote: "Social work's own peculiar function—the end it accomplishes that differentiates it from the organized systems of activities—was found to consist of giving assistance to individuals in overcoming the difficulties that stand in the way of their playing their expected roles in organized groups or making use of those groups' services."[3] Around this function, or, more properly speaking, purpose, social work has been built with standards and specifications which are the basis of determining what activities should be included. Institutional criteria have developed and involve organization, professional personnel, special equipment, values, methods, and rules.

On the basis of these criteria "the numerous efforts of individuals

[3] Helen Leland Witmer, *Social Work: An Analysis of a Social Institution* (New York: Rinehart and Company, Inc., 1942), p. 487.

to relieve social and economic distress on their own responsibility and on their own conceptions of what is good for people"[4] are clearly excluded. By the same token, however, institutions which operate on the fringes of social work and the social service activities of institutions with other primary functions are also excluded.

This is the general basis on which social work is conceived and operated. It does not, however, provide a sufficiently specific definition to indicate either the functions or the types of organizations which are to be found. The picture of what social work in cities looks like is complicated by two things both related to the very nature of social work.

Social work is primarily work with individuals; consequently, its patterns of operation are determined by the needs of the individuals, not by any pattern inherent in the techniques of social work itself. For example, a social worker on the staff of an agency established for service to the blind may be assisting an individual blind person to work out the problems of adjustment involved in his blindness. But, in the course of her work, she discovers that the blind person has a problem of health or needs a certain kind of educational experience. She may make arrangements for these services to be provided by health or educational agencies with which her agency has coöperative relationships; or circumstances may be such that the blind person may not be able to get to the other agency or the needed services are not available, in which case the original agency may have to provide the special services required. The agency's activities consequently become complicated by a service which in itself is not social work, but which is necessary for adequate service to individuals whose primary relationship to the agency comes through social work.

The second complication is in a more fundamental relationship of functions themselves. For example, medical care is not social work; and yet, in many cases, the care of an individual depends upon the understanding of his attitude, his family relationships, the conditions under which he lives, and other factors in his socio-economic circumstances and environment. This is particularly true with such physical conditions as tuberculosis and also with mental illness. Because of this, many hospitals have medical social workers and psychiatric social workers, for the job of dealing with these factors is social work. So case work becomes an adjunct of medical service.

[4] *Ibid.*, p. 62.

Similarly, counseling, which is recognized as a part of social work, is frequently carried on in relationship to organized education.

The Functions of Social Work. Although it is difficult to define the functions of social work from the point of view of its institutions, it is quite possible from the standpoint of its personnel. As a basis for the delineation of the areas of training and function of professional social workers, Joseph P. Anderson has made his definition: "Modern social work may be described as a professional service rendered to people for the purpose of assisting them, as individuals or in groups, to attain satisfying relationships and standards of life in accordance with their particular wishes and capacities and in harmony with those of the community."[5] He goes on to divide social work into five major specializations, representing the types of positions which social workers have: social case work, social group work, community organization, social research, and administration.

Social Case Work. This is a central function of social work because "social work's peculiar function consists of giving assistance to individuals in overcoming difficulties." Social case work is the term given to this function. It has been broken down into four things which the social worker helps the client to do: "(a) to understand his situation better, (b) to become acquainted with or use available resources, (c) to clarify his indecision, and (d) to discharge feelings and also to understand feelings which are obstructing constructive action or inducing destructive behavior." The approach, treatment, and emphasis of the social worker are determined by six variables: "(a) nature of the problem, (b) psychodynamics of the case, (c) actual life circumstances, (d) worker's capacities, (e) agency function, and (f) community resources available."[6] With such an array of variables, it is quite clear that every case with which a social worker deals must be unique.

Certain principles of social case work have gradually become recognized and accepted: "(a) the conviction that it is important to understand and to deal with the factors which cause social maladjustment, (b) an appreciation of individual difference and a realization that one must work differently individual by individual, (c) the importance of the family in the life of the individual, and (d) rec-

[5] Joseph P. Anderson, "Social Work as a Profession," in Russell H. Kurtz, *Social Work Year Book, 1947* (New York: Russell Sage Foundation, 1947), p. 513.

[6] Charlotte Towle, "Social Case Work," in Kurtz, *op. cit.,* p. 478.

ognition of the importance of the nature of the interrelationship between client and worker."[7]

As the techniques of social case work have broadened through the contributions of psychology, education, and especially psychiatry, and as it has increasingly focused its service on the development and adjustment of individuals, it has become useful in more and more agencies, for more and more purposes.

Social Group Work. This plays its part in the overall social work purposes "by providing group associations and experiences which afford persons a controlled environment within which they may be helped to adjust and relate to each other" and so develop their capacity and increase their skills as "to participate effectively in the groups and communities of which they are a part."[8]

Because of the changed conditions of family life and the variety of human relationships which have been a part of urbanization, this kind of experience has become very useful in helping children, young people, and adults to more adequate living within their social situation.

The role of the group workers or leaders, the interrelationships among group members, and the dynamics of interaction have been subjected to observation and research, the results of which form a substantial body of knowledge for the professional training of group workers. Several principles have had general acceptance: (1) Groups, like the individuals who compose them, differ in capacity, need, interest, and readiness to accept responsibility. (2) Groups are dynamic, but in the course of their change they must start where they are and progress at a pace they can negotiate. (3) Groups must be accepted by the worker as they are. (4) Groups have the right of self-determination in making their own decisions, devising their own plans, adopting their own programs, and accepting the responsibility for carrying them out. (5) In group work, process is more important than structure; so organization is developed only as a means of facilitating the group process and attaining the ends of the group. (6) The role of the professional is to help the group discover and define its needs and develop its program to accomplish its objectives in such a way that the members of the group will experience relationships in which they will have the maximum satisfaction and growth.[9]

[7] *Ibid.*, p. 479.
[8] Harleigh B. Trecker, "Social Group Work," in Kurtz, *op. cit.*, p. 485.
[9] *Ibid.*, p. 489.

Agencies specializing in group work have increased in the cities, and group work has become increasingly a part of the programs of many educational, religious, and other organizations. This testifies to its usefulness in urban communities.

Community Organization. This term in social work has a specialized meaning. It is used to designate the process whereby either social agencies or individuals or both are involved in developing organization through which social services may be more effectively carried out or through which the citizen of the community may attain a higher degree of social welfare in certain respects. Community organization is based on group work, but the focus of attention of the latter is upon the growth of the individual within its process, while the former is focused upon the development of the community through the accomplishments of groups of people who are working on the things which concern them.

The knowledge about and the techniques of community organization are far less developed than in the other functions of social work, but experience has been accumulating for about a quarter of a century. Although much of the experience has been equivocal, experience and research continue and have provided at least a tentative basis for training.

Community organization takes two forms: first, the coördination of social agencies and their respective services toward the more comprehensive planning of social work; second, the enlisting of community groups in activities to solve their community problems.

Social Research. This is especially important in social work because of its nature, dealing with problems of individuals and communities, and because of the stage of its development wherein the objectives of its services need to be more fully understood, the phenomena of problems and maladjustments need more adequate analysis, and the techniques and organization used need more complete evaluation. In one phase, the research grows out of the hypotheses which result from the observations of social workers and feeds back its results to them to increase the effectiveness and economy of practice. Another phase calls upon the results of research into human behavior and social institutions in the allied areas of psychology, biology, sociology, economics, and political science. A further phase is concerned with the constant collection of vital statistics and data on population, relief, delinquency, mobility rates, etc., etc.

Four main objectives for research in social work are given by Fletcher as follows: "The first is to improve and enlarge the techniques of diagnosis and treatment as they are used in social work practice. The second is to develop the efficiency and define the function of the social work agency as the medium through which social work is practiced. The third is to appraise and measure the community's needs for social work service and to disclose the steps by which these needs are to be met. And the fourth is to add to the general knowledge of the etiology of social pathology so the social action can be directed toward prevention as well as toward treatment."[10]

Research on more specific problems is usually carried on by large local agencies, by research departments of councils of social agencies, or by students and faculty in schools of social work. General problems and statistics are more likely studied by government— that is, the Bureau of the Census, the Bureau of Labor Statistics, the Children's Bureau, the Federal Security Agency—or by national organizations such as the National Tuberculosis Association, the Family Service Association of America, Community Chests and Councils, the Social Science Research Council, and the Russell Sage Foundation. All in all, a host of people are involved professionally in this function of social work.

Administration. The administration of social agencies differs from administration in other fields only in terms of the peculiarities of social work organizations, but these differences are sufficient to produce many unique and difficult problems. Dunham has designated nine major functional aspects or tasks: (1) the determination and clarification of objectives (both long-range purposes and more immediate goals), functions (the tasks which the agency undertakes to perform and the services which it seeks to give), and policies (the rules by which it operates); (2) the mobilization and maintenance of resources—personal, financial, material, even psychological—to the end that the agency may carry out its purposes and fulfill its functions effectively; (3) the development of a dynamic and fluid program in terms of the particular community, quality of staff personnel and of supervision, adequacy of budget, staff morale, community understanding, and many other factors; (4) organization, which is a conscious integration of human effort for a definite purpose, and coördination, which is the holding together of the parts of the enterprise and the encouragement and

[10] Ralph Carr Fletcher, "Research and Social Statistics in Social Work," in Kurtz, *op. cit.*, pp. 439–440.

production of teamwork; (5) leadership and direction, with established lines of responsibility, provision for evaluation, and supervision, which is teaching and sharing in professional thinking; (6) planning (the projection of activities), standardization (the establishment of criteria for operation and evaluation), measurement of the effectiveness of the work in terms of objectives; (7) recording, accounting, and related activities to assure the stability and continuance of operation; (8) processing, or the establishing of habitual routine procedures which assure the uninterrupted day-to-day material business; (9) public relations, the development of satisfactory and effective relationships between the agency and outside groups.[11]

Some would add two additional specializations: social action, which is coming to be absorbed in the group work and community organization, and coördination-and-planning, which is losing its special identity as it becomes increasingly involved both in community organization and in administration.

URBAN AGENCIES OF SOCIAL WORK

Although the inventory of any city's social agencies is unique, it always contains many and varied agencies. Certain types of agencies are always represented. The New York *Directory of Social Agencies* classifies thirty different kinds of agencies,[12] of which several have a number of subdivisions and a few put together under one heading from two to four different kinds of agencies which are similar in function.

Types of City Agencies. In any city there are likely to be some agencies of each of several very general types.

The *case work agencies*, ranging from the public welfare department of city governments and family service societies through the various types of children's service agencies to counseling and guidance services, are usually found in the greatest numbers. Clinics are essentially of this type.

The *group work agencies* include settlements, neighborhood

[11] Arthur Dunham, "Administration of Social Agencies," in Kurtz, *op. cit.,* pp. 15–16.

[12] *Directory of Social Agencies of the City of New York, 1946–1947,* prepared under the direction of the Committee on Information Service of the Welfare Council (New York: Columbia University Press, 1947), Table of Contents.

houses, community centers, the "Y's," and the different kinds of recreation agencies, which are usually considered of this type.

Agencies for the institutional care of individuals are of many varieties: orphanages, old people's homes, residences and transient quarters for homeless and unattached people, protective and correctional care. Sometimes homes for the chronically ill, for convalescent care, and for the mentally ill are considered to belong to this group.

Coördinating agencies of some sort are to be found in most cities: social service exchanges, councils of social agencies, community chests, research groups, and neighborhood councils. The growth of these agencies has been one of the marks of the development of social work in recent years, but not without difficulties, which will be considered presently.

Information and service agencies include general information services, information for travelers and foreign-born, information about various agencies (especially for contributors), homemaker service, legal aid, and employment services.

Adjunct social work is carried on by organizations whose primary activities are not social work—for example, group work in religious institutions and case work in hospitals. Such activities are increasing, are often carried on via collaboration with a city's social work organization, and are generally considered significant to the degree to which the social work activities are integrated with the total work of the organization.

These are purely descriptive groupings of agencies. Some particular organizations will not readily fall into any one classification, either because they operate with different kinds of functions or because they are different enough in their particular activities to seem to merit another grouping. The classification does, however, serve to indicate in a very general way a common denominator of any city's social work organizations.

Public and Private Social Work. That part of urban social work, called public or sometimes official, which is a part of the structure of city government and is paid for out of taxes has constantly increased over the years of urban development. Meeting the social problems of urban life has been and continues to be pioneered by private agencies, those organized and operated by groups of citizens who are concerned with a problem and supported by voluntary contributions. When, however, public opinion recognizes that a service

is essential to community life or that it should be available to all of
the people of the community, then it is taken over as a public service. One of the conditions which accelerate the crystalization of public opinion is the breakdown of private agencies at times of unusual
need for the service; thus the private relief organizations proved
wholly inadequate to cope with the great need for relief during the
depression years, and as a result the problem of relief was accepted
as a public responsibility; government agencies were enlarged or
created, and much larger amounts of public monies were made available, for this purpose. The need for social work which expanded so
greatly during the depression brought the federal government into
the picture, especially in the cities. The federal programs related to
relief and unemployment, such as WPA, ECC, and PWA, were temporary, but the subsequent Federal Security Act, with old-age assistance, unemployment insurance, etc., has become an established
part of social work which is backed by the federal government. Once
the pattern of public responsibility is established, it tends to continue.

Just what the final outcome of this trend may be it is not possible
to predict, but out of experience certain characteristics of the area
of operation of public and of private agencies can be denoted. Public agencies carry on those services which are universal in application
and/or are essential to the life of the community, when standards of
operation are well established. Private agencies, on the other hand,
carry on experimental programs, those of a highly specialized nature,
and those operated for the benefit of special groups in the population. They are also more particularly concerned with research, the
development of methods and techniques, and the raising of standards of operation. It is likely that this general distribution of labor
will continue in American cities because it is considered consistent
with the democratic principle of social organization, although the
pattern of particular services may continue to change with the shift
toward increasing public services.

COÖRDINATION OF SOCIAL WORK

Each of the many social work agencies in cities sprang up independently because a group of people was sufficiently concerned
about some problem to form an organization to do something about
it. It early became apparent that some sort of coördination was nec-

essary. This pressure of necessity has continued over the years and has increased the scope and the organization of coöperation and coordination.

Clearing House. The first coördination was in the area of relief. So long as agencies granting assistance to needy families and individuals operated independently, it was quite possible for a family to receive assistance from several different agencies at the same time. To protect themselves against such dissipation of funds and services, the agencies began to form clearing houses of information about what families were receiving assistance from which agencies, in the latter part of the nineteenth century. These social service exchanges, as they have in most instances come to be called, have taken on a more positive purpose to help the agencies offer better services to their clients.[13]

Associations. National associations of like organizations in the many cities, such as YMCA, YWCA, Salvation Army, and Red Cross, began to take form through the last half of the nineteenth century, though their largest increase was in the first quarter of the twentieth century. These associations affected the local agencies through the exchange of experience, the development of objectives and policies, the formulation of standards, and the expansion of services. In 1946, after a number of interorganizations in functional areas had been established, forty-four national associations joined together as affiliates in the National Social Welfare Assembly, with the National Education-Recreation Council, the Social Case Work Council of National Agencies, the National Committee on Service to Veterans, the National Health Council, and the Associated Youth Serving Organizations becoming the functional groups of the Assembly.[14]

Conferences. In the meantime, since 1874, the National Conference of Social Work has been providing the opportunity for professional workers and laymen interested in social welfare "to share experiences; consider and discuss current problems; report accomplishments and undertakings; submit the results of studies and research, raise questions and offer ideas, suggestions and recommendations; and sometimes to formulate platforms, endorse specific proposals, and engage in more or less vigorous social action." In late years the annual meetings have had a number of special sections. Forty-six states have state conferences, some operated by volunteers,

[13] Mary E. Samson, "Social Service Exchanges," in Kurtz, *op. cit.*, p. 509.
[14] Ray Johns, "National Associations," in Kurtz, *op. cit.*, pp. 331, 333.

others with budgets and staff. A number hold regional or local conferences. About half conduct institutes or refresher courses. A few have local chapters. Nearly half publish bulletins. Some have speaker bureaus, have research and study committees, or provide consultant services.[15]

The practitioners in the various project divisions of social work formed their respective professional societies, and in 1921 a comprehensive professional organization, the American Association of Social Workers, was formed.[16]

Councils. These important developments were but preliminaries to the real job of coördination, which exists on the level of the urban community. The movement toward city welfare councils began with the organization of councils of social agencies in Milwaukee and Pittsburgh in 1909. Some 350 cities in the United States have full-fledged councils of this type. Several hundred other cities, in one way or another, usually as a part of their community chests, carry on the principal functions of councils.

Councils are composed of delegates of all agencies, both public and private, operating in the field of health, welfare, and recreation, outstanding individual citizens, and representatives of any other organizations closely associated with social work. Their programs usually include coördinating activities ranging from getting acquainted to planning for more adequate community services; fact-finding, including the collection of routine information about agency programs, the gathering of facts about the community, and studies of specific problems; joint action, from improvement in community programs to sponsoring or supporting legislation; improving the quality of service through coöperative study and agreements; common services, usually not services to individuals except in demonstration situations, but rather such things as maintaining a directory of agencies, a social service index, a central volunteer bureau, or a joint publicity program; developing public interest through an educational program to improve the citizens' understanding of community problems, of the social work organization, of agency programs, and of the needs for coöperation and support.

Neighborhood councils have been organized in some of the larger cities which are little local replicas of the city-wide organization and

[15] Jane Chandler and Howard R. Knight, "Conferences of Social Work," in Kurtz, *op. cit.*, pp. 116–123.
[16] Anderson, *op. cit.*, p. 519.

operate in similar fashion on a more limited base. These neighbor-hood councils have representation in the city-wide council. They are made up, as a rule, largely of professional social workers, so that they maintain a direct but informal relationship to the agencies of which the professional workers are a part.

In a few cities, a different form of coöperative organization has developed, more accurately called a community council, which is primarily a people's organization rather than an organization of agencies and professional people. These councils are concerned with community problems on a broad base. The coördination and plan-ning of social work is just one area of problems and so takes its place by virtue of its importance in the consideration of the whole com-munity and its problems. In this plan the neighborhood council has tremendous significance. It has been "defined as 'grass roots' organi-zation of people living in and/or working in a natural geographic subdivision of a city, for the purpose of appraising local needs and developing resources to meet them. This activity involves the usual processes of community organization—study, planning, coordina-tion, and action. The neighborhood has, however, the special char-acteristic of being a group of people working together to eliminate problems directly affecting them in their work and homes. This per-sonal interest brings an urgent and dynamic quality to the neighbor-hood council."[17] These councils have been organized by local cit-izens' groups, special committees, local social agencies, councils of social agencies, and planning boards and other departments of local government.

Chests. Community chests, which are the organizations for co-operative fund-raising on the part of the private social agencies, got started a few years after the councils and have developed and spread along with them. The two are closely related; in fact, their compli-mentary functions are so essential to each other that when one does not exist in a community, the other includes some of the functions of the one which is lacking.

The community chest idea has appealed to American city people and has become firmly established as a part of urban social work. Chests have not always been successful, and there are some serious potential problems. Autocratic control of agency programs often happens when chests are dominated by conservative financial in-

[17] Merrill F. Krughoff, "Councils in Social Work," in Kurtz, *op. cit.*, pp. 130–138.

terests which have little understanding of social work. Arbitrary limitations are set on the total income of agencies, which must agree, in return for acceptance as participants in a chest, that they will make no appeal for operating requirements to the people of the community outside of the chest campaign.

In 1946 there were eight hundred community chests in American cities, which raised about $200,000,000. This was the largest number of chests ever reported, but the total raised was about 10 percent less than the year before, which was at the close of the war and included the various war funds. The general postwar letdown is reflected in the fact that in 1946 the chests fell 10 percent short of their goals, which is the poorest record for a decade; during the war years the goals were exceeded.

One important contribution of the chests to coördination is that a step has been taken toward social welfare planning in the cities: in drawing up the chest budgets, the work of each agency has had to be studied and appraised with reference to community needs in order that a fair apportionment of funds could be made.[18] This has encouraged the development of research departments, usually in the council of social agencies; however, in only a few cities have these departments even approached their possibilities, and nowhere have they yet been able to tackle any comprehensive planning for social welfare in the community.

Problems of Coördination. There are two fundamental and persistent problems of coördination and planning in social work in cities; both can and must be solved, but the solutions are not yet apparent.

The first problem lies in the fact that coördinating agencies, in the nature of the case, have no administrative authority. To give them any such authority is completely inconsistent with the democratic principle of social organization to which American society is committed. Coördination operates on the principle that working coöperatively will engender the will to coördinate and plan on the part of people and agencies. This is a slow process, and the force of institutionalization, with its established patterns and vested interests, works against it. The principle is sound, however, and it will operate effectively and creatively as there is developed within the institutions of social work a democratization of administration, with greater sensitivity to the problems of the community and the needs of peo-

[18] John B. Dawson, "Community Chests," in Kurtz, *op. cit.*, pp. 103–110.

ple. Such an inherent flexibility and adaptability can be used to achieve community welfare.

The second problem is that coördinating agencies are very difficult to finance. People give money, and cities appropriate money, for operations—that is, for doing things: rendering services, carrying out programs, and the like. Coördination is not an operation; it is a process. Operation, by principle, is left to the agencies which have been established for their respective operational purposes. Consequently, there is no tangible source of funds for the task of coördination and planning. There appear to be five plans or methods of financing coördination, all of which have been tried to some degree; the most promising has accumulated the least experience.

First is the "good angel" plan, by which a few people with money are convinced of the importance of this task and are asked to put up the necessary funds. This is a precarious method because people's interests in giving change as do their abilities. While this source of income is not yet played out, it is constantly declining in its potentialities. Grants from foundations fall into this category. Foundations, by and large, appropriate their funds for special projects; the launching of a coördinating agency might qualify, but seldom, if ever, do foundations accept any obligation toward the sustaining of an organization or program. This source, therefore, is available only from time to time for special endeavors. It must be recognized also that the "good angel" plan is inherently inconsistent with the very principle of the coöperative process.

Second is the operation of coördination and planning on a volunteer basis, without cost as such. This involves the investment of a great deal of time and effort on the part of professional people who are employed and paid to do the work of their respective operating agencies. It is not reasonable to expect that the magnitude and intricacies of conducting the coördinating and planning jobs can be bootlegged in this fashion. At any rate, the job requires executive responsibility to keep the machinery in operation and the results established. In a community of any size such serious business depends upon a thoroughly adequate and full-time staff.

Third is the support of the coördinating and planning function by the various agencies which are involved; that is, a percentage of each agency's budget is turned over to the coördinating agency. Again we have the problem of money given or appropriated for operation being, as governing boards are apt to think, sidetracked to what is still all too frequently considered a nonessential function. Such attitudes, plus the fact that operating budgets are at best too small, make such a source of support highly unlikely and impractical.

Fourth is the support of coördinating and planning by public or government funds. But this is an unlikely source since the appropriation of funds rests, in the final analysis, upon the acceptance of the function and operation for which the money is appropriated by the public. No such stage in the development of coördination and planning has yet been reached as could enable it to get public acceptance. Nor is city government fitted to operate a coöperative endeavor; its basis of operation is compulsion. The political aspects of city government, which contrive to be very powerful, would not be friendly to a genuinely coöperative enterprise.

Fifth is a comprehensive organization of the community: people's organizations on the neighborhood level coördinated into a community council in which a social welfare council, a health council, an education council, a research council, and a community chest are all completely integrated. Here would be the people working together in their own neighborhoods to understand and work out the solutions to their immediate problems and coöperating with other neighborhood groups on problems of the community. Among these problems would be coördination, planning, and raising the funds for the social service, health, and educational agencies of the community with a comprehensive budget. Through their participation in community affairs the people would have come to understand the financial needs of their organizations and would be ready to provide the money required by those enterprises which they had come to recognize as essential to the welfare of the people of the community. The cost of coördination and planning would be a part of the overall community welfare budget.

COST OF THE SOCIAL SERVICES

It has already been seen (p. 287) that health and welfare represent approximately 25 percent of the expenditure of cities. This, however, is only a part of the total cost. In 1944 a study was made of the total expenditure for health and welfare services of all kinds, including government and voluntary, chest and nonchest agencies, in fourteen cities. It was found that during that year the total expenditures averaged approximately $27 per capita. On this basis, the total cost for health and welfare in American cities would have been in the neighborhood of two billion dollars.

This study further found that, of the total amount, 7.7 percent was raised by community chests, 38.5 percent came from other voluntary sources, including fees, income from investments, sales, and other contributions, and 53.8 percent came from tax funds. When this is broken down to show the distribution among the various areas of the social services and the relative load on the three general sources indicated, the results can be seen in Table 53.

TABLE 53. Percentage Distribution of Total Expenditures for Health and Welfare Services in Thirteen Urban Areas, in 1944, by Kind of Service and by Source of Income[19]

| | | Source of Income | | | | |
Kind of Service	Percentage of Total Expenditures	Community Chests	Other Voluntary	Fees	Public Funds	
Relief and services to families and adults	41.2	4.7	12.7	4.5	78.1	100.0
Child welfare	8.4	15.0	14.5	13.1	57.4	100.0
Health	42.4	3.1	5.4	49.8	41.7	100.0
Group work and recreation	7.0	30.0	21.1	24.4	84.5	100.0
Planning, financing, and coördination	1.0	83.0	12.9	—	4.1	100.0
Total	100.0	7.7	10.1	28.4	53.8	100.0

It is clear that the burden of the cost of planning and coördination falls on community chests, that the bulk of relief is now paid from tax funds, that health activities are to the largest extent self-supporting, and that group work is, for the most part, still on the side of private support. Remedial programs absorb around 90 percent of the expenditures, and these are the programs which have come to have the backing of public funds.

The statistics indicate that the cost of health and welfare is about evenly divided between public (53.8 percent) and private (46.2 percent) funds, but the private include 28.4 percent from fees. The actual voluntary share was 12.2 percent, a slight gain over the 9.9 percent of 1942. On the whole, however, the part of private contribu-

[19] Community Chests and Councils, Inc., *Expenditures for Community Health and Welfare* (New York, 1946), pp. 2, 7.

tions has changed over the years from almost all to a minor item. Public funds are: local 24.3 percent, state 17.8 percent, and federal 11.8 percent; the last declined from 21.8 percent in 1942.[20] It is the federal part which fluctuates in accordance with the acuteness of the pressure of needs. This role of the federal government has developed since the depression period, when the extent of the problems made it necessary for federal funds and agencies to supplement the inadequate resources, in money and organization, of local communities and states. As a result, two roles of the federal government have become established and recognized: unemployment insurance, old-age pensions, and the other items under the Federal Security Act and similar legislation; and the cushion role just mentioned.

While social work is indigenous to the urban community, its development in cities has influenced in many ways the organizations and services in rural areas. Working amid the simple conditions of rural life, social work has gained new understanding and perfected methods of operation which have in turn fed back to urban social work many significant contributions.

Social work more than anything else reflects the effects of urbanization on people and the kinds of problems they must face. Because of this nearness to change and to people, social work has shown a relatively high degree of flexibility. There are growing evidences, however, that the grip of institutionalization has begun to tighten. With all its growth, development, and expansion, it lags behind the demands of the forces of change. It has not yet been able in a comprehensive way to put its knowledge and skills to the tasks of prevention and anticipation of community needs. When it becomes possible through more adequate research to understand the urban community and the trends which are taking place more thoroughly, and when the adaptability of the institutions of social work has been more completely attained, then through coöperation and a greater commitment to the objective of the welfare of the community's people, coördination and planning will be able to anticipate problems and foresee needs and so escape the kinds of difficulties which up to now have forced social work very largely into remedial patterns.

[20] *Ibid.*, pp. 2, 3, 7, 9.

CHAPTER 22

PATTERNS OF HEALTH
ORGANIZATION

IT IS to be expected that an organized area of urban life which ha:
responded extensively to the impact of the force of urbanization in
its adaptations and developments might also show certain phases of
its activity and organization which had lagged far behind. This is
true in the area of health. Special interests, concentrations of power,
areas of medical science where knowledge is still inadequate, lack
of appreciation and use of available health services, high cost of institutional operation, inadequacies of public funds, and many other
things have prevented health services from adequately meeting some
of the needs in urban communities. This is apparent in the organization of health services in cities. Some areas are highly developed;
others are far behind in their organization; and though there are
many interrelationships, there is no unity of total organization. As
a result, the patterns within the several areas must be considered
somewhat discretely.

PUBLIC HEALTH SERVICES

The area of paramount importance, because it deals with the
health of the community as a whole, is public health. This area of
health services is operated almost entirely as a part of government,
paid for out of the public treasury. The most advanced program and
the highest development of organization are found in public health.

The Stern report,[1] in a historical inventory, reports the extensive
services now being directly and indirectly provided by agencies of
government on local, state, and federal levels. The Mustard report[2]

[1] Bernhard J. Stern, *Medical Services by Government* (New York: Commonwealth Fund, 1946).

[2] Harry S. Mustard, *Government in Public Health* (New York: Commonwealth Fund, 1945).

emphasizes the trends in the expanding health services of government and points out the next steps in public health and medical care.

Smillie points out, however, that the development of public health has been an ebb and flow. Up to 1800 little more than the application of quarantine to combat contagious diseases in local communities was done, and this was largely a failure. The next fifty years, dominated by a disbelief in the contagious nature of disease, were "the dark ages of public health in the United States." There was an awakening from 1850 to 1875 of the "simple principle of community responsibility for health protection," and organization began. The next quarter century was a "golden era of communicable disease control," during which "practically all the basic information upon which our present system of communicable disease control depends was discovered and developed." Following the turn of the century, however, the public health services became a part of the political spoils system, resulting in inefficiency and incompetence. But these years gave rise to a new philosophy, "related to the importance of community action in the protection of the health of the individual." This came through the emergence of voluntary health agencies and the formation of foundations. These agencies experimented with methods and procedures, usually in special fields, and sought to demonstrate ways "to prevent illness and improve the health of the individual, and thus promote the health and happiness of the community." Since 1925 the nationalization of public health has brought great developments in all levels of government. Through publicity, promotion, consultation, subsidy, etc., the impact on the extension of public health organizations and programs in the cities has been very great. People have become aware of "the importance, from the community point of view, of health promotion of the individual because of the fact that the ill health of the individual is a direct menace to the economic security of the community."[3] Some general statements regarding the areas in which public health in American cities is now operating follow.[4]

Vital Statistics. All communities are required by law to gather the current data on births and deaths. A local office with a registrar

[3] Wilson G. Smillie, *Preventive Medicine and Public Health.* Copyright 1946 by The Macmillan Company and used with their permission; pp. 7–10.

[4] The material for these sections is drawn largely from Smillie, *op. cit.*, and from the article "Public Health," by Wilson G. Smillie, in Russell H. Kurtz (editor), *Social Work Year Book, 1947* (New York: Russell Sage Foundation, 1947), pp. 387–391.

is established for this purpose, and the attending physicians are responsible for making a report of each case. The various forms of communicable disease also must be reported, and the Bureau of the Census has recommended that data on marriages, divorces, annulments, and adoptions also be included in the records. While the statistics are forwarded to state offices, in the cities they are extensively used to keep track of health conditions, to compute trends, to check on the effectiveness of controls and of programs, and as a basis for geographical concentration of programs and program emphases. These data are the very foundation of the work of public health and are used to great advantage.

Sanitation.   Sanitation has come to be a highly technical matter operated in cities under the direction of trained sanitary engineers. It includes not only sewer systems and sewage disposal and furnishing and maintaining a sufficient and pure water supply for the community, but also food, meat, and milk inspection, the last often involving the inspection and certification of dairy farms throughout the entire milkshed of the city, vermin control, and fumigation and disinfection. More lately the sanitary aspects of housing have been included. Sometimes garbage collection and disposal and street-cleaning are included, although usually these are done by other agencies of the city government. For the larger cities, where water supply is very complicated and involves sources, transmission, and storage over large areas, it is operated by a separate department.

Communicable Diseases.   The health departments of cities not only keep track of contagious diseases through reporting by the physicians of every suspected case, but they carry out control through the isolation of cases and the quarantine of contacts. They also endeavor to search for the source of the disease. Much attention is given to vaccination against an increasing number of diseases and other preventive measures. In the spring of 1947 a few cases of small-pox in New York City brought a mass vaccination plan into play by the Department of Health, with the result that about 5,000,000 were vaccinated by the city at its expense.

Venereal Diseases.   Cases must be reported, isolation is used when necessary, tracing of infection is carried out, laboratory service is provided, free drugs are furnished, and clinics are operated. In the states where they are required, premarital examinations and blood tests on every pregnant woman are given.

Tuberculosis. Tuberculosis services involve clinics (because a large proportion of cases are poor), early diagnosis (frequently using mobile equipment for mass chest x-rays), the tracing of infection, and the isolation of patients (preferably in hospitals, for the protection of other family members). In the cities there is usually close coöperation with the Tuberculosis and Health Association and the department of hospitals of the city and the state. Remarkable progress has been made in lowering the incidence of tuberculosis, especially in children and young people. A concentrated campaign in the city of Detroit some years ago demonstrated the amazing improvement that could be made when sufficient funds are made available, resulting in a very large long-term saving in cost of treatment. One of the crucial phases in fighting tuberculosis is an educational program.

Maternal and Child Health. The premature death of children has been a problem and a challenge to public health programs. The successes have been striking, but there still remains much to be done. In the process of developing the program it has become very largely preventive in nature, involving clinics (prenatal, neonatal, postnatal, and well-baby), health conferences, classes, pamphlets, publicity, and home visits of nurses for instruction and care. This program has been the most successful in bringing to bear all of the resources of cities on a problem, including many voluntary agencies and doctors in private practice. Most cities have school health services where children are under the daily surveillance of a nurse and in which diagnostic services over the whole range of child health are given.

Laboratory Services. Extensive and modern laboratories are maintained by health departments in larger cities so that the best possible services can be immediately available. They are engaged in the routine examination of water and milk. They examine blood specimens for physicians. Diphtheria cultures and other types of specimens are examined without cost. Foods, drugs, and other products of potential danger are examined. All vaccines, sera, etc., are assayed, and sometimes some of them are produced on special farms. Intensive research is carried on in reference to any disease or situation dangerous to the health of the community.

Public Health Nursing. Fully one-third of all the public health budget is allocated to nursing service. Public health nurses have special training and experience in addition to their regular nursing training. They work throughout the whole of the public health program with many special functions. Their work is considered primarily educational, making their unique contributions through personal service, in considerable measure by home visitation. This visiting nurse service is operated by health departments but often participated in by voluntary organizations. There are two phases to the work, (1) preventive and instructional service and (2) bedside care, for which a nominal charge is made to those who can afford to pay. Nurses greatly facilitate the successful operation of public health services by finding cases, procuring early diagnosis, and following up prescribed treatment.

Dental Services. While the problem of decayed teeth faces all in the community, public dental services have so far generally been made available only to children, usually as a part of the school health program, for which financial grants are available from the federal Children's Bureau. Most of the larger cities maintain dental and oral hygiene clinics for preschool and school children, though they are seldom adequate to meet the needs.

Other Services. In a section of his book entitled "Adult Health Protection and Promotion," Smillie[5] has chapters with the following titles: Geriatrics, Mental Hygiene, Malnutrition and Its Prevention, Control of Cancer, Preventive Aspects of Peptic Ulcer and Appendicitis, The Role of Public Health and Preventive Medicine in Heart Disease and Hypertension, Preventive Aspects of Obesity and Diabetes, Preventive Aspects of Arthritis, Preventive Aspects of Allergic Conditions, Preventive Aspects of Alcoholism, Industrial Hygiene. These represent phases of activity which may or may not be specially organized, but which come within the scope of the concern of public health.

PUBLIC HEALTH ORGANIZATION

In each city will be found a department of health. Over this department there is usually a board of health, consisting of from three to five citizens selected by the city executive to carry out the municipal health functions. Membership on the board is an honorary position without salary, with overlapping terms of from three to five years. In some cities the board has only advisory powers, but usually

[5] *Preventive Medicine and Public Health*, Chaps. XXVI–XXXVI.

it has the power to select the health officer, to make policies, and to formulate the sanitary code.

The health officer is a physician with special training and often a graduate degree in public health. He is usually employed for a definite period of years. Standards for training and experience have been set up by the American Public Health Association for different classes of cities. Heads of divisions are also M.D.'s. A chart of organization for a city of around 100,000 population is shown in Figure 36. The health officer may also have the responsibility for one of the

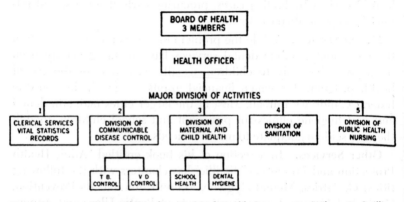

Figure 36. Organization Chart of a Municipal Health Department. (Wilson G. Smillie: *Preventive Medicine and Public Health.* Copyright 1946 by The Macmillan Company and used with their permission, p. 508.)

divisions. Health education will operate through all divisions and probably be administratively related to statistics and records. Nutrition may be in Division 1 or 3, and laboratory services would be in Division 4. More than half of the staff will be nurses. In a city of this size there would likely be a director of nurses, from twelve to fifteen nurses, and an assistant educational director trained in nutrition, health education, and perhaps child psychology.

The total personnel is drawn from many specialists. In addition to medicine, nursing, engineering, and dentistry, there might be those trained in nutrition, health education, bacteriology, entomology, statistics, parasitology, and veterinary medicine.

Larger cities have a more complex organization, with more divisions or bureaus, and a more extensive staff, including a greater variety of specialists. A chart of the organization of the Department of Health of New York City is seen in Figure 37.

Decentralized Services. In the larger cities it has been found that one public health center is too far removed from most of the people to be of any real service. Consequently, the city has been divided into health districts, in each of which a health center has been established. In New York City, for example, thirty such service areas have been laid out, which makes a population of about 250,000 to be served in each. These district health centers are replicas, in organization and program, of the department of health, with clinics, child health stations, district nursing offices, health education units, and

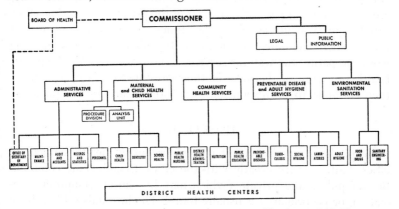

Figure 37. Organization Chart, Department of Health of New York City.

whatever other services are required to meet the peculiar needs in their respective areas. Each is in charge of a district health officer. Before the war fifteen new, up-to-the-minute buildings had been erected for health centers, and plans for the other fifteen await their turn for construction. In those areas where the need for health services is especially great, the centers are supplemented with substations. There are, in addition, sixty-four child health stations scattered throughout the city. All of them are coördinated through the central office.[6]

In some of the health centers district offices of the other health agencies have also been located and a close working relationship established. Some have formed community health councils whose headquarters and secretary have also been given offices in the same building. With close coöperation between health programs, services, and citizens' activities, real progress is being made.

[6] Rebecca B. Rankin, *New York Advancing* (New York: Municipal Reference Library, 1945), pp. 147–156.

Some centers operate in connection with great medical centers and their schools of medicine. In New York City this is true of several of the district health centers which house the departments of public health and preventive medicine, where graduate students in public health work, observe, and attend classes.

Voluntary Agencies. The large private health agencies, such as the Tuberculosis and Health Association and the Red Cross, as well as many smaller, more specialized groups, coöperate with the general public health programs in the health centers. Sometimes they are responsible for particular aspects of the program; sometimes they supply special equipment; at other times they supply personnel or funds. These voluntary agencies, in the main, do the pioneering work, preparing the way for services to be taken over by the public health program; or, because of their prestige and large resources, they continue to be responsible for distinct parts of the program.

HOSPITALS

Hospitals are an important part of organized health services in cities. Patterns vary greatly with the cities, though some combination of public and private (which may be church, nonprofit association, or proprietary) is usually found. The hospitals seldom have formal relationship beyond simple arrangements of reciprocity or occasionally a united campaign for funds, and even here not all are likely to coöperate.

City Hospitals. Most cities of any size have hospitals which are operated on tax funds for the care of indigents and those with contagious diseases, which private institutions endeavor to avoid if possible. In the largest cities this becomes a sizable task. Take New York, for example; it has, to be sure, the largest and most complicated task because it is the largest of the cities, but it shows what is involved and what other cities must deal with on a smaller scale with less resources, which makes in many ways a more difficult problem.

New York since 1929 has had a Department of Hospitals. Under its jurisdiction are operated twelve general hospitals, four contagious disease hospitals, three tuberculosis hospitals, a neurological hospital, a cancer hospital, a hospital and school for mental-defectives, a hospital for children with bone, joint, and gland (surgical) tuberculosis, and two homes for the aged and infirm. The total bed capacity is 20,500. In addition, the admission of many patients to private hospitals at the city's expense (on special below-cost rates) is authorized.

The department also directs and supervises a coördinated ambulance and emergency service covering the whole city, using its own, and also private, hospitals. It licenses all private hospitals and convalescent homes. It maintains a morgue in each borough of the city.

There are seven schools of nursing. Close working relationships are maintained with the five medical schools of the city. Some 4000 visiting physicians and surgeons, both general practitioners and specialists, serve in the hospitals without pay. Volunteer auxiliaries of various sorts also render much service. The paid employees normally number approximately 22,000, a number exceeded only in the Board of Education.[7]

Private Hospitals. The number and kinds of private hospitals in any city depend on many things: size of the population, average income of the people, nationality and religious backgrounds of major elements in the population, educational backgrounds of the people, occupational patterns of the city's labor force, and special needs for medical service (for example, a heavy proportion of industrial workers subject to accidents or other work-induced incapacities).

Many of the major religious denominations operate hospitals in cities where groups of their people are found in large numbers: Roman Catholic, Protestant Episcopal, Presbyterian, Methodist, Jewish, Lutheran, and others have their names attached to famous hospitals in one city or another. Many nonprofit associations also operate hospitals. In the larger and wealthier cities proprietary hospitals, operated often by groups of doctors, are also found. Though most hospitals do not discriminate among those they admit, it is clear that religious and economic groups tend to be served by this distribution of hospitals.

Larger cities are able to have specialized hospitals: orthopedic, children's, etc., where services of a particular kind can be concentrated.

Medical Social Work. Since its beginning in Massachusetts General Hospital in Boston and Bellevue Hospital in New York in 1905,

---

[7] The City of New York, *Official Directory:* "The City Record"; Rebecca B. Rankin, *op. cit.*, and *Guide to the Municipal Government: City of New York* (New York: Eagle Library, 1939).

the use of medical social workers in city hospitals has gradually increased. "There is now a growing belief that patients can be more satisfactorily and permanently restored to health when medical study and treatment are combined with treatment of unfavorable social and emotional factors." This is the job of the medical social worker—direct case work services to individual patients carried on in medical institutions in association with physicians, with its focus on social problems incident to illness, physical handicap, and medical provision.

More recently medical social workers have come also to serve in the development of community health programs and as consultants where expanding health services have come to include additional large groups of people.[8]

HEALTH EDUCATION

Health education has already been referred to, but it is so important in the growing edge of health organizations in cities that it should have more than incidental reference. It is coming to be infused into all public health activities, even to be a vital part of the work of clinics. It is taking its place as a regular part of the curriculum of public elementary and secondary schools and even of colleges.

Much mass education, using all of the means of mass communication, is being done not only by the city departments of health, but also by the major private agencies, such as the local organizations of the Tuberculosis and Health Association, the Red Cross, and the Cancer Society.

Training of health educators is a regular part of many schools of education, and there is increasing demand for people trained in this field. Certainly one of the crucial points in the advance of health in cities is the education of people in a greater appreciation of health, the development of better health habits, and an understanding of the uses of the available health facilities.

MEDICAL CARE

Medical care, for the most part, is provided through the private practice of individual physicians and surgeons. There are more doc-

[8] Grace White, "Medical Social Work," in Kurtz, *op. cit.*, pp. 310–311.

tors per 100,000 population in cities and more in those areas where per capita income is high. That is to say, the availability of medical care is highly related to the ability of people to pay and bears little relation to needs for medical services. This is true from neighborhood to neighborhood within cities also.

This method of organization is coming more and more to be challenged. Perhaps the two greatest single factors in this changing attitude have been the findings of the Committee on the Costs of Medical Care[9] and the astounding numbers that were turned down by the armed services in World War II on account of physical disability.

Following the passage of the workmen's compensation laws in the various states, there were set up in many industrial cities offices where groups of general practitioners and specialists worked together to provide the services required by those suffering industrial accidents. This method of organization proved satisfactory, efficient, and profitable. But the extension of the experiment has been slow.

Many examples of group medicine can be found in cities, but it is still a minor element in medical care. In a few cases, such as the Ross-Loos Clinic in Los Angeles, group medical practice has been combined with prepaid medical care on a complete basis and made available to large groups of people. In spite of the great success of these scattered enterprises, such organization is actually available to only a small number of city people.

The Blue Cross, which is an organized prepaid hospitalization plan, operates in many American cities and does serve some millions of people. More recently prepaid surgical service has been added to many hospital plans. This is an excellent advance in one area of health organization, though it comes far from meeting the needs.

The Wagner-Murray-Dingell Bill, turned down by Congress, is still to be reckoned with. If it should pass, the whole pattern of the organization of medical care throughout the country would be changed. This seems inevitable, not only because of the rising demand, but because the present system has broken down even where it has had the best chance, in the cities; it cannot work in a highly urbanized society. The forms which the new organization will take are still to be wrought.

Mustard conservatively states: ". . . no plan for improvement of

[9] Committee on the Costs of Medical Care, *Medical Care for the American People: The Final Report* (Chicago: The University of Chicago Press, 1932).

public health services in the nation as a whole or in any given state may be approached, realistically, without a recognition of the fact that the administration of a public medical care program may become the responsibility of the health department. If this should come to pass, much that is done in one way now would then be done in another . . . a public medical care program would need an administrative mechanism just as badly as does the present conventional public health system."[10]

Supplementary Reading

Mustard, Harry S. *Government in Public Health*. New York: Commonwealth Fund, 1945.

    An analysis of the trends in the expansion of government health services and of the next steps in public health and medical care.

Smillie, Wilson G. *Preventive Medicine and Public Health*. New York: The Macmillan Company, 1946.

    A comprehensive analysis of the whole field of public health.

Stern, Bernhard J. *Medical Services by Government*. New York: Commonwealth Fund, 1946.

    A historical treatment that deals with the medical functions and services carried on by Government at its various levels.

[10] Mustard, *op. cit.*, p. 191.

CHAPTER 23

THE STRUCTURE OF EDUCATION

EDUCATION, which is society's means of transmitting its culture, is an excellent example of what happens to the organization and operation of the functions of community life under such dynamic circumstances as are to be found in cities. While the function of education assumes proportionately about the same significance it holds in smaller communities, its bulk is so great that on the one hand it can operate on a broader base and on the other hand it is subject to the serious difficulties of bigness. The tables in Chapter 15 showing the percentage distribution of city expenditures indicate that health, welfare, public safety, and education are in an unstable equilibrium and that public safety, which for many years took a considerably smaller proportion of city expenditures than schools, in recent years has taken a larger proportion.

Specialization has reached a high degree of development in city school systems. Because there are so many schools, such a large staff, and so much money, it is possible to employ many different kinds of people for all sorts of specialized services and even to maintain specialized schools. This makes available to some of the children and young people of the cities a great variety of educational experience and makes it more nearly possible to meet the many different special needs among the students.

Such programs require many specialists who are highly trained in the areas of their narrow specialized functions. Inevitably, as these people work in limited areas, they grow more and more out of touch with the general operation of the schools. Many schools and many specialists require complicated organization and competent administrators. As administration becomes a highly technical job, the result is that professionals not only operate but also control the schools which perform the community function of education. The

435

special functions for which all of these people are responsible absorb their attention and energies, and the schools tend to become increasingly out of touch with their environments and less sensitive to the needs and desires of the people of their communities.

This insulation of schools from their communities in turn creates two new and serious problems. As the understanding of the learning process and of education has grown, it has become increasingly clear that the accomplishments of education depend to a considerable extent upon the conditions under which children live in their homes and upon the influences exerted upon their lives by their communities. So further specialists are needed to deal with this problem, home teachers, school social workers, and community workers—important additions in so far as they can be provided, but at best an artificial solution to the real problem.

The second problem is even more fundamental. The American tradition holds zealously to a close relationship between the people and their schools. It has been a part of the concept of democracy, but trends work against this tradition. The closeness of schools to the people of their communities also bears a close relationship to the quality of education which the schools can produce. The importance of the economics of the community, the demographic characteristics, the type of community, and the cultural backgrounds of its people to the adaptability of public schools was brought to light by Mort and Cornell.[1] The support, both financial and moral, which a community gives its schools is involved, and this rests upon the people's understanding of what the schools are doing and what they can and should do. Such an understanding depends upon the actual participation of the citizenry in the formation of public school policy and the participation of schools in the affairs of the community. Pierce,[2] in an endeavor to analyze the factors which contribute to good schools, in terms of their relative significance, found that 64 percent of the contributing factors had to do with the community outside the schools themselves. This necessitates the addition to the corps of specialists in the schools of those who are trained in public relations, community organization, and adult education.

[1] Paul R. Mort and Francis G. Cornell, *American Schools in Transition* (New York: Bureau of Publications, Teachers College, Columbia University, 1941).

[2] Truman Mitchell Pierce, *Controllable Community Characteristics Related to Quality of Education* (New York: Bureau of Publications, Teachers College, Columbia University, 1947), pp. 8–13.

THE GREAT MACHINE OF URBAN
PUBLIC EDUCATION

City school systems are big business. They employ some 500,000 people and spend approximately $1,500,000,000 annually. Large cities (over 100,000 in population) in 1945–1946 had, on the average, about 125 school buildings, slightly more than 100 on the administrative and supervisory staff, nearly 1800 teachers, some 58,000 pupils, an annual cost of $8,250,000, an indebtedness of $5,750,000, or approximately two-thirds of the annual cost, and school property valued at a little over $31,000,000. The range, however, is very great because the average includes New York City, with an annual budget of more than $200,000,000 and a pupil enrollment of nearly 900,000. A summary of the major facts of city school systems by city size groups is given in Table 54.

Big Administration. The administrative machinery for the operation of city school systems is complicated, extensive, and costly. Unified and centralized organization is a relatively new experiment which was introduced around the turn of the century. It was an attempt to overcome the inadequate and bad spots in the many local school districts and took the form of big business, which, at that time, was thought to be the solution of most problems. Like all great enterprises, it has been found to be costly, unwieldy, dissipating time, energy, and money in keeping the machinery in operation, and ultimately relatively ineffective in providing the best educational experience for individual children. It has been successful in equalizing educational opportunity, but it must be remembered that equalization is averaging; while it brings the lower end of the scale up, it also brings the higher end down. In more recent years the responsibility for equalization has been taken over by the states.

Complexity, however, does not come all at once. It develops gradually as city populations increase and spread out and as the service of schools is extended to a broadening age range and a greater variety of young people. As a result, in many cities, the administration which has been added bit by bit, as required, has become chaotic, overlapping, and clumsy. A scientific study of a school system, therefore, must begin by straightening out the administrative structure. An illustration of such a proposal for one of the larger cities, giving an idea of the complexity of administration in a large public school system, is shown in Figure 38.

TABLE 54. Summary of Major Facts About Public School Systems in Cities of 2500 Population or More, by Size Groups, for 1945–1946[3]

Item	All City Systems	Cities of			
		100,000 Population or More Group I	30,000 to 99,999 Population Group II	10,000 to 29,999 Population Group III	2,500 to 9,999 Population Group IV
City school systems	3,464	92	257	728	2,387
School buildings in use	32,862	11,323	5,487	6,804	9,248
Administrative and supervisory staff	25,864	9,562	4,648	5,223	6,431
Teachers	397,268	164,059	70,597	76,461	86,151
Pupils	11,970,043	5,295,445	2,011,736	2,201,602	2,461,260
Current expense	$1,528,644,864	$758,256,372	$260,561,496	$249,777,443	$260,049,553
Indebtedness	$1,224,728,951	$531,280,956	$265,574,000	$228,232,000	$199,141,995
Value of school property	$5,825,532,000	$2,860,778,000	$1,026,678,000	$995,432,000	$942,644,000
Average current expense per pupil in average daily attendance	$150.65	$171.92	$150.78	$131.49	$123.60

[3] Adapted from the 1944–1946 *Biennial Survey of Education in the United States: Statistics of City School Systems, 1945–46*, Chap. III (Washington: Government Printing Office, 1949), Table I, pp. 19–23, and Table XII, p. 13.

City school systems can and do set high standards for the selection and promotion of personnel. The great variety of teachers, specialists, and administrative officers necessitates many different specifications, examinations, and licenses. This, in turn, requires a board of examiners, or its equivalent, and a personnel department. All of the standards and machinery, however, cannot solve the fundamental problems of teaching personnel in public schools, inbreeding and inexperience: inbreeding because cities can usually supply technically qualified persons for the whole range of positions from their own people, and inexperience because young people tend to have more adequate training and find it easier to pass examinations—but this is no guarantee that youngsters will turn into good teachers.

Professional personnel is protected by probationary periods, salary scales with regular increments, tenure, and pensions. So-called "alertness" courses are often required as a condition of receiving salary increments. These things provide a stability of personnel which is all to the good, but it also makes serious problems. An aging teaching force makes changes in curriculum and innovations more difficult, and the infusion of "new blood" in the teaching force becomes impossible when school populations are rapidly declining, as they have been in many large cities. In New York City, from 1935 to 1943, because of a decline in school enrollment of about 27 percent, the number of teachers decreased nearly 17 percent, which decrease was made up of resignations and retirements without additions to the teaching force. A 22 percent increase in the next seven years made just as serious a problem in the other direction.

The proportionate cost of administration increases as the size of the city increases. Leggett and Vincent, in their study comparing New York with other communities, concluded: "When the schools of New York City are compared with schools in a group of communities of approximately equal wealth, that spend about the same amount of money to educate each child, and that have about the same kind of people as has the City, it becomes apparent that the children in those comparable communities get a better educational break than the children in New York City."[4] The great cost of overhead was shown primarily in the ratio of teacher to pupils: it would take between 9000 and 10,000 additional teachers to bring New York up to

[4] Stanton F. Leggett and William S. Vincent, *A Program for Meeting the Needs of New York City Schools* (New York: Public Education Association, 1947), p. 3.

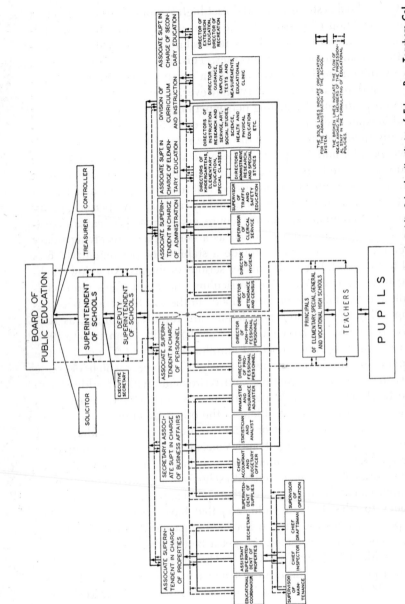

Figure 38. Proposed Reorganization of the Administrative Staff of the Pittsburgh Public Schools. (Institute of Educ. Res., Teachers College, Columbia Univ. *The Report of a Survey of the Public Schools of Pittsburgh, Pennsylvania*, 1940, p. 294.)

the average of the other communities. But there were also deficiencies in other personnel (dental hygienists, nurses, doctors, librarians, field administrative personnel), in buildings and equipment, in supplies, and in plant maintenance and operation. All in all, it was computed that to make up these deficiencies would cost about $100,000,-000, an increase in the annual budget of 50 percent. It is unlikely that any such increase could be obtained when, each year, education must fight to get the budget as it is.[5] Whenever slight increases are obtained, they are swallowed up for new buildings, which are obviously necessary, or by increases in the salaries of present teachers, whose large number and organization enable them to exert great pressure.

Big Schools. City schools operate in large units, sometimes with as many as 5000 students. While a variety of courses are offered, there tends to be relatively little flexibility within the accepted patterns. Other aspects of regimentation become necessary in the operation of such large schools and such an extensive system.

School buildings cost more in cities. They must be larger and of stronger construction. They must meet the safety and fire standards of their cities. They are built for a long time, and, though they may be constructed according to the best standards of use in their day, a half century later they are entirely unfitted for changed patterns and standards of education. For example, the development of the teaching of hygiene and health includes the frequent washing of hands, and yet many an old city school building has no equipment by which children can wash their hands at all. Types of classrooms in vogue fifty years ago are great handicaps to accepted programs of today. Space is expensive in cities, and so many city schools have been built right against the sidewalks, with no play space except the street in front of the school.

Experimentation. In spite of the difficulties, however, experimentation is carried on. Specialized personnel is available, and usually some manipulable margin of funds. Coöperation with universities and other special agencies is from time to time arranged for experimental purposes. Occasionally a number of projects are going on simultaneously. Greater difficulties come, however, in infusing patterns developed in successful experiments throughout the school system. Such adaptations make slow headway when the regular

[5] *Ibid.*, pp. 3, 6, 8, 9.

teaching staff must be depended on to make the adaptations. When additional staff is provided, changes come more quickly. This occasionally happens, as when in New York City, a few years ago, community coördinators were provided for some schools. As great bodies move slowly, so do changes take time in city schools. There tends to be a considerable lag between educational practice and the best knowledge and understanding of education.

THE STRUGGLE FOR THE CONTROL OF PUBLIC EDUCATION

Education is unique among the functions of urban communities, as it is throughout the whole of the democratic society of the United States. People place a different valuation on education which is expressed in special laws which provide separately for the organization of education distinct from all other government functions, and also special bases for taxation for schools. These give to education unique independence and stability. In spite of the trends in urban communities, many of which work against the continuation of the distinctiveness of public education, its uniqueness persistently continues in some respects.

Public administrators would like to simplify city operations according to their standards of efficiency by putting education on the same basis as a police department, as fire protection, or as public welfare. They have never felt, however, that the public would support them in establishing the type of organization, appointments, and operations in the area of education which prevails in other departments.

In small cities boards of education are still often elected by the people in the tradition of keeping education in the hands of the people, but in the larger cities the difficulties involved in knowing candidates tend to make election a matter of party politics, so that the board of education has generally come to be appointed by the mayor, who has been elected by the people. Then the superintendent of schools is elected by the boards, not appointed by the city council or the mayor. Where boards of education are still elected by the citizens, the voting is at a different time from other elections, and not on a party basis, in order to keep the schools as far from politics as possible.

The uniqueness of the financing of education is not always apparent. The fact that schools are included as an item—in fact, the largest item—on city budgets gives no indication of their separateness. There are, however, many laws which prescribe the financing of education. State laws specify the minimum support which communities can give to their schools, the conditions and amount of state aid which can be obtained, and the maximum of local tax levy which can be used for school purposes. These conditions establish the independence of school budgets and accounting. Some cities permit their school boards to levy separate taxes or to veto the levy made by city governments for school purposes. More and more, however, city financial departments have interfered with and sought to control the financing of schools.

A number of studies have been made of various aspects of dependent and independent boards of education. The results of these studies support the conclusion of most school administrators and educational observers that boards of education which are fiscally independent generally spend their money more efficiently and effectively than boards which are dependent upon municipal officials in matters of the budget.[6]

Not only is it practically impossible to fix responsibility for school administration where school boards are fiscally dependent, but inefficiencies show up at almost every point in the administrative procedures.

Where non-school officials have the power to interfere they usually will interfere. No aspect of the educational system is likely to be immune. The orderly hiring, promoting or transferring of school personnel will frequently be interrupted. The establishing of necessary supervisory positions which involve higher salary brackets often will not be tolerated. The reduction in class size to permit more adequate individual attention will be questioned. The value of guidance services, school social workers, and other specialists will not readily be appreciated. The importance of curriculum research and experiment, of visual and audio aids and other modern requisites of effective teaching will not be fully grasped. Repairs, rehabilitation and replacement of buildings will often be guided by political or other extraneous considerations rather than educational purpose.[7]

[6] Frederick C. McLaughlin, *Fiscal and Administrative Control of City School Systems, New York State* (New York: Public Education Association, 1949), p. 50.
[7] *Ibid.*, p. 51.

Mort has indicated five basic control principles[8] which operate in public education:

1. The integral character of the educational enterprise: School government must be viewed as an integral whole; through family, community, state, and nation, it operates under distinctive government treatment giving the structure of education a separateness which results in many conflicts between educational administration and the public administration concerned with the balance of governmental operations.

2. Education a state function: Education is specifically recognized in the constitutions of the states as a public responsibility to assure to all children a satisfactory foundation education by whatever means are necessary.

3. Home rule: Changing laws have maintained a bias in favor of local power to keep education close to the people in order that the right to make decisions on the character of education will be maintained in local communities.

4. Independence of finance and control: Financing and control have no inherent relationship; much of the financing of education can best be done through the agency of the people called state government, but this does not in any way modify the carrying out of control through the agency of local government.

5. Fiscal responsibility of school boards: The integrity of the school system should not be diluted by entangling fiscal relationships between boards of education and municipal governments; both simplicity and effective operation demand that the educational responsibility placed on school boards be supported by fiscal responsibility.

Although the principles of control for public education can be set down with great clarity, this provides no escape from the problems inherent in the present conditions in cities. The primacy which education holds in city life by tradition, by law, by importance, and by public acceptance cannot free it from the inevitable competition with other essential functions of cities which becomes more acute as needs for more functions increase, as the resources of cities decrease, and as the cost of operation mounts.

[8] *Fiscal Policy for Public Education in the State of New York,* Report of a Joint Committee Representing the New York State Educational Board and the Public Education Association of New York City (Albany: New York State Teachers Association, 1947), pp. 74–91.

EDUCATIONAL OPPORTUNITIES OF CITIES

Public schools are the first consideration in dealing with education in American cities because they are recognized as a major function of the corporate community. They do not by any means, however, comprise the whole of education in any city. A complete picture of urban education is impossible to obtain since many of its activities are tucked away in the nooks and crannies of community life and are known only to a few people who are directly concerned with them. It is possible, however, to point out the various kinds of educational activities likely to be found in an American city. For convenience they will be catalogued in four groups: the varieties of activities in public education, quasi-public educational institutions, kinds of private schools, and adult education.

Varieties of Public Education Activities. The broad base of public education in cities manifests itself in two ways: in the variety of programs in the usual elementary and secondary schools, and in various separate schools established to serve special interests or special groups of students.

Most city elementary schools now have kindergartens, so that children can begin to attend school at five years of age. The programs in the grades supplement reading, writing, and arithmetic with projects of interest to children, with trips into the neighborhood, with art work, and with music. Much material and a variety of equipment are usually available, and visual aids of various kinds are customarily used. Hand work of various kinds is a regular part of classroom programs; libraries are extensive and are frequently used. Secondary schools have a greater variety of courses of study, so that students can concentrate their work in areas of their special interests. More electives are usually possible, with opportunities for classes in the various arts and music under trained leadership, often including participation in orchestras, choruses, and dramatics. Laboratories are available for classes in the home economics subjects. Wood work, metal work, and sometimes radio and photography are offered and encouraged. Physical and health education, recreation, and games are a part of the curriculum or extracurricular activities. Many kinds of activities and clubs are carried on in addition to the regular curriculum: student government, school newspapers, hobby groups, debating societies, athletic teams, socials, dancing and many others.

Special schools and classes are many. Vocational preparation has greatly influenced secondary education. In sizable cities there will be an academic high school for college preparatory work, a commercial high school for preparation in the many business vocations from stenography and typing to accounting and advertising, and a technical, or trades, high school for vocational training for a variety of crafts and industrial jobs. In the largest cities these schools become highly specialized; music and art, science, food trades, needle trades, metal trades, seamanship are illustrations. These schools often operate in the daytime for regular high-school-age students and in the evening as continuation schools for those who have already gone to work. Vocational training is combined with the basic high-school requirements for those who seek graduation.

Schools may have classes for slow learners, for those with high IQ's, for the hard of hearing, for those with limited vision, for the crippled. Teachers are sent to city hospitals to conduct classes for the chronically ill and convalescents, or they go to the homes of children who are confined to the house for some reason. These teachers have special training to deal with their respective groups. City school systems have replaced truancy and attendance officers with visiting teachers who are trained case workers and whose job is to find the causes of a child's truancy and help to work out a solution.

Some cities also operate colleges as a part of the public school system, though they usually have a separate organization and their own board. The city of New York has a Board of Higher Education under which are operated four colleges: City College, with two centers in the Borough of Manhattan; Hunter College, with centers in Manhattan and the Bronx; Brooklyn College, in the Borough of Brooklyn; and Queens College, in the Borough of Queens. All of these colleges have many departments, large student bodies, and large and well-qualified faculties. They are exceedingly costly institutions and find it difficult to meet the demands for higher education. A few cities have added junior colleges which offer two years of post-high-school education to their public school systems. These schools are usually intended to provide a "terminal education" for those who do not expect to go to college. In some instances, however, they have become the equivalent of the first two years of college work.

City public school systems also carry on adult education, generally confined to adult elementary education, evening high schools, and vocational schools. City colleges usually have evening sessions and sometimes offer programs of informal and noncredit courses. In some cities adult education in the public schools has branched out into experimental forms and programs, such as adult schools, forums, and discussion of public affairs.

The vast expansion of the curriculum and the broadening of opportunities in public education in American cities is the response of the institution of education to the trends already discussed—pressures of the advancing technology, which has created new jobs for which people must be trained, and pressures of the public on its institution of education to meet new needs arising out of new conditions. The pressures have come from organized labor and organized business as well as organized parents; as an example, the pressure to expand vocational education to the distributive occupations by additional federal support through the George-Deen Act was largely from business organizations.

Quasi-Public Education. Cities maintain a number of institutions which are not operated as educational institutions in the way that public schools are, but which provide many educational services to city people. Many of these institutions are privately supported, though some receive subsidies from city budgets; others are entirely paid for out of public funds and are operated by the cities. Such institutions as libraries, museums, zoos, and botanical gardens are to be found in this group.

Public libraries, though always forced to operate on very limited funds, have managed to broaden their services greatly in recent years. They have spread out through branch libraries even to the extent of serving newer and remote neighborhoods with libraries on wheels. Specialized libraries have also been set up where such services are specially needed. There has been not only a geographical expansion but also a broadening of services. Pictures, musical scores, motion-picture films, slides, phonograph recordings, and so forth have been added to books. Reference works have been specialized, with qualified reference librarians in charge. Children's sections have been set up, and story hours are conducted. Readers' advisers and/or adult educators have been added to staffs. Forums, film forums, and discussion programs are conducted. Where there are auditoriums and rooms for group purposes, they are usually made available for community groups. Many city libraries maintain a directory of adult education opportunities in the community.

Museums are giving attention to educational services. Some have educational departments which serve school groups and carry on lecture, motion-picture, musical, art, dance, and other programs. Some carry on various types of activity programs. Guided tours are often provided, film and slide collections are maintained for loan, and various extension services are given. A few of the larger cities have planetariums, which not only offer scheduled performances but carry on classes of various sorts for study of the heavenly bodies and navigation.

All in all, the educational service of this type of institutions is a highly significant part of a city's educational opportunities.

Private Education. Public education is supplemented in most American cities by an extensive array of private schools of many different sorts. Some of these are experimental; others fill needs of one kind or another which public education is unable to meet; still others are operated as business enterprises for profit.

The large part of private schools are elementary and secondary schools. Parents who can afford it and who are dissatisfied with the public schools send their children to private schools. These schools must meet the same basic standards as public schools, but otherwise are free to operate according to their own policies. Many of these schools provide a very progressive education for their students; some are operated by university schools of education as experimental schools, although this number is declining; others are traditional college-preparatory schools which have established good reputations with the major colleges and so are in demand by parents who want their children accepted in these colleges; some are operated by religious institutions and combine religious and secular education; a few are for exceptional children of one sort or another; and there are those which undertake to get through school pupils who have had difficulties in public schools. In the past there have been girls' finishing schools, but with the increasing numbers of girls attending colleges these have either become junior colleges or ceased to exist. In most cities, private schools serve only a small part of the children and young people; in quality of education, they run the whole gamut from the best to the worst.

Most cities now have many nursery schools, which are privately or coöperatively operated. These schools serve younger children one or two years before they are permitted to enter public schools. This has been a pioneering job, and the acceptance and usefulness of this type of schools have already given evidence of a trend toward their acceptance as part of the public school systems.

City people support many private business and commercial and other vocational schools. The quality offered varies greatly from excellent training in thorough, first-class, long-established schools to very bad training in small, insufficiently equipped, poorly staffed, fly-by-night concerns. In most cases these schools have proved to be highly profitable to those who own and operate them.

Most of the great universities are located in cities. In some of the larger cities several universities may be found. Usually these include the high-grade professional schools of medicine and dentistry, law, education, engineering of various kinds, journalism, business, theology and religion, nursing, and so forth. The opportunities for higher education are very great in American cities. One of the most interesting developments in recent years is illustrated by the Cincinnati University School of Engineering, which operates what is called a coöperative education plan, under which students spend part of the year in classes and part of the year in actual work situations. This plan of education has begun to get into other areas of higher education.

Adult Education. Adult education is far more extensive in American cities than most people realize. It is carried on by all sorts of institutions: public schools, settlement and neighborhood houses, community centers, the various kinds of "Y's," churches, clubs, labor unions, industrial and commercial establishments, colleges and universities, political organizations, libraries, museums, and various associations and organizations.

The participants in adult education activities are all kinds of people. They range in age from the late teens to the nineties, with approximately half in the twenties and somewhat more above thirty than twenty and below. This indicates what is generally true, that the strongest motivations for further education are those connected with vocations. The variety of subjects ranges from agriculture to zoölogy and from art to sociology.

When the New York Adult Education Council had collected the data about adult education opportunities in New York as completely as possible and had put into operation its information service for adults, an analysis of the data was made. There were 9643 offerings of 1402 organizations listed, which "represents not the maximum but rather the minimum of units offered in all fields partly because it is impossible to collect one hundred percent information about anything in New York and partly because two or more units of the same offering by any one organization are listed as a single unit."⁹

The organizations were classified into five groups: businesses which operate for financial profit (22 percent); projects whose objectives are prestige, self-satisfaction, promulgation of ideas or ideals, or program experimentation (10 percent); associations for the furtherance of common interests around which the group is formed (34 percent); functions of government as service to the population (25 percent); and unclassified organizations outside New York used in the information service to supplement local resources and national organizations with headquarters in New York, and, therefore, relevant for local use (9 percent). Nearly 60 percent of the agencies which provide adult education opportunities in New York are community and special interest, age, or other group service organizations or government services, particularly through the public education system.

The subject classification was made by eight groupings (which are not mutually exclusive): (1) philosophy: those subjects which interpret man's relations to his fellow man, to the physical world, and to the universe; (2) religion: including subjects endeavoring to assist people in their efforts to find relationships to realities supreme to them; (3) the arts: both those subjects which provide an experience of beauty and those which give opportunity for creative expression in the various media of the arts; (4) human relationships: including the study of problems of various relationships with other people and also the fundamental study of social sciences, history, language, and so forth; (5) science: both the scientific method and the study of particular sciences; (6) training for work to assist people in increasing vocational competence; (7) recreation: educational experiences arising out of recreation or engaged in as recreation; (8) information: educational activities of adults not otherwise classified.

These classes lean heavily on the factor of motivation, which is of preëminent importance in adult education. The grouping worked out by subject and organizational distribution as shown in Table 55. In terms of offerings the same two kinds of organizations, associations and government services, account for two-thirds, and nearly 80 percent of the opportunities are related to three general motiva-

---

⁹ *A Picture of Adult Education in the New York Metropolitan Area* (New York: New York Adult Education Council, 1934), pp. 6–13.

Table 55   Distribution of 9643 Adult Education Offerings in New York by
Subject Classification and Organization Groups[10]

Subject Classification	Organization Group				Total	
	Business	Project	Association	Government	Number	Percent
Occupation	740	696	1,176	1,742	4,354	45.2
Human relations	299	281	474	702	1,756	18.2
Arts	251	236	398	590	1,475	15.3
Science	145	142	231	343	861	8.9
Recreation	153	140	236	352	881	9.1
Philosophy	8	7	14	18	47	.5
Religion	7	7	12	18	44	.5
Information	38	36	61	90	225	2.3
Total { Number	1,641	1,545	2,602	3,856	9,643	100.0
Total { Percent	17	16	26	40	100	——

tions: the desire to develop increased vocational competence—that is, to get better jobs and larger incomes; the desire to understand the problems of human relationships and get along better with other people; and the desire for appreciation of the arts and for creative expression.

While the extent of adult education opportunities in New York is impressive, and the picture is undoubtedly proportionately similar to that in other American cities, if a very generous estimate of twenty-five persons per offering were made, the total number of participants would be around a quarter of a million, which is approximately 7.5 percent of the adult population at that time. This, in reality, bespeaks an extremely meager attempt to provide educational assistance to adults, all of whom need some kind of help in the present complex and rapidly changing urban culture.

PROBLEMS OF URBAN EDUCATION

The chief problems of urban education fall into three areas: public education, the education of older youth, and adult education. These problems arise out of the intensification of urbanization.

Problems of Public Education. Public education in American cities faces problems of great difficulty which are inherent in the conditions and forces within which it must operate.

[10] *Ibid.*, Tables 2 and 3, p. 12.

Finances. Perhaps the greatest of these problems is money. Having the largest item on the city budgets, education is in a vulnerable position, and any attack on high taxes focuses its attention on education and what are called its "frills." While parents want the best education which can be had for their children, they, too often, do not understand what "good education" is; nor are they well enough organized to fight for what they want. Those who seek lower taxes, on the other hand, know how to organize and exert pressure on the administration of their cities. Only where there is well-grounded public understanding of the importance of education and what money can buy in good quality of education is the threat of attack on the education item in the city budget removed. Otherwise, education will not fare well in the competition with other urban needs and their budget items, which have strong supporters.

Staffing. Without enough money, an adequate teaching staff in public schools is not possible, and yet large cities especially have serious deficits at this point. The solution of this problem becomes very complicated because it involves the fundamental problems of city financing, the independence of education from municipal fiscal control, the value the people of cities put on education, and the machinery for the actual control of education by the people. There are other problems of staffing. Selection has not been solved, even with the complicated machinery. Inbreeding, the "alertness" of the teaching staff to new needs and new methods, and the increasing dead weight of tired oldsters provide conditions which must be coped with.

Local Control. Small boards of education appointed by city mayors to be representatives of the people in determining educational policy make a fiction of the control of education by the people. The actual restitution of the participation of the citizenry in determining educational policy is essential to preserving the great tradition of American free democratic education. The discovery of the form and functions of local boards under present-day conditions is a paramount problem. Fortunately, research toward this end is under way.

Fluctuation in Public-School Enrollment. This is another serious problem because it involves great numbers of children, comes with greater suddenness, and has a wider variation in cities. The number enrolled in city public schools has, in general, been declining for some years, in part because of the declining urban birth rates and the declining rate of growth in cities. With all of the difficulties involved, this problem could be met if a steady trend could be counted on, but it cannot be from year to year in any city.

In New York City, elementary-school enrollment from 1935 to 1943 decreased 27 percent, from 720,664 to 524,280; by 1950, it had increased 3 percent, to 539,804. Secondary-school enrollment in the same period declined 26 percent, from 247,108 to 183,800, and then rose to 283,702, an increase of 54 percent. So the changes in birth rate, migration, economic conditions, and the value of education in the minds of people are reflected in school enrollments and provide serious problems for boards of education.

The fluctuations in birth rates over the second postwar period are making a serious problem for education. Just before the United States entered the war, there was a rise in birth rates, during the war years the birth rates declined greatly, and following the war they went up so that an all-time high in number of births was experienced for several years, until the rates began to decline again. Each phase of this change is exaggerated in most cities. It takes five years for schools to feel the effects of such changes; in 1950 the public schools are experiencing the largest elementary-school enrollments they have ever had, but this will last for only a few years, until enrollments begin to decline rapidly again. This peak will follow through elementary schools and then high schools, putting a serious strain on public-school buildings, equipment, personnel, and budget. This is especially serious because it follows a long period of declining enrollments, when few teachers were added to the staffs and eligible lists of city school systems, and the war period, when many teachers left the profession, so that increasing enrollments meet a shortage of teachers. Economic conditions also contribute to fluctuation of public-school enrollments. When times are good and jobs are plentiful, more students leave school for jobs when they reach the age when the compulsory school attendance laws no longer compel them to attend, and more families find it possible to send their children to private schools. When depression hits the community, young people stay in school longer, and fewer children can be put in private schools. These are problems which public-school systems must meet, and they seriously complicate any plans to improve education through the increase of special services and the building of new schools, both of which are costly in money.

Local Adaptation. The bigness of city school systems, with their standardization and centralized administration, tends to develop stable patterns of operation in the schools because they can be highly routinized and so carried on with the minimum of difficulties and interruptions in the administrative line. Innovations interrupt the routine and often involve administrative exceptions; so they are discouraged. The great bulk of the routine, which involves a stream of directives, many reports, much paper work, a great deal of incidental and questionable research, and a lot of peripheral odd jobs plus the minor daily problems, absorbs the energies and concerns of local school staffs. Consequently, the framework of inflexibility is produced by the system. Changes do make their way, however, into large centralized systems.

Cillié studied the relative friendliness of centralized and decentralized school systems to various adaptations in their operation. He found that 30 percent of the adaptations, those that had to do with immediate flexibility and adaptation and democratic operation, prospered best under the conditions of decentralization; 12 percent of the adaptations, those that had to do with general security and efficiency, were more frequently found in centralized systems; the remaining 58 percent, dealing with such things as teacher improvement, broadening and enrichment of curriculum, were found under both types of administration.[11] This study showed clearly that the large centralized city school systems did not prevent innovations in general, but they did discourage adaptation at very vital points. It substantiated an earlier hypothesis of Mort and Cornell—that, while certain types of adaptation prosper best in a decentralized system of school administration, other types prosper best in centralized systems, and many types prosper regardless of the kind of administration[12]—but leaves a balance in favor of decentralization, or, perhaps more realistically, sets another hypothesis—namely, that adaptation can reach its best potentialities under a new pattern combining various aspects of decentralization with certain factors of centralization.

Later Westby made a study of local autonomy for city school systems and found that, although more leeway for local action would be desirable, there was already sufficient so that, "if properly uti-

---

[11] François S. Cillié, *Centralization or Decentralization: A Study in Educational Adaptation* (New York: Bureau of Publications, Teachers College, Columbia University, 1940), p. 96.

[12] Paul R. Mort and Francis G. Cornell, *Adaptability of Public School Systems* (New York: Bureau of Publications, Teachers College, Columbia University, 1938), p. 100.

lized, broad and significant changes in the practices of schools could be accomplished without the express approval of the central office." He went on to say that "the trouble isn't so much that the assistant superintendents or high school principals don't have the authority to act as it is that they are not prompted to act. The extension of their authority to act is not going to solve the problem." Westby goes on to suggest that local autonomy in the operation of city schools can be developed by the organization of local advisory groups of carefully selected leaders in the community who are alert to community opinion, interests, and needs, capable of interpreting the reactions of the community to what the schools do or propose, and ready to assist the school staff to make the schools more adaptable to community needs.[13] So would the force of democratic participation be set up to counteract the lethargy of institutionalism in making schools alive to the necessities for change in their changing cities. In fact, experimentation and research are endeavoring to find the feasibility of local boards, with powers of making policy, truly representative of, and elected by, the people in their own neighborhoods.

Educational Needs After Secondary School. The education of older youth is a serious problem in American cities because of their great numbers and the special problems in their adjustment. The establishment of city colleges has taken care of only a small part of these young people because, even though they have materially increased the number attending college, the large proportion do not go to college. The desirability of high-school graduation has been generally accepted in the United States, especially in cities, so that most employers will not hire anyone who does not have a high-school diploma. Such a diploma, however, is no guarantee that its holder will make a satisfactory employee. In part, the large number of young people who lose their jobs because they do not know how to work in an organization, or accept responsibility, or get along with bosses and co-workers, arouses the suspicion that the schools have significant weaknesses. Then there are still many who drop out of school before high-school graduation. These facts, coupled with the great variation in the rate at which young people can be absorbed into the work of the community, have led to experimentation with what have

[13] Cleve O. Westby, *Local Autonomy for School-Communities in Cities* (New York: Bureau of Publications, Teachers College, Columbia University, 1947), Chaps. IV and V.

been called junior colleges in a number of city public-school systems. These newer schools provide two years of post-high-school education, principally for those who do not intend to go to college. Three types of experiments have been tried: (1) The junior college offers the same type of programs as the first two years in the traditional liberal arts college. This type has served only the same young people that the established colleges have served. Because they are local public institutions, they have made part of a college education available to larger numbers of young people, but they have done little to solve the more basic problem of the education of older youth. (2) Technical institutes, such as those developed by New York State, offer basic training in the various fields of mechanics and agriculture, combined with a general education intended to meet the special needs of these young people. These have been more successful in meeting the problem. (3) Community colleges have built their offerings around the great variety of needs, not only of out-of-school young people, but also of adults. The understanding of and adjustment to the life of the community have been the central points of focus rather than technical training. While this experiment is more recent, where it has been tried it gives promise of great usefulness.

In some cities this problem has been attacked by a radical revision of the secondary-school curriculum to fit directly the needs of the young people rather than carrying on the traditional subject-matter-centered courses of study. To illustrate: A new superintendent of schools in a New England city a few years ago found that all was not well in the education which the high school in his city was providing for the young people of the community. He quietly gathered information regarding what the high-school graduates do. He found that a few went to college, some left the community and took a wide variety of jobs, but the majority were employed in the local industries and businesses. He went to see the personnel people of the establishments which employed the larger groups and asked them if their new employees were satisfactory and what sort of preparation they thought the high school might give students to better prepare them for the jobs they would get. The personnel directors were frank and coöperative and outlined the weaknesses they had found in their new employees, which were chiefly in their general background of understanding of mechanical processes, of working in an organization, and of getting along with people. The superintendent reported to the board of education, a plan was worked out to change the high-school curriculum to serve the various groups of students, the plan was presented and explained to the people of the community, and the changes were made with most satisfactory results.

Another approach to this problem is being made by a national organization of teachers who are working on a reorienting of the secondary-school curriculum in terms of life adjustment to the real problems of living.

Education of Adults. Adult education has become a necessity under the conditions of an increasing urbanization. Adults can no longer escape the requirements of continuing learning. To live and work in this age necessitates an increasing facility with the skills of communication and a broader base of general knowledge. The changing vocational patterns demand readjustment and retraining. The growing complexities of human relationships call for a high degree of ability in getting along with people under various circumstances. The great opportunities which are provided for enriching life and for growing satisfactions are sterile without the capacities to use them. The growing demands on individuals as citizens in a democratc society are not easily understood or fulfilled without co-operative study and action.

The educational job which these requirements involve is coming to be increasingly recognized by public education as a part of its responsibility. Public schools have been greatly assisted in expanding their services by financial aid for adult education, which more and more states are making available. The total resources of city public-school systems, however, are infinitesimal compared with the stupendous job which needs to be done. In fact, the multiplicity of private adult education offerings in cities, plus the maximum of services by public schools, are still woefully inadequate and will doubtless continue to be for some time to come. The problem is to coördinate and plan the whole job so that the greatest possible services can be obtained from the total private and public resources combined. This is a serious and difficult problem which cities must face, and it is logical to assume that the public institution established to carry on education has a responsibility for the initiation of the coördinating and planning process.

PROMISING EDUCATIONAL EXPERIMENTS

One of the most important experiments in the development of adaptability in public schools has been carried on by Professor Paul R. Mort of Teachers College, Columbia University, through the Metropolitan School Study Council. This organization is composed of some seventy school systems, largely in the four-state New York metropolitan area. It considers itself a research organization in public-school administration, but research is broadly interpreted, not only as the coöperative study of common problems, but also as the devising and carrying out, in communities and classrooms, of experiments planned to solve these problems.

The Council has found a formula whereby a graduate school of education through its faculty and students can work with public-school systems through administrators, teachers, and lay people of the communities, using the schools as a laboratory in which to procure data, discover and study problems, work out plans, and carry on experiments. In the few years of its existence it has called upon the services of more than 3000 skilled teachers and administrators and has affected the school life of 300,000 children. In the process of its operation it has issued fifty-six different publications and four motion pictures and has published a magazine with a circulation of 20,000. These have been instruments for use in its many projects, but have been made available to a wider audience.[14]

The plan of operation provides for working groups, composed primarily of teachers and administrators, where facts are gathered and interpreted. The four continuing research policy committees are on lay understanding, educational dynamics, intercommunity information, and unmet needs. Temporary subcommittees work on particular problems. Reports are published as working documents, which in turn are used by local action committees of lay and professional people. These groups have studied such things as what makes a good school, newer educational practices, and the unmet educational needs of their communities.

Teachers report that they have come to have a feeling of responsibility for school development, to appreciate the importance of their

[14] "A Progress Report of the Metropolitan School Study Council," *Teachers College Record*, Oct., 1948 (Bureau of Publications, Teachers College, Columbia University). The material for this section is taken from the various sections of this report.

own personal and professional growth, and to see more effective ways of helping children to grow. Students have found new interests in their school experiences and the wide contacts which have been made possible and have come to look on teaching as a vocation offering possibilities for creative work. School board members have found a new challenge and fascination in their responsibilities and potentialities, as they have come to understand education and its community relationships more adequately. To the school administrators work in the Council has opened the avenues to creative administration by helping them to understand problems better, to recognize creative work, and to see their job as creating conditions under which creative teaching can take place. The people of the community have become more informed about their school systems, have participated in the studies of problems of their schools, and have become not only supporters of their schools but the instigators of growth and improvement in their school systems.

After six years of activity the accomplishments of the Council were modestly stated around four points:[15]

1. The identification and diffusion of educational procedures that give promise of improving the operation of schools. This has been done primarily through the editing, publication, and distribution of *The Exchange*[16] as a regular periodical and the preparation and local use of the compilation of the descriptions of the better practices in public-school education which had been accepted and were on the way toward establishment in the form of an instrument to be used by lay groups in appraising their own schools.[17]

2. The identification of new problems facing education and the promise of efforts to solve them (including efforts to achieve solutions and try out such solutions in practice). This was carried out by intensive work of some nine special committees studying problems and working out new inventions in areas such as human relations, emotional stability, citizenship, and communication. Some of the committees worked through to carrying out local experiments, others reached the planning stage, and a few found prolonged difficulty in defining their problems.

3. The identification, development, and diffusion of procedures

[15] *Ibid.*, pp. 53–55.

[16] *The Exchange,* bimonthly (Metropolitan School Study Council, 525 West 120th Street, New York 27, New York).

[17] Metropolitan School Study Council, *What Schools Can Do* (New York: Bureau of Publications, Teachers College, Columbia University, 1944).

for increasing the degree of public participation in educational planning. This developed through various stages of study and experimentation in the development of lay understanding and communication to the publication of an analytical guidebook for community use.[18]

4. The identification of factors that make the provision of good schools easier, including the legal setting, administrative arrangements, staff selection, methods of working with pupils, character and potentialities of community groups, and community development; from a basic manual for the use of local groups in studying the educational needs of their communities[19] to a series of studies dealing with the particular points enumerated.

There is a long and fascinating story of experiments in the adaptation of schools to their communities. Many of the successful ventures have been in cities and have left their deposits, which are a part of the record already seen. The story includes the progressive education movement, the early activities in both recreation and education of the Russell Sage Foundation, as well as imaginative activities of scattered, enlightened educators who became obsessed with the purpose of using education as the instrument to develop the latent capacities of individual children rather than to spread over them a smattering of knowledge.

Progressive education is a product of the city. The changed conditions which were manifested in the development of urban communities were such that old patterns of education no longer obtained. In the early days of America, education had consisted in the development of children through bearing their responsibilities as a part of the coöperative family life within which the things and the experiences which were needed were produced. Schools were merely adjuncts for the purpose of conveniently giving all the children together the skills of communication. Cities turned things upside down and made schools the centers of education. Progressive education undertook, in the strictly adult world of the city, to stimulate a living situation within which the potential resources for enriching experience which cities afford could be made to some degree the real life framework within which education might operate and children develop.

[18] Committee of 14 (Norton L. Beach, Secretary), *Public Action for Powerful Schools* (New York: Metropolitan School Study Council, 1949).

[19] Will R. Begg, *The Techniques of Study Groups Concerned with Unmet Needs* (New York: Metropolitan School Study Council, 1947).

The school-community movement came later and recognized the school as only a part of the experience of children as they lived in communities and so endeavored to integrate schools into the whole of community life by relating them to community organizations, taking the children out into the community and bringing the community into the schools in an effort to develop capacities and personalities of children through their coöperation in the total life of the community. Marks of these efforts can be seen in city school buildings planned for community use, in lighted windows of these buildings in evenings where community programs of recreation and education for young and old are carried on, in school-community coördinating committees, in coöperative activities in which school children and community people work together to make better communities. Unfortunately, one must look for such bright spots, but they can be found in most American cities, although they are far from being universal. Again, all the difficulties of bigness and lethargy conspire to keep such adaptations from coming quickly, but changes come, and another quarter of a century will likely turn public schools into the centers of the active participation of community people in educational and community affairs, of continuing education for all people, and of well-developed programs of community recreation and of community development.

These experiments not only represent the most forward-looking approach to the problems of urban public education, but also illustrate an intelligent, organized approach to the very basic problem which all urban institutions face—the problem of increasing capacity for adaptability in the midst of intensified urbanization, with its rapidly changing patterns of invention, both mechanical and social, of population, in both number and composition, of organization, especially in the direction of specialization, and of human needs as their character and relative significance reflect the impact of other changes.

Supplementary Reading

Cook, Lloyd Allen and Cook, Elaine Forsyth. *A Sociological Approach to Education.* A Revision of *Community Backgrounds of Education.* New York: McGraw-Hill Book Company, 1950.

A sociological treatment of the school-community developments in American education, with much case material and analysis.

CHAPTER 24

HOW RECREATION OPERATES

So LONG as people's lives were reasonably well integrated and they were directly involved in the various aspects of living, there was little consciousness of the parts which made up the whole of life. When, however, the conditions of living changed to the point where there was an imbalance in the different parts of living, as happened under the circumstances of urban life, people became conscious of those things which are lacking in their experience of living. So working in factories, stores, and offices for long hours and living in cramped, dismal, and inadequate city dwellings began to make city people self-conscious about recreation needs.

This awareness took a long time to develop, partly because leisure time was not available and partly because the remnants of the medieval emphasis on "good mind" and "evil body" coming through the tradition of puritanism still affected the patterns of people's living and of the organization of cities. In the meantime, cities were growing up without making provision for recreation—no open spaces, no playgrounds, schools without play spaces. It was the mid-nineteenth century (1853) before the land for the first municipal park was purchased—Central Park in New York City. But this was not the beginning of recreation in American cities.

COMMERCIAL RECREATION

Those who saw the possibility of making a profit through their own enterprise by catering to the recreational need of city people started recreation activities in cities. Among the early commercial ventures were taverns, such things as bearbaiting in New England, street fairs and carnivals and the theater. From small beginnings, commercial recreation has grown over the years to a several-billion-dollar industry. If travel, including the various forms of transportation and automobile touring, with those things which go with them, resort hotels, lodging, meals, amusements, and the equipment for sports, games, and other forms of recreation are added, the total recreational industry would amount to upwards of ten billion dollars per year.

The catalogue of commercial recreation includes a large variety of items of many kinds. There are athletic contests, with the great American game of baseball, in its professional form, the most widespread, but including also both professional and college football, basketball, track indoor and outdoor, swimming, and hockey. Racing, with its concomitant of betting, has long been a popular form; the most extensive type continues to be horse racing, but dog racing has more recently been developed, and auto racing is an occasional major event, with midget auto racing becoming more widespread. Carnivals, circuses, fairs, and public exhibitions are occasional events which have long drawn great crowds, while amusement parks operate through the summer season adjacent to most of the large cities. Dance halls of various kinds are ever present in cities. Night clubs, roadhouses, and taverns are frequented by some people, with similar functions performed for young people by the soda and sandwich bars in the corner drug store. Pool and billiard halls, though declining, are still found in great numbers in the cities, and bowling alleys and skating rinks are also popular. The theater has declined and represents a minor item in recreation in all but a few of the largest cities. It has been replaced and added to by the movies, which have become the greatest single type of commercial recreation in terms of money invested, people employed, and attendance, which, at its peak, has approached a weekly attendance close to the total population of the United States. In the last couple of years, television has made some inroads on movie attendance. Radio continues to be a very significant part of commercial recreation, with more than one and one-half receiving sets per family in the country. Travel has been highly commercialized by transportation concerns, resorts, and hotels. Ski trains, week-end and holiday excursions, trains for hikers, and the like are highly promoted. Automobile touring is exploited and encouraged by national parks and forests. While commercialized recreation is by no means confined to city people, it is overwhelmingly a phenomenon of urban communities.

It has been pointed out that commercial recreation has three characteristics. First, it is predominantly spectator rather than participant recreation. In some forms, it does provide the facilities where individuals can participate, as in pool halls and skating rinks, but where the large numbers are involved, as in professional baseball and the movies, those who enjoy the recreation are passive as spectators. Second, those forms of recreation which do not conform to the accepted mores, such as horse racing, with its betting, and others which are related one way and another to vice, are to be found in the commercial field. Third, some recreation requires a large capital investment, which can be provided only when it can be used to make a profit.[1]

RECREATION IN HOMES AND ASSOCIATIONS

Perhaps more recreation than is supposed still takes place in homes, by individuals under their own initiative, and in associations which are formed for various recreational purposes. Most young children spend a large part of their time around their homes and in their own back yards, when they have back yards. Some of the modern recreational devices, such as radio, television, phonographs and records, are used largely in homes. Playing games, entertaining friends, parties, and conversation are home- and family-centered. The automobile has encouraged family trips for many purposes. A great many hobbies are carried on by individuals usually at home: reading, creative writing, sketching, painting, sculpturing, gardening, caring for pets, making things of wood and other materials, collecting of all sorts, and many others. Most of women's recreational activities, like knitting, embroidery, and fancy cooking, are home activities.

Many agencies have made a special point of promoting home recreation by putting out special pamphlets and even by giving instruction in recreational activities in homes. They have also organized services for giving various kinds of help to shut-ins. Contests for the best back-yard playgrounds have been carried on, and toy-loan centers have been set up. The radio has been used to help home recreation, and home beautification, landscaping, and gardens have been encouraged in various ways.

The number of social clubs is legion. Bridge clubs and their like are for social recreation. Golf and country clubs are the same thing

---

[1] Earl E. Muntz, *Urban Sociology* (New York: The Macmillan Company, 1938), pp. 631–632.

on the large scale, with emphasis on physical recreation, but used as much for social gatherings. There are many types of athletic clubs, from the swanky city athletic clubs to the small neighborhood basketball or baseball clubs. The cellar clubs of boys and young men (see pp. 373 f.) in the less favored areas of cities are similar. There are special-interest and hobby clubs and neighborhood clubs and associations. Many kinds of lodges, brotherhoods, and sisterhoods are to be found in cities. Women have clubs of many kinds, and men lean toward the luncheon or service clubs. All of these and many more involve a host of people in the cities.

PRIVATE AGENCY RECREATION

To get back to the story of the development of recreation, the early steps were taken by those people and agencies which concerned themselves with the welfare of underprivileged people, particularly children. In the last quarter of the nineteenth century, in Boston, Chicago, and New York, playgrounds were developed so that children could get off the streets and have space to play in a wholesome atmosphere with some direction and supervision. From this beginning came the playground movement.

The "Y's" began to acknowledge the importance of recreation by giving it a larger place in their programs. With gymnasiums and swimming pools the basis of recreation, activities were physical, but outdoor activities, hobby and other groups, club and general social events and camping were included. Settlements, neighborhood houses, and community centers have given much of their programs to recreation, largely in group activities with emphasis on art, music and drama.

Education and recreation usually come together. Many of the programs are, in reality, both. When they are carried on by agencies which consider themselves recreation and by people trained as recreation leaders, they are usually considered recreation; the educator or the educational group worker, however, would count them as part of the educational program. This is not important except to show how closely education and recreation are related. It has usually been found that voluntary educational programs tend to develop in the direction of recreation and that stable recreation programs carried on through group work tend to become more and more educational. This close relationship is apparent throughout

Chicago. In the six years following the organization of the association, 158 cities started playgrounds. In 1917 the association, whose name had been changed to Playground and Recreation Association, was asked by the War Department to organize recreation programs in the cities adjacent to military camps, which it did through the War Camp Community Service. This job involved more broadly trained leadership, working with citizen committees, the mobilization and coördination of community resources, the development of a more broadly conceived recreation program. The success of the efforts opened up new concepts of community recreation on the part of the organizations and community leadership and aroused new demands on the part of the men in the army, which they began to express when they returned to their homes.

In 1926 the association organized the National Recreation School for the training of professional leaders. In 1930 the name of the association was changed to National Recreation Association. In 1931–1932, under its auspices, the British education leader, Dr. L. P. Jacks, made a lecture tour of the United States preaching the gospel of recreation. In 1932 the first International Recreation Congress was held in Los Angeles. In 1933, as one of the depression measures, the federal government established the nation-wide WPA program, in which the expansion of recreation facilities and programs played an important part. By this time a high level of recreation development was attained. World War II made a contribution similar to that of World War I, but the effect was intensified because more communities and more people were involved; consequently, more widespread demands were engendered, and more communities were aroused and prepared to carry on community programs. One specific contribution came as a result of the USO (United Service Organization) program, which had provided buildings for recreation services to those in the armed service in many communities near military establishments. Following the war, these buildings, in many cases, were sold to the communities at much less than cost, so that the local organizations which had developed to carry on the USO activities could continue to serve their own communities.

The annual report of recreation activities in the United States for 1948 lists recreation activities in 1917 communities spending approximately $94,000,000, with more than 48,548 employed leaders in 1645 cities. There were 5899 full-time year-round leaders in 701 cities, and 89,234 volunteer leaders in 1133 communities. The 23,067 playgrounds, buildings, and centers reported for the year 1948 is an increase of 50 percent in the ten years since 1938.[4]

The National Recreation Association has played an important role in the advance of recreation. While it is a private agency serving all phases of recreation, it has come to be most closely related to public recreation because it has concentrated its efforts on promoting, assisting, and consulting in the organization of independent city boards of recreation. One of the important services in this connection has been conducting recreation studies of cities to which it was invited. The general NRA services include acting as a clearing house for recreation in America, publishing a monthly magazine, *Recreation*, and many pamphlets and monographs on various phases of recreation, initiating and carrying on a school for the training of recreation leaders until training programs had been established in a number of universities, carrying on various types of research, and generally promoting recreation.

By 1938 the number of professionals in the field of recreation had increased to the point where a professional organization was organized, originally called the Society of Recreation Workers of America, now the American Recreation Society. Besides being concerned with the problems of raising professional standards and of gaining recognition for the profession, attention has been focused on the community approach to recreation and the closer integration of education and recreation.

RECREATION IN PUBLIC SCHOOLS

Schools have been a part of developing recreation, but by and large they have lagged behind. Many things which were at least in part recreation came within the scope of school programs—physical education, athletics, playground games, extracurricular activities, art, music, dramatics. These additions were made, not as recreation, but rather as the result of a broadening conception of education and the school curriculum. This was an important indirect contribution to recreation, but did not help in the provision for recreation programs in the communities.

In the early days, school buildings were used without question for various forms of public gatherings, but as cities grew and all institutions became specialized and legal sanctions were established set-

[4] *Recreation*, Year Book Issue, June, 1949, and June, 1939.

ting the patterns for the use of public property, the functions of schools and the uses of school buildings were defined by state legislation. Enabling legislation, consequently, had to be passed before schools could engage in recreation or school buildings could be put to community use. Piecemeal legislation began in the mid-nineteenth century, permitting the use of school buildings by community groups. Practically all states have gone this far. Later laws began to permit schools to engage in recreation, particularly on playgrounds after school hours, on Saturdays, and during the summer. These programs were generally at first operated by private agencies. Comprehensive enabling legislation putting recreation in all its forms under home rule in the cities did not appear until 1915 and by 1947 had been passed in one form or another in only thirty-four states.

It was a big step from permitting various community groups to use school buildings occasionally to the point where schools themselves operated their buildings regularly as neighborhood centers for recreation programs. When people began to desire this type of program, they became aware of the fact that school buildings, in which there was a large community investment, were unused a large portion of the day and that they were well located for community programs. It was not until the 1930–1940 decade, however, that any significant number of school buildings began to be used as neighborhood recreation centers in the cities. Even now only a relatively small proportion of city schools are so used.[5] Where recreation has developed in this pattern, it has been generally very successful and people have participated in large numbers, especially where programs have been a combination of recreation and adult education. In some cities the integration of these neighborhood programs, including playground activities during afternoons, Saturdays, and summer vacations for children and young people, and evening programs for adults, into the school system has been complete, with professional leaders given status, salary scale and increments, and tenure like teachers in the schools. Newark (New Jersey) is perhaps the best example.

PUBLIC RECREATION

Public recreation has three principal phases: it is operated by park departments, by boards of education, and by recreation boards.

[5] George Hjelte, *The Administration of Public Recreation* (New York: The Macmillan Company, 1940), pp. 75–95; Butler, *op. cit.*, pp. 73, 423–428.

Basically, their spheres of activity are different, but they overlap at many points. Not all cities have all three public agencies operating recreation, but some do, and the patterns of organization differ widely because they have developed out of particular situations or conditions.

The main responsibility of park departments is to procure land, to put it into condition for use by landscaping, construction, and various other types of improvements, and to maintain the property. Altogether, a great variety of developments have been made by park departments: parks, playgrounds, athletic fields, stadiums, picnic grounds, bridle paths, bicycle trails, walks, golf links, tennis courts, lakes for boating, swimming pools, bathing beaches, yacht harbors, buildings for various recreational uses, skating ponds, ski trails, toboggan slides, aviaries, zoos, botanical gardens, and nature museums. Some of these demand special services, as bathing beaches require both house attendants and life guards; others, as bridle paths and picnic grounds, can be used by individuals or groups without assistance or supervision. Some others, however, must have qualified direction and supervision if they are to be used to their full advantage for recreation, but this type of leadership is outside the sphere of the usual park department affairs.

Boards of education have public-school buildings and playgrounds which they use, as has been described, by adding trained recreation leaders to school staffs to develop programs which will meet the interests and needs of individuals and groups in the school neighborhoods.

Recreation departments sometimes have their own playgrounds and recreation buildings, but more often their programs are carried on in the properties of park departments and schools and occasionally in private places. This makes them dependent upon park departments and boards of education for their recreation facilities. The chief job of recreation departments, however, is to organize recreation and provide recreation leaders who will develop, in the many neighborhoods, a wide variety of opportunities for individual participation, for group activities, for programs for mass enjoyment, and for city-wide activities and programs such as orchestras, choral societies, athletic leagues, and special events.[6] When they use their own property, coöperation is essential if coördinated community programs are to be obtained.

[6] See Butler, *op. cit.*, pp. 221–227, for a six-page double-column list of possible activities.

Four types of organization of municipal recreation have been developed:

1. *Recreation commission or department independent of the school and park department and controlling its own facilities.* Advantages are specialization, greater recognition on the part of people and government and, consequently, more adequate budgets, more likelihood of better qualified professional leadership, and more comprehensively and efficiently planned and organized programs. Disadvantages are difficulty in coördinating programs in schools, parks, and recreation centers, frequent misunderstanding between departments, and duplication of service. This plan is suited only to the largest cities.

2. *Recreation division as an integral branch or bureau of a park department.* Advantages are facilitation of use of all park properties for recreation purposes, and economy. Disadvantages are a tendency to subordinate recreation to traditional park functions and complete separation from school programs. Usually the result of adoption of recreation by a strong park department and found in various sizes of cities.

3. *Consolidated park and recreation department or commission organized on a functional basis.* Structural improvement over second type, to balance and coördinate functions and encourage coöperative relationships with public schools.

4. *Coordinated organization linking parks, schools and recreation in a unified program.* There are four types:

    A. *Recreation department separately constituted from school and park department, controlling no facilities of its own but using facilities of school and park department.* This plan accentuates the importance of recreation as such, but makes it completely dependent on the coöperation of park departments and school branches for its facilities. This coöperation can be withheld and usually results in inferior facilities because they are used by another agency than that responsible for them. Duplication is not overcome. This plan is considered a temporary expedient.

    B. *Organization under which schools conduct certain activities on school properties and a park and recreation department conducts other activities on municipal properties; but, by agreement, both agencies employ, each on half-time, the same executive.* This plan assures coördination and makes possible a more competent recreation executive. Few people, however, have the great variety of competencies which are required. The job becomes too complex and difficult to be attempted in very large cities.

    C. *Recreation commission, constituted in part by representatives of the school department and in part by representatives of the mu-*

nicipal government, which conducts a coordinated recreation pro-
gram using facilities of the schools, and parks, its own properties
and churches and other places available for public use. Coördination is assured, recreation holds a more independent and important position, and all of the resources for recreation in the community are more likely to be utilized. The school department,
however, is relieved of the direct responsibility for recreation,
which tends to leave uncultivated the important relationship between education and recreation.

D. *Quasi-public agency conducting the community recreation pro-*
gram, supported in part by private funds and using school, park
and other facilities available for public use. Usually the result of a
well-developed community recreation program under private agencies, and involves community chests. It hinders the development of
public recreation under both park departments and public schools
and is usually a transitional development.[7]

Public recreation has taken many forms in American cities. Some
represent adaptations to the particular situations and others are
compromises to meet strong political forces. All types of organization have been successful in some cities, and all have been unsuccessful in other cities. It is clear that the successful operation of
recreation in American cities is not primarily due to the type of organization which it has, but rather to the understanding of the functions, problems, and objectives of recreation on the part of the people and their leaders, based upon a conviction that recreation is a
vital part of urban living which should be made available to all
people in the community.

Butler has listed twenty-five criteria for a community recreation
program.

Every community recreation program should: 1. Provide equal opportunity for all; 2. Provide a wide range of individual choices in different
types of activities; 3. Continue throughout the year; 4. Serve all ages;
5. Provide equally for both sexes; 6. Encourage family recreation; 7. Uti-
lize fully all existing facilities; 8. Include passive as well as active forms
of recreation; 9. Provide activities for different periods of free time;
10. Be related to other programs in the city; 11. Carry over the leisure-
time skills and interests developed in the schools; 12. Provide activities of
a progressive nature; 13. Include activities that will persist at the adult
level; 14. Offer possibilities for varying degrees of skill, aptitude and ca-

[7] Hjelte, *op. cit.*, pp. 59–74. The italics are Hjelte's classification and the
comments a condensation of his statements regarding it.

pacities; 15. Encourage individuals and groups to provide their own activities; 16. Furnish outlets for the satisfaction of the desire for social relationships; 17. Recognize the different tastes and interests of the individual; 18. Give people who participate a share in the planning and control; 19. Place recreation opportunities within the financial abilities of all the people; 20. Make possible the wisest use of available funds; 21. Provide outlets for creative expression; 22. Assure safe and healthful conditions for recreation activity; 23. Afford opportunities for developing good citizenship; 24. Be based upon the specific interests and needs of the people in different parts of the city; 25. Be sensitive to changing conditions and needs.[8]

This might well be a charter for recreation in American cities, for it includes a basis for its organization, principles for its program, and the goals toward which it works.

RECREATION IN CITIES

The necessity for recreation in urban life is no longer a moot question. It grows out of the process of urbanization and the conditions which have come to exist in American cities. It is part and parcel of the promise of good living which the potentialities of cities make for their citizens.

The development of organized recreation has come relatively late in cities but has made rapid strides. There are many problems to be solved. Much jealousy and animosity still exist among the various agencies which are involved in community-wide programs in some cities; adequate funds are by no means yet available; many people have yet to attain an adequate conception of the character and values of recreation. What Steiner pointed out more than fifteen years ago is still true in spite of great interim developments—namely, that large sections of population are still not adequately provided with wholesome leisure-time activities, that park areas and playgrounds are far too limited to meet the needs of urban people, and that neighborhood programs fall far short of being adequate for young people living in crowded areas.[9]

One of the most hopeful signs for the further development of rec-

[8] Butler, *op. cit.*, pp. 229–232.
[9] J. F. Steiner, "Recreation and Leisure Time Activities," in President's Research Committee on Social Trends, *Recent Social Trends in the United States* (New York: McGraw-Hill Book Company, 1933), Vol. II, p. 955.

reation is found in the fact that it has become one of the major aspects around which city-planning is being done.

Supplementary Reading

Butler, George D. *Introduction to Community Recreation*, second edition. New York: McGraw-Hill Book Company, 1949.

    A comprehensive treatment of recreation as it is conceived, organized, and carried on in American cities.

Hjelte, George. *The Administration of Public Recreation*. New York: The Macmillan Company, 1940.

    An analysis of the organization, administration, problems, and relationships of publicly supported recreation in American cities.

Jacks, L. P. *Education Through Recreation*. New York: National Recreation Association, 1932.

    A statement of the philosophy generally accepted by recreation leaders in the United States, giving special emphasis to the inherent relationship between recreation and education.

Muntz, Earl E. *Urban Sociology*. New York: The Macmillan Company, 1938. Part V, "Urban Recreation."

    An exposition of the varieties of recreation, private, commercial, and public, as they are found in American cities.

CHAPTER 25

THE ORGANIZATION OF RELIGION

ORGANIZED religion reaches its highest forms in American cities. This, however, does not mean that all churches are well-developed organizations. Actually the range is from small, simple churches with meager programs to great enterprises with large constituencies, extensive buildings and equipment, multiple professional, business, and custodial staffs, and a great number of activities.

The needs of city people and the pressures of urbanization have combined to develop many churches as complex social institutions; to form denominational organizations for planning strategy for the total work of their denominations in the urban communities, for providing services to their many churches, and for granting financial aid to churches just beginning or those unable to pay for costly adaptations in the local congregations; and to establish interdenominational agencies of the Protestant churches to deal with problems of relationships and to develop coöperation in the churching of their cities.

Approximately one-third of the churches of the United States, but two-thirds of the church members, are in urban communities, or some 83,300 churches and nearly 45,000,000 members. In contrast to rural churches, which average 133 members, urban churches have an average membership of 541.[1]

Some denominations are largely urban. On the basis of church membership in 1926,[2] those with the highest proportion in cities were: Jewish congregations, 99.5 percent; Church of Christ, Scientist, 93.5 percent; Protestant Episcopal, 83.6 percent; and Roman Catholic, 80.1 percent. At the other end of the scale of the principal denominations were: Methodist Episcopal Church, South, 35.1 per-

[1] J. Frederic Dewhurst and Associates, *America's Needs and Resources* (New York: Twentieth Century Fund, 1947), p. 327.

[2] The 1926 Census of Religious Bodies gives the latest available complete data on churches.

476

cent;[3] Southern Baptist Convention, 27.1 percent; Norwegian Lutheran Church of America, 24.2 percent; and Churches of Christ, 24.3 percent. Most of the major denominations, however, are more than half urban in total membership.[4]

IMPACT OF CITIES ON THEIR CHURCHES

Not all churches have reacted to the impact of urbanization by developing complex social institutions; in fact, quite the reverse is true in many instances; but no urban church has escaped the impact of its immediate environment.

Rural Churches in the Cities. City churches are evolved rural churches, with their backgrounds in the simple traditional patterns of a gathering of people for worship. Since many city people are not far removed from their rural backgrounds, it is not surprising that their churches, in considerable numbers, cling to the simple rural patterns. This becomes clearer when it is realized that many communities have only recently grown over the line which separates rural from city communities. Village people do not change their ideas, their habits, or their institutions just because a few more are added to their population. Then, too, many villages have been absorbed as the cities have extended their boundaries, but neither does this make their people city people or their institutions city institutions. Some denominations are predominantly rural, and the patterns of their ideas are rural, so that their churches which happen to be in cities are considered no different from those in the country. The fact that many city-dwellers are but recent migrants from the country is also an important factor. These people, in many cases, have brought their churches with them to the city.

Store-Front Churches. In those parts of cities where rural migrants tend to settle, usually on the side streets, on the fronts of stores or houses will be found signs—Ebenezer Baptist Church, The Only True Church of God, Jehovah's Witnesses, etc.—denoting the meeting places of small groups of people. The feeble enterprises so designated are scarcely worthy of being considered churches. Their activities consist almost entirely of preaching services and Sunday

[3] Since 1926 the Methodist Episcopal Church, South, and the Methodist Episcopal Church have united into one denomination.
[4] C. Luther Fry, *The U.S. Looks at Its Churches* (New York: Harper & Brothers, 1930); the data are from the 1926 Census of Religious Bodies.

School. Their ministers usually have no training and little education. They make their living at other jobs and do their preaching as an avocation. While the budgets of these enterprises are very small, the per capita cost is very high.

These are the simplest of rural churches; in fact, in many cases they have been transported, name, organization, pastor, and members, from a former rural location, when the people came to the city. This is especially true among Negroes who have come from the rural South.[5] And yet these churches perform an important function, for they are the point at which rural people, bewildered by and lost in the city, can stick together with their friends and acquaintances in keeping alive their own institution as a place of refuge, stability, and security where all else fails them.[6]

Churches on Wheels. As cities have changed and the neighborhood environments of churches have become infiltrated with different kinds of people, sometimes foreign immigrants, sometimes people of lower social and economic status, sometimes people of other races, people whose problems were different and whose needs called for other services than the churches were accustomed to give, the churches have sought to escape by moving to new locations. It may be assumed that, when a church takes a location and becomes an institution of the community, it accepts the obligation to serve at that point so long as people are there to be served, as the Roman Catholic Church does; nevertheless, many a Protestant church, when the going gets tough, or its people face the prospect of associating with foreigners or Negroes or people from the farms, "takes it for granted that its duty is to reproduce its own religious culture for its children and to preserve the social ties and sympathetic interests of its women. In order to accomplish this it searches for an area affording conditions equivalent to those which created the church's original members. In such a locality it resettles and tries to repeat its past."

So, by moving in the direction of prosperity to a select neighborhood nearer or in the suburbs, many churches have gained a new building and facilities and a renewed life, with a better program and a new constituency. "Such migrations have actually taken place

[5] Benjamin E. Mays and Joseph W. Nicholson, *The Negro's Church* (New York: Harper & Brothers, 1933), p. 35.

[6] Wilbur C. Hallenbeck, "Churching of the Negro Population in a Northern City," manuscript report to the Home Missions Council of North America of a study made in Cleveland (Ohio), 1931, pp. 19–23.

by scores in city after city until they have worn trails as plain as trade routes from the worst neighborhoods toward the best. Groups of churches have done this three or four times, landing each time as neighbors and rivals in the same area, the area being always the one that was best in a given generation or decade."[7] In one American city the first church of one of the leading denominations is now located beyond the far boundary of a contiguous suburban city.

Graveyard of Churches. Many churches have been unable or unwilling to meet the demands of the changing city either by adaptations of their programs to new needs of new people or by retreating to other locations. "Their life dwindles away as old members pass on." Finally "they die because they seek to be what they have been, and this they cannot be in a growing city with new populations surrounding them." With traditional programs, in which the members carry on for their own sake, churches face declining membership and death. "The mortality is most serious in the great inner-city region. But graphs of the total Protestant membership by natural areas, arranged from downtown out to and including the suburbs, indicate that the graveyard of white American Protestant churches has pushed farther out as the city has grown. Though there are factors which cause the behavior to vary from church to church intensive case studies over a period of years reveal great similarity in the processes of decline of these institutions, and give us what might be called the behavior sequence of dying churches."[8]

Some years ago the research department of the Chicago Church Federation made a spot map of that city showing the locations at which Protestant churches had died during the life of the city. Some three hundred spots, with great density at the center of the city, were scattered all over the map. It was interesting to note that during the same period of time only three Roman Catholic churches had died. The Roman Catholic Church not only has had a greater genius for adaptation, but with centralized resources and some measure of administrative control has met the changing needs of cities with greater success.

Like Environment, like Church. As goes the neighborhood, so goes the church, is a general rule which was established by a study

[7] H. Paul Douglass, *The City's Church* (New York: Friendship Press, 1929), pp. 94–96.
[8] Samuel C. Kincheloe, *The American City and Its Church* (New York: Friendship Press, 1938), pp. 106, 107.

of nearly 2000 churches in cross-sectional sectors of sixteen American cities made by Sanderson and Hallenbeck.[9] The rule was found to be substantially true for all cities and for all denominations.

The sociological analysis of change through which the neighborhood areas of the cities were rated relatively in terms of change for the better or for the worse, has already been described (Chap. 11).

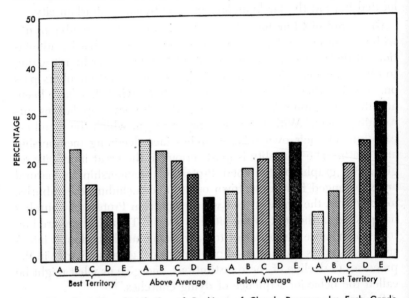

Figure 39.   Percentage Distribution of Rankings of Church Progress, by Each Grade (A—E), by Four Divisions of Neighborhood Social Trends, by 1950 Churches, in Sixteen Cities of over 100,000 Population. (Ross W. Sanderson, *The Strategy of City Church Planning* [New York: Institute of Social and Religious Research, 1932], p. 89.)

A corresponding measure of each church was made in terms of growth or decline over the same decade in church membership, Sunday School enrollment, and total expenditures. There was a very pronounced correspondence. Most churches in neighborhoods which were improving were growing, most churches in neighborhoods which were deteriorating were losing ground, and most churches in areas which were for the time being static were standing still. The distribution of the five grades of church progress with reference to the four kinds of territory is shown in Figure 39.

[9] Summarized in Ross W. Sanderson, *The Strategy of City Church Planning* (New York: Harper & Brothers, 1932), pp. 3–28.

There were, however, exceptions which proved the rule: sub-modal churches, or those that fail in the midst of favorable social trends, and supermodal churches, which, in the midst of unfavorable social trends, are making striking progress. Good environment does not make all churches good; it rather produces strength only in those churches which are capable of capitalizing it; nor does poor environment make all churches poor, for to those determined to retain their strength it becomes a stimulus.

By and large, churches are localized institutions, although they are becoming less so. The differences, however, are great. On the one hand, more than one church in five has 90 percent or more of its members living within a mile; at the other extreme are the churches at the heart of the city, more than half of which draw less than half of their membership from within a mile. Supermodal churches, in general, had scattered parishes, if their adaptations were in the nature of specialized services, or they had compact parishes, if their adaptations were for the purpose of meeting needs of people who lived in their own neighborhoods. The youthful vigor of a church is related to the pattern of its parish and varies directly with the compactness of the parish; it is also related to the chronological age of the church, as might be expected, for youthful sign varies inversely with the chronological age.[10]

An appraisal of the distinctive characteristics of supermodal and submodal churches was made by comparisons with the respective modal churches by means of a schedule of 207 items classified under eight headings: (1) composition and character of community as related to church; (2) characteristics of community; (3) church as related to community structure; (4) church as related to social process; (5) institutional characteristics; (6) program and equipment; (7) internal attitudes and relationships; (8) ecclesiastical and external relationships. The differences become clear.

Supermodal churches were larger and were increasing in size and so had the advantage of greater resources of people with which to work. They had exceptional lay leadership and larger and better professional staffs which had been longer on their jobs. They had greater financial strength of their own or by virtue of subsidies from

[10] F. Stuart Chapin, *Contemporary American Institutions* (New York: Harper & Brothers, 1935), Chap. XI, "The Protestant Church in an Urban Environment." This chapter gives an extended analysis of the relation of churches as social institutions to their environment. See also Chaps. XII and XVII.

their denominational city mission societies. They had little competition in their areas or in the kind of services they were rendering. They had more varied programs, which demonstrated their adaptability, but also had the will to adapt and were coöperative in their relationships. All of these characteristics were evidence of a high degree of group solidarity and cohesiveness.

Submodal churches, on the other hand, were too small to gain any momentum. They lacked lay leadership and also strong ministerial leadership, which changed more frequently. They were financially weak. There was a slight tendency toward competition. Programs were very limited. Adaptability was lacking. Group solidarity was seldom present; in fact, squabbles occurred twice as frequently and schisms four times as frequently as in supermodal churches.[11]

It is clear that the qualities of adaptability and administrative capacity and strength are required if churches are to succeed amid the pressures of urbanization.

VARIETIES OF CITY CHURCHES

On the basis of the factor of adaptability, Douglass devised a scheme by which he was able to classify 1044 city churches.[12] Taking a known representative sample of churches and a list of activities representative of the things churches do, he found a definite order of frequency of occurrence of the activities. Groups of activities related as to frequency indicated the stage of development of the churches. Table 56 gives the selected list of activities in order of frequency, together with the range of frequencies. This range of frequencies, together with a scale of the number of activities, formed a two-dimensional classification of seventeen groups of churches. The main groups of the 1044 churches distributed themselves, as shown in Figure 40, along with a definite curve of increasing complexity. Working from the modal group, it was clear that there were three possible directions of development: balanced development, increase of both range and size; increase of range of program, direction of novelty; increase of size of program, direction of conservatism. This is seen in diagrammatic form in Figure 41. The result was a classification of the seventeen subtypes into five main types: I, slightly

---

[11] Sanderson, *op. cit.*, Chaps. V and VI.
[12] H. Paul Douglass, *1000 City Churches* (New York: Harper & Brothers, 1926), Chaps. II and III.

TABLE 56. Frequency of 33 Organizations and Activities in 357 Churches[13]

Order of Frequency	Organizations and Activities	Range of Frequency %
33	Civics and Economics Classes	
32	Dispensary or Clinic	
31	Day Nursery	
30	Dramatic Classes	
29	English Classes	
28	Health Classes	1–10
27	Visiting Nurse	
26	Music Classes	
25	Employment Office	
24	Domestic Science Classes	
23	Kindergarten	
22	Sewing Classes	
21	Gymnasium Classes	
20	Dramatic Club	11–20
19	Young Women's Organization	
18	Mothers' or Parents' Organizations	
17	Girl Scouts or Equivalent	
16	Concerts	
15	Girls' Club (not Scouts)	
14	Library	
13	Lectures	21–40
12	Boys' Club (not Scouts)	
11	Orchestra or Band	
10	Organized Welcome	
9	Mission Study Classes	
8	Boy Scouts	41–60
7	Men's Organization	
6	General Social Events	
5	Chorus Choir	61–80
4	Young People's Society	
3	Women's Missionary Society	81–100
2	Ladies' Aid or Guild	
1	Preaching and Sunday School	

adapted churches; II, unadapted churches; III, internally adapted churches; IV, socially adapted churches; V, widely variant churches. The classification, with the distribution of the 1044 churches by number and percentage, is shown in Table 57.

[13] *Ibid.*, p. 56.

This study was followed by a series of intensive case studies of twenty-six city churches in thirteen different American cities. These churches represented planned and relatively successful adaptations to pressures of the environmental currents which unmake and re-make cities. The case studies were based on objective measurement; they were institutional, descriptive, and contemporaneous. Sixteen of them were published.[14]

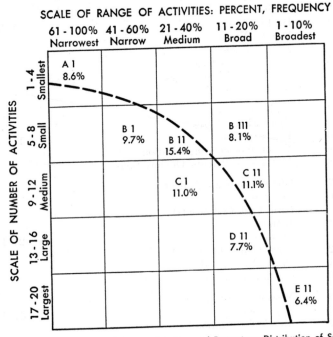

Figure 40. The Main Statistical Groups: Location and Percentage Distribution of Subtypes Which Constitute 5 Percent or More of the Total. (H. Paul Douglass, *1000 City Churches* [New York: Harper & Brothers, 1926], p. 66.)

These case studies illustrate the wide range of ways in which city churches met the impact of the changing city, from the complete avoidance of the necessity for change by moving to a new location in which a congenial population made a well-supported traditional program possible, to an institution with an extensive social and edu-cational program developed to minister to a polyglot, underpriv-ileged neighborhood. The adaptations are essentially of two types:

[14] H. Paul Douglass, *The Church in the Changing City* (New York: Harper & Brothers, 1927).

first, centrally located churches which have developed services to a particular kind of people drawn from the whole city and even the suburbs; second, those churches which have developed their programs to minister to the people who dwelt around them. The cases show these adaptations not only in their simple form but also in various combinations, including those which serve two and three distinct constituencies of both types.

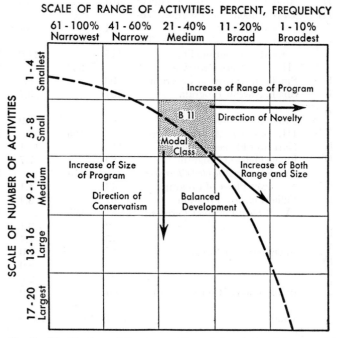

Figure 41. Possible Directions of Development Toward Complexity of Program. (H. Paul Douglass, *1000 City Churches* [New York: Harper & Brothers, 1926], p. 67.)

An extreme example of adaptation to immediate surroundings is found in Olivet Institute in the polyglot area of Chicago's lower north side, a sort of superchurch with broad and basic social ministries, modern community-service plant, large staff (37), and big budget. There are some two hundred meetings and activities per week, about three-quarters of which are groups of many different kinds not designated as religious activities. A constituency of some 6000, with a high percentage of men, families, adolescents, and children, roll up an aggregate attendance of nearly 150,000.[15]

[15] Douglass, *The Church in the Changing City*, pp. 414–443.

TABLE 57.   Classification of 1044 City Churches by Types and Subtypes[16]

Statistical Designation	Types and Characteristics of Subtypes	Number		Percent	
		Sub-types	Types	Sub-types	Types
	I. *Slightly Adapted Churches*		360		34.5
B II	Modal Subtype (Most Frequent)	161		15.4	
B III	Development of Program Toward Novelty	84		8.1	
C I	Development of Program Toward Conventionality	115		11.0	
	II. *Unadapted Churches*		253		24.2
A I	Smallest, Narrowest Program	90		8.6	
B I	Small, Narrow Program	101		9.7	
A II A III	Other Unadapted	62		5.9	
	III. *Internally Adapted Churches*		196		18.8
C II	Narrower Phase of Program	116		11.1	
D II	Fuller Phase of Program	80		7.7	
	IV. *Socially Adapted Churches*		110		10.5
D III	Narrower Phase of Program	43		4.1	
E II	Fuller Phase of Program	67		6.4	
	V. *Widely Variant Churches*		125		12.0
A IV A V B IV C III	In Direction of Novelty	32 15 11 30		3.1 1.4 1.0 2.9	
D I E I	In Direction of Conservatism	27 10		2.6 1.0	
	Total	1,044	1,044	100.0	100.0

Another type of adaptation to people's needs in a local area is seen in the Central Lutheran Church in Minneapolis, which started from nothing with a dozen families concerned about the multitude of young people of Scandinavian and Lutheran backgrounds who had come to the city "to make their fortunes," rented a building whose church had gone out of business because it was unable to adapt itself to a changed environment, and in ten years had built up a membership of 3000, had bought a whole block, including the old church, which was turned into a parish house, had built a beautiful Gothic sanctuary, was carrying on an extensive program through the whole

[16] Douglass, *1000 City Churches*, p. 54.

week, with many kinds of activities, and had sent a stream of new-formed families into other churches in the city.[17]

The specialized services are illustrated by the centrally located churches along Woodward Avenue in Detroit: Central Methodist, with its educational program for intellectuals; St. John's Protestant Episcopal, with its civic service and the use of its rooms and buildings by many organized groups in the city; Woodward Avenue Baptist, with a widely promoted program of conservative evangelism; First Unitarian, with its ministry to religious liberals; First Presbyterian, with service to three constituencies, the old wealthy membership, the young newcomers to the city who live in the area, and the underprivileged of the neighborhood; St. Paul's Protestant Episcopal Cathedral, with its diocesan services; and First Congregational, with its aesthetic worship and well-appointed social center for young people.[18]

DENOMINATIONAL CITY ORGANIZATIONS

Early in the nineteenth century, almost as soon as cities began to be self-conscious, church people realized that many of the poor did not have churches or the benefits of religion; so they began the formation of city mission societies, usually of denominational groups, to do something about it. More and more of these organizations have been formed in the larger cities by the major Protestant denominations. As the cities have changed, so have their purposes, organization, relationships, and functions changed. From simple organizations of missionary-minded people they have become in many instances the official administrative and supervisory organizations of the local denominational bodies, vested with considerable authority over the churches.[19]

Through these organizations denominational groups of churches have been able to work together, to develop a unified program, to meet acute needs where the impact of the changing city has been great, to equalize to some extent the resources of the whole group of

[17] Wilbur C. Hallenbeck, Minneapolis Churches and Their Comity Problems (New York: Harper & Brothers, 1929), pp. 75–76.

[18] Douglass, The Church in the Changing City, has case studies of three of these churches: Central Methodist, pp. 151–177; First Presbyterian, pp. 246–268; St. John's Protestant Episcopal, pp. 269–291.

[19] Wilbur C. Hallenbeck, Urban Organization of Protestantism (New York: Harper & Brothers, 1934), Chaps. II and V, especially pp. 107–110.

churches by assisting those which, through circumstances and the great need for services, were not self-sufficient, to use the methods and processes of scientific research as a basis for planning and strategy in churching their cities, and to coöperate effectively with other denominations and with other agencies in city-wide programs.

The product of urbanization, these societies have become "the bottlenecks through which the development of the churching of the city must flow," and they "can either facilitate or hinder the flow." One important aspect of their organization is that they "have been organizations of laymen, and in consequence have been free from the inhibitions and inelasticity of ecclesiasticism."[20]

The scope of the activities of these societies is very great. They act as denominational headquarters administering denominational affairs, serving as a clearing house for all denominational matters, and carrying on much office work in the process of serving the churches and their people. The first responsibility of the societies is to carry on local home-mission projects: to grant and administer home-mission aid to new churches in new fields, to assist churches that are not able to become independent, to provide backing for enlarged programs of rehabilitation and adjustment, to maintain institutions for special services, and to make grants and loans for church buildings. Another area of activity is doing things for particular churches, such as giving service in connection with church finances, rendering assistance in solving particular problems, helping with programs, doing office work that individual churches are not equipped to handle. In addition, many general programs are carried out: organizing and promoting programs of evangelism, developing religious education through leadership training, promoting special programs such as vacation schools and week-day schools, consultation services, social services, women's work, young people's work through city-wide organization and summer conferences, boys' and girls' work, summer camps, survey and research, and a variety of special and incidental activities.[21]

The diocesan organizations of the Roman Catholic Church, through a more comprehensive organization, combine all their churches and their social agencies in a single enterprise, which makes possible a unified program under single administrative control, through which coördination and planning are implicit. Jewish

[20] *Ibid.*, pp. 6, 23.
[21] *Ibid.*, Chap. III.

congregations, on the other hand, operate as units, but their people have established various city-wide organizations for community service and social work.

One of the important outcomes of the Protestant denominational city organizations has been their implementation of interdenominational agencies in cities.

ORGANIZATIONS FOR INTERDENOMINATIONAL COÖPERATION

In all of the cities, over 300,000 in population, in some between 150,000 and 300,000 in population, and in a few between 50,000 and 150,000 in population, church federations or councils of churches have been organized for Protestant church coöperation.[22] Cities had developed an immense complexity of religious organization, which inevitably expressed itself in various points of conflict. Against these pressures, though with some measure of idealism, Protestant coöperation in American cities began to take form after the turn of the century, with the hope that the religious needs of heterogeneous urban populations might be more adequately met through a coöperative approach. These organizations were voluntary associations, constituted without authority, whose membership consisted of local churches, in the main, but of denominational units in a few cases.[23]

The federations differ widely in proportion of churches participating, number of paid staff, amount of annual budgets, extent of programs, facilities, and complexity of organization. The most frequent pattern of activities is similar to that of denominational city societies, extended to a city-wide basis of operation, such as Lenten or Holy Week services under evangelism. There is usually emphasis given to agitation for reform on specific issues and advocacy of specific measures of international good will.

The unique function is church comity; though not carried on by all federations, in some it preceded the formation of the coöperative agency. Comity, in essence, is coöperative church extension; its primary concern is coöperation in the general field of home-mis-

[22] H. Paul Douglass, *Protestant Cooperation in American Cities* (New York: Harper & Brothers, 1930), p. 4.
[23] *Ibid.*, Chaps. I–VI.

sionary enterprise and goes on to many phases of church-planning in various concrete forms.[24]

The experience of a single federation in a single year adequately illustrates the range and wide variety of situations . . . in which the institutional expansion of one church or denomination may affect that of others, and which cooperating churches may need to deal with through joint machinery. [This is] fairly typical of what most comity committees find to deal with sooner or later.

During this period the comity committee of this federation dealt with the following *new situations:* (1) a religious survey of new suburban areas; (2) proposed organization of congregations; (3) location or purchase of church sites; (4) organization of Sunday schools; (5) organization of missions or branch churches; (6) selection of location for outdoor preaching.

Situations relating to existing churches which came up for joint consideration within the year were: (7) relocations of churches; (8) merger of two churches of the same denomination; (9) federations of local churches of different denominations; (10) transfer of churches from one denomination to another; (11) responsibility for fields abandoned by removing churches; (12) splits in local congregations and problem of whether or not to recognize seceding groups.

Comity situations relating to new policies of work included the following: (13) undertaking of special work for foreign-speaking groups by churches of American antecedents; and (14) abandonment of foreign-language services by churches of foreign antecedents which thus come into more direct competition with the neighboring churches.

Among general *matters of common concern* dealt with by the committee were: (15) a cooperative real estate holding company to acquire church sites; and (16) methods of making adequate surveys to determine proper church location.[25]

A large proportion (80 percent) of cases considered by comity committees had to do with church location and relocation and were brought to the committee by the churches concerned or their denominational city societies. Consequently, the greatest activity was in the more rapidly growing cities. Committees had not attained the stage of development which enabled them to study out the problems involved in the adequate churching of their cities. In fact, the basic standards for planning were largely lacking. Douglass states:

[24] H. Paul Douglass, *Church Comity* (New York: Harper & Brothers, 1929), pp. 5, 6.
[25] *Ibid.*, pp. 4, 5.

The church federation movement as a whole has omitted or failed to give due weight to the following factors closely related to the practice of comity in cities: (1) The characteristic mobility of urban population as determining the normal place for its churching; (2) the determination of actually available population for the churches of any location; (3) the legitimacy and advantage of clustering churches in many if not most urban situations; (4) the importance of a complementary denominational distribution of churches; (5) the varied principles governing the churching of down-town areas; and (6) consideration of institutional adequacy as determining the number, as well as the program, of churches.[26]

To determine some of these basic principles for planning, and to point out the specific problems to be found in one city, an intensive case study was made of the south sector of Minneapolis by using the resources and research staff of the Institute of Social and Religious Research as an adjunct of the comity committee of the Minneapolis Church Federation. The study included an analysis of population and its distribution, the social geography of the area, the location of churches and their constituencies, the geography of the churched and unchurched people, and a detailed study of each church as an institution.[27] From the facts accumulated the principles of churching the newer residential areas and the stabilized residential areas, and of adapting churches to the changing religious needs at the heart of the city, were deduced and applied to the specific problems which needed to be faced in planning for the better churching of the city.

In addition, norms of adequacy of size, finance, plant, and staff were computed on the basis of the average performance of the group of churches studied. These norms are shown in Table 58. Here are the average institutional characteristics of first-, second-, third-, and fourth-class churches.

The basis of predicting the possible attainment of a church as an institution is the potential number of people which it can serve. This is a matter of population per church, but not of gross population, because of the mobility of city people and the many patterns of their habitual movements. These movements must be taken into account in computing the available population for each church. "The resident population less the non-Protestants; less the people that go

[26] *Ibid.*, p. 143.
[27] Wilbur C. Hallenbeck, *Minneapolis Churches and Their Comity Problems* (New York: Harper & Brothers, 1929).

TABLE 58. Norms of Size, Finance, Plant and Staff Based on a Cross Section of Minneapolis Churches[28]

Items of Comparison	Classes of Churches			
	D	C	B	A
Church-membership	151 or less	152–297	298–650	651–3,196
S. S. Enrollment	116 or less	117–230	231–274	274–2,083
Current Expenses	$3,250 or less	3,251–6,215	6,216–12,500	12,501 and over
Per Capita Contributions	$15.19 or less	15.20–21.07	21.08–29.48	29.49 and over
Value of Plant	$15,500 or less	15,501–40,250	40,251–88,750	88,751 and over
Number on Staff	1 or less	1½–2	2½–5	over 5

out of the district to church, less the same proportion of the unchurched, plus the people who come into the district for churching, plus the same proportion of the unchurched, gives the available population. This, divided by the number of churches, gives the available population per church in each district."[29] Then it is possible, on the basis of the norms and the ratio of church membership to population, the cost of a church, and the per capita giving rate, to compute the

TABLE 59. Numbers Necessary to Provide Different Classes of Churches at Different Rates of Giving Based on a Cross Section of Minneapolis Churches[30]

Per Capita Giving Rate		C Class (Minimum Cost $3,200)	B Class (Minimum Cost $6,300)	A Class (Minimum Cost $12,500)
$15	Members	213	420	833
	Adherents	283	559	1,108
	Population	944	1,861	3,690
$21	Members	152	300	595
	Adherents	202	399	791
	Population	673	1,329	2,636
$29	Members	110	217	431
	Adherents	146	289	573
	Population	487	961	1,909

[28] *Ibid.*, Table IV, p. 84.
[29] *Ibid.*, p. 119.
[30] *Ibid.*, Table X, p. 91.

possibilities of a church. Table 59 shows this worked out for Minneapolis churches. When this scale was applied to the churches, it was found that, under the circumstances which prevailed at the time of the study, "only one-third of the churches have a fair chance of becoming adequate and one-quarter of the churches, even if the highest rate of per capita contributions were possible to them, could only achieve third-class status."[31]

Church comity, under interdenominational Protestant coöperation, lagging, as it does, far behind the pressures of urbanization, marks the greatest measure of adaptation which religious organizations have yet attained. It has been strengthened in recent years by the many partial church unions which have been effected and has promise in the diminishing sense of religious distance which is coming among church people.[32]

At best, the recognition of the function of the church as a social organization with its religious sanctions is a difficult matter. The best resolution of this seeming dilemma is in a statement of Douglass and Brunner:

All told, then, the church's function is determined, first by what the social group is and by the things which its nature requires it to do. Secondly, the church's function is determined by what its transcendental insight and relationships demand, and is interpreted, on the one hand, by accepted tradition and on the other, by the innovating prophetic consciousness. Thirdly, the church's concrete functioning is the work of thoughtful experimentation which devises and sets before the church its practical program. It is the function of the church to be and to do all things which the co-working of these three-fold forces brings forth as its total expression in the modern world.[33]

OTHER RELIGIOUS ORGANIZATIONS

As the cities developed, after the middle of the nineteenth century, church people organized Young Men's Christian Associations and Young Women's Christian Associations. These agencies were completely independent of the churches, but were prompted by the desire to provide Christian influences for young men and young

[31] Ibid., p. 91.
[32] H. Paul Douglass and Edmund deS. Brunner, The Protestant Church as a Social Institution (New York: Harper & Brothers, 1935), pp. 266–267 and Chap. XV.
[33] Ibid., p. 324.

women who were unattached and alone, working in business and in other jobs in the cities. In addition to religious programs, residences were established, physical activities in gymnasiums and swimming pools were carried on, many clubs, group activities, and educational programs were included, and various services were rendered, notably employment bureaus.

Somewhat later the Jewish people established Young Men's Hebrew Associations and Young Women's Hebrew Associations very much on the same general model.

These agencies have broadened their programs to include all ages of men and women and boys and girls of school age. The YMCA was the outstanding pioneer in vocational education and later in vocational guidance. The YWCA has been especially active in general education and in social and political action. Activities and programs have changed as the needs of their constituencies have changed with the changing city[34] and as leisure time has increased and the constructive use of leisure time has been given more consideration.

The New York City YMCA conducted a survey, 1925–1926, of its whole enterprise.[35] In general, the recommendations were in the direction of more specialized services at more centrally located buildings to serve youth in the metropolitan area. This study has influenced greatly the policy not only of this particular organization but also of this type of organization in American cities. More recently, however, there has been a trend toward greater emphasis on neighborhood service in the New York YMCA, which had become neglected in following the principle of adaptation emphasized in this study.

The Roman Catholic Church has no agencies which exactly correspond to these Protestant and Jewish organizations, though in its better-developed parish services and its many social services, which are a part of the overall diocesan organization, it makes available most of the activities in its city work.

In more recent years the Jewish people have organized many Jewish community centers in American cities located in those areas which are heavily populated with Jewish people. These agencies, as

[34] Owen D. Pence, *The YMCA and Social Need* (New York: Association Press, 1939), pp. 53 ff., 113 ff., and Chap. VIII.
[35] Arthur L. Swift, *The Survey of the Young Men's Christian Association of the City of New York* (New York: Association Press, 1927), Chap. II, especially pp. 42–43.

their name implies, have developed a broad community service. A recent study of their organization and activities has raised the issue of basic policy: whether these agencies should be primarily given to a religious service to their own group or to a broader community service.

There are many social and health agencies which are operated by religious bodies in cities, but these are not religious organizations in the sense in which they have been discussed here. In fact, the "Y's" and community centers have come to be considered as social agencies rather than as religious organizations.

Supplementary Reading

An exploration of the books noted in the references has much possibility for specialized study.

Kincheloe, Samuel C. *The American City and Its Church.* New York: Friendship Press, 1938.
     A popular presentation of the impact of cities on their churches and the functions of the church in the urban community.
Sears, Charles Hatch. *City Man.* New York: Harper & Brothers, 1936.
     An analysis of the religious needs of city people and the response of churches to these needs.

PART VI

PEOPLE IN CITIES

CITIES have had a profound impact upon their people. They have brought about great changes in the functions and structure of urban families and created the necessity for new forms of families (Chap. 26). They have surrounded people with conditions of living with which it has been difficult to cope and out of which have come certain characteristics of people, many crises with accompanying maladjustments, the disintegration of personality, and the social stratification of people (Chap. 27).

CHAPTER 26

URBAN FAMILIES

INDUSTRIALIZATION and its concomitant urbanization destroy the unity of the family and divorce it from society.[1] It is no wonder that in the cities divorce rates have been rapidly rising, that family service agencies find a growing proportion of their case loads made up of families with serious problems which do not involve relief, and that delinquency has come to involve many young children.

It would be folly, however, to let such headline news characterize urban families, for the large majority still get along with reasonable success—not without problems, but with problems which they have been able to solve without disrupting or destroying family life. They manage somehow because it takes a good deal of doing to withstand and counteract the forces which work against the integrity of the family. Traditional concepts of family life are of little help where circumstances require different kinds of families. The inherent stability, common sense, and flexibility of most people make it possible to work out difficulties from day to day without much understanding of what the basis of the difficulties is or why they have arisen. How much more promising it would be if the members of families knew what they were trying to do and why.

On every hand one can observe desertion, separation, divorce, cruelty to children, and even violence, which would make it appear that urban families are disintegrating. In reality, however, such things are largely evidences of the inadequacies of families which have a serious lag in their capacities to adapt themselves to the changed conditions of urban life. Families in cities would have begun to disappear if there were no longer use for them as society discards its useless forms, but families are increasing. Urban society has need for families; there are essential functions for them to per-

---

[1] Peter F. Drucker, "The New Society: I, Revolution by Mass Production," *Harper's Magazine*, No. 1192 (Sept., 1949), p. 26.

form. The personalities of urban people are, and will continue to be, primarily formed within the framework of family life; that the job is not adequately done is clear. If urban families are to be reëstablished, it is necessary to understand what the job of the family is in urban communities and why or how it differs from the traditional ideals of family life.

TRADITIONAL CONCEPT OF THE FAMILY

The ideal of family life which has become a tradition in America was formed in colonial days and was strengthened during the period of the pioneering of the West. Circumstances made strong family units necessary. Families were very largely on their own. Those things which were needed by the members of each family had to be provided almost entirely by their own efforts and resources. Not only food, clothing, shelter, heat, implements, and other material things, but also education, religious training and observance, recreation, and protection were included in the requirements.

So it was that social circumsttnces molded the patterns of families into large, coöperative, producing units which were strong by virtue of the mutual interdependence of the members and the headship of the father. They were large because there was much work to be done, and everyone had his tasks to perform within the activities of family life. Each new child was welcome because he was an asset to the family in that he made another pair of hands to take their share of the work. So, also, footloose kin, maiden aunts and unmarried uncles, grandparents and even cousins, were readily absorbed into the family unit because each one increased the capacity of the group to produce. They were coöperative because the many tasks to be done depended upon the assumption of responsibility on the part of each member of the household and the thorough organization of the group in their responsibilities and relationships so that the needs of all and of each could be met.

Early American families have frequently been characterized as patriarchal, but this term is misleading. It was the administrative function of the father, not his dominance as ruler of the family, which made him important and his family strong. A more truly patriarchal family, in which the father exerted control over the members of the group, came later in America and was the first symptom of the impact of change on the family. It was a defense, and a feeble one it proved, against those forces, inherent in industrialization, which began to break down the unity of the family. The older families were, for the most part, very democratic organizations.

This picture has persisted and become idealized in America. People continue to try to make their families after the pattern which fitted the circumstances of colonial and frontier days. Such families could not possibly exist under the conditions of modern urban life. It is necessary to determine what sort of family is suitable to these conditions.

IMPACT OF URBANIZATION

As industry began the process of providing goods through manufacturing in factories, home production was relieved from pressure. But factories had to have workers; so opportunities became available for people to get jobs outside their homes. More factories, more employees, more products, more things to be distributed; so more stores became necessary, and greater demands were put on transportation, all of which absorbed more and more people as workers. Factories tended to congregate in the embryonic cities because the resources for power were at hand, more potential workers were available, and transportation was accessible. Cities grew, more activities of government became necessary, and so more jobs. Services of many sorts were required and became possible with more people to serve; another new category of jobs began to develop. The larger communities began to be cities; as they grew, their power to draw people from the rural surplus and from the newcomers to America increased.

Men were the first to go out of their homes to work for money. Thus began the transformation of the very basis of family life. The close-knit coöperative family unit, which had been completely absorbed in "making a living" for its members by providing those things and those experiences which they needed, was broken. The father and husband "had gone to work," often to do something which had no direct relationship to his own needs or the needs of the members of his family, "to earn money" to buy things he and his family needed which had been produced in factories by other people, he knew not whom. "Earning a living" and "making a living" are two quite different things.

Young people followed the men into the jobs which cities offered. So they came to be "on their own." No longer were they dependent upon family units for their place to work, to live, and to supply their needs. This freedom opened up to them all sorts of new possibilities of ordering their lives in their own terms. They could set up their own families; they could join the pioneers who opened up the West. They could go to other cities to work and to live. All of these things they did, and much was gained, but the old established type of family was lost.

TABLE 60.   Married Women Employed in 1890, 1940, and 1950

	% of Gainfully Employed Women Married	% of Married Women Gainfully Employed
1890[a]	13.9	4.6
1940[b]	37.5	11.8
1950[c]	50.0	23.0

[a] Bureau of the Census, special release.
[b] Bureau of the Census, special release.
[c] Bureau of the Census, estimate, reported in the New York *Times*, Feb. 13, 1950, p. 23.

The circumstances which had made it necessary for families to be large coöperative units had so changed that such families were no longer possible except on the frontier and in rural farm areas. But now the frontier has disappeared, and most rural farm areas have come under the influence of cities to such an extent that only a very few remote and isolated areas have any semblance of the early American conditions.

As jobs in the cities continued to increase through the expansion of women's occupations, married as well as single women had opportunities to work outside their homes for wages. While the proportion of married women who are gainfully employed has never been large, it greatly increased in the half century from 1890 to 1940 and is estimated to have doubled between 1940 and 1950. It represented over one-third of the female working force in 1940 and is expected to reach one-half in 1950, as can be seen in Table 60. The employment of women is very largely an urban phenomenon because the jobs available to women are almost all to be found in cities; consequently, the proportion of city married women in the labor force is greater and the proportion of nonwhite more than twice that of white. Percentages are given in Table 61.

The fact that many married women in cities are gainfully employed, and that many more have had work experience or were trained for jobs before marriage, has had two far-reaching effects upon family life. In the first place, it has established the independence of women; they can take care of themselves. In the old days the only alternatives women had were marriage or remaining a part of their original large families. When they married, they had to stick it out no matter what degree of happiness or congeniality they found in their new relationships. Today women do not have to submit to unbearable conditions in the marriage relationship. To be sure, this has been an important contributory factor in the increase in divorce,

TABLE 61. Percentage of Families with Wife in the Labor Force, 1940[2]

	All Families	White Families	Nonwhite Families
Total U.S.	11.9	10.8	24.3
Urban	15.0	13.7	32.9
Rural nonfarm	10.9	10.1	22.9
Rural farm	4.7	3.3	13.9

but, what is more important, the independence of women has established a basis upon which it is far more possible to create a happy and creative family life.

In the second place, it has tended to change the focus of interest and association of wives and mothers, who have been the central figures of family life, from within to outside the home and family. This means that the trend in cities is for all members of the family to find the center of most of their interests and relationships outside of their family circle because their principal activities are outside the home.

Those wives and mothers who stick to the job of home-making find their responsibilities less exacting under the circumstances of modern urban life. Small dwellings, families of limited size, members of the family with many outside interests, children "on their own" at an early age, leave the home-makers before they are forty with time on their hands. Unless they have cultivated outside interests, they grow out of touch with the others in their families and lose the capacity to meet with them on common ground.

[2] 16th Census of the United States, 1940: Population: Families: Employment Status, Table 11, pp. 56–61.

So the conditions of urban life have wrought profound and fundamental changes in families—changes in the relationship of the members, changes in organization and operation, and changes in the
functions which are performed.

STRUCTURE AND FUNCTIONS OF URBAN FAMILIES

The structure or organization of social institutions never stands
by itself; no more that of families. Structure is an auxiliary of function and develops as a means of carrying out function. Structure,
moreover, is influenced by cultural and social environment; consequently, the form of the family has been found to differ widely
according to the places and the times in which it has been observed
and studied. The function of a social institution, however, is also
determined by its cultural and social environment. This is clear with
reference to the relative complexity of various cultures. In a simple
culture where institutions are few, an institution will likely have
many functions, but in a complex culture where there are many
institutions, they will be specialized with single or few functions. So,
also, the culture determines the ideas of what functions are and the
ways that functions are carried out.

When a culture is developing rapidly, it is becoming more and
more complex, and a part of the process is the changes which its
institutions undergo to adapt themselves to their changing environment. Since such changes in institutions are in the direction of increasing specialization, the phenomenon has been called "growth by
loss of function"; that is, an institution loses its auxiliary or secondary functions to new institutions in the community and thereby
is able to focus its attention and activity on its primary function.

This has been happening to families under the pressures of urbanization, although it has seldom been recognized. The difficulty is that
it has often been assumed that the traditional complex of family
functions in American culture is an essential part of its existence.
Consequently, when patterns of family life are seen to be changing
and some of the traditional functions are being taken over by other
institutions in the community, many people draw the conclusion, as
they have about American urban families, that the family is disintegrating, when in truth the reverse may be the fact.

Since structure and function are closely related, they should
change together, but this does not always happen. Sometimes very

gradual and imperceptible changes in function cause changes in structure which can be readily observed, but great structural changes can come about without any realization that basic changes in function have taken place. On the other hand, structure becomes so set that it resists those changes which radical changes in function require. Both of these things have happened in urban families; so people neither understand what their families should do nor realize that they are unable to maintain the organization of their families according to their traditional ideas of what families ought to be be-

TABLE 62. Percentage of the Population Fifteen Years Old and Over Married in the United States, by Sex, 1890–1949

| Year | Percentage Married | |
	Male	Female
1890[a]	53.9	56.8
1900[a]	54.5	57.0
1910[a]	55.8	58.9
1920[a]	59.2	60.6
1930[a]	60.0	61.1
1940[a]	61.2	61.0
1949[b]	68.3	66.1

[a] *16th Census, 1940: Population*, Vol. IV, Part 1, Table 5, p. 16.
[b] Bureau of the Census, Current Population Reports, Series P-20, No. 25 (Aug. 19, 1949); the figures are for fourteen years old and over, hence lower than the true comparative percentages.

cause they are in a different world—the city. Out of these conditions the problems of city families arise.

Some of the changes in structure and in function which urban families have undergone are clearly seen in the facts.

Changes in Structure of Families. With all the changes which have taken place in American families, the proportion of those over fifteen years of age who are married has constantly increased during the last sixty years, the period of increasing urbanization. The most striking change is that the increase from 1940 to 1950 will exceed that of the previous fifty years. The percentages for census years are shown in Table 62. A further breakdown of the marital status of the population over fifteen years, by age groups and by sex, is given in Table 63. Several revealing things about city marriages can be noted from these data. Rural people, especially rural nonfarm, marry at earlier ages than city people. Women marry much younger than

TABLE 63. Marital Status of the Population Fifteen Years Old and Over, by Percentage, in Age Groups, by Sex, for Urban, Rural Nonfarm, and Rural Farm People, in the United States, 1940[3]

Age Group		Single Urban	Single Rural Non-farm	Single Rural Farm	Married Urban	Married Rural Non-farm	Married Rural Farm	Widowed Urban	Widowed Rural Non-farm	Widowed Rural Farm	Divorced Urban	Divorced Rural Non-farm	Divorced Rural Farm
Total	M	32.6	31.4	36.4	61.8	62.7	58.3	4.2	4.6	4.5	1.4	2.3	0.8
	F	27.4	22.6	24.3	58.1	64.5	66.3	12.4	11.6	8.8	2.1	1.3	0.6
15–19	M	98.6	98.0	97.9	1.4	2.0	2.1	—	—	—	—	—	—
	F	91.0	84.4	85.1	8.8	15.3	14.6	0.1	0.1	0.2	0.2	0.2	0.1
20–24	M	74.5	66.6	71.5	25.1	32.8	28.0	0.1	0.2	0.2	0.3	0.4	0.3
	F	52.9	37.2	39.4	45.6	61.3	59.2	0.5	0.6	0.8	1.0	0.9	0.6
25–29	M	37.8	29.8	37.3	60.9	68.9	61.6	0.3	0.4	0.6	1.0	0.9	0.5
	F	26.6	16.3	16.8	70.0	81.0	81.0	1.2	1.3	1.4	2.2	1.4	0.8
30–34	M	21.5	16.7	22.7	76.3	81.3	75.4	0.6	0.7	1.0	1.6	1.3	0.9
	F	17.3	10.4	10.3	77.0	85.5	86.6	2.6	2.3	2.1	3.1	1.8	1.0
35–39	M	15.8	12.8	16.4	80.9	84.3	81.0	1.2	1.3	1.5	2.1	1.6	1.1
	F	13.1	8.3	7.3	78.4	85.3	88.5	5.0	4.4	3.3	3.5	2.0	0.9
40–44	M	12.9	11.6	12.8	82.7	84.2	83.8	2.1	2.2	2.3	2.3	2.0	1.1
	F	11.1	7.5	5.9	77.5	83.3	88.4	8.0	7.1	4.9	3.4	2.1	0.8

Age	Sex												
45–49	M	1.1	2.2	2.2	3.2	3.3	3.2	85.0	83.1	83.3	10.7	11.4	11.3
	F	0.8	2.0	3.0	7.0	10.6	11.9	87.2	80.2	75.0	5.0	7.2	10.1
50–54	M	1.3	2.3	2.1	4.8	5.3	5.2	83.4	80.5	81.8	10.5	11.9	10.9
	F	0.6	1.7	2.5	10.5	15.9	17.7	83.9	74.9	69.5	5.0	7.5	10.3
55–59	M	1.2	2.1	2.0	6.9	7.7	7.5	81.4	78.3	79.9	10.5	11.9	10.6
	F	0.6	1.6	2.1	15.0	22.3	25.0	79.3	68.5	62.7	5.1	7.6	10.2
60–64	M	1.2	2.0	1.8	10.0	11.6	11.5	78.6	74.8	76.4	10.2	11.6	10.3
	F	0.6	1.3	1.6	22.3	30.9	34.4	71.6	60.0	53.0	5.5	7.8	11.0
65–69	M	1.1	1.8	1.7	14.6	16.6	16.9	74.7	70.4	71.1	9.6	11.2	10.3
	F	0.6	1.0	1.2	34.2	42.4	46.1	59.4	48.9	41.6	5.8	7.7	11.1
70–74	M	0.9	1.4	1.3	21.9	23.6	24.9	67.8	64.2	63.9	9.4	10.8	9.9
	F	0.3	0.6	0.8	48.3	54.2	58.0	45.0	37.4	30.2	6.4	7.8	11.0
75–79	M	0.9	1.2	1.1	31.9	32.2	34.6	58.0	56.3	55.1	9.2	10.3	9.2
	F	0.3	0.5	0.5	63.7	66.1	68.8	29.6	25.7	20.1	6.4	7.7	10.6
80–84	M	0.6	0.8	0.8	44.3	42.7	46.0	46.4	47.1	44.8	8.7	9.4	8.4
	F	0.2	0.3	0.3	76.5	76.5	77.5	16.7	15.5	11.7	6.6	7.7	10.5
85 and over	M	0.5	0.7	0.6	59.2	55.8	59.5	32.6	34.9	32.2	7.7	8.6	7.7
	F	0.7	0.1	0.1	86.0	84.9	85.0	7.9	7.6	5.9	5.9	7.4	9.0

³ Data are from *16th Census, 1940: Population, Volume IV: Part 1, "U.S., Summary,"* Table 6, pp. 18-20.

men. The proportion of men who are married is greater from the age of forty on in cities, but only above the age of fifty-five on the farms. There are always more single men than single women in the country, but in cities, after sixty, there is a larger proportion of unmarried women than of unmarried men. There is little difference between the proportion of men in city and country who are widowed, but the proportion of widows in cities is considerably greater up to the age of eighty. There are proportionately more divorced people in cities than on farms and, during the years in which divorce is greatest, up to fifty, more than in the villages. With all of the great increase in divorce during recent years (from 1887 to 1937, while population and marriages each increased 211 percent, divorces increased 610 percent), in 1940 only 1.3 percent of the population fifteen or more years of age was divorced, and the highest proportion was among city women from thirty-five to forty-five years of age, 3.5 percent. Divorce reached an all-time peak in 1946 with 610,000, a crude rate of 4.3 per 1000 of population; the rate dropped to 3.4 in 1947 and to 2.8 in 1948, which was just under the 1944 rate, but well above the 1940 rate of 2.0, which was the highest up to that time.[4] It should be noted that some 80 percent of divorced people remarry.

The lag in marriage in cities exists in part because city young people demand a higher standard of living at marriage, in part because cities make it difficult for young people of marriageable age to get acquainted, and in part because single people with ambition make their way from the country to the city. Especially do unmarried women go to cities because there they can find jobs and independence. So also do widows go to cities, where the conditions of life are more conducive to convenience and satisfaction. Marriages in 1946 increased 42.0 percent over 1945, to a rate of 16.4 per 1000 of population, then dropped to 13.9 in 1947 and 12.3 in 1948.[5] This increase in marriage appears to have been disproportionately in cities, which temporarily discounts the lag. It is probable that this unusual situation will not continue; in fact, the return to a normal marriage rate in 1948 seems to indicate that the same circumstances which prevailed before the war have come back into control.

One of the most striking changes which have taken place in the

---

[4] Federal Security Agency, Public Health Service, National Office of Vital Statistics, *Provisional Marriage and Divorce Statistics, United States, 1948,* Special Reports, Vol. 31, No. 16 (Nov. 4, 1949), Tables 1, p. 221, and 9, p. 229.

[5] *Ibid.,* Tables 1, p. 221, and 8, p. 228.

structure of American families is in size. In the 150 years of the census records, families have decreased 40 percent in their average size, but the most frequent size of family changed from five persons in 1790 to two persons in 1940. Table 64 gives some additional details of this drop in size. In spite of the increase in marriages, the size of families continues to decrease.

TABLE 64. Changes in Size of Household in the United States, 1790, 1900, 1940, 1947, 1949[6]

| Year | Median Size of Household | Modal Size | | Size Range of about ¾ of Households | |
		No. of Persons	% Total Households	%	No. of Persons
1790[a]	5.43	5	13.9	72.8	3–8
1900[a]	4.23	3	17.6	74.6	2–6
1940[b]	3.29	2	24.8	73.0	1–4
1947[b]	3.18	2	27.2	76.3	1–4
1949[c]	3.11	2	27.2	78.4	1–4

[a] Bureau of the Census, A Century of Population Growth in the United States, 1790–1900, Table 28.
[b] Bureau of the Census, Current Population Reports, Series P-70, No. 1; Historical Statistics of the United States, 1789–1945.
[c] Bureau of the Census, Current Population Reports, Series P-20, No. 26, Table 6, p. 19.

The decrease in size of families in the United States is largely due to the influence of cities. The rapid drop followed the beginning of the industrial age and the accompanying rapid growth of cities. The distribution of families by size in 1940 and 1949, given in Table 65, shows the larger proportion of small families in cities and the larger proportion of large families on the farms, but the median size is decreasing everywhere, even since the war.

The number of small children at home is a further factor of family structure which is significant. Seven-tenths of urban families have no small children, and only a little more than one-tenth have two or more children under ten years of age. Table 66 shows the distribution of families with small children for 1940 and 1930, during which period there was a marked change. The 1950 census will undoubtedly show considerable increase in the proportion of families with young children, but this will work itself back to the pattern shown here, in all likelihood, several years before the 1960 census. In 1940 more than half (53.0 percent) of the city families had no

[6] This table was specially prepared by the Chief of the Population Division, Bureau of the Census.

TABLE 65.   Percentage Distribution of Households in the United States, by Size, Urban, Rural Nonfarm, and Rural Farm, 1940 and 1949[7]

No. of Persons	Total U.S.		Urban		Rural Nonfarm		Rural Farm	
	1940	1949	1940	1949	1940	1949	1940	1949
1	7.7	8.0	8.1	9.2	9.0	7.3	5.1	4.8
2	24.8	27.2	26.4	28.5	25.2	26.9	19.5	23.1
3	22.4	24.1	23.3	24.5	22.1	24.5	19.9	22.5
4	18.1	19.2	18.5	19.3	17.6	19.9	17.8	17.7
5	11.5	10.4	11.0	9.6	11.1	11.3	13.3	12.4
6	6.8	5.5	6.0	5.0	6.6	4.7	9.2	8.4
7	3.8	2.7	3.1	2.0	3.7	2.7	6.0	5.2
8	2.2	1.3	1.7	0.9	2.1	1.3	3.9	2.6
9 or more	2.7	1.5	1.9	1.0	2.5	1.5	5.3	3.4
Median size	3.28	3.11	3.16	3.00	3.21	3.15	3.81	3.48

children under eighteen years of age at home, while only about one-third (39.4 percent) of the rural families were without children under eighteen.

This changed pattern since the close of World War II is due to the many new families which have had children, as indicated by the great increase in birth rates. Cities appear to have more than their share of this increase. In large part it is due to delayed births, those which would have occurred during the war period; so there may be little change in the decade except in the total age structure of the

TABLE 66.   Percentage Distribution of Families with Children Under Ten Years of Age, Urban, Rural Nonfarm, and Rural Farm, in the United States, 1940 and 1930[8]

No. of Children Under 10	Urban		Rural Nonfarm		Rural Farm	
	1940	1930	1940	1930	1940	1930
None	70.2	62.4	62.4	57.4	57.1	50.7
1	17.6	19.4	19.0	18.8	18.7	19.1
2	8.2	10.9	10.8	12.3	12.3	13.7
3	2.7	4.6	4.8	6.7	6.8	8.8
4	0.9	1.9	2.1	3.3	3.4	5.0
5 or more	0.4	0.8	0.9	1.5	1.8	2.7

[7] Bureau of the Census, Current Population Reports, Series P-20, No. 26 (Jan. 27, 1940), Table 6, p. 14.

[8] 16th Census, 1940: Population and Housing: Families: General Characteristics, Table 3, p. 14.

population. At any rate, population experts are of the opinion that this temporary change will have no significant effect upon the long trends.

The roles of family members have become different in cities. Men are not so exclusively heads of families. Table 67 shows that nearly one-fifth of urban families have a woman at their head. This, however, does not tell all of the story, for there is a tendency for women to take over more and more completely the management of family finances and affairs, including the responsibility for bringing up children. This is especially true with the families which live in suburbs, where the men commute and are away from home from early morn-

TABLE 67. Family Heads in the United States, 1940[9]

	Urban Percentage		Rural Nonfarm Percentage		Rural Farm Percentage	
Male head	81.7		86.2		92.2	
Wife present		73.4		76.7		82.0
No wife		8.3		9.5		10.2
Female head	18.3		13.8		7.8	

ing to evening. These families have been called, by some, "neomatriarchal" families. It is probably more accurate to recognize these things as evidence of a growing democracy in family life which is a positive response to changing conditions which call for new patterns of sharing family responsibilities. Another evidence of this sharing is to be found in the fact that many city families have more than a single breadwinner. In 1940 one-third of urban families had two or more members gainfully employed.[10]

The two-person family became the predominant type of urban family by 1930. It has been estimated that this type comprises from one-quarter to one-half of the families in the various American cities.[11] This is a radical change in the structure of the family, which has been thought of largely in terms of children. It is the result of the impact of urbanization upon the family, but it represents several quite different things.

Unstable families are among the number. Those which have never been able to catch on to the urban way and pace are some of them.

[9] *Ibid.*, Table 2, p. 10.
[10] *Ibid.*, Table 13, p. 36.
[11] See Tables 64 and 65. See also M. F. Nimkoff, *The Family* (Boston: Houghton Mifflin Company, 1934), p. 262.

Because of either lack of educational background, lack of marketable skills, or physical or mental illness, the employment and income of the breadwinner are precarious. These families usually live in furnished rooms or light-housekeeping quarters. But there are others among the unstable families by choice. Zorbaugh, in his study of those living in furnished rooms on the lower North Side of Chicago, found 23 percent of the roomers were unmarried couples while 15 percent were regularly married couples.[12] It is not likely that Chicago differs from other large cities, and in all probability the number of those who involve themselves in these unstable alliances has increased in the period since this study was made. The important point would seem to be that even those who shun the responsibilities and patterns of the legalized contractual marriage find the need for a form of family existence.

There are also many stable families in the two-person group. Some of these are older people whose children have left home. Others are husbands and wives who are both gainfully employed, many times professional people, who find it necessary, or who choose, to pool their incomes in order to maintain a higher standard of living than they otherwise could. Between these two are other couples who are unable to have children, but who may desire to have them very much. There is a hypothesis in some quarters that the conditions of urban life make for sterility. It is not likely that this can ever be proved, but a significant comment on family life is the fact that there are long waiting lists for babies from adoption agencies, and that a considerable black market in babies has grown up in American cities.

A corollary of the changing structure of families is their changing dwellings. Home ownership is growing less in cities, and it is much less than in rural areas, as can be seen in Table 68. It is difficult to say whether this reflects the increasing difficulty involved in owning homes in cities or the decreasing desire to have homes of their own on the part of city families. Both are probably the case. This is also seen in the trend in types of dwellings in cities. While the majority of families in even the largest cities still live in single-family dwellings, about 18 percent of all city families in the United States live in multifamily dwellings, and the proportion is much greater in the larger cities. In New York City, for example, in 1940, in the Borough of Queens 35.9 percent of the dwellings were single-family residences and 23.5 percent were two-family dwellings, while in the

[12] Harvey Zorbaugh, "Roomers," *Survey*, No. 56, p. 461 (July 15, 1926).

Borough of Manhattan 78.8 percent were multifamily dwellings. In the large cities, in recent years, the new dwellings which have been constructed have been multifamily dwellings, in large proportion. This has been especially true in the city housing projects, both public and private, which have been erected since the end of the war. The unit dwellings in these newer structures are predominantly three- and four-room apartments. These small apartments are in keeping with the increasing two-person families, but they are also

TABLE 68. Percentage of All Dwelling Units Occupied by Owners in the United States, Urban and Rural, 1930 and 1940[13]

	1940	1930
Total U.S.	43.6	47.8
Urban	37.5	43.4
Rural nonfarm	51.7	53.7
Rural farm	53.2	53.9

an influence in keeping families small because there is no room for more than a child or two, at most.

It has frequently been stated that small families are the result of the increasing use of birth control. This hardly seems consistent with the general picture of the impact of urban conditions upon family life. It is more accurate to recognize that the economic and social circumstances of urbanization make for small families, and that birth control is the device which has been developed to facilitate this adaptation of families. This analysis is confirmed by the fact that families grow smaller even in those groups which have been bitterly opposed to the use of birth control.

Changes in Functions of Families. MacIver has defined the family as "a group defined by a sex relationship sufficiently precise and enduring to provide for the procreation and upbringing of children."[14] This functional definition includes three things: (1) the establishing of a continuing, socially (and in most societies also legally as a contractual matter) recognized relationship of two individuals of opposite sexes, with arrangements for living together in a "home" so that (2) sex relationships can be stabilized because of their in-

[13] *16th Census, 1940: Housing:* First Series, "U.S., Summary, Table 11, p. 10.
[14] R. M. MacIver and Charles H. Page, *Society: An Introductory Analysis* (New York: Rinehart and Company, Inc., 1949), p. 238.

volvement in this intimate relationship, and (3) the procreation and rearing of children, which is a prolonged process among humans, can be provided for.

How are these things to be carried out? The patterns are determined by the time and place of the cultural environment. In America the patterns, established in the early days of a simple rural culture, involved necessarily a number of secondary functions so inseparably interwoven with the primary functions that they have become distinguishable only in the light of the changes which have taken place in the cultural environment in more recent times. These secondary functions have been variously catalogued. Six such—economic, protective, religious, recreational, educational, and status—are given by Ogburn in his study of the recent social trends in the American family.[15]

Ogburn's thesis, which is supported by a great deal of evidence, is that these six functions, which were formerly an integral part of family life, in the process of industrialization and urbanization have been taken over from families by other institutions of the community.

The economic functions of early American families consisted largely in production for direct use. This was the central and most time- and energy-consuming family task, and it involved the coöperative activity of all members of the family group. The loss of these productive functions was gradual and extended over a long period of time. The factories early took over the making of metal products, implements, and furniture; later, spinning, weaving, and the making of clothing; the making of medicines, soaps, and the like also went to the factories; and more recently baking, canning, laundering, cleaning, dyeing, and even sewing have, in the main, left the home. The great increase in the number of restaurants and delicatessens, where much ready-to-eat food is available, has greatly decreased the work of cooking in the home. Modern central heating has simplified the maintenance of the home, and living in apartments has removed this responsibility altogether from the family. Many of the household duties have been made easier by the great variety of electric appliances, from toasters and irons to vacuum cleaners and refrigerators. A considerable number of housekeeping tasks are still left for women to do, but in small dwellings, with few people and the many

[15] William F. Ogburn (with the assistance of Clark Tibbitts), "The Family and Its Functions," in President's Research Committee on Social Trends, *Recent Social Trends in the United States* (New York: McGraw-Hill Book Company, 1933), Vol. I, pp. 661–708.

aids, they have become immensely simplified and less time-consuming.

Protective functions were an important part of the activities of families until recent times, when they have become, in large measure, community responsibilities. Public health, sanitation, and hospitals are among the agencies developed to protect against illness. The state has largely assumed responsibility for the care of the feeble-minded, the insane, the chronically ill, and the indigent. Many homes for the aged have been established, and, in more recent years, other forms of care for the aged are found in old-age and other kinds of insurance. The number of persons engaged in police and fire protection in cities is very large. Further protection of families is provided by mother's aid out of public funds, child-labor legislation, juvenile courts, and the great variety of family services which are available through many social work agencies.

The traditional family religious functions, consisting of ceremonials, family prayers, reading of the Bible, grace at meals, and so forth, seem to have been declining in urban communities. Religious observances are more and more left to the religious institutions of the community. No data are available to determine trends in this area, nor would the interpretation of the facts be easy even if they were available. It is clear, however, that the circumstances of family life in cities, which make it difficult for the members of families to get together and to have common interests, are not conducive to carrying out religious activities.

Commercial recreation has been a growing and profitable business in cities. As working hours have been reduced and leisure time has increased, the places and activities of recreation in the cities have greatly increased. This is true of both commercial and public recreation. The expenditures of city government for recreation have increased at a much greater rate than the increase in families. This would seem to indicate that people look more and more to places outside their home for their recreation. Some recreation, however, continues even in city families. Reading aloud, playing games, singing, playing musical instruments, and family visiting are still found in some families. The family automobile has contributed somewhat to keeping members of the family together by its use for trips and picnics. Radio listening goes on in the home, but there is a tendency for the various members of the families to have their own radios, so that this is more of an individual than a family activity. Television, on the other hand, bids fair to be more of a family affair because it requires coöperative group use.

The educational functions of early American families were very important. In fact, the education of children and young people took place largely within the framework of the family activities. Schools provided the basic communication skills, chiefly reading, writing, and arithmetic. In modern cities there is little education in the home. Institutions of the community have been established for this purpose, from nursery schools for the two-year-olds to schools for adults of all ages. Manual training, the household arts, and vocational training are included in the public schools. Most city children are in school: in 1940, of those from five to nine years old, 80.2 percent; of those from ten to fourteen, 97.1 percent; of those from fifteen to twenty, 52.7 percent. The number of days on which schools are in session has increased, and there has been talk of doing away with the long summer vacation in city schools because it was started to fit agricultural conditions and has no meaning in cities. This removal of the educational functions from the home to the community is one of the most significant changes in families, and the great variety of educational experiences offered by city schools is testimony to the great effect of urbanization on this function of the family.

"Who is your father?" was the question which used to be asked in order to place a person. This question, however, has been replaced in American cities by "what do you do?" This is testimony to the change in the basis of status from the family to the community. Changes in the laws over the years have recognized the individualization of the members of the family by giving married women the right to property and the right to make a will, giving women the vote, and so forth. The family function of determining status is growing less, especially in cities.

So the secondary functions, formerly a vital part of family life, have gradually slipped away until there is little left of them in city families. This change of the focus of people's lives to the community has made fundamental changes in the place and responsibilities of families.

FAMILIES AND THE COMMUNITY

Just as the lives of its members are centered in their communities, so is the life of the family centered in the community. The fact that the responsibilities which were once a great part of family life have been transferred to the community cannot mean that families are no longer concerned with them, but that their involvement must take the form of coöperative interrelationships.

There are, however, inherent difficulties in the development of close relationships between urban families and the institutions of the community which carry on those functions which families formerly had, for these newer institutions have become highly specialized and are operated by professionally trained people. The institutions, consequently, tend to operate and be administered with reference to their technical services, under boards which are self-perpetuating, in fact or in effect, and are made up of that element of the community which is most able to cope with the problems of the maintenance of the institution. Seldom are the families served represented on the boards or given a voice in determining policy. That is to say, there has come to be little if any relationship between families and those community institutions which carry on the functions long a part of family responsibility. Logically, and also to be consistent with the principle of democratic social organization, there should be a close relationship, which would consist in the voice of the families saying "what to do" or determining policy, and the professional being responsible for "how to do it" through the application of technical knowledge and skill.

Actually, many things have happened in recent years to compensate for the isolation of families in their communities which has resulted from the impact of urbanization, though there is still much to be done. Many community social service agencies, such as neighborhood houses, community centers, and "Y's," have added representatives of the families in their communities to their boards of directors or have organized advisory committees made up of community people. Community councils have been organized by the people of the community, composed of their representatives, to consider the problems of their community and work with the agencies serving their community. In some cities, however, councils are composed of representatives of the social agencies themselves, which is a good thing because it works toward the coördination of community services, but it contributes little to the solution of this problem. Community health committees and the like have also been developed in some cities.

In education, where the relationship between families and the schools which their children attend is more direct and obvious, more has been accomplished. Parent-teacher associations are widely organized. At best, they are groups of parents and teachers working together to understand children better and to plan to solve their problems through coöperation between homes and schools. At worst, they are groups of parents which are used by teachers to provide extra equipment, etc., for the classrooms. They are, too often, almost entirely mothers. It has never been possible to get a large proportion of the parents into the activities. There are still too many principals who have discouraged these associations because they have not appreciated their possibilities. Another recent development is very promising for closer relationships between families and schools. It has come from the discovery by school administrators that one of the major factors in making good schools is the understanding on the part of the people of what their schools are like and what good schools can do. The activities which have grown out of this discovery are developing mutual understanding and coöperation (see pp. 458–461).

Labor unions are organizations which operate in the relationship between members of families and the economic institutions. Since the mass-production revolution in industrial production, management has come into control, but its control is inherently geared to the efficiency of the productive sources. It becomes necessary, therefore, as Drucker says, for strong and stable labor organizations to make management legitimate—that is, to make it operate in the interests of its workers while it operates in the interests of society and as an efficient productive unit. The full measure of its responsibility has not yet been attained, though much has been accomplished.[16]

Another type of situation has arisen, in the process of the shift of the secondary functions of the family to institutions of the community, which involves family-community coöperation. This involves the deficiencies which exist in the urban arrangements. Some of these are inadequacies in community services, and others are due to conditions which make certain desirable results very difficult to obtain. With regard to the latter, here is an illustration bearing on the development of children. In the coöperative life of early American families engaged in productive activities, children had important work to do. In doing their jobs, they developed their capacities and

[16] Peter F. Drucker, "The New Society: II, Is Management Legitimate?" *Harper's Magazine*, No. 1193 (Oct., 1949), pp. 74–79.

a sense of responsibility. When production went out of the homes, it was logical that children should go on with their work under the new circumstances. It was soon found, however, that children in factories could be badly exploited; so, in time, child-labor laws were passed. Social changes have left no important place of responsibility for children in their homes, society prevents them from being employed outside the home, and communities have assumed no responsibility for the integration of children in the responsibilities of community life.

Other problems of this type are found in the lack of adjustment, retraining, and placement services in helping people at work where vocational patterns are constantly changing; making available to families the health services which have been developed; the proper and adequate use of the specialized social services; and many others.

FUNCTIONS OF PRESENT-DAY URBAN FAMILIES

With all the shifts in function of urban families, the primary functions remain untouched, although they have been disturbed in the changing patterns. On the assumption that families are no longer needed in a highly urbanized industrial society, serious proposals have been made to do away with the family. While the proposals have met with limited intellectual assent, they have been completely discarded by behavioral patterns. "People do not marry because it is their social duty to perpetuate the institution of the family, or because the preacher and Mrs. Grundy both recommend matrimony, or even because they fall in love with each other, they marry because they lived in a family as children and still cannot get over the feeling that being in a family is the only proper, indeed the only possible, way to live."[17] This is not tradition, but experience. The conditions of urban life have greatly increased the need for and the importance of the affectional functions, as the primary functions of the family have been called. These have two concomitants, a quite different type of economic functions and a complex of socio-psychological functions.

The Affectional Functions. The establishment and maintenance of a home are of paramount importance under the circumstances of urban life. This is testified to by the increasing proportion of the

[17] John Levy and Ruth Monroe, *The Happy Family* (New York: Alfred A. Knopf, 1938), p. 3.

population which is married, by the independent individuals who marry and continue in their business or professional lives, and by the great attention which is given to more and better housing for all families as places where effective homes can be established. Homes provide the chief compensation for the confusing complexity of urban life, in which many human relationships and dependencies exist, and where people are regarded in terms of their capacity to function and produce rather than as individuals. In homes, people can be individuals who are regarded as individuals and are surrounded with affection for what they are. Without this center of life, human personality can scarcely withstand the disintegrating forces of the urban environment.

Amid the circumstances of home, stable sexual relationships are possible. Medical scientists, psychologists, and pychiatrists, through their more recently acquired knowledge and understanding, recognize this as basically important to stable and growing human personality.

These are the circumstances under which procreation and the rearing of children are most promising. There is growing evidence that the potentiality of a child's physical, social, mental, and emotional development can be attained only in the environment of the intimate affectionate relationships of home and family life. An institutional environment at best is limiting and at worst is crippling in all of these areas of maturation.

The Economic Functions.   Maintaining a home was not difficult under the old economy, where production was for use and so closely related to consumption. Now, however, there is no relationship whatever. Money intervenes, so that the problems are much more complicated and difficult. There is the problem of family income. Many times more than one member of the family group, by his or her earnings, contributes. Often incomes are sporadic, or at least interrupted from time to time by instability of employment, by sickness, or for other reasons. In spite of uncertainties of income, however, family budgets must be made, for the costs of food, shelter, clothing, recreation, and the like go on even though income may stop. Some of these, like medical expenses, are unpredictable. This family budgeting is an operation which requires great knowledge and skill.

Beyond this, the family faces all of the consumer problems, for the money budgeted must be used to purchase goods which will meet the needs of the members of the family, collectively and individually. Getting the best and the most for the money that is spent is no easy task. It involves a knowledge of the basis of value, both qualitative and quantitative, and how to apply this knowledge to the goods which are available. There are the standards of producers and of merchants and also the standards of use, and they seldom agree. The basis of value is different in every kind of goods purchased. In food, there are staples, fresh fruit and vegetables, meats, canned goods, frozen foods, processed foods, etc. Then comes the problem of nutrition and peculiar dietary needs. In clothing, there are kind of materials, quality of materials, durability, style, etc. Then there is the problem of use with reference to the social circumstances in which each member of the family will use the clothing. There are also implements, household appliances, and equipment, from furniture to towels. Each has its own problem of the most for the money to meet the particular needs and use of each family and its members. This is a stupendous job if it is to be done conscientiously and well.

Because of the close relationship of families to their communities, growing out of the shifts in function, there comes the whole range of how to use community institutions. This involves not only retail establishments, financial institutions, and services, from repair shops to beauty parlors, but also governmental agencies, private social service agencies, and health services. There are also matters of transportation, communication, recreation, and others.

Taking it all in all, the range and complexity of the economic functions involved in maintaining a home have come to be vastly more difficult and demanding, and they require highly specialized knowledge and skills.

The Socio-Psychological Functions. Research in the fields of psychology, sociology, child development, and cultural anthropology have provided a substantial body of facts concerning maturation, the conditions of physical, intellectual and social growth, and personality development. It has been discovered that the bases of child development are laid in the first weeks of life, when the feeling of security is experienced, and continues through the early years as the sense of belonging continues. Here are indicated some of the other important factors which designate family responsibilities in the socio-psychological functions.

Infants are essentially individuals, but they are destined to live in a world of many human relationships. This is particularly true in cities. Their capacity to adjust to other individuals and to be effective social beings depends upon their experience of relationships in their first little worlds, which are their families.

Health habits and patterns of behavior are formed at a very early age, and they tenaciously persist throughout life. In the atmosphere of security, with sympathetic guidance, habits and patterns can be formed which will be of lifelong helpfulness.

Reactions to early learning experiences build the attitude that a child will have toward learning. If there are satisfying experiences, those attitudes will be developed which will make the child teachable and make him interested in learning. The reverse, however, may be true, as many teachers will testify.

The capacity for happiness in the individual is closely related to the early experiences of happiness. In fact, Terman found that the best single item for predicting marital happiness or unhappiness was the marital happiness of the parents; that, where both the bride and the groom had had a happy childhood, happiness in marriage was very likely to ensue.[18]

These responsibilities of families require a high order of adjustment, stability, understanding, and wisdom on the part of parents. The development of these qualities is no small task, but it is rewarding, for the qualitative aspects of life (both good and bad) are self-perpetuating. Children learn their values, their attitudes, their ideals, and their objectives from those with whom they are surrounded in their homes, and in turn they create experiences for their children through which they are carried on.

FAMILIES IN TROUBLE

It is in the failures of families in these functions for which they are responsible that the roots of family troubles are to be found. Koos, in his study of sixty-two low-income families on the East Side of New York City over a period of two years, found that forty-six families had a total of 109 troubles during this period.[19] One-third of these problems were financial, resulting from death,

---

[18] Lewis M. Terman, *Psychological Factors in Marital Happiness* (New York: McGraw-Hill Book Company, 1938), p. 372.

[19] Reprinted from Earl Lomon Koos, *Families in Trouble.* Copyright 1946 by Earl Lomon Koos. ("Trouble" here means the real disruption of family life, not the ordinary troubles which all families have.)

illness, poor management, and unemployment. While these troubles which arose from causes external to the family life brought great difficulties, they did not disturb family relationships. The other two-thirds of the troubles, however, were interpersonal. Though they arose out of a variety of situations, it was the inability of the family to adjust to the situation within itself which made the trouble. It was apparent that "the less adequate the organization of the family the more frequent and important are the interpersonal problems as causes of trouble."[20] In these cases, moreover, troubles resulted in changes in the roles of family members; "one-fourth of the troubles occasioned no lasting change in interaction, only one was beneficial to the family, and three-fourths occasioned lasting damage to the inter-action of the family. The high-frequency of the latter condition among the below-average (in adequacy of organization) families indicates the importance of adequate family organization if the family is to survive in the low income environment."[21]

At the root of the inadequacies of family organization was some form of internal conflict: conflicts due to cultural disparity between parents and children, conflicts due to religious differences, conflicts arising from adolescent sex behavior, conflicts due to uneven assimilation of husband and wife, parents' conflicts over children, conflicts resulting from sexual maladjustment, conflicts over attachment to an earlier generation, conflicts over the economic status of the family, conflicts over the social life of the family, and conflicts over the handling of money.[22]

The families which had no troubles had four characteristics of strong family organization: (1) Every member of the family had a recognized role, and each one accepted his own role and the complementary roles of the others. Unity served as a buffer against events. (2) This unity enabled each member of the family to accept the common good of the family as a whole over his own individual good, not by compulsion, but by the desire to pull together. (3) There was a continued effort by the family to provide for its members' interests and satisfactions within the home; where there was participation in activities outside the home for special interests, they were looked upon and treated as extensons of the home

[20] *Ibid.*, p. 63.
[21] *Ibid.*, p. 111.
[22] *Ibid.*, pp. 33–55.

and not as substitutes for the home. (4) There were family goals toward which they moved by planning for the future. Even though the objectives were small, they were recognized by all the members, and each shared in the efforts to attain them.[23]

Where these factors operated in an atmosphere of mutual respect and interchange of ideas and opinions in a genuine democratic coöperative life, the families were strongest.

Koos further observed that, since families had troubles and needed help, assistance should be available in the community, but that, in spite of many services which the agencies of the community provided, they were not actually available to the families. This was partly because of the almost complete ignorance on the part of the families of the agencies which existed, the kind of help which they could give, and how to go about obtaining help. It was also due, however, to the kind of institutions, their methods, and the attitudes of their professional personnel, who were, by and large, not in close enough contact with families to discover when and how they could be helpful. The people, on the other hand, had developed the attitude that obtaining help was charity, which their pride made them refuse except as a very last resort.

The first need is the reconstitution of the family on the basis of an understanding of what the functions of urban families are, and the organization of communities so that these functions can be carried out. This will have to start with a realistic education of young people in such things as the family and its functions, the psychology of family relationships, the organization of the community and the work of its institutions, and family-community relationships.[24]

FUTURE OF AMERICAN URBAN FAMILIES

Families in cities are increasing at a more rapid rate than population. There can be no doubt that they will continue as the fundamental social unit. Many difficulties, however, assail them under the conditions of urban life, as seen in the increase in separations, in divorce, and in troubles.

In cities, families take many different forms to meet the different patterns of need which people have, although a basic pattern of functions for all families in cities is becoming more and more clear. The shifts in function which have taken place, however, bring fam-

[23] *Ibid.*, pp. 58–60.
[24] *Ibid.*, pp. 122–128.

ilies into closer relationship and interdependence with their communities. There is, consequently, greater responsibility on the communty and its institutions to operate so that these interrelationships can go on with greater facility and that mutual understanding of the relationships can develop.

The complexity of family functions and the intricacies of family-community relationships cannot be taken lightly, nor can people who marry be expected to understand them by some mysterious revelation at their marriage. This means that preparation for the responsibilities of home and family life are more necessary in cities than ever before. Young women and young men, as a part of their education, should be given adequate preparation for this important part of their lives. Until public education recognizes this responsibility and finds out how to meet it adequately, it will be necessary for community institutions, both public and private, to expend much of their efforts, which should be given to constructive activities, in devising remedies for the failure of their families.

Supplementary Reading

Elliott, Grace Loukes. "The Home in Transition." *Social Action*, Oct. 15, 1937.
> A brief statement of the major changes in the American home.

Hill, Reuben. *Families Under Stress*. New York: Harper & Brothers, 1949.
> A study of the adjustment of families to the crises of war separation and reunion, showing practical principles for families to rely upon in meeting crises, and highlighting the importance of the sense of interdependence, of family integration, and of adaptability.

Koos, Earl Lomon. *Families in Trouble*. New York: King's Crown Press, 1946.
> A study of the impact of crises on families in cities, showing the significance of family organization.

Levy, John, and Munroe, Ruth. *The Happy Family*. New York: Alfred A. Knopf, 1938.
> A psychiatrist looks at the basis of successful family life.

Nimkoff, M. F. *The Family*. Boston: Houghton Mifflin Company, 1934.
> A good basic text on the family.

President's Research Committee on Social Trends. *Recent Social Trends*. New York: McGraw-Hill Book Company, 1933. Chap. XIII, "The Family and Its Functions," by William F. Ogburn.
> Presents basic data on the changing functions of American families.

CHAPTER 27

CITY PEOPLE

THE hobos and the playboys, the slum-dwellers and those in the social register, the bohemians and the "do-gooders," the politicians and the panhandlers, the reformers and the criminals, and many, many other types are to be found in the cities. Most of them have been studied and written about as such. They represent an unlikely conglomerate of disparity in which to find any common denominator. Could there be anything common to them except that they are pieces in the mosaic of city life? Perhaps they may be different results of the impact of the forces and circumstances of urban life on people with different backgrounds, different opportunities, and different personalities. With all the differences, however, the city environment imposes certain conditions upon its people, within which they must live. It is in the light of these conditions that the characteristics, relationships, adjustments, and stratification of city people should be viewed.

CHARACTERISTICS OF CITY PEOPLE

Already certain observable human characteristics of cities have been noted (p. 41 f.): heterogeneity in the marks of many social and national backgrounds on the faces and in the names of people; anonymity in the extreme dilution of personal contacts in the city's hordes and in the extreme of impersonal contacts; and similarity in the clothes and styles and make-up of people. Beyond this, the adjustment to the conditions of urban life gives city people certain characteristics in common. Four of these conditions seem to leave their special marks: controls, the immediacy of living, being shut in, and the necessity for immunities.

To get along in the city, man must accommodate himself to living under many different kinds of controls. Because there are so many people, in so many relationships, and so many activities, necessity has developed a complex of legal codes by means of which orderly procedures can be maintained. Laws control traffic, crowds, peddlers, dogs, marriages, business, building, use of sidewalks, placing of advertising signs, killing of animals, leases and contracts, liabilities, responsibilities of parents to children, of landlords to tenants, requirements for obtaining public services, taxes, and a host of other things, including details of behavior considered criminal. Since ignorance of the law is no excuse, city people have to know what they are doing, and there are police all around to remind them. Besides legal control, there are conventions and folkways that set limitations on what the individual does and the kind of clothes he wears on the streets, in theaters and movies, on crowded public conveyances, in stores; on whom he can speak to and under what conditions; on cashing checks, opening a bank account, or obtaining credit without being vouched for; and many other things.

City people are slaves to clocks and calendars. Almost everything operates on a time schedule. One must be at work at an exact time, have a designated period for lunch, and quit at a prescribed hour. Transportation operates on a schedule; deliveries of milk, newspapers, mail, are at certain times. Entertainment, games, and celebrations take place according to a specified schedule. Meetings, luncheon dates, parties, all run by the clock. Telephone conversations are paid for by the minute, comings and goings are calculated to meet appointments precisely, a day may be badly upset by an unusually long line at the grocery store or the bank. Calendars are essential, for days must be planned and appointments kept clear. While sunrise and sunset may be real to farmers, they are but poetic terms for the city-dwellers.

Clocks and calendars do not account for all of the pressures under which city people live. There is an immediacy to life peculiar to the city. None, except perhaps the wealthy, can escape the intense pressures of day-to-day existence. The immediate necessity of making ends meet is unrelenting to low-income people, but only a little less stringent for the middle-income group. Then there is the constant fear of emergencies—death, sickness, accidents, unemployment—which create immediate situations so serious and costly that the very existence of people is threatened. When income ceases, a person's family cannot eat, or cannot obtain clothing, or will be evicted from their dwelling. If death removes the bread-winner, families are often in desperate straits. Sickness or accident may involve costs which cannot be borne. There are also particular pressures which affect everyone. Workers operate under the constant pressure of mass-production methods. Employees forever fear the loss of jobs. Businessmen are under the stress of terrific competition. Social workers and health workers must carry impossible case loads. Housewives can never escape from the care of little children, from getting meals, from combating dirt. All people must struggle with immediate things from which there is no escape.

City people must become accustomed to being closed in. Besides the psychological reactions to the impact of the controls under which they must live and the pressures of the immediacy of living, there are material things and social experiences which close in upon them. Most city-dwellers live in small quarters, some so small that privacy is impossible. If there are any yards around their dwellings, they are very limited. The majority do their work inside of buildings; they come and go through canyons of brick walls over pavements of asphalt. Open spaces and the green of trees and grass must be sought out, and when found they are filled with signs: "keep out" and "keep off the grass." In buildings places marked "no admittance" or "restricted area" are frequently encountered. Although people often find themselves in crowds, their social contacts are very limited. Those who live near by are almost never seen; casual acquaintances seldom happen. One meets people, becomes acquainted, finds associations, only when one makes special efforts to join groups in work, in churches, in lodges, in clubs, in community organizations, in educational or social groups. This usually involves membership in organizations, but the proportion of city people who have such memberships is exceedingly small. In a few cities, services have been organized to facilitate acquaintances and friendships between people. So the city closes in upon its people and confines them to little worlds, psychologically, socially, and physically. An incipient claustrophobia becomes a characteristic of urban-dwellers, and some break under the strain.[1]

Another condition of city life is the necessity for developing im-

[1] James S. Plant, M.D., *Personality and the Cultural Pattern* (New York: Commonwealth Fund, 1937), states, in the section entitled "Crowding and the Individual," that crowding results in lack of self-sufficiency, the destruction of illusions, sexual maladjustment, mental strain, negativism, instability, and lack of objectivity.

munities. Disease germs are thick in the crowded cities, and woe to him who is not fortified against them. Suburban children who come to the city on Saturdays to attend the movies or the theaters, or to shop, usually return home with colds. Other kinds of immunities, however, are also necessary: to the close contact with other human bodies in crowded conveyances and gathering places; to the unusual and exciting happenings and events; to the sensationalism of newspapers and the flamboyance of advertising. The immunity to temptation is perhaps the most difficult to attain, for one can live anonymously in a city, and no one else need know what one does. One is far removed from the influence of the conventional pattern of ethics which influences people's behavior greatly in small communities.

Prejudice is by no means absent from city life; in fact, it occasionally flares into conflict between various groups; but, on the whole, city people tend to become tolerant because they are accustomed to many kinds of people with their varying habits and opinions. One of the assets of city life is that it exposes its people to much information, many ideas, and a variety of experiences. Metropolitan daily newspapers carry a great variety of news and many features, though some are very one-sided in their reporting and editorial policy; a majority of the people read at least one newspaper a day. City radio stations carry much news and many informational programs. There is a wide variety of opportunities in cities for all sorts of experiences for those who will take advantage of them. And the city is a stimulating place, with many things to challenge attention, many places to go, much activity all about. It is no accident that, since the days of ancient Greece and Rome, there has been attributed to city people a characteristic—in this day called urbanity, which is a synonym of sophistication, worldly wisdom, knowing one's way about—that carries with it a certain tolerance of alien modes and customs and the ability to get along with a minimum of conflict and discomfort.

CRISES AND MALADJUSTMENTS

How do city people stand up under the strains and stresses of city life? In all fairness the answer must be: far better than might be expected. The resiliency of the human organism is more amazing than its vulnerability, as witnessed by the adjustments which

people can make to crises like depression and war, without notice-
able increase in mental illness. The people of the English cities
were able to adapt to the effects of the continuous air raids without neurotic disturbance. So also do individuals and families stand
up under the grievous blow of bereavement, are able to adjust to
crippling and the loss of sensory functions, without mental breakdown.[2]

It has been generally accepted as a hypothesis that the incidence
of mental disease is greater in cities, although this has not yet been
proved. Statistics on mental disorders usually indicate higher rates
in cities, but these statistics account for the cases which can be
identified by virtue of being under treatment. It is known that the
facilities for diagnosis and treatment of the mentally ill are far
greater in cities, and it is generally not possible to care for those
suffering from mental illness in city homes; consequently, a large
proportion come to light. In rural areas, on the other hand, there
are many people living at home who are merely considered "queer"
but who would be recognized as mentally ill in cities. Moreover,
rural people are, for the most part, less hospital-conscious than city
people, and also the rural community, where ties are much stronger
than in cities, tends to look with disfavor upon families which do
not take care of their unfortunate and aged relatives within the
home.

This is borne out by investigations of patients admitted to mental hospitals. Landis and Page,[3] analyzing the first admissions to
the state mental hospitals in 1933, found that the average rural
rates per 100,000 of general population were: women 44.6, men
69.5, combined 58.0. The corresponding urban rates were: women
94.1, men 134.8, combined 113.5. The differences held for the various psychoses except for an exaggeration of alcoholic psychoses
among urban women. There was also a corresponding age pattern.
Sex appeared to determine age distribution, and the factor of environment determined incidence. When incidence was analyzed with
reference to size of city, it showed a tendency for first admissions
to increase as the size of cities increased; but, more importantly,
the critical increase of incidence came at the 2500 population

[2] D. B. Klein, *Mental Hygiene* (New York: Henry Holt and Company,
1944), pp. 433–435.

[3] Carney Landis and James D. Page, *Modern Society and Mental Disease*
(New York: Farrar and Rinehart, 1938), pp. 44–55.

point, which is used to differentiate rural and village communities from cities. The authors warn their readers, however, that in the few instances where limited data are available for total cases of mental disease, including those cared for at home as well as in institutions, no differences can be found between rural and urban rates. They conclude that their analysis shows only differences in hospitalization.

It has long been acknowledged, however, that the social environment of the individual is an important factor in the etiology of mental illness. Such conditions as those which have been outlined as characteristic of city life are among those which have been found conducive to mental breakdown. The isolation of the city person, which lessens his contacts with other people and decreases his capacity to communicate with his fellows because of his highly specialized experiences; the many impersonal relationships with people who are different in background, education, and even language; the hostility of the city, its controls and its restrictions; the problems which one must face without the capacity to solve them; the strain of noise, hurry, and insecurity; the inability to deal with the forces which exert determining influences on life; and many other aspects of city life are sufficient to cause the breakdown of the individual, especially when there are no compensations. In the light of the available facts, there are two tenable hypotheses: first, that, as cities produce the conditions which produce mental disease, so do they force the development of immunity; second, that, if a lower threshold for designating mental disease could be determined, cities would show a definitely higher rate of personality disintegration. Perhaps both may be true. Further understanding can be obtained, however, by looking within a particular city.

In their study of the social geography of mental disorders in Chicago, Faris and Dunham shed considerable light on the relationship between the city and the breakdown of its people. They found that the geographical distribution of total insanity rates followed the pattern of the social sturcture of the city (see p. 174 f.), that the highest rate occurred in the central business district, and that there was a steady decline in rates from the center to the periphery of the city,[4] as shown in Figure 42. This is essentially the same as the radial pattern of juvenile delinquency shown in Figure

[4] Robert E. L. Faris and H. Warren Dunham, *Mental Disorders in Urban Areas* (Chicago: The University of Chicago Press, 1939), pp. 23–37.

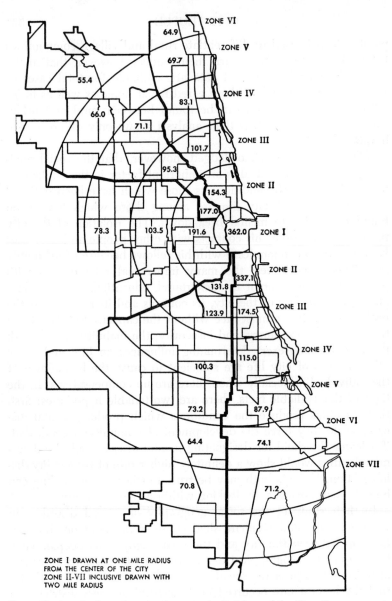

ZONE VI
64.9
ZONE V
69.7
55.4
ZONE IV
83.1
66.0
71.1
ZONE III
101.7
95.3
ZONE II
154.3
177.0
78.3 103.5 191.6 362.0 ZONE I
ZONE II
337.1
131.8
123.9 174.5 ZONE III
ZONE IV
115.0
100.3
ZONE V
73.2 87.9
ZONE VI
64.4 74.1
ZONE VII
70.8 71.2

ZONE I DRAWN AT ONE MILE RADIUS
FROM THE CENTER OF THE CITY
ZONE II-VII INCLUSIVE DRAWN WITH
TWO MILE RADIUS

Figure 42. Insanity Rates from the Center to the Periphery of the City. Here are represented the insanity average rates, for 1922–1934, by zones and divisions of the city. The
rates are based on 100,000, 1930 population, age 15 and over. The subcommunities are
based on census tracts of Chicago. (Robert E. L. Faris and H. Warren Dunham, *Mental
Disorders in Urban Areas* [Chicago: The University of Chicago Press, 1939], Map VI,
p. 36.)

21 (p. 176). So again it can be seen that social ills tend to go to-gether.

When they came to break down insanity into the various types of mental illness, much more was revealed. Schizophrenia followed the pattern of total insanity and showed the same general relation-ships,[5] but when the manic-depressive psychoses were distributed geographically, the pattern was distinctly different. In the radial distribution of rates, the center of the city was still the highest, but the outer zones had higher rates than the inner zones. When manic-depressive rates were compared by neighborhood areas, however, a relationship was found to the higher cultural and economic lev-els.[6] So also did other types of mental disorders show particular relationships. The paranoid type of schizophrenia had its highest rates in the rooming-house areas of the city, while the catatonic type was predominantly found in the neighborhoods of first immi-grant settlement in the city, where a high proportion of foreign-born and Negroes, the latest newcomers, was located[7] Alcoholic psychoses were found to be concentrated in the apartment-hotel and hotel area.[8] The geography of general paralysis, the result of syphilitic infection of the brain, shows it to be related to rooming-house and hotel areas where there are Negroes, which are the vice areas of the city.[9] The senile psychoses are related to the areas of lowest percentages of home-owners.[10]

At the close of their study Faris and Dunham propose the hy-pothesis that communication is essential for normal mental devel-opment and that social isolation makes for mental breakdown.[11] This tends to indicate an important additional significance of those conditions of urban living which make human relationships and understanding difficult, and circumscribe people in their little worlds of specialized activity and immediate problems.

PERSONALITY DISINTEGRATION AND COMMUNITY DISORGANIZATION

The social integration of cities becomes an important considera-tion if there is a relationship between the well-being of a human

[5] *Ibid.*, pp. 38–62.
[6] *Ibid.*, pp. 63–81.
[7] *Ibid.*, pp. 82–109.
[8] *Ibid.*, pp. 110–123.
[9] *Ibid.*, pp. 124–133.
[10] *Ibid.*, pp. 134–142.
[11] *Ibid.*, pp. 154–159, 177.

personality and the character of the communities in which it develops. This relationship is difficult to study. Angel, however, has
broken the ground.[12] He found twenty-eight of the larger cities in
the United States for which he could get comparable health and
welfare statistics. Proceeding on the hypothesis that the cities
which shoulder a large proportion of their welfare responsibilities
are better integrated, he derived from these statistics a composite
number made up of the per capita amounts obtained from local
sources for welfare purposes, the local level of living, and the percentage of the total funds provided locally, which he used as a welfare effort index for each city. These were negatively checked by
an index of crime, which is generally considered one of the best indications of social disorganization, obtained by combining data
from the Uniform Crime Reports on murder, robbery, and bur-
glary, properly weighted. The hypothesis was that a community
which is sufficiently well integrated to accept responsibility for the
health and welfare of its citizens would also have mores strong
enough to keep the citizens from committing crime. The correlation of the two indices for the twenty-eight cities was −.393, too
low to validate the relationship of the factors but high enough to
justify further analysis. When the cities were looked at individually,
however, they were seen to fall into four groups: well integrated,
moderately integrated, poorly integrated, and inconsistent.

This exploration was continued by Angel in a study of the social
integration of forty-three independent cities over 100,000 in population for which comparable data were available.[13] A welfare index, essentially the same though differently devised because of differences in the data which could be obtained, and the same crime
index were supplemented by a mobility index combining in- and
out-migrants for each city and a population composition index
made up of the proportion of foreign-born and other races in the
population. The results of the correlation were as follows: welfare
index and crime −.43; crime and mobility +.45; crime and population composition +.58; welfare index and mobility −.57; welfare
index and population composition −.20. When the welfare index
and crime index were combined in an index of integration, the cor-

[12] Robert C. Angel, "Social Integration of American Cities," *American
Journal of Sociology*, Vol. XLVII, No. 4 (Jan., 1942), pp. 575–592.
[13] Robert C. Angel, "Social Integration of American Cities," *American
Sociological Review*, Vol. 12, No. 3 (June, 1947), pp. 335–342.

relations were: integration and mobility −.49; integration and population composition −.59. It was determined that mobility and composition of population were independent factors by a correlation of −.06. The multiple correlation of integration with mobility and population composition was −.79, with a coefficient of determination of +.63, showing that the factors of mobility and population composition account for about two-thirds of the variation of integration in these cities of over 100,000 population. No factors were found to account for the other one-third of the variation.

This exploration seeking the indices of social integration in American cities has turned up the principal negative factors which work against integration. It opens the way for a more positive approach, which will doubtless have to be carried on by case studies, as Angel suggests. There are still many things to be learned before we shall know what can be done to effect the better integration of communities that will provide the environment for wholesome development of human personality. The studies of Shaw, Faris and Dunham, and others would seem to indicate that units of urban environment smaller than whole cities provide the most powerful influences on human life. It seems likely, therefore, that more positive results can be obtained when it becomes possible to apply these methods of analysis to neighborhoods within cities because variations within cities are greater than variations between cities, and that measures to develop better community integration will need to be applied to neighborhoods.

HUMAN RELATIONSHIPS

The paradox of human relationships in cities rests upon the high degree of interdependence which people with specialized functions necessarily have and the great impersonality of city life. Many of those on whom city people must depend are remote, seldom if ever seen—the workers in the wholesale produce markets, the telephone cable splicers, the transportation workers, and many others—and yet they are all important to daily life. There are others who are seen about their important tasks, but with whom relationships are still entirely indirect—garbage-collectors, street-cleaners, policemen, firemen, and other kinds of service workers.

Direct relationships are both personal and impersonal. Many people serve others through direct contacts—bus-drivers, waiters,

cashiers, telephone-operators, clerks in stores, barbers, beauty op-
erators, and the like. These contacts are for the most part impersonal, although occasionally they are highly personalized, as the
barber or grocery-store clerk or apartment-house elevator man who
serves a person for years becomes interested in his work, his family, his vacations, and even his personal problems. These contacts
quantitatively represent the bulk of the relationships of city people. They are, for the most part, superficial and make little, if any,
impression on people, but potentially any one of them may become
very disturbing or very helpful. A cheery elevator-operator with a
bright "Good morning" may give one a lift to meet the problems of
the day; an indifferent clerk may arouse anger which persists for
hours; a gruff and inconsiderate bus-driver may create a situation
whose frustrating effects may wreck one's poise for the balance of
the day. A city-dweller must be able to cope with whatever comes
through the welter of a continuous stream of direct, but impersonal, relationships.

The direct personal relationships are by far the most important,
but they are relatively limited in number, partly because any individual has a limit to his capacity to maintain direct personal relationships (though the capacity differs with the individuals), partly
because city life tends to make personal contacts difficult, and
partly because living and the kinds of work people do in cities are
so time-consuming that the small margins of time which are left
make many intimate personal relationships impossible. These relationships are found in four areas: families (and many city people
live alone, outside of family groups); work associates, who vary
greatly in the degree of their intimacy; small informal friendship
groups, which are largely simple social relationships; and associations or groups with special purposes. These last, in their great
numbers and variety, are particularly characteristic of cities and
are most significant, although it is probably true that considerably
less than half the people in cities are involved in such associations.

City people tend to form their personal groups on the basis of
interest rather than proximity. As a result, each group membership
may involve an individual with entirely different people; participation is costly in time (for often transportation is involved) and
money (for, besides the cost of transportation, usually dues or fees
of some sort are required). Associations outside the home, in addition to work away from home for all but the home-makers, leave

little time for family life but intensify the importance of family relationships in the basic family functions.

The associations of city people, however, are not entirely free. There are lines of social cleavage which surround them with certain limitations.

SOCIAL STRATIFICATION IN CITIES

Those who belong to racial groups and those whose backgrounds are in other nations tend to have their personal relationships largely within their own group, partly because they find a more substantial basis of congeniality and understanding among their own people, but also because prejudices among other groups make association across these lines almost impossible. Such prejudices are blind, unjustified, and artificial; nevertheless, they make very real limitations on the free associations of people. In his study of a southern town, Dollard found the position of Negroes tantamount to caste.[14] In the cities of other sections of the country prejudices and discrimination continue to impose rigid limitations upon the relationships of Negroes in general, although among intellectuals and professionals prejudices are breaking down. This situation, however, is pointed out by Myrdal as one of the most vulnerable points in American democracy.[15]

Several recent researches[16] have studied the social stratification in the life of small, relatively static cities. The evidence shows a series of social levels in which people could be located. Where people belonged was a matter of family, money (especially inherited wealth), and the vocations of the men. Five (Elmtown) or six (Yankee City) distinct strata were defined. By and large, the social relationships of people were confined to the stratum to which they belonged and to the strata immediately adjacent. That is to say, associations were with people of like kind, the phenomenon which Giddings pointed out long ago. As a result, the social stratification

[14] John Dollard, *Caste and Class in a Southern Town* (New Haven: Yale University Press, 1937), Chap. V.

[15] Gunnar Myrdal, *An American Dilemma* (New York: Harper & Brothers, 1944).

[16] Especially the Yankee City Series: W. Lloyd Warner and Paul S. Lunt, *The Social Life of a Modern Community* (New Haven: Yale University Press, 1941); August B. Hollingshead, *Elmtown's Youth* (New York: John Wiley and Sons, 1949); W. Lloyd Warner and Associates, *Democracy in Jonesville* (New York: Harper & Brothers, 1949).

tended to perpetuate itself because the ideas, conventions, standards, values, types of work, patterns of recreation, and extent of
education of each social stratum were passed on from generation
to generation through the discipline of the limited social environment in which each rising generation found itself. This process was
accentuated because it resulted in marriages taking place within
the social group, not only because it naturally happened that way,
but also because the mores frowned upon marriages outside the
social group.[17] A further result was the concentration of wealth
and property ownership in the upper strata through inheritance.
This, together with the positions of financial and political importance, kept within these upper groups, resulted in a very substantial control over the life of the whole community.

This power was used to protect the ideas, the values, the conventions, the positions, and the property of the power group. Such
conservatism, moreover, became oblivious of social problems and
social needs in the community. The difficulties in which those in
the lower strata found themselves were considered to be due to
their own indifference and lack of ambition. What was really happening, however, was that the perpetuation of an old, academic
secondary-school education was meeting the interest and needs of
only the young people who were headed for college, and that the
others, who were made to feel out of place, dropped out of school
at the earliest possibility. The jobs to which they went, moreover,
were the inferior and menial jobs, partly because they did not have
enough educational background, partly because the good jobs were
kept for the young people of the upper strata, and partly because
of the stereotypes fastened on the families from which these young
people came.

This restricting situation probably exists in hundreds of the
small-to-medium-sized cities which are growing only slowly if at
all. The only saving factor is that the capable and ambitious young
people get themselves out of such social strait jackets by migrating
to the larger cities. The students of this social stratification and
many others have called it class structure. The use of the term
"class," however, has been subjected to much criticism because of
the lack of precision in its definition[18] and the problem of applying

[17] August B. Hollingshead, "Class and Kinship in a Middle Western Community," *American Sociological Review,* Vol. 14, No. 4 (Aug., 1949), p. 475.
[18] Llewellyn Gross, "The Use of Class Concepts in Sociological Research,"
American Journal of Sociology, Vol. LIV, No. 5 (March, 1949), pp. 409–421.

any definitions operationally to separate the people of a community into their respective classes,[19] but a further reason for avoiding the use of the term "class" in American society is that it tells just part of the story—too large a part, perhaps, but how large is not known because no comparable studies of social mobility have yet been made. While there can be no doubt that social stratification does exist in the larger cities, it has far less significance than in smaller cities, for it is lost in the bigness. Most cities have their "Four Hundreds" and their social registers, but apart from those who belong it makes little difference, and their power and control are highly diluted by political organization. At any rate, opportunity is sought and found by young people of all backgrounds in education and in work in the larger cities.

So city people live in the midst of problems and difficulties imposed by the city itself. They are subjected to conditions of strain and stress conducive to mental breakdown, but show amazing resiliency. The foci of community disintegration in cities, however, provide the circumstances in which personal disintegration of all sorts develops and grows. The human relationships of city people have severe limitations. They are bounded by space far more than would be expected. The lives of individuals tend to be confined to the neighborhood in which they live; when this is a "bad" neighborhood, the restrictions are often determinative in the development of the individual's personality and his opportunities. Relationships are also bounded by social stratification in many ways, so that social mobility can come only to those who through their own efforts and capacities can take advantage of the city's opportunities and make a place for themselves outside of the environment in which they have been born and raised.

Supplementary Reading

Faris, Robert E. L., and Dunham, H. Warren. *Mental Disorders in Urban Areas*. Chicago: The University of Chicago Press, 1939.
    A comprehensive analysis of the socio-geographic distribution of mental disorders in a large urban community.
Hollingshead, August B. *Elmtown's Youth*. New York: John Wiley and Sons, 1949.

[19] Milton M. Gordon, "Social Class in American Sociology," *American Journal of Sociology*, Vol. LV, No. 3 (Nov., 1949), pp. 267–268.

A study of the social stratifications in a small, static city.

Warner, W. Lloyd. *Democracy in Jonesville.* New York: Harper & Brothers, 1949.

An analysis of what democracy is like in an average small city in terms of human relationships and social organizations.

PART VII

CITIES AND THE FUTURE

A SUMMARY with a look toward the future begins with a consideration of the contribution of foresight through planning as it has developed over the years, as it operates in the present, and as it might work in the future with greater commitment and coöperation (Chap. 28); then inventories the assets and liabilities of cities as the setting for democratic life (Chap. 29); and finally seeks to foresee the future form of cities and briefly reviews the part cities play in the American scene (Chap. 30).

CHAPTER 28

CITY-PLANNING

MOST cities have just grown up by the accidents of circumstances, the pulling power of their opportunities, and the enterprise of their real-estate promoters. The physical expansion of cities has already been discussed (pp. 149–154). Harris and Ullman call attention to three general forms which cities have taken: first, the concentric zone type, with its five zones: (1) central business, (2) transition, (3) workingmen's homes, (4) better residence, and (5) commuters (cf. Fig. 14, p. 153); second, the sector-arranged type, with the same divisions in the form of sectors rather than concentric circles (the generalized pattern is shown in Fig. 43); third, the multiple-nuclei type, with ten identifiable types of areas: (1) central business, (2) wholesale or light manufacturing, (3) low-income residential, (4) medium-income residential, (5) high-income residential, (6) heavy industry, (7) outlying business, (8) residential suburb, (9) industrial suburb, (10) commuters' area (a conventionalized diagram of this type is shown in Fig. 44).[1] Most cities of any size, however, are a combination of these types and have features of each in their layout.

While these various parts of American cities are fairly clear when analyses of the social geography are made, they have developed through a natural process rather than by intention. For the most part, the geography of American cities is amorphous and unintegrated.

If the observer views it from an airplane, the typical American city will appear as a sprawling mass of structures of varying size, shape and construction, criss-crossed by a checkerboard street pattern which here and there assumes irregularities. The cells or blocks into which the city is di-

---

[1] Chauncy D. Harris and Edward L. Ullman, "The Nature of Cities," *Annals of the American Academy of Political and Social Science,* Vol. 242 (Nov., 1945), pp. 7–17.

vided seem to lack any organic grouping into units, even though the variations of the terrain may suggest the articulation of series of blocks with one another. The general impression to be derived from the arrangement is that of unimaginative, stereotyped, mechanical monotony. Only rarely will one find even a partially organic pattern throughout. Upon closer inspection it will appear that portions of the area are devoid of structures, and consist of green open spaces or parks. Other vacant space will turn out to be public squares, railroad yards, or merely unutilized land areas of varying shapes and sizes. The observer will note that the rectangles or

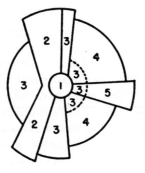

SECTOR THEORY

Figure 43. Diagram of Sector-Arranged Type of City. (Chauncey D. Harris and Edward L. Ullman, "The Nature of Cities," *Annals of the American Academy of Political and Social Science*, Vol. 242 [Nov., 1945], p. 12.)

other shapes that make up the horizontal pattern of the city are generally built up around the edges and are hollow in the middle, indicating that the structures line up along the streets.

More intensive examination of the city of medium or large size will show that the city is more densely built up at the core, where, even if it is only a few square miles in area, one or more tall structures will loom up grotesquely, marking the location of the central business district. If the city is large the number of these skyscrapers will be correspondingly multiplied and they will reappear irregularly at places somewhat distant from the city center, indicating the location of subcenters. The central business district will flatten out abruptly toward the edges where the city's light manufacturing and warehouse areas may be recognized, interspersed by ramshackle structures constituting the blighted areas and slums. Adjacent to this belt are to be found the tenements and workingmen's homes, and beyond are the more densely built apartment house sections tapering off rather unsymmetrically and stretching fingerlike along the main traffic streets into areas of single homes with small yards and open spaces. Along these radials that follow the main transportation lines and, like a web between them, will cluster other less intensively built up settlements. The city will thus approximate a circular or semi-circular pattern at the edges of which tentacles will protrude, tending to stretch the circle into a star-shaped outline. The symmetry of the total configuration is sometimes warped by waterfronts, rivers, elevations and depressions in the topography, and by the proximity of other cities.

Beyond the built-up parts of the city, there are to be found great open spaces, on which the occasional structures reveal the location of truck

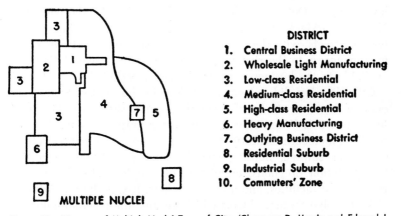

DISTRICT
1. **Central Business District**
2. **Wholesale Light Manufacturing**
3. **Low-class Residential**
4. **Medium-class Residential**
5. **High-class Residential**
6. **Heavy Manufacturing**
7. **Outlying Business District**
8. **Residential Suburb**
9. **Industrial Suburb**
10. **Commuters' Zone**

MULTIPLE NUCLEI

Figure 44. Diagram of Multiple-Nuclei Type of City. (Chauncey D. Harris and Edward L. Ullman, "The Nature of Cities," *Annals of the American Academy of Political and Social Science,* Vol. 242 [Nov., 1945], p. 12.)

farms, nurseries and gardens, country clubs, and abandoned or unsuccessful subdivisions, marked by pavements and sidewalks and other improvements, but showing no, or only a few, scattered buildings. At the most favorable sites, partly obscured by woods, nestle imposing mansions with large fenced-in grounds resembling the feudal estates of the European countryside. At intervals along the railroad lines and through-highways, often as uninterrupted extensions of the city proper, more densely settled areas are distributed. These are the suburbs and satellite towns. Some of these immature cities will be clearly recognizable as industrial sites and others, but for the abundance of yards and trees and the absence of building concentration, might be mistaken for residential sections of the city itself.[2]

[2] National Resources Committee, *Our Cities* (Washington: Government Printing Office, 1937), pp. 4–6.

HISTORY OF CITY-PLANNING IN AMERICA

Early Developments.　Limited planning occurred in a few early American cities. In 1682 William Penn laid out the checkerboard street system for Philadelphia which has served as the basic pattern for plotting American cities. In 1791 L'Enfant drew up the plans for the new national capital of the United States, Washington, which combined radial streets with the rectangular pattern, a European idea. While this plan was not accepted for over a century, it has dominated the development of the city. In 1807, following a fire, Detroit was laid out with radial major thoroughfares. New York (Manhattan Island) in 1811 was plotted in the grid pattern of streets, with the more frequent east-and-west streets giving greater access to the rivers, the only means of transportation then available to the business area on the lower end of the island.

City-planning did not come into use in the United States early enough, however, to be of more than minor significance in building new cities. When cities began to grow rapidly in the last half of the nineteenth century, they encountered a great variety of problems: sewage, housing specifications, population congestion, transportation of goods, circulation of people, railroad terminals, recreational facilities, and a host of others. It was the rebuilding of cities to solve these problems which became the chief stimulus and the main task of city-planning.[3]

Beginning of Modern City-Planning.　A significant influence on the modern acceptance of planning cities was exerted when Frederick L. Olmsted laid out a large area in the middle of the extension of the New York street system for Central Park. This idea was taken up by other cities. Another influence was the ideas which wealthy Americans had picked up in their European travels, which were given expression in the carefully ordered arrangement of classical buildings in the Chicago World's Fair in 1893, which was used as the basis for emphasis on the "city beautiful." This seemed to set off a new movement of city-planning centered on the architectural aspects of cities, parks as centrally located as possible, and parkways in relation to street layouts. A revival of the old New England plan of centering community life in the village green was

---

[3] Robert A. Walker, *The Planning Function in Urban Government* (Chicago: The University of Chicago Press, 1941), pp. 4–8.

soon added by the civic center idea. Among the plans which grew out of these developments and which in turn exerted much influence were those of Roanoke by John Nolen and Los Angeles by Charles Robinson.[4]

The greatest advance in the expansion and spread of city-planning came with the first national conference on city-planning, held in Washington in 1909. Here the idea of overall planning with reference to the solution of particular problems of cities was developed. Consideration was given to the economic implications of planning and the need for comprehensive and coördinated treatment of their various problems by the cities. In this same year the Burnham plan for Chicago recognized these new ideas in its statement of the objectives of planning.[5]

During the next decade more and more cities began to employ city-planners as consultants. This was done first by privately organized civic improvement associations and then by an increasing number of official city-planning commissions.

Zoning. The development of ideas and experimentation had progressed to the point of practicality. The need then was for legal sanction and implementation. Preliminary steps were taken in several cities when fire districts were established regulating the construction of wooden buildings. The Massachusetts state legislature had passed a law specifying the allowable building heights for certain streets in Boston. In Los Angeles the permissible use of structures in various areas was established. The first inclusive zoning law in America, however, was passed in New York in 1916. The immediate stimulus for the New York law was the problem of the concentration of people caused by the number of high buildings in a small area and the consequent congestion of street traffic and inadequacy of transportation facilities.[6]

Zoning laws divide their cities into areas which have been determined by studies of present land use, of probable future needs, and of the most convenient and desirable arrangement for the required activities. Certain areas are set aside for industry, others for business, and others for residence. Often the industrial areas are divided into those where heavy industry may be located and those where

---

[4] *Ibid.*, pp. 9–11.
[5] *Ibid.*, pp. 12, 17–19.
[6] Edward M. Bassett, *Zoning* (New York: Russell Sage Foundation, 1936), pp. 22–23.

only light industry is permitted, and the residential areas into sections where multiple dwellings may be built, those where two-family houses are allowed, and those where only single-family homes are permitted.

Along with these use designations there are usually other factors which are controlled. The percentage of a lot which can be built upon differs with use; for example, industry and business may cover as much as 100 percent of the land, single-family residences as little as 30 percent of the land. Maximum building heights are also frequently specified, by a fixed limit in feet in business areas, or by number of floors in residence areas. The Los Angeles height limit of 150 feet has made the roof tops of the downtown business area almost level. Another method of specifying height is in relation to street width, as in New York, where, in different districts, building heights 1, 1¼, 1½, 2, and 2½ times the width of the street are permitted. Certain extensions of height are permitted when setbacks are used, which has made the downtown area in some places look like rows of giant steps. Often there are also certain specifications with regard to building materials and types of construction for the various zones.

Powers for the enforcement of zoning laws are among the police powers and have been specified by enabling acts passed by state legislatures. The pattern for most of the state acts has been the Standard State Zoning Enabling Act published by the United States Department of Commerce in 1924 and thoroughly revised in 1926.[7] By 1949, comprehensive zoning was established in all 14 cities of over 500,000 population, in 21 of the 23 of 250,000–500,000, in 45 of the 55 of 100,000–250,000, in 82 of the 106 of 50,000–100,000, in 142 of the 212 of 25,000–50,000, and in 343 of the 662 of 10,000–25,000, or in nearly two-thirds of the cities over 10,000 in population. Slightly fewer had official planning agencies.[8]

Until recently it had been assumed that zoning cannot be retroactive. The tendency now, however, is to specify a time limit within which buildings erected before zoning laws were passed must be made to conform to the laws. Many difficulties have been encountered in the enforcement of the laws, particularly on the fringes of zones. Through the use of various forms of pressure many individ-

[7] *Ibid.*, pp. 27–29.
[8] International City Managers' Association, *Municipal Year Book, 1949*, p. 261.

uals who considered that the zoning requirements interfered with their interests have been able to cause planning boards to make unsound exceptions and so detract from the effectiveness of the zoning plans and add to the confusion and instability of the cities.

These situations most frequently arise in areas zoned for residence which lie adjacent to areas zoned for business. Owners of such older residential property have often been holding on to it for years with the expectation that they could profit greatly by selling it for business purposes when retail business areas expanded with the growth of their cities. This is sometimes a false hope, betraying ignorance of the trends in city development. A striking illustration of this occurred in St. Louis. A better-than-average older residential area southwest of the retail business center was zoned for residence in the zoning law which was a part of the original city plan. About two years later, through the activities and influence of some of the property owners in this area, the zoning law was changed to permit business establishments and light industry. Some five years later there was occasion to map what would have been infringements of the original zoning ordinance. It was found that local corner stores and small industrial establishments had infiltrated the whole area. No significant commercial enterprises had been located there. It was clear at that time and has been subsequently demonstrated that this area would be by-passed to the north by the expansion of the business center. But the damage was done—a good, substantial residential area was ruined for residence and would never become a part of the commercial center of the city.

While zoning can do little to repair past mistakes, it can protect and stabilize the areas of cities. It seems very difficult for many people to see that the stability and social good of the whole city are, in the long run, to their protection and advantage. Zoning is only a first step; however, its significance is summed up by Justement: "It is now evident that zoning is only capable of restraining some of the more glaring abuses of the unrestricted uses of private property, and that it will have relatively little positive value in creating a more efficient city."[9]

The Master Plan. In 1928 the United States Department of Commerce issued a pamphlet entitled *Standard City Planning Enabling Act*, prepared by its Advisory Committee on City Planning and

[9] From *New Cities for Old*, by Louis Justement, p. 29. Copyright 1946. Courtesy of McGraw-Hill Book Co.

Zoning. The pamphlet was for the purpose of guiding those engaged in drafting planning laws which would bring together the results of investigations in the various phases of city activities as a basis for planning. The pamphlet emphasized the *master plan*, the combined and coördinated objectives and plans for all phases of the physical aspects of a city. Bassett points out that the master plan is dynamic and should always be capable of constant change and revision. He limits its scope to seven specific elements: streets, including pedestrian and vehicular bridges and tunnels; parks and parkways; sites for public buildings; public reservations; zoning districts; routes for public utilities; pierhead and bulkhead lines.[10] The thinking and developments since this statement, however, have expanded the scope of the master plan considerably.

The Regional Plan. The regional plan has already been discussed as an evidence of the emerging metropolitan community (pp. 235–236 and 246–247). It is also important because it marks an important stage in the development of planning. The pioneer job of this kind was done by a group of forward-looking individuals who formed the Regional Plan Association of New York in 1921. The chairman of the group, all of whom became well known in the field of planning, was Charles D. Norton, who had come to New York from Chicago, where he had been inspired by the Burnham Chicago Plan. With a grant of $1,000,000 from the Russell Sage Foundation, the group began a comprehensive series of surveys of the New York area under the direction of "Nelson P. Lewis, former Chief Engineer of the Board of Estimate and Apportionment, who had helped develop the McClellan Plan of 1903. . . . Thomas Adams, of London, later became general director, and Lawrence M. Orton, now a member of the New York City Planning Commission, became secretary."[11]

The surveys were completed and the plan prepared and published in 1929. It was the most comprehensive plan made up to this time. It analyzed twenty-two urban counties in New York, New Jersey, and Connecticut from the standpoint of a metropolitan area and their respective importance and relationships; it appraised the resources and needs of each in relationship to the whole, and it

[10] Edward M. Bassett, *The Master Plan* (New York: Russell Sage Foundation, 1938), p. 142.

[11] Cleveland Rodgers and Rebecca B. Rankin, *New York, the World's Capital City* (New York: Harper & Brothers, 1948), p. 243.

proposed a plan to unify the whole region. While the plan was not official and has depended upon acceptance by the public and their elected officials for its execution, it has been a major influence in the development of the metropolitan area.[12]

The three subsequent reports made by the New York Regional Plan Association, *From Plan to Reality*, published in 1933, 1938, and 1942[13] described the progress toward the accomplishment of the plan which had been made in the four-, eight-, and twelve-year periods. The construction of highways, railroad and port developments, the improvement and extension of park systems, the increase in planning councils, and the completion of many special projects show a creditable record.

There has been severe criticism of the New York regional plan among the more advanced thinkers in planning. One of the most outspoken has been Lewis Mumford.[14] He challenges the assumption of continuous growth and expansion of the city and the accompanying two-hour, forty-mile commuter zone. This has shown no evidence of working out (cf. pp. 232 f.). He considers that to plan a metropolis providing for a flow of population from the crowded center to the fully urbanized and dependent outlying sections is in no way to control the forces which wreak havoc on the center of the city. He says: "Mr. Benton MacKaye has pointed out that to remove a traffic snarl from Times Square the planners may have, not to build double-decked streets or belt line railroads . . . , but to reroute the movement of wheat . . . through the eastern ports," and he adds that a city like New York is not a self-contained entity; "it is what it is because of continental and world-wide conditions."

Mumford further criticizes the suggested building of large neighborhood units are impractical because ground parcels are too badly chopped up and the cost is beyond financial interests; the proposal for developing garden cities in expensive suburban areas without industrial bases makes them merely more suburbs; and the concentration of traffic, transportation, and high buildings in Manhattan below 59th Street, like the plan of 1811, neglects the sociological facts of the city—"a collection of groups, within a limited

[12] *Ibid.*, p. 243.
[13] Cited in full on p. 236.
[14] Lewis Mumford, "The Plan of New York," *New Republic*, June 15, 1932, pp. 121–126, and June 22, 1932, pp. 146–154.

area, housed in appropriate structures, serving the common life in related institutions." If buildings, streets, transportation systems, etc., constituted the city, the New York plan, though inadequate, would be real, but, since physical structure is only one aspect of the city, the plan is inadequate in its very scope. Mumford sums up his criticism: "In short, the Regional Plan, since it carefully refrains from proposing measures which would lead to the efficient control of land, property values, buildings and human institutions, leaves the metropolitan district without hope of any substantial changes, or more than minor and necessary improvements."[15]

Newer Plans. While the majority of plans, even those prepared in the 1930's and 1940's, followed the prevailing pattern of primary emphasis on physical repair and face-lifting, a few have been built on more fundamental concepts.

The plan of Richmond (Virginia), though purporting to deal with physical development, recognizes the dangers involved: "We hope through the city plan to avoid a policy of laissez-faire, to substitute for expediency a positive plan of action so far as control of growth is concerned." This plan proposes housing improvements on a large scale, with particular emphasis on developing good neighborhood environments in which single-family units can be protected. Emphasis is also placed on the city's economic ties and the various factors of social living for its people.[16]

The Los Angeles plan starts with the premise that the city is "a method of living—a mechanism or device for getting satisfactions out of life. The city, too, must have an objective—which may include comfort, beauty, happiness, or distinction in some field of joint endeavor." The plan dismisses decentralization as a ready-made solution of the problem, especially when it does not provide for the use of the city center. It sums up its basic principle: "The key to the effective way of life in the Los Angeles area would appear to be the furtherance of numerous, well-rounded, semi-sufficient communities grouped about the central nucleus which performs the essential services for all and which binds many segments into an integrated metropolitan structure."[17]

[15] *Ibid.*, p. 154.

[16] *A Master Plan for the Physical Development of the City: Richmond, Virginia* (Richmond: City Plan Commission, 1946), pp. 21, 24.

[17] George W. Robbins and L. D. Tilton (editors), *Los Angeles: Preface to a Master Plan* (Los Angeles: Pacific Southwest Academy, 1941, Publication No. 19).

In an annual review of planning for the year 1947 Segoe commented extensively on the master plan of Cincinnati, which had designated its objective as "the realization of the maximum potentialities of the area in terms of the economic well-being of its people, and in terms of the most satisfying conditions of living attainable." The plan, which involves thirty-two cities and villages in Ohio and twenty-one in Kentucky, was built on three principles: (1) a gradual readjustment of land-use patterns to separate producing, distributing, and living areas, which will be insulated from each other, by assembling industry into belts or corridors with railroads and trunk-line motorways; (2) organization of existing and new residential sections into self-contained communities of 50,000–100,000 population, corresponding roughly to junior-high-school districts, where the everyday needs of the people can be met and from which there is easy access to the central district for special facilities and services, each community having its local business and service institutions and a community civic center; (3) improvement in the "texture of the city's development through conservation and rehabilitation on a sound density standard which redistributes the congestion of population and buildings in the central areas to a stabilized pattern of community and neighborhood organization."[18]

The principles involved in these newer plans have been expressed also by Segoe: "The master plan, while it must be thoroughly practical and sound economically, must give expression to other than the purely materialistic operations of the community. It must be: (1) balanced and attractive as a general design best suited to the present and probable future needs of the community, (2) in scale with the population and economic prospects of the community, and (3) in scale with the financial resources available."[19]

The London County Plan. Although it is outside the borders of the United States, reference must be made to what is probably the most comprehensive, realistic, and daring adventure in city-planning—the London County Plan. The great destruction in London during the war provided a most unusual opportunity for a funda-

---

[18] *Planning, 1947* (Chicago: American Society of Planning Officials, 1947), pp. 57–62.

[19] Ladislas Segoe, *Local Planning Administration* (Chicago: International City Managers' Association, published for the Institute for Training in Municipal Administration, 1941), p. 43.

mental reconstruction of the city. The plan accepts the principle of "conditioned yet comprehensive replanning." It proceeds to build upon the preservation and reconstruction of the established community areas and the development of new community areas divided into neighborhood units of from 6000 to 10,000 people related to elementary schools as the focal points of neighborhood life and services. It proposes a moderate decentralization involving slightly more than half a million people and the integration of residence, business, and industry as a basis for removing the necessity for much extensive "journey to work." Around this are the planning of thoroughfares for the relief of traffic congestion, the removal of obsolete and depressed housing, the establishment of more adequate and better-distributed open spaces, the provision for a coherent architectural development, and a coördination and modernization of the railways.[20]

The London plan is criticized by Mumford upon the basis of what he terms "the fundamental matter that had been neglected: the relation of population growth to city design." He points out that the only reasons for retaining the prewar population in the County of London are political and economic: the enormous amount of money invested in the elaborate transit system, sewers, waterworks, and other services, in trades, industries, and public works, in educational and health services, in power and prestige, and in the monopoly of cultural resources, all of which depend on the quantity of population. He questions the accepted density of population and shows that the decentralization of population planned is at a rate less than that already experienced in the unplanned development. He decries the perpetuation of highly urbanized conditions which have been demonstrated to be unfriendly to reproduction and which give families model flats when their great desire is for single-family houses. A truly great plan would have been for a constellation of garden cities. He adds: "Metropolitan London, even the County of London, is too small a unit for re-planning and re-building, indeed, the essential provincialism of the metropolis is one of the chief obstacles to its reformation."

The preconditions which Mumford lays down for the replanning of London are worthy of further consideration, aside from any question of their immediate application:

[20] J. H. Forshaw and Patrick Abercrombie, *County of London Plan* (London: Macmillan & Co., 1943), especially the Preamble, pp. 1–20.

1. A National Population Policy, looking toward its stabilization, if not its increase, instead of permitting the threatened decrease of population to go unchecked.

2. A Policy of Urban Land Nationalization which will liquidate the present structure of urban values and permit large-scale reconstruction to be economically carried on, in a fashion favorable to family life and balanced communal relationships.

3. A National Policy of Industrial Decentralization along the lines laid down in the Barlow Report: a policy which will progressively move population out of London and other large centers until a net reproduction rate close to 1.0 is achieved.

4. Regional administrative units that will undertake the task of resettlement and building outside the existing municipal or county areas and will co-ordinate the work of the municipalities themselves.[21]

In the intervening years the British Parliament has passed three laws which are far-reaching in their implications and have put a solid foundation under city-planning.

The Distribution of Industries Act of 1945 was for the purpose of securing a proper national distribution of industry by means of decentralization. It provided for financial assistance in the form of subsidies and loans to facilitate relocation and the construction of new plants.[22]

The New Towns Act of 1946 added another member to the British cabinet, a Minister of Town and Country Planning. It also implemented his responsibility and activities by establishing government corporations with power to acquire land for town sites, to prepare the land for development, to build housing, to make other improvements, to lease land for private developments, to provide the required utilities and other services, and ultimately to transfer the land and improvements to local authorities when they were established and were ready to take over. By this law the machinery was provided for starting the development of twenty new towns which were deemed desirable. These were to follow the principles of Howard's garden cities. The cities would be planned for a maximum population of from 50,000 to 60,000 people. They would be self-sufficient communities for all day-to-day needs, including industries, retail business, purveyors of services, schools, churches, and other social institutions, public utilities, and the various public

---

[21] Lewis Mumford, *City Development* (New York: Harcourt, Brace and Company, 1945), p. 239.

[22] Distribution of Industries Act, 1945, 8 and 9 George VI, Chap. 36.

services. The cities would be located a sufficient distance from the city of London to preserve a green-belt area between them and the city.[23]

The third law, passed in 1947 and entitled the Town and Country Planning Act, not only extended the planning program to include the redevelopment of all kinds of urban areas, but also provided a basis on which planning could be effective through the establishment of a new code of physical planning and land tenure. The law had two complementary parts. In the first the government assumed the prerogative of control over the use of all land. Thereafter all landowners were required to get permission to change the land use. Unearned increment and profit derived from community improvement were appropriated by the government; that is, the government acquired the development rights of the whole country and thereafter landowners had to pay for the right to put improvements on their land. Against this the government set aside three hundred million pounds, the estimate of the total possible development value for fifty years, for compensation in properly adjudicated hardship cases. This arrangement has been accepted by all interests. The second part of the law required all counties to prepare master plans, which must be revised every three years. These plans must deal with the size and density of the various areas and designate land use zones. They must be based on adequate surveys. When they are accepted, they become the statutory plans.[24]

It is important to check the realism of the student of planning against the practical experience of the planning process. The criticisms which Mumford made of the London County Plan were not likely taken seriously enough to form the basis for the subsequent action on the part of the British Parliament, though his analysis may well have influenced the thinking of British planners to some degree. It is clear, however, that the problems which were encountered in the execution of the plan led to action on three of the four fundamental points which he made. Regional administrative units as a function of government have been established. The bases for industrial decentralization have been laid down. To all in-

[23] New Towns Act, 1946, 9 and 10 George VI, Chap. 68. See also *Final Report of the New Towns Committee* (London: His Majesty's Stationery Office, 1946).

[24] Town and Country Planning Act, 1947, 10 and 11 George VI, Chap. 51.

ents and purposes, for practical operation, land nationalization has been effected. Mumford's other suggestion, for a population policy, is of another order, but the steps already taken may very well bring more definite results, as they create the circumstances under which a balanced population growth may develop, than any national edict could.

Not often do circumstances compel action so close on the heels of the pronouncements of planning students, but the function of the analysts, students of city problems, and creative thinkers in planning is clear.

PHILOSOPHY AND OPERATION OF CITY-PLANNING

Through the experience of many years what might be termed a working philosophy of city-planning has emerged. It has never been written down as such, but it is clearly implicit in the principles on which city plans are constructed. There are six points of major importance in this philosophy, some of which are of long standing while others are just now coming into general acceptance.

Principles of City-Planning. City plans must be *comprehensive*. The definition of what is included in comprehensiveness is not, however, static. This can be seen in the increasing scope of city plans. Early plans dealt chiefly with parks, street layouts, zoning, monuments, and public buildings; then civic centers, transportation, etc., were added; later, housing, school locations, and other social features. This broadening base has grown steadily from the consideration of only the physical features of a city to the consideration of the city's people and their convenience in living, working, and playing. The master plan is a big step in this direction. While as such it is still, perhaps, too largely confined to physical features, yet it is built as a basic layout, not as rigid as the old gridiron street pattern, but rather establishing a functional design with use and unit areas, and consequently subject to adaptation.

City plans must be *flexible*. It is recognized that the future needs and requirements of cities cannot be anticipated; so planning should take a form which on the one hand establishes stability for the development and redevelopment of a city and on the other hand enables development to take the specific form which future change may demand. The newer concepts on which city plans are built and the newer forms they are taking make flexibility possible to a far greater degree than formerly.

City-planning should be based on the *planning of unit areas*. While this has not yet had universal acceptance, it is becoming rapidly recognized as of basic importance. In fact, recent plans have been built on the principle, whether or not it has been stated as theory. The sociological significance of the neighborhood as the limited area within which most city people live and move, and the high degree to which convenience must be localized are major factors in planning. On the other hand, the congestion of central areas and the overloading of transportation have intensified the use of near-at-hand facilities.

City-planning must have *popular support*. Plans will be successful only when they are of, by, and for the people. Many good plans have fallen by the wayside because the people had nothing to say about them. One of the most notable was a recent plan for Toledo. It had behind it outstanding men in the city. A large amount of money was spent for the services of the best experts obtainable. A magnificent model was prepared at great expense to show the plan which had been made. But the people voted it down, for they had not been consulted, they were not able to see in it the needs which they recognized through experience, and they did not understand its advantages. Since it was their money which would pay for the execution of the plan, they would not accept it. Unless the people of the city are involved in working out the plan, it will probably not adequately meet the needs; and, unless the people understand it and want it, it is not likely to be accepted.

City plans must provide for *gradual development*. So much reconstruction is required for any planned redevelopment of cities that the job obviously cannot be done all at once. It must be gradually accomplished by stages over a long period of time. As the plan is carried out, the cost must be spread over years, and the life of the city cannot be disrupted. As the contractor for the Grand Central Terminal in New York was instructed, "Build the great new station, but keep the traffic moving."

Operation of City-Planning.   Through the long experience of city-planning there has evolved a *modus operandi*. The various steps are taken in different ways and sometimes in a different order, but the successful development of planning in a city includes them all.

Community commitment to a planning process is the basis and beginning of planning. This involves not only publicity, public meetings, and discussion, but actual participation in working out plans, as was done in Philadelphia with great effect. Many times the process is initiated by a group of people who arouse widespread interest, form an association, raise funds, and employ experts to work out plans. In other situations the official body comes first and then attacks the problem of community commitment along with its other duties.

Establishment of an official planning agency must come sooner or later, for a continuing, responsible group of capable and enthusiastic people which is a part of the local government is essential if plans are to become reality.

Accumulation of facts about all pertinent aspects of city life by experts in research and interpretation is the stuff out of which substantial plans are made. No idealistic picture of a "city beautiful" will do the job of solving the real problems of making a particular city useful and beautiful as a means to better living for its citizens. The quantity of facts acquired is stupendous, for problems must be precisely defined, the factors and implications analyzed, and the resources for solution appraised. This is a job for experts; it is time-consuming and requires the coöperation of all concerned in the community.

The master plan is the interpretation of the facts and the objectives into the general, comprehensive plan for what ought to be. Some cities have published their city plan and after the approval of the city council put it to the vote of the people to make it the "law of the city." The trend, however, is away from this practice toward getting the basic approval of the council and having the community first accept the policy of planning and subsequently approve sections of the plan, with the budgets involved.

A *program of priorities,* or the plan for the execution of the plan, is essential. Since no plan can be carried out all at once, it is necessary to establish a program of things to be done on the basis of the relative need for them. This is good strategy, for it demonstrates to the people of the community the results of their city plan at places where they know the need. It is good practice because it keeps an orderly control on opportunism, which always has to be used.

Order is the essence of the city plan, and accomplishments, no matter how slowly they may have to be made, add up to progress when they are according to the priorities and the plan. A few years will make great changes.

THE FUTURE AND PROBLEMS OF CITY PLANNING

Though many are working and writing on this pressing matter of stepping up the process of urban redevelopment, there are a number of things which stand in the way. The newer ideas, consequently, tend to be related to the problem areas, several of which are of major importance.

Congestion. Most thinking about city planning begins with the congestion of people, living so jammed together in buildings which fill up all the space except for streets that there is no chance for fresh air or any light or room for grass or trees, or a place for children to play. These desirable things for good living everyone thinks a city should provide for all its people. These conditions are quite characteristic of the central areas of large cities and although the number of people in these areas has been decreasing for many years, the conditions of congestion persist.

The matter of density of population, already discussed,[25] is a moot question. There are widely differing opinions with regard to what is desirable in different parts of cities and wide variations in densities in the different cities.[26] The solutions of this problem which have been proposed have a wide range. On the one hand, there are Frank Lloyd Wright's Broadacre City,[27] in which he would coördinate factories, farms, professions, and services in a countryside community where each family can have its house and land up to five acres according to its needs and desires, and Raymond Unwin's system of satellite towns, planned for a whole metropolitan area after Ebenezer Howard's ideas of garden cities, on the basis of his proof that there was nothing gained by overcrowding.[28] On the other hand, Le Corbusier's "ville contemporaire" pro-

[25] Cf. chapter 20, p. 287.

[26] Sanders, S. E. and Rabuck, A. J., *New City Patterns*. New York: Reinhold Publishing Corporation, 1946, pp. 102–119 gives an extended discussion of population density in cities.

[27] Frank Lloyd Wright, "Broadacre City: A New Community Plan," *Architectural Record*, April, 1935, pp. 243–254.

[28] Raymond Unwin, *Town Extension Plan*, Warburton Lectures, 1912 (Manchester: University Press, 1912), pp. 25–62.

poses to get rid of congestion by greatly increasing the density at the center of the city, with skyscrapers for business, industry, and residence arranged around a highly developed transportation center which would give access to the single-family residences which radiate in all directions from the center. The skyscrapers, which would accommodate hundreds of thousands of people, would still be surrounded with parks and open spaces.[29] And there are many ideas and combinations which lie between these extremes.[30]

Density is not only a matter of how many people dwell on an acre of ground, but also the kind of structures in which they dwell, how these structures are arranged, the amount of open space, parks, and playgrounds which are included in the arrangement, the height of buildings, the space between them, the kinds of roofs they have, their compass line with reference to the sun, the latitude of the city, the shape of the buildings, the room arrangement, the street system, the use of superblocks, the topography of the land, the direction of prevailing winds, the relationship to the location of industry, transportation facilities and the journey to work, the availability of stores, services of all kinds, and people's institutions, and the accessibility of natural recreation areas.[31]

In most of the larger American cities housing projects have been built which have materially increased the density of population by replacing single-family units with multiple dwellings or smaller buildings with many-floored apartment houses. To the degree to which this complicated array of factors has been taken into account, living has been found to be very satisfactory by those who have settled there.

The resolution of the question of density and the solution of the problems of congestion will likely be a by-product of city redevelopment on sound functional principles. Such a procedure is illustrated by Saarinen,[32] who proposes what he terms "organic decentralization." This scheme involves a basic plan for an area

[29] Charles Édouard Jeanneret-Gris Le Corbusier, *The City of Tomorrow and Its Planning* (New York: Payson and Clarke).

[30] L. Hilberseimer, *The New City* (Chicago: Paul Theobald, 1944), pp. 55–74, gives a review of and a comment on many of these ideas.

[31] Hilberseimer, *op. cit.*, pp. 74–128, discusses these and other items pertaining to density.

[32] Eliel Saarinen, *The City: Its Growth, Its Decay, Its Future* (New York: Reinhold Publishing Corporation, 1943), pp. 200–266.

extending beyond the settled city, with scientifically determined unit areas within which the facilities for the "everyday activities" of the residents can be developed, including the opportunities for work for those who choose to rid themselves of the daily journey to work. Redevelopment of the city would take place over a long period of years in a paired relationship, by which a new unit would

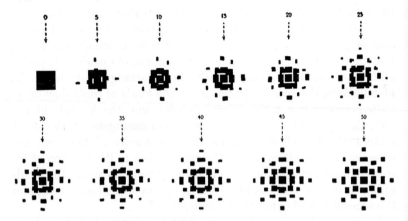

Figure 45.   Diagram of Organic Decentralization.

"Assumptions: The concentrated city is compactly built. Fifty percent of the city is decayed and must be rehabilitated in accordance with a preconceived decentralization pattern. This process takes fifty years—the number of years being a mere symbol—during which period of time the city's size will be doubled. This decentralization process is divided into ten five-year programs, as the above diagram indicates.

(Eliel, Saarinen, The City: Its Growth, Its Decay, Its Future [New York: Reinhold Publishing Corporation, 1943], facing p. 288.)

be developed and an old area would be remade, thus gradually increasing the housing capacity and compensating any loss of value with added value at the same time each individual project contributed toward making over the whole city. Saarinen's diagrammatic scheme of the process is shown in Figure 45, which shows in conventionalized pattern what could be accomplished in half a century. "The ultimate result of this transformation is that there has been gradually formed, around the nucleus of the original compactness, an organic grouping of new or reformed communities of adequate functional order according to the best principles of forward town-building. The ultimate result is: organic decentralization."[33]

Klein, in his plan for a new city of 50,000 population on the shore of the Mediterranean in Israel, uses several new principles. All services for the production or distribution of goods, workshops, commercial centers, markets, and transportation terminals usually found at the center of cities are placed on the periphery; the system of vehicular streets connecting with the outer ring and the pedestrian ways radiating from the center are entirely separated; daily trade, schools for small children, and other services are available in the small residential units; public buildings are along a central axis; residences are in unit areas accessible to an outer transportation line; the geographical size of the town is established by fixed boundaries which also predetermine the number of inhabitants. This centrifugal city is inside out from the traditional pattern and is planned for the benefit of human beings to meet their social, cultural, and recreational needs.[34]

Neighborhood Units. The sociological significance of neighborhoods in city-planning has only lately come to be recognized, and even yet its basic importance for urban redevelopment has not been fully appreciated by city-planners. Experience, however, has pushed in the direction of this recognition. The very nature of the case, which necessitates the redevelopment of cities piecemeal, has forced city plans into patterns of unit development. This has been accentuated in more recent years by the large-scale housing projects, which, for the most part, have been built without regard for the necessities of living beyond the dwelling units themselves. The needs for community services, schools, churches, transportation, retail establishments, and many others, not provided for in the planning, have had to be met subsequently at considerable cost and difficulty by the cities. These experiences have shown the consideration of neighborhoods to be a very practical matter in planning.

Neighborhoods have other points of significance, however, which should be and doubtless will be taken into account as city plans come more directly to grips with the living patterns and habits of people. Some of the more important factors are: the tendency to-

[33] *Ibid.*, pp. 216–217.
[34] Alexander Klein, "Man and Town," in *Technion Yearbook, 1947* (New York: American Technion Society [154 Nassau St.], 1947).

ward a greater degree of homogeneity among the people of neighborhoods; the tendency of all sorts of problems—for example,
delinquency, health, dependency—to be related within neighborhoods; the great extent to which urban neighborhoods are the experience worlds of a large proportion of their people, especially
women and children; the neighborhood character of most institutions which involve people, such as churches, neighborhood houses,
parent-teacher organizations, improvement associations, social
clubs, and of most institutions which serve people, such as health
centers, welfare services, educational programs; the development of
democratic participation through action groups, which is likely to
become effective and inclusive of more people when it operates on
a neighborhood basis. The study of factors of this kind as a part of
the basic research of planning can be of great assistance in determining fundamental neighborhood units, for which more practical
planning can be developed, not only to locate the proper units for
planning, but also to discover the particular complex of problems
within each unit area with reference to which the particular plan
must be worked out. In addition, such a basis of planning makes
possible the participation of people in the planning process and the
support of the citizenry for the city plan which has been found to
be vital to the success of city-planning.

There has been a continuous movement in city-planning toward
the recognition of the sociological unity of areas, from Howard's
garden cities, through Unwin's decentralization in a number of
satellite cities, to the development of the green-belt suburban communities and Wright's Broadacre City. These have largely been
with reference to new communities. Saarinen applies the idea as a
practical principle for the redevelopment of cities, as do many of
the later planners. The London County Plan accepted this principle,
but it was difficult to put into operation until the legal basis was
established in the new laws already discussed. The difficulties in
operating planning on this basis in American cities are chiefly in the
inadequacies of the legal basis of planning.

Control. Four problems form the key to the weaknesses in the
necessary controls for planning in American cities: land use, obsolescence, speculative land values, and limited geographical jurisdiction.

While zoning has been practiced in American cities for thirty
odd years, it has been only partially successful in the control of
land use. Zoning laws are built on past experience and consequently

tend to perpetuate past mistakes and prevent any comprehensive program for redevelopment. The right of eminent domain has been used in connection with certain major city improvements and occasionally in connection with large housing developments, but under the prevailing concepts connected with the private ownership of land it is used in only a limited way and with great reluctance. Plans which are broadly conceived for the reconstruction of cities still meet the opposition of uninformed officials in various administrative departments and have not yet attained the full support of the citizenry. Upon a change in public opinion, the provision of adequate legal powers, and a close relation to the legislative bodies, the chief executive and the administrative departments must wait. Revisions in the structure of city government can then unify the many local government agencies which are involved in planning and reconstruction. Cities, unfortunately, are subject to their states and the limitations of the state statutes. This has been a serious handicap, as has also the lack of coördination of local, state, and national governments in urban affairs.[35]

It has never been possible to define obsolescence in practical terms, let alone make legal provision for the destruction of outworn structures. So long as it is not economically feasible to tear down old buildings and replace them with new ones which will be more profitable investments, and so long as structures, no matter what their age, will hold together and be used, they continue. It is often the case in cities that relatively new buildings are replaced on account of a marked rise in land values and changes in pattern of use, while in other parts of the cities decrepit tenements, lofts, and warehouses remain. It is obvious that all buildings wear out in time. Though the length of time may vary according to the type of construction and use, it is much more logical that they should be replaced on this basis than on the basis of the value of the land on which they are situated. No basis, however, exists on which this can be done, or on which outworn structures can be destroyed. Until a way of controlling obsolescence is found, the physical framework for blight and slums will continue to exist.

The fact that urban land has a speculative value is a controlling factor in its use. The potential unearned increment in city locations is more determinative of its recognized value than the stable income from its use. So long as this condition persists, it is possible

---

[35] National Resources Committee, *op. cit.*, pp. 60–70.

neither to stabilize land use nor to carry on extensive planned re-development, for a fictitious value creeps in whenever there is a market for land for any purpose. Since land as space is the basic natural resource of any city, some means of treating it as such must be found. The British Town and Country Planning Act of 1947 (see p. 556) and such plans as that made by Justement[36]—who proposes that cities purchase all of their land at the fair market value over a period of approximately fifty years, demolish structures which are obsolete, and lease the land for private development in accordance with a comprehensive plan—are suggestive of various practical and fair methods by which cities can gain control over the use of their land.

The jurisdiction of cities extends only to the city limits, but the urban community knows no such bounds. It reaches out in all directions to include an extended area in which the relationships of people and the functional life are so closely enmeshed that the artificial boundaries are meaningless. "The greatest obstacle to the full emergence of a metropolitan community is the great number of conflicting and overlapping political and administrative units into which the area is divided."[37] Facts showing the many municipal governments in the metropolitan areas have been given in Chapter 13. Further complications are found in counties, townships, school districts, sanitary districts, sewer districts, library districts, health districts, park districts, forest-preserve districts, street-lighting districts, utility districts, water districts, and even mosquito-abatement districts, each of which is a separate body politic and corporate body. This is an odd picture of independent units performing related or even identical governmental functions with some degree of coöperation, but with a great degree of competition for municipal revenues, for administrative prestige, and for legal powers. To make it worse, some of the metropolitan districts straddle state lines. This will be one of the most difficult problems to solve. A federal bureau for the continuous compilation of a more extended array of facts about cities and a national urban policy would help.

Cost. The cost of rebuilding American cities cannot be estimated on the basis of data which are available, but we know enough to indicate that it would be a staggering sum. But the cost

[36] Justement, *op. cit.*, pp. 37–38. See also Hans Heyman, *Property Life Insurance* (New York: Harper & Bros., 1939).

[37] National Resources Committee, *op. cit.*, p. 67.

of World War II was a staggering sum, and yet the war was carried on. The cash required to pay the bills was accumulated, and the debt which was left is by no means fantastic in terms of American resources. The cost of rebuilding the cities of America is small by comparison, and, when it is broken up into the total number of cities involved and a long period of time, say fifty years, the pieces are relatively small.

Whether or not the job will be undertaken is, in the final analysis, a matter of value and wisdom. If the basic human values of democracy are really accepted, then providing the conditions of life and work in cities which are up to the standards of knowledge and technology could scarcely be other than fully accepted. Wisdom and good business, moreover, require that the facts and understanding of cities which have been accumulated, inadequate though they may be, be used for planning and prevention to cut down the costly items of urban budgets which are caused by lack of foresight in the past.

Three things seem necessary to meet the cost of reconstructing cities. First is establishing an adequate tax base for cities and straightening out the tax structure (cf. pp. 291 f.). One aspect of this problem is determining the real urban community in the case of each city and building this total community, without regard for present city limits, into a corporate whole so that all members of the real urban community can participate in planning and paying the cost of the new cities.

Unless, therefore, the boundaries of the political city can be stretched to include its suburban and satellite industrial and residential colonies, the economic and social base, upon which rests the welfare of both those who remain in the city and those who seek a partial escape from it, will eventually disintegrate. For no community in a democratic society can long remain a sound functioning organism, if those among its members who gain the greatest benefits from it, escape from most of the obligations communal life imposes, and if those who obtain the least returns in the way of the necessities and amenities of life are left to bear the brunt of civic responsibility and taxation. If an orderly development and a higher level of life for the people of the imposing supercities are to be attained, some measures calculated to endow them with the capacity to act collectively as a political unit are indispensable.[38]

[38] *Ibid.*, p. 68.

The second necessity is federal assistance. Adequate collateral and an equal distribution of help on the basis of the acuteness of the problems and local capacity to meet them can only be made against the total common resource and the use of the common treasury. Long since has the principle been accepted in America that it is the responsibility of the community to assist families in trouble to get on their feet and become self-supporting and self-respecting. In fact, this principle has been extended to various social groups in American society; for example, rural areas, through many kinds of expert services and financial assistance, have been solidly reëstablished and stabilized. Currently, there are a number of forms of federal assistance available to cities—for highways, hospitals, and planning—and the latest and most significant is through the Housing Act of 1949. These efforts need coördination and supplementation to give cities the full help which is now necessary.[39] It is not that American cities are unable to take care of themselves, but they are in trouble, serious trouble, and to get firmly established and well started on the way to redevelopment, they, too, need help. In January, 1950, the Committee on Land Policy of the American Institute of Planners recommended (1) a strong national policy for urban development, (2) federal, state, and local action to redevelop central cities and establish new communities, and (3) establishment by states of machinery to plan and develop entire urban districts.

The third necessity is planning. Great Britain has found that the help required by local cities for their redevelopment, in spite of national laws, could not be given until adequate and comprehensive planning had been made by the cities. No longer is piecemeal and opportunistic planning able to meet the far-reaching and inclusive problems which cities face. Every phase of urban life must be included and related, and plans must include priorities and timetables which can be consistently worked upon.

With such a base it becomes possible to handle the problem of cost realistically. Justement estimates that the total cost of urban redevelopment, including purchase by the cities of all land and improvements, would be approximately $5,100,000,000 a year for fifty years. Of the $2,200,000,000 annual expenditure for the purchase of land, $1,600,000,000 would be written off because of lower

---

[39] *Federal Assistance to Cities* (Chicago: American Municipal Association, 1950).

recapitalization. This might be taken care of by a grant of $1,000,-000,000, and a 2 percent government loan, the interest on which could be paid from the annual income of the land.[40] The Twentieth Century Fund study of America's needs and resources estimates that a fifteen-year program, to provide good housing for people and the removal of all blight in American cities, would cost around $79,500,000,000.[41] Planning would itemize, schedule, and discover the ways and means for doing the job of redevelopment in each urban community.

So, both in theory and in practice, city-planning in America moves toward a more adequate conceptual basis and more promising plans. The recalcitrant planners who tenaciously cling to the outmoded inadequacies of opportunism in their outlook and procedure are gradually growing fewer. America is on the way to remaking her cities. It will, at best, take a long time. Patience and persistence are of the essence.

Zoning, master plans, surveys—these are instruments, not ends. The end is a livable city, suited to modern technologies of living. Until the planners know by what methods the ends are to be achieved, what the purpose of the city is, what those who live in it (not just those who "own" it) want it to be, planning will continue to be merely the means of livelihood of planners. A city plan is the expression of the collective purpose of the people who live in it, or it is nothing. For in the last analysis, planning is not just yielding to the momentary pressures of fugitive groups, nor is it even the making of beautiful maps encompassing future hopes. It is something far more subtle; something inherent and ineluctable—the unspun web in the body of the spider.[42]

Supplementary Reading

The various references indicate books which are well worth considerable perusal.

Construction and Civic Development Department. *Zoning and Civic Development.* Washington: Chamber of Commerce of the United States, 1950.

[40] Justement, *op. cit.*, Chap. 7, especially p. 50.
[41] J. Frederic Dewhurst and Associates, *America's Needs and Resources* (New York: Twentieth Century Fund, 1947), Chap. 18, especially pp. 428–429.
[42] Henry S. Churchill, *The City Is the People* (New York: Harcourt, Brace and Company, Inc., 1945), p. 186.

A statement of the present concepts and problems of zoning. (See also the Hillman reference at the end of Chap. 29.)

Dahir, James. *The Neighborhood Unit Plan: Its Spread and Acceptance.* New York: Russell Sage Foundation, 1947.

The progress of planning toward the use of a neighborhood basis, with an extended bibliography on neighborhoods from the point of view both of planning and of sociology.

Geddes, Patrick. *Cities in Evolution,* new edition. New York: Oxford University Press, 1950.

The ideas of one of the great pioneers in city-planning.

"Some Helpful Books and Pamphlets on Community Planning and Development." Reprint from *The American City,* March, 1950.

Exactly what the title indicates, with the addition of references to more detailed planning bibliographies.

Stein, Clarence. "Toward New Towns for America." *The Town and Planning Review* (edited at the Department of Civic Design, University of Liverpool), Vol. XX, No. 3 (Oct., 1949) and No. 4 (Jan., 1950).

A review of the most advanced examples of city-planning in the United States.

Walker, Robert A. *The Planning Function in Urban Government.* Chicago: The University of Chicago Press, 1941.

Brief history and analysis of city-planning in the United States, and an interpretation of the broader aspects of planning.

CHAPTER 29

DEMOCRACY IN URBAN LIFE

THE appraisal of democracy in any social situation must have two points of reference which grow out of the concept of democracy itself: first, the extent to which that society provides the opportunities for good living to its citizens; and, second, the extent to which the citizens participate in the determination of policy and in the affairs of their communities. This chapter undertakes to briefly summarize material already discussed for the purpose of reviewing the advantages which cities offer to their people and of appraising the active interest which people take in the conditions, the statutes, the organizations, and the programs which affect their lives, in order to estimate the extent to which urban life facilitates or deters the extension of democracy in America.

OPPORTUNITIES FOR GOOD LIVING IN CITIES

The character of cities makes greater provision for meeting human needs both necessary and possible. The very proximity in which urban people live creates the problems which this book has discussed and many others. Problems and needs which seem small and individual in small communities loom large in cities because of their very bulk. Many people have many varieties of needs and wants, any one of which, though infrequent, becomes quantitatively significant within a large concentration of population. The resources of many enterprises make possible a great variety of activities. The broader organization which results provides more latitude for specialization of all sorts, and specialization requires many kinds of experts. Out of these circumstances which exist in cities a greater variety of problems can be tackled and a greater variety of needs of people can be served.

Many of the advantages of city life which are the result of these conditions and the processes which grow out of these conditions have already been mentioned in connection with the discussion of various aspects of urban life. Consequently, by way of summary, to indicate the scope of the opportunities afforded to people in cities, they will be merely inventoried here under a series of general categories of opportunities.

Government. One of the essentials of good living is orderly housekeeping. This goes for communities as well as families. The facility and adequacy with which city government operates are basic to the satisfactory life of its citizens. Within its various forms and in spite of its many failures, city government has developed to the point where it operates reasonably well. Community business can, on the whole, be carried on expeditiously and well. Legislative processes are highly organized; legislative bodies meet as long and as often as required, and they are able to consider thoroughly and take action immediately upon problems which arise. City budgets are highly controlled, and the community money is meticulously accounted for, though sometimes this results in too great inflexibility. Cities are costly as the variety of operations increases and the organization and activities grow larger. Not only the money required, but also the cost of accounting, increases. In spite of the great cost, citizens of cities get more for their tax money than for any other money they spend. Civil service has been developed, partly as a means of protecting civic funds, and partly to assure trained and capable people for the increasingly skilled and specialized jobs. While civil service is far from perfect, it has made great improvements and has removed most of the city positions of any importance from use as political patronage.

The services of city government are all too frequently taken for granted, and yet they contribute, immeasurably, to the safety, welfare, and comfort of the city's people, things which it would be impossible for individuals to provide for themselves. Sanitation provides for disposal of waste, hauling of garbage, rubbish, and ashes, cleaning streets, and removal of snow in northern cities. There is inspection of foods and other products and also of the health and safety factors of dwellings. Not only do the police carry on their regular duties in maintaining order, but special departments supervise traffic. There are detective bureaus, homicide squads, and special laboratories to work with the many details of crime. Emergency squads of various kinds are operated with special equipment.

Fire-prevention is also specialized and operated with full-time well-trained personnel, and modern equipment of all sorts is well distributed throughout the city. Streets, highways, bridges, and tunnels, essential to modern life, are constructed and maintained. Parks are developed and kept up; playgrounds are set aside and equipped. There are fields for outdoor sports such as baseball, football, and hockey, also tennis courts and golf links, and sometimes bridle paths, toboggan slides, ski trails, and skating ponds. Swimming pools and bathhouses are operated. Many cities have bathing beaches and some anchorage for private pleasure boats. Planning commissions make the plans for the orderly development and improvement of the cities and supervise the operation of zoning laws, which are the basic protection for all types of privately owned property. These and many more incidental services are a part of the day-to-day operation of city government. All of them directly or indirectly lay the basis of satisfactory living for the people of the cities.

Public Utilities. The utilities which are the necessary conveniences for operating homes are provided in the cities on a community-wide basis, sometimes by the coöperative efforts of the citizens through government and sometimes by private enterprise. Water and gas are piped through the streets, and wires, overhead or underground, bring electric power to each house. In some sections of a few cities steam can be had through a meter. Various types of transportation are operated to provide means for the necessary movements of people. Communication is also provided by telephones, newspapers, and radio.

Professional and Business Services. In the cities a great variety of professional people are located—doctors, lawyers, engineers, architects, educators, clergymen, scientists, financiers, and many others. Many specialists are available when their services are required.

So also are the services of an amazing variety of mechanics, craftsmen, and service workers to be had—from plumbers to beauticians, from bankers to shoemakers.

A great amount and a great variety of merchandise are available in cities. Besides great stores with many different departments, each with its own type of goods, there are many specialty shops with large stocks of a single kind of product. There are convenient vending machines dispensing gum, candy, peanuts, drinks, stockings, music, insurance, and what not. There are financial institutions of many sorts, from pawnshops to brokers. Whatever may be desired in material things can be had in most cities.

Education. Public education gives the children and young people of the city a better chance through the enriched and broader curriculum of the schools and through special schools of various kinds. This is supplemented by private schools of many sorts on the primary, secondary, and vocational levels. Higher education is to be found in most cities, often as a part of the system of public education.

Educational experience of many kinds under various circumstances is also available to meet the many needs and interests which arise from the problems of adult living in the present day. Essert is quoted as saying that a new pattern of American education may be emerging in which more adults than children will be studying. He estimates that already some 30,000,000 persons are touched by the many facets of adult education.[1]

Health Services. Cities have established extensive public health services. They maintain health centers with many kinds of clinics, equipment, and specialists and conduct classes for instruction in health care, habits, and problems. Their visiting nurses are everywhere assisting in cases of illness and problems of health in homes. They render special services of many kinds, such as vaccination and inoculation, and they conduct research laboratories.

There are many hospitals, both public and private, especially in the larger cities. Some of these are specialized and have the highest-skilled specialists on their staffs. Most hospitals also conduct special clinics.

Schools have doctors, nurses, and dentists, and many large industrial establishments maintain accident and health services. There are hospital insurance plans, and some medical service insurance programs and many other services and activities which contribute to the improvement of the health of the people and the environmental conditions conducive to health.

Social Services. Many kinds of social services are to be found in cities. Welfare departments of city governments have been greatly enlarged in recent years and carry the main load of family assistance. In addition, there are usually a number of private family case work agencies whose primary work is to help dependent families

---

[1] New York *Times*, June 27, 1949, p. 29.

become self-sufficient. These are frequently supplemented by case work service to special groups.

All sorts of institutions are maintained—for the aged, for orphans, for homeless men, for predelinquent children, and for many others—all using personnel trained for their special work.

There are consultation and guidance centers, employment agencies, psychological and psychiatric services, marriage and planned parenthood clinics, legal consultants, and others.

Group work agencies and neighborhood centers are operated by many different organizations in various sections of cities; they serve children, young people, and adults in the development of coöperative group life in recreation, education, and community action.

There is scarcely any type of social service which cannot be had somewhere, from some agency, in the cities.

Recreation.   The opportunities for recreation in American cities are very great. A large part of them, however, are commercial and are for spectators rather than participants. There are baseball, football, basketball, boxing, swimming, hockey, and other athletic contests which draw large crowds. There are operas, theaters, movies, concerts, lectures, exhibitions, and galleries. But each of these which are for spectators has its counterpart in which those sufficiently interested may engage as participants in the activity.

Many cities have recreation departments which carry out organized recreation programs throughout their cities. Sometimes they use school buildings and playgrounds and at other times parks and playgrounds of the park departments. These programs have a wide variety of activities, from basketball to amateur symphony orchestras, and from painting to the discussion of current political and social issues.

There appears to be a strong tendency for recreation and education to grow closer and closer together, and, consequently, city school systems have extended their recreation programs and have in some places developed close relationships with recreation agencies. Recreational opportunities become increasingly difficult to classify because the interests of individuals lead them into all areas of living for the pursuit of their leisure-time activities.

Religion.   Organized religion has taken on many forms in cities in its endeavor to serve all kinds of people. They range from great, beautiful, and costly churches on the avenues, where the great preachers can be heard and fine professional music can be enjoyed, to the simple, small, modest meeting places where neighborhood people gather to worship; from store-front churches with little organization and few activities to institutional churches with large buildings, excellent equipment, and extension programs of education, recreation, and social work.

Almost anyone's bent in religion can find opportunity for expression in cities, not only in the larger denominations, with their wide variations in ritual and theology, but also in the whole gamut from the highly emotional sects to the ethical societies.

Associations.   The gregarious instinct of people can find expression in countless organizations in cities: social clubs, lunch clubs, country clubs, cellar clubs, lodges, nationality societies, service clubs, veterans' associations, political organizations, labor unions, social action groups, and many others. Some are large and important enough to get their activities reported in the newspapers; others are so small and insignificant that they are unknown except to the few people who belong to them.

Cultural Opportunities.   If we take cultural opportunities to mean those opportunities which provide intellectual and aesthetic experience, we must admit that they are, to a considerable degree, concentrated in cities.

Literary opportunities depend primarily on the availability of books. Library resources in cities are far more extensive and much more available through branch libraries. There are also usually private lending libraries in cities. Bookstores are also confined largely to cities. Cities usually have historical societies, often with museums and documents and other historical materials.

The study and understanding of current affairs and of social, economic, and political problems are facilitated by the greater adequacy in these areas of metropolitan daily newspapers, by frequent lectures and discussion groups, as well as by the accessibility of many special materials.

Even when the radio is considered as a source of opportunity, it must be remembered that a majority of radio stations are located in cities. Programs are produced by city technicians and are keyed to the interests of city people.

The resources for scientific study are also greater in cities. There are technical schools and libraries, scientific museums, lectures, and demonstrations. Study on any level, from the purely avocational and amateur to the highly technical and professional, is possible.

In the graphic and plastic arts, there is a great range of opportunity: hobby groups with instruction, special schools, galleries with fine collections to be viewed and studied. Both appreciation and participation are available.

Music offers symphonic, chamber, and vocal concerts in many combinations. There are also opportunities to study professionally and as amateurs, as well as opportunities for participation and performance. Music appreciation is also the objective and study of many different groups. Both the enjoyment of music and self-expression through music can be had in the cities.

These items give a general indication of the scope of opportunities for good living which American cities provide for their citizens. The larger the city, the greater the range of opportunity. It is often argued with considerable logic that the opportunities are insufficient, but a more serious difficulty exists—the failure of a large proportion of the people to take advantage of the opportunities which exist.

Distribution of the Cities' Opportunities. Some of the facilities for good living in cities are organized and distributed so that they are made available to all or almost all of a city's people—water, sewers, utilities, etc. People take these for granted and tend to forget their importance and how much they contribute to comfort and convenience. There are still, however, some families in American cities who do not have the use of these things.

A large group of services, social and professional, for example, are not of everyday use, but stand ready when needs arise. Although many people know of these services and how to obtain them and use them when they are required, there are still a large number of city people who neither know that they need these services, nor are aware of their existence, nor are acquainted with how to obtain them. The professional, privately operated services become available to people not only when they know about them and that they have use for them, but also when they are able to pay for them; consequently, many are deprived of them because they do not have money enough to buy them.

Another group of services, those which are more often thought of in the category of opportunities because they are largely educational and cultural advantages, are distributed entirely on the initiative of the individual. A person not only must know about such opportunities and how to avail himself of them, but also must have an awareness of need for them or sufficient interest in them to be motivated to take advantage of the opportunity.

It is in the last two groups that distribution breaks down; there, in spite of the existence of opportunities, a great number of city people do not take advantage of the opportunities which exist. The first problem of distribution is, in reality, a problem of education by means of which people can become aware of the possibilities of better living and how they can take advantage of them and be motivated to do something about them under their own steam. To be sure, when greater numbers of people want these opportunities, there will not be enough to go round, and new needs which seek fulfillment will arise, but the problem of the extension of opportunities can be faced when the first problem of getting the opportunities which are already available adequately used is solved.

CITIZEN PARTICIPATION IN COMMUNITY AFFAIRS

The participation of city people in the affairs of their communities has come to be a serious problem. In the embryonic New England cities of the seventeenth and eighteenth centuries this important aspect of democracy was very real. Not only did the town meeting provide the opportunity for every citizen to have his say about even the details of community action, but it also created a sense of responsibility in the people for what went on in their communities and a sense of being an important part of the community.

It was inevitable, however, that the town meeting as a political and social mechanism should disappear as these small centers grew into full-fledged cities. The simple fact of bigness made the direct participation in the affairs of the community on the part of the citizen quite impossible, and so the individual grew more and more out of touch with community affairs. The high degree of specialization of function of people and of institutions, which is a characteristic of cities, focuses the attention and energy of the citizens on their particular vocational responsibilities. Their time is given to the small world of their primary relationships. So the very circumstances of people's lives work against any interest in the broad concerns of their communities.

The very forms of city government discourage the active participation of the citizens. Elected representatives of the people constitute the policy-making, legislative part of the government, but, even

where council members are elected by districts, they soon lose identification with their districts as they find it necessary to deal, for
the most part, with problems of the city as a whole. About the only
contact which can be maintained with the people of their districts
is through the political organization, and even that is largely with
their constituency.

The proportion of municipal officials voted for is small because
cities must have highly trained specialists to carry out their many
activities and these people must be selected on the basis of their
qualifications through civil service and appointment, not on the
basis of their popularity and the support of political organization.
Consequently, there is little basis for a sense of responsibility for
the operation of urban government on the part of the citizen. It is
not surprising that under these circumstances so many citizens of
American cities do not take the trouble to vote in city elections and
so make it all the easier for political machines to control the cities,
though few realize that this is true.

The bigness of city government, its many highly specialized activities, the lack of direct control between people and government
even in elections, all contribute to a sense of remoteness on the part
of people. They speak of government as "it" or "they" and have little
sense of being a part of it. When they encounter problems which
involve them with their city governments, they do not even know
where to go, and, when they do succeed in getting to the proper
place, they find it all very complicated and impersonal.

So people find themselves up against the social forces of the city
—big, organized, impersonal. They cannot cope with them; they can
do, it seems, nothing about the things which affect their living. A
social worker who had worked for some months to help a group of
people in East Harlem in New York get some improvements in their
exceedingly bad housing conditions described the situation in this
graphic fashion:

> In looking back I was struck by the tremendous amount of effort put
> in by the people, true a few people, and how somehow along the line,
> their attempts to get a window fixed, to get some heat, to fill a hole in
> the ceiling, were to no avail.
> Nobody said "No." The Department of Housing and Buildings sent in-
> spectors; the court held the rents; the landlord came to a meeting; the
> political club had a lawyer represent the tenants in court—and ten apart-
> ments were painted.

But I am wondering how much we can expect of people. How much must they do to get a window fixed, heat in the radiator. The people have jobs, families. They have to cook, clean, shop. They have to take time off to listen to the ball game, play the numbers—have some fun. This leaves little time for social action—little time to fix the window. But surely fixing a window won't take too much time. . . .

Mr. R says, "I told you, landlord, about the window. Was it a month ago? No! Was it a year ago? No! It was two years ago, landlord, I told you two years ago and the window is still broken."

The Department of Housing and Buildings says, "We have thousands of complaints . . . takes time to inspect . . . sure the windows are loose, but if we record every violation we'd be here a week . . . once we report the violations we do not have any enforcing powers, the courts have this power." Takes time, a day, week, year, two years.

Certificate of Violation—one buck . . . very cooperative . . . takes time, a month, maybe two—three . . .

Withhold rent—excellent . . . pay rent to court . . . How long . . . takes time, one month, maybe two, three . . .

What's wrong? What does it take to fix a window? A radiator heater?

How long can a group of people participate in an action aimed at change when nothing changes?[2]

The individual is helpless in the city; his only hope is in organization, in participation with others in working at their common problems, the affairs of their community.

EXPERIMENTS IN PARTICIPATION

Community workers have recognized the problem of participation for a long time. They have seen it not only as crucial to the revitalization of democracy in American cities, but also as essential to counteracting the deadening effect of urbanization upon the personalities of city people. Many experiments have been made toward the solution of this problem, and some of the experiments have met with remarkable success, both in terms of their accomplishments through organized action in doing something about common neighborhood problems, and in terms of the releasing and energizing of the people who participated.

One of the early experiments in organization to involve city people in activities to solve their common problems was made in Cin-

[2] From a field worker's report to the Neighborhood Center for Block Organization, Union Settlement Association, New York.

cinnati, where the social unit plan was first put into operation. It had a stormy life, but left such a mark on the city that it has enabled Cincinnati to attain a degree of democratic concern and participation not found in many other cities.[3]

An exciting story is told by Agnes E. Meyer in her articles about the Back of the Yards Neighborhood Council in Chicago.[4] It is a report on how 120,000 people living in the area of Chicago adjacent to the stockyards formed a council of the representatives of business, labor, nationalities, religions, and all other groups for exchange of ideas and for coöperative action. This organization not only dissipated the many group conflicts which had torn the community apart for years, but welded the people together so that they could be victorious in their clashes with the most powerful political machine and industrial organization in Chicago.

The people have decreased the infant-mortality rate by supporting the Infant Welfare Station. They have overcome a bad malnutrition condition among the children by getting state and federal support for free-milk and hot-lunch programs. They have largely done away with juvenile delinquency by understanding help: getting jobs and making the young people a responsible part of the council. They have established a credit union through which they have gotten people out of the clutches of loan sharks and been able to help them in the management of their finances. They maintain an office where all sorts of help may be obtained by anyone, at any time.

Saul D. Alinsky, the instigator of the back of the yards movement and of people's organizations in a number of other cities, has given the philosophy and the methods of this kind of organization, together with many illustrations, in a recent book. He believes in people, all kinds of people, and their worth to a democratic society, and in the necessity of their active participation in the affairs of their communities to make democracy real, to remove the frustrations from people, and to use the power of coöperative action to extend opportunity to all people.

Built out of the people's own organization, within the framework of their traditions, developed by the natural native leadership, these

[3] Wilbur C. Phillips, *Adventuring for Democracy* (New York: Social Unit Press, 1940).

[4] Agnes E. Meyer, *Orderly Revolution,* a reprint of a series of articles printed in the Washington *Post,* June 4, 5, 6, 7, 8, and 9, 1945.

councils carry out the programs which the people themselves decide upon. Since the power of democracy is in the people, the people's organizations become power organizations, and in the wielding of their power they use the tactics and strategy of power, but always in accord with the basic values of democracy. Education permeates the program, in association with many kinds of people, in learning to respect and understand different points of view, in the experience of action, and in rationalization.

The People's Organizations built according to the methods and philosophy described here stand today as the strongest people's groups in the nation. They have been locked in mortal combat with some of the most notorious power blocs in America and always emerged victorious. They have shown by positive, concrete action, in every field of human endeavor from housing to food, from wages to health, from child welfare to civic administration, that an organized people can achieve limitless objectives through the democratic process. They are great by their accomplishments, and glory in the deadly hatred and fear in which they are held by all native Fascists.[5]

In some city neighborhoods, people have been helped toward organizations and action by community workers supported by neighborhood houses, denominational city mission societies, local urban leagues, or other organizations. Through the discovery of local leadership, helping people find the resources they needed, using methods of organization and pressure, and prodding them toward action, these workers have been able to help people to participate in cooperative action.

Another type of development is represented by the work of the Southside Community Committee in Chicago. "The story of how the plain people of Chicago's South Side, in the face of an unparalleled problem of juvenile delinquency, undertook to build a community life in which all children could find that fulfillment which alone can reach and destroy the root causes of delinquency."[6]

The Southside Community Committee is an overall group of citizens numbering over a thousand paid members. The Board is a body of delegates from nine neighborhood committees and six gen-

[5] Saul D. Alinsky, *Reveille for Radicals* (Chicago: The University of Chicago Press, 1946), p. 74.

[6] *Bright Shadows in Bronzetown* (Chicago: Southside Community Committee, 1949).

eral subcommittees. It has had the help of the Chicago Area Project, the state government, various city-wide organizations, and the community chest, but it remains an activity of the people themselves. The neighborhood committees have carried on various projects, especially in recreation, have developed and used volunteer leadership of many kinds, and have worked directly with young people and their families when problems have arisen. There has come about a marked change in the attitude of people toward delinquents and their problems, and there has developed a coöperative effort to change the conditions under which delinquency has thrived. Many young people in trouble have been helped to get on the right track, and there is a general conviction that the people of the South Side are on the way toward building a better community. Behind the work of this committee was the influence of the South Side Planning Board.

Throughout the cities, much has been accomplished by the active participation of people in various types of specialized citizens' organizations, such as groups affiliated with the Government Research Association, local Bureaus of Municipal Research, Leagues of Women Voters, Citizens' Housing and Planning Councils, Citizens' Committees on Schools, and many others. These groups, while involving relatively few people in their particular activities, have had a decided impact on determining particular policies and courses of action in many cities.

During World War II, based on a very successful program in the rural areas, a plan for the participation of all the citizens of American cities in the war effort was developed by the Office of Civilian Defense.[7] The organization proved very effective in those cities where it was developed because it established lines of direct communication with all family units and so resulted in a high proportion of coöperation on the part of city families in the various programs of civilian war services. The plan of organization is shown in Figure 46.

While the operation of this plan was greatly facilitated by the war situation, which made it possible to organize from the top down with a program determined by war needs, it has much to suggest as a scheme for the development of participation on the basis of

[7] Office of Civilian Defense, *The Block Plan of Organization for Civilian War Services* (Washington: Government Printing Office, 1942).

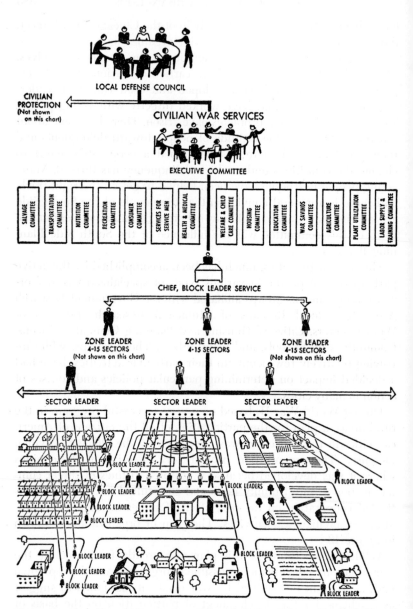

Figure 46. Block Plan of Organization. (Office of Civilian Defense, *The Block Plan of Organization for Civilian War Services* [Washington: Government Printing Office, 1942], p. 8.)

local problems and community affairs. The purposes stated for the plan were:

1. To carry forward civilian war activity, quickly and effectively.
2. To get vital war information into every home, rapidly and accurately.
3. To collect information which may be needed for community war planning, and to bring back to the homes answers to questions which have been raised.
4. To promote a spirit of cooperation in neighborhood enterprises, such as block discussion meetings, rallies, car-sharing plans, the sharing of scarce mechanical and household equipment, and any other activity of the community war services.[8]

These are, in part, the purposes of citizen participation expressed in war terms. The program anticipated laying a foundation for the development of indigenous neighborhood groups in which people would be active in dealing with their own problems. The whole civilian war service program was intended to marshal the various community resources and through coördination and planning relate them most effectively to community needs.

The training of the volunteer block leaders, who were the key people in the whole organization, gave not only information about the organization and its operation, their responsibility, and community resources and organization, but also instruction in community surveying and in the skills of interviewing, discussion leading, and teaching.[9]

One of the war casualties is that much which was learned about community organization under the necessity of war seems already to have been largely lost.

THE ENIGMA OF PARTICIPATION

The tremendous difficulties in extending participation to anything like what would logically be expected in a democratic society seem to stem from a widespread apathy which exists among city people. Alinsky reports that a careful study of participation in the most powerful and deeply rooted people's organizations in this country revealed that the degree of popular participation varied between 5 and 7 percent of the people in the community, but that this was

[8] *Ibid.*, pp. 5–16.
[9] New York State War Council, Office of War Training, *Block Leader: Instructor's Manual* (1942).

many times as great as participation in political organizations, in labor organizations, or even in religious organizations.[10]

A recent five-year experiment on the block-plan principle, with professional community workers, while in many respects very successful proved to be discouraging in terms of the extent of the participation which developed.[11]

It is too easy an explanation, however, to say that the indifference of people is the cause of nonparticipation. The conditions of urban life work against participation. Specialization, with its circumscribed experience, prevents the sense of community. Compartmentalization of living around different kinds of foci makes for many unrelated activities. Bigness, with its complexities, remoteness, and slowness of operation, makes effective relationships difficult. Socioeconomic stratification, with its limited environments, emphasizes differences, limits acquaintance and understanding, and arouses conflicts. All of these conditions create in urban people a psychology made up of a sense of isolation, frustration, fear, potential prejudice, conflicts of values, preoccupation with the immediacy of life, and a protective shell against the distracting stimuli on every hand. These are behind what seems to be indifference on the part of most people and accounts, in part, for the fact that community councils often shake down to the participation of professionals and top lay leaders who consider such activities within the responsibilities of their positions.

Perhaps the ideas of participation are too narrow. It may be that many new patterns of participation must be recognized and taken into account. At any rate, it would seem at this juncture that, if this crucial problem of our democracy is to be solved, it will need a large investment in thoroughly trained professional community workers to get the fires lighted and the needed movement under way.

One thing, however, seems eminently clear: the great variety of welfare resources of the modern urban community, without the participation of the citizens in community affairs, may rob democracy of its greatest potential value—the development of the personalities of its citizens. As Alinsky puts it:

[10] Alinsky, *op. cit.*, pp. 198–200.
[11] Report of the Neighborhood Center for Block Organization, Union Settlement Association, New York.

There is a much more profound basis for the passionate desire of all human beings to feel that they have personally contributed to the creation and the securing of any objective they desire. It is a part of what great religious schools of thought call the dignity of man. It is living in dignity to achieve things through your own intelligence and efforts. It is living as a human being. To live otherwise and not to share in the securing of your own objectives but simply to receive them as gifts, or the benevolent expression of either a government which does not consult with you, or a private philanthropist, places you in a position of a pauper. While to be given life's essentials may be physically pleasant, it is psychologically horrible, and the recipient, though outwardly expressing appreciation, is inwardly filled with revulsion.[12]

Supplementary Reading

Alinsky, Saul D. *Reveille for Radicals*. Chicago: The University of Chicago Press, 1946.

> The story of people's organizations and the results of their activity in civic improvement, better human relations, and better living.

Hillman, Arthur. *Community Organization and Planning*. New York: The Macmillan Company, 1950.

> A presentation of community organization and its merging with the active processes of community planning. "The methods by which communities deliberately change their way of life is the theme of this book."

Southside Community Committee. *Bright Shadows in Bronzetown*. Chicago: Southside Community Committee, 1949.

> A report on the objectives, organization, program, and accomplishments of the people on Chicago's South Side.

[12] Alinsky, *op. cit.*, p. 193.

CHAPTER 30

THE ROLE OF CITIES IN
AMERICAN CULTURE

BEFORE reviewing the part which cities play in American culture, it is well to look briefly at the ills which present cities have bred. Cities seem to be much like the giant redwood trees whose hearts have decayed or been burned out and which live on the healthy, youthful, and vigorous rings on their periphery. It is chiefly in the decaying zone around the central business centers that the evils have concentrated: poverty, delinquency, squalor, disease, mental breakdowns, unemployment, instability, wretched housing, congestion, drunkenness, prostitution, crime, and all sorts of social maladjustment.

While many things are involved in causing these evils, there is unanimous agreement that the environment in which these evils breed must be destroyed. A united attack on the form of cities is gaining momentum. Urban sociologists, social workers, city-planners, and many others are using their knowledge and experience to replan American cities. Not all ideas of what ought to be done agree, but the predominant view is that cities should be decentralized.

DECENTRALIZATION OF CITIES

At first thought it seems fantastic to consider decentralizing cities, but there are pressures and possibilities that have brought the idea already into the realm of practical planning.

National Security. From its first report the Atomic Energy Commission has decried the concentration of population and industry in the great American cities as points of great vulnerability. The National Security Act of 1947 described one duty of the National

Security Resources Board as "the strategic relocation of industries, services, government, and economic activities, the continuous operation of which is essential to the Nation's security." The Board is urging that the decentralization of industry begin with the location of new plants and new equipment, on which from twelve to fourteen billion dollars is being spent annually, outside the highly concentrated industrial areas.

A Process Already Under Way.   This trend, however, has been under way for some years. In its study *Decentralization of Industry,* the National Industrial Conference Board states: "There is a trend toward locating manufacturing plants in the smaller cities and towns. Cities and towns with 10,000 to 100,000 population are reported to be the most popular places for plants established from 1940–1947. Only one-third of the plants built or acquired since 1940 are in cities of 100,000 and over. For plants established prior to 1940, close to half were in cities of that size. On the other hand, almost 30 percent of the plants established since 1940 are in towns of 10,000 or less, against only 20 percent of the plants built before 1940."[1]

Because of the great cost of the terrifically destructive weapons of modern warfare, the strategic objective of their use must be calculated to bring commensurate results. The National Security Resources Board states in a pamphlet: "If the industrial facilities of the United States were effectively dispersed, that fact alone would make an incalculable contribution toward the maintenance of peace because of the prohibitive expense of any enemy attempt to destroy this country's ability to defend itself. Dispersion could contribute significantly toward outlawing war."[2]

So fear, adding its urgency to the force of changing conditions, to the pressure of technological advances, and to the desire for better standards of living for more people, contributes toward a radical change in the form of modern cities. Now that time has become the costliest ingredient in the productive process, the center of a great city, with the loss of time in elevators and in loading and unloading, with the paralysis of movement in narrow streets packed solid with vehicles, with the time-consuming errands and the journey to and

[1] *Decentralization of Industry* (New York: National Industrial Conference Board).

[2] National Security Resources Board, *National Security Factors in Industrial Location* (Washington: Government Printing Office).

from work (even with rapid transit), together with people's growing consciousness of their conditions of living, as well as their wages, hours, and conditions of work, is the most impractical and most costly place in which to carry on industry. To this can be added the mounting cost of operating the supercities, which must inevitably be reflected in an increase in taxes. Moreover, the technological advances (particularly the application of readily transmitted electricity as power), the relative cheapness of the protracted use of motor trucks, and the extensive use of the telephone make the decentralization of factories completely feasible.

The Practicality of the Idealist. So the prophetic idealism of an Ebenezer Howard becomes the practical solution of a complex of serious problems a half century after his proposal of garden cities. What great difficulties might have been avoided, what countless costs might have been saved, what abundance of human welfare might have been realized, if society could have capitalized on the foresight of the "dreamer" instead of having to wait a half century and more to be forced to the same solutions by the pressure of necessity, Even though the developments which have come in this half century have increased the practicability of the plan, it was practicable even when it was set forth.

IDEAL CITIES

The ideal city is still in the stage of speculation, but it is not beyond the realm of possibility. It is partly a matter of standards and partly a matter of calculation. In the final analysis, it boils down to size of population and relationships between cities, and between cities and their hinterlands.

Standards. Any idea of standards must begin with the concept of a city, first, as a means to provide good living for its citizens, and, second, as an instrument to produce goods and services—the economic base of the city. Standards cannot be absolute because people have different ideas of satisfactory living; not everyone prefers a single family dwelling with ample grounds as a home, though most families with children do. They must also be flexible, for standards rise with new facilities and with increasing appreciation. Nor can the economic machine be rigid, for patterns of production, to meet human needs, have a way of changing, and technological developments change methods and the kinds and numbers of workers.

Certain general standards, however, can be set down. The conditions of living should be such as would provide a good and satisfactory life for all the people. Homes should be substantial, well equipped, convenient, adequate, and attractive. They should be located so that they would be convenient for the daily going and coming to and from work, shopping, and school. There should be accessibility to recreation, to the open country, and to a central city where special services of all kinds are available, where durable goods can be had, and where the great museums, universities, opera, and the like are located. There should be proportion and beauty, as well as convenience and comfort, and neighborhoods should be as thoroughly planned as the whole city.

Commerce and the services should be planned to adequately meet the needs of the city's people. Controls should be sufficient to assure success and prevent crippling competition, but they should not hamper private enterprise. Adequate transportation facilities should be provided to obtain supplies of dairy products and fresh fruits and vegetables from the countryside, and manufactured goods from distribution points. But industry, commerce, and the services must be planned together because they all will depend on the same labor force. There should be enough jobs to employ all who want to work at wages high enough to give a reasonable standard of living to the people of the city. Employment should be stable, both as a basis of the security of the people and also to provide a total income for the city's families which will continue to keep business in successful operation. Industrial production, in most cases, will be the backbone of the city and should use all available technological development and the minimum of man power per factory (and that of a high order of skill) so that a high rate of man-hour production can be maintained. Arrangements should be made to facilitate the receiving of raw materials and the movement of manufactured products. Factories will likely be placed for more efficient operation on the periphery of the city rather than at its center. They can be built—and, in fact, many have been—to add to the attractiveness of the city.

Government is one of the most determinative factors in the size of a city. The population must be large enough to require all of the desirable services and to pay for them, but it must be small enough so that these services can be provided with simple organization and minimum personnel. There is a crucial point of size beyond which the machinery of government must become complicated and costly. In order to get the maximum returns for taxes, a city must be below this crucial point of size.

Schools require a large enough number of children so that the many special services found useful in modern education can be provided in units small enough for intimate coöperative groups of teachers and students, and with elementary schools located conveniently for small children and related to neighborhoods. Under the circumstances of such cities, the social services, operating chiefly within neighborhoods, will be able to concentrate on the more constructive aspects of their activities: counseling, group work, and community organization working toward the effective participation of people in solving their own problems and working out their own destinies through democratic action. Health services, similarly organized, can make their major activities preventive measures and health education.

A Statistical Problem. All of these items are subject to calculation. It is not a simple statistical problem because it involves the balancing of many items, but it is completely soluble. It is similar to a simple problem worked out a number of years ago to determine the future possibilities for growth and development of Protestant churches in Minneapolis.[3] From the range of various items of the churches under study, the four quarters were taken on the norms of as many classes of churches. The result is shown, by way of illustrating the method, in Table 58 (p. 492). Then, from an analysis of population and church relationships, it was determined what numbers of church members, church adherents, and population[4] were required at the various levels of per capita giving to obtain A, B, or C classes of churches in terms of the norms of cost from the earlier computation. This is shown for Minneapolis in Table 59 (p. 492).

By this type of calculation, starting with government and its cost, continuing through the analysis of retail trade, the services, and industrial production, taking into consideration wages and income, adding the social services and education and their cost, it would be possible to compute, in terms of the experience of American cities, the specifications for various classes of cities.

[3] Wilbur C. Hallenbeck, *Minneapolis Churches and Their Comity Problems* (New York: Harper & Brothers, 1929), pp. 83–91.

[4] The population item includes the membership and adherents of the particular church, the membership and adherents of other churches, and the balance of unchurched or available population.

TABLE 69.   Comparison of Population, Median Income, Per Capita Total Revenue of Government, and Percentage Per Capita Government Revenue Is of Median Income, by Rank, for the 37 Cities of 250,000 or More Population in 1940

	Population, 1940[a]		Median Income, 1939[b]		Per Capita Total Revenue of Government, 1937[c]		Percentage Per Capita Govt. Revenue Is of Median Income[d]	
	Number	Rank	Amount	Rank	Amount	Rank	Percent	Rank
New York	7,454,995	1	1,083	17	107.77	1	9.95	1
Chicago	3,396,808	2	1,093	14	80.67	8	7.38	10
Philadelphia	1,931,334	3	1,004	24	56.88	23	5.67	20
Detroit	1,623,452	4	1,237	4	68.46	17	5.53	22
Los Angeles	1,504,277	5	1,094	13	79.84	9	7.30	11
Cleveland	878,336	6	1,055	20	68.55	16	6.50	15
Baltimore	859,100	7	942	28	65.78	18	6.98	13
St. Louis	816,048	8	945	27	49.85	27	5.28	26
Boston	770,816	9	1,040	22	99.77	3	9.59	3
Pittsburgh	671,659	10	1,083	16	81.28	6	7.51	8
Washington	663,091	11	1,264	2	70.50	14	5.58	21
San Francisco	634,536	12	1,239	3	73.10	12	5.90	19
Milwaukee	587,472	13	1,132	8	75.37	11	6.66	14
Buffalo	575,901	14	1,086	15	81.23	7	7.48	9
New Orleans	494,537	15	721	34	61.72	20	8.56	6
Minneapolis	492,370	16	1,139	7	71.33	13	6.26	17
Cincinnati	455,610	17	1,055	21	75.38	10	7.15	12
Newark	429,760	18	978	26	97.03	4	9.92	2
Kansas City	399,178	19	979	25	53.34	25	5.45	23
Indianapolis	386,972	20	1,071	19	48.56	28	4.53	32
Houston	384,514	21	901	29	53.80	24	5.97	18
Seattle	368,302	22	1,175	5	58.46	22	4.98	29
Rochester	324,975	23	1,097	12	96.65	5	8.81	5
Denver	322,412	24	1,074	18	68.62	15	6.39	16
Louisville	319,077	25	848	31	43.61	32	5.14	28
Columbus	306,087	26	1,030	23	47.85	29	4.65	31
Portland (Ore.)	305,394	27	1,114	10	59.02	21	5.30	25
Atlanta	302,288	28	709	35	38.22	33	5.39	24
Oakland	302,163	29	1,314	1	50.18	26	3.82	36
Jersey City	301,173	30	1,152	6	107.24	2	9.31	4
Dallas	294,734	31	817	32	34.17	35	4.18	34
Memphis	292,942	32	686	36	35.47	34	5.17	27
St. Paul	287,736	33	1,102	11	47.83	30	4.34	33
Toledo	282,349	34	1,126	9	46.78	31	4.15	35
Birmingham	267,583	35	752	33	22.76	37	3.03	37
San Antonio	253,854	36	601	37	28.85	36	4.80	30
Providence	253,504	37	852	30	65.26	19	7.66	7

[a] 16th Census, 1940: First Series: *Population: U.S. Summary*, Table 12, p. 24.
[b] 16th Census, 1940: *Population*: Series P-14, No. 3 (Sept. 28, 1942), Table 1, p. 5.
[c] Bureau of the Census, *Financial Statistics of Cities, 1937*, Table 4, p. 43.
[d] Computed.

This would be a composite picture, for many inconsistencies can be seen in Table 69, which takes the thirty-seven cities in the United States which had populations of 250,000 or more in 1940 and shows their rank in size of population, in median income, in per capita total revenue of the city government, and in the percentage that the per capita total revenue of city government is of the median income. While it is clear that, the larger the city, the more it costs a person to live in it, a correlation of .43 between size of population and per capita total revenue of city government shows that there are other important variables. One of these variables is *not* the incomes of the people, however; the correlation between median income and per capita total revenue of city government is .09. Both of these relationships might well be closer in an ideal situation. Many hypotheses can be drawn from this table. There is a strong suspicion that business might be better and standards of living higher if the cost of government in some cities were more in line with the capacity of people to pay for it. Or, again, some cities notorious for their political machines stand very high in per capita cost of government. One hopeful note is found in Oakland, a well-governed city, which heads the list in median income, but is next to the bottom of the list in the ratio of government cost to income.

Size. While the calculations are yet to be done, some significant estimates of the best size for cities have been made. The National Security Resources Board, for purposes of strategic security, considers it desirable that urban concentrations of more than 50,000 people be avoided. This estimate has an entirely negative basis. "The scarcity of the essential materials for the manufacture of an atomic bomb makes production so costly that we may reasonably assume that no country in the foreseeable future will ever have enough to afford to use one on each city of as few as 50,000 people, or on a congested industrial area of less than five square miles."[5] The Board's case will be greatly strengthened when it shows the positive advantages and possibilities of cities of the suggested size.

For the limited decentralization of the London Country Plan the population has been set at approximately 60,000, although there seems to be no indication that this is more than an arbitrary figure.

Clarke and Renner have made general preliminary calculations on the basis of which they set a population of about 30,000 as the maximum for good living and efficient operation.

Howard's plan for garden cities, at the turn of the century, set a maximum population of 32,000, a city area of 1000 acres, and a surrounding area of 5000 acres of agricultural land. His principle provided that the cities be laid out so that it would not be possible for them to exceed this population. Howard set this maximum size

[5] National Security Resources Board, *op. cit.*

on the basis of the arrangements which his observations and study had convinced him were best for good living and efficient operation. Apparently in fifty years his estimate has not been improved.

Constellations of Cities.   Decentralized cities of moderate size not only must be built according to such standards as have been suggested, but must also be well-balanced, adequately organized, and self-sufficient. This, however, will not be in the same way that the independent cities of a half century or more ago were self-sufficient, but rather under the circumstances of the present day, in which specialization has even come to be a characteristic of cities, which in turn makes them interdependent.

The great developments of recent years have come through specialization in the various areas of human activity, and it is in specialization and its accompanying research that further advances will come in science, technology, administration, organization, methods in business, industry, government, community organization, social services, education, and all the other aspects of life. It is the great bulk of population in the large urban centers, however, which has facilitated and made possible the development of specialization. It would be highly undesirable to remove the conditions under which specialization flourishes. The way toward resolving this apparent dilemma between the desirability of decentralizing cities into smaller units and maintaining great numbers of people in proximity is already clear.

It has been seen that one of the characteristics of urban growth has been the growth of the smaller medium-sized cities which fall within the influence of the larger urban centers, and the growth of the areas outside the central cities in the metropolitan districts. The studies of metropolitan communities have indicated a complex of relationships between the cities which are located within these areas even at considerable distances from the major central cities.

The solution seems abundantly clear in the planning of constellations of cities within metropolitan communities, which may be much more extensive in their total geographical area than would be expected from looking at the metropolitan districts which have been selected for the census enumeration. Such a plan would permit various types of specialization in the particular decentralized units and at the same time preserve a sufficient total bulk of population to facilitate further developments of specialization. The present large central cities would be neither denuded nor essentially changed in character, though they would gradually grow smaller and be given over more completely to the focal centers for highly specialized activities. They would become the location of the administrative centers for widespread business and industry, the points of distribution of goods and of power, the seats of metropolitan and regional government and planning, the places for dispersing highly specialized and perhaps major durable goods, the location of highly specialized services in health and social work, especially institutions, an urban university, major museums, art centers, the legitimate theater, professional symphony orchestras, opera, and ballet, major league baseball, and other activities. Subcenters in the smaller cities in the constellations might take certain forms of specialization, even some of those which would ordinarily gravitate to the centers. With adequate transportation between the decentralized cities and the central city and among the various smaller cities, together with the use of automobiles, little difference would be experienced in the operation of the total community except that daily commuting would tend to disappear, though undoubtedly it would continue as a minor factor operating in many directions rather than, as now, into the centers from all directions.

Again, it must be recognized that Howard foresaw such a pattern as the proposed constellations of garden cities around a central city. This plan, like Howard's plan, differs greatly from the present situation, for it would do away with the whole pattern of suburbs or parasite communities as they now exist.

ROLE OF THE CITIES

Through all of the criticism of the form of cities there has been no dissent as to the functions of cities. As America has developed into a commercial and industrial society, cities have grown and come into prominence because this kind of civilization operates in and through cities.

Cities are the focal points through which energy and materials flow so that their lines of service and influence reach far. Some of the great cities serve the whole nation, some cities serve particularly as the centers of the great regions of the United States, and the smaller cities have more limited outreach. Around the major urban centers, however, has developed an area of constant interrelationship making up metropolitan communities, and within these a large proportion of the smaller cities play their lesser roles.

So the social and economic machinery of the present day operates, giving to cities an essential role. An important concomitant is that the influence of cities on the ideas, the habits, and the patterns of living of the nation's people is very great. Not only does the nation depend upon the cities, but the cities depend upon the nation; yet this interdependence has never been fully appreciated, and all too often conflicts arise where there should be mutual understanding and coöperation.

Yet cities have never been able to get their own houses in order. This is partly because their job is too big for them and they have been expected to do it themselves. The adequacy of cities to fulfill their functions is the whole nation's business because all suffer to the extent to which cities are inadequate. It is costly to operate cities, and no way has yet been found to pay the cost. But it is also because of a lack of foresight and adequate planning based on an understanding of the role of cities in American culture and the forms which they should take to play these roles well.

Cities, however, are more than vital elements in the social and economic machinery of the nation; they are also instruments to provide a livelihood and good living for the cities' people. This is the people's business, and until they are ready to increase their understanding of their cities and accept the responsibility of participation in the cities' affairs, the cities must wait for their fulfillment.

INDEXES

NAME INDEX

SUBJECT INDEX

604